THE

BORDER TOWERS OF SCOTLAND:

Their History and Architecture

THE WEST MARCH

(Dumfriesshire & Eastern Galloway)

by

Alastair M. T. Maxwell-Irving

2000

To

Margery Salmon and

an anonymous friend,

whose generous help has

made the publication

of this work possible

First published 2000

© Publication Copyright Alastair M. T. Maxwell-Irving

© Copyright of individual photographs, where applicable, remain with the photographer.

Typeset, designed and printed by Solway Offset the Printers, Dumfries, for the publisher, Alastair M. T. Maxwell-Irving, Telford House, Blairlogie, Stirling, FK9 5PX.

ISBN 1 899316 31 0

THE
BORDER TOWERS OF SCOTLAND:

THE WEST MARCH

Dick

With best wishes and fond memories
of a mutual friend, Nigel Tranter,
from
    Alastair Maxwell-Irving

Amisfield Tower.

CONTENTS

FOREWORD

Journeying by road or rail across the Solway Plain north of Carlisle or descending from the Lowther Hills into the lush farmlands of Lower Annandale, modern travellers in their haste may catch only the briefest of glimpses of the tangible reminders of the time when this area – the West March of the Anglo-Scottish Border – was once a veritable cockpit of local feuds and national wars. Even from a brief, fleeting passage, however, they are likely to gain the impression that this was land of a quality and strategic value that was worth defending or fighting for, while closer inspection would begin to reveal just how much evidence of building – the most obvious and telling indicator of human activity from prehistory to the present-day – lies embedded in the surrounding countryside.

Conspicuous among such buildings is the tower-house, a multi-storeyed house-type of an immensely versatile design which struck just the right balance between the needs of security and domestic amenity, and which for more than three centuries from the 14th century onwards proved enduringly popular in the northern and western parts of the British Isles. Few areas can boast more such towers, both past and present, than the West March.

The author – my friend and fellow-enthusiast, Alastair Maxwell-Irving – brings far more to this major and substantial work of reference than a close and detailed knowledge of the region. To the study and analysis of the architecture, including the historical illustrations, he applies the acuity of an engineer, his recording and observation skills having been honed over many years to a precise accuracy (in horology as well as historic architecture), and to the study of the documentary background he draws upon a long-standing familiarity with the subtleties and complexities of Scottish family history, particularly of the Borders, the homeland of his own family. Evaluating and balancing carefully the strands of evidence presented by the architecture and the documents – including those recording turbulent episodes affecting what we might now describe as the quality of life in the Borders – demands a cool head and disciplined scholarship of the kind which the author has long evinced.

There could be no better informed, nor more reliable guide to these buildings and to what they tell us about the history of the West March than that which he presents here. It is my confident prediction that this book will cause at least some of the more discerning travellers through the region to halt awhile, and to consider, for example, why the banks of the otherwise unremarkable Kirtle Water should have attracted one of the densest concentrations of tower-houses in Scotland. But, as befits an area where tower-houses once grew like mushrooms, this work has a much wider importance and interest, laying claim to be the first published study of its kind relating to mainland Britain.

Geoffrey Stell
Head of Architecture,
Royal Commission on the Ancient and
Historical Monuments of Scotland

ACKNOWLEDGEMENTS

I am immensely grateful to the owners and tenants of all the properties covered by this work for their kindness and hospitality in giving me unrestricted access to both the sites and the towers, many of which are also their homes. They are too numerous to mention individually, but without their co-operation and forebearance a book of this kind would not be possible. I am particularly indebted to Patrick, Earl of Annandale, who let me have the facilities for clearing the Lochwood site of its dense vegetation and carrying out a limited excavation in the 1960s, and to all those owners and occupiers who let me have the free run of their homes while preparing the plans, especially Mr. M. A. Armour, His Grace the Duke of Buccleuch & Queensberry, Mrs Peter Buckley, John and Julia Clarke, Archie Donaldson, Robert Greenshields, Dr. Bruce Irving, the late Mary and William Johnstone, Sandra Lammie, Francis Maxwell, the late Lady Pigott, the Hon. Sir Steven Runciman, CH, Count Rutger von Seth, David Shields, George Stewart, Sophia Weatherall and James Williams.

I owe a great debt to John Dunbar, OBE, former Secretary of the Royal Commission on the Ancient and Historical Monuments of Scotland (RCAHMS), for all the help he gave me in the early days, as well as for his ongoing interest and encouragement, and to Geoffrey Stell, Head of Architecture at the RCAHMS, who took over his mantle and with whom I have now had the privilege of working on innumerable occasions for more than twenty years. Geoffrey has also very kindly contributed the Foreword to this work. I would also like to thank all the other staff at the RCAHMS who have assisted me in my researches, both in the National Monuments Record and on site. Christopher Tabraham and Miss Doreen Grove of Historic Scotland have provided generous help in respect of the properties in the care of that body.

I am also indebted to the late Dr. Robert C. Reid and Alfred Truckell, MBE, formerly Curator of the Dumfries Museum, both of whom were for many years Joint Editors of the Transactions of the Dumfriesshire and Galloway Natural History and Antiquarian Society. It was Dr. Reid, one of the greatest authorities on the West March, who first guided me in the transcription of early titles more than forty years ago, while Mr. Truckell's tireless enthusiasm and encyclopaedic knowledge of the region have proved of immense value. More recently, I have had both help and advice from Bill Cormack, MBE, and James Williams, the current editors of the Transactions. In addition, the staff of the Scottish Record Office have generously assisted me with their time and expertise in transcribing some of the more complex titles.

Figures 145, 290 and 365 are Crown Copyright, reproduced by kind permission of the Royal Commission on the Ancient and Historical Monuments of Scotland. Figure 1 is reproduced by kind permission of the Trustees of the National Library of Scotland; figure 11, the Trustees of the National Museums of Scotland; figure 252, Sothebys; figure 359, the late Mrs Elsie Graham of Mossknowe; and figure 369, His Grace the Duke of Buccleuch and Queensberry. Figures 169, 174, 219, 323 and 336 are taken from *Picturesque Antiquities of Scotland*, by Adam de Cardonnel; figures 111, 126, 168, 220, 230, 242, 259, 273, 293, 299, 328, 352 and 367 from *The Antiquities of Scotland*, by Francis Grose; figures 50, 51, 121, 173, 177, 215 and 346 from *The Castellated and Domestic Architecture of Scotland*, by David MacGibbon and Thomas Ross; figure 344 from *The Book of Carlaverock*, by Sir William Fraser; figure 338 from *The Book of the Irvings*, by John Beaufin Irving; and figure 362 from *Liddesdale, Eskdale, etc.*, by Robert Bruce Armstrong.

The drawing of Threave on the title page is by Geoffrey D. Hay, formerly of the RCAHMS, and is reproduced with his kind permission.

GENERAL NOTES

1. All structural dimensions are given in feet and inches, as these were the units used by the masons who built the towers. In the majority of cases the principal structural dimensions are found to be multiples of 3 or 4 inches. To convert the dimensions to metric measurements would not only give long strings of decimals, but it would give no idea of relative size without converting the dimensions back. 2ft 9in, for example, would become 0·838m, which gives neither an immediate, nor a clear, idea of size.

2. One aspect of land ownership that often causes confusion, even to the experts, is the feudal system of land tenure and all its ramifications. In the first instance, the feudal superior held his lands directly of the Crown. He could then lease any part of those lands either to a feuar – to be held in blench-ferme or feu-ferme – or to a tenant. But it becomes more complicated, and confusing, when mid-feuars (or subinfeudation) enters the picture. This is when one or more additional layers of feudal holding are established between the feudal superior 'holding of the Crown' and the ultimate feuar 'in actual possession'; and without a knowledge of the property's overall history, it is not always apparent from the titles exactly what the status of the title-holder is.[1]

3. Another practice that affects most properties – although rarely mentioned in this work – derived from marriage contracts. It was normal practice for the owner of land to grant his spouse a liferent in all or part of his lands for her future security. It was also common for a father to sease his eldest son in the family's lands, whilst reserving a liferent interest for himself and his spouse. This was often necessary for the security of an intended daughter-in-law on marriage. It could, however, lead to friction within a family at a later date, and in rare cases led to physical violence and litigation between a son and his mother, or, more likely, step-mother.[2]

4. Prior to 1st January 1600, each calendar year started on the 25th March. This means that the 17th March 1564, for example, would be 17th March 1565 by our modern reckoning. To avoid confusion, therefore, such dates are shown in this work as 1564/5.[3]

---

1   See Dickinson, 84; and Gouldesbrough, P. *Formulary of Old Scots Legal Documents* (The Stair Society, Edinburgh, 1985).
2   See, for example, Shirmers Castle at the turn of the 18th century.
3   England did not follow suit until 1752, when both countries fully adopted the Gregorian calendar.

Hoddom Castle in 1789.

INTRODUCTION

'The seeds of our destiny are nurtured by the roots of our past' (Chinese proverb)

It was the Treaty of York in 1237 that finally established the Border between Scotland and England along its present line.[1] Prior to that, Scotland had from time to time also possessed Cumbria and occasionally part of Northumbria;[2] and even after 1237 there were parts of the Border that were unresolved, notably Berwick-upon-Tweed, which kept changing hands before finally resting with England in 1482,[3] and an area in Lower Eskdale, known as 'The Debateable Land', which was for long a source of dispute.[4] It was not until 1552 that a Commission, set up by the two kingdoms, finally agreed to partition the Debateable Land along a line defined by 'boundary stones' and a substantial earth bank, known as the 'Scots Dike',[5] and this has remained the boundary ever since.

Following the Treaty of York, laws were drawn up for the administration of the frontier and adjacent territories. These 'Border Laws' were first issued in 1249, and were subsequently modified and extended many times during the next three and a half centuries.[6] Among many clauses covering such diverse subjects as criminals, fishing, shipwrecks and even the cutting of trees, it was decided that the Border should be divided into three Marches on either side — an East March, a Middle March and a West March — , each of which was to be administered by a Warden and one or more deputies; in addition, on the Scots side there was to be a Keeper of Liddesdale based at Hermitage Castle.[7] The Wardens and their deputies were responsible for the administration of justice, and for the resolution of all cross-Border disputes there were to be 'Days of Truce', at which the respective Wardens were to meet to resolve their differences, exchange grievances and mete out justice.

Such was the theory: the reality was often very different. While some of the Wardens were most diligent in bringing criminals to justice, others procrastinated,[8] countered one charge with another,[9] or ignored their duties altogether.[10] Nevertheless, while the two countries remained at peace, many meetings were held and many differences resolved, but life in the Borders was often far from peaceful. Not only were the two countries repeatedly in a state of war with each other, either with a view to conquest, reprisal, or support for another friendly country — such as France or Spain — or cause, but the very existence of a hostile frontier led to its own way of life within the territory. Bands of lawless men, families or clans on both sides regularly raided their neighbours far across the frontier, burning and pillaging all in their path and carrying off the livestock, sometimes even with the connivance of their own officials.[11] Others either took advantage of the unsettled state of affairs to further their own ends, or were victims of it. Families living in the Debateable Land before 1552 had the worst of both worlds, as neither country would tolerate any settlement in a territory that was still under dispute.[12] Thus the Eskdale Armstrongs and the Border Grahams[13] were for long in a particularly invidious position. Even the former's kinsmen in Liddesdale declared that 'they woolde not be ordoured, naither by the king of Scottes, thair soveraine lorde, nor by the king of Einglande, but after suche maner as thaire faders had used afore thayme'.[14]

While a few of the lawless families and reivers served only their own interests, others looked to much larger clan groups, or even powerful chiefs, for protection; and as the chiefs themselves fell out with one another, especially on the Scottish side of the Border, so feuds developed that escalated to involve nearly all the clans in the March. Thus when the Johnstons and Maxwells fell out over the office of Warden in the 16th century, a dispute fomented at first by Sir Thomas (later Lord) Wharton, who thereby sought to de-stabilize the region,[15] and later by the Regent Arran in furtherance of a personal grievance,[16] other families drawn into the net included the Irvings, Bells, Carlyles, Elliots, Grahams and Scotts, who sided with the Johnstons, and the Douglases of Drumlanrig, Armstrongs, Carruthers, Charteris, Crichtons, Kirkpatricks and Murrays, who joined the Maxwells.[17] By 1585 the situation had developed into virtual war;[18] and eight years later the dispute came to a climax at the battle of Dryfesands, the last clan battle fought in the Borders, where Lord Maxwell, the Warden, was killed.[19] But feuds were rarely static, and during the course of this dispute the Bells and Carlyles fell out with the Irvings, their neighbours, as a result of which they changed sides and joined the Maxwells.[20] Not all the Maxwells, however, were involved, for Sir John Maxwell, 4th Lord Herries, who was Warden for a total of some twenty-one years and one of the most distinguished statesmen of the age, was strenuous in his efforts to maintain the peace. It has also to be said that, despite the many protestations of the Johnstons, the Lords Maxwell were more often than not acting in their official capacity as Wardens and Justiciars. Meanwhile, in Galloway, another feud had developed between Lord Maxwell and the Gordons of Lochinvar.[21]

It was against this background that the various families and clans had to lead their daily lives. It was also the reason why the tower-houses of the Scottish Border — with which this work is concerned — developed their own particular characteristics, and were once almost as common a feature of the landscape as fermtouns were further north. The invaluable maps prepared at the end of the 16th century by Timothy Pont show just how dense that distribution was.[22] To survive in such a hostile environment, one had to have a 'tower', however small.

It is with the tower-houses of the *Scottish Border* that this work is concerned, and for this reason it only deals with the tower-houses of the West March within the county of Dumfries and the eastern part of Galloway, as far as the valleys of the rivers Ken and Dee. This is not the whole of the West March as officially defined in the 16th century — which included all of the Stewartry of Kirkcudbright as far as the river Cree[23] —, but it includes all the territory that was affected, and influenced, by the Border and its way of life. By the time one reached the Ken–Dee valley, the troubles of the Border seemed very remote. Life was generally more tranquil, and small, strong 'towers' were giving place to more commodious, and less outwardly aggressive, 'castles', with less provision for firearms. English invading forces never penetrated further west, nor did the army of the

Regent Morton when, in 1568, he made a progress through the West March to impose his rule upon the supporters of Queen Mary.

The aim of this work is to give a concise history and description of those tower-houses that have survived, whether complete or ruinous, and of the families who built and lived in them, as well as some background information about the property's earlier history, where known. There are, however, a number of other properties, no longer in existence, which have been included, because enough is known about them to merit attention: these include Auldgirth, Bogrie, Castlemilk, Friars Carse, Lochinvar, Lockerbie, Maxwell's Castle and Terregles. But while the architecture is described in detail, both for the record and for the benefit of those with a specialist interest in the subject, the historical background has been reduced to brief 'vignettes', — though for the larger and more important properties and their owners, the histories have been condensed rather more than for those of the lesser dwellings about which little is known, and where even the smallest detail may help to fill the picture. No attempt has been made to write a 'history' of any of the families concerned; such an undertaking would alone fill one or more volumes, as, indeed, it has in the past for the Armstrongs, Bells, Cairns, Carruthers, Douglases, Irvings, Johnstones, Maclellans, Maxwells, Scotts and other families.[24] Cadet branches of families are only mentioned where relevant, while the daily pursuit of family feuds and other incidental details rarely get a mention. All known public offices have, however, been included to show the part played by the various lairds in the everyday administration of both national and Border life.

Despite the lengths to which the author has gone in researching the various properties, including exploratory excavations at a number of sites, the scope for further work in this field

is still vast. Nobody, for example, has ever fully researched all the surviving records held by the burgh of Dumfries, of which there is a vast number. Then there are all the records, such as Acts and Decreets, Protocol Books of Notaries, land titles, estate records, etc., held by the Scottish Record Office and the Registers of Scotland,[25] as well as the countless original titles and other records still in the hands of individual families,[26] solicitors, banks and building societies, many of which have over the generations become divorced from the properties to which they relate.[27]

One of the reasons for including much more history than would normally appear in a book on Scottish architecture, is to provide a better understanding of the properties as a whole. Such monumental works on Scottish architecture as MacGibbon and Ross's *Castellated and Domestic Architecture of Scotland*, the Royal Commission on the Ancient and Historical Monuments of Scotland's *Inventories and Reports*, Nigel Tranter's *The Fortified House in Scotland*, John Gifford's *Dumfries and Galloway* (in *The Buildings of Scotland* series), Mackay Mackenzie's *The Mediaeval Castle in Scotland*, Stewart Cruden's *The Scottish Castle*, and many lesser works, make no more than passing references to the occasional owner or historical context. The authors had neither the time, nor the resources, at their disposal to embark upon pure historical research; their approach was first and foremost that of 'architectural' historians. More recently, however, the Royal Commission has adopted a different approach, and in their latest volume on *Eastern Dumfriesshire* they have employed a broader brush to demonstrate the correlation between the region's social and political history and its architectural legacy; and a similar approach has been adopted in another recent work, *Kirkpatrick Fleming, Dumfriesshire: An Anatomy of a Parish in South West Scotland*.

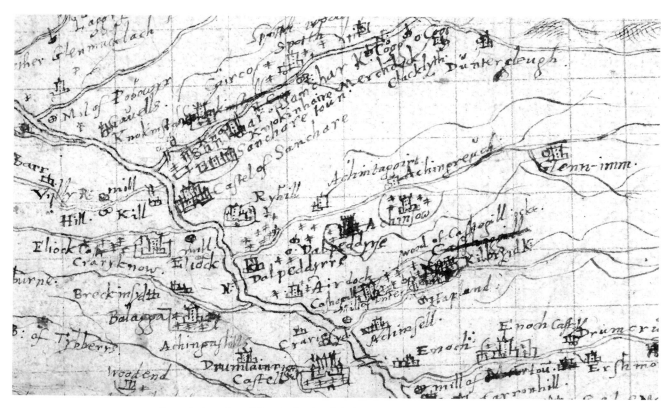

Figure 1 A portion of Timothy Pont's original survey of Upper Nithsdale, *c*.1595,
showing the castles of Sanquhar, Eliock, Coshogle, Drumlanrig and Enoch.

During nearly half a century that the author has been researching Border towers, there have been considerable changes in the towers themselves. The relentless process of decay has continued unabated, all too often assisted by mindless vandalism. At two towers, Lochar and Torthorwald, there have been major collapses. Features that were once clearly visible have disappeared under new heaps of rubble. Lochwood, on the other hand, which was once almost buried and overgrown with trees, has been cleared and largely opened up during several seasons of excavations by both the author and a later team, though, sadly, the 17th century garden has recently 'disappeared'. Towers such as Barscobe, Elshieshields and Lochhouse, which were beginning to suffer badly from neglect, have found new owners and been completely refurbished; and towers that were roofless shells, such as Abbot's, Hollows and Spedlins, have been totally restored. On the other hand, Breconside and Kenmure, both of which the author remembers when they were still inhabited, have been abandonned and fallen into ruin, and Lockerbie has been deliberately demolished.

Although most of the towers and sites are no longer held by the families who built them, there are exceptions. Lochwood is still held by the Earls of Annandale, Chiefs of the Johnstones, and Drumlanrig by the Duke of Buccleuch, a cadet of the Douglases of Drumlanrig. Bonshaw is held by a cadet of the Irvings, Closeburn by a Spanish branch of the Kirkpatricks, and Kirkconnell by a branch of the Maxwells, albeit a different line from the original Maxwells of Kirkconnell; and the ruins of Kenmure have been acquired by a Gordon descended from that house. At the end of the 19th century the ruins of Sanquhar Castle were acquired by the 3rd Marquess of Bute, lineal descendant of the Crichtons of Sanquhar, and restoration commenced; but after his death in 1900, work stopped, and decay has once again set in, although the family still owns the property. Drumcoltran, Maclellan's, Orchardton and Threave are the only ruins guaranteed protection, as they are all under the guardianship of the Crown.

---

1   Dickinson, 80.
2   Ibid, 75-77.
3   Ibid, 226-7.
4   There is also a reference to some 'debateable ground' between the East March of England and the Middle March of Scotland in 1565 (Border Papers I, No.6).
5   RPC I, 120-2, 125; Scottish Papers I, No.392.
6   Nicolson 1705, 1-170.
7   Rae, Appendix 2. See also Border Papers, I, 30-1.
8   Border Papers I, No.40.
9   Ibid, Nos.72, 241.
10   William Ker of Cessford, Warden of the Middle March, on being informed by Sir John Forster, the English Warden, that certain Kers had taken stock from his cousin, countered that the Halls of Gristonstell still had his sheep (Border Papers I, 113 (No.180)).
11   Ibid, No.176; RPC I, 149, passim; Reid, R. C. 'The Border Grahams', TDGAS, 3rd Ser., XXXVIII, 105-6.
12   Armstrong 1960, 49.
13   'Long Will' Graham 'of Esk' and his eight sons were banished from Scotland and settled in the Debateable Land c.1515 (Reid, 'The Border Grahams', op. cit., 104-5).
14   Armstrong 1883, 267.

15   Fraser 1873, I, 213.
16   Ibid, 261.
17   Irving 1907, 37.
18   Fraser 1873, I, 261-2; Border Papers I, Nos.303, 304, 321, 327, 425.
19   Fraser 1873, I, 289-91; Border Papers I, No.918.
20   Border Papers I, 394; Hope-Johnstone MSS, 32 (No.62).
21   Fraser 1894, I, xl.
22   Blaeu, 53, 55, 57, 59, 61, 65, 66; Stone 1989, 187-96.
23   Rae, 23.
24   See Bibliography.
25   The Registers of Scotland, being a self-financing government Agency, make a substantial charge for every entry looked up, with no concessions for historical researchers. Financial constraints, therefore, make it impossible to pursue any detailed research into their records.
26   The records of Annandale Estates, for example, are vast, and although the Historical Manuscripts Commission have twice (in 1895 and again c.1968) spent many hours poring over them, there are many records relating to the last three centuries that have never been looked at.
27   The titles to Bonshaw, for example, also include titles to a number of other properties which have at various times passed through the family's hands (See Reid, R. C. 'The Bonshaw Titles', TDGAS, 3rd Ser., XXXVII, 48-61).

CHAPTER 1

FAMILIES OF THE WEST MARCH AND THEIR LANDS

When David I became king in 1124, he determined to introduce the order and discipline of the Anglo-Norman system of government to Scotland. This was the 'feudal' system, with which he had become familiar during his youth at the English court, and which he had subsequently employed in the administration of his English estates as Earl of Huntingdon. To assist him in this task, he invited various Normans and other friends, whom he had met at court, or who were his English vassals, to come north to Scotland, where he gave them generous grants of land on which to settle.

Foremost among these newcomers was Robert de Brus, a powerful Yorkshire lord and close friend, with whom David had been brought up at the English court. To Brus, David granted 'Estrahanent [Annandale], and all the land from the march of Dunegal de Stranit [Nithsdale] even to the march of Randulf Meschin [Lord of Carlisle, and later Earl of Chester, who held a large part of Cumberland]'.[1] How much time Brus spent in Annandale is not clear, but he and his younger son, Robert de Brus, who succeeded him in Annandale in 1136, in turn granted large tracts of their lands to friends and vassals from their English estates, many of whom were themselves of Norman origin. These grantees became vassals of the Bruces in Annandale, and thus, as Croft Dickinson relates, 'a French-speaking aristocracy was established which administered a new, precise and orderly rule'.[2]

THE 12th AND 13th CENTURIES

Familiar names in Annandale in the 12th century, most of whom were followers of the Bruces, were Bosco (or Bois), Corri, Carnoto (Charteris), Crossebi (Crosbie), Dunwithie (Dinwiddie), Flamanc (Fleming), Franciscus (French), Heriz (Herries), Hodelm (Hoddom), Gardin (Jardine), Joneston (Johnston), Kirkpatrick, Locard, Ross and Torthorald. Some of these families, such as Carnoto, Graham, Heriz and Locard brought their Anglo-Norman names with them, occasionally passing them on to their lands (e.g. Locard to Locardebi, or Lockerbie); some, such as Fleming and French, took names descriptive of their origin; and some, such as Johnston and Kirkpatrick, took their designation from their lands (John's-Toun) or a feature there (Kirk-Patrick).

The Bruces themselves settled first at Annan, but later moved to Lochmaben in Central Annandale. They also built a stronghold at Castlemilk and another at Auldton, near Moffat.[3] All these castles were of the motte-and-bailey variety. Other families found in Lower Annandale were the Crosbies, Herries, Richard de Penresax, Udard de Hodelm, and Gilbert de Johnston (2nd of Lochwood), who, c.1194, acquired the use of some land near Annan.[4] Early in the following century Adam de Crosbie quitclaimed some land at Cummertrees in exchange for a tenement at Gretna,[5] and about the same time Robert de Crossebi received a right of commonty in the wood of Stapleton.[6] The Flemings settled a little further east in Kirtleside, where they are later found in possession of lands in the vicinity of Kirkconnel, as well as giving their name to the old parish of Kirkpatrick-Fleming, further down the Kirtle. It was during the 13th century

that a branch of the Murrays settled at Murraythwaite, near Dalton.

The first incomers to settle at Lockerbie were evidently the Locards, who gave their name to the lands; but they did not stay long, and c.1150 Robert de Brus granted the lands to Robert de Carlyle. Then, in 1198, following a dispute over their lands, the Carlyles quitclaimed Lockerbie to the Bruces in exchange for the lands of Kinmount, near Annan.[7] Other families who settled in Central Annandale included the Corries, who took their name from the lands of Corrie;[8] Henry de Graham, who held the lordship of Hutton before 1214;[9] the Jardines of Applegarth; the Dinwiddies; and the Rosses, a Norman family from Yorkshire who acquired lands along the Kinnel Water. The Boscos held the lordship of Dryfesdale, and during the 13th century they also obtained possession of some lands in the Kinnel valley.[10]

Further up Annandale were the Johnstons, who evidently acquired their original lands of 'John's toun' – where their caput later became known as 'Lochwood' – from the Bruces.[11] Beyond them was Ivo de Kirkpatrick, who is also said to have come north with the Bruces, and by them was granted the lands of Kirkpatrick (Juxta), also on the west side of Annandale.[12] There the Kirkpatricks built the strongholds of Garpol motte and, later, Auchencass.[13] Another family who settled in Upper Annandale was the Frenches, who acquired some lands at Moffat from the Bruces,[14] though little is heard of them there until several centuries later, when they held Frenchland.

The lands between Lochmaben and Dumfries were acquired by the Torthorwalds of that Ilk, who took their name from the place, and the Mandevilles of Tinwald. Roger de Mandeville was a Norman, who was granted the barony of Tinwald after his marriage to Affrica, a natural daughter of William the Lion.[15] Adjoining his lands to the north was the barony of Amisfield, which had been acquired by the Carnoto, or Charteris, family, probably from the Bruces, during the time of David I.

Nithsdale was the territory of Dunegal – referred to in the Bruces' original grant –, a Celtic lord whose principal stronghold is said to have been at Morton, near Thornhill.[16] It was from his eldest son, Rodolf (or Randolph) of Stranid (Nithsdale), that the family of Randolph were descended, and from Edgar, the son of Dunegal's second son, Duvenald, that the Edgars likewise took their name.[17] The Edgars inherited the castle and half the barony of Sanquhar in Upper Nithsdale, as well as Dunscore and other lands further south, while the other half of Sanquhar came into the possession of the Rosses, from Helmsley in Yorkshire, following the marriage of Robert de Ros to William the Lion's daughter, Isobel. The Rosses' caput seems to have been at Ryehill.[18]

During the 13th century other families began to settle in Nithsdale. These included the Herries, who already had lands in Annandale, and Sir John Comyn of Badenoch, who added the lands of Dalswinton and Duncow to his already vast estates in the north. It was probably Sir John who built the castle of Dalswinton to assist him as Justiciar of Galloway, an office to which he was appointed c.1258.[19] Further north lay the extensive lands of Closeburn. These had passed from Dunegal to his younger son Duvenald, but by 1232 they had come into the possession of Ivo de Kirkpatrick, who received a charter of confirmation of the lands from Alexander II in that year.[20]

Galloway was held by Fergus, Lord of Galloway.[21] After his death in 1161, the lordship was shared between his sons, Uchtred and Gilbert, until Uchtred's murder by his brother in 1174, when Uchtred's son Roland succeeded as Lord of all Galloway. Roland had married Elena, the heiress of Hugh de Morville, Constable of Scotland, and through her inherited both the lands of Senwick, on the west side of Kirkcudbright Bay, and the office of Constable. In due course Roland was succeeded by his son Alan (d.1234), whose youngest daughter, Dervorguilla, was to become the celebrated wife of John Balliol of Barnard Castle. It was as part of Dervorguilla's patrimony that the Balliols acquired the lands of Buittle.

Meanwhile, Alan's second, but eldest surviving, daughter, Helen, married Roger de Quincy, Earl of Winchester. By this marriage, De Quincy acquired the hereditary office of Constable of Scotland, that part of northern Galloway which included The Glenkens and Lochinvar, and the lands of Senwick;[22] and it was through the marriage of their daughter and co-heiress Elizabeth that the Forest of Glenken ('The Glenkens') came into the possession of the Comyns, Earls of Buchan,[23] while Senwick was shared equally between the three De Quincy heiresses. The 7th Earl of Buchan subsequently granted half The Glenkens and Lochinvar to John Maxwell, younger of Caerlaverock, who in 1297 granted them to Sir Adam Gordon of Stitchill, the progenitor of the Gordons of Lochinvar, later Viscounts Kenmure.[24] Although the lands of Earlstoun also formed part of The Glenkens, they were not included in the grant, and there is no evidence as to who possessed them at this time.

At the eastern extremity of the West March lay Liddesdale, Eskdale, Ewesdale, Wauchopedale and what became known as 'The Debateable Land', a disputed tract of land on the border between Scotland and England. A large part of Lower Liddesdale was granted by David I to Ranulf de Soulis, his cup-bearer, a powerful Norman lord from Northamptonshire, who built there the great motte-and-bailey castle of Liddel.[25] His descendants subsequently acquired another stronghold at Hermitage, further up the valley,[26] and by the end of the 13th century they were also in possession of the lands of Westerker in Eskdale and the castle and barony of Durisdeer in Nithsdale.[27]

Lower Eskdale was granted to the Rosedales. Very little is known about the family, but they are thought to have come from Rosedale in Yorkshire. Further up the valley, David I granted the barony of Wauchope to Walter de Lindsay; the barony of Staplegorton to Geoffrey de Coningburgh;[28] and a large part of Upper Eskdale and Ewesdale to Robert Avenell, an Anglo-Norman from Northamptonshire, who is thought to have had his caput at Westerker.[29] It was at Staplegorton c.1240-50 that David I gave to Robert de Brus a charter of the 'forest' of Annandale, 'as far as his land stretches towards Stradnitt [Nithsdale] and towards Clud [Clyde]'.[30] Roger Avenell granted some of his lands in Eskdale to the abbey of Melrose, a grant that was confirmed by William the Lion c.1165-71.[31] These included Tanlawhill, which was later united with other lands into the barony of Dumfedling. On Roger's death in 1243, the remainder of his property in Eskdale passed by marriage to the Grahams of Dalkeith. Some of the lands are then said to have passed by marriage to the Douglases, while Westerker was disponed to the de Soulis (supra). A large part of Ewesdale, however, was acquired by the Lovels, possibly by marriage, when they obtained the lands and manor of Unthank.[32] The Lovels, who are thought

to have come from Somerset, had held the adjacent Lordship of Hawick since the previous century.

It was c.1266 that the Maxwells first received a grant of land at Langholm from Sir William de Coningburgh. However, in 1281 this land was resigned in favour of Sir John Lindsay of Wauchope, and it was not until two centuries later that the Maxwells were again in possession.

THE CHURCH

Another important landholder at this time was the church. In 1142, David I founded the monastery of Dundrennan on the Galloway coast, and endowed it with a generous grant of lands.[33] His example was later followed by Uchtred, who, in 1174, founded the convent of Lincluden at Dumfries;[34] he also gave the extensive lands of Kirkewinni (Kirkgunzeon) in south-east Galloway to the abbey of Holm Cultram in Cumbria.[35] In addition, Holm Cultram received a grant of the lands of Conheath and Caerlaverock from Ranulf of Nithsdale;[36] but c.1225 the abbey gave up these lands and granted them to Sir John Maxwell of that Ilk.[37] Later in the century, Caerlaverock superseded the Maxwell's original lands of Maccuswell, in Roxburghshire, as the family's principal seat.

The thirteenth century saw the founding of two more abbeys in the West March: Holywood and Sweetheart. Holywood is said to have been founded by the Kirkconnells of that Ilk,[38] who later in the century gave the abbey of Holm Cultram several grants of land from their Kirkconnell estates. Sweetheart Abbey was founded by Dervorguilla c.1273 in memory of her husband, John Balliol.[39] It was endowed with various lands, including the churches of Buittle, New Abbey, Loch Kinder, Kirkpatrick Durham, Crossmichael and Kirkcolm.[40] There was also a priory at Canonbie, which was founded by Turgot de Rosedale sometime before 1220,[41] and a friary at Dumfries, which is said to have been founded by Alan of Galloway, and was certainly supported by his daughter Dervorguilla.[42]

Other abbeys further afield also acquired lands in the West March, though the exact date of these acquisitions is rarely known. One of these was the abbey of Melrose, founded by David I in 1136. Towards the end of the 12th century, Thomas Colville leased the abbey the lands of Kar, or Keresban (Carsphairn), which formed a part of the lands of Dalmellington.[43] Alan, Lord of Galloway, subsequently exchanged these lands for some lands in the the Lammermuirs, and then let Kar to the abbey of Vaudey in Lincolnshire, who later gave the lands back to Melrose. Melrose also acquired some land at Friars Carse, in Nithsdale, where they established a cell,[44] and the lands in Eskdale already referred to.

Churches held lands too, and some of these were tied to religious foundations. The Bruces, for example, gave a number of churches in Annandale to the priory of Guisborough in Yorkshire, which they had founded;[45] Fergus, Lord of Galloway, and his son Uchtred granted a number of churches in Galloway to the abbey of Holyrood;[46] and the first of the Edgars is said to have given the churches of Dalgarnock and Dunscore to the nearby abbey of Holywood, or Dercongal.[47] The abbey at Kelso was also the recipient of many churches, including Dumfries and Morton in Nithsdale, Dumgree and Trailflat in Annandale, and Staplegorton.[48]

As a direct result of the Crusades, two new orders of knights were established, the Knights Hospitaller and the Knights Templar. The former, who were founded in 1092 when they built their first hospital in Jerusalem, were dedicated to looking after and providing hospitality for pilgrims to the Holy Land, while the Templars, who were founded in 1118, had the task of building and guarding the roads to the Holy Land. Both are said to have been introduced into Scotland by David I, who presumably gave them their first grants of land. In the West March, the Hospitallers established a hospital at Trailtrow,[49] while the Templars held lands at Lochmaben, Templand, Moffat, Dalry, and at least a dozen other locations.[50]

THE WAR OF INDEPENDENCE AND THE 14th CENTURY

The War of Independence and associated events wrought considerable changes in land ownership in the West March, quite apart from the lands and offices granted by the English to their vassals and supporters during the period of English occupation. The accession of the Bruces to the throne meant that the lordship of Annandale became merged with the Crown, until it was conferred by Bruce, first on his brother Edward, who was killed in Ireland in 1318, and then, in 1324, on his nephew, Sir Thomas Randolph, Earl of Moray and Lord of Nithsdale.[51] On the death of the 3rd Earl without male issue in 1346, Annandale was divided between his two daughters, the elder of whom, Agnes, married Patrick, Earl of Dunbar and March, who became Lord of Annandale.[52] He was succeeded in Annandale, as well as in Morton and Tibbers in Nithsdale, by his son George, 10th Earl of Dunbar; but in 1409 George finally forfeited the lordship of Annandale, which was then granted to the Earl of Douglas.[53] Tibbers had been held by the Siwards, a Saxon family, during the latter half of the 13th century, but had been forfeited by them for siding with the English.[54]

At the beginning of the 14th century, the lands and castle of Cockpool, with the lands of Ruthwell and Comlongon, on the Solway coast, were held by the Duncurrys. From them they passed to William Murray, nephew of Sir Thomas Randolph, who received a charter of half the lands from Sir Thomas c.1329; and his descendants, later Earls of Annandale, and successors, the Viscounts Stormont and Earls of Mansfield, continued to hold them until the latter half of the twentieth century.[55]

One of William Murray's neighbours was Thomas de Carruthers of Mouswald. He was granted the lands of Mouswald and Appletreethwaite by Robert the Bruce c.1320; and in 1351 his son received a charter of the lands of Middlebie from David II. The family subsequently obtained further lands at Mouswald from John de Raffles – whose family had been in possession of the adjacent lands of Raffles since before 1245[56] – , and extensive estates elsewhere in Dumfriesshire, including the lands of Cornal and Logan-tenement[57] near Moffat. Another branch of the family was the Carruthers of Holmains, descended from Roger de Carruthers, who received a charter of the lands of Little Dalton and Holmains from the Lord of Annandale in 1375.

The Carlyles seem to have settled in the West March early in the 14th century, when they are found in possession of the lands of Luce, Locharwood and Kinmount;[58] and it was probably not long after when they also acquired the lands of Brydekirk. The Corries were also expanding their territory around this time; by the middle of the century they had split into two distinct branches, the Corries of that Ilk and the Corries of Newbie and Kelwood, near Annan.

In Upper Annandale, the Moffats, who took their name from the town, had become an established family, two of their number rendering homage to Edward I in 1296,[59] while, c.1315, the Lindsays of Crawford were rewarded by Bruce with a grant of the lands of Blacklaw and other lands in Evandale. Meanwhile, the Kirkpatricks' castle at Auchencass had been destroyed

by the English. It was partly in compensation for this, and reputedly partly through his wife, that Sir Humphrey de Kirkpatrick received a grant of the lands of Torthorwald from Bruce in 1321, the Torthorwald family having forfeited them for supporting the English. Later, the Kirkpatricks also acquired the lands of Kirkmichael.

Great changes were also taking place in the east of the March at this time. William de Soulis of Liddesdale forfeited all his estates in 1320, and his uncle, Sir John de Soulis, Guardian of Scotland, died about the same time, leaving no issue.[60] This left a large part of Upper Eskdale, as well as Liddesdale, nominally without a superior. William had held half the barony of Westerker, while the other half, together with the barony of Durisdeer in Nithsdale, had been leased to Sir John by Sir Ingram de Gynes.[61] William's lands were now granted by Bruce to the 'Good Sir James' Douglas, while Sir John's portion of Westerker was granted to the abbey of Melrose; then in 1324 Sir James acquired the latter portion too.[62] Sir James also acquired the lands of Polmoody, near Moffat, in 1318; the barony of Staplegorton from the Lindsays c.1319; and the barony of Buittle in 1324, the last having been forfeited by the Balliols.[63] Later, Sir James's brother Hugh, 'the Dull', who succeeded to the lordship of Douglas in 1333, granted Liddesdale and Westerker to his kinsman, Sir William Douglas of Lothian, 'the Knight of Liddesdale'.[64] Sir William also acquired the Ewesdale lands of the Lovels after their forfeiture in 1341.[65] It was from the Douglases that the Glendinnings obtained the lease of Westerker.

Another family who first appeared on the Scottish side of the Border around this time was the Armstrongs, who began to settle in the Debateable Land and in the area around the confluence of the rivers Esk and Liddel. Theirs was a precarious and violent existence, especially as the English were bitterly opposed to any occupation of the Debateable Land, so the Armstrongs looked first to the Douglases, and later to the Maxwells, for protection.

In Galloway, one of the unwitting victims of the War of Independence was the abbey of Holm Cultram, which lost all its possessions north of the Border. Some of their lands were subsequently held by the Balliols, until their forfeiture, when they were granted to the Douglases; others were acquired by the Herries. However, although Bruce granted the superiority of the lands and castle of Buittle to Sir James Douglas in 1324/5, the Balliols retained intermittent possession until 1354, when they were finally ousted, a year after the Earl of Douglas received a new charter from David II. The Douglases also held the lands of Terregles for a while. Then in 1357/8 David II granted the lands of Terregles to Sir John Herries, and in 1367 the lands of Kirkgunzeon.[66] These two properties thereafter became the principal residences of the family, later Lords Herries of Terregles.

Not long afterwards, in 1369, David II granted to Sir Archibald Douglas, 'the Grim', later 3rd Earl of Douglas, 'all our lands of Galloway' from the Cree to the Nith. He was charged with bringing the unruly Gallovidians to order, and in effect made Lord of Eastern Galloway. He built Threave Castle as his base. Three years later, he purchased the other half of Galloway from the Flemings to become Lord of (all) Galloway, and received a new charter from Robert II confirming his lordship. He also served the church well, for in the same year that he became Lord of Eastern Galloway he built a hospital at the abbey of Holywood, which he endowed with lands at Troqueer and Crossmichael;[67] and in 1389, the same year that he succeeded as Earl of Douglas, he founded the magnificent collegiate church of Lincluden to succeed Uchtred's earlier convent on the site.[68]

Other lands in Nithsdale obtained by the Douglases during the 14th century included the barony of Preston, on the Solway coast, and Drumlanrig. Preston was acquired by the 'Good Sir James' Douglas c.1325, and, in 1374/5, granted by his nephew, the 1st Earl of Douglas, to his kinsman Sir James Douglas of Dalkeith. The barony then remained with Sir James's descendants until the forfeiture of the 4th Earl of Morton in 1581, when it was granted to the Maxwells.[69] The lands of Drumlanrig had formed part of the estates of the Earls of Mar until, sometime before 1333, they came into the possession of the 1st Earl of Douglas's father, Sir Archibald Douglas. They were subsequently given by the 2nd Earl to one of his natural sons, William Douglas, 1st of Drumlanrig, whose descendants – now represented by the Dukes of Buccleuch and Queensberry – have held them ever since. It was from the Douglases of Drumlanrig that the Douglases of Coshogle sprang. Coshogle had been in the possession of the Lorrain family until their forfeiture early in the 14th century, when it was granted to the Blairs of that Ilk. Then in the 15th century Coshogle passed to the Wallaces before being acquired by Archibald Douglas, 1st of Coshogle, a younger son of Drumlanrig.

On the forfeiture of the Comyns, the barony of Dalswinton was granted by King Robert the Bruce to Sir Walter Stewart, a younger son of Sir John Stewart of Bonkyl, and his descendants continued to hold it until it was finally sold to the Romes in 1624. The old castle, however, never fully recovered from the War of Independence, and sometime around the turn of the 15th century the Stewarts moved their principal residence to Garlies, another of their properties, in Galloway.

At the beginning of the century, the barony of Glencairn formed part of the Nithsdale estates of the Earls of Dunbar. The lands subsequently came into the possession of the Danielstons, from whom they passed by marriage to Sir William Cunningham of Kilmaurs, whose descendants became Earls of Glencairn. The Cunninghams also acquired the neighbouring lands of Snade, which had been granted by Robert the Bruce c.1320 to one John, son of Lochlan.[70] Early in the following century, Snade was made a barony in its own right, before passing by descent to the Hays of Yester.

Other families who first appeared in Upper Nithsdale in the 14th century were the Eccles, the Crichtons and the Menzies. The Eccles were a small family, who held the lands of that name near Thornhill at the beginning of the century.[71] In 1500 they also acquired the lands of Lochrutton and Hills.

The Crichtons obtained one half of the barony of Sanquhar through the marriage of William Crichton to Isabella, daughter and co-heiress of Sir Robert de Ros of Sanquhar. These lands fell into the hands of the English during the War of Independence, but were later recovered by Crichton; and he subsequently also acquired the other portion of the barony, which, together with the principal manor, had been acquired by Richard Edgar through his marriage to Sir Robert de Ros's elder daughter, Margaret.[72] The Crichtons also obtained some lands near Moniaive, including the lands of (Old) Crawfordton. They were the ancestors of the Lords Crichton of Sanquhar, Earls of Dumfries and Marquesses of Bute.

It is not clear how Sir Ingram de Gynes lost the barony of Durisdeer (supra), but sometime before 1329 it was granted by King Robert the Bruce to Sir Alexander de Meyners (Menzies);[73] and at the same time, or very shortly afterwards, Sir Alexander also obtained the lands of Enoch, where he built himself a new stronghold. Thereafter the combined lands became known as the barony of Enoch, and it was as such that Robert Menzies received a new charter of the lands from Robert II in 1376.[74]

THE ARMS OF THE BRUCES

One interesting sidelight on the Bruces' association with Annandale is the number of families in the West March whose 'arms' are derived from those of the Bruces. The arms of the Bruces were: *Or, a saltire and chief gules*. It is not surprizing that this became the arms of the Lordship of Annandale and of the town of Annan; but the saltire and chief also became the basis for the arms of the Drysdales, Griersons, Jardines, Johnstons, Kirkpatricks, Moffats and Torthorwalds,[75] with differences of tinctures and charges to identify each family.

THE 15TH CENTURY

The most significant event to occur in the fifteenth century was the fall of the Douglases, and the subsequent rise of the Maxwells and Johnstons and their allies. It was also during this century that the smaller families began to make their mark on history, as records of their activities and land tenure became more frequent.

The Earl of March forfeited the lordship of Annandale in 1400 for his support of Henry IV of England, but it was restored in 1408, only to be finally taken away the following year.[76] It was then granted to the 4th Earl of Douglas.[77] But after the 9th Earl of Douglas and his brothers rebelled against the Crown in 1455, they forfeited not only the lordship of Annandale, but also Threave Castle and the lordship of Galloway, as well as their estates in Eskdale.[78] The Earldom of March and lordship of Annandale were then bestowed on the King's second son, Alexander Stewart, who was made Duke of Albany; and he continued to hold Annandale until he too joined the Douglases and rebelled against the Crown in 1483, when the lordship of Annandale was again forfeited.[79] Thereafter it remained with the Crown.

Soon after the Earl of Douglas acquired Annandale in 1409, he appointed Sir Herbert Maxwell hereditary Steward of Annandale. This was confirmed by the Crown in 1440.[80] Thus, when the Douglases suffered forfeiture in 1455, the 2nd Lord Maxwell, who had sided with the Crown, retained the office of Steward, and not long afterwards he recovered the family's former lands in Eskdale. It is not clear whether he had any control over Lochmaben Castle at this time, but when, a century later, his possession of the castle was challenged, he argued that the keeping of Lochmaben was hereditary as the Steward of Annandale's residence.[81]

Other properties which were acquired by the Maxwells during this century included Carnsalloch, which they obtained from the Stewarts of Dalswinton;[82] Kirkconnell, which they acquired by marriage with the heiress of the Kirkconnells of that Ilk; and Tinwald, which they acquired partly by marriage with one of the heiresses of the Mandevilles, and partly by purchase from the other three heiresses.[83]

The 3rd Lord Maxwell's brother John became Abbot of Holywood, and his son John Abbot of Dundrennan. It was while the elder John was in office, in 1495, that Lord Maxwell was appointed bailie of all the abbey's lands,[84] and eight years later he was also made bailie of all the lands belonging to Sweetheart Abbey.[85] His son, the 4th Lord Maxwell, subsequently added bailiery jurisdiction over the lands belonging to the abbeys of Dundrennan and Tongland, the Provostry of Lincluden and the Preceptory of Trailtrow.[86] Many of these lands were later granted to the Lords Maxwell in liferent, and ultimately converted to feus.

While the Maxwells recovered their former lands in Eskdale, the lordship of Eskdale itself was granted by the Crown to George Douglas, 4th Earl of Angus;[87] and in 1472 the bailieship of the lands of Liddesdale, Eskdale and Ewesdale was granted by the 5th Earl to David Scott of Buccleuch and his eldest son, David, who, the previous year, had married the Earl's sister.[88] In 1484 Buccleuch also acquired from Melrose Abbey bailiery jurisdiction over the abbey's lands in Eskdale,[89] an office that became hereditary in 1524 and, after the Reformation, a temporal lordship.[90]

The Johnstons were another family who benefitted from the forfeiture of the Douglases and their allies, and in particular from the forfeiture of the Corries for their part in the Douglas rebellion of 1484. They seem to have acquired the major share of the Corries' lands in Annandale and Kirtleside, including the lands of Kirkpatrick-Fleming and Gretna, though the Corries of Newbie and Kelwood did not suffer forfeiture.[91] The Johnstons were also granted some of the Douglases' lands in Galloway, including Buittle and Senwick, for their part in the siege of Threave in 1455.[92]

Although the Bells first appeared in Dumfriesshire early in the 14th century, it was not until the second half of the 15th century, when they acquired lands in the parish of Middlebie, that they became established. They soon spread to dominate the whole parish, the principal branches being the Bells of Kirkconnel and the Bells of Blackethouse. Later, Kirkconnel passed first to the Irvings, and then to the Maxwells.

The Irvings had been settled at Bonshaw, in Kirtleside, at least since the latter half of the 13th century, but it was not until after the battle of the Kirtle in 1484, when the Johnstons became their new superiors – and no doubt helped by the very handsome sum obtained for the ranson of William Musgrave of Edenhall[93] –, that their fortunes were transformed, and the family began its rapid expansion, until, by the middle of the following century, the Johnston-Irving alliance became one of the dominant powers in the West March.[94] Another family that appears in possession of lands in Kirtleside at this time is Glencorse of that Ilk, who held the lands of Woodhouse.

Meanwhile, the Grahams continued to expand their territory in Dryfesdale, the Grahams of Mosskeswra, Gillesbie and Thornik being the most prominent branches of the family.[95] The Grahams of Fintry, in Stirlingshire, also apparently acquired by marriage early in the century some of the Lovels former lands in Ewesdale, but in 1457 they disponed them to the Earl of Angus.[96] Another family found in Ewesdale early in the century was a branch of the Frasers of Teviotdale. Their lands passed to the Littles in 1426.[97]

In Nithsdale, William Carlyle, eldest son of Sir John Carlyle of Kinmount, inherited the lands and barony of Torthorwald through his wife, Elizabeth Kirkpatrick, co-heiress of Torthorwald and Kirkpatrick, c.1425.[98] Then, in 1436, William agreed an exchange with his brother-in-law, Thomas Graham of Auchencass, the spouse of Elizabeth's late sister, Janet Kirkpatrick, whereby William agreed to give up Elizabeth's share of the Kirkpatricks' ancestral lands of Auchencass in return for Janet's interest in the lands of Roucan.[99] William must, however, have retained a share in some of the lands in Upper Annandale, as Kinnelhead, Holmshaw and Cogrie were still included in the estates of the Lords Carlyle in 1575.[100]

There was a third Kirkpatrick sister and heiress, Isobel, who, in 1412, married Gilbert Grierson, younger of Lag, and

brought to that family the lands of Rockhall and Collin.[101] The Griersons first appear in the West March c.1400, when Gilbert Grierson was granted the lands and barony of Aird, in Galloway, by the Earl of March.[102] Not long afterwards, Gilbert purchased the lands of Lag and Bardonan. Lag became the family's principal residence, and so it remained until it was finally eclipsed by Rockhall early in the 17th century.

In 1372 Sir James Douglas, 1st of Dalkeith, married Agnes Dunbar, sister of the 10th Earl of Dunbar, and received as part of her dowry the lands and castle of Morton.[103] Sir James was granted a charter of these lands by Robert II in 1401,[104] but his superior was still the Earl of Dunbar until 1434, when the 11th Earl forfeited his estates. Then in 1440, Sir James Douglas, 2nd of Dalkeith, received a new charter of the lands of Morton, which were henceforth to be held directly from the Crown.[105]

On the west side of Nithsdale, the Kirkhaugh family – later contracted to 'Kirko', and finally 'Kirk' – first appeared in Glenesslin, where they quickly spread to dominate the valley.[106] The principal branches of the family were the Kirkos of Chapel, Bogrie and Sundaywell.

Further west, the Gordons of Lochinvar were consolidating their position. Soon after the turn of the century, the 4th Earl of Douglas granted Sir Alexander Gordon of Stitchill a new charter of his lands and lordships in the Forest of Glenken,[107] and he also gave him the lands of Kenmure, the barony of Balmaclellan, and Shirmers, on the east side of Loch Ken. But nearly half a century was apparently to pass before the family finally left Berwickshire and settled in Galloway. William Gordon then moved to Lochinvar, while his eldest son, Sir John, built himself a new stronghold at Kenmure.

Meanwhile, the neighbouring estate of Earlstoun, which had also formed part of the Douglas Lordship of Galloway, came into the possession of the Hepburns of Hailes; and sometime before 1482, the 1st Lord Hailes granted it in feu to John Sinclair of Herdmanston.

By the end of the century, the lands of Dundeugh and Kar to the north, which had formerly been held by the abbey of Melrose, were in the possession of the MacNaughts. They were an old-established Galloway family, who had other lands elsewhere. They remained in possession until the middle of the 17th century, when Dundeugh was acquired by the Gordons.

Other families that first come on record in Eastern Galloway at this time include Cairns, Campbell, Livingstone, Morison and Lindsay. It is not known exactly when the Cairns family first acquired lands in Galloway, but it was in 1456 that John Cairns, Collector of Customs at Linlithgow, resigned the office that both he and his father before him had held, and retired to his Galloway estates. There he built Orchardton Tower. The lands remained with his descendants until 1560, when the male line ended with three daughters. Thereafter, the lands remained divided for nearly sixty years, before the Maxwells of Spottes were able to purchase the various parts and once again reunite the estate.

The Campbells of Loudon were in possession of the lands of Edingham and Culloch in the middle of the 15th century. It is not known when or how they acquired them, but in 1465 they granted the superiority to Alexander Livingstone of Duchray, in exchange for his lands in Ayrshire, and the lands remained with the Livingstones of Little Airds (later called 'Livingstone') until finally sold, first to William McClellan of Crofts, and then to Alexander M'Ghie of Balmaghie, in 1591. The lands themselves were held in feu by the Morisons.

A branch of the Lindsay family acquired the lands of Dunrod, in the parish of Borgue, sometime during the 14th century.[108] From them are said to be descended the Lindsays of Fairgirth, who first appear on record in the following century; and it was John Lindsay, a younger son of James Lindsay of Fairgirth, who settled at Auchenskeoch, beside the Southwick Water, late in that century, and became the first of the Lindsays of Auchenskeoch.

The Maclellans first appeared in Galloway at the beginning of the 14th century, and a century later are found settled in and around Kirkcudbright, where they were soon taking an active part in the civic life of the burgh. The Maclellans of Bombie came to be recognized as the senior branch of the family, and in 1466 William Maclellan of Bombie was elected Provost of the burgh.[109]

In the same year, another branch of the Maclellans acquired some of the barony of Balmaclellan from the Griersons of Lag, who had earlier obtained it from the Gordons; but although the lands of Barscobe formed part of the barony, it is not clear whether they were included at this time. Barscobe is not mentioned as being in the possession of the Maclellans before 1502.

Although the families of 'de Cumstoun' and 'de Twynholm' are on record c.1300,[110] Walter de Twinham being Robert the Bruce's Chancellor in 1329,[111] possession of the lands of Cumstoun and Twynholm subsequently passed to the Crown, possibly after the forfeiture of the Douglases, and it was the Crown which granted them to John Kennedy of Blairquhan when he was made Steward of Kirkcudbright in 1463.

THE 16th CENTURY

With the Reformation in 1560, the vast landholdings of the church, and of the monasteries in particular, finally came to an end. It was a change that had been forseen since the end of the previous century, when the process of transferring ownership to the lay lords had begun. In the West March, the Maxwells were one of the principal beneficiaries, the main concentrations of monastic lands being in Nithsdale. There the Maxwells added to their already extensive estates such properties as Cowhill, Portrack and Fourmerkland, all of which had belonged to the abbey of Holywood, while in Annandale they acquired the lands that had belonged to the Preceptory of Trailtrow.[112]

In 1510, the Maxwells were also granted, under reversion 'for great sums of money', many lands in Annandale that had come into the Crown's possession by forfeiture or default.[113] Three years later, following the Scots' disastrous defeat at Flodden, Lord Maxwell was made Captain and Keeper of Threave Castle and Steward of the Stewartry of Kirkcudbright; and in 1522, in addition to his hereditary office of Steward of Annandale, he was made Keeper of Lochmaben Castle.[114] He also acquired a lease of Wauchopedale in 1525, which five years later was converted to a grant on condition that he 'build and repair the house, tower and fortalice of Wauchope', and retain it for the King's service;[115] and in 1529 James V granted him the lands of Spottes, which had been resigned by Patrick Sinclair of Spottes.[116]

In 1527, Edward Maxwell, a great-grandson of the 2nd Lord Maxwell, purchased the lands of Lochrutton and Hills from Douglas of Drumlanrig, who in turn had purchased them from the Eccles five years earlier. It was his second son, Edward, who subsequently acquired the lands of Drumcoltran from Lord Herries. Drumcoltran, which had at one time formed part of the lands of Kirkgunzeon held by the abbey of Holm Cultram, had been granted to Sir John Herries of Terregles in 1367.

The other family who made enormous gains of territory during this century was the Johnstons. The forfeiture of the Douglases and their allies after the battle of the Kirtle, in 1484, had been the turning point in their fortunes, but it was during the 16th century that they rose to compete with the Maxwells, both for land and the power of public office – a situation that was to be ruthlessly exploited by the English, who thereby sought to weaken the unity of the Scots' resistance to their inroads.[117] By the end of the century, lands held by the Johnstons included the whole of the parish of Johnston; Biggarts, Easter Kinnelhead, Craigielands, Chapel, Lochhouse, Milton, Boreland, and other lands in Kirkpatrick Juxta; Raecleugh, Mellingshaw, Blacklaw, Craigieburn, Cornal, Breconside and most of Moffat, in the parish of Moffat; Kirkbriderig, Glenae, Hutton-under-the-Moor, Corrie, Sibbaldbie, Elshieshields, Broats, Wauchope, Staplegorton, and much of the parishes of Annan and Gretna.

The Corries still held the lands of Newbie and Kelwood; but sometime in the 16th century the male line at Newbie died out, whereupon Newbie was purchased by the Johnstons of Gretna, and from them it passed to the Johnstons of that Ilk early in the following century. Kelwood was finally sold c.1610, when that branch of the family moved to Ayrshire.[118]

On the death of the 3rd Lord Herries without male issue in 1543, the family's vast estates passed to his three daughters, the eldest of whom, Agnes, Baroness Herries of Terregles, married Sir John Maxwell, the Master of Maxwell. Eventually, Sir John acquired the shares of the other two daughters, thereby reuniting the lands,[119] and became 4th Lord Herries. The estates at this time comprised the lands of Terregles, Kirkgunzeon, Ur, Hoddom, Ecclefechan, Warmanbie, Scales, Tundergarth, Hutton, and parts of the lands of Lockerbie, Morton, Evandale and Moffatdale.[120]

It was from Lady Agnes Herries, in 1549, that 'Duke Richie' Irving, of the Irvings of Trailtrow, received a grant of one third of the lands of Hoddom.[121] There he built his stronghold, 'Duke's Tower',[122] and from him were descended the Irvings (later Bell-Irvings) of Whitehill and Knockhill, both of which stood on the lands granted.[123] Meanwhile, another branch of the Irving family was consolidating its position in Eskdale at Irvine and Auchenrivock, and over some of the former Debateable Land immediately to the west.

One of the smaller families to appear in Upper Annandale were the Weirs. In 1510/11 the new barony of Crawford-Lindsay was granted by the Crown to George Douglas, eldest son of the Earl of Angus,[124] and five years later he let the lands of Raecleugh, which formed part of the barony, to the Weirs. The lands were forfeited by the Earl of Angus in 1528, and in 1542 leased to the Johnstons; but Angus was restored soon after, and in 1546 he granted the Weirs a new charter. Later, however, the Johnstons again got possession, and this time the Weirs disappeared from the scene.

On the forfeiture of John Lindsay of Wauchope for treason in 1505/6, his lands in Wauchopedale and Ewesdale were granted to Lord Home.[125] Wauchopedale was eventually restored to the Lindsays in 1593, and was then retained until 1707.[126]

Another family that was common in Ewesdale, Upper Eskdale and Wauchopedale in the 16th century was the Batesons, Beatisons or Beatties. Among the many properties they held in the latter part of the century was Tanlawhill, which in the following century passed first to the Scotts and then to the Elliots. Another property that eventually passed to the Elliots was Arkleton, in Ewesdale, which had been granted to the Armstrongs in 1537.

In Lower Eskdale, 'Long Will' Graham and his eight sons, who had been banished from Scotland c.1515, settled, and quickly established an unenviable reputation as a thorn in the flesh of both kingdoms.[127] In 1578, Lord Herries reported that they had built 'upoun the verray fronteiris . . . aucht or nyne greit stane houssis, inprynnabill for the Warden of Scotland his power'.[128] However, by this time at least one son was respectably settled in business in Carlisle, and in due course the rest of Long Will's descendants also became respectable. Indeed, Long Will himself was granted lands on the Border by the English Warden on condition that he served the English interest,[129] and it is from his eldest son, Richard Graham in Netherby, that the Grahams, baronets of Esk and Netherby, are descended.[130]

One of the smaller families in Nithsdale that benefitted from the Reformation was the Browns of New Abbey and Carsluith. They appear to have been established in Galloway at an early date, and by the beginning of the 16th century held the tenure of many lands in south-east Galloway, including Landis, from the abbey of Sweetheart.[131] It was at Landis that they built Abbot's Tower. Not long after, Richard Brown, brother of Thomas Brown of Landis, acquired the lands of Carsluith by marriage with Elizabeth Lindsay, Lady Carsluith.[132] Thomas's younger son, John, became abbot of Sweetheart in 1538, and in 1565 he was succeeded by his cousin Gilbert Brown of Carsluith, who was to be the last abbot.[133] It was during the abbacies of John and Gilbert, with the impending arrival of the Reformation, that the abbey's lands were progressively feued out, and, not surprizingly, their kinsmen were among the principal beneficiaries.[134]

Amongst the other smaller families in and around Nithsdale who first appear on record in the 16th century were the Wallaces of Breckonside, in Cairndale, and the M'Millans of Brockloch, in Glenesslin. The latter family were probably a cadet of the M'Millans who occupied the northern part of The Glenkens, where they also had another property with the same name.[135] In each case the amount of land possessed was small, and in consequence the tower-houses which the families built for their own protection were but simple peles. There were other peles in the same area, such as at Auchenfedrick, but the names of the owners have not been discovered.

Meanwhile, in Galloway, the Sinclairs continued in possession of Earlstoun until the end of the 16th century, when the male line failed and the estate passed by marriage to John Gordon of Airds. The Gordons (later Baronets of Earlstoun) took up residence there, and remained in possession until 1745.

At the southern extremity of the valley, the Crown feued half the lands of Balmangan to William Brown, March Pursuivant (and later Albany Herald), and the other half to David Purves, Macer. The feus were later acquired by Gilbert Maclellan of Barmagachan, whose second son settled at Balmangan, and his descendants continued in possession until the end of the 17th century, when the property passed to the Carsons.

The barony of Twynholm, which included Cumstoun, remained with the Kennedys of Blairquhan until 1588, when John Kennedy excambed it with William Maclellan of Gelston for the barony of Remiston in Wigtownshire. It was subsequently acquired by John Hay, Clerk Depute of Edinburgh, and sold by him in 1614 to Sir Robert Maclellan of Bombie.

It was in 1569, a century after William Maclellan of Bombie was first elected Provost of Kirkcudbright, that his descendant, Sir Thomas Maclellan of Bombie, also Provost, acquired the site and remains of the old friary in Kirkcudbright. On this land he built his magnificent new castle, Maclellan's Castle. He also obtained many other lands; but within a century all was lost to the creditors of his descendants.

1 Lawrie, 48-9, 307-10; Gladstone, R. 'The Early Annandale Charters and their strange resting place', TDGAS, 3rd Ser., VI, 145-6.
2 Dickinson, 83.
3 RCAHMS 1920, xxiv; 1997, 194.
4 Bain I, No.606.
5 Ibid, No.1685.
6 Fraser 1894, I, 5.
7 Bain I, No.2666.
8 Johnston, C. 'The Early History of the Corries of Annandale', TDGAS, 3rd Ser., I, 86-98.
9 Reid, R. C. 'The Border Grahams, their Origin and Distribution', TDGAS, 3rd Ser., XXXVIII, 85-113.
10 Reid, R. C. 'De Boys of Dryfesdale', TDGAS, 3rd Ser., XXIII, 82-3.
11 Fraser 1894, I, i-iii.
12 Reid, R. C. 'The Early Kirkpatricks', TDGAS, 3rd Ser., XXX, 61-110.
13 See RCAHMS 1920, Nos.384, 397; 1997, 195-6, 199, 201-3.
14 Bain I, No.705; Macquarrie, A. 'Notes on some Charters of the Bruces of Annandale, 1215-1295', TDGAS, 3rd Ser., LVIII, 73.
15 McDowall 1986, 24.
16 Scots Peerage VI, 286.
17 Ibid, 286-7; RCAHMS 1920, xxv.
18 RCAHMS 1920, xxvi.
19 Scots Peerage I, 507.
20 Reid, 'The Early Kirkpatricks', op. cit., 77.
21 See Scots Peerage IV, 135-143.
22 Scots Peerage IV, 142. See also 'Balmangan Tower'.
23 Complete Peerage II, 374-5.
24 Fraser 1873, I, 92; Scots Peerage V, 99.
25 RCAHMS 1956, No.64; 1997, 190, 192. See also Reid, R. C. 'Some Early de Soulis Charters' and M'Michael, T. 'The Feudal Family of de Soulis', TDGAS, 3rd Ser., XXVII, 150-193.
26 RCAHMS 1956, 82-3.
27 Bain II, No.1452.
28 Reid, R. C. 'Staplegorton', TDGAS, 3rd Ser., XXXI, 167-173.
29 RCAHMS 1997, 196. See Reid, R.C. 'The Scottish Avenels', TDGAS, 3rd Ser., XXXVII, 70-8.
30 Bain I, No.29.
31 Barrow 1971, Nos.104, 264.
32 See Ralegh Radford, C. A. and Reid, R. C. 'Unthank, a Manor of the Lovels', TDGAS, 3rd Ser., XXXVII, 26-35.
33 Easson 1957, 64.
34 Ibid, 120.
35 Reg. Holm Cultram, No.133a; Barrow 1971, No.88; M'Kerlie IV, 212.
36 Reg. Holm Cultram, No.133a.
37 Ibid. The reason for the grant to the Maxwells is not clear. It has been suggested that it was given up to settle a dispute with Dundrennan (Reg. Holm Cultram, No.133), but it may have been connected with the lavish gifts being handed out by Abbot Kendal to win favour for his nomination for the bishopric of Carlisle (Victoria History: Cumberland, II, 169).
38 Dugdale, Sir W. Monasticon Anglicanum, II, 1057, cited in McDowall 1986, 39.
39 Easson 1957, 66.
40 McDowall 1986, 248.
41 Easson 1957, 75.
42 Ibid, 105; Shirley, 17.
43 See 'Dundeugh Castle'.
44 Grose I, 148-9; Melrose Regality Records III, 385, etc.
45 RCAHMS 1920, lxvi; Thorold, 189-190; Barrow 1971, No.450.
46 Barrow 1971, No. 485.
47 McDowall 1986, 17. – There was also land and a fishery at Dalgarnock that had been granted by Edgar to the abbey of 'Holyrood', and confirmed by William the Lion c.1210 (Barrow 1971, No.492). This suggests that there

may have been some confusion between Holywood and Holyrood, either when the original documents were transcribed, or in a subsequent typographical error.

48 HAS, 43, 156-7; Barrow 1971, Nos.183, 367, 379.
49 Ibid, 47, 160.
50 Many of these are listed in McDowall 1986, 249.
51 RMS I, App.1, No.34.
52 Scots Peerage III, 266; VI, 296.
53 Ibid, III, 270-2. He had earlier forfeited Annandale in 1400, but had it restored in 1408.
54 Sir Richard Siward built the 'Edwardian' castle, whose ruins may still be seen.
55 See 'Comlongon Castle'.
56 Black 1946, 679.
57 Logan-tenement is in the parish of Moffat (Carruthers 1934, 51). It is not to be confused with the lands of Logan in the parish of Half Morton (as mistakenly done in RCAHMS 1997, 207).
58 Scots Peerage II, 379.
59 Bain II, 198, 206.
60 M'Michael, op. cit., 189; DNB, 680.
61 Bain II, No.1452.
62 See 'Westerhall'.
63 Scots Peerage III, 144-5.
64 Ibid, III, 147; Maxwell 1902, 70.
65 Reid, 'Unthank', op. cit., 34.
66 See 'Corra Castle'.
67 Scots Peerage III, 160.
68 Easson 1957, 182.
69 See 'Wreaths Tower'.
70 RMS I, No.31.
71 ALHT II, 10. One branch of the family is said to have changed its name later to Maitland (McDowall 1986, 25).
72 It is not clear how the Edgars lost possession of their original share of Sanquhar, but they seem to have been supplanted by the Rosses at an early date (See 'Sanquhar Castle').
73 Menzies MSS, 688-90; RMS I, App.2, No.146.
74 Menzies MSS, 691.
75 Bain II, 537.
76 Scots Peerage III, 272.
77 Complete Peerage IV, 434.
78 APS II, 42; Maxwell 1902, 192-3.
79 Complete Peerage I, 80.
80 Fraser 1873, I, 123.
81 Ibid, 241.
82 Ibid, 125.
83 Ibid, 597.
84 Fraser 1873, 165.
85 Ibid.
86 Ibid, 174.
87 RMS II, No.670.
88 Fraser 1878, II, 73 (No.74).
89 Ibid, 82 (No.84).
90 RCAHMS 1997, 224.
91 Reid, R. C. 'The Bonshaw Titles', TDGAS, 3rd Ser., XXXVII, 48-52.
92 ERS VI, 203; Fraser 1894, I, xix.
93 Reid, R. C. 'Bonshaw', TDGAS, 3rd Ser., XX, 152.
94 The Crown was so concerned about the strength of the alliance that, in 1564, they forbade the marriage of Johnston's daughter with the eldest son of Irving of Bonshaw (RPC I, 306).
95 Reid, 'The Border Grahams', op. cit., 87-98.

96 Ibid, 85; Scots Peerage VI, 218..
97 RCAHMS 1920, xxv.
98 Reid, 'The Early Kirkpatricks', op. cit., 76-7.
99 Buccleuch MSS, 44-5 (No.82).
100 RSS VII, No.263.
101 Lag Charters, 3.
102 Ibid.
103 Adams 1921, 5.
104 RMS II, No.993.
105 Ibid, No.224.
106 Hamilton-Grierson, Sir P. J. 'The Kirkos of Glenesland, Bogrie, Chapel and Sundaywell', TDGAS, 3rd Ser, III, 222-41.
107 Fraser 1885, III, 405 (No.357). The Gordons had been appointed keepers of the new Forest of Glenken in 1358 (Scots Peerage V, 99).
108 M'Kerlie III, 215.
109 Scots Peerage V, 258.
110 Black 1946, 192, 785.
111 Ibid, 785.
112 RMS IV, No.2311.
113 RMS II, No.3522.
114 Fraser 1873, 204. He already had possession under a previous grant.
115 Hyslop, 225. See RCAHMS 1997, 190, 194, 200.
116 RMS III, No.841. The ownership of Spottes is complicated. John Gordon of Lochinvar had been superior when he sub-infeudated the lands to Andrew M'Dowall. James IV, however, annulled this grant and gave the lands to Patrick Sinclair (RMS II, No.3065), but in 1516/17 Gordon's superiority was itself revoked and M'Dowall reinstated (RMS III, No.131). Sinclair nevertheless remained in possession, and it was on his resignation that Lord Maxwell acquired the superiority.
117 Fraser 1894, I, xli.
118 Johnston, C. 'The Early History of the Corries of Annandale', TDGAS, 3rd Ser., I, 94-97; Fraser 1894, I, cccxl.
119 Scots Peerage IV, 410.
120 RMS IV, Nos.405, 1728.
121 Irving 1907, 120-1.
122 Duke's Tower almost certainly stood at Knockhill, where Aglionby's platte of 1590 shows 'Knockhill ye dukes howse'. The oft-made suggestion that is stood at Hallguards is effectively disproved by the fact that Hallguards was the site of old Hoddom Castle, which was demolished to provide the stones ('Hoddomstanes') for the present Hoddom Castle. In any case, Old Hoddom Castle was apparently excluded from the Irvings' grant (See pp. 153, 275). A tower of the Irvings of Hoddom certainly stood at Knockhill until the 18th century (Adamson, D, 'The Hearth Tax for Dumfriesshire', TDGAS, 3rd Ser., XLIX, 66; Irving 1907, 127), and there was presumably another at Whitehill.
123 Irving 1907, 120-32.
124 RMS II, No.3532.
125 Armstrong 1883, 196.
126 Ibid, 168.
127 Reid, 'The Border Grahams', op. cit., 86, 104-5.
128 RPC III, 78.
129 Reid, 'The Border Grahams', op. cit., 105-6.
130 Burke Peerage 1959, 976, 'Graham of Esk'; 978, 'Graham of Netherby'.
131 M'Kerlie IV, 244; Stewart, F. D. and Reid, R. C. 'The Early Browns in New Abbey', TDGAS, 3rd Ser., XXXVII, 93.
132 RMS III, No.3284. Elizabeth was probably the daughter of John Lindsay of Fairgirth, who received a new crown charter of Fairgirth, Carsluith, and other lands in 1527 (RMS III, No.519).
133 Stewart, 'The Early Browns in New Abbey', op. cit., 94, 101.
134 Ibid, 93-110; Stewart, F. J. 'Sweetheart Abbey and its Owners over the Centuries', TDGAS, 3rd Ser., LXIV, 58-70.
135 See M'Kerlie III, 301-7.

CHAPTER 2

THE DEVELOPMENT OF TOWER-HOUSES IN THE WEST MARCH

The concept of the tower as a means of defence is almost as old as civilization itself. From the time of the earliest organized societies, there has been a need for communal defence, and it was the effectiveness of that defence that determined whether a society would survive and flourish, or fail. It was in those defences that towers came to play a vital role. At first they were usually incorporated into the walls surrounding communities or guarding frontiers, but later they were built to stand alone as a self-contained, defensive retreat - albeit often as the final citadel within a fortified enclosure.

It was evidently not until around the 10th century A.D. that individual towers started to appear in southern Europe, when they were built in towns as the private fortresses of feuding families and in the mountain passes of the Alps and Apennines for more communal defence against an outside aggressor.[1] The idea rapidly spread northwards, where the Normans adapted it to produce their much-larger and more-sophisticated keeps; and for the next five hundred years the Norman keeps were to dominate the defences of north-western Europe as much as the smaller towers were to dominate those further south.

THE EARLIEST TOWER-HOUSES

The earliest tower-houses in Scotland are thought to have owed their origin to the towers of southern Europe, which had been seen around the Mediterranean by Earl Sigurd and Earl Hakon while on pilgrimage to the Holy Land, and which were not too demanding of skills or materials in their construction. They appeared, not on the mainland, but in the Norse territory of the Orkneys, where the remains of one – Holbein Hruga's (or Cubbie Roo's) Castle – may still be seen. Built c.1145, it is some 26 feet square, with walls 5ft 6in thick bonded with lime mortar, and had the entrance above ground level.[2] But this form of tower-house never seems to have been taken up by the Scots on the mainland, where the more familiar tower-house probably owes more to the influence of the Normans and their keeps south of the Border.

The earliest known tower-house of the type familiar to us seems to have been the one built at St. Andrews by Bishop Roger de Beaumont c.1200, the remains of which may be seen incorporated in the 14th century fore-tower of the castle.[3] But if this was the progenitor of the tower-house in Scotland, it was very much alone for half a century or more, until tower-houses began to appear in Aberdeenshire, first at Dunnideer and then at Drum. The great tower-house castle at Drum is the earliest complete example to survive. It was evidently built for Alexander III by Richard Cementarius, the King's master-mason, and served partly as a hunting lodge in the royal forest of Drum and partly to protect one of the most important fords over the river Dee.[4]

Although these castles undoubtedly drew inspiration from the Norman keeps, with which their builders must have been acquainted, they were not a direct development, nor was their purpose quite the same. Indeed, the very location of Drum, with adjacent rising ground, is contrary to fundamental Norman principles of defence. And while the Norman keeps bristled with elaborate facilities for their defence, the early tower-houses were clearly designed as passive, impregnable retreats, following the same principles as the earlier brochs and round towers, but on a much grander scale. Their primary purpose was to provide accommodation, whilst at the same time being able to resist the unwelcome attentions of a local rival, or contender for the throne, or an unexpected attack by a marauding enemy or sea-borne invader.

Drum is a massive but almost featureless tower, measuring 52ft by 39ft on plan and rising just over 70ft to the parapet. Built of granite rubble, with rounded corners, it has walls 12ft thick at the base and contains three vaulted chambers, one above the other, the upper two of which were provided with entresol floors. The entrance, which was at first floor level, communicated with the other floors by means of straight stairs contained within the thickness of the walls – except for the uppermost floor and parapet, which were apparently reached by a wooden stair or ladder. The only means of defence was provided by the crenellated parapet; this projects on crude, single-stage corbels, and runs around the entire wall-head.

With the onset of the War of Independence in 1296, work on the building or repair of castles in the south-west seems to have been confined to the English and their supporters. Their strongholds were almost exclusively castles of enclosure of the type that became known as 'Edwardian', after the castles being built by Edward I in the Welsh Marches,[5] the design of which seems to have owed its origin to the castles seen by the Crusaders in the Near East.[6] Examples of these Edwardian-type castles could be found at Kirkcudbright and Tibbers. A solitary exception seems to have been the 'great tower' erected by Edward I at Lochmaben.[7] This is believed to have been of timber.[8]

However, with the introduction of Robert the Bruce's 'scorched earth' policy, which had the avowed intent of making every stronghold uninhabitable, and thus preventing the English from gaining, or keeping, a foothold in the country, the building of new strongholds soon came to an abrupt end. It was as much as the English and their allies could do just to keep the existing castles in repair; and it was not until long after Bruce's death, when the English had finally been driven out of Scotland, that the building of strongholds recommenced. It is not certain when the earliest 14th century strongholds were built, as there are no precise records, but what is certain is that, when they arrived, a new era had dawned. The age of the great castles of enclosure had gone – nobody could now afford to build them – , to be replaced by tower-houses, or indeed great tower-castles, the lineal descendants of Drum and St. Andrews.

THE GREAT TOWER-HOUSE CASTLES

The earliest of the new generation of tower-houses in the West March was probably the small tower at Sanquhar, measuring a mere 24ft square on plan, but it was the massive keep of Threave, built by Archibald 'the Grim', later 3rd Earl of Douglas, immediately after he was granted Eastern Galloway in 1369, that really set the pattern for the future. It is rectangular in plan, and rises sheer from the foundations to the wall-head, where provision is made for a wooden hoarding for defence. Despite the tower's massive size – it measures 61ft by 39ft 6in, and was some 74ft high –, its layout was in fact quite simple, comprising a barrel-vaulted basement with entresol floor and three floors above. Mural chambers were confined to three garderobes in the SW corner. The tower did not, however, stand alone. Recent excavations have established that there was also a separate hall for the garrison and other buildings on the site, all of which were contained within outer earthworks and a palisade. On the other hand, the defensive wall and corner towers now to be seen on the S and E sides, with their generous provision of arrow-slits and early types of gun-loops, were not added until the middle of the next century.

The oldest part of the present castle of Torthorwald may belong to the same period, or be even earlier. It too was a simple tower, measuring some 47ft by 39ft 3in on plan, which was later extended and raised in height. It was contained within an irregular enclosing wall, which had at least two circular corner towers; but the date of these features has not been established. Like Sanquhar, it was founded on a splayed plinth course, a feature seen earlier at Loch Doon.

At this time the older castles of Caerlaverock, Dalswinton and Buittle were being repaired and refurbished as best their owners could, but the latter two were evidently never restored to their former selves, and were eventually abandonned. Meanwhile the old castle of Staplegorton was retained by the Douglases as an occasional residence until at least 1389, but it too was later abandonned. Little is known of how the other lords and chiefs lived at this time, though it would appear that the many mottes in the region continued to serve their original purpose until well into the next century; and there may have been some other, early, stone castles, of which little or no trace now remains, which continued to soldier on.[9] There is, for example, evidence that the Johnstons built some form of stone stronghold at Lochwood at an early date to supersede their original motte there, but again we have no details and cannot be more specific as to date. It was probably not until well into the next century that another tower-house appeared in the West March.

One of the earliest of the 15th century tower-castles was Closeburn, another simple tower, with three vaulted storeys, an intermediate floor and an attic beneath the roof vault. It was only marginally smaller than Torthorwald, and like both Threave and Torthorwald had immensely thick walls with its entrance high above the ground at first floor level. The walls were broken only by the wheel-stair to the upper floors and, probably, a garderobe or two.[10] Like Threave, the parapet is flush with the wall below, but as the tower has been altered at this level more than once during the last two and a half centuries, one cannot be certain that this was the original arrangement.

Another tower of the same general period was Castlemilk, though, as no trace now remains, our only knowledge of it is what can be gleaned from old records. Notable among these is an English survey and drawing of 1547.[11] This states that the castle was eleven yards square and eleven yards high, with walls two and a half yards thick; but clearly these dimensions cannot be relied upon.[12] The drawing also tells us that the entrance was at first floor level, where it was reached by a wooden ladder, which is shown, and there was a crenellated parapet around the wall-head.

Spedlins dates from the latter half of the 15th century, although only the lower two storeys belong to this period, the upper floors having been added in 1605. It is typical of the early tower-castles, apart from the unusually low, vaulted basement. It also has a pit-prison, a feature found in earlier castles else-

where, but previously absent in the West March. The fact that the upper floors were not added until later, as at Torthorwald and many other early castles in Scotland, raises an interesting question. Why were the original upper walls demolished, if they were immediately going to be rebuilt? Such an operation would have been both difficult – the masonry was strongly bonded – and unnecessary. Could it be that the original superstructure was in fact of timber, as is known to have been the case with some mediaeval town-houses,[13] where a balance had to be struck between cost and vulnerability to fire?

The ultimate development in the great tower-house castles is to be found at Comlongon, which has been described as 'perhaps the ablest thing of its kind in Scotland, and in it the plain rectangular tower-house . . . may be thought to have reached its climax'.[14] Built c.1501, it has a vaulted basement, with pit-prison and entresol floor, and three upper floors culminating in a boldly corbelled-out parapet and look-out turrets; but the feature which distinguishes it most from the earlier towers is its myriad of mural chambers, of which there are no less than twelve.

That there were no further developments in this type of tower-house after this time can probably be attributed to Scotland's disastrous defeat at Flodden in 1513, and the subsequent distressed state of the kingdom.

ORCHARDTON TOWER

The tower at Orchardton is something of an anomaly, not just in the Borders, but in the country as a whole. Not only is it the only example of a round tower-house in Scotland, but, whilst in essence its layout follows the same basic concept as the great towers that preceded it, it is a tower in miniature. Built soon after 1456, it is only some 29ft in diameter at ground level, and comprises a vaulted basement and three upper floors, with walls averaging about 5ft 9in in thickness. An entrance at ground level admitted to the basement, while a second doorway at first floor level served as the principal entrance to the tower, there being no internal connection between the two. From the first floor, a very small wheel-stair, contained entirely within the thickness of the walls, rose to serve the upper floors and parapet-walk, a mere 33ft or so above the ground. This tower did not, however, always stand alone, for it was ably supported by a substantial, stone, secondary building of uncertain date, parts of which, including a vaulted undercroft, have survived.

LESSER TOWERS

By this time, other small tower-houses, the 'lesser towers', had begun to appear in Scotland. It is not possible to be certain when the earliest ones were built, as, by their very nature, they were even less likely to appear in documentary records. Indeed, to this day land titles are only concerned with the ownership of *land*, not with the buildings that stand on it. Many of the earliest towers were also of timber, so no trace of them has survived. One early example of a lesser tower built of stone in the West March is to be found at Lochwood, though its precise date has not been established. It must not, however, be confused with the earlier stone castle on the site (*supra*), masonry from which was re-used in its construction. Other lesser towers which would also appear to date from an early period, at least in part, are Cumstoun, the Tower of Lun (or Corrie), Amisfield (basement), Elshieshields (basement), Gillesbie and Lag, though one cannot be more specific.

In, or soon after, 1525, Johnnie Armstrong of Gilnockie built a 'strong house' on land that he had been granted in Eskdale. The English, however, claiming that it was built on part of the

Debateable Land, crossed the Border in 1528, and burned it. This suggests that the tower was probably of timber. Another tower, this time presumably of stone,[15] was later built in the same area by Sandy Armstrong. It is illustrated by a thumbnail sketch on the *Platte of Castlemilk*, a survey carried out by the English in 1547, where it is described as 'sande arme stronges new hous'.[16] It stood on, or near, the site of the present tower of Hollows, which may even incorporate part of it. The building of Cornal Tower is referred to in 1532, when Adam Johnston of Corrie cheekily asked the owner of the lands to reimburse him for the cost of its construction (even though it had been built without permission!); and Lockerbie, another Johnston tower, may have dated from the same general period.

For some years after the Scots disastrous defeat at Flodden, James V actively discouraged the building of tower-houses in the Borders, both to avoid antagonizing the English further and in an attempt to suppress lawlessness. Indeed, in 1528, the Council ordered the demolition of a partly built tower south of Coldingham 'sen it stands so nerr the bordouris of Ingland and may turne this realme to hurt and dampnage'.[17] Before long, however, it was realized that this was also damaging the security of the Kingdom, so in 1535 an Act was passed that required 'evry landit man duelland in ye Inland or upon ye bordouris havand yare ane hundreth pund land of new extent' to build 'ane sufficient barmkyn . . . of Stane and lyme contenand thre score futis of ye square ane Eln thick and vj Elnys heicht' for himself and his tenants and their goods in time of trouble 'wyt ane toure in the sami for him self gif he thinkis It expedient', and 'all uthir landit men of smallar Rent and Reuenew' shall build 'pelis and gret strenthis' as they please; and all the said strengths, barmkins and peles were to be completed 'wtin twa zeris [years] under ye pane'.[18] It is thought that it was after this date that the building of the lesser towers really started in earnest, though even then numbers were small compared with half a century later. In general, the characteristic that distinguishes the earliest of the lesser towers from those built after *c*.1550-60 is the absence of gun-loops and shot-holes, which only begin to appear after the hand-guns for which they were designed became generally available.

The most complete of this new generation of towers is Hills, a plain rectangular tower with a vaulted basement and three upper storeys terminating in a corbelled-out parapet-walk. There are no gun-loops in the basement, just crude ventilation slits. It is of particular interest, because it retains its barmkin, which, although partly rebuilt, is approximately of the size laid down in the Act of 1535. It also retains its fine, slightly later gatehouse and the adjacent house that was added in the 17th century when the threat of hostile neighbours had receded, and more comfortable accommodation came into demand. Lag also retains fragments of its gatehouse, which was recorded in a less advanced stage of decay by both Cardonnel[19] and Grose[20] in the 18th century.

One of the features that distinguishes the majority of the lesser towers from their grander predecessors is the arrangement of the stair well. Whilst a few of the early examples of lesser towers had straight flights of stairs contained within the thickness of the walls – as, for example, in the early work at Amisfield –, the usual arrangement was a wheel-stair in one corner, just as in the earlier tower-castles. But because the main walls of these towers were significantly thinner, the stair now encroached upon the rooms at each floor; and the thinner the walls, the greater the loss of living space. This is well demonstrated at Hills. To overcome the problem, some of the towers incorporated a separate wing for the stair, producing an 'L–plan'. Early examples of this arrangement are to be found at Lochwood and Kirkconnell. Another example is found at Drumcoltran, which was built by the younger son of Edward Maxwell, the builder of Hills, and which was clearly based upon the experiences of his kinsman at nearby Kirkconnell. Both these towers included a look-out chamber at the top of the wing, access to which was gained by a small, secondary wheel-stair partly corbelled-out from the wall below. This arrangement was subsequently developed further to provide additional rooms in the wing by corbelling-out the stair in the re-entrant angle for the full height above first floor level, as at Buittle, Abbot's Tower and Earlstoun, or having the entire stair in the re-entrant angle, as at Rockhall. Barjarg, which was built *c*.1587, is exceptional in having had the wheel-stair to the upper floors contrived within the re-entrant angle in such a way that there was no external projection, and yet, apparently, it did not encroach upon any of the rooms in the main block or the wing either.

By far the largest and most important tower to be built in the West March in the 16th century was Hoddom, which was built by Sir John Maxwell, later 4th Lord Herries, in 1565. It was designed primarily as a garrison fortress for the control of lawlessness in the region, although, together with the new look-out tower of Repentance, which was built in the same year, it was also to serve as a defence against the English should they ever again invade. Like the great tower-castles of the past, it was simple but massive, with walls 8ft 10in thick, a vaulted basement, three upper storeys and a separate wing for the unusually large (10ft 10in diameter) wheel-stair. But what distinguished it from its predecessors was the vast array of widely-splayed gun-loops that penetrated its walls at both ground and third floor levels; and this was supplemented by further gun-loops in the round towers which stood at each corner of the barmkin.

It is not known whether Hoddom was the first tower-house in the West March to incorporate such gun-loops, but from now on they were to become a normal feature, except in some of the smaller or more remote towers in the north and west of Dumfriesshire, and some of the towers in eastern Galloway furthest removed from the Border troubles. They are, for example, not found at Glenae, Boreland, Blacklaw, Breconside or Frenchland in Annandale, or Crawfordton or Sundaywell in Nithsdale, all of which are presumed to date from the latter half of the 16th century, nor are they found at Abbot's Tower, Edingham, Earlstoun or Shirmers in Galloway.

The earliest stone towers of the families closest to the Border, namely the Irvings in Kirtleside and the Armstrongs in Eskdale, were solid rectangular keeps, with walls up to 5ft 9in in thickness, penetrated by splayed gun-loops on each side, and with corbelled-out parapets at the wall-head. Such towers include Bonshaw, Robgill, Woodhouse, Kirkconnel, Stapleton and Hollows. A similar layout is found in the Johnstons' tower at Lochhouse, and is also recorded as having existed at Mouswald and Friars Carse; but another Irving tower in Eskdale, Auchenrivock, was evidently built on the L–plan. Lochar, a Maxwell tower which apparently dates from *c*.1568, is unusual in having relatively thin walls (3ft 2in) – no doubt due to the marshy ground on which it is founded –, and yet having splayed gun-loops. Moreover, there are two loops on each long side, not only at ground level, but also at second floor level, following the design at Hoddom. The original tower was rectangular in plan, the wing not being added until 1622. 'Mosstroops Tower' at Terregles and Barclosh also appear to have been rectangular on plan.

Apart from the early **L**–plan towers of Kirkconnell, Hoddom, Drumcoltran and Abbot's, already mentioned, there was another at Mellingshaw, though only part of its stair tower has survived. All the other, known, **L**–plan towers in the West March are the result of a stair wing having been added at a later date.

The normal arrangement in the basement of tower-houses was a single, vaulted chamber. Occasionally, however, the vaulting was omitted, as at Lochar, where the marshy nature of the site would not bear the load; Elshieshields, where the basement of the main block was of earlier date; and Abbot's. Variations on the basic arrangement were, however, found at Lochwood, Hoddom and Bonshaw, where prisons were incorporated into the original design, and at Lochwood, Crawfordton, Rockhall and Edingham, where the basements were subdivided into more than one vaulted chamber. Crawfordton and Rockhall also had the distinction of an interconnecting passage. The arrangement of the basement at the early 17th century tower of Dalswinton was more complex, as it also incorporated the kitchen, and so possibly was the basement at Auchenskeoch, of which we have no details. Dalswinton was also unusual in being built on the **Z**–plan, i.e. with two wings at diametrically opposite corners so arranged that they gave covering fire to all the main walls; and Auchenskeoch is also believed to have been built on the same plan, though all trace of the second wing has now gone.

By the beginning of the 1580s, it was no longer considered necessary to have parapet-walks around the wall-head. Instead, the attic floor was extended to the outer wall-face, and dormer windows inserted to give more light. The only concession now made to defence was the addition of turrets corbelled-out at the corners. In the case of the smaller towers, such as Isle (1587) and Fourmerkland (1590), these were only added at diametrically opposite corners, whilst Frenchland and Sundaywell may only have had a single turret at the corner facing down their respective valleys. The great tower-castle of Spedlins, on the other hand, the upper floors of which were not added until 1605, and the towers at Barjarg, Elshieshields and Amisfield, had a turret at each corner, though the last three omitted the turret at the corner occupied by the stair. The turrets at Amisfield were unusual in being two storeys in height, as were those later raised in height on the wing at Hoddom, while the turrets at Elshieshields had a unique 'higher' level. At Isle, Amisfield and Spedlins, the towers have shot-holes so arranged that they give covering fire to all the main walls at basement level, and the others may originally have been similarly equipped .

A design feature that was occasionally found in the Middle and East Marches was a second, smaller tower at the opposite side of the barmkin from the main tower. Examples could be found at Branxholme, Goldielands, Holydean, Corbet and Cowdenknowes. There is, however, no known instance of such an arrangement in the West March. It is, however, just possible that the various old buildings now incorporated in the present house at Westerhall originated in a late example of this arrangement.

The ultimate development of the 'lesser tower' is to be found at Amisfield, where, in 1600, a simple rectangular basement, of earlier date, was extended and developed upwards through a succession of stairs and chambers corbelled-out from the E gable to terminate in a watch-turret perched nearly 80 feet above the ground. There are four storeys below the wall-head, plus a garret and upper attic high in the steeply pitched roof, while the corbelled-out tower in the SE corner provided another two, small rooms. There was also a small chamber, or 'laird's lug', overlooking the great hall. The tower was unusual for a lesser tower in having a guardroom just inside the entrance. This belonged to the earlier building, though a not dissimilar guardroom was incorporated in the later tower at Lochhouse. Despite Amisfield's late date, defence was not overlooked: apart from the shot-holes in the corner turrets already mentioned, gun-loops were inserted into the earlier ventilation slits in the basement and guardroom; a substantial machicolation was built over the entrance; and a shot-hole was built into the watch-turret to cover the ground below.

BASTLE-HOUSES AND PELE-HOUSES

Less conspicuous than either the great tower-castles or the lesser towers were the bastle- (or bastel-) houses, pele-houses and peles, each of which – as they are now defined[21] – had its own particular characteristics. These were not the strongholds of great lords or chiefs, or even of their more affluent cadet families, but the stone-built homes of those who eked out a living farming in the upland valleys; for bastle-houses and pele-houses were in reality nothing more than 'strong' farmhouses with integral cattle-sheds, though on the English side of the Border, where bastle-houses were much more common and farming generally more prosperous, some of their owners were considered to be men of some consequence.[22] These fortified farmhouses were not exclusive to the Borders, but it was largely due to the unsettled state of the Borders that they owed their existence, and it is in the Borders, both in Scotland and in England, that their greatest concentration is found. They were only built like 'strongholds', in an age when farm buildings elsewhere were generally much more rudimentary, because that was what local conditions dictated.

Very few bastle-houses or pele-houses have survived in Scotland, even in outline, although more sites are now coming to light, including some as far afield as Upper Clydesdale;[23] but on the English side of the Border many have survived virtually intact, providing an excellent idea of how they were built and how they appeared to their enemies.[24] It is also of interest to note the way in which they are sometimes found in small groups, whilst at others they are totally isolated high on remote hillsides.

Bastle-houses and pele-houses were very similar in design, but the former was the more superior dwelling. Indeed, on the English side of the Border it has been said that the 'vaulted bastles roofed with stone' belonged to 'lairds' and 'yeomen proprietors', while the 'unvaulted ones [pele-houses] roofed with thatch' belonged to tenants.[25] There is also plenty of scope for confusion in the use of the terms 'bastle' and 'pele', because there was no consistency in the way the officials and chroniclers of the 16th and 17th centuries used the various terms. Thus the English reports of bastle-houses destroyed in 1543-4,[26] such as the '16 strong bastell houses' burnt in Lessudden in November 1544,[27] could as well refer to pele-houses as bastle-houses, but in all probability referred to neither, as at that time they were more likely to have been their timber antecedents. None of the bastle-houses surviving today is believed to pre-date the second half of the 16th century. The terms now used are but a modern expedient to differentiate clearly between the various types of building.

Bastle-houses were two storeys in height, with a vaulted basement and separate entrances at each level, the upper being reached by a removable ladder. In times of trouble, and perhaps also each night, the livestock (horses, cattle and sheep) would be secured in the basement, which in effect served as the barmkin, while the owner and his family lived above, where they could feel more secure as well as benefitting from the heat rising from

the animals below.[28] The masonry was generally fairly rudimentary, being of roughly hewn blocks or rubble, bonded with
lime mortar. The only decoration used was either a bold chamfer or a crude QER moulding on some of the surrounds. The
entrance to the basement was normally in a gable wall, while the
upper entrance was in a side wall; both were secured with strong
wooden doors, reinforced with one or more drawbars, but there
was no yett. The only other openings in the basement were small
ventilation slits, and even at first floor level the only windows
were a few, small, unglazed apertures, reinforced with one or
two vertical iron bars or a small grille. There is rarely any surviving evidence of a fireplace, though rudimetary fireplaces are
known to have existed in some of the English buildings,[29] and
they may have been more common than is now evident. In a
few instances the two floors were connected internally by a stair;[30]
in the others a hatch was provided so that the man securing the
livestock could then reach the living quarters above by ladder.
At least one bastle-house in England is known to have had a
watch turret or beacon on one of the gables.[31]

No bastle-houses as such have been identified in the
Scottish countryside close to the Border. This no doubt reflects
the fact that the Scottish hill farmers were poorer than many of
their English counterparts, and thus the only 16th/17th century
farmhouses to have survived in this area are pele-houses. What
were often called bastle-houses did, however, exist in some of
the towns, such as Jedburgh and Peebles. Only one of these, the
so-called 'Queen Mary's House' in Jedburgh, has survived, albeit much altered.[32] It is, however, most unlikely that any of
these ever served as a farmhouse, unlike some of the examples
to be found in the English farming villages. Despite the similar-
ity in design, it is much more likely that they were stone town-
houses, with vaulted basements, typical of the type to be found
in many towns and cities, which the richer merchants and officials built for themselves, and which stood out in sharp contrast
to the humbler timber dwellings round about.

As already related, bastle-houses have been found further afield in Upper Clydesdale, and re-appraisal of the existing
evidence makes it fairly certain that the 'tower' at Kinnelhead,
in Upper Annandale, was in fact a bastle-house too. The dimensions of Raecleugh, also in Upper Annandale, suggest it may
have been another, later enlarged, though excavation would be
needed to confirm this.

Pele-houses were, in essence, very much the same as
bastle-houses in their design and layout, the principal differences
being the absence of a basement vault, thinner walls, and the use
of clay mortar instead of lime. There was a group of them NW
of Carter Bar in the Middle March, two of which are almost
complete,[33] and the ruins of a number of others are known in the
East March; but none has so far been identified in the West March,
where the diminutive 'peles' seem to have taken their place.

PELES

What is now defined as a 'pele' was the smallest and
simplest form of tower-house. In general it seems to have been
the home of the poorer tenant farmers, and was thus commonly
found on high ground overlooking the more remote valleys; but
as none has survived other than as a collapsed ruin, little is known
about their construction or features. It is only because of their
portrayal as tower-houses by Pont[34] that we know they qualified
as 'towers'.

The one characteristic that immediately distinguishes a
pele is the use of clay mortar instead of lime, like the pele-houses;
and it is this feature more than any other that has led to their

wholesale demise. They were not vaulted either. Unlike the
pele-houses, however, their much smaller size shows that they
could not have provided accommodation for livestock in the lowest storey, except possibly for their most prized beasts in an emergency, but there were other buildings on the site that could be
used as byres, etc. Another characteristic of the majority of peles
is that they were almost square, the ratio of the long side to the
short side in an average pele being about 1·16:1, compared with
1·33:1 in a typical 'lesser' tower. Brockloch and Stewarton fall
into this category, but Breckonside and Auchenfedrick I and II
were exceptions, where the ratios were 1·23:1, 1·42:1 and 1·28:1
respectively. The walls, which were made entirely of local rubble, varied in thickness, but were always substantial. Brockloch,
at 4ft thick, has the narrowest walls of any recorded pele in the
West March (it also has the smallest overall dimensions, 22ft by
19ft), while those at Stewarton are nearly 7ft thick. Peles also
differ from pele-houses in having the entrance at or near the
middle of one of the longer sides. No doorways or windows
have survived intact, nor is there evidence that there were any
mouldings.

URBAN STRONGHOLDS or 'PALACES'

Whilst the castles and tower-houses of both nobles and
lesser lairds were normally situated in the midst of their lands or
estates in the country, some of the more affluent of their number
also had town-houses, either in the local county town or in the
nation's capital, and in a few instances these town-houses were
built as veritable strongholds in their own right. There were two
such houses in the West March: Maxwell's Castle in Dumfries
and Maclellan's Castle in Kirkcudbright.

Maxwell's Castle was finally demolished early in the
18th century, and old accounts of it are somewhat sparse. It is
on record, however, that the castle comprised '3 large stories',
with four vaulted basement chambers, a corbelled-out parapet
and 'bartisan[s] covered with lead', as well as having a courtyard and stables. It was evidently large enough to accommodate 50 footsoldiers and 12 horse. And although probably more
symmetrical than Maclellan's Castle, it would have provided
similar facilities.

Maclellan's Castle, on the other hand, has survived almost complete and unaltered, providing a perfect picture of what
was intended, although the courtyard and outbuildings have long
since gone. Built on the L–plan, with an additional, two-stage
projection in the re-entrant angle, where the main entrance and
stair were located, and an additional tower at the corresponding
outside angle, it comprised three storeys and a garret, with
corbelled-out corner turrets at the four principal, outside angles.
The basement accommodated a range of cellars in the main block,
a large kitchen in the wing, and another chamber in the corner
tower, all of which were vaulted; and on every side, except the
N end of the kitchen, there were splayed gun-loops to deter any
would-be aggressor. The principal living chambers were on the
first floor, including a magnificent great hall in the centre of the
main block, with private hall beyond and a separate 'laird's lug',
and there were further chambers on the floor above. Communication between these various chambers and floors was either by
direct access or by means of one of three wheel-stairs, which
rose from this level to serve the upper floors: there were no cor-
ridors, except in the basement. There was a short parapet walk
at the wall-head above the main entrance.

1   Many of these early towers may still be seen in the cities (e.g. Florence, San Gimignano, Lucca, Bologna, etc.) and mountain passes of Italy, and in southern France and the Tyrol.
2   Marwick 1973, 56.
3   Cruden 1960, 21-2.
4   See also Slade, H. G. 'The Tower and House of Drum', *PSAS*, 115 (1985), 297-356; Thompson 1986.
5   Caerlaverock (*c.*1277) was one of the precursors of this style in Scotland, just as Caerphilly (1268) was in Wales.
6   The castles of the Near East owed their origin to the ancient Roman strongholds, of which Constantinople was a supreme example.
7   Bain II, Nos.1101, 1112, and p.535.
8   The motte-and-bailey strongholds in S.W. Scotland were probably all of timber, and so were many of the lesser tower-houses built before the 16th century.
9   The form and extent of early buildings at Auchenfranco, Kirkgunzeon and Wamphray, for example, is not known, nor whether they were of stone or timber.
10 Any original garderobes have been obscured or lost during modernization.
11 Merriman, M 'The Platte of Castlemilk, 1547', *TDGAS*, 3rd Ser., XLIV, 181.
12 Three different English accounts, for example, give three different thicknesses for the walls, ranging from 7ft 6in to 11ft.
13 See Naismith, 74-5, and Fawcett, 283.
14 Simpson, W. D. 'Comlongon Tower, Dumfriesshire', *TDGAS*, 3rd Ser., XXIII, 20-9.
15 It has been suggested recently that it too may have been of timber (RCAHMS 1997, 215).
16 Merriman, *op. cit.*, 181.
17 Hannay 1932, 277. Armstrong's interpretation of the report of this case in *Balfour's Practicks* as a general inhibition on building in the Borders is not, however, supported by the original record (Armstrong 1883, 245n).

18 APS II, 346.
19 Cardonnel, 'Lagg: Plate I'.
20 Grose I, 155-6.
21 In the 16th and 17th centuries, the terms were often interchanged, leading inevitably to a certain amount of confusion; but the definitions have now been standardised by the respective Royal Commissions for Ancient Monuments in Scotland (RCAHMS) and England (RCHM).
22 RCHM 1970, 65, citing Hodgson, J. *History of Northumberland*, II, i, 147.
23 Discovery & Excavation in Scotland 1990, 37-8; 1991, 69; 1992, 66; etc.
24 See RCHM 1970, 61-95.
25 RCHM 1970, 65, citing Hodgson, J. *History of Northumberland*, II, i, 189.
26 Armstrong 1883, lv-lxxi.
27 Ibid, lxx.
28 The same arrangement is still found in the Tyrol today, where the large timber farmhouses are so constructed that the lower floor is used to house the animals in the winter months, while the farmer and his family live in the floors above.
29 RCHM 1970, 63.
30 Stairs existed at the bastle-house of Woodhouses in the Coquet valley of Northumbria and at the neighbouring pele-house of Crag (RCHM 1970, 86-8), and they have also been found in the recently excavated bastle-house ruins at Glenochar and Wintercleugh in Upper Clydesdale (Discovery & Excavation in Scotland 1991, 69).
31 At Melkridge, now demolished (RCHM 1970, 89 and Plate 18).
32 RCAHMS 1956, No.418.
33 Ibid, Nos.561, 562; RCAHMS 1994, 11-12.
34 e.g. Brockloch and Stewarton (Pont MS. No.35 in National Library of Scotland).

CHAPTER 3

FEATURES OF THE TOWERS

One of the most endearing features of tower-houses is their individuality, for, despite the simplicity of the basic concept, each has a character that is uniquely its own. Not only do they reflect the fashions of the day, they also incorporate the whims of the owner or his master-mason, or there may be a style common to a particular family or area. Thus, while each of the Irving towers in Kirtleside[1] may be seen to follow a common pattern, they still exhibit features that are unique to each tower. On the other hand, the various Maxwell towers[2] – although admittedly built over a much longer period – are more a product of the architectural fashions of their time, and the limitations of the local materials, than of any family preference, for no two are alike.

MASONRY

The nature of the local stone had a very profound influence on the structure of the towers, and on their ability to survive to the present day. The sandstones of Lower Nithsdale, Annandale and Kirtleside were not only easy to split to form ashlar or coursed rubble, but they were also easy to cut for mouldings, and were in fact the only stone in the region suited to this purpose. Thus they are found being used for the mouldings of doorways, windows and armorial panels even in areas where sandstone is not the local stone, although the cost of transportation meant that they were unlikely to be found in the humblest towers or peles. The one disadvantage of sandstone is that most of the varieties found in the West March are soft when wet, and therefore easily disintegrate once exposed. There is, however, one form of sandstone that is very hard. It is a form of gritstone which is found in use for dressings at Closeburn, Lag, Hills and Edingham.

The granite of Criffel and Dalbeattie is also very hard. It was mainly used in its natural boulder form, and as such constituted the basic building material at Kirkconnell, Abbot's, Auchenskeoch, Barclosh, Edingham and Orchardton. Where used for arrises and mouldings, the margins are usually fairly crude. The one exception is Kenmure, where some of the later work employs machine-cut granite from the Dalbeattie quarries.

The other stone that is widely used in the region is the Silurian greywacke of the upper valleys. More than half the towers in the West March are built of it. It is hard to break and the line of fracture is quite unpredictable, like flint, so that in the main one has to rely on the strength of the mortar to bond it all together: it is almost impossible to dress or mould. Towers built of greywacke were often harled for added protection.

Where sandstone was the principal building material, it was rarely cut into fine ashlar – unlike at the earlier castles of enclosure, such as Caerlaverock, Lochmaben and Tibbers –, but was fashioned into roughly finished blocks. These were then used to build the walls at 'random', sometimes with the addition of other local rocks – as, for example, at Wreaths, where granite was also used, or Lag and Isle, where greywacke was used –, or were 'roughly coursed' – as, for example, at Closeburn, Hoddom, Repentance and Dalswinton. A notable exception was the second period of construction at Torthorwald, where fine ashlar was

Fig. 2 Torthorwald Castle: rebated joints.

used for all the external walling and the stair-wells, although instead of being regularly coursed throughout, many of the joints were 'checked' or 'rebated'.[3] Ashlar was also widely used for quoins, mouldings and vaults, and was sometimes finely dressed for such features as corner turrets (Amisfield and Spedlins), parapet walls (Hoddom and Bonshaw) and the look-out turret at Elshieshields. An unusual feature of the earliest dressed work at Spedlins is that some of the stones were deliberately cut on the bias instead of following the natural layering of the rock.

The greywacke, or Silurian rock, in some areas is especially hard and difficult to split. This is known locally, if sometimes incorrectly, as whinstone. When this is used for walling, it is liberally pinned with much smaller stones for packing and stability. Examples of this are found at Amisfield and Lag. The same technique is also found where the principal building material was granite.

An unusual combination is found at Corra. Here the main walling is greywacke rubble, while the quoins are of granite, which, although hard to work, was easier to shape than greywacke and more readily available than sandstone. Granite is also used at nearby Drumcoltran for the principal dressings and, uniquely in the Borders, for the inscribed panel over the entrance.

Another source of masonry was older buildings in the neighbourhood that were no longer required. This was especially true of dressed stone and mouldings, and permission to use the existing material was often written into the mason's contract. There is evidence of this practice at both Orchardton and Lochwood, while the popular name 'Hoddomstanes' for Lord Herries' new castle at Hoddom spoke for itself. The practice was later documented at both Barscobe and Hills. At Barscobe (q.v.), William MacLellan of Barscobe had permission to take from Threave Castle 'as manie of the forsaid friestane . . . as will serve for his use'; and for the new house of Hills (q.v.), in 1721, the contract stipulated that the mason could 'take down the [old] house . . . and to fit and prepare the stones, timber and slate thereof for building the new house so far as they will serve'.

It was a practice that had existed throughout the Middle Ages, and which has continued to this day. Indeed, the absence of dressed stone at many ruins is a direct result of the stone being taken for use elsewhere.

COURTYARDS

Most of the tower-houses in the Borders now stand alone, with little or no indication of the courtyard or other buildings that formerly existed on the site. It is easy, therefore, to forget that each was once a bustling community of men and beasts, with additional accommodation for lesser clansmen or servants, stables for horses, storage for meat, grain and fodder, a brew-house, and, usually, a separate kitchen. Hills is a notable exception, as it retains its original gatehouse and barmkin, albeit much restored, and excavations in 1970 revealed that the original cobbled surface of the courtyard was also still *in situ*. The forecourt at Orchardton was also cobbled, and recent excavations in the area immediately outside Abbot's Tower have revealed granite setts.[4]

Fig. 4 Hoddom Castle: tower at NW corner of barmkin, with 19th and 20th century restoration and alterations.

Fig. 3 Hills: gatehouse.
Late 16th century.

Lag was another tower that still retained much of its gatehouse and barmkin when recorded in 1788-90,[5] but little of the former remains and the wall is now reduced to its foundations. Kenmure also retained its curtain wall and gateway in 1790,[6] though these probably only dated from the 17th century restoration. Neither Lochwood nor Hoddom retain a gatehouse, but substantial sections of their barmkins have survived; Hoddom also has the remains of a corner tower, complete with gun-loops in the vaulted basement, and a wide gateway, though in its present form the latter feature probably only dates from the 17th century. Hoddom was recorded in detail in the 18th century, when there were still three corner towers[7] and various buildings along both the north and south sides of the courtyard.[8] Bonshaw is another tower where the remains of the barmkin and a postern

Fig. 5 Threave Castle: gatehouse.

Fig. 6 Threave Castle: SE corner tower in 15th century defences.

gate have been retained in the modern restoration. The line of the barmkin and the various outbuildings, kilns, etc., can usually be traced at long-abandoned sites too. Notable examples are Blacklaw, Kinnelhead, Cornal and Brockloch.

None of the great tower-castles has retained its original curtain wall or outbuildings, though the overgrown outline of some of their foundations can be traced at Torthorwald. Excavations carried out at Threave in 1974-8 revealed details of an external great hall and a second building, several lesser works of indeterminate date, and further information about the harbour and enclosing earthworks and palisade.[9] They also provided further information about the existing outer wall and corner towers of the artillery fortification, which was added in the middle of the 15th century. It would appear that corner towers also existed at Torthorwald and Lun, and perhaps also at Spedlins.

Orchardton was unusual, though not unique, in having a substantial stone building of at least two storeys only a few feet away from the tower. No doubt there was a barmkin too, but without excavation it can no longer be traced.

The earliest tower-houses usually had a well within the basement of the tower itself (*infra*), but some of the later ones had a well in the courtyard. An example of the latter, built of fine ashlar, survives at Maclellan's.

PLINTHS

Unlike the great Norman keeps in England, where the base of the walls was commonly provided with a massive batter to resist undermining and battering by a besieging force, the splayed plinth to be found at the base of many Scottish tower-houses appears to have served no other purpose than to distribute the weight over the ground beneath. Indeed, when the Ministry of Works explored the foundations of Bonshaw in 1960, they were amazed, and somewhat alarmed, to find that there weren't any! The tower had been built on the surface, with no attempt to strengthen the ground between the walls and the bedrock of the cliff many feet below.[10]

QUOINS AND CORNERS

The normal arrangement at the corner of a tower, as in a stone building of any other period, was to have quoins with the long and short sides alternately disposed. An obvious exception was Orchardton, which, either from considerations of strength, or because the stone was difficult to fashion into quoins, was completely circular and thus had no corners. But there were other towers which, apparently because of the difficulty of fashioning quoins from the local greywacke, were provided with rounded corners for part or all of their height. These included Boreland, Lockerbie, Gillesbie and Lochhouse. Rounded corners are also found at some of the corners of the two barmkins at Lochwood, where, unlike the tower itself, which has fine sandstone quoins, the walls are made entirely of random greywacke.

A unique variation of the rounded corner is found at Drumcoltran. There, the corners are rounded with a small radius at basement level, and then neatly chamfered, or 'canted', for the upper floors.

ENTRANCE DOORWAYS

In the earliest tower-houses, the entrance was normally high above the ground at the level of the basement entresol or first-floor, where it was reached by a removable wooden ladder. This is where the entrance originally was at the great tower-castles of Threave, Torthorwald, Closeburn and Spedlins; and at Threave one can still see the corbels, later cut almost flush, that were used to support the 'ladder'. First floor entrances also originally existed at the smaller towers of Orchardton and Elshieshields.

The usual arrangement at the entrance doorway was to have a double-rebate at the rear of the jambs to house an outer door of wood reinforced with an inner door of iron. This left the

Fig. 7 Torthorwald: original first floor entrance, with arched head, later converted into a window.

outer arrises free for decoration according to the fashion of the
period. Some towers, however, such as Comlongon, had the
rebate for the wooden door on the outside of the jamb, such that
the door was flush with the outer wall face, and in these instances
the decoration was omitted.

The head of the doorway was usually square, but semi-
circular heads are, or were, found at the earlier castles of Threave,
Torthorwald, Closeburn, Comlongon and Coshogle, while a segmental arch with a more elaborate, leaf-and-stalk ornament on a
QERH moulding is found at Stapleton. Both Bonshaw and Repentance have a motto immediately above the door; and some
towers, notably Hoddom and Coshogle, have, or had, an elaborate hood-moulding, which in the case of Hoddom was in the
form of a rope, or 'cable', with a knot at each end – though this
may be a later replacement.

Another feature that was found above the entrances to
many towers was an armorial panel, though it is comparatively
rare for the arms themselves to have survived. Exceptions are
Hills, MacLellan's, Isle, Fourmerkland, Amisfield and Barscobe.
The armorial panel has also been preserved at Kirkpatrick – even
though all trace of the tower has long since gone –, and the panel
commemorating the modernization of Lochar in 1622 was still
in situ at the end of the 19th century.[11] Drumcoltran has an elaborate Latin motto on a separate stone above the armorial panel.
There is a widely-held belief that some of the panels never in
fact had any arms added.

Throughout the period of the tower-house, wooden doors
were almost invariably made from an outer layer of close-jointed,
vertical planks securely bonded to an inner layer of similarly

Fig. 9 Fourmerkland: entrance doorway and armorial panel. 1590.

Fig. 8 Maclellan's Castle: main entrance doorway
and armorial panels. 1581-2.

Fig. 10 Hoddom Castle: old door with feather jointing and clencher
nails.

Fig. 11 Amisfield; carved door, dated 1600.

Fig. 12 Closeburn: inner side of entrance door and yett. 15th century.

Fig. 13 Isle.
Yett seen from inside, with portion of original cobbled floor
(found beneath later flagstones). 1587.

close-jointed, horizontal planks by clencher nails (i.e. nails with large heads and long tails), which were bent over and hammered flat for strength. The closing stile was usually a single plank, the full thickness of the door, into which the top, middle and bottom horizontal planks were dovetailed. Sometimes the vertical planks had the added refinement of 'feather-jointing'. Doors of this type have survived at Closeburn and Hoddom, though the latter is no longer in its original position, and there are the remains of a third at Amisfield. Both Amisfield and Terregles also had magnificent examples of carved doors, which, although no longer in their respective towers, have been preserved. They were clearly made by the same craftsman, and are dated 1600 and 1601 respectively.[12]

YETTS

Grated iron doors, or 'yetts' as they are known in Scotland, are first recorded at Edinburgh Castle in 1377.[13] Thereafter they quickly became a standard component of the defences at the entrance to every major tower-house in the land, and the same method of construction was used for the grilles protecting windows.[14] Made of iron bars forged together in an intricate pattern about a central point, which gave them immense strength, they were usually situated immediately behind the outer wooden door to reinforce it, as well as being invincible to fire. They were carried on heavy hinges, and had one or more strong bolts that could be secured with a padlock or chain. The licence granted to John Murray of Cockpool for the construction of Comlongon *c*.1501 included permission 'to mak apone the sammyn . . . irnezettis [iron yetts] and windois'.[15]

At Comlongon, Closeburn and Isle, the yetts have survived *in situ*, and the same is probably true of at least one of the three preserved at Drumlanrig; but the one at Barjarg has been shortened and re-hung outside, while the one from Lochwood is now preserved at Raehills.

To give the whole still more strength, the yetts were usually reinforced with one or two drawbars, which were strong bars of wood or iron that could be slid into a slot, or tunnel, in the adjacent wall when not in use. These slots were usually lined with wood, and, together with the drawbars themselves, were built into the towers when they were being constructed. In a few instances, the arrangement was more elaborate. One such example is to be found at Isle. Here the conventional drawbar was situated *between* the wooden door and the yett, while two further bars, held by hooks fixed to the wall, could be dropped into place behind the yett.[16] Lochwood, on the other hand, was found to have no means of reinforcing the yett. This was probably because the entrance has been altered or rebuilt at some later date.

Barscobe, being of much later date than the other towers, was not provided with a yett.

Fig. 15 Comlongon: details of yett, showing bolt and reinforcing ring for drawbar.

MOULDINGS

The mouldings found at the main entrance are usually repeated on the surrounds of other doorways and windows. In the great tower-castles of the 14th and 15th centuries, the principal moulding was usually no more than a bold chamfer – although at both Threave and Torthorwald it had the added refinement of being a hollow-chamfer – , and the chamfer was still being used at Comlongon at the beginning of the 16th century. Later still, a diminutive hollow-chamfer is found on the arrises of the doors and windows at Hills. It was not until the middle of that century that other forms of moulding began to make their appearance.

By far the commonest of the new mouldings was the quirked-edge-roll (QER), which continued in common usage for a century or more. Early variants of it were the roll-and-hollow, the quirked-edge-roll-and-hollow (QERH) and the quirked-edge-roll-and-fillet (QERF). The roll-and-hollow moulding was used for the great fireplace on the fourth floor of Hoddom's wing; for the entrance at Lochhouse; and for the entrance and buffet at Bonshaw; while, with the added quirk (QERH), it was used for the entrances at Robgill, Frenchland and Barjarg, for some of the fireplaces and windows at MacLellan's (though in an unusual, embellished form in the case of the windows), and for the dormer window at Elshieshields. Early in the following century, a more complex variant of it is found at Dalswinton. The QERF moulding is the principal decoration used at Hoddom, where it is found on all the principal doorways and windows as well as around the great hall fireplace. It is also found on some of the windows at Kenmure and on the doorways at Abbot's, while one of the windows at Kenmure has the even more elaborate QERFH moulding.

Fig. 14 Drumlanrig Castle: great yett inside main entrance.

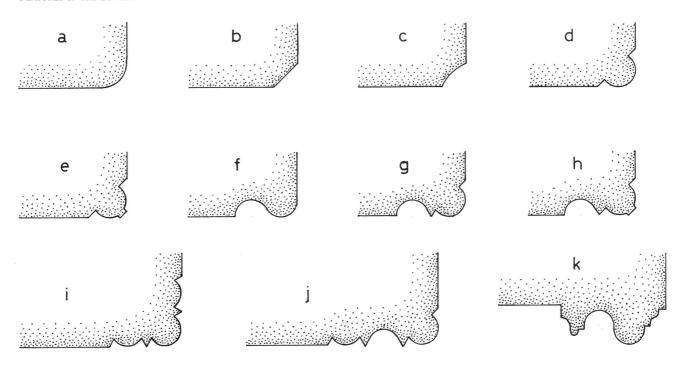

Fig. 16 Mouldings: (a) Edge roll; (b) Chamfer; (c) Hollow Chamfer; (d) Quirked-edge-roll (QER), or Bowtell;
(e) Quirked-edge-roll-and-fillet (QERF); (f) Roll-and-hollow; (g) Quirked-edge-roll-and-hollow (QERH);
(h) Quirked-edge-roll-and-hollow-with-fillet (QERHF); (i) QER with an additional quirked-roll (Hollows Tower);
(j) QERH with an additional quirked-roll (Dalswinton); (k) Bolection (Bonshaw).

A more elaborate form of the basic QER moulding is found at the entrance to Hollows, where the quirked-edge-roll is repeated a second time on either side of the arris, although elsewhere in the tower only the basic QER moulding is used. An extra quirk is also found on some of the windows at Abbot's and on an internal doorway at Dalswinton. In addition, Dalswinton has some unusual quirked ornament around the windows of the surviving entrance tower. MacLellan's Castle in Kirkcudbright is another building that has some unusual and very ornate mouldings. These include the elaborate surround at its entrance doorway, which is based on an embellished QER combined with a bolection roll-moulding.

The mouldings around armorial panels are usually fairly simple. They include several forms of edge-roll, such as the simple half-round moulding found at Hoddom and Fourmerkland, and a cavetto, or hollow-chamfer, moulding. The latter is found at both Bonshaw and Drumcoltran. Stapleton has an added nail-head course. MacLellan's Castle is alone in the West March in having a very fine and elaborate frame around its armorial panels. It is in a sophisticated, early-Renaissance style, with a pedimented head; and there is a similar surround framing a nearby window on the same level, except that the window has added dog-tooth ornament.

Towards the end of the 16th century, nail-head mouldings were also incorporated around some windows, as at Barjarg and Amisfield, while other forms of ornamental moulding began to appear as an additional string-course at the wall-head and around such features as the new dormer windows. Amisfield has a string-course with a chequer, or billet, moulding around the SE turret and at the main wall-head, and a slightly larger version of the same ornament is found at the wall-head of the reentrant angle at MacLellan's Castle. The smaller version of the same moulding is found again in the upper works at Elshieshields, on the gatehouse at Hills, and amongst the fallen masonry from

the 1603 alterations at Lochwood. Another popular ornament was the cable moulding, which is found at the wall-head at Hollows, on the dormer window and gablet at Amisfield, on the turrets at Spedlins, and in an explosion of ornamentation around doorways, heraldic panels, windows and as string courses at

Fig. 17 Bonshaw: pendant boss with IHS monogram
in vault of entrance vestibule.

Fig. 18 Sanquhar Castle: entrance to pend in Keep-Gatehouse.
Mid 15th century.

Fig. 19 Sanquhar Castle: pend in Keep-Gatehouse.

Kenmure. The cable hood-moulding over the entrance at Hoddom is probably a later replacement.

Some fireplaces and some early buffets had much more elaborate mouldings. These will be dealt with presently.

ENTRANCE VESTIBULES

The vestibule immediately inside an entrance was rarely little more than a passage through the thickness of the wall, with the main stair leading off it, but in some cases even this had features worthy of note. Several towers have a large open-aumbry behind the door, which in some instances may have been used as a seat by a door-keeper, while Amisfield and Lochhouse have separate guard-rooms, the former with the added facility of a slop-sink. Kirkconnell had a guard-room contrived beneath the stair. In some cases the vestibule was extended into a mural passage serving more than one basement chamber, as at Kenmure, Hoddom, Crawfordton, Edingham, MacLellan's and Rockhall; and at Hoddom this also gave access to the prison and guard-room opposite.

Both Bonshaw and Robgill are distinguished in having a cross vault, in the centre of which is a pendant boss bearing the sacred monogram 'IHS'. The former is finely wrought, but the example at Robgill is crude and looks as if it were added later.[17]

Sanquhar is unique, in that the main entrance to the 15th century keep-gatehouse admitted to a pend leading into the inner courtyard. While a door-way in the pend led directly into the basement, the upper floors could only be reached from a separate entrance in the inner courtyard.

BASEMENTS

The basements of tower-houses were normally vaulted, partly to give the walls added strength at ground level, but primarily as a precaution against fire. It was a common ruse for besiegers to stuff straw or gunpowder through every available aperture and then set fire to it,[18] hence the need to keep basement apertures to an absolute minimum. Before the advent of handguns, the only apertures found in basements were narrow

Fig. 20 Threave: N end of basement, showing prison in NW corner.

Fig. 21 Comlongon Castle: E end of basement
and entresol floor level. *c* 1501.

Fig. 23 Spedlins: slit-window in basement. 15th century.

ventilation slits, with the occasional small window for light high up in the end walls; and in some large towers, such as Threave, even the ventilation openings were located high in the walls, with steeply stepped sills on the inside, to serve the combined purpose of providing both light and ventilation.[19] It was also quite common for the larger towers to have high vaults, which were subdivided to provide an entresol floor beneath the Great Hall. Examples of this arrangement are found at both Threave and Comlongon.

With the introduction of hand-held guns in the middle of the 16th century, the ventilation slits gave way to splayed gun-loops, though it is noticeable that they did not become so universal in the west of the March. Perhaps some of the lairds there considered themselves sufficiently far-removed from the troubles of the Borders not to need such protection. Whatever the reason, gun-loops are not found at Abbot's, Sundaywell, Earlstoun, Shirmers or Corra – though the date of Corra is uncertain.

Torthorwald was alone among the early towers in having no vault, the present vault being a later addition. Later, several of the lesser towers were built without vaults, sometimes because the soft ground could not bear the weight – as at Abbot's and Lochar – and sometimes for less obvious reasons. Among the latter were Lag, Elshieshields, Glenae, Frenchland, Auchenskeoch, Cumstoun and Barscobe. Except in the case of Auchenskeoch and the 17th century house of Barscobe, it may have been because the tower started life as a more basic structure. Repentance did not have a vault either, but it was only built to serve as a watch tower.

At Lochwood, Hollows, Bonshaw and Robgill, the vaults are made of well-cut ashlar, but elsewhere they are only made of roughly coursed sandstone or slabs of greywacke. In some instances the vaults are keyed into the end walls, while in others they were built to abut them, as if added later; it was a difference of building technique. In either case they would appear to have been built using timber formwork, but without wicker centering.[20]

Although the majority of basements were a single chamber, some had the vault subdivided to form two chambers – as, for example, at Lochwood and Edingham –, and some – such as Crawfordton and Lockerbie and probably also Rockhall – were built with two or more separate vaults, connected by a passage. The vaults at Lockerbie were at right angles to one another. The basement at Barscobe was probably subdivided from the outset, but the partitions at Spedlins and Hoddom are later insertions.

Much the most complex basements were those of Kenmure, MacLellan's and Dalswinton, though, because of sev-

Fig. 22 Spedlins: slit-window in basement.

Fig. 24 Bonshaw: S end of basement, showing prison in SW corner,
gun-loop and later, stone storage-bin. *c*1570.

eral phases of destruction and rebuilding over many centuries, there is now no certainty as to which periods the various surviving parts of Kenmure belong. MacLellan's, on the other hand, was all built at the one time, *c*.1581-2, and, as befits a large town-house of that period, has a basement that is provided with a series of vaulted cellars, a kitchen with a vast fireplace and oven, and another vaulted chamber that is reputed to have served

Fig. 25 Hills: basement 'window'. Early 16th century.

as an 'ice-house'. These were all interconnected by passages, and communicated directly with the hall above by means of a service stair.

The transitional tower-house at Dalswinton is considerably later in date. It is also the earliest tower-house to have a basement that was truly subterranean. This served as the kitchen, with a fine fireplace behind a wide arch at one end and steeply-angled shafts on the other sides to let in the light from above. It was covered with a barrel-vault of coursed ashlar, and was evidently subdivided into two chambers, as well as having a third, smaller chamber in the basement of the SE corner tower.

Basement floors were covered in a variety of materials. Some were left as the bedrock, rubble or mud, probably covered in straw, while others were cobbled or paved with greywacke or flags of sandstone. The floor at Isle was originally of cobbles, which are believed to be still *in situ* beneath the later flags, while Lochwood, Drumcoltran and Bonshaw had sandstone flags. At Bonshaw, the flags are graded to drain towards the prison in the SW corner, where a channel through the tower's walls connected with the external drain leading from the garderobe to the cliff edge.[21] This is a clear indication that the basement was designed to be used by horses or other livestock, at least in an emergency.

It was not uncommon for the great tower-castles to have a well within the basement. This ensured that they were self-sufficient for water in the event of a protracted siege, as well as having the means to quench any fires started by besiegers. Threave, Spedlins and Sanquhar had wells, and there is said to be one underneath the present rubble at Torthorwald. The well at Threave is rock-cut and was originally lined with oak, while those at Spedlins and Sanquhar are lined with ashlar.

Occasionally there was a small hatch in the top of a basement vault, which communicated with the floor above. The precise reason for these is not clear, but examples may be seen at Lochwood, where there are two, Bonshaw and Fourmerkland.[22]

The only other feature of note in some basements is a slop-sink. These will be discussed later.

GUN-LOOPS AND SHOT-HOLES[23]

The earliest example of firearms being used in defence in the West March is at Threave, where an artillery wall was added *c*.1450. This gave additional protection on the S and E sides, and included three corner towers, each equipped with both inverted-keyhole and vertical dumb-bell loops, on two levels, for the use of small cannon. A feature of these loops is the inclusion in the sills of a transverse slot, in which a wooden beam could be mounted to support the guns and take the recoil.

It was another century before gun-loops were incorporated in the towers themselves, when the smaller hand-guns, known as 'arquebuses' or 'hagbuts', became widely available. These early loops were widely splayed through the thick walls, and were usually so arranged that the narrowest part, or 'throat', of the opening was in the middle of the wall. This gave the widest angle of fire with minimum weakening of the walls. At

Fig. 26 Threave: dumb-bell and inverted key-hole gun-loops
in SE corner tower. Mid 15th century.

Fig. 27 Threave Castle: SE corner tower of 15th century artillery
curtain, showing gun-loops.

Fig. 28 Lochar: gun-loop in basement.

Fig. 29 Bonshaw: field of view through east gun-loop.

Hoddom, for example, where the thickness of the walls is 8ft 6in, the angle of fire is 44°, while at Bonshaw and Hollows, where the thicknesses are 5ft 9in and 5ft respectively, the corresponding angles of fire were 53° and 45°. Some towers of the same period, however, such as Woodhouse, provided only half as much cover, leaving a wide area of 'dead' ground over which an enemy might advance in comparative safety. It was to overcome this handicap that the Z-plan towers, such as Auchenskeoch and Dalswinton, were devised. Not only did this arrangement provide cover for those areas of the outfield not covered by the main block, but it also provided flanking cover for the walls of the main block itself; and similar protection was also incorporated into the more elaborate ground-plan found at Maclellan's. Some towers, such as Bonshaw, Robgill, Stapleton, Kirkconnell, Drumcoltran, Lochar, Maclellan's and Dalswinton, also provided additional protection for the entrance. Hoddom seems to have been alone in incorporating slots for wooden supporting beams in the sills of the loops – as found earlier at Threave –, possibly suggesting more powerful guns than used elsewhere.

Another feature to re-appear at Balmangan and Dalswinton was the dumb-bell loop, though it was now mounted horizontally to provide the same wide field as the splayed loops. The dumb-bell shape had been used in the north at both Tolquhon, in Aberdeenshire, and Muness, in the Shetland Isles, in the 1590s, and is believed to have been adopted partly for ornamental reasons and partly to reduce the 'funnelling' effect of the splayed loops, where the splay could actually guide an enemy's shot through the opening. A dumb-bell shaped gun-loop has also been found on the Bonshaw site,[24] where it presumably came

Fig. 30 Hoddom Castle: gun-loop in basement, showing sliding wooden beam in sill with hole to support hakbut.
(See also Cruden, 219.)

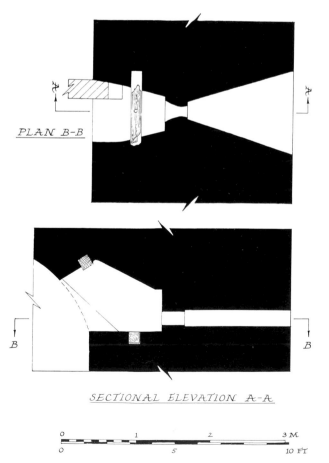

PLAN B-B

SECTIONAL ELEVATION A-A

Fig. 31 Hoddom Castle: plan and elevation of gun-loop in basement.

Fig. 32 Dalswinton: dumb-bell gun-loop. Early 17th century.

from the demolished secondary works, but unfortunately neither its original position nor date are known. Small, vertical, dumb-bell-shaped openings are also found in the garderobes and stair-well at Hills and in a garderobe at Amisfield, where their sole purpose appears to have been to provide light and ventilation.

Kirkconnell is unique in the Borders in having 'crosslet' shot-holes in the basement instead of splayed gun-loops. It is a form that is found elsewhere only in Aberdeenshire, and which consists of an inverted keyhole with a horizontal slot near the top. It has been suggested that the shape may have had some religious significance.[25] Another uniquely-shaped opening, now largely filled in, is found beside the N entrance at Kenmure. It is in the form of a double-cross, arranged horizontally, and one

Fig. 33 Kirkconnell: crosslet gun-loop.

Fig. 34 Hoddom: shot-holes in corner of parapet.

can only presume that it was intended to be more ornamental than practical, especially as there is a conventional, splayed gun-loop in the W wall opposite.

At Amisfield, where the basement pre-dated the introduction of hand-guns, the ventilation slits on the S and E sides were later modified to incorporate splayed gun-loops. However, this was only done on the outside, where an enemy could see it, so that, although it gave the appearance of providing a wide angle of fire, the actual angle was in fact very narrow, being as little as 6° on the E side. Here it was the psychology of its apparent strength that mattered, rather than what could be achieved in practice.[26]

One of the problems with gun-loops at basement level was that, on at least two sides, they could only fire on an enemy after he was inside the barmkin. This limitation was overcome at Hoddom and Lochar by having a second array of gun-loops at a higher level, which could fire over the barmkin. In addition,

Hoddom had corner towers which were also equipped with gun-loops, so arranged that they covered the angles not adequately covered from the towers themselves as well as providing flanking fire along the barmkin itself; and similar arrangements may also have existed at some other sites. Hills, for example, had shot-holes at two levels in the gatehouse.

In addition to the substantial gun-loops at basement level, provision was increasingly made for the use of lighter hand-guns from the wall-head and occasionally also from window-breasts on the intermediate floors, though no example of the latter arrangement is known in the West March.[27] Hoddom has an unusual arrangement of shot-holes in its parapet wall, while towers with turrets, such as MacLellan's, Kenmure, Isle, Elshieshields, Amisfield and Spedlins have shot-holes in the turrets themselves. Elshieshields and Amisfield also have shot-holes in their look-out turrets, at the highest point.

PRISONS

None of the earliest towers appear to have been provided with prisons, the one at Threave having been inserted later. When they did eventually appear in the West March, in the second half of the 15th century, they were built in the form of pit-prisons, contained within the thickness of the walls and only accessible from the floor above. Such were the prisons at Spedlins and Comlongon. The only other towers to have prisons were Lochwood, Hoddom and Bonshaw. The one at Lochwood, which is partly subterranean and partly encroaches on the basement, is reached by a short, low, mural passage. The one at Hoddom, which is situated in the wing, is also in part below basement level; it is accessed through a low door and then down two steep steps. It is unusual in being provided with a lamp-shelf. Bonshaw's prison is above floor level, and is partly contained within the thickness of the wall and partly encroaches on the

Fig. 35 Spedlins: corner turret with flanking
shot-hole adjacent to wall. 1605.

Fig. 36 Threave: vaulted prison with garderobe in NW corner.

Fig. 37 Comlongon: prison guardroom, with dungeon below,
window on left, and steps leading up to hall. *c.* 1501.

basement. It too is entered through a low door; and both it and
the prison at Hoddom have floors of very large, thick slabs to
prevent prisoners from tunnelling out.[28] All the prisons, except
apparently Spedlins, have very small ventilation flues that rise
up within the thickness of the walls: there are no windows or
other openings and only Threave has any garderobe facilities.

Fig. 38 Lochwood: prison, showing passage to basement.

Fig. 39 Sanquhar: window with segmental, ribbed arch in SW tower.
14th century. (There were originally three ribs. A second fell recently.)

WINDOWS

Threave is almost unique among the surviving towers,
in that, having been built shortly before the general introduction
of iron grilles, its two principal floors were provided with large
windows divided into four by handsome mullions and transoms,
and another, much smaller window of this type and period may
also be seen in the SW tower at Sanquhar. Shortly afterwards,
the distinctive, Scottish style of interlaced iron grille was uni-
versally adopted for all but the smallest windows in all but the
humblest towers.[29] At the same time the windows themselves

Fig. 40 Comlongon: iron grille in hall window. *c.* 1501.

Fig. 41 Comlongon: window with stone seats on N side of hall.

Fig. 42 Comlongon: window of upper prison with stone seats.

became smaller, partly because of the cost of the grilles and glazing, and partly for reasons of defence. Many of these windows were subsequently enlarged, especially by lowering the sill, and this can clearly be seen – as, for example, at Hoddom, Bonshaw and Kirkconnell – where there is an absence of socket holes for the grilles around part of the present frames. Although most of the grilles have long since been removed, some have survived at Spedlins and Comlongon.

The usual arrangement for the windows themselves was for the upper half to be glazed, while the lower half was closed by wooden shutters that could be opened for ventilation or to admit more light in fine weather: opening, glazed windows as such were unknown this early in the Borders. It was also common, especially in the earlier towers, to incorporate stone seats in the side walls of the window recesses, where people could sit and have a confidential chat, or the ladies could see better to do their needlework. There are fine early examples at Spedlins and Comlongon, and later examples at Hills, Hollows, Bonshaw, MacLellan's, Isle and Amisfield, while Blacklaw is almost unique in having stone seats on either side of a small slit-window only 6in wide.[30]

The scoinson-arches, which carried the massive walling over the window recesses, were usually in the form of a segmental arch. Threave, however, is an early exception, where the recesses have semi-circular heads, and a similar arrangement is found at Cumstoun, while those at Comlongon are almost semi-circular. Lag is unique in the West March in having pointed arches. Another method of distributing the load is the use of the 'Caernarvon Arch', a lintel supported by corbels at each end. This is not found in any of the tower-houses, but it is found in the hall-house at Morton Castle in Upper Nithsdale. Where timber beams are used, it is invariably an indication that the recess has been inserted later or enlarged.

Fig. 43 Bonshaw: typical wheel-stair.

STAIRS

By far the most common form of stair in Scottish castles and tower-houses is the wheel-, or turnpike, stair, where the treads radiate from a central newel, rising in a clockwise direction. It was easy to construct, took up a minimum of space, and, as a last resort, could – at least in theory – be easily defended by a single swordsman. Should the builder be left-handed, then the stair rose anti-clockwise, as may be the case at Balmangan, where the stair is currently inaccessible. Exceptions to the wheel-stair are found in all periods. There is a straight flight of stairs at the S end of Torthorwald; between the basement and first floor in the earlier work at Amisfield, and for the main stair at MacLellan's; and at Repentance. There are also two flights of straight stairs at Spedlins.

Fig. 45 Amisfield: original stair to first floor, with wheel-stair added in 1600 to serve upper floors.

Fig. 44 Amisfield: looking down stairs to entrance vestibule and guardroom beyond. Early 16th century.

In the early tower-castles, the walls were so massive that an entire stair could be contained within their thickness. However, as the towers and their walls got progressively smaller in later years, the space taken up by the stair increasingly began to encroach upon the rooms. This was a nuisance. To overcome the problem, some of the towers, such as Lochwood, Mellingshaw, Auchenrivock, Kenmure, Earlstoun and Barscobe, were built with a separate wing for the stair, while at both Blackethouse and Frenchland, which were originally oblong in plan, a wing was later added to achieve the same object. A stair tower was also added at Rockhall. A further development was the incorporation of a look-out chamber at the top of the wing, with a smaller, secondary stair corbelled-out to reach it. This is the arrangement found at Kirkconnell, Drumcoltran and Elshieshields. Still more accommodation could be provided in the wing by stopping the main stair at first floor level, and then

Fig. 46 MacLellan's Castle: main staircase leading up from entrance. *c.* 1581-2.

Fig. 47 Earlstoun: corbelled-out stair turret.

Fig. 48 Amisfield: top of main wheel-stair with chambers above.

reaching the upper floors from a secondary stair-turret, supported either by corbels – as at Buittle, where there are no less than seven courses, and Earlstoun – or a squinch arch – as at Abbot's –, in the re-entrant angle. One of the secondary stairs at MacLellan's is different, in that it is corbelled-out from the middle of the E wall, and there is another stair similarly corbelled-out at the top of the SE tower in the same castle. Barjarg was exceptional amongst the later towers in managing to accommodate the secondary stair in the re-entrant angle without any projection or, apparently, intrusion upon the rooms, while the upper floors and look-out turret added at Amisfield in 1600 are served by an amazing arrangement of no less than three wheel-stairs of diminishing size.

It was during the 17th century that the fashion for wheel-stairs finally died out. Then one finds new staircases, such as that already referred to in the new wing at Frenchland, being built in the much more spacious, and elegant, scale-and-platt form. But even as late as 1648, when tower-houses were all but a thing of the past, Barscobe was still built with a traditional wheel-stair; and at least one wheel-stair at Kenmure is almost certainly even later. Another feature of the new generation of stairs was the introduction of projecting, so-called 'bottle-nosed' treads, which gave more surface area for the feet as well as being considered more refined.

THE GREAT HALL

In every mediaeval stronghold there was one public room where all the family, their retainers and visitors met for meals and general socializing. This was the 'great hall' or 'hall', which in tower-houses was almost invariably on the first floor. Rare

Fig. 49 Threave: N end of great hall and upper floors.

Fig. 50 Comlongon: the Great Hall, by Thomas Ross, *c.* 1887.

exceptions to this arrangement were found at Threave and Lochwood. At Threave, in addition to the great hall on the first floor of the tower, there was an even larger hall for the garrison in a separate building, while at Lochwood the hall was not in the tower at all but, apparently, on the first floor of one of the adjacent building ranges, probably above the kitchen.

Not surprisingly, it is in the hall that the largest and finest fireplace is normally found, though Amisfield has an almost identical one in the family's private room on the floor above,

Fig. 51 Threave: the Great Hall, showing reconstruction of floor timers.

Fig. 52 Comlongon: carved lamp bracket on left of hall fireplace. The arms are those of Stewart impaling Murray.

Fig. 53 Comlongon: heraldic corbel in great hall supporting beams for floor above. The arms are those of Lord Maxwell.

above. Another form of decoration is found at Comlongon, where the royal arms are found on a panel above the fireplace and the shields of various other families on the corbels supporting the floor above. These have now been painted in strong heraldic colours, very much as they would have appeared when the tower was first built.

Fig. 55 Comlongon: detail of moulding over great hall fireplace.

and Elshieshields also has a large one on the second floor.[31] Another feature in some of the finest halls is a 'buffet', or mural sideboard, while Comlongon, and perhaps also Frenchland, are alone in the West March in also having a separate kitchen fireplace at the opposite end of the hall. These features will be dealt with presently. And just as modern houses have painted walls, decorated with pictures and finished off at the top with friezes and cornices, mediaeval halls were sometimes plastered and painted, were often hung with tapestries and other hangings, and, by the 16th century, were beginning to have friezes and cornices. Amisfield was a fine example: it has traces of a contemporary cornice in the hall and of a painted frieze[32] on the floor

FIREPLACES

Apart from the kitchen, the most important fireplace in any dwelling, whether fortified or not, was that in the principal living room, which in the case of the tower-houses was the great hall. It was usually vast, and anyone who has experienced such a fire can attest to the heat that it generates. The largest to survive was that in the great hall at Comlongon, which was originally 10ft 10in wide. This was only marginally greater than the fire in the great hall at MacLellan's, which was 10ft 7in wide, and compares with 9ft at Threave and rather less in such 16th century towers as Hollows, Hoddom and Bonshaw (all 7ft 4in), Kirkconnell (6ft 10in) and Hills (6ft 8in). The fireplace at Spedlins was rebuilt in 1605 in classic Renaissance style, but is still 7ft 6in wide.

The majority of hall fireplaces have simple QER, roll-and-hollow or, in the case of Hoddom, QERF mouldings; but a few are much more ambitious. The one at Comlongon, for example, has shafted jambs with moulded bases and embellished capitals, while above the lintel there is an elaborate, vine-scroll cornice; and at Amisfield, a century later, the jambs of both the hall and second floor fireplaces are also shafted with moulded bases and capitals. In each case the lintel was usually a single, massive stone, with the weight of wall above taken by a relieving arch, but at Threave the surviving second-floor fireplace has a 'joggled' lintel with a slightly pedimented top. The second floor fireplace at Orchardton also has a compound lintel, in this instance of three stones, with the central keystone cut to produce a 'flat arch'.

Fig. 54 Comlongon: great hall fireplace. c. 1501.

Fig. 56 MacLellan's Castle: great hall fireplace, showing aperture for 'Laird's Lug' behind. 1581-2.

Fig. 57 Bonshaw: S end of great hall. *c.* 1570.

Apart from the very late tower-house at Barscobe and the kitchen fireplaces at MacLellan's and Dalswinton, none of the towers had a fireplace in the basement, those at Robgill and Drumcoltran being later insertions, and only some of the towers had fireplaces on one or more of the upper floors. Despite the huge size of the hall fire at Bonshaw, there were evidently no fireplaces on the upper floors before the 18th century, not even in the laird's private chamber; and the same was apparently true at Stapleton, another Irving tower. The fine fireplace on the third floor at Elshieshields appears to be a later insertion, as is the present hall fireplace there and the Renaissance fireplace in the hall at Earlstoun, as well as some of the fireplaces at Comlongon, Hoddom, Drumcoltran, Kirkconnell, Stapleton, Isle and Rockhall. The unique and massive fireplace on the fourth floor of the wing at Hoddom, however, is original, although now reduced in size, and was evidently intended to provide boiling liquids for the castle's defence.

Salt was a very precious commodity in the Middle Ages, and to keep it dry special aumbries, or 'salt boxes', were built into the wall adjacent to the principal fireplaces. In a few instances, as for example at Amisfield and MacLellan's, one or more were actually built within the fireplaces themselves. There is also one in the hall at Amisfield that has the unique feature of five holes in its side wall to let the hot air from the fire circulate freely within the box itself.

Fig. 58 Amisfield: second floor fireplace with salt box in jamb. 1600.

Fig. 59 Hoddom: fireplace on 4th floor of wing. 1565.

KITCHENS

Very few of the Border towers had a kitchen as such within the tower, though it is probable that some cooking was carried out over the hall fire. The kitchen was usually in an outbuilding, and in some instances this was probably fairly rudimentary. The remains of a fine example can be seen at Lochwood; it was in a substantial outbuilding with a vaulted roof, and has a large fireplace, 14ft 3in wide, with what may well have been a larder with an aumbry next door. There were also two ovens adjacent to another outbuilding on the site, one of which is brick-lined and has survived almost complete. A kitchen building with a plinth for an oven has also been identified amongst the rubble remains at Blacklaw,[33] and the vestiges of another may be seen at Sanquhar.

Only Comlongon, MacLellan's, Dalswinton, and possibly Frenchland, had their kitchens within the towers themselves. The ones at MacLellan's and Dalswinton were in the basement, as already described, while that at Comlongon is on the first floor, at the opposite end of the great hall from the main fireplace and segregated from it by a partition with a hatch. The fireplace, which is 14ft wide, is fronted by a fine arch, 11ft 5in wide, of well-cut voussoirs. Similar arches existed in the kitchens at Maclellan's and Lochwood, but only the two ends of the latter have survived, and another such arch formerly existed in the kitchen at Sanquhar. The ruins at Frenchland suggest that it too may have had an arrangement similar to Comlongon, though on a much smaller scale.

BUFFETS, AUMBRIES AND WALL-SAFES

Even in the 16th century, the furniture to be found in a laird's house was very rudimentary. Chests of drawers were unknown, and free-standing cupboards rare. Items that had to be stored, such as linen, clothes, charters, and even books, were usually kept in either coffers (plain chests) or clothes-presses. There was, however, one other option: the aumbry, or wall-cupboard.

Aumbries could be either 'open', like a large lamp-shelf,[34] or 'closed', with a wooden door. 'Open-aumbries' were normally just plain recesses within the thickness of the wall, but a few had moulded surrounds, such as the two in the great hall at Elshieshields. One of these has at some time been subdivided by shelves,[35] while the other, with its more elaborate head of two moulded semi-circles, is really a diminutive buffet.

Fig. 61 Comlongon: buffet in great hall. *c.* 1501.

Fig. 62 Bonshaw Tower: buffet. *c.* 1570.

Fig. 60 Elshieshields Tower: buffet in great hall.

Fig. 63 Amisfield: closed aumbry with projecting shelf in great hall.

'Buffets', which were normally only found in the most sophisticated castles and tower-houses, were grand recesses, with richly carved ornamentation, designed for the display of items such as silver and plate. Most of the finest examples date from the 15th century. The large one in the hall at Comlongon, though of slightly later date and less refined, is among the most ornate. There is a simpler, but graceful, buffet with a fine ogee head at Bonshaw, and possibly the closed-aumbry with projecting shelf in the hall at Amisfield was intended to serve a similar purpose; while even simpler examples, without moulded surrounds, are found at Stapleton, Isle and Fourmerkland. It is not clear whether the 'piscina' at Orchardton was really intended as such, or whether it came from some religious establishment nearby and was being re-used as a miniature buffet, especially as the wall opens out behind the moulded façade.[36]

Fig. 66 Hoddom: aumbry. 1565.

Fig. 64 Orchardton: aumbry with piscina, possibly re-used from a religious building.

Fig. 67 Amisfield: salt-box beside great hall fireplace.

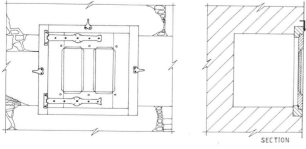

16TH CENTURY AUMBRY AT HODDOM

Fig. 65 Hoddom Castle: 16th century aumbry.

Fig. 68 Amisfield: wall-safe in NE corner of hall, showing double rebate for inner iron grille and outer wooden door.

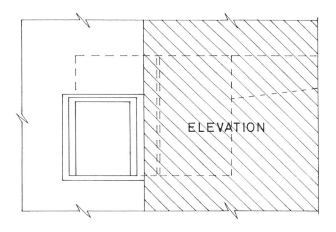

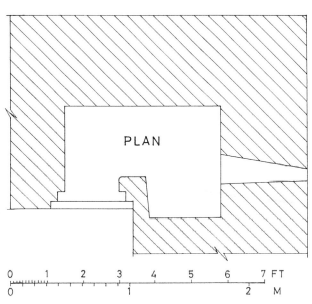

WALL-SAFE AT AMISFIELD

Fig. 69 Amisfield: wall-safe in great hall.

It is very rare to find an aumbry with its original pan-elled door. There is, however, an example at Hoddom, which was found concealed by later plasterwork and only exposed again comparatively recently. The door comprises two vertical, fielded panels within a broad, bevelled and rebated frame, which was supported within the outer frame by two strap-hinges of iron, with simple decoration. A few other closed-aumbries have been restored – as at Isle and Elshieshields –, but the rest are now no more than recesses. One can, however, always tell whether a mural recess has been a closed-aumbry by the presence in the masonry of a rebate for the frame. Indeed, the moulded oak frame for one of the closed aumbries at Amisfield (in fact a salt box) is still *in situ*. When closed-aumbries were situated either inside, or immediately adjacent to, a fireplace, they were invari-ably intended for the storage of salt, which had to be kept dry, as already mentioned (*supra*). Although most aumbries were sim-ple box-like recesses, there were a few which opened out within the thickness of the wall – as on the fourth floor at Hoddom –, or into the adjacent corner – as in the hall at Frenchland –, to pro-vide greater storage capacity. A rare variant is found at Isle, where an opening in the top of one of the hall's aumbries gives access to a secret upper chamber where valuables could be kept.

The two 'wall-safes' at Amisfield are a unique form of aumbry, and provide something of a puzzle, as their true pur-pose has never been established. Situated in corners of the great hall, each is 6ft 9in above the hall floor; opens out within the corner of the wall to a sizeable chamber, the NE one, for exam-ple, measuring 4ft 6in long by 2ft 1in wide by 3ft 4in high; and has a small ventilation slit in the outside wall. Instead of the usual, single, wooden door, each was closed by a small, inner, iron door or 'yett', 2ft 7in wide by 2ft 2in high, fastened by a single bolt, and an outer door of wood. For what were they intended? Not only does it require a ladder to reach them, but the presence of the ventilation slits would presumably make them too damp for the storage of perishable items such as charters; and why the need for the iron doors?[37]

SLOP-SINKS

One or more slop-sinks were to be found in most tow-ers. As their name suggests, they were used for the disposal of waste water and other liquids, and comprised a small, mural basin with a drain through the wall to a spout outside. They could be situated anywhere on the lower floors. At Threave, Spedlins and MacLellan's, there is one in the basement; Amisfield has one in the guardroom; many are situated off the wheel-stair; and some are on the first floor, either near the floor or, as at Lochwood, in a window-breast, while the one in the keep-gatehouse at Sanquhar is in a mural recess off the hall. Sanquhar also had one in the separate kitchen building, as would, no doubt, have been the case at Lochwood and in other kitchen outbuildings.

Fig. 70 Spedlins: slop-sink in basement.

Fig. 71 Amisfield: slop-sink in guardroom.

Although slop-sinks were basically intended for the disposal of waste, the location of some of the outlets immediately above the entrances cannot be accidental. Examples are found at Elshieshields and Fourmerkland, and that may also have been the arrangement in the keep-gatehouse at Sanquhar. One can only presume that these were intended for the secondary purpose of discouraging unwelcome visitors!

GARDEROBES

Garderobes, or mediaeval privies, were a normal feature of tower-houses. They were of two types: Open-garderobes, which had flues, and Close-garderobes, which did not. Some of the latter may originally have had flues too, which were later blocked up. In other cases, such as at Spedlins and Amisfield, close-garderobes were used in the later superstructures where there were no existing drains in the earlier work to connect into.

Fig. 72 Bonshaw: slop sink in Stair-well.

Fig. 74 Amisfield: close-garderobe in great hall.

Fig. 73 Sanquhar: slop sink on first floor of gatehouse.

Close-garderobes are also found at MacLellan's Castle, perhaps because it stood in the middle of the town, where open drains may have presented a problem. The only other option was to have a corbelled-out flue. This arrangement, where the flue is corbelled-out from the outer wall-face at the garderobe itself and discharges freely at that level, was used at Closeburn and Lag.

Garderobes were normally provided with a door, a lamp shelf and a small slit-window. In the great tower-castles of the earlier period, garderobes were relatively plentiful to cater for the larger households, but in the lesser towers of the 16th century it is rare to find more than two or three, one of which was adjacent to the laird's private apartment. As far as practical, they were located so that the flues could be grouped together,

Fig. 75 Threave: outlet chute from garderobe flue.

Fig. 76 Bonshaw: looking down garderobe flue.

Fig. 77 Amisfield Tower: 'Laird's Lug' above great hall.

MacLellan's, it comprises a small room immediately behind the great hall fireplace, with a small aperture that looks through the back of the fire itself, while at Amisfield it comprises a small room off the stair between the great hall and second floor, with a similar small aperture that overlooked, and overheard, the hall below.

PRIVATE APARTMENTS

The laird's private apartments were usually on the second floor, and were, as their name implies, for the exclusive use of him and his lady. It was where he slept, and where his children were born. In the lesser towers, they often comprised no more than one room with a fireplace and garderobe, but in some of the towers – such as Kirkconnell, Drumcoltran and Elshieshields –, the floor was divided in two, with the room remote from the stair being reserved for the lady of the house in her confinement, the arrival of new children being an almost annual occurrence. In the larger towers, the private apartments were also sometimes divided in two – as at Threave –, and sometimes not – as originally at Comlongon and probably Closeburn. Comlongon, however, had the additional feature of two mural chambers, one of which was used, certainly early in the 17th century, as a 'scholehous' (schoolhouse). By this time the main chamber had been subdivided, and the outer room become the 'lairds chalmer'.

Where partitions did exist, some were made of stone, which, being heavy, had to be supported by one means or another. This was achieved for the upper floors at Spedlins by building two huge, transverse arches, which took the weight off the hall vault below.[38] The majority of partitions, however, com-

either for discharge through a common chute just above ground level – as at Threave, Orchardton and Abbot's –, or into a stone drain below the ground – as at Hills, Bonshaw and Elshieshields.

In the great tower-castles, even the better prisons were provided with garderobes, but none of the pit-prisons had one except the inserted prison at Threave, nor did any of the prisons in the later towers of the 16th century.

'LAIRD'S LUG'

A feature more commonly associated with castles further north is the 'Laird's Lug', or 'Luggie'. This was an architectural device that enabled a laird to overhear the private conversations of his guests without himself being seen. Such an arrangement exists at both MacLellan's and Amisfield. At

Fig 78 Comlongon Castle: mural chamber at hall level.
(The steel supports are modern.)

Fig. 79 Threave: put-log sockets and access 'windows' for
wooden bretasche at wall-head.

Fig. 80 Comlongon: south parapet walk.

prised no more than wattle and clay. This, by its very nature, has not survived in the ruinous towers, although this method of construction continued in use well into the 17th century.[39] Barscobe was a late example. Such partitions were not only used to divide floors into two or more rooms, but also – as at Abbot's, Drumcoltran and Kirkconnell – to partition off semi-mural garderobes or bed recesses where it was not possible to contain them entirely within the wall's thickness.

UPPER VAULTS

In the early tower-castles, it was quite common to find a barrel or pointed vault over one or more of the upper floors.[40] The reason for this is not always clear, especially as there is no consistency in their location. They may have been included to give added strength and stability to the walls in the event of a siege, or to support a heavy roof, or they may merely have been a fire precaution. Torthorwald, Closeburn and Spedlins all have vaults over their great halls, and Closeburn has a third vault to support its roof.

By the 16th century, upper vaults had become rare, and were probably only inserted when it was considered essential as a fire precaution. Thus the chamber on the third floor of Hoddom's wing had a vaulted ceiling to protect it from the large fire and molten liquids being prepared on the floor above, and Repentance Tower had a vaulted roof to protect it from the beacon.

PARAPETS

The earliest mediaeval castles in Britain, the great Norman keeps with their massive enceinte walls, did not have corbelled-out parapets, but walls that rose sheer to the crenellated wall-head;[41] and this was the usual form in Scottish castles until late in the 13th century, when simple parapets, carried on single-stage corbels, began to make their appearance.[42] A century later, however, Threave still chose to follow the earlier arrangement, with walls rising sheer to the wall-head. The only difference was the inclusion of put-log holes for a projecting timber gallery, or bretasche, which could be erected or dismantled at will.[43] Closeburn would also appear to have had sheer walls.

Sometime early in the 15th century, the continental fashion of replacing timber hoardings and simple corbelled-out parapets with boldly corbelled-out, machicolated parapets of stone was adopted in Scotland too. This was a major advance in defensive warfare, for it allowed missiles to be dropped through

Fig. 81 Hoddom: machicolation over entrance.

same time, more ornamental, 'embellished' corbelling was beginning to appear. This was individual corbelling with smaller corbels set between, giving a patterned effect. Examples of this are found at Hills, Hoddom, Hollows, Stapleton, MacLellan's and Amisfield. Less common at this time was the simple, single-stage corbelling found at Drumcoltran, the unique arrangement of single corbels at Lochhouse, and the continuous corbel courses at Repentance.

From the earliest times, parapets were usually crenellated, and where this feature is now missing – as at Kirkconnell and Bonshaw –, it is almost certainly due to later modifications or restoration. Indeed, the breaks in the mouldings at Kirkconnell prove this to have been the case. The purpose of the merlons was to give added protection to the defenders when firing through the crenels, or embrasures. It was for the same reason that shot-holes were sometimes inserted in the parapets of later towers, as they were at Hoddom.

Fig. 82 Bonshaw: parapet walk,
showing machicolations over entrance.

the machicolations on to any enemy who got too close to the walls, without the danger of the defensive platform being set alight or shot to pieces. The corbelling of the great tower-castles of the 15th century was commonly of three stages, as found in the keep-gatehouse at Sanquhar[44] and at Comlongon,[45] whilst that of the smaller towers, such as Orchardton, although also machicolated, had only a single stage.

Later in the 16th century, the corbelling employed for the lesser towers usually comprised two-stage corbels with a smaller, continuous course below, while machicolations became rarer. However, the more important towers, such as Hoddom and Bonshaw, did incorporate machicolations over the more vulnerable features, such as the entrance and gun-loops. At the

Fig. 84 Hills: crenellated parapet walk.

ROUNDS AND TURRETS

It was soon realized that corbelled-out parapets could be further improved by adding 'rounds', or bartizans, at the corners. These were circular projections, which were corbelled-out still further in such a way that they provided much more effective cover against any attacker who reached the base of the walls, as well as providing better cover for the corner itself. The rounds were also crenellated, and in some later examples shot-holes were incorporated in the sills of the crenels.[46] Rounds are found at Hills, Hoddom, Hollows and Stapleton, though the latter two are modern restorations where only the corbelling had survived.[47]

After about 1580, corbelled-out parapets began to disappear, to be replaced by pitched roofs covering the full width of the building. In place of the rounds, there were now corbelled-out corner-turrets, though often only at diametrically opposite

Fig. 83 Bonshaw: machicolations seen from below.

Fig. 85 Isle: corner turret, showing shot-hole
to left of window.

Fig. 87 Amisfield: two-storied corner turret.

Fig. 86 Elshieshields: corner turret, showing look-out platform
at top of wing beyond.

Fig. 88 Spedlins: corner turret before restoration,
showing shot-hole (lower right).

corners and occasionally only at a single corner, while the roof was penetrated by one or more dormer windows to give more light to the top storey. This was presumably in recognition of more peaceable times. But defence was not abandoned altogether; not only did the towers continue to be built with yetts and ground level defence, but, as already related, the new turrets almost invariably incorporated shot-holes to cover the walls and ground beyond. Thus the turrets at MacLellan's, Isle, Elshieshields, Amisfield and Spedlins all had shot-holes, and so probably did Kenmure and Barjarg. In addition, the turrets at Amisfield were two storeys high, while the earlier turrets at Elshieshields had an unusual arrangement of two levels. Hoddom was different, in that the original arrangement seems to have comprised single-storey turrets to which a second storey was added sometime in the 17th century. Buittle and Abbot's also had turrets, but only the corbelling has survived, while at Frenchland the surviving corbels would seem to indicate that it had a corner turret of the much rarer, square form.

GARGOYLES

Gargoyles were used to direct the water from parapet-walks well away from the walls below, just as they did in the great churches and cathedrals; but sadly very few original examples have survived unbroken, perhaps because of the soft and

Fig. 89 Hills: cannon-shaped gargoyle.

friable nature of the sandstone usually used. There is, however, a notable set of original gargoyles at Hills. These are made in the form of cannons, with two pronounced 'bands' carved around them. They are made in two parts, with the upper half carved in

Fig 90 Bonshaw: gargoyle.

sandstone and the lower half, most unusually, carved in a very hard gritstone.

Bonshaw retains two original gargoyles, one carved with a flange at the outer end and the other with three rings cut in it. The remains of a third, quite remarkable gargoyle, has also been found on the site. It is circular, apart from the water channel cut in it, and is carved in such a way that the outer end is a continuous succession of fluted spirals, turning anti-clockwise, and the inner end a similar succession of concave spirals, turning clockwise, on either side of a central band. MacLellan's Castle is another stronghold that retains a gargoyle with an outer flange.

CAP-HOUSES

Where a wheel-stair rose directly to an open parapet-walk, it was necessary to provide protection from the weather. This was achieved by enclosing the head of the stair in a small cap-house with a pitched roof. Cap-houses of this sort are found at Orchardton, Hills and Repentance, and would have existed at many other towers that are now ruinous. There is also a cap-house at Comlongon, but it has a flat roof that serves as a watch-turret, and there was one on the top of the wing at Hoddom, where there is now a 19th century replacement. The cap-house at Closeburn has a flat roof too, but this may not always have been the case. Bonshaw avoided the need for a cap-house by turning the stair-head so that it emerged on to the parapet through the gable,[48] and there is a similar arrangement at Hollows and Lochhouse.

Fig. 91 Orchardton: cap-house.

Fig. 92 Hills: parapet walk and cap-house.

Fig. 93 Drumcoltran Tower: top of stair wing.

L-plan towers were built such that, where the main block had a parapet walk, the wing rose above that level. Thus the upper floor, or floors, of the wing took the place of the caphouse, with the stair opening straight on to the walk.

ROOFS

Although slate was in use for roofing throughout the Middle Ages, it did not occur naturally in the Borders, and, even as late as the 16th century, was very costly if it had to be transported any distance. Accordingly, many of the roofs in the Borders were originally covered with slabs of sandstone, which required strong rafters and purlins to support the enormous weight,[49] while some of the lesser towers and peles may have had nothing more than thatch. It was only later that these roofs were recovered with slates. Sandstone slabs have, however, been retained at both Closeburn and Repentance, where there are vaults to support the timbers. The slabs at Closeburn are about 13in thick, and some are more than 3ft square; they are fixed to the

Fig. 95 Amisfield: timbers for garret floor and roof in NW corner.

timbers with wooden pegs. Those at Repentance are of similar thickness, and measure up to 5ft by 2ft. When the stone roof at Bonshaw was removed in the 19th century, the new roof was built at a lower pitch, and this can be seen from both the steeper gables and the position of the water-tables on the chimney stacks. The position of the water-tables is, in fact, often a good indication of where there has been a change. Hills is another tower where the change of the roof-line is clearly visible.

Few of the original roof trusses have survived, but where they have – as, for example, at Hoddom, Amisfield and Barscobe –, they are all of double collar and rafter construction, with the trusses numbered in sequence with Roman numerals for identification during assembly.[50] So great was the roof span at Hoddom that each rafter had to be made from two timbers, joined with a scarf joint, and the lower collar was reinforced with braces. Amisfield also has braces on its lower collar. Smaller roofs, such as the one over the wing at Barscobe, only have a single collar.

Fig. 94 Hoddom Castle: main roof timbers.

Fig. 96 Elshieshields: dormer window.

DORMER WINDOWS

Dormer windows first appeared in tower-houses at the same time as parapets disappeared, and were provided to give more light to garrets. The earliest examples in the West March were probably those at MacLellan's, which was completed in 1582. Other examples that soon followed included those at Isle (1587), Elshieshields (*c*.1590), Fourmerkland (1590)[51] and Amisfield (1600). The dormer at Amisfield, which is immediately over the entrance, is unusual in that it projects beyond the wall-face and has a machicolation in its sill. When Lochar was modernised in 1622, one or more half-dormers[52] were inserted into the new roof.

Fig. 98 Barscobe: dormer window. 1648.

Fig. 97 Amisfield: dormer window with machicolation over the tower's entrance.

CROW-STEPS AND SKEWPUTS

From a very early date, it had been traditional in Scotland for the coping stones on a gable to be 'crow-stepped', i.e. built up with 'corbel-stones' or 'corbie-stanes', giving a stepped appearance. This has been exploited at both Comlongon and Hoddom, where access was required to the look-out posts and beacon respectively on the tops of the roofs, by widening a section of the crow-stepping to form a stair. At Comlongon it is 2ft 6in wide, and at Hoddom 2ft 4½ in.

The lowest stone of a crow-stepped or coped gable was known as a skewput. In the earlier towers it was usually cut square, but later in the 16th century it became the custom to give the underside a cavetto moulding. There were, however, a few instances where the moulding was made more elaborate by the addition of a billet or other ornamental moulding. An example of this is found at Spedlins. But much stranger are the carved heads to be found on a single skewput at Kirkconnell, Spedlins and Shirmers, especially as they could scarcely be seen from the

Fig. 99 Shirmers Castle: carved skewput
preserved in wall of later farmhouse.

Fig. 101 Elshieshields: look-out turret on top of wing,
showing shot-holes just below coping.

ground. Were they a mason's whim, or was there some deeper religious or masonic significance?[53]

Barscobe is unique in that, instead of the traditional crowsteps, it has plain coping, broken by two, evenly-spaced, additional skews on each sloping surface.

WATCH-TURRETS, BELLS AND BEACONS

Whilst L-plan towers were usually designed such that the top floor of the wing could be used as a look-out, and Amisfield had a special watch-turret perched on the very top of one of its steep gables, complete with its own fireplace, there were other towers where the duty of sentry was not so congenial. One of these was Comlongon, where two look-out posts were perched on the E gable – the side from which any English invasion was most likely to come. It is, however, unlikely that these posts were constantly manned, and it was presumably to make the duty of sentry more bearable that parts of the parapet-walk were later covered over and provided with a small fireplace. Another tower which had an exposed look-out post on top of the roof was Elshieshields. This was, in effect, a prototype for the watch-turret subsequently built at Amisfield.

In the event of impending danger, depending on its nature, bells were rung or beacons lit. The principal reason for

Fig. 100 Comlongon: NE look-out turret and steps up gable.

Fig. 102 Amisfield: look-out turret on top of E gable.

having a bell was to warn one's clan of some local danger, the bell's range being somewhat limited, while a beacon, or series of beacons, could carry news over great distances.[54] The bell on Repentance, however, may have had a wider use than just giving warning of a local disturbance, for the tower was in a commanding position and its primary role was to warn the country of an English invasion. When the tower was first built in 1565, Thomas Randolph reported that it had 'a bell *to warn the country at need*, and beside the same a "becone"'.[55] Lochwood is also reputed to have had a bell, and so is Bonshaw, the present one there being a modern replacement, and there will have been bells at other towers that went unrecorded.[56]

The principal beacons, or 'bale' fires, in the West March were those set up by the Earl of Douglas and confirmed by parliament in 1448.[57] Positioned on strategic hilltops throughout the lengths of Annandale and Nithsdale, and deep into Galloway, they were designed to give speedy warning of any English invasion in the west, so that a large force could be quickly mustered to meet the threat; and before long these beacons were supplemented by secondary ones to serve the smaller valleys, where the names 'Bail Hill', 'Beacon Hill', 'Watch Hill', etc., survive to this day. When, in the 16th century, the building of stone towers became widespread, it was deemed much more expedient to incorporate the look-out and warning system in the towers themselves. Thus, one finds that the sites of many of the towers were chosen not solely for their own defence, but also as signal stations to provide a visible line of communication from one tower to the next. This enabled any clan, or group of clans, to summon help, either by bell or beacon, depending upon the distances involved, without delay. Although most of the towers

Fig. 104 Hoddom Castle: beacon platform on N gable of main block, with steps leading up to it.

Fig. 105 Hollows: remains of beacon on south gable.

are now no more than sites, one can still clearly follow the lines of communication.[58]

Despite their known existence, there is little more evidence left of the beacons than there is of the bells. The beacon on top of Repentance is a 19th century reconstruction, but it is evident from the reference *c*.1566 to its 'Beaken in the Fire-pan . . . with ane Bell to be on the Head of the Fire-pan' that the original beacon and bell were on the tower itself.[59] There is also a platform on the roof at Hoddom that was clearly intended for a beacon, with steps to reach it, and another 'beacon' on top of one of the gables at Hollows. There is, however, no obvious explanation now of how the latter beacon was reached, nor indeed of how the adjacent roof was protected against fire. A similar arrangement of corbels on the surviving gable at Brydekirk suggests that it too had a beacon. Apart from their smaller size, these latter beacons are very similar in design to the so-called

Fig. 103 Repentance: stone hipped roof and restored beacon.

'look-out' turrets to be found on the English strongholds of Drumburgh Castle, just across the Solway, and the recently destroyed bastle-house at Melkridge.[60] On the other hand, an edict issued by the Earl of Sussex to his Wardens in the East and Middle Marches of England in 1570 was quite unequivocal about the use of beacons: it states that 'everie man that hath a castle or towre of stone shall, upon everie fray raysed in the night, give warning to the countrie by fire *in the topps of the castle or toure*'.[61]

MASONS' MARKS

It has been the practice for masons to 'mark' or 'sign' their work with their own distinctive symbol from the earliest years of the Middle Ages. The reason for this may not always have been the same – for example, it has been suggested that, on some sites where many masons were working, they were paid according to how many stones they had cut –, but it can be a useful way of identifying a number of sites where a particular mason has been employed. It would be even more helpful if each mark was unique to one, and only one, mason; but despite the ingenuity displayed in their design, it is clear that this was not so, for some of the simpler marks are found in work many decades, and even centuries, apart. It is also regrettable that the

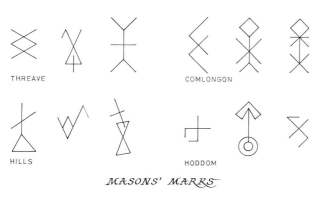

Fig. 106 Examples of masons' marks.

use of marks was very erratic, and fell off during the later years of the 16th century. Apart from such prestigious works as Hoddom Castle, where the principal features are generally marked, there are very few examples in Border towers built after about 1540. This may well be because, during the period when tower-houses were being erected in such great numbers, the majority of masons simply did not have, or use, 'marks'.

Few towers can boast such an abundance of masons' marks as Borthwick Castle in Midlothian, but masons' marks are found in the West March at Threave, Comlongon, Hills and Hoddom. They may also have been used at other sites where the ruinous and weathered state of the stonework has since obliterated them; but at other sites there is no evidence of any mark at all.

FURNISHINGS

Mention has already been made of the primitive nature of the furniture to be found in a typical Scottish castle even as late as the 16th century, whilst discussing aumbries (*supra*), and even in a royal household or elsewhere in Europe it was little different. There were tables, benches, a few primitive chairs, and simple coffers, cupboards and presses; but chests of drawers, desks, bureaux and domestic bookcases had yet to be invented; floor coverings were almost exclusively confined to rush

matting; paintings were rarely seen outside a church; and clocks and watches were virtually unknown before the latter half of the 17th century. On the other hand, there were colourful curtains, bedhangings and tapestries, and there was a certain amount of silver and plate, and perhaps a few books, depending upon the owner's wealth and status. There were also more mundane domestic utensils. By modern standards, however, the overall picture was one of spartan living, and this is amply demonstrated in the Inventories that have survived. Appendix A gives two examples.

DEER PARKS

Throughout the Middle Ages, the Crown and some of the most powerful nobles retained hunting forests that extended over vast tracts of the countryside. These provided them with both sport and meat for the table. What is less well known is that a great many lesser gentlemen also kept smaller deer parks to provide venison for their own consumption. It is not known when many of these were first established, though the earliest, the park of Stapleton, was first so designated by Robert de Brus early in the 13th century; and the park at Lochmaben is mentioned in 1333/34.[62] It was not, however, until the 16th century that parks apparently became more widespread. They are sometimes mentioned in land titles, and a great many are recorded in the surveys of Timothy Pont *c*.1595. There were, to take but a few examples, deer parks at Kenmure, Cumstoun, Terregles, Glencairn, Drumlanrig, Sanquhar, Mouswald, Cockpool, Castlemilk, Duke of Hoddom's, Stapleton and Bonshaw, but none are recorded in Eskdale.

It is not clear how all these parks were enclosed or even their extent. Whilst one might have expected high dykes of stone, the absence of any surviving traces, with the sole exception of Sanquhar, suggests that they may have been partly constructed of timber. The dyke at Sanquhar, a high drystone wall, with 'embattled' coping stones, encloses an area of some 70 acres. This was probably one of the larger parks, being associated with one of the most important strongholds in the region. It is, however, worth noting that another deer park further north – at Laighwood, in Perthshire –, whose massive drystone dyke still survives in part, enclosed no less than 385 acres.[63]

Fig. 107 Sanquhar: wall on SW side of deer park with 'castellated' coping. The castle can be seen behind.

1   Bonshaw, Kirkconnel, Robgill, Stapleton and Woodhouse.
2   Corra, Drumcoltran, Fourmerkland, Hills, Hoddom, Kirkconnell, Langholm and Lochar. Caerlaverock Castle, although not a tower-house, also represents a number of different building periods and styles employed by the Maxwells over more than four centuries.
3   Checked or rebated joints are also found at Loch Doon and Lochmaben castles.
4   When the writer excavated the south tower at Cramalt (Selkirkshire) in 1979, the forecourt there was also found to be cobbled, with larger slabs used for the path to the entrance (Maxwell-Irving 1982, 415).
5   Cardonnel, 'Lagg: Plate I'; Grose I, 155-6.
6   Grose II, 21-2.
7   The SW tower was rebuilt and the SE tower demolished in the 19th century.
8   Grose I, 141, 144. There is a view of the castle, painted by Sir John Clerk of Eldin c.1750, in the National Gallery of Scotland.
9   Good and Tabraham 1981.
10 When R. W. Billings was working at Dalzell Castle in the 19th century, he found that the massive walls of the old tower had been built 'on the natural surface of the ground . . . on a sloping bank of clay . . . with moisture enough continually passing over its face to have slipped the whole mass at any moment' (MacGibbon & Ross III, 317-8).
11 Fraser 1873, I, 621; MacGibbon & Ross V, 233. The panel was removed long before the wing collapsed, and its whereabouts is not known.
12 The Amisfield door is in the National Museum of Antiquities in Edinburgh, while the one from Terregles is preserved at Traquair.
13 ERS II, 554.
14 See Maxwell-Irving 1994, 433-54.
15 RSS I, No.692.
16 See Christison, D 'On the Grated Iron Doors of Scottish Castles and Towers', PSAS, XVII, 107-9.
17 This may only be because the joints are loose, or the whole stone may be a crude, later replacement.
18 Gunpowder was used by the English during the siege of Cessford in 1523 (RCAHMS 1956, 128).
19 The hall-house castle of Morton, in Upper Nithsdale, also has steeply stepped sills leading up to a row of very small apertures that served to provide both light and ventilation.
20 Wicker centering was a characteristic of vault construction in Ireland. See Leask 1986, Fig.52; Hist Mon NI 1987, Fig.47.
21 The basement in the south tower at Cramalt, which was floored with slabs of greywacke, also drained into a central channel (Maxwell-Irving 1982, 416, Fig.5).
22 Such hatches are not common, but they are also found in the Borders at Carfae and Whiteside in Berwickshire, at Oakwood in Selkirkshire, and at Lanton and Smailholm in Roxburghshire.
23 See also Maxwell-Irving 1974 (II), 192-224.
24 Maxwell-Irving, A M T 'A Recently Discovered Shot-Hole Block at Bonshaw Tower', TDGAS, 3rd Ser., XLIV, 224-6.
25 Bryce, I B D and Roberts, A 'Post-Reformation Catholic symbolism: further and different examples', PSAS, 126 (1996), 905-8.
26 Maxwell-Irving 1974 (II), 212-14.
27 The nearest examples were at Oakwood in Selkirkshire and Drumelzier (now demolished) in Peeblesshire.
28 In 1579 the magistrates of Dumfries remarked on the disadvantages of ground-floor cells, because of the sandy and stony ground beneath, which was easily undermined.
29 See Maxwell-Irving, A M T 1992 (II), 433-454.
30 The guardroom and upper prison at Comlongon also have stone seats on either side of their small windows. Duart Castle, in Argyll, is another castle that has large window recesses with stone seats and very small windows.
31 Cardoness Castle, further west, has similar fireplaces on both the first and second floors.
32 See RCAHMS 1920, Fig.143, for a coloured reproduction.
33 RCAHMS site survey, 1991.
34 Lamp-shelves were small square recesses designed to hold a small candlestick or lamp. They are commonly found in vestibules and garderobes, where there was no other free surface.
35 It is not clear whether the shelves were original, or a later addition.
36 There is evidence of masonry being re-used elsewhere in the tower, as, for example, in the first floor garderobe, where the doorstep started life as a window sill or lintel in another building. It has, however, been suggested that most castles had oratories before the Reformation, even though few have yet been identified as such (Proudfoot, E and Aliaga-Kelly, C 'Excavations at Niddry Castle, West Lothian, 1986-90', PSAS, 127 (1997), 833.
37 Suggestions have even included cages for falcons or pet monkeys. Safes, or strong rooms, are not unknown in Scottish castles, but where they exist elsewhere, such as at Melgund (MacGibbon & Ross, IV, 312-3) and Leslie (Ibid, II, 198-9), they are in a separate room built for the purpose. There is, however, a large aumbry with a double rebate and two sets of hinge sockets in the restored Drumlanrig's Tower in Hawick.
38 A similar arrangement may be seen at second floor level in the ruinous interior of Cardoness Castle, near Gatehouse-of-Fleet (See MacGibbon & Ross, I, 246, Fig.202).
39 Beaton, 18-19.
40 The earliest surviving tower-house, at Drum in Aberdeenshire, has three vaulted storeys, the upper two of which have entresol floors.
41 Typical examples in England are the Tower of London, Rochester and Hedingham, while in Scotland the same arrangement was found at the early castles on the west coast, such as Sween, Rothesay and Skipness.
42 Carew (in Wales) and Drum are early examples.
43 A similar arrangement was found in the early mediaeval towers of Italy. It is debateable whether the hoardings at places like Threave were in fact ever dismantled.
44 Cardonnel, 'Sanquhar: Plate I'.
45 Caerlaverock Castle is also a fine example.
46 An example of this feature is found at Bemersyde in Berwickshire, but none is known in the West March.
47 Cardonnel also shows Friars Carse with rounds, but Grose does not.
48 Although the stair-head was rebuilt in the 1890s, the arrangement is original.
49 Rather surprisingly, the RCAHMS found, when working in the far north of Scotland in the 1970s, that the timber trusses used for stone roofs were neither stronger nor more frequent than those for slate or thatch.
50 The trusses were first made and assembled on the ground, before being raised to the roof for re-assembly in their final position.
51 The NW dormer is modern, but the SE dormer, although partly rebuilt, is original.
52 A half-dormer is one where the lower half of the window is below the wall-head while the upper half projects through the roof.
53 This form of ornamentation was not new; at the top of each of the huge corbels supporting the battlements of the Palazzo Vecchio in Florence there was originally either a human or an animal head, some of which survive. The corbels date from c.1300, two years before the palace was finally completed.
54 The Romans are reputed to have been able to carry news throughout their empire by this means.
55 Scottish Papers II, 155.
56 Roxburgh Castle had 'a great bell called "Watchebelle"' on record in 1411 (Bain IV, No.810), and the Platte of Roxburgh Castle prepared in 1547 shows 'The Bell Mowntte' (RCAHMS 1956, Fig.518).
57 APS I, 714-6.
58 They are also self-evident from the surveys of Timothy Pont around the 1590s (Pont MSS; Blaeu, 55, 57, 59, 65 and 66).
59 'Order to be observed in the Stewart-Court of Annandale', issued sometime between 1565 and Mary's abdication two years later (Border Laws, 197).
60 RCHM 1970, 89 (No.53), Plate 18.
61 RCAHMS 1956, 417.
62 RCAHMS 1997, 206.
63 RCAHMS 1990, 94.

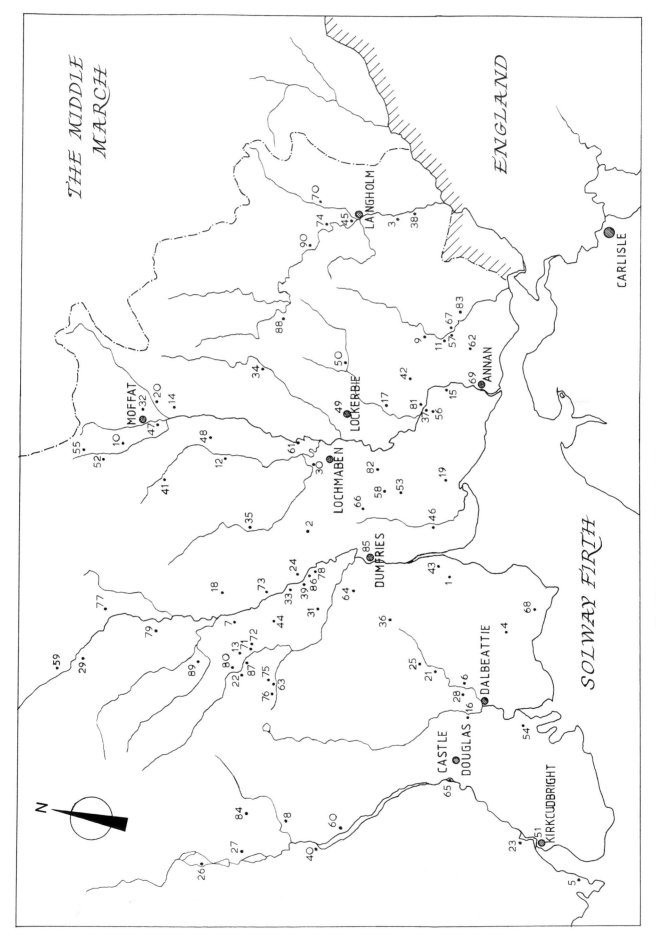

Fig. 108 The West March: locations of the towers referred to in the text.

CHAPTER 4

TOWER-HOUSES OF THE WEST MARCH

1. ABBOT'S TOWER
(³/₄ m ENE New Abbey)   (NX972666)

Contrary to what its name implies, this tower was never the home of an abbot, despite its close associations with the nearby Sweetheart, or 'New', Abbey founded by Lady Dervorguilla of Galloway in 1273. Indeed, the name 'Abbot's Tower' does not seem to have appeared until late in the 18th century, by which time the tower was already a ruin.[1] Prior to that, it was the manor-place and tower of the lands of Landis, or Lawne.

Situated only half a mile NE of the abbey, Landis was one of the many properties belonging to the abbey that were latterly leased out. Early in the 16th century the tenant was one Thomas Brown, a kinsman of the Browns of Carsluith.[2] He had at least two sons, the elder of whom, Cuthbert, succeeded him, while the younger, John, in 1538 became Abbot of Sweetheart.[3] Three years later, in return for 'certain sums of money paid to the Abbot in his urgent necessity', Abbot John converted his brother's tenancy of the '40 shilling lands of old extent called ye Land, the 20 shilling lands of Barbeth, the 20 shilling lands of Glen and the 20 shilling lands of Colyngach . . . in the barony of Lochindelocht' into a feu,[4] and in 1548 the family was granted a lease of more abbey lands.[5] By this time the Reformation was well advanced, and the abbey, finding itself increasingly unable to manage all its lands, was steadily feuing them out. The abbot's family received a generous share, with the Browns of Landis benefitting by further grants in 1559, 1563, 1578 and 1586.[6] The

Fig. 109 Abbot's Tower: view from NW before restoration.

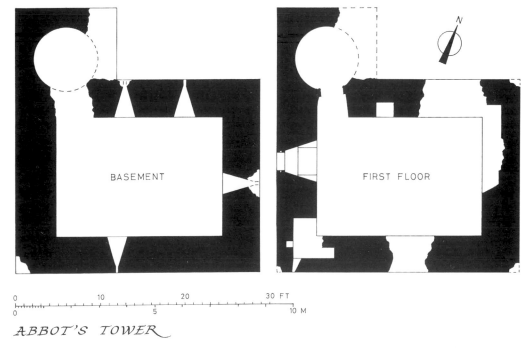

ABBOT'S TOWER

Fig. 110 Abbot's Tower: plans of basement and first floor before restoration.

following year, upon the annexation of all church lands by the state, the crown became the new superior.[7] Meanwhile, by 1578 Cuthbert had been succeeded by his eldest son, John, who in 1585 was included in a general amnesty for those charged with rebellion.[8]

It is not certain when the present tower was built. Although Cuthbert Broun might well have desired a more substantial house after he acquired security of tenure in 1541, there are various features which suggest a date much later in the century. The absence of a vaulted basement is probably a reflection on the ground beneath,[9] but the larger than usual stair, the use of turrets instead of a parapet walk,[10] and the comparative sophistication of some of the mouldings, all point to a later date. The absence of gun-loops, however, is not, perhaps, as significant in Eastern Galloway as it would have been further east. Clearly defence was not a priority, as no-one with an eye to defence would have chosen a site immediately under a steep slope, even if it was bounded by marshland on the other side. All that seems certain is that the present tower existed c.1595 when the tower of 'Lawnn' appears on Pont's survey of eastern Galloway.[11]

The **TOWER** has recently been restored, but prior to that it had been a ruin for more than two centuries. It is built on the L–plan, with the re-entrant angle facing NE, and comprises three storeys and a garret, with diagonally-opposed corner turrets, while the wing contained a generously-proportioned stair and terminated in a cap-house. Both the main roof and that on the cap-house had crow-stepped gables. The main block measures 23ft 6in from N to S by 29ft from E to W over walls 4ft 6in thick, while the wing, which is 12ft wide, extends 8ft 3in towards the N. The masonry comprises local granite boulders, with quoins, dressings and mouldings of red sandstone, all bonded with shell mortar. The original entrance has gone, and there is no record of its details; but the doorway leading into the hall at first floor level has a QERF moulding on its surround, while the slit-windows at basement level have QER mouldings and the larger windows at higher levels a QER moulding with an extra quirk around the outside. The entrance admitted directly to the wheel-stair, 7ft 6in in diameter, and a doorway leading into the un-vaulted basement.[12] The only features in the basement are solitary slit-windows on the N, E and S sides, and an additional slit-window on the N side to cover the entrance.

The first floor was supported on massive beams, each about 9in square and built up to 3ft deep into the side walls. It has window recesses on the N, S and W sides, but not on the E side, where the hall fireplace was situated. The fireplace was about 4ft 6in wide, and on its left, in the NE corner, both walls were inset, possibly for a press.[13] Whilst the window recess on the W side was the most complete, including stone seats and bar holes for an iron grille, the arrangement was peculiar in that the window itself was too high above the recess and seats for anyone looking out to see more than the sky. Other features are a large garderobe in the SW corner, which extended beyond the thickness of the wall into the room, and an open aumbry in the N wall. The former is provided with the usual lamp-shelf and slit-window, and has a drain that discharges below.

On the second floor, the entire central section of both the N and S walls had fallen, but much detail still remained. This floor had always been divided into two chambers, each with its own fireplace, with QER-moulded surround, in the respective gable walls. The W chamber had a garderobe in the SW corner, similar to the one below and sharing a common drain, and between it and the fireplace in the W wall there is a small,

horizontal window with sockets for an iron grille. This room also has a lamp-shelf in the N wall, and there was probably a second window on the S side. The E chamber has a window in the E wall, on the left of the fireplace, and in the S wall there was a vestige of the ingo for another window recess; it is likely that there was also a window in the N wall. This room does not appear to have had a garderobe.

Little remained of the garret, although it was apparently fairly complete when Grose drew it in 1790.[14] At that time the turrets at the NE and SW corners, though roofless, still remained, but by 1970 all that remained were the four stages of continuous corbelling that supported them. The only other feature to survive was a small section of the W gable, containing a small fireplace, with plain jambs, and an open aumbry. In the wing, part of the cap-house remained; this projected beyond the wall-head on each side, being supported on a continuous course of moulded corbels, and had a window with rounded arrises facing W.

Investigations in 1990-91 revealed vestiges of two secondary buildings and other external walls on the site.[15] These included a wall, some 4ft 9in thick, running W from near the SW corner of the tower for some 40ft and then N for about the same distance. It was built of shell mortar like the tower, and so in all probability formed part of the original barmkin. Another corner of an enclosing wall was exposed NE of the tower. If this was also part of the barmkin, as is tentatively suggested, it would establish an overall size for the barmkin of about 130ft from N to S by 70ft from E to W. Within this enclosure, and only 17ft to the N of the tower, were found the remains of another building. Its purpose is not known, but it had apparently been altered and extended at some time re-using 16th century material. The ground between it and the tower was paved with granite slabs.[16] Outside this complex, and some 100ft to the SW of the tower, there are the remains of a third building, which is thought to have been a cattle shed or stable. It was oblong in plan, of dry-stone construction, and measured about 40ft by 21ft over walls 4ft 6in thick. The entrance to this building was originally on the S side, where there was another area of granite paving, but this was later closed up and a new entrance made near the middle of the N wall.

In 1611 John Broun was served heir to his father in the forty shilling lands of Lande and others,[17] and the following year he sold them in feu to his brother, Gilbert Broun of Largis.[18] John apparently had financial problems, for only three days later the lands, having been annexed by the crown, were mortgaged to a burgess of Edinburgh.[19] Then, in 1613, Gilbert sold the feu to John Hay, Clerk-Depute of Edinburgh.[20] This may have been a wadset, as Hay was granted another charter and sasine of the same lands by Cuthbert Brown, son of the late John Brown of Land, in 1627.[21] Hay took the title 'of Landis' and remained in possession until he surrendered the lands to the crown in 1633. Landis, 'with the manor-place and tower', and various other properties in the neighbourhood were then united into the bishopric and free barony of Edinburgh,[22] which was confirmed, again 'with the manor-place and tower of the Landis', in favour of William Forbes upon his provision to the bishopric the following year.[23] These are the first mentions of a tower as such.

Five years later, following the signing of the National Covenant, the superiority of the lands reverted to the crown, and in 1641 the forty shilling lands of Landis and the twenty shilling lands of Colingach, 'with the manor-place and tower', and various other lands were incorporated into the free tenancy of Landis and granted to William Hay (later designated 'of Aberlady'),

Fig. 111 Abbot's Tower: view from NE in 1790.

one of the Clerks of Council and Session and son of Sir John Hay of Landis.[24] The superiority, however, was now incorporated into the enlarged Barony of New Abbey and granted to Sir Robert Spottiswood.[25] By this time it is not clear who was actually occupying the lands. Thomas Hay of Aberlady, William's son, had sasine in 1658.[26]

The superiority of the lands changed hands several more times before being successfully reclaimed by John Spottiswood in 1740.[27] The crown then renounced all claim to the lands, except the ultimate superiority. Spottiswood later broke up the estate and sold it off. Landis was acquired by the Maxwells of Kirkconnell, who were in possession in 1790;[28] but by this time the tower had been abandoned and was roofless, and a new farm of Landis had been built on the hillside above. Thirty years later, the property was purchased by Robert Carrick, a banker in Glasgow.[29]

In 1989 the ruined tower was purchased by Peter Kormylo, and the following year he started its restoration for habitation once more.

1   Grose II, 13.
2   Hornel MSS, cited by Truckell, A.E. 'Three Sweetheart Abbey Charters', *TDGAS*, 3rd Ser., XXXVII, 171. See also M'Kerlie IV, 242-5.
3   Stewart, F.J. 'Sweetheart Abbey and its Owners over the centuries', *TDGAS*, 3rd Ser., LXIV (1989), 60.
4   Hornel MSS, *op. cit.*, 171. Sasine, however, was not given until 1555 (Laing Charters, No.632), and two years later, the Papal See held an enquiry before finally confirming the charter (Laing Charters, No.669).
5   Stewart, F.J. & Reid, R.C. 'The Early Browns in New Abbey', *TDGAS*, 3rd Ser., XXXVII (1960), 94.
6   M'Kerlie V, 14; RMS V, No.1127.
7   Stewart (1989), *op. cit.*, 60.
8   APS III, 388.
9   c.f. Lochar Tower (q.v.).
10 The earliest dateable turrets in the Borders were built after 1580, e.g. Greenknowe (1581), Isle (1587) and Barjarg (c.1587).
11 Blaeu, 66, 'The Steuartrie of Kircubright, The most easterlie part of Galloway'.
12 The comments in MacGibbon & Ross, V, 215, and RCAHMS 1914, 210, that the vault has fallen are in error, as there never was one.
13 The N wall was inset by 1ft 6in and the E wall by 2ft 3in. This seems to be a feature of tower-houses in the area, as similar recesses are found on the second floor at both Kirkconnell and Drumcoltran (q.v.).
14 Grose II, 13.
15 The RCAHMS made a survey in 1990, and in 1991 the Scottish Urban Archaeological Trust carried out exploratory excavations.
16 These were irregular in shape and varied in size from about 1ft 3in to 3ft, with smaller stones filling the gaps.
17 Laing Charters, No.1624; M'Kerlie V, 15.
18 RMS VII, No.728; Laing Charters, Nos.1641-3 – John Hay was a witness.

19 RMS VII, No.731.
20 Ibid, No.830; Laing Charters, No.1650.
21 Laing Charters, No.2000.
22 RMS VIII, No.2225.
23 RMS IX, No.21.
24 Laing Charters, No.2295; M'Kerlie V, 16.
25 Stewart (1989), *op. cit.*, 63.
26 Laing Charters, No.2521; M'Kerlie V, 16.
27 Stewart (1989), *op. cit.*, 64.
28 Grose II, 13.
29 M'Kerlie V, 17.

2.   AMISFIELD TOWER
(5m NNE Dumfries)   (NX992838)

Of Norman descent, the family of Charteris, or in Latin 'Carnoto', came to Scotland in the reign of David I, and acquired the lands of Amisfield, probably from the Bruces, some time before 1200.[1] The first of the family on record is Robert de Carnoto, who witnessed William the Lion's charter confirming the grant of Annandale to Robert de Brus in 1166.[2] He was succeeded by Walter de Carnoto, reputedly his younger brother, who, c.1180, granted the churches of Trailflat and Dumgree to the abbey of Kelso;[3] and this was confirmed in 1266 by Sir Robert de Carnoto of Amisfield.[4]

Sir Robert was succeeded in 1288 by his son Andrew, though, presumably because Andrew was still a minor, the 'ward of Amysfeild' was granted to his uncle, Thomas de Carnoto, who had recently been appointed Chancellor of Scotland.[5] In 1296 Andrew swore fealty to Edward I.[6] Two years later he rebelled against the English, and forfeit his lands, whereupon Edward granted 'the castle of Amesfeld and land of Drungrey' to the Earl of Warwick.[7] Submitting to Edward again in 1303/4, Andrew

Fig. 112 Amisfield Tower: view from SE

had his lands restored, including his estates in Wiltshire,[8] and in 1306 he is included in a list of 'squires' holding Dumfries Castle for the English.[9] By 1314 Andrew had been succeeded by his son, Robert de Chartres, who sided with the Scots at Bannockburn. For this 'rebellion', the family again forfeit its English estates, this time for good.[10]

All trace of the original castle has long since gone, so we do not know what form it took. At one time it was thought that the quadrangular enclosure 100m W of the present tower represented surviving earthworks from this period, but excavations carried out in 1957 established that this was in fact a romantic 'folly' of the late 18th, or early 19th, century.[11] However, in the absence of any motte, it is possible that the earliest castle was some form of moated manor.

Apart from a short break in the 17th century, the Charteris continued to live at Amisfield for the next five centuries. During this time their feudal superiors were evidently the Lords of Annandale, a title conferred by Robert the Bruce on his nephew

Thomas Randolph *c*.1312, and subsequently inherited by the Earls of March.[12] After the defection of the 3rd Earl of March to England in 1400, their lands were acquired by the 4th Earl of Douglas, who was formally granted the Lordship of Annandale in 1409;[13] and the lands and Lordship continued to be held by the Douglases until their forfeiture in 1455, when they reverted to the Crown.

The Charteris were often prominent in public life, especially in the administration of justice, and were recognized as Chiefs of the name. In 1434 the lands of 'Aymisfelde, Trailflat and Elyok' were held in ward for Robert Charteris, son and heir of Roger Charteris.[14] He (or a son of the same name) was eventually given sasine in 1454;[15] but the Crown deemed this to be 'in error', so took the 'farm lands and cot lands of Amysfelde' back into ward,[16] and it was not until 1461 that Robert finally had legal sasine of the lands of 'Amysfeild, Charteris and Elyot'.[17] Three years later, Robert agreed to exchange the lands of Eliock (q.v.) and others with Sir Robert Crichton of Sanquhar in return

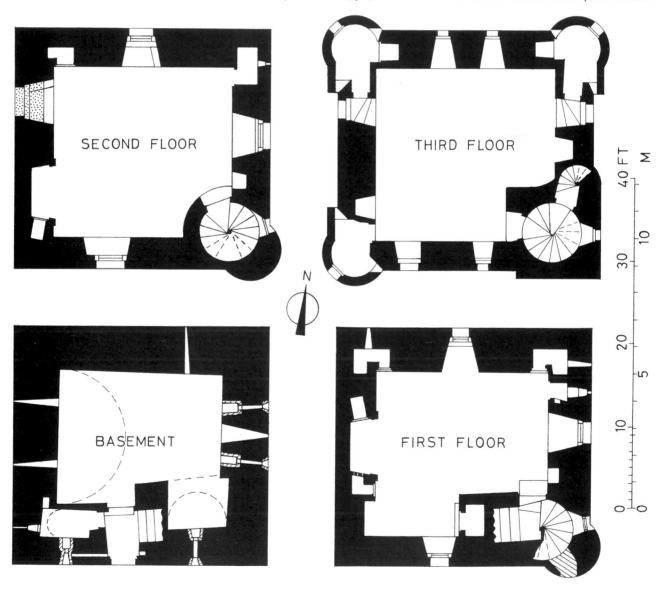

AMISFIELD TOWER

Fig. 113 Amisfield Tower: plans.

for an annualrent of £20 and lands in East Lothian.[18] It was presumably this Robert, later knighted, who became armour-bearer to James III, and took part in the battles of Lochmaben (1484) and Stirling (1488);[19] he also represented the barons of Dumfriesshire in the parliaments of 1481, 1487 and 1505.[20] In 1481 he was appointed Captain to take charge of Castlemilk, Annan and Bell's Tower (Kirkconnel) in time of war, with himself and two deputies to be based, one at each stronghold.[21] For his faithful service, James III granted him, in 1487/ 8, the lands of Pulchree in Galloway, which had at one time been held by his great-grandfather;[22] and this was confirmed by James IV in 1501.[23]

Sir Robert was succeeded by his grandson, John Charteris, who was served heir in Amisfield, Dalruscan and Duchra in 1506.[24] In 1525 John was appointed sheriff-depute of Dumfries and steward-depute of Annandale.[25] His son Robert, who is believed to have succeeded c.1527, was one of the Commissioners charged with organizing redress in the West March in 1531 and 1532.[26] Two years later, he sold an annualrent from the £10 lands of Amisfield to Lord Carlyle.[27] On his death in 1535, the ward of all his estates was given to John Carmichael, Captain of Crawford, and Ninian Crichton until his son and heir, John, came of age.[28] Later, Carmichael transferred his interest in the wardship to Robert's younger brother, John Charteris,[29] and in 1540 the Crown appointed John the sole ward.[30]

According to an old Border tradition, James V came to Amisfield in disguise in 1530 on behalf of a poor woman, who had in vain sought the laird's assistance, and was refused admission. It was only after a second servant brought the message that 'The Gudeman of Ballengeich' – a name used by the king when travelling incognito – had long been awaiting admission that Charteris realized his mistake, and begged forgiveness. For his contemptible conduct, he was ordered to recover the woman's only son, who had recently been taken by a band of marauding Englishmen, under pain of death; to reimburse her other losses tenfold; and to provide accommodation for the King's retinue at his own expense. The story is recorded by Grose,[31] but to what extent it is true remains an open question.

When the English overran Dumfriesshire in 1547, John Charteris of Amisfield submitted and pledged the service of 163 men.[32] He eventually had sasine of Amisfield in 1549/50.[33] The next laird, Sir John Charteris, who succeeded his father in 1577, was one of the Commissioners appointed in 1593 for establishing good order in the West March.[34] He took an active interest in the affairs of the burgh of Dumfries, being elected Provost in 1607/8.[35] In 1610 he was again appointed a Commissioner of the Peace for Dumfriesshire and Annandale,[36] and in 1612 a Judge Delegate and Commissioner for Peace.[37] In 1613, Sir John received from James VI a new charter of the lands and barony of Amisfield, which was formally ratified by parliament in 1633.[38] He died c.1616.

The oldest part of the present tower appears to date from the time of Sir Robert Charteris (d.1506), or his son, and there is evidence of another building period before all the upper floors were rebuilt by Sir John Charteris in 1600. On his survey of Nithsdale c.1595, Pont shows 'Hemsfeld Cast.', which he also labels 'Hemisfeeld',[39] while on his map of Annandale he calls it 'Amsfield',[40] which he shows as a significant tower. The tower stands high on the E side of Nithsdale, where it also commands the old route between Dumfries and Upper Annandale.

The present **TOWER** is justly considered to be one of the finest examples of corbelled progression, certainly in the S

Fig. 114 Amisfield: slit-window in W wall of basement, similar to those later 'converted' to shot-holes on the E and S sides.

Fig. 115 Amisfield: vaulted recess under stair with later, inserted gun-loop.

of Scotland. From an almost square base, 31ft 2in by 28ft 8in, a succession of corbel courses rise up the SE corner and E gable to carry the upper stairs, secondary chambers and, ultimately, a watch turret terminating some 77ft above the ground, whilst at the other three corners the wall-head is penetrated by 2-storey turrets of unusual design. What is not so often appreciated, though, is that, far from representing a single design, the present tower represents the cumulative result of at least three different periods of building and alterations.

The earliest period is represented by the basement, which appears to date from late in the 15th or early in the 16th century. The masonry is whinstone boulders, heavily pinned, with quoins and margins of dressed, red sandstone.[41] On the N, E and S sides the walls average 5ft 8in in thickness, but on the S side this

Fig. 116 Amisfield: gun-loop throat inserted into existing
slit-window in basement.

Fig. 118 Amisfield: S window of hall with nail-head
moulding and sockets for iron grille. 1600.

is increased to cater for the entrance passage and associated mural features. The entrance itself was defended by the usual wooden door and yett, backed by a stout wooden drawbar. Immediately inside, a door on the left admits to a small, vaulted guardroom, equipped with a slit-window, lamp recess and slop-sink, while on the other side of the passage a straight stair, 4ft 1in wide,[42] rises within the wall's thickness to the floor above. The vaulted basement is a very dark chamber, only 8ft 4in high, with slender ventilation-slits on all sides and a single, small window high up in the E wall; the floor is cobbled. In the SE corner a barrel-vaulted recess has been contrived beneath the stair. Although only 4ft 2in high, it is equipped with a lamp-shelf and slit-window. When firearms came into more general use later, the two slit-windows on the S side and ventilation-slits on the E side were modified to serve as gun-loops. The wide splay of the loops on the outside was, however, a bluff, as the actual angle of fire was restricted by the earlier slits to a mere 6° on the E side.

The first-floor hall represents a later period of reconstruction. Prior to this work, however, there is evidence of an

earlier change at this level, where several courses of ashlar masonry survive in the N and E walls. The hall is an L-shaped chamber, with a large fireplace, 7ft wide, in the W wall and windows on the other three sides. There is evidence to suggest that the S window may occupy the position of an earlier, first-floor entrance.[43] The jambs of the fireplace have an unusual form of moulded shaft, with cap and base, and originally there was a moulded shelf above the massive lintel. The latter feature, like the similar one on the floor above, has at some time been deliberately broken off. In the right ingo there is an aumbry, while on the opposite side five, well-cut holes provide heat to an L-shaped salt-box in the adjacent wall; both retain their original wooden surrounds, the latter one being moulded. A third aumbry over the stair has a projecting sill in front, and opens out behind to provide a substantial storage-space. Immediately above it, and accessible only from the stair above, is a private chamber, 5ft

Fig. 117 Amisfield: splayed gun-loop inserted into outer
face of existing slit window in late 16th century.

Fig. 119 Amisfield Tower: great hall fireplace (with broken lintel)
showing salt boxes.

8in by 4ft 5in, that overhears, rather than overlooks, the hall below through a very small opening, or 'laird's lug' as it is called. In the hall's E wall there is a close-garderobe, with a lamp-shelf and slit-window in the form of a vertical dumb-bell,[44] and an open aumbry. Perhaps the most remarkable features on this floor, however, are two wall-safes, situated at either end of the N wall and 6ft 9in above the floor.[45] Generally similar in construction, although almost a mirror-image of each other, the one in the NE corner is dog-legged on plan and has an overall measurement of 4ft 3in long by 3ft wide and is 3ft 4in high; it has a slit-window, 11in high and 4in wide, at the top of its E wall: the safe in the NW corner has the window on the N side. Access to these safes was through a small doorway, 2ft 3in wide by 2ft 1in high, with a double rebate in the surround where they were secured by an outer wooden door and an inner iron door or grille. Some of the hall's plaster cornice has survived *in situ*.

The straight stair from the basement ends four steps below the first floor. It then continues as a wheel-stair, 7ft 6in in diameter, rising to third floor level. But whilst the SE corner of the tower is corbelled-out as if to support this stair, the two do not actually correspond, and it appears that the corbelling has been retained from an earlier arrangement. A doorway, now blocked, on the S side of this projection at first-floor level may have given access to a wall-walk on the barmkin; it is 11ft above ground level.

The second floor was the family's private hall, a spacious chamber made larger by the reduction in wall thickness at this level to 4ft 8in for the E and W walls and 4ft on the other sides. It also has the largest windows in the tower. There is one in each wall, those on the N and W sides having a stone seat along the right ingo; all were originally protected by iron grilles.

The W window is now blocked. The fireplace in the W wall is the same size as, and has identical mouldings to, the one in the hall below; it has an aumbry in the left ingo. There is an open aumbry, or lamp-shelf, beside the door in the E wall, and another, L–shaped aumbry in the NW corner, while a close garderobe with slit-window but, unusually, no lamp-shelf occupies the NE corner. Traces of a painted frieze may still be seen around the plastered walls.[46] Outside the S wall, and on either side of the window at this level, there are two, well-preserved, heraldic panels. They are dated 1600 and bear the arms of Sir John Charteris and his wife Agnes, daughter of Sir John Maxwell, 4th Lord Herries,[47] who completed the tower as it now stands in that year.

The third floor was originally divided from N to S by a timber partition to form two chambers, each with windows on

Fig. 120 Amisfield: bottom of stair turret with blocked doorway, which probably led on to the barmkin wall. 1600.

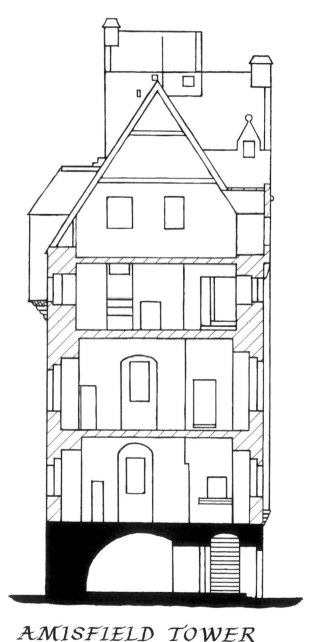

AMISFIELD TOWER

Fig. 121 Amisfield Tower: sectional elevation (after MacGibbon & Ross).

Fig. 122 Amisfield Tower: access,
on two levels, to NE corner turret.

three sides and a small fireplace in the gable wall. The only other features on this floor are the 2-storey, corner turrets. These are corbelled-out from the NE, NW and SW corners and have the rare, if not unique, feature of squared extensions along the gable walls. Being some 3ft 6in higher than the adjacent floor, access to those on the N side was arranged by way of a quarter-turn stair within the adjacent window-recesses in the gable walls, while the SW turret was probably reached by a wooden stair or ladder. Each has a single window facing outwards and two shot-holes angled downwards to cover the adjacent walls. In addition, the NE and NW turrets were each provided with a close-garderobe within the thickness of the N wall.

Above this level a smaller wheel-stair, 4ft 8in in diameter, is partly corbelled-out from the E gable to give access to the two, attic floors originally contained within the steeply pitched roof[48] and the two, small chambers corbelled-out, one above the other, over the main stair. The smaller stair is lit by windows in the form of a cross and a quatrefoil. The lower attic has a fine dormer-window, with elaborately moulded jambs and pediment, corbelled-out over the S wall-head such that a large machicolation in its sill covers the tower's main entrance. There is also a window in each of the gables and a small fireplace at the W end. It is from this floor that the upper level of the corner turrets is reached. Each of the rooms over the main stair has a small fireplace and a generous provision of windows, those on the E and W sides of the upper room being dormers. The walls of these rooms are of finely dressed ashlar.

Higher still, and perched upon the apex of the E gable, is the watch-turret, a 2-storeyed building, also of well-dressed ashlar, with a pitched roof. To provide more space the side walls

Fig. 123 Amisfield: top of middle wheel-stair, with chambers
over main wheel-stair beyond.

Fig. 124 Amisfield: N side of watch-turret, showing stairhead and
small fireplace for use by look-out when the stairhead is closed off.

are corbelled-out from the gable, while a half-turn stair, some 2ft wide, connects the two levels at the N end. When used in earnest, it was arranged that the stair could be floored over to provide a self-contained chamber with its own tiny fireplace. Shot-holes, angled steeply downwards, covered the ground immediately to the E and also the head of the upper wheel-stair, while windows on all sides gave a commanding view of the surrounding countryside, as far as Lochar Moss and the Solway to the S and across Nithsdale to the W.

Fig. 125 Amisfield: ?shot-hole in watch-turret angled down to cover approach from E.

The dressed masonry of the tower has further enrichment, especially on the S and E sides. This includes double-roll mouldings separated by a nail-head enrichment around the larger windows, while the other windows and outside doorways have plain, rounded arrises; a double-roll separated by a double row of nail-heads around the heraldic panels; a double row of mini-ature corbels separated by nail-head enrichment at the wall-head, and repeated as a string-course higher up the stair-turret; and a cable-moulding around the pediment of the S dormer-window and adjacent gable and chimney above the stair-turret.

There is a fine, oak door from Amisfield in the Royal Museum of Scotland. It bears the initials of Sir John Charteris and his wife, Agnes Maxwell, with their quartered arms and the date 1600. Almost the entire panel is taken up by a relief carving of Hercules grappling with the Nemean lion; these figures were originally painted.[49] The hanging stile is extended at each end to form wooden hinges, probably for incorporation into a wooden screen or partition wall. The following year the same craftsman made a similar door for Sir John's brother-in-law, Lord Herries, at Terregles.[50]

The next laird, Sir John Charteris, was served heir to his father in 1616.[51] Later that year he was appointed Sheriff of Dumfries,[52] though it was not until the following year that he formally accepted the office.[53] He subsequently led an active career as a Commissioner of Justice and Commissioner for the Middle Shires,[54] as well as holding various other Crown appointments from time to time.[55] He represented the county in parliament in 1621,[56] and again from 1628 to 1633.[57] He also represented the county at the Convention of Estates in 1625.[58]

In 1631, with the need for 'houses of fence' being a thing of the past, Sir John decided to build a new house at Amisfield, immediately to the south of the tower.[59] This forms the north part of the present mansion. However, the cost of the house, together with other debts, proved too much, and in 1636 he had to wadset the £10 lands and barony of Amisfield, with the castle and manor-place, to John Dalzell of Newton;[60] and two years later he had to raise additional funds against the security of the rest of the estate.[61] He died a year later.

His son, Sir John Charteris, represented Dumfriesshire

Fig. 126 Amisfield: view of tower and 17th century house in 1789.

and Annandale in parliament from 1639 to 1641.[62] He was also a Commissioner for Keeping the Peace in 1641,[63] a Commissioner for War in 1643 and 1644,[64] and on the Committee for the South in 1644.[65] Later that year he joined Montrose as Captain of a troop of horse, but was captured and imprisoned in Edinburgh Castle.[66] He was eventually banished, before submitting to the General Assembly in 1647.[67] He fared no better with his finances, and in 1649 he finally had to sell the lands and barony of Amisfield, which also included the lands of Glenae, to Sir John Dalzell of Newton. Sir John Dalzell, who subsequently took the designation 'of Glenae', was then granted a crown charter of the lands[68] and, in 1666, a further charter of novodamus to himself and his eldest son, Sir Robert.[69] This was confirmed by parliament three years later.[70]

Eleven years later, in 1677, Thomas Charteris, a burgess of Dumfries and third son of the last Sir John Charteris of Amisfield (d.c.1654), bought the estate back from Sir Robert Dalzell, 1st Baronet of Glenae.[71] A year later he was appointed a Commissioner of Supply for Dumfriesshire,[72] an appointment that was renewed in 1685.[73] In 1683 he took the Test.[74] He was succeeded in 1692 by his daughter, Elizabeth, and her descendants, who took the name Charteris, continued to live at Amisfield until the family was forced to sell it again in 1834.[75] Three years later the front half of the present mansion was built to a design by the local architect Walter Newall.[76]

In 1894, Robert Charteris-Thomson, a Canadian descendant of the laird who died in 1616 by a younger son, purchased Amisfield, but in 1904 his son sold it again to a Mr. W. R. Farish.[77] Shortly afterwards, Amisfield was purchased by William Johnstone of Roberthill, St. Andrews, and his descendants have lived there ever since. In the late 1920s, William's son, Major William Johnstone, restored the tower. By that time the windows were all missing, and what was left of the floors was unsafe; and although the roof was weatherproof, several of the timbers had to be replaced. It is now maintained in excellent order.

---

1 RCAHMS 1920, xxix; McDowall 1986, 24.
2 Bain I, No.105.
3 Burke L.G. 1952, 421, 'Charteris formerly of Amisfield'.
4 Ibid.
5 ERS I, 35. See also Bain II, No.524; V, Nos.79, 115; ERS I, 47, 49.
6 Bain II, 198, No.730. The Robert de Chartres who also swore fealty (Bain II, 202) is said to have been his son, but if Andrew was a minor in 1288, his son would have been too young.
7 Ibid., No.1009
8 Bain II, No.1481.
9 Bain IV, 390.
10 Bain III, No.366.
11 Birley, R. E. and Fildes, D. C. 'An Excavation at Amisfield Tower, 1957', TDGAS, 3rd Ser., XXXV, 81-2.
12 Complete Peerage I, 81n(a); IV, 508.
13 Fraser 1885, I, 362. That the barony of Amisfield formed part of those vast estates is shown by a charter of the 4th Earl granting 'his lands of Drumgrey in the barony of Amisfield' to William de Johnston in 1408 (Hope-Johnstone MSS, 9 (No.1)).
14 ERS IV, 562, 600.
15 Burke, op. cit. The genealogy given by Burke should be treated with caution, as some of the dates, and generations, do not correspond with contemporary records.
16 ERS VI, 167-8.
17 ERS IX, 668.
18 RMS II, Nos.815-16; Scots Peerage III, 221.
19 Fraser 1873, I, 154, 162; Burke, op. cit. According to Burke, this was yet another generation, but the dates make this unlikely.
20 APS II, 175, 180, 262.
21 Ibid, 140.
22 RMS II, No.1714.
23 Ibid, No.2592.
24 Burke, op. cit.
25 Ibid.
26 Rae, 257.
27 RMS III, No.1458.
28 RSS II, No.1918.
29 Ibid., No.2558.
30 Ibid., No.3542.
31 Grose I, 158-9; McDowall 1986, 183. In the story the laird is called John Charteris, but by 1530, when the incident is said to have taken place (during James's judicial expedition to the West March in July that year), John had been succeeded by his son Robert.
32 MS of Richard Bell, Warden's Clerk, cited in Irving 1907, 32, and Armstrong 1883, lxxiv. Another contemporary list gives 111 men (Armstrong, lxxvii).
33 RSS IV, No.2663.
34 Fraser 1873, I, 293n.
35 RPC VIII, 109.
36 Ibid. IX, 77.
37 Ibid., 419.
38 APS V, 148-9.
39 Pont MS. No.35 in National Library of Scotland.
40 Blaeu, 57, 'THE STEWARTRIE OF ANNANDAIL'.
41 The rubble walls were originally harled (Mackenzie 1927, 136).
42 The break in the treads suggests the stair was widened on the outer side when the first floor was rebuilt.
43 A similar arrangement existed at nearby Elshieshields (q.v.), Newark (Selkirk) and Kirkhope.
44 Hills (q.v.) has several similar slit-windows.
45 It is evident from the rebates and hinges of the hall doorway that the original floor was lower than the present flags.
46 See RCAHMS 1920, Fig.143, for colour illustration.
47 See Hoddom Castle.
48 The roof is of double-collar rafter construction. Although restored in the 1920s, the majority of the timbers are original and still bear their assembly reference numbers.
49 Grose, I, 158.
50 RCAHMS 1967, 314, Pl.96c. The door was moved to Traquair in 1961, when Terregles was demolished.
51 Burke, op. cit.
52 RPC X, 677.
53 RPC XI, 2; RPC 2nd Series, I, 659.
54 RPC XI, 345; XII, 106, 650; XIV, ci, 692-711; RPC 2nd Series, I, 373, 659; et al.
55 RPC XIII, 141; 2nd Series, I, 138, 423n, 615, 667; et al.
56 APS IV, 593; RPC XII, 549n.
57 APS V, 3, 8.
58 Ibid, 166.
59 Grose, I, 157; Stell 1986, 89.
60 RMS, IX, No.609.
61 Ibid, Nos.844, 846, etc.
62 APS V, 252, 258, 426.
63 Ibid, 685.
64 Ibid, VI, Part I, 51-7, 199.
65 Ibid, 91.
66 Parl. of Scot., 118; Burke, op. cit.
67 Burke, op. cit.
68 RMS IX, No.2102.
69 Scots Peerage II, 408.
70 APS VII, 643.
71 Forman, S. 'Amisfield', Scottish Field, February 1947, 18.
72 APS VIII, 225.
73 Ibid, 465.
74 RPC, 3rd Ser., VIII, 640.
75 Forman, op. cit.
76 MacKechnie, A 'Walter Newall Architect in Dumfries', TDGAS, 3rd Ser., LXIII, 83.
77 Burke, op. cit.

3.   AUCHENRIVOCK TOWER

(2½ m S Langholm)   (NY372805)

The earliest mention of Stakeheugh, which is commonly thought to have been the old name for Auchenrivock, is in 1513, when Sir Christopher Dacre burned 'the Stakehughe (the manor place of Irewyn)',[1] and the following year Lord Dacre reported a further raid into the West March when many townships in Eskdale were destroyed, including Stakeheugh.[2] Stakeheugh was the principal stronghold of the Irvings of Eskdale – often called 'Kangs' after their leader 'Williame Irwing callit Cang'[3] – , whose subsequent lawlessness alongside their Armstrong neighbours became notorious. From 1528 until well into the 17th century, they are increasingly on record for burning, rieving, killing and treasonable activities.[4] Richard Irwin of Staikheugh was also mentioned in a charter of 1532 as claiming another small property granted to Lord Maxwell.[5]

Fig. 127 Auchenrivock Tower: ruins viewed from NW.

The present tower was built sometime during the second half of the 16th century, and probably late in that period. The name 'Auchenrivock' first appears on record in the 1590s, and it may be that this is when the present tower was built, possibly on a slightly different site from the earlier stronghold of Stakeheugh, the name of which continued to be used, intermittently, for several more decades. Aglionby's Platte of 1590 calls the tower 'Steakhugh', but Pont's survey some five years later calls it 'Achinriffack'.[6] In 1592 Lord Maxwell complained that

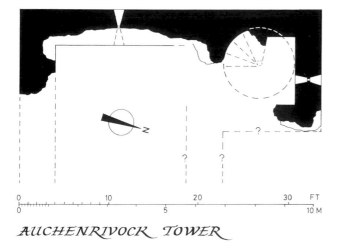

AUCHENRIVOCK TOWER

Fig. 128 Auchenrivock Tower: plan of basement.

Thomas Carletone had taken John Irvinge in Starkhewghe 'out of his house' and kept him imprisoned in Carlisle Castle.[7]

Standing on high ground overlooking the confluences of the Tarras Water and Irvine Burn with the River Esk, Auchenrivock had a commanding view along Eskdale to the N and S and up the Tarras valley to the NE.

Only a vestige of the **TOWER** now remains, built into the garden wall of the former farm. It was originally thought that the tower, whose E half is completely missing, had been oblong in plan like other towers in the area and the Irving towers in nearby Kirtledale, with the W wall forming one of the long sides; but more recent investigations show that the tower was in fact almost certainly an **L**–plan structure, with the main block lying E–W and a stair wing at the W end of the N side.

Fig. 129 Auchenrivock: gun-loop.

The remains, which reach a maximum height of about 8ft in the NW corner, comprise the W end of the main block and most of the wing except the re-entrant angle, where the entrance was probably located. Neither the width of the main block nor the projection of the wing are known, but their overall length was 33ft 7in: the width of the wing was evidently 13ft 6in. The masonry is large, irregular boulders, crudely dressed and bonded. The walls of the main block are 4ft thick,[8] while those of the wing are 3ft, except where the curvature of the stair well, 7ft 10in in diameter, reduces the W wall to a minimum of 2ft. There is a recess beneath the stair-well in the NW corner. The only other features to have survived are a rectangular gun-loop with splayed inner and outer jambs in the W wall and a smaller one in the N wall of the wing.[9] Due to the crude nature of the masonry the splay was exceptionally narrow for walls of this thickness, the one in the W wall opening out from a central throat-block, with a 3in diameter aperture, to 14½ in wide by 8in high on the outside, giving an angle of fire of only 25°. The basement is said to have been vaulted.

In 1606, James VI rewarded two of his servitors, James Maxwell and Robert Douglas, with a grant of various lands that had previously formed part of 'the Debateable Land', and which were now incorporated in the free barony of Tarras.[10] These included the lands of Auchinriffock. He also granted a commission to 'certain barons and gentlemen in Nithisdaill and Annanderdaill' to survey the lands. Not surprisingly, the families already there, such as the Irvings and Armstrongs, did not take kindly to such an intrusion. The lands were their home;

they had fought for them and held them against all comers for generations, and were not going to give them up now just because someone else had been given a charter. The following year, Maxwell and Douglas complained to the Privy Council that the survey had been impeded by the occupiers, including 'Richie Irwing in Auchinriffeck', 'Eckeis Richie Irwing in Staikhewch' and 'Willie Irwing callit the Cang', who had all vowed to debar them from the lands.[11] They were charged to appear before the Council, and failing to do so were denounced as rebels.

In 1643 the lands of 'Staikheuche' and others 'now called Irving' were included in the extensive estates granted to the 2nd Earl of Buccleuch[12]; and twenty years later, in 1663, they were included among the lands resigned by the Countess of Buccleuch and regranted to her and the Duke of Monmouth on the occasion of their marriage.[13] They have remained a part of the Buccleuch estates ever since.

1   State Papers, Henry VIII, I, No.4529.
2   RCAHMS 1997, 239-40.
3   'William Irwin alias Gang' was finally executed for murder at Jedburgh in
     1617 – Household Books of Lord William Howard of Naworth. Although
     Willie Kang was leader in the field, the chieftain of this family was Richard
     Irving in Stakeheugh (Hope-Johnstone MS, 37 (No.78); Fraser 1873, II, 498).
4   MS in Record Office, London, cited in Armstrong 1883, 249, xxvii; Armstrong
     1960, 73; Fraser 1873, I, 216; Border Papers, II, (8/6/1595), (23/6/1600); etc.
5   RMS III, No.1199.
6   Blaeu, 53, 'Lidisdail'. The exact date of Pont's survey is not certain, though
     he is said to have been in Dumfriesshire and Galloway in 1595-6.
7   Border Papers, I, 423.
8   Although the inner face of the W wall has fallen, its original thickness can be
     confirmed by the symmetry of the gun-loop.
9   A third gun-loop was recorded still in situ in the S wall in 1902 (Irving Note
     Book No.2, 220 (28 Oct 1902), by the writer's grandfather, John Bell Irving
     of Beanlands).
10   RMS VI, No.1802.
11   RPC, 2nd Ser., VIII, 292; RPC VII, 339. The presence of both Auchenrivock
     and Stakeheugh in the same document suggests two separate dwellings.
12   RMS IX, No.1341.
13   Fraser 1878, II, 473; RMS XI, No.673.

4.   AUCHENSKEOCH CASTLE

(5¹/₂ m ESE Dalbeattie)   (NX918589)

'Achinskeauch' first comes on record in 1462, when the lands were held by the Crown and the fermes payable amounted to £4:6s:8d per annum.[1] Thereafter, the lands continue to appear in the Exchequer Rolls intermittently until 1481,[2] when Mr. Richard Robert[son], rector of Southwick, who had a four year lease, agreed to the tenure being transferred to Robert Herries, son of David Herries.[3] A few years later, the lease of the lands of Auchenskeoch and Redbank was given to Montrose Pursuivant for three years. However, in 1488, before that term had expired, the lease was again transferred, this time to John Rerik of Dalbeattie.[4] Then in 1490, Auchenskeoch, Auchinhay, Clonyard 'and other lands' were granted in feu by James IV to John Lindsay,[5] son of James Lindsay of Fairgirth.[6] Lindsay was 'falconer to the King',[7] and the grant, which constituted a sizeable estate, is understood to have been part of his fee. The position of master falconer was one of considerable importance in mediaeval times, and it brought rich rewards. In February 1498/99, Lindsay was granted a formal renewal of the gift of the lands of Auchinskeauch, Auchinhay, Clonyard, Glenstoken and Auchenlosh, in the lordship of Galloway, to be held in liferent

Fig. 130 Auchenskeoch Castle: view from the N.

as previously, with all the profits pertaining thereto.[8]

John Lindsay died sometime before 1508, when the lands and fermes were let to his widow, Marion Bonkle, and her son James Lindsay, who succeeded his father as master falconer.[9] Four years later, Marion received a new grant of the lands for life, with all the mails, etc., 'for her good and thankful service done to the Queen'.[10] At the same time, Marion was granted a special 'Protection and safeguard . . . because the king has commanded her to remain in service with the queen'.[11] She was still at court three years later,[12] and was still in possession of Auchenskeoch 'for service to the King and Queen' as late as 1532.[13] After her death, Auchenskeoch passed to her son James.

James Lindsay first appears as 'Keeper of the King's Hawks' in 1529, when he was given 'the usual class of livery'.[14] Thereafter, there are regular payments to James Lindsay, Master Falconer to King James V, for fees, 'pension',[15] travelling expenses, etc., until the king's death in 1542.[16] He then disappears from the royal accounts until 1554, when he became master falconer to Queen Mary,[17] and he continued in that office until he finally retired in 1562,[18] though he is still called 'master falconer' in the Exchequer accounts for 1574.[19]

In the meantime, in 1553, William Cairns of Orchardton sold the 'merkland of Auchenskeoch' to Peter Cairns and his spouse;[20] while a further charter in 1575 refers to a grant of the 40 shilling lands of Auchensheen and Auchenskeoch, formerly belonging to John Cairns of Orchardton, to Robert Herries of Mabie.[21] These lands would appear to be a different, or much smaller part of, Auchenskeoch,[22] for, in 1562, James Lindsay, 'Master of hawks to the queen', paid his annual tax to the crown for the lands of Auchenskeoch, etc.,[23] and the following year Queen Mary gave him and his son John, a new grant of the lands of Auchenskeoch, etc., in liferent.[24] In 1585 John Lindsay of Auchenskeoch was included in the general amnesty for those charged with rebellion.[25]

The castle stands on the NE shoulder of a low hill overlooking the Southwick Water. There is no firm evidence of who the builder was, although it has been suggested that it was James's son John (d.1628).[26] It may, however, have been James himself, for although the architecture is unique, the gun-loops could point to any date after the middle of the century.

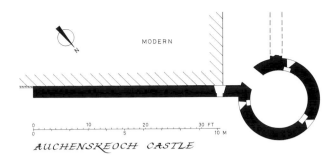

Fig. 131 Auchenskeoch Castle: plan of surviving basement walls.

The **CASTLE** is generally believed to have been built on the **Z**–plan,[27] and as such it was the only example in Galloway.[28] All that now remains is a round tower, 14ft 3in in diameter, which stood at the N corner, and an adjoining wall of the main block, which runs SE for a distance of 36ft 10in[29] and is some 20ft high. When the RCAHMS visited the site in 1911, the corresponding wall running SW from the tower still existed for a distance of 6ft, but this has since disappeared and only the tusking remains.[30] The masonry is water-worn boulders of the local grey granite, which has been roughly dressed for the margins of windows and gun-loops and, where necessary, for other surfaces. The walls are unusually thin, varying in thickness between 2ft and 2ft 6in. There was no vaulting. Unfortunately it is not possible to establish what the full extent of the castle originally was, but the overall effect of the main block is more akin to a hall-house than a tower-house, with a simple basement, a principal floor of several rooms, probably with timber partitions (as there is no stone tusking), and one upper, garret floor.

Apart from its wooden floors and roof, the corner tower is almost complete. It comprised two storeys and an attic, and was reached at each level through a doorway in the corner of the main block. The only openings in the basement were three, rectangular, splayed gun-loops, one facing out to the N, while the other two provided flanking cover along the adjacent walls of the main block. The floor above was not circular internally, but had six, irregular sides, with a fireplace to the NE, a lamp shelf to the SE, an aumbry to the W, and three irregularly spaced windows, each only about 1ft square. The chimney stack serving the fireplace still rises to a height of some 8ft above the wall-head, while immediately below the wall-head there are three slit-windows which served the attic.

The overall arrangement of the main block is most unusual, if not unique. The only opening in the surviving NE wall at basement level is one small window near the N end. This was provided with two horizontal bars, in contrast to the three small windows on the principal floor above, each of which was provided with two vertical bars. The latter windows, which each measure only about 1ft high by 1ft 4in wide, are evenly spaced along the wall. This floor was supported by beams let into the side walls, whilst, for the floor above, crude granite corbels were provided to support runners. At its N end, this wall continued upwards to form a gable, containing a slit-window. Immediately adjacent to this, the wall-head still carries coping for some 12ft along the inside, suggesting that there was a parapet walk here.

Early in the 17th century a deadly feud developed between the Lindsays of Auchenskeoch and their cousins at Fairgirth, and it continued until 1621.[31] The laird at the time was John Lindsay, who is on record in 1612 as Stewart-Depute

of Kirkcudbright.[32] In all probability this was the only time in the castle's history when it was needed as a place of strength.

In 1628 James Lindsay was served heir to his father.[33] He was soon in financial difficulties, and three years later he had to mortgage the estate of Auchenskeoch to Patrick Young, chirurgeon in Dumfries.[34] His affairs did not improve. The lands were apprised from him in 1648, the same year in which he was appointed a Commissioner of War for the Stewartry,[35] and in 1654 the Protector gave Young and his spouse a new grant of the lands.[36] The lands were still to be held under reversion, but they were never redeemed, and the Youngs continued in possession until c.1780, when they sold Auchenskeoch to Thomas Crichton.[37] In 1704 William Young of Auchenskeoch was appointed a Commissioner of Supply for the Stewartry,[38] and the following year he was made Steward-Depute.[39]

Crichton's forebears are said to have held lands in Glencairn, but had forfeited them for their part in the Jacobite rebellion of 1715.[40] Thomas Crichton had subsequently gone to England, where he had had a very successful career as a merchant, restoring the family's fortunes and enabling him to purchase Auchenskeoch. Having no issue, he left Auchenskeoch to his nephew, Robert Crichton, who had sasine in 1783.[41]

Robert's eldest son, Thomas, who eventually succeeded to the property, was a member of the Faculty of Advocates and a Major in the Dumfriesshire militia.[42] He subsequently became Chamberlain to the Duke of Buccleuch and Queensberry, and went to live at Dabton, near Thornhill, the Chamberlain's official residence.[43] He was admitted a burgess of Sanquhar in 1811, was elected to the Council in 1812, and was Provost from 1815 to 1832.[44] He retired as Chamberlain in 1843, and died five years later.[45]

Major Crichton was succeeded by his nephew, Thomas Crichton; but he did not long survive his uncle before being succeeded in turn by his brother Robert, who, having no issue, sold Auchenskeoch to one Edward M'Kenzie, a railway contractor from Henley-on-Thames, and M'Kenzie's descendants were still in possession in 1912.[46]

It is not known when the castle was abandonned, but a 'considerable portion' of it was taken down in the 19th century, when the present steading was built.[47]

1   ERS VII, 114.
2   Ibid, 603; VIII, 340, 417; IX, 18.
3   ERS IX, 584.
4   ERS X, 657.
5   Ibid, 220.
6   Fairgirth was a small estate 3 miles SW Auchenskeoch. The Lindsays had held lands elsewhere in Galloway since the previous century.
7   ERS XI, 191.
8   RSS I, No.343.
9   ERS XIII, 600.
10   RSS I, No.2477.
11   Ibid, No.2478.
12   ALHT V, 66.
13   ERS XVI, 210.
14   ALHT V, 382.
15   'Pension' here seems to have meant the same as 'Fee'. In 1533, for example, he was paid a fee of £33;6s;8d and a pension of £33;6s;8d, whilst in 1534 he received a yearly pension of £66:13s:4d and no fee, and in 1537 a fee of £66:13s:4d and no pension.
16   ALHT V, 435; VI, 47 et al.; VII and VIII.
17   ALHT X, 294, et al.
18   ALHT XI, 165, 166.
19   ERS XX, 166.
20   RMS IV, No.871.
21   Ibid, No.2410.
22   Auchensheen, although in the same parish, is quite a different property, 4½ miles WSW of Auchenskeoch.

23 ERS XIX, 152.
24 Ibid, No.1462.
25 APS III, 388.
26 Reid, J 'Auchenskeoch Castle', *TDGAS*, 3rd Ser., XIV, 217.
27 RCAHMS 1914, No.115.
28 The nearest examples are at Kelburn and Knock in Ayrshire, and elsewhere in the Borders at Dalswinton in Dumfriesshire (q.v.) and at Drochil in Peeblesshire.
29 It is not clear whether this wall was originally longer, as there are no conclusive quoins at the S end.
30 The 25-inch O.S. map of 1893 shows both this NW wall and a short return to the SE, which was too close to have been the beginning of the SW wall.
31 Reid, *op. cit.*, 218.
32 Laing Charters, No.1624.
33 M'Kerlie III, 343.
34 RMS VIII, No.1821; Reid, *op. cit.*, 218; Adams 1921, 299.
35 APS VI, Part II, 35.
36 RMS X, No.253.
37 M'Kerlie III, 345.
38 APS XI, 150.
39 Fraser 1873, I, 422.
40 M'Kerlie III, 345; Wilson & McMillan, 258. Thomas Crichton's ancestors are said to have lived at Breckonside, in the Cairn Valley (q.v.).
41 M'Kerlie III, 345.
42 Ibid; Wilson & McMillan, 258.
43 Ibid.
44 Wilson & McMillan, 258.
45 Ibid.
46 County Directory 1912, 24.
47 M'Kerlie III, 346.

---

5.   BALMANGAN TOWER

(2m SE Borgue)   (NX650457)

The lands of Balmangan, or Grange of Senwick, formed part of the lands of Senwick (or Sannak), which together with other lands in the parish of Borgue, were granted by David I to Hugh de Morville, Constable of Scotland, some time prior to 1150.[1] Hugh was the founder of Dryburgh Abbey.[2] The male line of the de Morvilles subsequently died out, when Elena (or Eva) de Morville became heiress of her father William and brother Richard.[3] Elena married Roland, Lord of Galloway, who thus inherited the lands, and from him they passed first to his son Alan and then to Alan's eldest surviving daughter and co-heiress, Helen, who married Roger de Quincy, Earl of Winchester.[4] Through his wife, de Quincy became Constable of Scotland. He was succeeded by his three daughters and co-heiresses, Margaret (also known as Agnes), Elizabeth (also known as Marjory) and Elena, who married respectively the Earl of Ferrars & Derby, the Earl of Buchan and Alan de la Zouche.[5] They became heirs-portioners of their father and evidently shared the lands of Senwick,[6] which included the £10 lands of Grange of Senwick. An Account in 1266 recorded that the Earl of Buchan was keeper of 'two parts of the park lands of Roger de Quency in Galwethia (Galloway)',[7] while an Inquisition in 1296 found that Lady Elena la Zuche, the widow of Alan de la Zouche, held a 'third part of the vill of Sa'nayk';[8] but nowhere is it made clear who held the Grange.

The War of Independence wrought a complete change. All the former owners forfeited their lands, which were then granted by King Robert the Bruce to Isobel of Atholl and her son Alexander Bruce.[9] Later, David II granted Senwick and other lands, first to Andrew Buttergask[10] and then to Dougall M'Dougall,[11] while the church was gifted to the abbey at Tongland.[12]

Nothing more is heard of Balmangan until 1456, when Grange of Senwick appears in the Exchequer Rolls as part of the

Fig. 132 Balmangan Tower: view from the E.

extensive Crown lands in Galloway for which the fermes were £14.[13] Thereafter, it features frequently in the Rolls until 1588.[14] Sometimes the tenants are named, as for example in 1459, when it was Sir John Carlile,[15] 1490, when it was Patrick Earl of Bothwell,[16] and 1500, when it was Thomas M'Clellan of Bombie.[17] Then in 1512 James IV granted 'half the lands of Sannak called Balmangane' to William Brown, March Pursuivant, in feu for life,[18] and Brown continued to hold them after he became Albany Herald in 1516.[19] This is the first mention of 'Balmangan' as such. Although described as half the lands, it actually comprised two thirds of the property, being a £20 land of old extent, while the other 'half' only comprised a £10 land. The latter 'half' was, in 1517, granted to David Purves, Macer, in feu for life 'for his good and faithful service to the King and his governors'.[20] It was on this portion that the tower was later built. David Purves was succeeded in 1527 by Andrew Purves, Macer, presumably his son, whose feu was on the same terms.[21] Andrew Purves held office until 1546,[22] but evidently he had given up his feu by 1534, for in that year Grange of Senwick was let to Gilbert McClellan of Barmagachan and his second son William.[23] The fermes for the Grange subsequently appear in the Exchequer Rolls for 1538,[24] 1561[25] and 1588, when it was let in feu to William Seton, brother of Lord Seton.[26] Meanwhile in 1540, following the death of William Brown, the Crown granted the other portion of Balmangan in liferent to John Balfour in Leith for services rendered;[27] and in 1571 William McClellan gave his wife, Margaret Gordon, a liferent of his portion.[28]

William Seton's lease of Balmangan was very brief, for in the same year that he obtained it, 1588, he resigned it again in favour of William McClellan in Balmangan, who had presumably continued to farm the lands. McClellan was then given a charter of novodamus of the '£10 lands of Balmangan, *alias* the Grange of Sannik, of old extent, with the fortalice, manor-place, [etc.] . . . and with special power [to take] *wrak and wair*[29] from the sea to the other part of the said lands (occupied by the said William and others, his sub-tenants),'[30] and this was subsequently confirmed by John Gordon of Lochinvar, the superior of the lands.[31] It would appear, therefore, that William had also obtained at some earlier date the portion of Balmangan previously held by John Balfour. It is also the first mention of a fortalice, which must, therefore have been built by William. It is situated on rising ground, facing E across Kirkcudbright Bay and the mouth of the Dee estuary. It appears on Pont's map c.1595 as 'Balmangan Cast.'[32]

The **TOWER**, which stands on a small outcrop of rock, is oblong in plan, and measures 22ft 9in from NE to SW by 30ft 3in from SE to NW over walls that are 3ft 6in thick on either side and 4ft 6in at the ends. All that now remains is the vaulted basement and the lower part of the hall above, rising to a maximum height of about 18ft at the S corner. The masonry is Silurian rubble, including the roughly-shaped quoins, but a re-used QER moulding in the modern entrance in the SE wall would suggest that such mouldings were probably used for the door and window surrounds, which are now missing.

It is not certain where the original entrance to the basement was located. It was probably in the middle of the NW wall, where the basement has a mural recess with an original relieving arch and, on the outside, a blocked doorway that formerly communicated with the adjacent, later cottage.[33] The W ingo of this doorway has a mural recess, 1ft deep, similar to the landing for a drawbar, although no drawbar slot is now evident on the other side. On the other hand, the tower had an entrance in the NE wall that admits to a mural passage, leading to a wheel-stair serving the upper floors in the N corner, and across the passage there has at some period been a doorway to the basement. Both the outer doorway, which has been first enlarged[34] and then reduced again, and the inner one are now blocked, so there is no longer any access to the passage. What is not clear is when the inner doorway was built, nor whether it served as an entrance to the basement, or was added to give direct access to the stair and upper floors from the basement and cottage at a later date.

The basement itself has a barrel vault 8ft 4in high, formed from Silurian rubble of all shapes and sizes. On the W side of the NW doorway there is a large open-aumbry , and at the E end of the NE wall a mural recess with a pointed arch about 6ft high. The middle of the SW wall is occupied by a splayed gun-loop with a horizontal dumb-bell opening, formed from two sand-stone blocks, in the outer wall-face. Any opening that may have existed in the SE wall was lost when the modern doorway was inserted. The mural passage and stair encroach upon the NE side and in the N corner. Neither is now accessible, but the way the stair encroaches upon the basement suggests that it has the rare feature of rising anti-clockwise.

What is left of the first floor hall is completely ruinous and overgrown, but fortunately a record of the remains was made by the RCAHMS in 1911. This shows a small mural chamber, probably a gardrobe, with a lamp shelf in the W corner; an open-aumbry in the middle of the SW wall; and a splayed window-recess with stone seats in the middle of the SE wall. There is no direct evidence of a fireplace, which could only have been a small one either in the NW wall or the NE wall, where there are breaks in the masonry.

In 1605, William McClellan, who was by then a very old man, granted the lands of Balmangan, with the tower and fortalice, to his eldest son Thomas.[35] He died later that year. Then in 1615 Thomas sold a quarter of the '£5 land of Balmangan' to William Gordon of Holm.[36] Thomas died some time after 1618, and was succeeded first by his son James, who died c.1637-9, and then by his grandson Robert. Meanwhile, in 1631, John Gordon of Lochinvar received a crown charter, under reversion, of the superiority of many lands that had pertained to Sir Robert Maclellan of Bombie, including 'the £10 lands of Balmangan with the mansion-house', which Sir Robert had had to wadset because of debt.[37]

Robert McClellan of Balmangan was admitted a burgess of Kirkcudbright in 1661.[38] Four years later he acquired Borness, but the following year had his estates apprised when Lord Kirkcudbright, for whom he had stood surety, failed to pay his debts.[39] Thereafter, Robert found himself in increasing financial difficulties, with many wadsets being taken out against

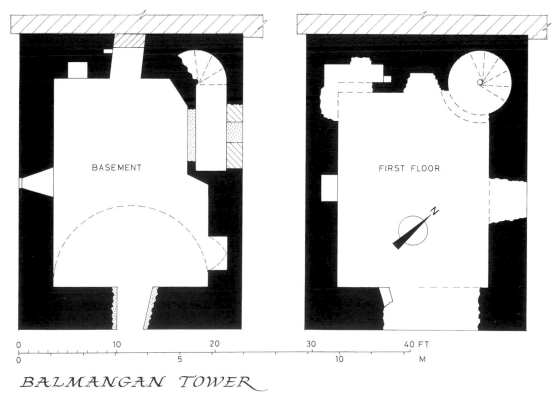

BASEMENT

FIRST FLOOR

0   10   20   30   40 FT
0   5   10   M

BALMANGAN TOWER

Fig. 133 Balmangan Tower: plans of basement and first floor. (The stair is conjectural, as it is inaccessible.)

his lands. The principal beneficiaries were John Carson and his son Andrew, who obtained titles to the lands of Senwick and Balmangan in 1676, 1677, 1678 and 1694.[40] On his death in 1690, Robert McClellan was succeeded at Balmangan by his third son, Robert, while his eldest son inherited Borness. Robert, who is said to have been a Writer to the Signet in Edinburgh, had sasine in 1704.[41] He was the last of the family to possess the property.[42]

By 1689, however. the Carsons must have had all but possession of Balmangan, for in that year 'John Corsane of Balmangan' was appointed a Commissioner of Supply for the Stewartry of Kirkcudbright, and he was re-appointed again the following year.[43] Then, in 1695, Andrew was served heir to his father, who is again designated 'John Carson of Balmangan',[44] and in the same year Andrew was himself appointed a Commissioner of Supply.[45] Andrew was in turn succeeded by his son John, who was appointed a Commissioner of Supply in 1704,[46] and grandson Hugh, who had sasine in 1743.[47] Hugh had two daughters, Margaret and Agnes, who were his heiresses, but by then the Carsons were themselves in financial trouble, and the estate had been mortgaged away.[48]

Alexander Blair of Dunrod then acquired the £10 land of Balmangan, having sasine in 1751.[49] From him the lands passed to Dunbar Douglas-Hamilton of Baldoon, who had succeeded in 1744 to the Earldom of Selkirk;[50] and thereafter the lands remained with the Earls of Selkirk and their descendants until the 20th century. It is not known when the tower was abandonned as a residence, but it was described as being in ruins in 1845.[51]

---

1 M'Kerlie III, 174, 177.
2 Anderson II, 249.
3 Scots Peerage IV, 139.
4 Complete Peerage XII/2, 753. See also Bain I, No.1372.
5 Scots Peerage IV, 142.
6 Bain I, No.2565; RMS I, App.2, No.319.
7 ERS I, 31, 33.
8 Bain II, No.824(4). See also Bain III, No.386.
9 RMS I, App.2, No.319.
10 Ibid, No.792.
11 Ibid, Nos.1006, 1176.
12 M'Kerlie III, 175. Tongland Abbey had been founded in 1218 by Alan, Lord of Galloway (Easson 1957, 88).
13 ERS VI, 192.
14 ERS VI, 345, 453, etc.; VII; VIII; X; XI; XII; XIII; XIV; XV; XVI; XVII; XIX; XXI.
15 ERS VI, 572.
16 ERS X, 704.
17 ERS XI, 454.
18 RMS II, No.3771.
19 ERS XIV, 135; ERS XVI, 26.
20 RSS I, No.2794; ERS XIV, 234-5. It states in the Exchequer Roll that David Purves had been granted the lands under the Great Seal, but there is no such record in the Great Seal Register.
21 ERS XV, 317, 426, 486; XVI, 26, etc. ERS XVI, 99, also refers to a Great Seal charter, which does not appear in the Register.
22 RMS III, 1054.
23 ERS XVI, 344, 506; M'Kerlie III, 203-4; Torrance, 46. The McClellan's lease was renewed in 1565 (M'Kerlie III, 204).
24 ERS XVII, 73.
25 ERS XIX, 152.
26 ERSXXI, 352, 362.
27 RMS III, No.2220.
28 Torrance, 46.
29 Kinds of seaweed.
30 RMS V, No.1505.
31 Torrance, 46.
32 Blaeu, 66, 'The Steuartrie of Kircubright, The most easterlie part of Galloway'.
33 It is unlikely that the cottage would have been built abutting this wall unless it was intended that they be interconnected.
34 The wide relieving arch over this doorway is puzzling, unless it was inserted when the doorway was widened; and the very existence of an unusually wide door here is in itself unusual.
35 Torrance, 47.
36 Ibid, 48.
37 RMS VIII, No.1775.
38 Torrance, 49.
39 Ibid; M'Kerlie III, 205; Scots Peerage V, 271..
40 PRS Dumfries II (1672-1702), Index, 47-8.
41 Scots Peerage V, 271.
42 M'Kerlie III, 206; Torrance, 51.
43 APS IX, 74, 144.
44 M'Kerlie III, 207.
45 APS IX, 375.
46 Ibid, XI, 149-50.
47 M'Kerlie III, 207.
48 Ibid.
49 Ibid.
50 Ibid.
51 NSA IV, 54.

---

6.   BARCLOSH CASTLE
(1½ m ENE Dalbeattie)   (NX855625)

The lands of Barclosh formed part of the extensive estates of 'Kircwinnyn', or Kirkgunzeon, granted to Holm Cultran Abbey in Cumbria c.1170 by Uchtred, Lord of Galloway.[1] Thereafter, the history of the lands was very much the same as for the other lands of Kirkgunzeon and Corra (q.v.) until the closing years of the 16th century, when the present tower-house, or 'castle', appears to have been built. Although Sir John Maxwell (d.1582/3), later 4th Lord Herries, built or enlarged a number of major strongholds, including the house of Kirkgunzeon, Barclosh was apparently built later, for there is no stronghold shown at 'Barclossh' on Pont's map c.1595.[2]

There is very little on record about the tower-house itself, which stands on a ridge on the E side of the valley of the stream known as Kirkgunzeon Lane, and some 270ft above it. From there it had a commanding view across the valley and its confluence with the Water of Urr to Buittle, 2½ miles to the WSW, and up the valley towards Corra, which lies 2½ miles to the NNE. It thus formed another link in a chain of Maxwell strongholds stretching across East Galloway from the Water of Urr to Dumfries.

Fig. 134 Barclosh Castle: remains of SE corner.

The **TOWER** was oblong in plan, and, according to the RCAHMS, measured about 15ft in width between walls 'averaging 3ft in thickness' and 'not more than 12ft in height'.[3] At the time of the Commission's visit in 1911, there were still portions of the two side walls (NE and SW) surviving.[4] It is, however, impossible to reconcile their report with the remains standing today, which comprise a substantial section of walling, 4ft thick and 27ft high. The masonry is a mixture of local pink and grey granite and red sandstone rubble, with quoins of roughly shaped pink granite. The surviving wall formed part of the E wall of the tower, and extends from the SE corner northwards for some 12ft, at which point, at basement level, there is a remnant of a splayed jamb, probably for a slit window. Higher up, but also at basement level, the wall bears the vague outline of an arc, which encroaches slightly into the fallen S wall. If this represents the line of a vault, it would indicate that this was the gable wall and confirm that the basement was vaulted. At second floor level, there is the S jamb of a window with a boldly chamfered arris. The S wall was also 4ft thick. Although it is now missing, there are the remains of a window recess at first floor level, immediately adjacent to the SE corner. The recess is 2ft deep, and in the adjacent wall there are the holes where the lintels were supported.

A thumbnail sketch of the ruins as they were *c.*1878 is reproduced by M'Kerlie.[5] It shows one gable wall virtually complete and an adjacent section of one side wall. No doubt part of the other side wall, as recorded by the RCAHMS, was also standing, hidden behind the gable. If this sketch is compared with the 1893 edition of the large scale Ordnance Survey map of Barclosh, which shows the remains of three walls, it is apparent that the surviving wall is indeed the E gable wall, and it is the longer section of the N (or NE) wall that has since fallen completely. From M'Kerlie's sketch, it would appear that the tower had three storeys and a garret.

It is not known, either who occupied the tower, or for how long it was in use. In 1770 it was the property of Lady Winifred Maxwell, granddaughter and heiress of the 5th and last Earl of Nithsdale and wife of William Constable of Everingham Park, Co. York.[6] The land later became a separate farm unit, but still apparently within the estate of Kirkgunzeon,[7] until it was finally sold by Herbert Constable-Maxwell-Stuart to Maxwell Murdoch, the tenant farmer, in 1920.[8]

---

1   M'Kerlie IV, 212; Gillespie, J.E. 'Notes on the parish of Kirkgunzeon', *TDGAS*, 2nd Ser., XXIV, 177.
2   Blaeu, 66, 'Praefectura KIRCUBRIENSIS'.
3   RCAHMS 1914, No.277.
4   The E wall is 17° out of true, N to S, which could lead to it being described as the SE wall, but the RCAHMS only refer to NE and SW walls.
5   M'Kerlie IV, 223.
6   Directory of Landownership, 196.
7   M'Kerlie IV, 220.
8   Reg. Scot., Kirkcudbright, No.2206.

7. BARJARG TOWER
(3¹/₂ m SE Penpont)   (NX877901)

The lands of Barjarg, or Parkjarg as it was often known of old, formed part of the extensive estates that once belonged to the abbey of Holywood. The Lords Maxwell obtained bailiary jurisdiction over these properties in 1495,[1] and in 1522 Abbot John (Maxwell) granted various lands, including the £16 lands of Keir and the £3 lands of Barjarg, Ferdyne James and Barboy, to Lord Maxwell in consideration of counsel and help given, and to be given, to the abbey by him, his heirs and successors.[2] In 1556/7 Lord Maxwell's grandson, John, 7th Lord Maxwell, had sasine of these lands from Abbot Thomas (Campbell),[3] and in 1587 he granted the 20 shilling lands of Parkjarg and others in feu-farm to one Thomas Grierson, reputedly a kinsman of the laird of Lag.[4]

John, 8th Lord Maxwell, had sasine of the superiority of the lands of Keir, Barjarg, etc., in 1605;[5] but following his forfeiture four years later,[6] James VI granted many of these lands, including the £3 lands of Parkjarg, to Sir Robert Ker, later Earl of Somerset;[7] and after Somerset's fall from favour, the £3 lands of Parkjarg, Ferdingjames and Barbey were granted, first, in 1618, to John Murray of Lochmaben,[8] and then, in 1621, to Robert Maxwell, 1st Earl of Nithsdale.[9] Meanwhile, in 1613, the crown granted to Sir William Grierson of Lag and his heirs in feu-farm various lands, including the 53s 4d lands of Parjarge and Barboyes, in compensation for an outstanding caution on behalf of the forfeited Lord Maxwell.[10]

It is not certain when the oldest part of the tower was built, but all the evidence would indicate that it was the work of Thomas Grierson soon after he acquired the property in 1587.[11] His 'duelling' (dwelling) of Barjarg is first mentioned ten years later,[12] and it is also shown on Pont's map of Nithsdale *c.*1595.[13] Standing on a gently rising slope on the W side of the Nith valley, it overlooked a wide expanse of Nithsdale to the N and E, but had no direct communication with any other strongholds in the vicinity. Nothing survives of the barmkin or outbuildings.

Fig. 135 Barjarg Tower: view from NW.

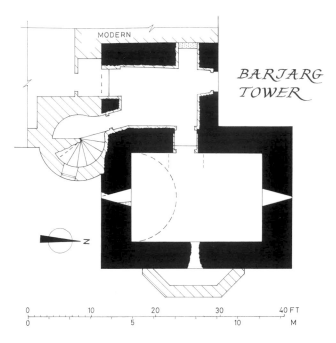

BARJARG TOWER

Fig. 136 Barjarg Tower: plan of basement.

more than once during the last three centuries, it appears that the main block was originally four storeys high, with corbelled-out corner turrets,[14] while the wing rose one storey higher. The entrance is in the N wall of the wing; it has a QERH moulded surround. Immediately outside, there is a fine iron yett, which was evidently moved to its present position comparatively recently. Originally, it would have been on the inside and was taller, one bar having been cut off the bottom. Inside, the wing has been completely modernized, so no original details survive. It would seem, though, that a relatively large stair rose from the entrance to the first floor, while the higher floors were reached by a small wheel-stair partly contained within the wall's thickness in the re-entrant angle. The slit windows that lit the latter stair may still be seen on the outside. Later, both these stairs were superseded by a spacious new wheel-stair, 8ft 2in in diameter, that was provided in a large, circular tower added on the S side of the building. The basement of the main block is vaulted. It was provided with light and ventilation by a single slit-window at each end. A small, ragged opening in the E wall appears to be of recent origin, probably added in connection with the new bay-window immediately outside, and not a former gun-loop.

Above this level the tower was completely modernised internally in 1914, and integrated with the later additions on the S and W sides. Nevertheless, in the main block, original windows with QER mouldings may still be seen built up at first floor level in the S wall and at first, second and third floor levels in the W wall. In addition, the moulding around the third floor window also incorporates a nail-head surround, similar to Amisfield. All that remains of the original turrets at the NW, NE and SE corners of the main block are the corbelling that supported them and between five and nine courses of the

The **TOWER** was built on the **L**–plan. It comprises a main block, measuring 29ft 8in from N to S by 22ft 1in from E to W, from the S end of which a wing, 18ft 2in wide, extends 13ft 1in to the W. The walls of the main block measure 4ft 2in in thickness along the sides and 4ft 8in at the ends. The masonry is local red and grey sandstone rubble, with dressed quoins and margins. Although the roof-line has been greatly altered

Fig. 137 Barjarg: yett. The yett is now mounted outside the original entrance.

Fig. 138 Barjarg: restored corner turret.

roughly-shaped rubble walling. Above this level, both the turrets and roof have been entirely rebuilt, with the roof of the wing being brought down to a common level.[15] The present corbelled-out parapet, false garderobe projection and dormer window were only added late in the 19th or early in the 20th centuries. Barjarg is credited with a total of eight fireplaces in the Hearth Tax returns c.1690.[16]

Although a stone with the date 1603 and initials 'R M' (for ?Robert Maxwell) has been noted nearby,[17] there is no known record of a Maxwell living here at that period. On the other hand there were Thomas Griersons recorded here, father and son, and possibly also grandson, between 1587 and 1642.[18] Six years later, according to Gray,[19] the family sold Barjarg to one John Grierson, of another branch of the family, and it was he who built the first extension to the tower in 1680. His initials and those of his wife, Grizel Kirkpatrick, are on a date-stone now over a window in the modern W wing. John was appointed a Commissioner of Supply for Dumfriesshire in 1696 and again in 1698.[20]

Early the following century, Barjarg passed by marriage to the Erskines of Alva, when, in 1712, Grizel Grierson married Charles Erskine of Tinwald, third son of Sir Charles Erskine, 1st Baronet of Alva.[21] Charles, who was an advocate by training, was Member of Parliament for Dumfries from 1722 to 1741.[22] He became Solicitor-General for Scotland in 1725, a King's Advocate in 1737, a Lord of Session as Lord Tinwald in 1742, and Lord Justice Clerk in 1748.[23] He died in 1763. Barjarg passed to his second son, James, who later also acquired the Alva estate.[24] James became a Lord of Session in 1761 as Lord Barjarg, and later as Lord Alva.[25] In 1772 he sold the Barjarg estate to Dr. Andrew Hunter of Abbotshill (Co. Ayr).[26]

Dr. Hunter was Professor of Divinity at Edinburgh.[27] He was succeeded in 1809 by his eldest surviving son, William, an Advocate, who, following his marriage to Jane St. Aubyn, the eventual co-heiress of the Arundells of Tolverne and Truthall in Cornwall, took the surname Hunter-Arundell.[28] William was succeeded in 1827 by his elder surviving son, Godolphin, who was a Justice of the Peace for Dumfriesshire.[29] His descendants, the Hunter-Arundells, continued to live at Barjarg until 1985.

It was during the 18th, 19th and present centuries that the house was progressively enlarged by further extensions on the S and W sides to become the large and fine mansion it now is, with a wing at the W end that is almost a mirror-image of the original tower.[30] The central part of the house was added in 1806-7 for Dr. Andrew Hunter to the designs of John Cook, possibly replacing an earlier addition,[31] and the symmetrical W end was added by James Barbour in 1864 for William Francis Hunter-Arundell, J.P., who had succeeded his brother Godolphin in 1847.[32] John Bowie, of Barbour and Bowie, then modernised the entire house and made major additions at the rear in 1914.[33]

1   Fraser 1873, I, 165, 175: II, 450.
2   Buccleuch MSS, I, 70-1, Nos.169, 170.
3   Ibid, 74, No.176.
4   RMS V, No.1683.
5   Buccleuch MSS, I, 74, No.176.
6   Complete Peerage, VIII, 598.
7   RMS VII, No.217.
8   Ibid, No.1817.
9   RMS VIII, No.228.
10 Lag Charters, No.180; RMS VII, No.941.
11 The tower is clearly shown on Pont's MS map of Nithsdale, where it is called 'Barjarg' (Pont MS. No.35 in National Library of Scotland).
12 RPC V, 424.
13 Pont MS. No.35 in National Library of Scotland.
14 Neale's 'View' in 1824, drawn after the tower had been completely modernized inside, shows corner turrets, but no parapet (Neale 1824, Vol.VII).
15 Some of the wing's original upper walling is retained in the W gable.
16 Adamson, D. 'The Hearth Tax', TDGAS, 3rd Ser., XLVII, 172.
17 RCAHMS 1920, No.327.
18 RMS V, No.1683; PRS Dumfries, I.
19 Gray 1894, 37.
20 APS X, 29, 131.
21 Burke Peerage 1959, 1940, 'Rosslyn'.
22 Ibid.
23 Ibid.
24 Ibid.
25 Ibid.
26 Burke L G 1910, 36, 'Hunter-Arundell of Barjarg'.
27 Ibid.
28 Ibid.
29 Ibid.
30 The tops of the turrets, as they now appear, were added in 1914, at the same time as those on the old tower. This was when the last major refurbishments were carried out and the dated rainwater heads added.
31 Gifford, 120.
32 Wolffe, A. 'James Barbour', TDGAS, 3rd Ser., LXXI, 154; Burke L G 1910, 36, 'Hunter-Arundell of Barjarg'.
33 Gifford, 120.

---

8.   BARSCOBE CASTLE
(2¼ m NE New Galloway)   (NX660806)

The lands of Barscobe form part of the parish and barony of Balmaclellan, which takes its name from the 'house' or 'village' of MacLellan. Balmaclellan first comes on record in 1408, when Sir Alexander de Gordon received a charter of various lands 'in the barony of Balmaclelane' from Archibald, 4th Earl of Douglas;[1] but although the MacLellans are found in possession of Barscobe later in that century, there is no record of them in the parish this early, nor any reliable information as to when, or from whom, Balmaclellan got its name.[2] In 1422, the Earl granted a charter of 'half of the lands of Bordland, of Balmaclelane, and le Farchiere' to his squire, Robert de Gordon, Sir Alexander's son, and this was confirmed in 1437 by the Earl's widow, Princess Margaret, Duchess of Touraine and Countess of Douglas.[3]

Some of the lands in the parish subsequently came into the possession of Vedast Grierson of Lag, who, in 1466, granted the 12 merk lands in Balmaclellan commonly called Ironmaccanny, Troquhain, Blairinnie and Blackcraig to John M'Lelane, son of Dougall M'Lellane (or Johnsone)[4] of Gelston.[5] This is the earliest surviving record of a MacLellan in the parish. Later, when his daughter Janet got married, John MacLellan gave Troquhain as her dowry;[6] but the fate of the other lands is not clear, as they are never again mentioned in connection with the MacLellans. Barscobe is first mentioned in 1502, when John MacLellan had sasine of the lands of 'Barsqweib'.[7] This John was probably the son of the earlier John, as, when he died in 1515, his own son and heir, John, was still a minor. The following year, the ward of the lands was given to Sir Robert Gordon of Glen,[8] and it was not until 1524 that John MacLellan had sasine of the 'five merk lands of Barsquib'.[9]

There are few references to the MacLellans of Barscobe in the 16th century, and no mention of their fortalice or dwelling. Pont's map c.1595 only shows 'Barskuob' as a settlement, not as a tower-house.[10] John MacLellan of Barscobe, probably a son, is on record in 1562,[11] and in 1577 John MacLellan gave a charter of the 5 merkland of Barscobe to his grandson, William MacLellan, to be held of the Crown.[12] John was still alive in

Fig. 139 Barscobe Castle: view from SW.

1611.[13] Eight years later, William married Margaret, daughter of Alexander Gordon of Troquhain.[14] William had a brother James MacLellan of Marscaig, who had a son William; and it was to the latter William, who was still a minor, that his uncle disponed Barscobe in 1625, on condition that he might redeem the lands at any time.[15] That there was probably no dwelling of note on the lands at this time is supported by the fact that, in 1633, the elder William brought an action against one John Gordon to remove from his lands.[16] This William died shortly afterwards.

The nephew, William, was admitted a burgess of Kirkcudbright in 1644,[17] and was a member of the Committee for War in 1648 and 1649.[18] It was he who built the present house in 1648. After John M'Ghie of Balmaghie was ordered by the War Committee for the Stewartry to 'slight' Threave,

William MacLellan applied to the committee for permission to take the stones from the castle, as he had 'use for certaine friestane for building' his new house at Barscobe.[19] The committee's Minute Book records: 'Anent the supplicatioun presented by William McClellan of Barscoib et. etc. ordaines the said lard of Barscoib to tak as manie of the forsaid friestane of the said hows, as will serve for his use, and to be in the Committee's will for the prye thereof'.[20] Freestone was precious at Barscobe, where the local stone is greywacke, but it is not clear how much eventually came from Threave.

The castle stands on a bluff of rock, which is defended to the W by marshy ground, though by this time defence was clearly no longer a major consideration, despite the civil war. There was almost certainly a barmkin or walled garden on the plateau immediately to the S.[21]

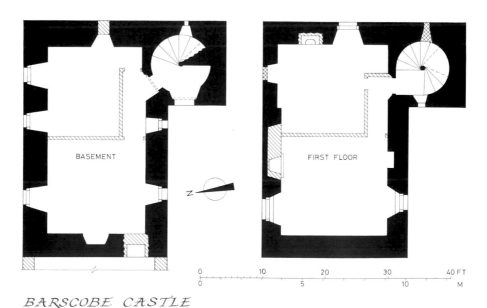

BARSCOBE CASTLE

Fig. 140 Barscobe Castle: plans of basement and first floor before restoration in 1971.

The **CASTLE** is built on the L–plan, and comprised two storeys and a garret, with an additional chamber above the stair in the wing. The main block measures 37ft 10in from E to W by 23ft 3in from N to S, over walls averaging 3ft 9in in thickness, while the stair wing, which is 13ft 6in wide, projects 9ft 1in from the E end of the S wall. The masonry is local greywacke rubble, with sandstone dressings and some sills and lintels of re-used granite. Most of the sandstone dressings around the door-ways and windows have QER mouldings. There was no vault-ing.

It is not clear what the original arrangement was inside the castle, nor what windows there were. There are, however, records of the basement layout in 1911[22] and the first floor in 1971,[23] immediately prior to the restoration. Several of the win-dows had clearly been enlarged at some period, at least one had been added, and the dormer window on the S side, now restored, had been replaced by a smaller window below the wall-head, and the pediment built into a nearby farm building.

The original entrance to the castle is in the re-entrant angle, where it is overlooked by a small window in the main block. The surround is unusual in that the lintel is a flat arch of three stones. Above it there is an armorial panel bearing the arms of MacLellan[24] and Gordon[25], side by side, with the initials 'WM' and 'MG' for William MacLellan and his wife, Mary, natural daughter of Sir Robert Gordon of Lochinvar,[26] above their respective shields and the date '1648' below. This panel has now been painted in brilliant colours, much as it would have

Fig. 141 Barscobe: entrance doorway and armorial panel.

appeared originally. There is no evidence that the door was re-inforced by either a yett or a drawbar. Inside, a small vestibule admits to the wheel-stair, which is a generous 9ft in diameter at this level, and what was probably a short passage connecting the two rooms in the basement. The room at the E end was lit by a small window in the N wall and an even smaller window high up in the E wall, the third window immediately to the W of the former one being almost certainly a later insertion. Both this room and the entrance vestibule retain their floors of stone flags. The room at the W end was probably the kitchen. It had a fire-place[27] in the middle of the W wall and windows in the N and S walls, both of which have been enlarged, if the former is not wholly a later insertion. The N window was converted into an-other entrance doorway in 1971, but is no longer in use.

The first floor was the great hall, or principal living room. It had a massive fireplace, 9ft wide, in the middle of the N wall with windows on either side of it, and there are further windows in the S and E walls and a mural recess near the middle of the S wall. At some period this floor has been subdivided into two chambers, with a small fireplace being inserted into the original fireplace to serve the W room, while another fireplace was in-serted in the E wall to serve the E room. It was probably at this time that the two windows serving the W room were enlarged, and perhaps also when the N window of the E room was blocked.[28] In 1971 this floor was once again restored to a single chamber with a central fireplace. However, instead of reinstat-ing the original fireplace, a new one was built, 5ft 6in wide, extending 18in further into the room and with a flat arch of three stones as the lintel.

The top floor is a garret, which was divided into two rooms, each heated by a fireplace in its respective gable wall. The fireplace in the E gable has a later surround. The W room was lit by two dormer windows, one on each side, with moulded pediments. The pediment above the N window was plain, while the one on the S side, now built into a nearby farm building, bears on its tympanum the arms of MacLellan and Gordon with the initials 'WMMG' and the date '1648' similar to the armorial panel over the entrance.[29] The latter was dispensed with at some period when the window was rebuilt at a lower level, but it was restored in 1971 using the pediment from the N window, while in its place on the N side there is a new pediment bearing the date '1971' and the initials 'HW' for Sir Hugh Wontner, who restored the castle in that year. The E room has a dormer win-dow on the N side and another window in the E gable wall. The pediment above the N window bears the date '1648' and the initials 'WMG' beneath a solitary 'C'.[30]

The main roof is of double-collar-and-rafter construc-tion, and retains its original oak trusses, though they are not all in the same sequence as the carpenter's incised numbers. The attic thus contained, although not fitted out as a proper room, was provided with a small window in each gable. It could only be reached by ladder. The gables themselves were finished with a rare, if not unique, arrangement of three equally spaced crow-steps, or skews, with plain coping between. In the wing, the wheel-stair finished at the level of the second floor. Above this there was a small chamber with a pitched roof and S facing ga-ble, equipped with a small window and dummy chimneystack. This chamber must have been reached by either a wooden stair or ladder, now missing.

Abutting the W end of the castle, there is a single storey extension with a steeply pitched roof. This is a 19th century addition,[31] which was at one time used as a byre.[32] At first the two buildings were connected by a doorway slapped through the end wall of the castle, but this was later closed up. It was opened again when the building was restored and modernized in 1971, and now serves as the everyday entrance to the castle.

William MacLellan died *c*.1654, and was succeeded by his eldest son, Robert, though Robert was not formally served heir until 1664.[33] Two years later, he had the 5 merk lands of Barscobe, Mark, Drumister and Corriedow apprised from him by his brother-in-law John Neilson of Corsock, under reversion, for debt.[34] An ardent Covenanter, he took part in the battle of Rullion Green in 1666 and Bothwell Bridge in 1679, for both of which he was declared a rebel and sentenced to forfeiture of life and lands, the Privy Council decreeing that no-one was to harbour or intercommune with him,[35] and this sentence was confirmed by parliament in 1669.[36] Nevertheless, William managed to elude his enemies, and in 1673 he gave sasine of three quarters of his lands to his cousin Roger Gordon of Troquhain, and the following year the other quarter to James Cannan of Barnshalloch, to avoid forfeiture.[37] He was finally captured by Claverhouse in 1682, tried and sentenced to death for treason.[38] His sentence was, however, repeatedly deferred,[39] and then, after he took the Test, he was released,[40] only to be murdered two years later by another Covenanter, Robert Grierson of Mylnemark.[41] After his death, the Privy Council ordered that 'the garrison which was formerly . . . in the house of Barscobe be put in the house of Earlestoune'.[42]

When Robert MacLellan died, his only son, Robert, was still a minor. His mother then married Gideon Murray, and they all went to live at Goosefords.[43] It was whilst they were there in 1689 that John Neilson, 'called of Corsock', and his brothers came 'in a hostile manner with swords, guns, pistols, etc., to the manor-house and mains of Barscob and took possession thereof, and still continue the same, though the property belongs to the said Elizabeth'.[44] The Neilsons then went to Goosefords, and carried off Robert. The Privy Council demanded his return, but, after hearing the Neilsons' case, agreed that they might have the rents and educate Robert at their own expense.[45]

After James II was deposed in 1689, William and Mary sought a reconciliation with the families who had previously suffered forfeiture. Accordingly, in 1690, parliament rescinded the sentence of forfeiture imposed upon the late William MacLellan of Barscobe in favour of his sons, Robert MacLellan of Barscobe and his brother Samuel.[46] Robert was evidently in serious financial difficulties by 1702, when he had to borrow a large sum of money.[47] He subsequently joined the Jacobites, and fought at the battle of Preston in 1715, where he was taken prisoner and marched to London.[48] He was later released, and died in 1734.

Robert's only son and heir, Robert, had a charter of the lands of Barscobe under the Great Seal in 1743.[49] The family's estates were, however, becoming increasingly encumbered by debt, so that when he died in 1761, his eldest son and heir, Major Robert MacLellan, who had sasine of Barscobe the same year,[50] had little choice but to dispose of them to satisfy his creditors. In 1764 he wadset his lands to Patrick Heron of that Ilk, who, two years later, bought Barscobe and several other properties;[51] but he renounced his title in favour of MacLellan the following year.[52] The whole estate was finally sold by roup in 1775.[53]

The next owners were the Carsons, who eventually sold Barscobe to William Forbes of Earlstoun some time after 1819.[54] The castle continued to be occupied by tenants until well into the 20th century, before being relegated to the status of a farm store. The estate was finally bought by Sir Hugh Wontner c.1970, and the castle restored in 1971,[55] with the internal decor being supervised by its new tenant, Dame Bridget D'Oyly Carte.

---

1   Fraser 1885, III, 405, No.354.
2   The earliest stronghold at Balmaclellan was the motte, which lies just N of the village (RCAHMS 1914, No.37).
3   Fraser 1885, III, 422, No.401.
4   Dougall is on record as both 'M'Lellane' and 'Johnsone', even in the same document (RMS II, No.907)
5   RMS II, No.907.
6   Adams 1921, 136; Torrance, 97.
7   ERS XII, 711.
8   RSS I, No.2814.
9   ERS XV, 624. The annual fermes are given as £6:13s:4d.
10   Blaeu, 66, 'The Steuartrie of Kircubright, The most easterlie part of Galloway'.
11   Torrance, 97.
12   Ibid.
13   Ibid.
14   Adams 1921, 137.
15   Torrance, 99.
16   Ibid, 100.
17   Ibid, 101.
18   APS VI, Part II, 35, 493.
19   McDowall 1986, 386.
20   Torrance, 101.
21   The Ordnance Survey map of 1854 also shows what was probably a formal garden to the SE.
22   RCAHMS 1914, No.35; NMRS: Plan of Barscobe Castle.
23   NMRS: Barscobe Castle - Survey of First Floor by G. Stell, May 1971.
24   Or, 2 chevronels sable. These are in fact the arms of MacLellan of Bombie, the head of the family (Nisbet, 157), but see Note 29 (*infra*).
25   Azure, 3 boars heads erased, Or.
26   Scots Peerage V, 117.
27   It was 4ft 3in wide in 1911, but the original opening was probably larger.
28   The relieving arch above this window is much wider than was necessary for the present opening, which raises the question, Why?
29   The only difference is that here the MacLellan arms have the addition of a mullet in the base, 'for difference'. It is quite likely, therefore, that the Maclellan arms over the entrance doorway originally also had a mullet, though this variant is not recognized by Nisbet (Nisbet, 157-8).
30   The significance of the 'C' is not clear.
31   It is not shown by MacGibbon & Ross in 1889 (MacGibbon & Ross III, 524).
32   RCAHMS 1914, No.35.
33   Torrance, 103.
34   Laing Charters, No.2606; RMS XI, No.924. It has been suggested that the transfer of the lands to Neilson was a ruse to prevent them being forfeited (Torrance, 102), but this is not supported by the dates. Moreover, Neilson was also a Covenanter, who forfeited his own estates.
35   RPC, 3rd Ser., II, 230, 348; VI, 260; VII, 488; APS V,
36   APS VII, 562.
37   PRS Dumfries, I, f.211, f.276.
38   Buccleuch MSS, 270 (No.198); RPC, 3rd Ser., VII, 217, 373.
39   RPC, 3rd Ser., VII, 394, 396, 445.
40   Ibid, 489; VIII, 640.
41   Ibid, VIII, 379.
42   Ibid, 523.
43   Torrance, 107.
44   RPC, 3rd Ser., XIV, 154.
45   Ibid.
46   APS IX, 164-5.
47   Torrance, 107.
48   Ibid; M'Kerlie III, 68.
49   Torrance, 108; PRS Dumfries, XIV, f.220.
50   PRS Dumfries, XIX, f.63.
51   Torrance, 111; PRS Dumfries, XIX, 489.
52   M'Kerlie III, 68.
53   Torrance, 111.
54   M'Kerlie III, 69.
55   To the designs of Ian G. Lindsay and Partners (NMRS drawing archive).

9.   BLACKETHOUSE TOWER
(¹⁄₂ m E Eaglesfield)   (NY243744)

A century after the first Bell appears on record in Dumfriesshire,[1] one branch of the family settled near Middlebie in Lower Annandale, where they soon spread to dominate the parish. At first the Bells of Kirkconnel appear to have been the senior branch,[2] but in the second half of the 16th century William Bell of Blackethouse, known as 'Red-Cloak', became prominent in Border life and the acknowledged chief of the clan.[3]

Blackethouse, or Blackwoodhouse, is first mentioned in 1459, when John Bell of Blackwoodhouse received remission of a fine levied on him at the justice ayre.[4] He received a further remission in 1465.[5] Blackethouse then seems to have sunk into obscurity until it came into the possession of William Bell, 'Red-Cloak', who is first designated 'of Blacathous' in February 1583/4.[6] He was the son of John, or 'Jok', Bell of Albie,[7] and a tenant of Douglas of Drumlanrig.[8] In 1585 he was one of those included in the general amnesty for those charged with rebellion.[9]

Although the name Blackwoodhouse would suggest a building of some substance in the 15th century, the present tower is no older than the second half of the 16th century, and was in all probability built by 'Red-Cloak'. It stands near the edge of a cliff on the right bank of the Kirtle Water, from where it had a commanding view along the Kirtle from Old Kirkconnel to Wyseby and Bonshaw. 'Ye Blacketthowse' is shown on Aglionby's Platte in 1590,[10] and 'Black-wood hous' on Pont's map of Annandale c.1595.[11]

The **TOWER** was oblong in plan, and measured 29ft 3in from E to W by 23ft 9in from N to S over walls 3ft 6in thick; it had three storeys and a garret. The masonry is red sandstone rubble, with dressed quoins and margins. Of the original building, all that survives is the ruinous basement – now choked with rubble and inaccessible – and most of the S wall, together with some adjacent portions of end walling, although the higher lev-

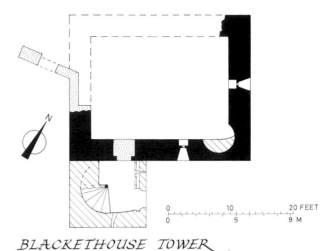

Fig. 143 Blackethouse Tower: plan of basement.

els of all these walls have been subjected to considerable patching and restoration in more recent centuries. The only features of the basement that may still be seen are two, splayed, rectangular gun-loops, with circular throats, which are preserved in the outer faces of the E and S walls, and a curved recess, later partly filled, in the SE corner, where the original wheel-stair rose to serve the upper floors. It is not clear whether the basement was vaulted. Unlike most towers, the entrance was not adjacent to the stair, but seems always to have been at the other end of the S wall, where the wing was later added. At first floor level there are the remains of one window recess at each end and an unusually large window on the S side, which was in all probability a secondary enlargement, possibly made when the wing was added. On the second floor there was one smaller window on the S side and, nearer the re-entrant angle, a slit window. The principal arrises in both the main block and wing have a simple chamfer. All the openings in the S wall were later built up.

The wing appears to have been added early in the 17th century, either by the same William Bell (d.c.1623) who built the main block, or his son William, who had sasine of Blackethouse in 1631.[12] Built to provide the tower with a more spacious stairway, 8ft 4in in diameter, it is 12ft 6in wide and projects 10ft 8in from the W end of the S wall. It also provided a new entrance in the re-entrant angle. But, although there is no additional provision for gun-loops or shot-holes in the wing, merely slit windows, the entrance's double rebate for the usual iron yett and wooden door, and the substantial slot, 6¹⁄₂in wide by 5in high and 4ft 6in long, for the reinforcing drawbar, show that strength was still important. At first floor level there is a slop sink, which discharges in the re-entrant angle, and a few steps higher in the same wall a slit-window with a lamp-shelf below the sill. The wing terminates one storey above the main block in a pitched roof with stone flags and crow-stepped gables. Where the SW corner of the main block meets the wing, there are the last vestiges of a parapet walk supported on three continuous courses of corbels, but as the wall immediately beneath has been rebuilt, one cannot determine whether the original parapet took the same form.

During the last two decades of the 16th century, there is frequent reference to bitter feuds between the Bells and Carlyles on the one hand and their Irving and Graham neighbours.[13] After one such incident in 1591, Drumlanrig complained to the

Fig. 142 Blackethouse Tower: view from SW.

Privy Council that Will Bell, his tenant in Blacathous, had been of late 'violentlie and per force dispossessd and ejectil' by Edward Irving of Bonshaw.[14] William Bell, 'Red-Cloak', died c.1625, and was succeeded by his son William, who was infeft in Blackethouse, Newlands, Johnstonestoun, Cushethill, and other lands, six years later on a precept by Viscount Drumlanrig.[15]

The next laird was John Bell, elder son of the younger William. John, who was a steadfast supporter of Charles I, is reputed to have been Governor of Carlisle in 1644-45, when it held out against Cromwell's forces for more than eight months. In retaliation, the parliamentarians are said to have burned Blackethouse, together with the family papers.[16] The following year, John was appointed a Commissioner of War for Dumfries-shire.[17]

It is likely that the tower was enlarged soon after the Restoration of 1660, for a lintel bearing the date 1663 and the initials IB and II, for John Bell and his wife Jean Irving, would seem to belong to the new wing, or house, that was added at the NW corner of the old tower. The two buildings were at an angle to one another. Only a fragment of the later building now survives, although it is shown on an old estate map.[18] Another lintel, which may have been the lintel of a fireplace, and which is also incorporated into the ruins, bears the date 1714 and the initials 'GB' and 'IK'. It is not known whence it came.

John Bell of Blackethouse was succeeded by his son William, who was infeft in the lands of Blackethouse, and others, in 1669 on a precept by the Earl of Queensberry.[19] William was laird for a great many years, before being succeeded by his son George, who was served heir to his father in 1719.[20] A lintel bearing the date 1714 and initials GB and IK, for George Bell and his wife Isobel Kennedy,[21] commemorates some additional building work undertaken by him. Both this stone and the lintel of 1663 were subsequently built into a "doorway" immediately W of the tower, when the ruins were converted into a 'romantic ruin', or folly, in the fashion of the 19th century.

George's elder son, William, who was formally served heir in 1734,[22] had in fact already sold the estate two years earlier, reputedly to meet the costs of a protracted lawsuit over some land at Kelso.[23] One part of the estate, comprising Bankhead, Craighead, Palmersgill, Blacketridge and Ashyards, was sold to Sir William Maxwell of Springkell, while the main portion, comprising Blacketlees, with the tower, Cushethill and Johnstoun, was sold to his kinsman Benjamin Bell in Woodhouselee, a younger son of George Bell of Godsbrig by his third wife, Isobel Bell.[24]

Benjamin, who died in 1762, was succeeded first by his son Thomas, who only held the estate in liferent, and then, after Thomas's death without issue in 1770, by his grandson Benjamin, the eldest son of Thomas's youngest brother, George Bell in Woodhouselee.[25] Benjamin became a distinguished surgeon in Edinburgh. Having no immediate use for an estate in Dumfriesshire, and a family to educate, he finally sold Blackethouse in 1775 to John Carruthers of Braes.[26]

The property has since passed through many hands. The tower was reported to be 'fast sinking into ruins' in 1835,[27] at around the time when the present dwelling-house was built just to the S of the old tower. Recently the house underwent extensive restoration. The stair wing of the old tower was last used as a doo'cot.

One of Blackethouse's dubious claims to fame is the tradition that one of the Bells of Blackethouse was the rejected suitor of 'Fair Helen [Irving] of Kirkconnel', who, in a fit of jealousy, shot Helen dead in mistake for his rival. The story was

well-known in the mid 18th century, when it was recorded by Pennant,[28] and was later included in Scott's Minstrelsy of the Scottish Border.[29]

1   One Thomas Bell was a juror in Dumfries in 1304 (Bain, II, 412).
2   The last Bell of Kirkconnel appears to have been Thomas Bell, whose 4 merk land of Kirkconnel was granted to Alexander Jardine of Applegarth by James V in 1515 (RSS, No.2660). – For notice of the old tower, see 'Kirkconnel Tower' at Ecclefechan.
3   RPC, V, 497. He was a younger son of Jok Bell of Albie (RPC, III, 42 et al).
4   Exchequer Rolls, VI, 554.
5   Ibid, VII, 310.
6   Hope-Johnstone MSS, 31 (No.56).
7   Steuart 1932, 27-8.
8   RPC, IV, 565.
9   APS III, 389-95.
10 Hyslop, 320.
11 Blaeu, 57, 'THE STEWARTRIE OF ANNANDAIL'.
12 PRS, Dumfries, III, 131.
13 Border Papers, I, Nos. 123, 127, 197, 743, et al.
14 RPC, IV, 565.
15 PRS, Dumfries, III, 131; Steuart 1932, 30.
16 Ibid, 31. The story was recorded in a manuscript family history, written c.1692, that used to be in the library of the Bells at Rammerscales.
17 APS VI, Part II, 32.
18 Mercer 1997, 92.
19 Steuart, 32.
20 Ibid, 34.
21 Ibid, 33. According to Steuart (p.34), George's wife was Janet Irving, but PRS Dumfries II (1672-1702), Index, 14, gives his (?first) wife as Isobel Kennedy.
22 Ibid, 34.
23 Ibid.
24 Ibid, 35, 41.
25 Ibid, 36. George Bell is believed to have been the George Bell who was provost of Dumfries during the 1745 rebellion.
26 Ibid.
27 NSA IV, 366.
28 Pennant, 88-9. The event is popularly supposed to have occurred in the reign of Queen Mary, but there is no general agreement regarding either the date or the players.
29 Irving 1907, 60-1. Wordsworth also put the story to verse.

10.   BLACKLAW TOWER
(2¹/₂ m WNW Moffat)   (NT052067)

The lands of 'Blaclau' are first recorded c.1315, when King Robert the Bruce granted these and the adjoining lands of Rivox, Mosshope, Middlegill, Greenhillcoats, Erickstane and Meikleholmside to Sir David de Lyndsay, younger of Crawford,[1] whose family already held the adjoining lands in Clydesdale. Blacklaw, which became the centre of a large estate in Upper Annandale and Evandale,[2] subsequently passed by marriage to the Herries of Terregles,[3] who held it until 1507/8, when the 4 merkland of 'Blakelaw' and other lands were apprised in settlement of a debt of £380 owed by Andrew, 2nd Lord Herries, to the Crown.[4] The following year, 'by special grace, and at the request of our dearest cousin the Queen of France', James IV discharged and quitclaimed Lord Herries of 'all manner of sums of money and debts owed' by him to the Crown, including the debt for which Blacklaw had been apprised;[5] but it appears that Lord Herries soon acquired further debts, and again had Blacklaw apprised, for only two years later, in return for 'great sums of money' paid to the Crown by Lord Maxwell, the 5 (sic) merk lands of Blacklaw, and others that had been similarly apprised, were granted under reversion to his eldest son, Sir Robert Maxwell of Park, Deputy Steward of Annandale.[6]

Fig. 144 Blacklaw Tower: ruins seen from the SE.

Some time later in the century Blacklaw came into the possession of the Johnstons, and it was presumably they who built the tower. In 1549 Gavin Johnston in Kirkton of Kirkpatrick-Juxta and his sons, James Johnston of Blacklaw, James (sic) Johnston of Middlegill and Andrew, were granted remission for having pledged themselves to Thomas Wharton, English Warden of the West March,[7] when the English overran Dumfriesshire in 1547. Later, in 1592, John Johnston of Greenhill bequeathed 6 nolt and 8 sheep and their lambs to Janet, daughter of James Johnston in Blacklaw.[8]

The tower stands on the edge of a small ravine on the E side of the Evan valley, from where it overlooked, and guarded, the main road north to the Clyde valley and beyond. On its S side the ground falls steeply down to the Blacklaw Burn, while on the other three sides there are the remains of a complex sys-

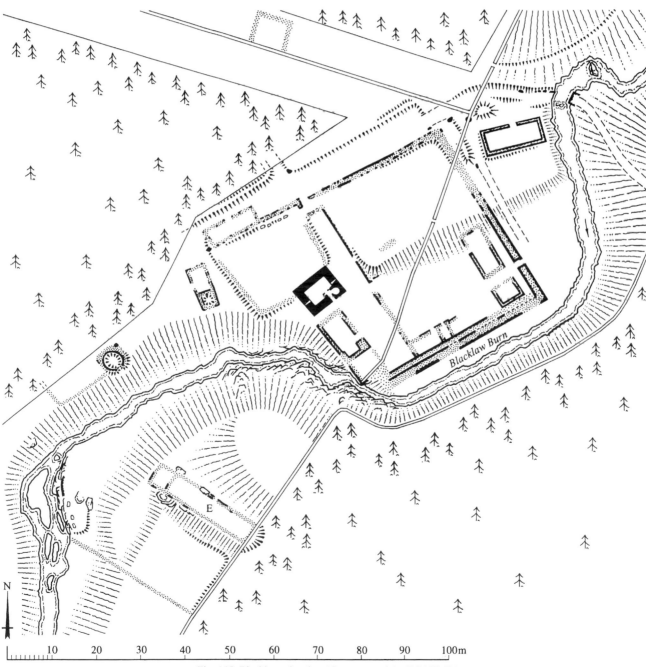

Fig. 145 Blacklaw: site plan. (Crown copyright: RCAHMS.)

tem of enclosures and secondary buildings, all of which are now reduced to little more than heaps of rubble. It is thus impossible without excavation to relate them with any certainty to the overall chronology of the site. It has, however, been suggested that the enclosure complex is 'perhaps without close parallel in Scotland'.[9] The largest enclosure, which extends beyond the tower to the NE and SE and measures approximately 160ft square, was surrounded by a wall that varied in thickness from about 4ft to 7ft. This was presumably the original barmkin. It was unusual in that, along the SE side, there was a secondary, apparently lower section of wall or a wall-walk, 3ft 9in wide, abutting it on the inside, which gave the wall an overall thickness of 10ft 9in at the base.[10] This arrangement would seem to have an affinity with the unusually broad NE wall at nearby Kinnelhead (q.v.). In the E corner of this enclosure there were two buildings, measuring about 40ft by 19ft and 19ft by 15ft, while running along the SE wall further W there are the remains of another small range of buildings. Immediately S of the tower was the kitchen, a building measuring approximately 38ft by 23ft, at the S end of which the base of the kitchen fireplace can still be discerned. Beyond this, in the S corner of the enclosure, there was another small chamber.

Between the tower and the main part of the enclosure to the E there is another wall, 4ft thick, which, apart from a gateway in the middle, divided the main enclosure from NW to SE and, at its southern end, formed the W gable of the range of buildings built along the SE side of the barmkin. A short distance NE of the barmkin, a road crossed the Blacklaw burn to give access to the site. The southern abutment of the bridge is still in situ; it is about 8ft wide. From here the road passed another building, measuring about 47ft by 20ft, before dividing at the N corner of the barmkin and passing along each side to enter the barmkin through two gateways in the NW and SE sides.

To the N and W of the tower, there is the outline of another, adjacent enclosure, which measures about 50ft from NW to SE and 65ft from NE to SW. Outside this enclosure, and

abutting its N wall, is another outbuilding, measuring about 40ft by 15ft, while a little to the W of the enclosure there is a kiln-barn. A second, circular kiln stands alone some 50ft further W, immediately above the steep bank of the burn. There was also another, much larger building on the other side of the burn, some 150ft SW of the tower, which may have been later in date; it measured about 90ft long by 18ft wide, and was partitioned near its NW end. It had an associated enclosure on its SW side.

Of the **TOWER** itself, only the ruinous basement and traces of the first floor walls survive. It is oblong in plan, measuring approximately 32ft 2in by 25ft 6in,[11] and is made of the local, hard, sedimentary sandstone rubble, varying in colour from brown to black.[12] The walls are 5ft 6in thick on the sides and 5ft thick at the ends. There is no surviving evidence of any dressings. The entrance, which is on the E side, admitted directly to a partly-mural vestibule (now completely blocked with rubble), which in turn gave direct access to the wheel-stair, 5ft 6in in diameter, in the NE corner and the vaulted basement beyond, the W end of which has collapsed. The latter chamber was lit by one small slit-window at each end, and had a maximum height of 8ft 6in. The only feature that remains on the first floor is the lower part of a narrow window recess on the S side. This was most unusual, for while there were generous stone seats on either side of the recess, the window itself was no more than a mere slit, 6½in wide and 2ft 2½in high.[13] The wall at this level is 4ft 8in thick.

In the title to some land at Bridgend of Dumfries recorded in 1632, one of the bounding properties is described as 'the tenement and yard pertaining to umquhile James Jonstone of Blaiklaw'.[14] Blacklaw subsequently came into the possession of James Johnston of Corehead, who, in 1647, sold the lands to Lieutenant-Colonel William Johnston, younger son of the 1st Earl of Hartfell.[15] By this time the tower had probably been abandonned.

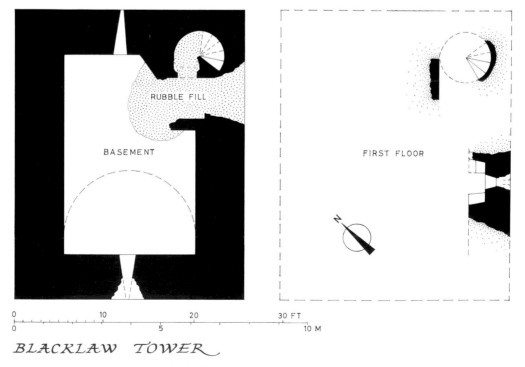

BLACKLAW TOWER

Fig. 146 Blacklaw Tower: plans of basement and first floor.

After his father's death in 1653, Colonel Johnston, being the sole male heir of his elder brother, the 2nd Earl, was known as 'the Master of Johnston'.[16] He died at Newbie four years later.[17] As he never married, Blacklaw passed to his brother, who later became 1st Earl of Annandale & Hartfell, and thus the lands became part of the vast Annandale estates. Blacklaw subsequently remained with the Earls and Marquesses of Annandale and their descendants until 1965, when it was sold to the Forestry Commission.

1   RMS I, No.34.
2   RCAHMS 1997, 212.
3   Sir John Herries of Terregles (d.1420) married Euphemia, daughter and co-heiress of Sir James Lindsay of Crawford (d.1397) – Scots Peerage IV, 400.
4   RSS I, No.1778.
5   Ibid. Lord Herries was in France at the time.
6   RMS II, No.3522. – Under the terms of the reversion, the original owner was to be given 'full re-entrance' if the debt was repaid within seven years.
7   RSS IV, No.497.
8   Hope-Johnstone MSS, 33 (No.69).
9   RCAHMS 1997, 212.
10   On the outside the wall survives to a maximum height of about 4ft 6in, while the inner section is about half as high.
11   The remains of the tower were recorded by William Lee Ferguson in 1900 when it was less ruinous (NMRS; Notebooks of W.L.Ferguson, No.10), but whilst the details portrayed are known to be correct, his measurements are, in the main, wildly inaccurate.
12   This kind of sandstone does not split into layers, and was too hard to cut for dressings with the tools then available.
13   This was measured in 1900 by William L. Ferguson, op.cit., when it was still complete, and is recorded in a photograph of about the same date (See Marchbank 1901, 70). There is no other example in the Borders of a south-facing slit-window provided with stone seats, but a good 15th century example may still be seen complete in the hall of Audley's Castle, Co. Down, in Northern Ireland.
14   PRS Dumfries III, 201v.
15   Fraser 1894, I, ccx. See also Adams 1921, 123n.
16   Ibid, ccxxv. The 2nd Earl of Hartfell, later 1st Earl of Annandale & Hartfell, did not have a son until 1660 (who died in infancy) and a son and heir until 1664.
17   Ibid.

11.   BONSHAW TOWER
(¹/₂ m SE Kirtlebridge)   (NY242720)

According to tradition, the William de Irwyn to whom King Robert the Bruce granted the lands and castle of Drum in 1323 was of the family of Irving of Bonshaw, neighbours and presumably vassals of the Bruces, Lords of Annandale.[1] 'The old mound and the syke', the principal messuage referred to in the earliest surviving title to the lands of Bonshaw (infra), was probably an old motte or moated manor dating from that period.[2] No trace of it now survives. Later, it appears, the Corries of that Ilk became the Irvings' feudal superiors, and so they remained until 1484, when, having supported the Douglas rebellion, they too suffered forfeiture, and the Johnstons of that Ilk acquired the superiority.[3]

There is, however, no contemporary record of Bonshaw before 1506, when William Irving of Bonshaw died and was succeeded by his eldest son, Edward,[4] – although there is a subsequent reference to an agreement entered into by the same William Irving of Bonshaw in 1484.[5] By 1522, Edward had himself died, for in that year 'Christopher Irwyng of Boneschaw' was infeft in the 'five merkland of Boneschaw and five merkland of Dunbratane' as his son and heir. It is this event that is attested in the earliest surviving title, a notarial instrument dated 1529.[6]

Fig. 147 Bonshaw Tower: view from the W.

The Irvings of Bonshaw were Chiefs of the Border Irvings, a small clan that greatly increased in size and importance during the 16th century. When Lord Maxwell, Warden of the West March, held a 'Wapinschawing' (weapon-show) at Burnswarkhill in 1541, 'the Lard of Boneschaw' attended with three score men;[7] and six years later, when the English overran Dumfriesshire, 'Cristie Irwen of Boneshawe', who had been taken prisoner at the battle of Dalswinton,[8] pledged 103 men to their service, while other branches of the clan pledged a further 303.[9] Yet within fifty years the Irvings had become one of the dominant clans in Dumfriesshire, almost as strong as their feudal superiors, the Johnstons of that Ilk, and with effective control over a vast tract of land stretching from Lower Annandale to the river Esk.

When Henry VIII was pursuing his policy of the 'Rough Wooing' in the 1540s, the tower at Bonshaw is presumed to have been a timber peel, typical of the lesser Border towers of the period. It was this that was burned by Lord Wharton in 1544, during his campaign in the West March, when among the many places reported 'burned' were 'Boonshaw [and] Robgyll, wyth all the corne fownde by the way'.[10] But whatever the extent of the damage, Bonshaw was repaired, and it was not until the latter half of the 1560s, or, at the very latest, immediately after the Earl of Sussex 'destroyit with gunpoulder . . . Bonshaw'[11] and other important strongholds in the West March, in August 1570, that the present stone tower was built. It was the work of Edward Irving, who had succeeded to Bonshaw c.1554.[12] The tower owes much in its design to the immensely strong new castle built at Hoddom (q.v.) in 1565 by Lord Herries, and also has an affinity with the earlier tower-house of the Johnstons of that Ilk at Lochwood. By this time the Irvings had become close allies of the Johnstons in their deadly feud with the Maxwells, a bond that had been further strengthened by the marriage, in 1566, of Edward Irving of Bonshaw's eldest son and heir, Christopher, to Margaret, daughter of John Johnston of that Ilk.[13] Indeed, this alliance may well signal the date when the present tower was built, especially as the reference to the use of gunpowder by Sussex would strongly imply the existence of a stone tower at

Fig. 148 Bonshaw Tower: view from the E.

Fig. 150 Bonshaw: gun-loop in basement.

Fig. 151 Bonshaw: gun-loop at foot of stair guarding entrance.

that date, and references to the 'throwing down' and 'destruction' of castles by Sussex should not be taken too literally: both
Hoddom and Caerlaverock were reported 'caist doun' and
'demoliest',[14] yet at Hoddom the tower itself was unscathed and
at Caerlaverock there is 'little evidence' of the damage done.[15]

    The site at Bonshaw is naturally strong, bounded on the
E by a steep cliff that drops some 70ft to the Kirtle Water and on
the S by a deep ravine, whilst protection on the other sides was
afforded by strong outer defences, probably in the form of a
ditch and rampart, reinforced with palisades. The latter were
finally destroyed when the present mansion was built and the
gardens laid out in 1770.[16] 'Ye Bonshawe' is shown on
Aglionby's platte in 1590,[17] and on Pont's map of Annandale
c.1595, although on the latter map the name 'Bonshaw' has been
inadvertently transposed with 'Bonshau syd'.[18] Pont shows a
substantial tower in its own, large deer-park.

Fig. 149 Bonshaw: 'dumb-bell' gun-loop block,
presumably from the outer defences.

Fig. 152 Bonshaw: entrance doorway with motto
'SOLI DEO HONOR ET GLORIA' and empty armorial panel.
The outer porch and both doors are modern.

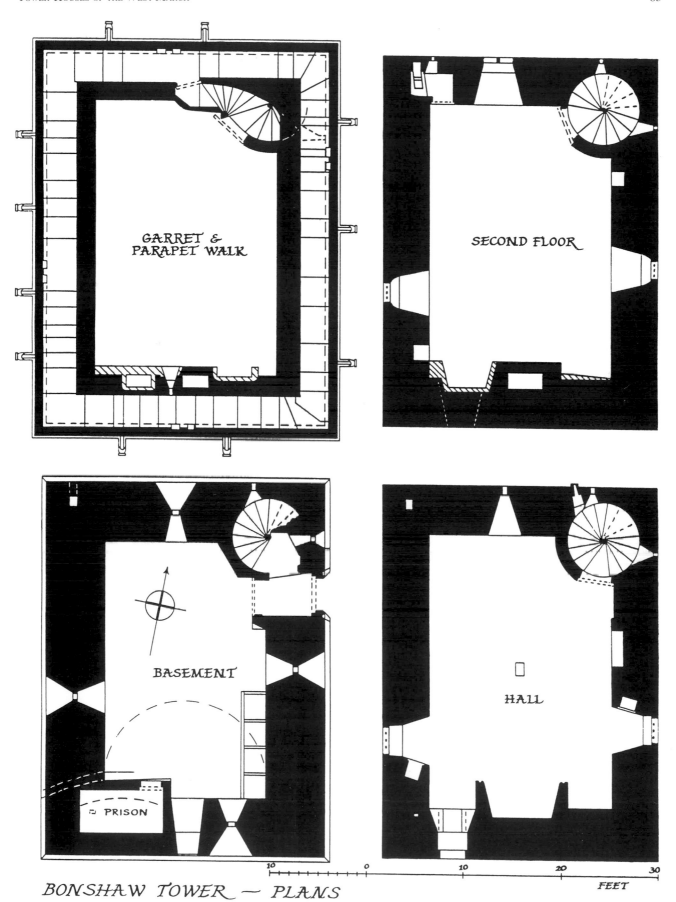

GARRET &
PARAPET WALK

SECOND FLOOR

BASEMENT

PRISON

HALL

BONSHAW TOWER — PLANS

Fig. 153 Bonshaw Tower: plans.

Within the outer enceinte at Bonshaw lay the **BARMKIN**, which enclosed the tower on the E, S and probably also the W side. A charter of 1582 refers to 'the gate of the . . . fortalice'.[19] All that now remains of these defences is the much reduced and altered walling along the cliff edge to the E and S of the tower.[20] This includes the lowest courses of an old postern near the SE corner.

The **TOWER** itself is unusually strong and refined for its period. Built of local sandstone rubble, with dressed margins, ashlar vaults and well-cut mouldings, it is oblong in plan, measuring 36ft 4in from N to S by 27ft from E to W above a splayed plinth course 2ft 8in high, and rises three storeys to a garret. The basement walls are 5ft 9in thick immediately above the plinth, where they are pierced on all sides by widely-splayed, rectangular gun-loops, with oval throats: for the upper floors the thickness is reduced to 4ft 8in. A smaller gun-loop at the foot of the wheel-stair gave added protection to the entrance, while machicolations in the parapet above gave further cover, on the E side to the entrance and on the other sides to the gun-loops. Despite a number of alterations and considerable renovation, the tower is still essentially the same building that successfully resisted the Maxwells in 1585.

The entrance was protected by the usual wooden door and yett, only the hinges of which survive. On the lintel outside, beneath an empty armorial panel, is carved the motto 'SOLI DEO HONOR ET GLORIA', whilst immediately inside, suspended from the keystone of the cross-vaulted vestibule, is a finely cut, octagonal boss bearing the sacred monogram 'IHS'. Beyond the vestibule were two further doors, one leading to the vaulted basement and the other to the wheel-stair, 7ft 6in in diameter, in the SE corner. The former retains its original floor of large flags, which slope down towards the SW corner, whence a drain passes through the wall to join the main drainage channel outside. This provision was almost certainly to cater for the stabling of horses or other prized animals in time of siege, should the need arise.[21] In the same corner, and partly within the wall's thickness, is a small but strong prison roofed with a segmental vault. This feature is remarkable in being one of only four prisons known to have been incorporated into Border towers in the 16th century.[22] It measures 8ft 1in by 4ft 4in and has a maximum height of 6ft. Its floor, which is 18in above that of the basement, is made up of massive stone slabs designed, like those at nearby Hoddom, to prevent prisoners tunnelling out. The only source of air was a small vent that rises up through the vault, but is now blocked higher up. There are two, well-documented instances of prisoners being held here.[23] Apart from the gun-loops, the basement's only source of light is a single window high up in the S wall, which, like the other windows, was originally protected by an iron grille. There is a hatch, now blocked, to the floor above. The large, stone storage-bin in the SE corner is a later addition.

The first floor was the great hall. In the middle of the S wall is a large fireplace, 7ft 4in wide, beneath a single, huge, stone lintel, 8ft 11in wide, with a moulded cornice above. To the right of this two steps lead up to a high window with stone seats, where the ladies would have sat, whilst on either side of the room there are more conventional window recesses with closed aumbries in the jambs. The window at the N end is very much smaller, presumably being outside the protection of the barmkin. Most of the tower's windows have QER mouldings, though a few have plain edge-rolls: the mullions are later additions. An outstanding feature in the E wall is a fine buffet with ogee-arched lintel, which, like the entrance doorway and hall fireplace has a bold, roll-and-hollow moulding on the surround.

This is one of only three examples of late 16th century, ornamented buffets known in the Borders – the other two, smaller examples are at Elshieshields (q.v.) – and recalls the very fine buffets found in the previous century.[24] A few steps up from the hall there is a slop-sink that discharges outside the N wall.

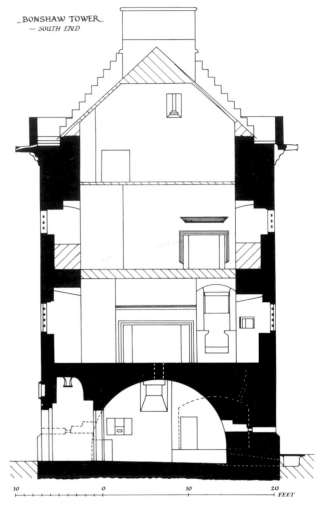

Fig. 154 Bonshaw Tower: sectional elevation
looking towards south end.

Above first floor level the S gable was considerably altered in the 19th century by the insertion of new fireplaces on the upper floors, that on the second floor, which has been re-used from another 18th century building, having apparently taken the place of an original window.[25] The windows on either side have also been altered, the lower part of the recesses having been filled in, while the stepped sill of the N window has been cut away. In the NW corner of this chamber is a mural garderobe. Its flue, which is joined at this level by another flue (infra) now closed off at parapet level, joins the main drain that runs around the W side of the tower and discharges into the gully to the S.[26] There are two open aumbries, or lamp shelves, on this floor. At the beginning of the 18th century this room was known as the 'Chamber of Dyre (or Dire)'.[27]

Although the stair-head was modified when the original stone roof was removed and replaced by a slate one of shallower pitch,[28] there was never a cap-house as such; access to the parapet walk has always been via the strangely-angled doorway in the middle of the N gable. This is an unusual arrangement, which

Fig. 155 Bonshaw: gargoyle.

gave rise to the uniquely-offset crow-step above, but it did give the defenders unrestricted access around the wall-head. However, it is not clear how the garderobe, or more primitive facility, which formerly existed at the NW corner at this level, was accommodated. The parapet itself, which is carried on 2-stage corbels 36ft 9in above the ground, has been restored; it would originally have been higher and almost certainly crenellated. Some of the original moulded gargoyles survive, each with a different design of bands, perhaps to simulate cannons. The garret, whose floor is lower than the parapet walk, has a slit-window high in each gable, but retains no other features of interest. However, although the clan bell at the top of the N gable is modern, there is a tradition that there was a bell here in the 16th century to warn the neighbouring Irving towers of impending raids.

In 1583 Sir James Douglas of Drumlanrig and his brother the Provost of Lincluden, with a following of some fifty friends and broken men from both sides of the Border, forcibly entered Bonshaw, and 'maisterfullie sett at libertie' some eighteen Bells and Irvings, 'notorious offendouris, rebellis and dissobedient personis', who had been placed in custody there by Sir John Johnston, the Warden.[29] Johnston promptly complained to the Privy Council, who ordered Drumlanrig and his brother to be held in ward until the prisoners were produced.

Some two years later, during 1585-6, when the Maxwell-Johnston feud was involving most of the region in bloody conflict, Bonshaw was twice besieged by Lord Maxwell and twice more threatened. The first incident was in April 1585, when Johnston fled to 'Bonshaw Castell' after the burning of Lochwood. Maxwell laid seige, and even brought up cannon, but when it looked as if the house was 'almost gotten' and might have to surrender, Lord Scrope, the English Warden, intervened and effected an agreement.[30] But the truce did not last long, for two months later Maxwell was again laying siege. Once more Johnston appealed to Scrope for assistance, 'seinge the house of the Bonshawes is in such extremitie'; but although Scrope reported the incident – when two or three of Maxwell's men were killed and four hurt – in detail to London, he did not deem it necessary to take any action.[31] It was at this time that Scrope described Bonshaw as 'one of the strongest howses of that border'. Clearly the damage reported, or inferred, on each occasion was greatly exaggerated, as was so often the case in these conflicts. Maxwell retired to lick his wounds, but two weeks later Scrope reported that he had again placed his forces about 'the house of Bonshawe';[32] and the following May Lord

Maxwell's brother returned 'neare unto the howse of Bonshawe . . . and burned the Bonshawsyde'.[33]

In 1592, Sir Richard Lowther, Warden of the English West March, reported that 'The Lard [Edward Irwen] of the Boneshaw . . . hathe delyveryd to the King his howse . . . , which howse shall taike no harme'.[34] Ten years later, in March 1602, James VI himself spent a night at 'Boneschaw' during a military expedition to the West March to punish rebels.[35] He then went on to Lochwood on his way back to Edinburgh. Three years later, Edward Irving died, having led his clan for fifty years, and was succeeded by his grandson, William.

In 1609, on the resignation of Robert Johnston of Raecleugh, his tutor, James Johnston of that Ilk received a crown charter of the superiority of the lands of Bonshaw and Dumbretton.[36] Three years later, the crown granted to John Murray of Renpatrick (later Earl of Annandale) the barony of Lochmaben;[37] this included an over-superiority right to the lands of Bonshaw. The grant was confirmed four months later, and again in 1617 and 1625.[38] On the death of the 2nd Earl of Annandale without issue in 1658, his estates devolved upon David Murray, 4th Viscount Stormont, who, in 1666, received a new crown charter of the barony of Lochmaben.[39] Meanwhile, in 1661, the crown granted the vacant Earldom of Annandale to James Johnston, Earl of Hartfell;[40] and the following year the Earl of Annandale received a new grant of many lands, including the lands of Bonshaw and Dumbretton, all of which were erected into the Earldom of Annandale & Hartfell.[41] The Johnstons continued to hold the superiority of Bonshaw until the 20th century.[42]

During all this time Bonshaw remained in the possession of the Irvings, though not always in the direct line of succession. After the death of William Irving in 1646, Bonshaw passed to his eldest son, Edward, who, two years later, handed the estate over, at least nominally, to a younger half-brother, Herbert Irving of Hairgills.[43] The reason for this is said to have been to save Bonshaw from the Covenanters.[44] Herbert was thereafter designated 'of Bonshaw', and as such he was appointed a Commissioner of Supply for Dumfriesshire later that year.[45] The following year Edward himself died, and was succeeded by his son James, 'The Wild Bonshaw', a notorious persecutor of the Covenanters,[46] who confirmed the disposition of the estate to Herbert.[47] However, with the subsequent change in the political scene, it was James himself who took sasine of Bonshaw in 1655, as heir to his grandfather,[48] before he granted Herbert a second charter confirming the sale of Bonshaw to him 'for great sums of money'.[49] This charter was confirmed by the Earl of Hartfell, as superior. Herbert died five years later, and was succeeded by his only son, William, who remained in peaceable possession until the death of James, 'The Wild Bonshaw', without issue in 1682.

Then, Sarah Douglas (the widow of John Irving of Woodhouse and daughter-in-law of William Irving of Rockhillhead, eldest son of William Irving of Bonshaw by his second marriage) and her brother, Sir James Douglas of Kelhead, began legal proceedings to recover Bonshaw for Sarah's young son, William Irving of Woodhouse, who had now become the heir-male of the family.[50] William finally won his case and obtained possession in 1696;[51] and it was presumably he, rather than the ousted William, who in the same year embarked upon a new house, or other building work, at Bonshaw. However, it did not survive long, or it may never have been completed – his finances had been drained by the protracted litigation –, before it was demolished and the masonry used elsewhere. Stones bearing the date '1696' and initials 'W.I' may be seen re-used in the walls of the nearby Bonshaw Mill, which was built in 1743, and the fire surround on the tower's second floor, the W doorway in the passage (built 1896) connecting the tower to the house, and various other moulded stones re-used on the site may also belong to this period, though some of the more classical mouldings would seem to belong to a later date. In 1699, William was granted a new charter of the lands of Bonshaw by the Earl of Annandale, as superior,[52] and five years later he was appointed a Commissioner of Supply for Dumfriesshire.[53]

William died in 1742, and was succeeded, first by his eldest son, John, who only survived his father by five years, and then by his grandson William. John, who was 'one of [the] Duke of Queenberry's chamberlans',[54] had been a Collector of the Land Tax since 1732, and was appointed to the committee in 1746;[55] and in 1760 William was also appointed a Collector of the tax.[56] To protect the succession to Bonshaw, William drew up an entail of the estate in 1765.[57] Then in 1770, three years after his marriage, he cleared the site immediately N of the tower and built the present house, recording the event on the tympanum over the entrance with the date '1770' and the inscription 'W. Irving J. Douglas', for himself and his wife, Janet, daughter of Sir John Douglas of Kelhead. He was succeeded in 1772 by his only son, John Robert Irving. John was admitted to the Faculty of Advocates in 1793, and subsequently became Professor of Civil Law at the University of Edinburgh, a post he held for 27 years.[58] During this time he rarely visited Bonshaw. He died without male issue in 1839.

Bonshaw then passed to the Reverend John Irving, an army chaplain and great-grandson of John Irving (d.1747) of Bonshaw, by his son Henry. John carried out various additions and alterations to Bonshaw c.1841-2,[59] including the reconstruction of the tower's roof at a lower pitch and possibly the insertion of the new fireplaces on its upper floors. He also completed the interiors of the new house and extended it.[60] In 1853 he disentailed the estate.[61] He died in 1870, leaving no male issue.

Bonshaw then passed to a distant cousin, Robert Nasmyth Irving, a great-great-grandson of the William Irving who had recovered Bonshaw in 1696.[62] As a young man, Robert had served in the Kaffir wars. When he died in 1894, having broken the entail, he left the estate to his housekeeper, which led to a long legal battle before the next heir-male, Colonel John Beaufin Irving, succeeded in obtaining posssession in 1896.[63] Colonel Irving had had a distinguished military career, including taking part with Napier at the capture of Magdala during the Abyssinian campaign of 1868, and ending as Colonel of the 3rd Battalion, The Manchester Regiment. He was also a member of the Royal Company of Archers, the Sovereign's bodyguard in Scotland. After acquiring Bonshaw, he devoted himself to its restoration, adding the passage connecting the old tower to the house.

Colonel Irving was succeeded in 1925 by his son, Sir Robert Irving, OBE, who had a distinguished naval career. On active service during the First World War, he served in the cruiser Yarmouth at the battle of Jutland and later in Palestinian waters, before rejoining the Cunard Line. After holding a number of important commands, he ultimately became Captain of the RMS 'Queen Mary' and Commodore of the Cunard White Star Line. He was a Deputy Lieutenant for Dumfriesshire.

After Sir Robert's death without issue in 1954, his nephew sold Bonshaw to Mrs Eileen Straton-Ferrier, a descendant of the last male Irving of Wyseby, who established a Trust for the preservation of the tower. After her death in 1986, it was acquired by Dr. Bruce Irving, a descendant of the Irvings of Dumfries and Gribton.

1   Irvine, 1678 (MS); Irving 1907, 93; Leslie 1909, 12, 14n. It is a tradition that has been maintained by both branches of the family since at least the 17th century.
2   See Reid, R.C. 'The Bonshaw Titles', TDGAS, XXXVII, 50.
3   Reid, 'The Bonshaw Titles', op. cit., 48. See also 'Tower of Lun'.
4   Reid, 'The Bonshaw Titles', op. cit., 51; Lag Charters, No.54.
5   Reid, R. C., 'Bonshaw', TDGAS, XX, 151-3.
6   Bonshaw Charters, No.2.
7   Buccleuch MSS, I, 66, No.135.
8   Irving 1907, 35.
9   Scottish Papers I, No.396; Armstrong 1883, lxxiv, lxxvi.
10 Hamilton Papers, II, 456; L & P, XIX, Part 2, Nos.191, 625.
11 Irving 1907, 43.
12 One account relates that he was killed near Bonshaw by some marauding Kirkpatricks in 1554 (Fitzmaurice 1899), while his son's retour in Stapleton states that he died in 1555 (Scottish Antiquary, VIII, No.29)
13 Irving 1907, 38, where the full text of the marriage contract is given. Two years earlier, in 1564, the Privy Council, fearing the added power and instability to the region that such an alliance would create, had ordered Johnston 'that he on na wayis allyat his dochtir with the said Edward Irrwingis sone' (RPC I, 306), but the marriage still went ahead.
14 Scottish Papers III, No.436; Irving 1907, 43.
15 Grove, 25.
16 Reid, 'Bonshaw', op. cit., 150.
17 Hyslop, 320.
18 Blaeu, 57, 'THE STEWARTRIE OF ANNANDAIL'.
19 Bonshaw Charters, No.10.
20 In all probability the loose, dumb-bell-shaped, shot-hole block that was found at Bonshaw in 1966 also came from these outer defences, though it would appear to have been of slightly later date (See TDGAS, 3rd Ser., XLIV, 224).
21 Another example of a basement floor with drainage facilities was found at Cramalt's South Tower, in Selkirkshire (See Maxwell-Irving 1982, 414-6; Plates 35-6).
22 The others are at Comlongon (where there is a late example of a pit-prison dating from c.1501), Lochwood and Hoddom, the latter two having a close affinity with the one at Bonshaw.
23 RPC, III, 607-8; RPC, IV, 55-7.
24 In view of the strong religious sentiments expressed by the builder at the tower's entrance, it has been suggested that it may also have been intended to double as an altar.
25 See MacGibbon & Ross, III, 400-1. The fireplace may have come from the house built in 1696.
26 Before the lawns were laid out, the ground level may have been lower and the drains open.
27 Irving 1907, 75-6.
28 MacGibbon & Ross, III, 401.
29 Fraser 1894, I, xc.
30 Holinshed, R 'The Historie of Scotland', 429-31, cited in Irving 1907, 45.
31 Border Papers I, No.321.
32 Ibid, No.327.
33 Ibid, No.425.
34 Ibid, No.760.
35 Scottish Papers XIII, No.778.
36 RMS VII, No.23. Robert was the son of Robert Johnston (d.1592), 1st of Raecleugh, second son of John Johnston (d.1657) of that Ilk.
37 RMS VII, No.683.
38 Ibid, Nos.764, 1600; RMS VIII, No.826.
39 RMS XI, No.965.
40 Ibid, No.39
41 Ibid, No.230.
42 Feu Register of Annandale Estates at Raehills.
43 Irving 1907, 66.
44 Ibid.
45 APS VI, Part II, 32.
46 Irving 1907, 72-3; RPC, 3rd Ser., VII, 431.
47 Ibid, 66.
48 PRS Dumfries, VI, f.68.
49 Bonshaw Charters, No.24.
50 Irving 1907, 36, 74.
51 Ibid, 36, 75.
52 Papers of J. B. Irving of Bonshaw, 1902, recorded in the Note Books of John Bell Irving of Beanlands.
53 APS XI, 142.
54 Prevost, W. 'Sir John Clerk's trip from Drumcrief to Carlyle in September 1734', TCWAAS, LXII, 247.
55 Sederunt Books of the Commissioners of Supply, Dumfries.
56 Ibid.
57 Irving 1907, 79-80.
58 Grant, Sir F. J. 'Faculty of Advocates in Scotland, 1532-1943', SRS, LXXV, 110.
59 See Historic Scotland: Statutory List of 'Buildings of Special Architectural or Historic interest', Annan Parish, No.5, 'Bonshaw Tower, House and Courtyard Walls'.

60   Mercer 1997, 166-70.
61   Reg. Scot. Dumf., 1853, Nos.686, 694.
62   See Irving 1907, 36 (pedigree).
63   Irving 1907, 82.

12.   BORELAND TOWER

(1¹/₂ m N St. Ann's)   (NY066957)

The lands of Dumgree, of which Boreland forms a part, belonged of old to the abbey of Kelso,[1] and the remains of the old church may still be seen on a hillside some 1200 yards NNW of the tower. In 1408 the Earl of Douglas granted the lands of Dumgree, in the barony of Amisfield, to William de Johnston.[2] Some fifty years later King James II granted the ward of the lands to John Johnston of that Ilk,[3] and in 1472 James III granted the lands in feu-farm to his armour-bearer, Gilbert Johnston of Elphinstone.[4] The superiority subsequently passed to the Charteris of Amisfield, who, in a new lease of the one merk church lands of Dumgree to Sir John Charteris of Amisfield in 1602, are referred to as 'former possessors' of the lands.[5] In the meantime, in 1594/5, there is a charter granting the lands in feu-farm to John Johnston, son of John Johnston of that Ilk.[6] It is presumed that by this time the tower had been built, but there is nothing to indicate by whom, nor is Boreland itself mentioned before a crown charter of 1605 confirmed to Sir John Charteris of Amisfield 'the lands of Drumgrene', comprising various properties including 'Bordland'.[7]

Fig. 156 Boreland Tower: view from the NE.

The **TOWER** stood on a low cliff at the confluence of the Kinnel Water and a small streamlet. Although not a site of any great strategic importance, it may have guarded an old ford. All that remains of the tower is the central portion of the vaulted basement and its E end. Built of sandstone and Silurian rubble, it averages 21ft 5in in width over walls 3ft 3in thick, and has a surviving length of about 28ft along the N wall. According to the RCAHMS, the original length was 30ft 9in.[8] The construction of the corners is most unusual in that they are square for the first 4ft and then rounded-off higher up.[9] There is now no trace of the entrance and stair, which must have been in the SW corner. High up at the E end there is a small slit-window, while on the S side, at a lower level, there are two more slit-windows with crudely-dressed, sandstone margins on the inside. The vault now has a maximum height of 9ft 6in. On the N, E and S sides of the tower, there is evidence of a fairly spacious courtyard and other foundations. The latter probably relate to outbuildings,

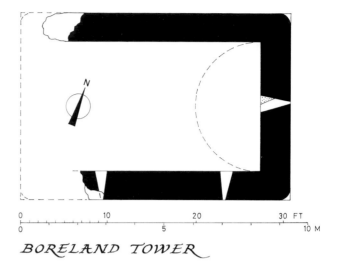

BORELAND TOWER

Fig. 157 Boreland Tower: plan of basement.

but there is nothing to indicate whether they were contemporary or of later date.

In 1634 Catherine Crichton, spouse of John Charteris, younger of Amisfield, had a crown charter of the lands of Dumgree, including Boreland;[10] but within four years the Charteris were in financial trouble and had to put up the lands as surety for various loans.[11] The barony of Amisfield, including these lands, was subsequently acquired by Sir John Dalzell of Newton.[12] It was later divided, and in 1662, when the lands of James Johnston, Earl of Annandale, were erected into the barony and earldom of Annandale and Hartfell, the lands of Dumgree, including Boreland, were included.[13] The Johnstones have held them ever since.

In 1845 the New Statistical Account mentioned a vaulted ruin at Boreland, but gave no other details.[14]

1   See HAS, 43, 156-7.
2   Hope-Johnstone MSS, 9 (No.1).
3   Fraser 1894, I, xx.
4   RMS, II, No.1058.
5   RMS, VI, No.1287.
6   Ibid, No.240.
7   Ibid, No.1683.
8   RCAHMS 1920, No.387.
9   The change could be due to later restoration.
10   RMS, IX, No.248.
11   Ibid, Nos.641, 844, 846, etc.
12   Ibid, No.2102.
13   RMS, XI, No.230.
14   NSA IV, 127.

13.   BRECKONSIDE PELE

(3¹/₂ m S Penpont)   (NX840889)

The lands of Breckonside[1] formed part of the barony of Snaid, or 'Snathe', the lands of which were granted by Robert the Bruce to John, son of Lochlan, c.1320.[2] At that time, Snaid was a part of the barony of Glencairn. Later, however, and presumably after the Cunninghams acquired the lands and barony of Glencairn (q.v.) by marriage c.1400, Snaid passed to a cadet branch of the family and became a barony in its own right.[3]

There was an early castle of Snaid, but nothing is known of its history, and all that remains on the overgrown site (NX846856) are vestiges of rubble walls and the suggestion of a round tower at the SE corner. In 1482, George Cunynghame of Belton, having no male issue, granted the superiority of the barony of Snaid to his grandson John Hay, later 2nd Lord Hay of Yester,[4] and it was still held by the Hays, Lords Hay of Yester and Earls of Tweeddale, in 1660.[5]

The first mention of the twenty shilling lands of 'Bracanside' was in August 1505, when these and various other lands in the northern part of the barony were sold by Sir John Hay of Snaid[6] to John Cunynghame of Westburns.[7] Only three months earlier, Cunningham had resigned these lands to Sir John, apparently under reversion.[8] There was no tower this early.

The lands subsequently passed into the possession of a branch of the Wallaces, who would seem to have resided there. In 1548 John Wallace 'of Brekandsyde' was witness to a deed,[9] and in 1556, John Wallace 'of Brakanesyid' received from the Crown the gift of the ward and non-entries of the lands of Brakanesyid within the barony of Snaid 'of all years and terms bygone since the decease of the late John, Lord Hay of Yester, that last deceased, or any others; and suchlike of all years and terms to come'.[10] It was presumably the Wallaces who built the present tower, though it is unlikely to have been their first dwelling on the site, as there is no tower shown on Pont's fairly detailed map of the area c.1595.[11] The tower was, in all probability, built shortly afterwards. The site is a small rocky outcrop surrounded by marshy ground in a secluded setting high above, and to the NE of, the Cairn valley. The old drove road from Tynron to Dunscore is said to have passed nearby.[12]

Fig. 158 Breckonside Pele: remains viewed from the N.

The **TOWER** is one of a group of towers in this area and nearby Glenesslin – others are at Over and Nether Auchenfedrick, Brockloch and Stewarton (q.v.) – that fall into the simplest category of tower-house, or 'pele'. They are all of the simplest form, built of local rubble bonded with clay mortar, not lime, and are located on relatively barren hillsides in the more remote valleys. Because of their remoteness, the sites have survived relatively unscathed, and have thus retained the remains of both contemporary and later outbuildings and their associated kilns and field systems.[13]

The tower was oblong in plan, and measured 26ft 3in from N to S by 21ft 3in from E to W over walls that varied in thickness from 4ft to 5ft. The entrance was on the E side. It is unlikely that any of these simple peles was vaulted. Although the tower is said to have been occupied less than 200 years ago, it is now reduced

to no more than the base of the walls, which reach a maximum height of about 4ft, and heaps of fallen rubble.

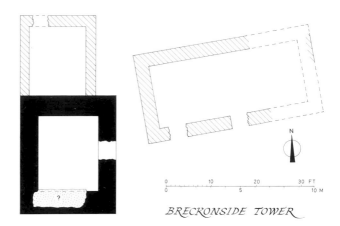

BRECKONSIDE TOWER

Fig. 159 Breckonside Tower (Cairn Valley): plan of pele and outbuildings.

There were two outbuildings; one, measuring 18ft by 16ft 9in over walls averaging 2ft 3in in thickness, abutted the N wall of the tower, and a second, measuring 39ft 6in by 20ft over walls 3ft thick, stood some 6ft further E. The latter building appears to have had two doorways in the S wall, although there is no surviving evidence to indicate that it was divided internally. The ground immediately S of this building has at some time been levelled, and beyond it to the S and E there is evidence of a barmkin or later enclosing wall. In the Hearth Tax returns for 1690-92, 'Breakinsyde' was credited with having two fireplaces.[14]

The Wallaces were still here during the first half of the 17th century. In 1615 John Wallace 'of Bracansyde' sat on an assize,[15] and in 1636 both John Wallace 'of Brekensyd' and his son Thomas were portioners of the property.[16] The previous year Stephen Laurie of Maxwelton acquired some lands at Breckonside, presumably from the Wallaces, and in 1636 John Wallace sold Stephen some more land at Breckonside.[17] Stephen died a year later, following which, in 1638, his son and heir John Laurie, 2nd of Maxwelton, was served heir to his late father's lands, including the '20s land of the 40s land of the £3 land of Brackansyde occupied by John Wallace, formerly of William Wallace his father' together with 'half of the 20s land, half of the £3 land of Brackansyde called 'the halff merkland of Muirhead, the halff merkland of Dykehead and ye halff merkland of Chappell mark', with all the buildings, etc., in the barony of Snaid.[18] By 1659 the Wallaces had been succeeded at Breckonside by Alexander Ferguson, who undertook to pay John Laurie of Maxwelton an annualrent of 36 merks out of the 30/- land of Breckonside.[19]

Six years later, in 1665, John Laurie of Maxwelton and his son Robert had a charter erecting the lands of Breckonside, Fleughlarg and others into the barony of Laurieston, to be held by John in liferent and Robert in fee.[20] In the Valuation Roll for 1671 the Threttie shillingland of Braikensyd' was valued at 90 merks.[21]

It has been said that the Thomas Crichton who bought Auchenskeoch (q.v.) c.1780 had forebears who were lairds (or ?tenants) of this Breckonside, and who forfeit the property for having joined in the rebellion of 1715;[22] but no evidence has been found of Crichtons living here.

The tower is said to have been still occupied early in the nineteenth century.[23]

---

1   Considerable confusion has been caused by the number of places called Breckonside in the region. There is one 8½ m N, NW of Drumlanrig; one 14m S, near Kirkgunzeon; one 19m ENE, SE of Moffat; and there was some land of that name 8m SE, near Holywood.
2   RMS I, No.31 and App.2, No.145.
3   RMS II, No.1411.
4   Ibid, No.1514.
5   RMS XI, No.22.
6   Sir John Hay was the second son of the 1st Lord Hay of Yester by his second marriage, to Elizabeth Cunynghame; but he was the only surviving son when his father died in 1508, and thus succeeded to the peerage.
7   RMS II, No.2872. The murder of Robert Fergusson 'of Braconsyde' and Alexander Fergusson, brother of the deceased John Fergusson of Craigdarroch, is on record in 1511, but there is no certainty as to which Breckonside is meant (RSS I, Nos.2259, 2333, 2338, 2703).
8   RMS II, No.2854; RSS I, No.1122. John Cunningham had sasine of the lands of Snade in 1503 (ERS XII, 714).
9   Hamilton-Grierson, Sir P.J., 'The Protocol Book (1541-1550) of Herbert Anderson, Notary in Dumfries', TDGAS, 3rd Ser., II, 213.
10   RSS IV, No.3225.
11   Pont MS. No.35 in National Library of Scotland.
12   Lennox, J 'The Castellated Remains of Dumfriesshire', TDGAS, 2nd Ser., XIX, 95.
13   RCAHMS 1994, 9, 13-17
14   Adamson, D 'The Hearth Tax', TDGAS, 3rd Ser., XLVII, 171.
15   RMS VII, No.1258.
16   PRS Dumfries I (1617-71), Index, 366-7.
17   Gladstone, 48.
18   Ibid, 60.
19   Ibid, 63.
20   Ibid, 73.
21   Corrie 1910, 33.
22   M'Kerlie, III, 345.
23   Lennox, J, op.cit., 95.

---

14.   BRECONSIDE TOWER
(2¼ m SE Moffat)   (NT108021)

The lands of Breconside originally formed part of the ancient 'tenement of Logane'. This was already in the possession of the Carruthers of Mouswald when the Earl of Douglas granted them a new charter of the lands in 1411,[1] and it continued in their possession until the death of Simon Carruthers, 10th of Mouswald, in 1548.[2] He was succeeded by his two young daughters, who were made wards of Douglas of Drumlanrig.[3] Two years later the lands of Breconside were being feued from Douglas by a branch of the Johnstons.[4] This is the earliest confirmed record of Breconside as a separate property.[5] James Johnston of Breconside subsequently obtained possession, and in 1576 his son James was served heir on precept from Sir James Douglas of Drumlanrig.[6]

There is no evidence of a tower or other building of substance as early as this, and it is evident that it was not until some time around 1591 that the present tower was built. It does not appear on Aglionby's Platte, which details other towers in the immediate vicinity c.1590, but by October 1592, when James VI spent a night at Lochwood, Sir John Carmichael was able to report that, of those accompanying the king, 'My Lord Maxwell [the warden] and Johnston [of that Ilk] was [staying] togidder in the Brekensyde'.[7] The laird at the time was James Johnston of Brakenside[8], who features prominently in local records during the last decade of the 16th century and early in the next.[9] The

position of the tower is deceptive, for, although it is situated low down and close to the burn in an apparently secluded valley, with steep hills rising high above, it did, in fact, have a good view down the Breconside burn to Poldean and Annandale to the south, whence any danger was most likely to come.

Fig. 160 Breconside Tower: view from the S in 1969.

The **TOWER** is oblong in plan, and measures 21ft 4in from N to S by 34ft 10in from E to W. In all probability it was always the same height as it is now, with three storeys and an attic; but over the centuries it has undergone several major changes, including at least one rebuilding of the roof, so that nothing is now known of the original arrangement at the wall-head. Built of local rubble, with sandstone dressings around

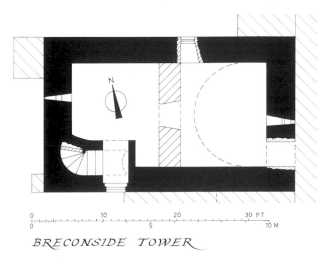

BRECONSIDE TOWER

Fig. 161 Breconside Tower (Moffat): plan of basement.

the doors and windows, the walls are 4ft thick at the gable ends and 3ft 6in thick on either side. The original entrance was on the S side, where it admitted to a vaulted vestibule, leading to the basement and a wheel-stair, 6ft 8in in diameter, in the SW corner. The jambs for this doorway are still in situ, and have the usual double rebate for a door and yett. Later, when the E wing was added, this entrance was converted into a window and replaced by a new doorway at the E end. The basement, which is vaulted, reaches a maximum height of 10ft above the present floor. It was originally lit by one, small slit-window high up at each end, the outer openings of which are now blocked. A larger window on the N side is a later addition, although it would appear to pre-date the 3ft thick wall that was built across the basement in the middle of the 18th century. It was at the latter date that the old wheel-stair was closed off, and a new, semi-octagonal, stair tower added on the S side of the tower to serve the upper floors. Because of the later works and decoration, it is not at present possible to ascertain whether the basement originally had any gun-loops or other windows.

Above basement level, the tower has been completely modernized. It was apparently when the new stair-tower was built that each of the upper floors was divided into two chambers, with separate fireplaces at each end. Some fine wooden panelling was also installed on the first floor at this time, but little of it remains, most of the panelling in the tower today being much more modern. During the 18th and 19th centuries, the original windows on the S side at both first and second floor levels were removed and replaced by much larger ones. Some old windows were also filled in, so that no window now faces N, E or W on the upper floors. This may well have been done at the time of the Window Tax, as, in 1758, Breconside was taxed on 14 windows, which was the maximum number permitted if one was not to be charged at the higher rate.[10] One small window may be seen filled up in the W wall at first floor level and another in the N wall at second floor level.[11] Both had moulded sandstone surrounds, and the former can be seen to have been chamfered. The roof was completely rebuilt in 1746, and it would appear that both the roof and chimneystacks were rebuilt again later. The only other features that can now be traced are two mural recesses at the E end of the first floor. One of these, in the E wall, is for a simple press, but the one in the N wall is considerably larger. Measuring 6ft 4in wide by 1ft deep, beneath a segmental arch rising to a height of 5ft 3in, it may have been used to house a sideboard, buffet or box-bed. The outside walls of the upper floors are all 4ft thick.

James Johnston of Breconside died shortly before 1621, when he was succeeded by his son James, who in that year, and again in 1622, was declared a fugitive and outlaw.[12] It was presumably a later James Johnston 'of Brekensyd' who is on record in 1683.[13] Six years later, the 'Laird of Brackenside' was appointed a Commissioner of Supply for Dumfriesshire,[14] but it is not clear whether this was James or his son John, who succeeded him. In the same year, he was commissioned as a Captain in the militia.[15] The 'laird's' appointment as a Commissioner of Supply was renewed the following year, but again the name is not given.[16] Breconside is not mentioned in the Hearth Tax returns for 1690.[17]

The Johnstons finally gave up the property in 1693, when John Johnston disponed Breconside to his nephew, Andrew Chalmers of Dam, in Dryfesdale.[18] On his death two years later, Breconside passed to his sister, Margaret, who married one William Carruthers.[19] It was presumably William who was the 'Laird of Breconside' named as a Commissioner of Supply for Dumfriesshire in 1698,[20] and it was certainly William who was named as a Commissioner of Supply for Nithsdale and Dumfries in 1704.[21]

It was Margaret's son, Captain John Carruthers, a shipmaster in London, who, in 1746, carried out extensive work on the tower and a small house nearby.[22] How the work progressed can be gleaned from a series of letters he sent to his neighbour, George Clerk of Dumcrieff, who was keeping an eye on his affairs locally. In one letter, in May, he refers to masons and joiners working on the tower, prior to a new roof being put on, and shows his frustration at the slow progress: 'I dont care how many men are sett to work to gett that house covered in before I come down'.[23] The new stair tower, the sub-division of the rooms, the original wooden panelling and the second floor windows all appear to date from this time.

In 1805 Breconside was bought by Dr. Rogerson, who had earlier bought Dumcrieff and Frenchland (q.v.), and on his death in 1823 it passed to his daughter, Elizabeth.[24] She later married Lord Rollo, and it was their son, the 10th Lord Rollo, who, although he never lived at Breconside, did much to improve the property further.[25] In 1877 he replaced the windows on the first floor of the tower with larger ones with mullions, and added the east wing and the new passage and entrance linking it to the stair tower.

Having gradually fallen into disrepair under successive, absent owners during the 20th century, the tower was finally abandoned in 1980.

1 Fraser 1885, III, 410, No.363.
2 Carruthers 1934, 68.
3 Ibid.
4 Ibid, 77. For details of the Johnstons' earlier connection with Logan-tenement, see 'Cornal Tower'.
5 There is an intriguing reference to one Thomas de Johnston of Breconside, said to have been a son of Adam Johnston of that Ilk, in 1448 (Reid MSS, 'Cadets of Johnston - Vol.1', 114). If correct, he was presumably a tenant of the Carruthers.
6 Reid MSS, 'Cadets of Johnston – Vol.1', 114. Sasine was not taken until 1607. Dr. Reid suggests that James Johnston may have been a descendant of the above Thomas de Johnston of Breconside.
7 Border Papers I, 414.
8 Variously spelt Brekensyde, Brekanesyid, Brakensyd, Braikansyd, Breckonside, etc.
9 e.g. Fraser 1894, I, xcix, 57, 79; Hope-Johnstone MSS, 33 (No.65); RPC XIV, 686.
10 Prevost, W A J 'The Lands and Tower of Breconside', TDGAS, 3rd Ser., LV, 127.
11 There may be other blocked windows, but details are obscured by a cement wash that has been applied to the walls sometime in the past.
12 RPC XII, 569; XIV, 677.
13 PRS Dumfries II (1672-1702), Index, 181.
14 APS IX, 70.
15 Ibid, 26.
16 Ibid, 139.
17 Adamson, D 'The Hearth Tax for Dumfriesshire', TDGAS, 3rd Ser., XLIX, 82-3.
18 Prevost, op. cit.,127.
19 Ibid.
20 APS X, 131.
21 Ibid, XI, 142.
22 Prevost, op. cit.,128.
23 Ibid,130.
24 Ibid, 131.
25 Ibid. This work was carried out to the designs of James Barbour, the Dumfries architect (Wolffe, A. 'James Barbour', TDGAS, 3rd Ser., LXXI, 156.

15. BRYDEKIRK TOWER

(2³/₄ m N Annan)   (NY187711)

The Carlyles are first recorded in the district early in the 14th century, when they held the adjoining lands of Luce, on the opposite bank of the river Annan.[1] A century later, Sir William Carlyle acquired the castle of Torthorwald, near Dumfries. His eldest son was in 1473/4 created Lord Carlyle of Torthorwald, while a younger son, Adam, is said to have been ancestor of the Carlyles of Brydekirk.[2] In 1529, the 4th Lord Carlyle was granted a new charter of all the family's lands. These included the lands of 'Bridkirk'.[3]

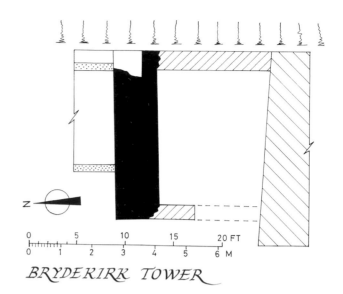

Fig. 162 Brydekirk Tower: view from NW.

The earliest of the family on record at Brydekirk was Alexander Carlyle, who was one of the local clan chieftains during the English occupation in 1547.[4] He was succeeded by Adam Carlyle, who, with his eldest son and heir, Alexander, is on record during the 1560s and 1570s.[5] After the death of the 4th Lord Carlyle in 1575, his second son and heir male, Michael, sold the superiority of the lands of Brydekirk to the 7th Lord Maxwell.[6] The Carlyles living at Brydekirk, however, continued in residence, and in 1590 Habye Carlile of Brydekirk was one of the landowners who was ordered to find surety under the Act of 1587.[7] Two years later, an English report on the Borders said of Brydekirk: 'a great surname of Belles and Carlilles, who hath bene longe in fede (feud) with the Irwins'.[8]

The earliest record of a **TOWER** at Brydekirk is in 1590, when it was shown on Aglionby's Platte.[9] On the other hand, Pont's map, some five years later, does not show a tower as such, only the church of 'Bryid kirk' and a small settlement a little further S, presumably where the present village stands.[10] It does, however, show a deer park at Brydekirk adjacent to the deer

Fig. 163 Brydekirk Tower: plan of surviving north end.

park of Turnshaw (Woodcockair) immediately to the north, and there can be no doubt that the tower shown by Aglionby existed by then. The present remains would appear to belong to that general period, the few surviving features suggesting a date somewhere in the second half of the 16th century. They comprise the N wall and a large part of the E wall of the original tower, which are now enclosed on the other two sides to form part of a range of outbuildings at the farm of Brydekirk Mains. A small, squat building, the tower stands on the left bank of the river Annan, where it is defended to the E by the steep river bank and to the S by a gully formed by a minor tributary. It measures 17ft 6in from E to W, and on the E side has a surviving length of 17ft. The walls are 4ft 6in thick. In the middle of the N gable, the tower rises some 25ft to the wall-head, where five, single-stage, moulded corbels survive. The two outer corbels are most unusual in being a course lower, as if to suggest a beacon platform. The masonry is local pink sandstone rubble, with dressed quoins. No evidence of any windows survives, but in the NW corner at first floor level there is a door jamb with a chamfered arris. This evidently admitted to a stair-well, now partly filled by the new W wall. The only other feature is the remains of a dressed recess, 2ft 9in deep, in the outer face of the E wall in the NE corner and above ground level. This may have been a garderobe chute discharging down the adjacent cliff.

Early in the 17th century, Alexander Carlyle of Brydekirk had an only daughter and heiress, Blanche, who c.1624 married Francis Irving, called 'of Kirkpatrick-Irongray', a lawyer in Dumfries.[11] He does not appear to have lived at Brydekirk, which must have passed to another branch of the family, as there were Carlyles in possession of Brydekirk for the rest of the century.[12] Adam Carlyle of Brydekirk took the Test in 1683,[13] and the following year he is on record as one of the heretors of the Stewartry of Annandale.[14] As 'Laird of Brydekirk', he was a Commissioner of Supply for Nithsdale and Dumfries in 1689, 1690 and 1696.[15]

Some fifty years later, William Currie of Cleughheads came into possession of Brydekirk, probably by marriage, and took the name Currie-Carlyle.[16] He was succeeded by his son James Currie-Carlyle of Brydekirk.[17] It is not known when the tower was abandonned.

1   RCAHMS 1920, xxvii.
2   Burke 1883, 'Carlyle – Lord Carlyle'; Complete Peerage, III, 41.
3   RMS, III, Nos.868, 871.
4   Irving 1907, 32.
5   eg. RMS, V, No.134; Irving 1907, 122.
6   RMS, V, No.136 (1580/1).
7   RCAHMS 1920, No.2.
8   Border Papers I, No.743.
9   Hyslop, 320.
10   Blaeu, 57, 'THE STEWARTRIE OF ANNANDAIL'.
11   Maxwell-Irving 1968 (III), 30.
12   Herbert Carlyle of Brydekirk and his son Lancelot, and Alexander Carlyle
     younger of Brydekirk, are all on record in the same deed in 1535 (PRS Dum-
     fries I (1617-71), Index, 29, 32).
13   RPC, 3rd Ser., VIII, 640.
14   Ibid, IX, 629.
15   APS IX, 70, 139; X, 29.
16   PRS Dumfries V (1761-80), Index, 35, 37.
17   Ibid; Irving 1907, 231.

---

16.   BUITTLE PLACE
(³/₄ m WNW Dalbeattie)   (NX819616)

Recent excavations in the outer bailey of Buittle Castle have shown that the site has been occupied at least since Mesolithic times, no doubt due to its importance as the lowest crossing point of the Water of Urr.[1] By the same token it was the highest navigable point of the river, and this must have given added importance to the site when the Romans arrived in the 1st century AD and used Buittle as their local base, to which they could bring in supplies by sea, perhaps from their major port at Caerlaverock, further along the coast.[2] It is not clear what occupation there was during the Dark Ages, but it has been suggested that the name 'Buittle' or 'Botel' originated in that period.[3]

Fig. 164 Buittle Place: view from SW.

Buittle subsequently appears to have been the principal seat of the Lords of Galloway at least since the 12th century, when they created a large motte-and-bailey castle out of the existing works on the W bank of the river. With its extensive earthen ramparts and ditches, it covered an area of some 5¹/₂ acres.[4] The palisades and other structures on the motte were later rebuilt in

stone. This work may have been started by Alan (d.1234), the last native Lord of Galloway,[5] or his successor, John de Balliol (d.1269), who married Alan's daughter, Dervorguilla; but the present remains are those of a typical 'Edwardian' castle dating from the end of the 13th century. The Balliols, who succeeded to the greater part of Alan's estate in Galloway, also used Buittle as their principal residence, and it was here, in 1282, that Dervorguilla sealed the Statutes for Balliol College, Oxford.[6] Four years later, after the death of Alexander III, Robert the Bruce attacked and took possession of Buittle as part of his campaign to establish his own claim to the throne.[7]

John Balliol, 2nd of Buittle – who succeeded to Buittle on his mother's death in 1290 – , subsequently became a contender for the Scottish Crown and, in 1292, King of Scotland. However, he soon rebelled against Edward I's claims of overlordship, and attempted to assert his authority, but in 1296 he was defeated at Dunbar. Soon afterwards he abdicated and retired to the continent. Edward I then put Buittle in the charge of Henry de Percy, who was succeeded the following year by John de Hodelston.[8] Then, in 1298, he granted the lands of Buittle to Sir John St. John, who was also given charge of the castle.[9] It was presumably under the supervision of one of these Norman knights that the new, Edwardian castle was built. It was quadrangular in shape, enclosing an area measuring approximately 150ft by 100ft, and had round towers at the corners and a strong gatehouse flanked by two drum towers, each 27ft in diameter with walls 6ft thick.[10]

In 1300 Sir John St. John was ordered to provision the castle, and to give no truce.[11] Two years later he was succeeded by his son, who was still in command c.1309 when Edward Bruce compelled an English force to take refuge in the castle, while he drove off the local cattle.[12] Robert Bruce attacked the castle in July 1312,[13] but it was apparently not until he laid siege to it again in February 1312/13 that it was taken.[14] Then in accordance with Bruce's avowed policy of leaving no foothold for his enemies, the castle was partially dismantled.

In 1324/25, Bruce granted 'all our lands of Botyll' to Sir James Douglas, 'The Good', but there is no mention of the castle, which at this time was uninhabitable.[15] The Balliols, however, still claimed possession, and after Sir James's death in 1330 it became the base of Edward Balliol's power. Balliol was crowned king two years later, and it must have been soon afterwards when Edward III formally restored to him Buittle and the other lands forfeited by his father.[16] Balliol repaired the castle, at least in part, including the construction of a new gatehouse and strengthened curtain walls,[17] and he resided there from time to time during his brief reign as King of Scotland.[18] He certainly dated two charters at his 'castle of Bottel' in 1352,[19] but finally lost possession two years later.[20] He renounced the Crown in 1356.

Meanwhile, in 1342, David II granted to Sir Hugh Douglas, Sir James's brother, a charter of the superiority of the lands of Buittle; and on Sir Hugh's death five years later, the title passed to his nephew William, later 1st Earl of Douglas.[21] William being then a minor, he was made a ward of Sir William Douglas, 'The Knight of Liddesdale', who evidently betrayed the trust placed in him, and appropriated the lands of Buittle for himself.[22] But after his death in 1353, instead of the lands passing to his daughter Mary as he had intended, David II granted them, together with many other lands, to Sir William Douglas, the future Earl of Douglas;[23] and the Douglases continued to hold them until their forfeiture in 1455.[24] Little is known about Buittle during this time, but in 1427 Henry VI of England complained

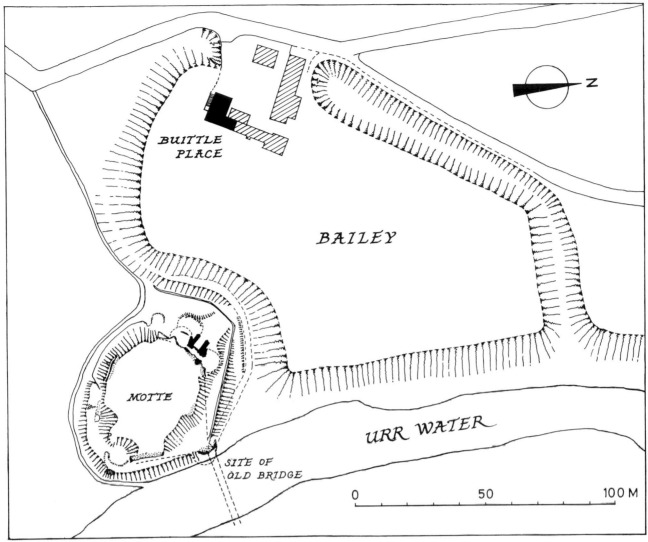

Fig. 165 Buittle: site of old castle and bailey and later tower-house.

to James I about the plight of some English fishermen imprisoned in the castle by William Carneys.[25] In 1452 the Earl of Douglas had sasine of these and other lands.[26] After the forfeiture of the Douglases, the lands passed to the Crown, who the following year granted the lands of Buittle and Sannak to Johnston of that Ilk for his part in the siege of Threave.[27] At the same time, there is also mention of a terce pertaining to the spouse of the lord of Caerlaverock from the lands of Buittle.[28] By this time the old castle was probably ruinous,[29] although it is still mentioned in charters of lands granted to Sir William Monypeny of Ardweny in 1458[30] and William Levenax of Caly, armour-bearer to James III, in 1485.[31]

During the 16th century, the feudal superiority of the lands of Buittle changed hands between the Douglases, Earls of Morton, and the Lords Maxwell with surprizing frequency as their fortunes changed. In 1516, the Earl of Morton was granted a 19-year tack of the lands and barony of Buittle,[32] and this was ratified by parliament eleven years later.[33] At the end of this period, Lord Maxwell received a crown charter of Buittle in feu-farm,[34] and this was confirmed in 1537.[35] Three years later, however, on the enforced resignation of the Earl of Morton, James V granted the lands of Buittle to Sir Robert Douglas of Lochleven;[36] but within three months Douglas was forced to give them back to the king, who now gave them to Lord Maxwell

again.[37] Then, in 1543, on the petition of the 3rd Earl of Morton, the Court of Session revoked the resignation of 1540, whereupon Queen Mary gave Morton a new charter of the lands, 'with the manor-places', etc.[38] This was confirmed in favour of the 4th Earl by charter in 1564 and parliament in 1567,[39] and again in favour of the 7th Earl in 1589.[40] This must relate to the superiority, for in 1550 the Crown granted to Robert Lord Maxwell the nonentries of many lands, including 'the landis and barony of Butill, that is to say, the toun of Butill and mylne thairof',[41] and in a charter of 1592/3 to Sir John Gordon of Lochinvar, it states that the lands and barony of Buittle belonged to Lord Maxwell.[42] In 1605 the 8th Lord Maxwell was infeft in the lands as heir to his father.[43]

By this time the new fortalice of Buittle had evidently been built, although it still does not appear on Pont's map as late as c.1595.[44] Nothing is known for certain about the builder. It may have been the work of either an Earl of Morton or one of the Lords Maxwell, but the original arrangement of a first floor entrance would tend to suggest an even earlier date for its foundation. It was under the Lords Maxwell that the Gordons subsequently came into possession.

In 1563, Sir John Gordon of Lochinvar married, as his second wife, Elizabeth Maxwell, daughter of John (1512-82), 4th Lord Herries, one of the most powerful men in the West

Fig. 166 Buittle Place: view from NW.

March.[45] By this marriage he had a third son, John, who became 'of Buittle', where he resided until his death, without issue, c.1611-14.[46] Buittle then passed to his brother, James Gordon of Barncrosh (d.1633), who is later referred to in charters as 'of Buittle'.[47] His eldest son, John, succeeded in 1639 as 3rd Viscount Kenmure, while his third son, James, appears to have inherited Buittle.[48] It was James 'of Buittle' who in 1649 was appointed a Commissioner of War for the Stewartry.[49]

Over the years of occupation, ruin, restoration and modernization, 'Old Buittle', or Buittle Place as it is now known, has undergone various structural changes that make it difficult to be certain of the exact building sequence. It evidently started life as a simple oblong house or tower, perhaps of three storeys and an attic – though its full height may not have been achieved until later –, and either at first, or later, this was provided with turrets corbelled-out at the N and S corners. To this was later added a wing, with a new entrance, and a corbelled-out stair-turret in the re-entrant angle. It was built on part of what had been the

outer bailey of the old castle, and no doubt there was originally a barmkin and various other buildings, but all that remains is the tower and some of the older earthworks.[50]

The original **TOWER** measures 36ft 7in from NW to SE and 22ft 7in from NE to SW, over walls 4ft 2in thick along the sides and 4ft 3in thick at the ends. It is probable that it is largely built of rubble quarried from the old castle. The basement, which is vaulted and has a maximum height of 8ft 4in, was provided with two slit windows on the SW side and one in each of the other three walls. That at the NW end was later converted into a doorway, while the original doorway to the basement on the NE side was blocked up. There is no evidence of any internal communication with the first floor, so it is presumed that in the original arrangement there was a separate entrance on the NE side at first floor level, which was reached by a ladder or, more likely, a forestair, similar to, but on the opposite side from, the present entrance. Above basement level the walls are 4ft 3in thick at the ends and 3ft thick at the sides. Illustrations of the ruined tower c.1790[51] show chimneys in each gable and two windows at each upper floor level on the SW side; in addition, it is likely that there was, as now, one window at each level on the opposite side.

The wing, which was added at the S end of the NE wall, may not have been added until late in the 16th or early in the 17th century. Slightly irregular in shape, it is 13ft 10in wide and has an average projection of 14ft 4in, over walls which vary in

Fig. 168 Buittle Place: view of tower from SW in 1790.

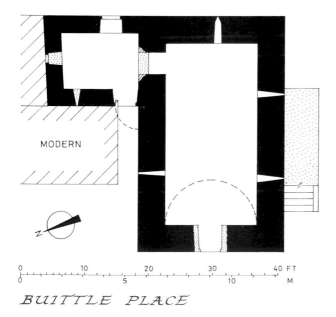

Fig. 167 Buittle Place: plan of basement level.

thickness from 2ft 6in to 2ft 8in. The purpose of this addition was undoubtedly to carry a stair up to the first floor – although this has now gone – and to provide further accommodation above, while a new stair-turret, carried on seven continuous corbel-courses in the re-entrant angle, rose to serve the upper floors. That this was not the original arrangement can be seen from: the SE wall of the building, where the walls of the main block and wing are integral at ground floor level,[52] but abut one another throughout the rest of their height; the re-entrant angle, where the wall of the wing at ground level abuts that of the main block; and in the much reduced thickness of the walls themselves. The jambs and lintel of the new entrance doorway carry a QER moulding. Within the wing there are three upper floors, the levels of which do not correspond with the floor levels in the main block.

BUITTLE PLACE

The upper floors have all been modernized, to the extent that no details survive of any original fireplaces, aumbries or garderobes that may have existed.

In 1609, the 8th Lord Maxwell was declared guilty of treason for the murder of the Laird of Johnston, and all his lands, including Buittle, were forfeited.[53] Five years later, his brother, the 9th Lord Maxwell, had his honours and estates restored.[54] In 1620 he was created Earl of Nithsdale, and the following year he received a new crown charter incorporating all his lands, including the lands, lordship and barony of Buittle, into the Earldom of Nithsdale.[55] But the Earl's subsequent adherence to Charles I cost him dearly, and in 1644 he eventually forfeited all his honours and estates.[56] This does not explain a charter of confirmation of the lands and baronies of Borgue and Buittle, with the castles, etc., granted to the Earl of Morton in 1638,[57] but Nithsdale's declining fortunes were apparently the reason for a crown charter of 1643 granting all the family estates to the Earl of Buccleuch.[58] On payment of a fine of 10,000 merks in 1647, the 2nd Earl of Nithsdale had his honours and estates restored.[59] Nevertheless, the Scotts of Buccleuch still laid claim to various Maxwell lands, including Buittle, and in 1664 the Duke of Monmouth and his spouse, the Countess of Buccleuch, received a crown charter of numerous lands, including the lordship and barony of Buittle.[60] But all the Scotts eventually retained were the Langholm properties.

It is not known when the Gordons' direct connection with Buittle came to an end, but it may have been a consequence of the marriage, in 1674, of William Maxwell of Kelton and Buittle, youngest son of the 3rd Earl of Nithsdale, to the daughter of Viscount Kenmure.[61] Although William evidently lived at Kelton, his kinsmen, the Maxwells of Breconside and Terraughty, appear to have acquired an interest in the property around this time, and it was at Buittle, in 1720, that the second son of John Maxwell, 3rd of Breconside, was born.[62] Four years later, on John's death, his widow, being in straightened circumstances, left Buittle and went to live at Kirkpatrick Durham.[63] This may be when the house was abandonned. The property subsequently passed to the Maxwells of Munches, who were still in possession in 1788 when the house is on record as being a roofless ruin.[64]

Fig. 169 Buittle Place: view of tower from SW in 1788.

Sometime during the following century, the Maxwells restored the old tower as a farm-house. It is as such that 'Old Buittle' is on record in 1877.[65] As part of this work, the basement of both the main block and wing were relegated to store rooms, and one of the first floor windows on the SW side was opened up to serve as the new entrance, reached by an unusually tall forestair. At the same time the turrets were removed, leaving only the first two courses of corbelling just visible below the wall-head. The house has since been further modernized.

———————————————

1   Penman, A. *Botel Bailey Excavation – Interim Report 1997*.
2   Maxwell-Irving, A. M. T. 'The Maxwells of Caerlaverock'.
3   Penman, *op. cit.*, 4.
4   Coles, F.R. 'Motes, Forts and Doons of Kirkcudbright', *PSAS*, XXVI, 132-5.
5   Alan's second wife, and the mother of Dervorguilla, was Margaret, daughter of David, Earl of Huntingdon, and great-granddaughter of David I.
6   Jones 1988, 281-3.
7   Oram, R. 'Bruce, Balliol and the Lordship of Galloway', *TDGAS*, 3rd Ser., LXVII, 30.
8   Reid, R.C. 'Buittle Castle', *TDGAS*, 3rd Ser., XI, 200.
9   Ibid, 200-1.
10 RCAHMS 1914, No.74. Similar castles in the area are to be found at Kirkcudbright and Tibbers.
11 Fraser 1885, II, 603.
12 Ibid.
13 Bain III, No.279. In 1311 Edward II had had letters under the Privy Seal delivered to Buittle and other castles in English hands in the SW, namely Lochmaben, Dalswinton and Dumfries (Bain III, No.218).
14 Oram, 'Bruce, Balliol and the Lordship of Galloway', *op. cit.*, 40. Fraser points out that the oft quoted statement that Bruce took Buittle in 1313 is based on a misreading of 'Bute' in Fordun's Chronica, which has subsequently been repeated. It is, nevertheless, a fact that many strongholds were destroyed by the Bruces as part of their deliberate, scorched-earth policy (Fraser 1885, II, 603; Nicholson 1978, 84).
15 RMS I, Appendix 1, No.37. According to one account, Douglas was first granted the lands in 1309 (M'Kerlie III, 237).
16 Bain III, No.1578. The precise date of the grant is not recorded.
17 Oram, R 'Bruce, Balliol and the Lordship of Galloway', *op. cit.*, 46. It has been suggested that the castle on the motte may have been too severely damaged in 1313 to be repaired, so that Balliol had to erect a new building, or restore an older one, in the outer bailey as his residence (Penman, *op. cit.*, 27).
18 RCAHMS 1914, No.74; Reid, *op. cit.*, 202; M'Kerlie III, 237. According to Cardonnel, in 1334 Balliol granted Edward III a great part of Galloway, reserving for himself only the castles of Buittle, Kenmure and Kirkgunzeon (See 'Corra Castle'). Oram states that Balliol provided the castle with a new gatehouse, as well as strengthening the curtain wall (Oram, 'Bruce, Balliol and the Lordship of Galloway', *op. cit.*, 46).
19 Reid, R.C. 'Buittle Castle', *TDGAS*, 3rd Ser., XI, 202.
20 Nicholson 1978, 161.
21 Oram, R. 'A Note on the Ownership of the Barony of Buittle', *TDGAS*, 3rd Ser., LXVII, 80.
22 Ibid.
23 RMS I, Appendix 1, No.123. Oram mistakenly believed they passed to Mary Douglas (Oram, 'A Note on the Ownership of the Barony of Buittle', *op. cit.*, 80).
24 Ibid, No.154
25 Bain V, No.1003. William Carneys, or Cairns, would have been one of the Orchardton family (q.v.).
26 ERS IX, 661.
27 ERS VI, 203.
28 Ibid, 209.
29 A sasine in 1406 refers only to the 'Chief place of the barony of Buittle' (Fraser 1885, 604). Little remains today, but vaults were still visible in 1845 (NSA IV, 203).
30 RMS II, No.626. Monypeny was granted the dominical lands of Buittle, with the enclosed space up to the castle.
31 Ibid, No.1627. In the same year, the town of Butil was let to Edward Maxwell and his son Herbert for 40 merks for 5 years.
32 RSS I, No.2835. Parliament confirmed his possession of the lands and barony in 1527 (APS II, 320).
33 APS II, 320.
34 RMS III, No.1475; Fraser 1873, I, 171.
35 RMS III, No.1692.
36 Ibid, No.2213; Scots Peerage VI, 360. It is not clear how they had passed from Maxwell to Morton during the years 1537-40.
37 Scots Peerage VI, 360; RMS III, No.2368.

38 RMS III, No.2901.
39 RMS IV, No.1535: APS II, 562-5. The Act of Parliament refers to 'the lands
    and barony of Buthill with the castles, manors', etc., while the charter only
    refers to 'the manor-places'.
40 RMS V, No.1674.
41 RSS IV, No.622.
42 Ibid, No.2278.
43 Fraser 1873, I, 300.
44 Blaeu, 66, 'Praefectura KIRCUBRIENSIS'.
45 See Maxwell-Irving 1988, 188-90, for a brief account of Lord Herries' life.
46 Scots Peerage V, 112.
47 Ibid; PRS, Dumfries, I, 108; M'Kerlie III, 238.
48 Scots Peerage V, 112.
49 APS VI, Part II, 493.
50 Coles, op. cit., 133. The SE wall of the wing, which is integral with the tower
    at ground level, may represent part of the original barmkin.
51 Cardonnel, 'Buitle: Plate II'; Grose II, 12.
52 The lowest courses of the wing's SE wall are unquestionably contemporary
    with the original tower, but whether they first formed part of the barmkin, or
    part of some other, single storey structure, cannot now be determined.
53 Complete Peerage VIII, 598.
54 Ibid, 599.
55 RMS VIII, No.228.
56 Complete Peerage IX, 560.
57 RMS IX, No.809.
58 Ibid, No.1341.
59 Scots Peerage VI, 487.
60 RMS XI, No.673.
61 Fraser 1873, I, 396. There are, however, references to the Gordons of Kenmure
    receiving sasine of Buittle in 1723 and 1777, which cannot readily be ex-
    plained (M'Kerlie III, 243-4).
62 Fraser 1873, I, 572.
63 Ibid.
64 Cardonnel, 'Buitle: Plate II'; Grose II, 12.
65 M'Kerlie III, 245.

17.   CASTLEMILK
(2½ m SSE Lockerbie)   (NY 149776)

The first known stronghold at Castlemilk was a motte-and-bailey castle built by the Bruces in the 12th century. It gave its name to the property, and as such was referred to by Pope Alexander III in 1170.[1] The site chosen was one of great natural strength, a high, triangular outcrop of rock on the left bank of the Water of Milk with steep scarps on two sides. Across the remaining side a deep ditch was dug. The Bruces continued to hold the lands throughout the War of Independence, but by that time the castle, which is not mentioned during the protracted hostilities, had probably fallen into disuse.

The lands of Castlemilk are said to have passed to Robert II when he ascended the throne in 1371,[2] and to have been granted by him, some time before 1388, to Sir John Stewart, eldest son of Sir Alexander Stewart of Darnley.[3] At first Sir John may have lived there, as he took the designation 'of Castlemilk'; but some time before 1402, having succeeded his father at Darnley, he feued two-thirds of the lands of Castlemilk (including the castle site) to Sir William Stewart of Jedworth and Castlemilk.[4] On Sir William's death in 1402, Castlemilk passed to his younger son, also Sir William, while the Stewarts of Darnley, later Earls of Lennox, retained the superiority.

It is not known which of the Stewarts of Castlemilk built the great tower. One of the earliest records of it is in 1481, when it was one of the four strongholds in the West March in which parliament decreed that 'men of war' were to be stationed.[5] 'In castelmylk [there were to be] xl men', and Castlemilk, Annan

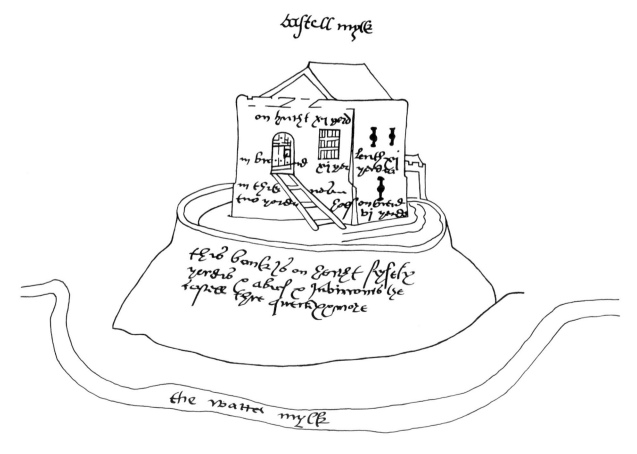

Fig. 170 Castlemilk (based on the Platte of Milkcastle, 1547).

and Bell's Tower (Kirkconnel) were to be manned by the Captain (Charteris of Amisfield) and his two deputies. The following year, when the Duke of Albany's forces raided Dumfries, Christopher Longcastle, one of the Englishmen involved, was taken prisoner by Alexander Stewart, younger of Castlemilk. He was subsequently taken to Castlemilk, and there he was held for the next five years.[6]

With the resumption of hostilities between the two kingdoms in the 1540s, Castlemilk once again became a strength of national importance. Shortly before the battle of Solway Moss in 1542, Wharton reported that 'the King of Scottes is repared . . . to the Castell of Mylke'.[7] Five years later, Lord Wharton was himself at the gates, accompanied by the Earl of Lennox, who only two years earlier had forfeit both the lands and superiority of Castlemilk for treason. They reported that, on being satisfied as to the Earl's identity, Castlemilk was delivered up to him by the captain, James Stewerd. Wharton and Lennox then camped there for the night, and put in one Fergus Graham with 20 foot (12 of them hagbutters) to keep it'.[8] They further reported that 'the wall is 9 feet thick, the roofs in decay. It stands in a country fit for fortifying, albeit we had no means therefor'.

By this time the Protector Somerset had need of a military map of SW Scotland, showing the lie of the land and the location of all important strongholds where English garrisons might be housed. The result was the 'Platte of Milkcastle', produced in November 1547.[9] It showed most of the West March from Lochwood in the N to the Solway in the S, and from Eskdale in the E to Dumfries in the W. At the centre was Castlemilk, surrounded by a barmkin with a gatehouse, and standing on a steep-sided hill, whose 'bank is on heitht fyfty yerdis & abuf & Invirronis the castell thre querlies & more'.[10] Castlemilk itself is described on the side with the entrance as, 'on heitht xj yerd, in breid xj yer, in thiknes two yerdes half', and on the adjacent side as, 'lenth xj yerdis, on breid vj yerd'. It is shown two storeys high, with a plinth course, an entrance at first-floor level reached by a wooden ladder, and a parapet-walk around the wall-head, with a pitched roof within. A relatively large window, with a grille, is shown to one side of the entrance, while on the other visible side are shown three windows of a comparatively rare, arrow-slit type found at Trematon (c.1250) in Cornwall and in some later mediaeval manuscripts.[11] But, although the English were in possession of Castlemilk at this time, one cannot place too much credence in the details given. For one thing, all but one of the castles and towers illustrated are shown, like Castlemilk, with only two storeys, yet both Caerlaverock and Comlongon, although shown with only two, did in fact have four main storeys. The width of the tower and thickness of the walls are other areas in contention. If the side had a 'length of 11 yards', what is meant by its 'breadth of 6 yards', when the walls are given as 7ft 6in thick? And what was the real thickness of the walls? The platte gives it as 7ft 6in, Wharton gives it as 9ft, and an English survey of the West March made c.1564-5 gives it as 'xi foote thyk'.[12] In 1550 the garrison is on record as comprising a captain, a trumpeter, a surgeon and twelve soldiers.[13] There was also a deer park, which is shown on Pont's map c.1595.[14]

In 1541 Archibald Stewart of Castlemilk had granted a lease of all the lands of Castlemilk to the 5th Lord Maxwell.[15] Then in 1545, on the forfeiture of the Earl of Lennox, the Regent Arran granted Castlemilk to John Johnston of that Ilk in compensation for all his misfortunes.[16] This was eventually confirmed by crown charter in 1550, after peace was concluded between the two kingdoms and the English garrison had left

Castlemilk;[17] but it soon led to a dispute over possession between the 6th Lord Maxwell and Johnston. The matter was referred to arbitration, when it was decided that Maxwell was to have possession of Castlemilk, with the tower and place thereof, and was to pay an annualrent of 44 merks to Johnston as superior.[18] In 1565 the forfeiture of Lennox was rescinded, and all his lands and honours restored.

Following Mary's defeat at Langside in 1568, the Regent Moray made several expeditions to the West March to restore good order. It was during one such visit in 1568 that he camped at Castlemilk for two days,[19] and the following year he held a court there.[20] Castlemilk next attracted attention in 1585, when Robert Maxwell of Castlemilk was included in the general amnesty for those charged with rebellion.[21] Three years later, the 7th Lord Maxwell returned from exile in Spain without permission while the Spanish Armada was in preparation. To forestall any rising by Lord Maxwell or his 'bastard' brother, Robert Maxwell of Castlemilk, on behalf of the Catholic cause, James VI led an expedition to the West March, burned the Maxwell castles of Langholm, Castlemilk and Morton, secured other Maxwell strongholds, and took Lord Maxwell prisoner.[22]

Castlemilk was subsequently repaired – 'Ye Cast. of milk' is shown on Aglionby's Platte in 1590,[23] and 'Castel milk' on Pont's map of Annandale c.1595[24] –, and Robert Maxwell continued to hold it until the forfeiture of his nephew, the 8th Lord Maxwell, in 1608.[25] It was then granted by the crown in feu-ferme to Sir Thomas Hamilton of Binney,[26] who shortly afterwards resigned it in favour of one John Johnston, advocate.[27] The next owner was Thomas Johnston, probably a son, who was at Castlemilk in 1617[28] and remained in possession until 1623, when it was purchased by John Murray, later 1st Earl of Annandale.[29] He assigned it to the Earl of Nithsdale, who in turn sold it to John Maxwell, eldest son of the deceased Robert Maxwell of Castlemilk, for 12,000 merks.[30]

By this time, however, Maxwell already had a tenancy interest in Castlemilk, for in 1622 it was as 'John Maxwell of Castlemilk' that he was nominated to assist the Earl of Nithsdale in administering justice in the late Borders.[31] He was an unusually wild character, even for those days, and he was forever in trouble.[32] Eventually, his extravagant lifestyle put him into debt, and in 1634 he was ordered to deliver up his house of Castlemilk,[33] though there is no evidence that he did so. During the Civil War, Castlemilk was besieged by Cromwell's forces, and is reputed to have held out for a considerable time, despite considerable loss of life.[34] Cannon balls found on the site in 1771 may belong to this period.[35] John died in, or soon after, 1667, and was succeeded by his grandson, John, the elder son of Robert, his eldest son, who had predeceased him.

In 1662, the year after James Johnston, 2nd Earl of Hartfell, was created Earl of Annandale, he received a new charter erecting all the lands of which he held the superiority, including the lands of Castlemilk 'with the tower thereof', into the new Earldom of Annandale.[36]

John Maxwell, being still a minor, his grandfather had appointed Alexander Jardine of Applegarth as his tutor. His uncle, Alexander Maxwell of Mellintaehead, however, had other ideas, and took possession of Castlemilk and the family charter chest, until the Privy Council intervened and ordered the Earl of Annandale to resolve the matter.[37] Nevertheless, the serious financial difficulties in which John found himself could not be resolved, and in 1688 his estates and rents were apprised at the instance of Lady Mary Maxwell, sister of the Earl of Nithsdale, and Robert Maxwell of Carnsalloch.[38] The Hearth Tax returns *c.*1690 record four fireplaces at Castlemilk.[39] Then, in 1697, Carnsalloch disponed the lands of Castlemilk to William Douglas of Dornoch, who was infeft in 1704.[40]

It appears that the old tower was finally demolished in 1707,[41] when a more modern house was built further down the outcrop, on the site of the original fosse.[42] This was later improved to become 'one of the most delightful and romantic situations which can well be conceived'.[43] Sometime in the middle of the 18th century, the property was acquired by John Lidderdale, eldest son of David Lidderdale of Torrs, in Galloway, and it was here that he died in 1777.[44] He was succeeded by his son William Robertson Lidderdale, who was commissioned as a Captain in the Scots Greys in 1775.[45] It was he who, in 1796, decided to clear the site and build a fine new mansion in the classical style, comprising an oblong central block with a bow at the back and two pavilion wings symmetrically disposed on either side.[46] It was finally demolished *c.*1870, after the present mansion was completed.[47] The four columns that flanked the entrance doorway were subsequently used in the garden to support a baldacchino over a fountain.

William Lidderdale eventually sold Castlemilk. It was in the possession of one Thomas Hart in 1845,[48] and from him it was subsequently purchased by George Armstrong, a merchant trading in Singapore.[49] Armstrong was in possession in 1851;[50] but three years later he sold the estate to Joseph Jardine, a younger son of Dr. William Jardine, who had founded the Hong Kong trading company of Jardine, Matheson & Co.,[51] and it has remained in the Jardine family ever since.

On Joseph's death without issue *c.*1862, Castlemilk passed to his youngest brother, Robert, who decided to build a completely new mansion on the site, on a much larger scale and in the latest fashion. Designed by David Bryce, the work lasted from 1864 to 1870 and cost £44,290.[52] In 1874 the estate comprised 7,714 acres.[53] Robert was Member of Parliament for the Dumfries Burghs from 1868-1874, and for the county from 1880-1892.[54] He was also a Deputy-Lieutenant for Dumfriesshire and a Justice of the Peace.[55] He was created a Baronet in 1885.[56] He died in 1905, and was succeeded by his only son, Sir Robert Buchanan Jardine, 2nd Baronet, who was named Buchanan after his mother, Margaret Buchanan-Hamilton, whose father, John Buchanan-Hamilton of Leny, was Chief of the Buchanan Clan.

Sir Robert served as a Major in the 1st Battalion, Dumfriesshire Volunteer Regiment, and as a Lieutenant-Colonel in the 3rd Volunteer Battalion, King's Own Scottish Borderers.[57] He also succeeded his father as Chairman of Jardine Matheson. He died in 1927, and was succeeded by his only surviving son, Sir John Buchanan-Jardine, 3rd Baronet, who served as a Captain in the Royal Horse Guards, and subsequently as Chairman of Jardine Matheson.[58] He was also a Justice of the Peace for Dumfriesshire and a member of the Royal Company of Archers.[59] He died in 1969, when he was succeeded by his elder son, Sir Rupert Buchanan-Jardine, 4th Baronet.

1   NSA IV, 203
2   Stat Acct, XI, 390.
3   Reid, R.C. 'Castlemilk', *TDGAS*, XIX, 173.
4   Ibid, 174.
5   APS II, 140.
6   Reid, R.C. 'The Merkland Cross', *TDGAS*, XXI, 216.
7   Hamilton Papers I, lxxx.
8   Scottish Papers I, 19.
9   Rutland MSS, I, 38. Reproduced in Merriman, M. 'The Platte of Castlemilk, 1547', *TDGAS*, XLIV, Plate XV.
10   The reference to 'three querlies' is obscure: one suggestion is a reference to the circumference of the outcrop; and another to 3 quarries nearby. - See Merriman, M. *op. cit.*
11   eg. René d'Anjou, 'Traité de la Forme et Devis d'un Tournois', *c.*1460 (Reprinted by Éditions de la Revue Verve, Paris, 1946).
12   Armstrong 1883, cxiii; RCAHMS 1920, lxi.
13   Merriman, M., *op. cit.*, 180.
14   Blaeu, 57, 'THE STEWARTRIE OF ANNANDAIL'.
15   Fraser 1894, I, lvii.
16   Ibid.; RSS III, No.1385.
17   RMS IV, No.448.
18   Fraser 1894, I, lviii.
19   Irving 1907, 122.
20   Reid, R.C. 'Castlemilk', *op. cit.*, 177; Fraser 1894, I, lxvii.
21   APS III, 388.
22   RCAHMS 1920, xliii.
23   Hyslop, 320.
24   Blaeu, 57, *op. cit.*
25   Complete Peerage VIII, 598. See also RMS VI, No.2005; Scots Peerage VI, 482.
26   RMS VII, No.221.
27   Ibid, No.296.
28   RPC XI, 226.
29   RMS VIII, No.826; Reid, R. C. 'Castlemilk', *TDGAS*, XIX, 176.
30   Reid, 'Castlemilk', *op. cit.*, 176; Reid, R. C. 'John Maxwell of Castlemilk', *TDGAS*, XIX, 192-3.
31   RPC XII, 695.
32   Reid, 'John Maxwell of Castlemilk', *op. cit.*, 187-204.
33   RPC, 2nd Ser., V, 347.
34   Stat Acct XI, 390.
35   Ibid. They are unlikely to date from the previous century as suggested.
36   RMS XI, No.230.
37   RPC, 3rd Ser., III, 318.
38   Ibid, 318.
39   Adamson, D. 'The Hearth Tax', *TDGAS*, 3rd Ser., XLIX, 72.
40   Reid, 'John Maxwell of Castlemilk', *op. cit.*, 204.
41   Masonry believed to belong to the tower was found during excavations undertaken *c.*1916. It lay between the top of the outcrop and the fosse (Reid, R.C. 'Castlemilk', *op. cit.*, 175).
42   Stat Acct XI, 390.
43   Ibid.
44   M'Kerlie IV, 182.
45   Ibid.
46   NSA IV, 211; Rowan, A. 'Castlemilk', *Country Life*, CLXII, No.4180 (August 1977), 350-1.
47   A photograph of it survives. It is reproduced in Rowan, *op. cit.*, 350.
48   NSA IV, 209.
49   Rowan, *op. cit.*, 351.
50   Post Office Directory (*c.*1851), 41.
51   Rowan, *op. cit.*, 351.
52   Ibid, 353.
53   Return of Landowners, 55.
54   Burke Peerage 1959, 1224, 'Buchanan-Jardine'.
55   Ibid.
56   Ibid.
57   Ibid.
58   Ibid.
59   Ibid.

18.   CLOSEBURN CASTLE
(2½ m SE Thornhill)   (NX907921)

When David I granted Annandale to the Bruces in 1124, the western boundary was defined as 'the march of Dunegal de Stranit', the powerful British chief and lord of Nithsdale, whose territory included the lands of Closeburn.[1] Dunegal was succeeded in much of his domain by his eldest son, Ranulf, ancestor of the Randolphs; but Dunscore and Closeburn appear to have passed to another son, Duvenald, who granted the church of Closeburn to the Abbey of Kelso.[2] Later in the century a man named Ivo, who is presumed to have come north in the train of the Bruces, first appears on record as the recipient of a charter of some fishing from Robert de Brus.[3] Not long after, Ivo received a grant of part of the lands of Kirkpatrick Juxta, near Moffat.[4] This became the family's principal seat, first at Garpol motte and later at Auchencass, and it was from here that they took their designation, later surname, 'de Kirkpatrick'.[5] 'Yvoni de Kirkepatric' received a charter of lands in the fee of Pennersax from William de Brus c.1194-1214.[6]

Fig. 171 Closeburn Castle: view from SSE.

It is not known how the lands of Closeburn passed from Duvenald, or Donald, to the Kirkpatricks, but in 1232 Alexander II granted to 'Ivone de Kyrkepatric' a charter of confirmation of 'all his lands of Kelosbern'.[7] He came to live here, and somewhere on the lands, quite possibly on the present site, he would have built himself some form of stronghold.[8] Ivone was succeeded by Sir Adam de Kirkpatrick, presumably his son, who had a dispute with the abbey of Kelso in 1264 over the advowson of Closeburn Church.[9] The next laird, Sir Stephen,[10] rendered homage to Edward I in 1296 and, as 'Sir Estevene de Killosberne', accompanied Sir John Botetorte, justiciar of Galloway, Annan and the Nith valley, on a foray against 'the enemy' in 1303/4;[11] but after the murder of the Red Comyn in 1305/6 he joined Bruce. Edward I promptly confiscated his lands, which were then given to John de Cromwell, and he did not recover them until after the battle of Bannockburn in 1314.[12] Sir Stephen died soon afterwards. He was succeeded by his son, Sir Thomas de Kirkpatrick, who, in 1319, was granted a twopenny land in the nearby toun of Briddeburgh, to be held by service of ward.[13] Brigburgh, which had been forfeited by the Comyns, was later made a barony and eventually combined with the barony of Closeburn. Little is known of Thomas's eldest son, Thomas, who succeeded him and who is believed to have died c.1394.

The next laird was the latter Thomas's eldest son, Sir Thomas Kirkpatrick of Closeburn, who fought at the battle of Homildon Hill in 1402, where he was taken prisoner. After his release he continued to pursue an active career, and in later life held various crown offices, including Joint-Custumar for the Borders, Sheriff of Dumfries, and one of the Conservators of the Truce with England in 1438.[14] He resigned his lands and barony of 'Kyllosbarne and Brygburghe' in 1409/10, and was granted a new charter of them by the Regent Albany.[15] He died c.1452. It is thought most likely that it was he who built the present castle, the tower of 'Killosbern', which is first mentioned as such in 1456.[16] The site was a promontory on the E side of Closeburn Loch. Originally some 70 acres in extent, the loch had been reduced to almost a tenth of that by the end of the 18th century, before finally being drained in 1859.[17] Additional defence was provided on the landward side by a wide moat cut across the neck of the promontory.

All that remains of the castle is the **TOWER** itself, a simple rectangular keep with solid walls and devoid of ornament. It is one of the smallest tower-houses of its period in the Borders; it is also the oldest that is still inhabited. Measuring 46ft from N to S by 33ft 9in from E to W, the walls rise sheer from the splayed foundation course to the top of the parapet wall, some 52ft above. There is no corbel-course.[18] The masonry is mainly light grey sandstone rubble, with some cream, pink and red sandstone and some dressings, including the entrance doorways, of a hard gritstone. At basement level the walls are 9ft 2in thick, but this is reduced to 7ft 6in at the level of the hall and to 6ft 6in at the upper floors. Inside, the tower comprises three vaulted chambers, one above the other, with the topmost one, which supports the roof, being subdivided into two floors and an attic.

The entrance to the basement is in the middle of the W wall. It has a round-arched doorway with chamfered margins, and is rebated on either side for an outer door of wood and an inner yett.[19] There is also provision for a drawbar. Both Cardonnel[20] and Grose[21] record a chevron-moulding on the surround, but a century later McGibbon & Ross record that no evidence of this could be found.[22] From here a mural passage leads directly into the basement, a low, featureless chamber with a segmental barrel vault, only 8ft high. There is no evidence now that the basement had any provision for ventilation, or communication with the floor above; but as late as the 18th century there was a 'small trap' linking the two floors.[23] According to one account, there was also a well.[24] The partitions, including the vaulted, prison-like chamber are modern.

The main entrance to the tower is at the N end of the W wall at first floor level, some 10ft 6in above the ground. Originally it was reached by a retractable wooden ladder; but this was later superseded by a stone forestair, which, together with the basement entrance below, has since been enclosed within a later addition. The doorway is similar to the one below, except that here the rebates for the wooden door and iron yett are both on the inside. Although the door is a replacement, the old yett, complete with twin bolts and hasps, has survived.[25] The drawbar recess behind is 5½in square and 6ft deep. From the entrance a short passage leads to the NW corner of the hall, while in the same corner another doorway admits to the wheel-stair, 5ft 6in in diameter, which rises within the thickness of the N wall to serve the upper floors and parapet-walk. The hall was originally a single chamber, with a barrel-vault 15ft high; but when Sir Thomas Kirkpatrick, 3rd Baronet of Closeburn, came to live here c.1748, he divided all the upper floors with a new, transverse wall, 3ft thick, incorporating fireplaces on either side and a central chimney stack. This arrangement was later copied at Hoddom (q.v.). It is not known where the original fireplace

Fig. 172 Closeburn Castle: view from NW.

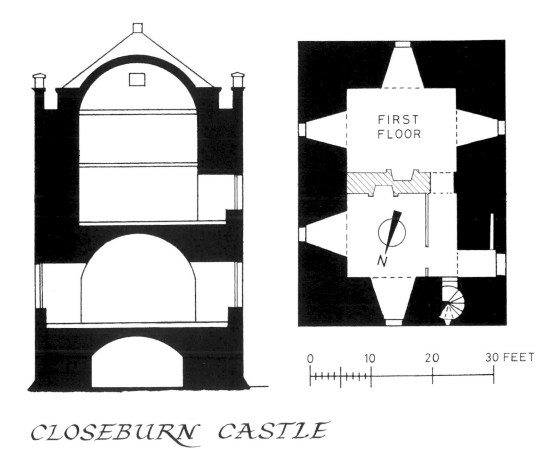

CLOSEBURN CASTLE

Fig. 173 Closeburn Castle: plan of first floor and sectional elevation (after MacGibbon & Ross).

was; it was either blocked up in the W wall or converted into a window recess at that time, and any surviving details are hidden behind the modern plasterwork. None of the windows, of which there are two in the E wall and one on each of the other sides, is original either. Those that existed have either been enlarged or, in the case of a small window with round arched head high up in the N wall, filled up; and some may have been added. More recently, lower ceilings have been inserted beneath the vault.

The second and third floors have been entirely modernized, and most of the windows enlarged. An exception is the slit window, with chamfered arrises, on the E side of the third floor. Both floors had a garderobe in the north wall, the recesses and small slit-windows for which may still be seen; and according to Cardonnel,[26] the upper one originally had a flue corbelled-out from the wall-face. To provide more room for the window recesses at this level, the parapet walk has been modified such that it rises towards the middle of each side, above the windows, and drains towards each corner. The attic is lit by windows in the end gables.

The wheel-stair terminates in a cap-house, which gives direct access to the parapet-walk on the N side. When Grose sketched the castle at the end of the 18th century, the cap-house had a pitched roof, while the parapet-walk, which continues around the other three sides of the tower, is shown with a round corbelled-out at the NE corner and a plain parapet.[27] Sometime during the 19th century this was all changed: the round was removed, probably with others at the other corners;[28] the upper portion of the parapet was rebuilt with fashionable crenellations; and the cap-house was rebuilt with a flat roof and matching crenels at the wall-head. The main roof was originally covered with stone flags, but when the tower was modernized and the central chimney added c.1748, these were removed and replaced with slates.[29] Then, early in the 20th century, the slates were discarded and a new roof of sandstone flags, some of which are more than 3ft square, put on. The flags are not supported directly on the vault below, but on heavy beams in between, to which they are fastened with wooden pegs.

Nothing is known for certain about the barmkin and outbuildings, which are said to have been cleared away when the new mansion was built in the 17th century.[30] On his manuscript survey of Nithsdale c.1595, Pont shows a substantial tower-house with a barmkin and arched gateway.[31] To some extent this is stylized, but he also shows what appears to be a wing or tall, secondary building. There is no evidence of any wing, but there is in existence an old sketch that shows a distant view of the castle, seen through an arched gateway, in which 'walls of enceinte with a round corner tower similar to those at Craigmillar' may be seen.[32] Some of the old foundations were exposed when a new water supply was laid in the mid 19th century.[33]

Sir Thomas Kirkpatrick's eldest son, Thomas, was granted a new crown charter of the lands and barony of Closeburn and of the barony of 'Birdburgh' in 1470.[34] Eleven years later, it was decreed that in time of war Thomas should be Captain in charge of Lochmaben Castle,[35] and in 1487 and 1488 he attended parliament.[36] Two generations later, the new laird, also Thomas, nearly lost the estate. Having become closely involved with the Earl of Lennox, who supported the English during 'The Rough Wooing', and having joined Lennox's expedition against Edinburgh in 1544, he forfeited all his moveable goods.[37] But although he was still in favour with Lennox in 1547, when the Earl asked the Protector Somerset to grant the Abbacy of Holywode to his 'cousin the laird of Cloisburn',[38] and in the

same year pledged 403 men to the service of England,[39] Thomas redeemed himself in 1548 by helping Drumlanrig rout the English at Durisdeer. A month later he received a remission from the Crown.[40] He died without issue.

The next laird, Roger, being still a minor when he succeeded in 1554, the Crown gifted the ward and nonentries of the lands and barony of Closeburn, 'with all castellis, touris, fortalices', etc., and of all the other lands that had belonged to the late laird, to Elizabeth Hamilton, daughter of Grizel Sempill, together with the marriage of Roger.[41] Nine years later, in 1563, Roger was one of the barons and gentlemen of the West March who took an oath to serve Queen Mary against any rebels, or in the event of an English invasion,[42] and in 1567 he was one of those asked by the Regent Moray for advice in keeping order.[43] He subscribed the Band drawn up by Mary's adherents at Hamilton in May 1568,[44] only five days before her final, decisive defeat at Langside. In 1570, Closeburn was one of the many castles reported to have been 'destroyit with gunpoulder' by the Earl of Sussex, when he invaded the West March,[45] though clearly, as elsewhere, the damage reported was greatly exaggerated.

Roger was succeeded by his son, Thomas, who was appointed a Gentleman of the Privy Chamber to James VI.[46] He was Sheriff-Depute of Dumfries in 1591,[47] and represented the county in parliament in 1593.[48] The following year, he was granted a charter of confirmation of his lands and barony of Closeburn and Brigburgh, and other lands, with the castles and manor-places, together with ratification of the original infeftment by Alexander II to Ivon Kirkpatrik, all to be held in alba-ferme for a quarter of a knight's fee.[49] Soon afterwards Thomas was knighted. Later in the 1590s the lands of Closeburn again became the scene of feud and raids. Following a dispute between the Kirkpatricks and Johnstons, a Bond of Assurance was agreed in 1596 between Sir Thomas and Johnston of that Ilk that neither they nor their kinsmen would harm or molest each other.[50] Two years later Sir Thomas lodged a complaint against some rebels of the name of Bell, who had invaded his lands,[51] and in 1599 some rebels from the West March of England were reported to have done likewise and killed six Scots.[52]

However, the more peaceful times brought about by the Union of the Crowns in 1603 did not bring an end to Sir Thomas's problems. Only four months after King James appointed him Provost of Dumfries in 1608,[53] he had to resign because of the demands made upon him at Court,[54] and no doubt it was the cost of this life that ultimately led him into financial difficulties. Two years later he was appointed a Commissioner for Justice in the Borders.[55] In 1615 Closeburn was apprised for debt;[56] and in 1622 it was apprised again, this time to be granted by the Crown to Brisius Sempill of Boghaugh.[57] Meanwhile, in 1619, and again in 1622, Sir Thomas was appointed a Commissioner for the Middle Shires.[58] Then in 1637, on the resignation of Brisius, now of Cathcart, the lands of Closeburn were erected into a new barony and granted to the late Sir Thomas's eldest son, Thomas, in liferent, and to Thomas's eldest son, John, in feu.[59]

The younger Thomas succeeded his father c.1630. He was appointed a Justice of the Peace for Dumfriesshire in 1634;[60] attended parliament in 1641;[61] and was a Commissioner of War for Dumfriesshire in 1643 and 1644.[62] He died shortly afterwards, when he was succeeded by his third, but eldest surviving son, Robert. Robert was a Commissioner of War for Dumfriesshire in 1645 and 1648,[63] and in 1663, shortly before his death, he was appointed a Justice of the Peace.[64] He was succeeded by his eldest son, Sir Thomas, who, in 1672, received from parliament a ratification of the lands and barony of Closeburn, with sasine to be taken at 'the tower, fortalice and manor-place of Closeburn'.[65]

Sir Thomas Kirkpatrick, who was created 1st Baronet of Closeburn in 1685, had a distinguished career in public life. He was appointed a Commissioner of Supply for Dumfriesshire in 1675,[66] and again in 1678.[67] Three years later, he was granted a warrant for holding two yearly fairs and a weekly market at the town of Closeburn.[68] He took the Test in 1683,[69] and the following year he was appointed a Commissioner for the Borders,[70] and also a Commissioner to act against the Covenanters.[71] He was subsequently commended for the diligence with which he pursued rebels in the South-West.[72] He was a Commissioner of Supply again in 1685,[73] as were both he and his eldest son, Thomas, in 1689, 1690, 1696, 1698 and 1704.[74] In 1689 Sir Thomas was a Captain in the Militia,[75] and two years later he was both a Commissioner for, and a Lieutenant-Colonel in, the force.[76] He was appointed as an additional Commissioner to parliament for Dumfriesshire in 1690,[77] and was elected to represent the county again in 1693, 1698 and 1700.[78] He voted against the new colony of Caledonia in 1701.[79] In 1693 he had been appointed to administer the Oath of Allegiance.[80]

It was apparently Sir Thomas who, in 1685, built a new house close to the tower, using the old buildings on the site for some of the materials.[81] Some idea of its size can be gained from the fact that Closeburn was taxed with 12 fireplaces in 1690.[82] The house did not survive long. It was accidentally burned down in 1748, after which Sir Thomas Kirkpatrick, 3rd Baronet, is said to have restored and modernized the old tower as his residence.[83] His son, Sir James, finally sold Closeburn in 1783.[84]

The new owner was the Reverend James Stuart-Menteth, from Barrowby in Lincolnshire.[85] He built himself a new mansion-house, Closeburn Hall, some 700 yards to the N, while the castle – which was shown by Cardonnel in the early stages of ruin in 1788[86] – was restored as the factor's house, a place much frequented by Robert Burns around this time.[87] In 1838 James's son, Charles, was created a Baronet, but he so burdened the estate with his various enterprises that in 1852 his son, Sir James, was forced to sell it.[88] The new owner was Douglas Baird, a wealthy industrialist, who was eventually succeeded by his two daughters.[89] It was Douglas who finally drained the loch.[90]

The castle remained the factor's house until well into the 20th century,[91] while the Hall was abandonned in 1903,[92] and now only a vestige remains. Later the castle was the home

Fig. 174 Closeburn Castle: view from NW in 1788.

of Sir Stephen Pigott (d.1955), who was Managing Director of the famous John Brown's shipyard from 1938-49.

1   Black 1946, 109; McDowall 1986, 17.
2   Scots Peerage VI, 287.
3   Buccleuch MSS, 38.
4   It is not known whether the grant was made by King William the Lion or the Bruces. – The 1d land of Kirkpatrick entailed in favour of Richard, son of Richard Edgar (a descendant of Duvenald), in the time of King Robert the Bruce, is thought to have been another Kirkpatrick, in Glencairn in Nithsdale (RMS I, No.94; App.2, Nos.208, 297, 530).
5   The terraced motte at Garpol, like the one at Lochwood, appears to date from late in the 12th century. It appears to have been succeeded by nearby Auchencass, a castle of enclosure, sometime during the latter half of the next century.
6   Buccleuch MSS, 39 (No.68); Fraser 1894, I, 2. – Roger de Kirkpatrick, Robert de Kirkpatrick and Humphrey de Kirkpatrick, Steward of Annandale, are mentioned in Bruce charters c.1200-20.
7   Ramage, 191-2, where the charter is given in full. It is reproduced in Reid, R.C. 'The Early Kirkpatricks', TDGAS, 3rd Ser., XXX, Plate 1.
8   Another possible site is the Motte of Dinning, 1½ miles SW.
9   Ramage 1876, 389.
10   'Stephanus, Dominus Villae de Closeburn, filius et haeres Domini Ade de Kirkpatrick militis' (McDowall 1986, 30).
11   Bain II, No.1437.
12   Reid, R.C. 'The Early Kirkpatricks', TDGAS, 3rd Ser., XXX, 78.
13   Ibid.; RMS I, App 2, Nos.295, 509; Ramage, 198-9. The service was the provision of 2 archers and 2 pleas in Bruce's court.
14   Reid, op. cit., 82.
15   RMS I, No.919; Robertson's Index, 164.
16   Reid, op. cit., 82.
17   Ramage, 242-3. A boat, 12ft in length, was found in the loch after it was drained.
18   Although the top of the parapet wall has been rebuilt, the lower part of the wall is original. The shallow corbel-course on the W side is apparently part of the rebuilding.
19   The yett was still in situ in 1788 (Cardonnel, 'Killosborn').
20   Cardonnel, ' Killosborn'.
21   Grose I, 153. Because the ornament is Norman in style, Grose incorrectly attributed the tower to the 12th century.
22   MacGibbon & Ross III, 130.
23   Cardonnel, 'Killosborn'. Watson also mentions a hatch (Watson 1901, 57).
24   Ramage, 182.
25   See Christison, D. 'Additional Notices of Yetts, or Grated Iron Doors, of Scottish Castles and Towers', PSAS, X (1888), 287, 295, 297. The style of the yett also helps to date the tower.
26   Cardonnel, 'Killosborn'.
27   Grose I, 152.
28   It is not clear from Grose's sketch whether there was a round at each corner.
29   Grose I, 153.
30   Ramage, 184.
31   Pont MS. No.35 in National Library of Scotland.
32   MacGibbon & Ross III, 131. The drawing was in the possession of the Royal Scottish Academy in 1889, but its present whereabouts is not known.
33   Ramage, 184.
34   RMS II, No.1007.
35   APS II, 140.
36   Ibid, 175, 180.
37   Reid, op. cit., 98.
38   State Papers, Scottish, I, No.64.
39   Armstrong 1883, lxxiv. Another account gives the number of men pledged as 378 (Scottish Papers I, No.396).
40   Reid, op. cit., 99.
41   RSS IV, No.1713. Burke's Peerage (1959), 'Kirkpatrick of Closeburn, Bt.' is incorrect in giving Roger as the son of Thomas's brother Henry; as this document clearly states, Roger was 'sone and air to the said umquhile Thomas'. See also Reid, op. cit., 100.
42   RPC I, 378.
43   Ibid., 570.
44   Scottish Papers II, No.650.
45   Irving 1907, 43.
46   Parl. of Scot., I, 401.
47   RPC IV, 614.
48   APS IV, 6.
49   RMS VI, No.155; Reid, op. cit., 104. The charter of 1232 had apparently been lost or mislaid for many years.
50   Hope-Johnstone MSS, 36 (No.75).
51   RPC V, 496.
52   Scottish Papers XIII, No.410.

53 RPC VIII, 36.
54 Ibid, 85.
55 Ibid, 814.
56 RMS VII, No.1258.
57 RMS VIII, No.277.
58 RPC XII, 45, 650.
59 RMS IX, No.761.
60 RPC, 2nd Ser., V, 380.
61 APS V, 308.
62 Ibid, VI, Part I, 53, 199.
63 Ibid, 559; Part II, 32.
64 Ibid, VII, 504.
65 Ibid, VIII, 154.
66 RPC, 3rd Ser., IV, 474.
67 APS VIII, 225.
68 Ibid, 441.
69 RPC, 3rd Ser., VIII, 639.
70 Ibid, 682.
71 Fraser 1894, I, cclvii.
72 RPC, 3rd Ser., IX, 288.
73 APS VIII, 465.
74 Ibid, IX, 70, 139; X, 29, 131; XI, 142.
75 APS IX, 26.
76 RPC, 3rd Ser., XVI, 289, 291.
77 Parl. of Scot., I, 401.
78 APS IX, 238; X, 113, 183, 196.
79 Ibid, X, 246.
80 Parl. of Scot., I, 401.
81 Ramage, 210.
82 Adamson, D 'The Hearth Tax for Dumfriesshire', TDGAS, XLVIII, 134.
83 MacGibbon & Ross III, 131; Watson 1901, 57.
84 Ramage, 210.
85 Burke Peerage 1959, 1529, 'Stuart-Menteth, Bt.'
86 Cardonnel, 'Killosborn'.
87 Grose I, 154; MacGibbon & Ross III, 131.
88 Ramage, 213.
89 Ramage, 216; Ordnance Gazetteer, 267.
90 Watson 1901, 56.
91 Lennox, J. 'The Castellated Remains of Dumfriesshire', TDGAS, 2nd Ser., XIX, 95.
92 3rd Stat Acct, Dumfries, 219.

19. COMLONGON CASTLE
(4m WNW Cummertrees)   (NY079689)

The earliest stronghold at Comlongon was the castle of Cockpool, or 'Cokpule', an Anglo-Norman motte dating from c.1200 and situated one mile SW of the great 15th-century tower-castle that eventually succeeded it. It is not known who the builder was, but, prior to its acquisition by the Murrays early in the 14th century, it had been in the possession of one Thomas de Duncurry, whose family were witnesses to several Annandale charters of the Bruces during the previous century.[1] The site lies at the confluence of two burns, tributaries of the Lochar Water, close to where the latter's estuary joins the Solway Firth. It was easily accessible from Cumbria by boat, a factor that seems to have been significant in the siting of a number of these early settlements.[2] The motte, which was some 90ft in diameter, stood within a great ditch 40ft wide, while on the landward side it was further defended by extensive marshland: there was no bailey.[3] The buildings and enclosures would have been of timber. At some later date the motte was cut down to fill up the ditch, so that little is now visible.[4] A farm now occupies the site.

The lands of Comlongon may have come into the possession of the Murrays by marriage.[5] Certainly it was on the resignation of Thomas de Duncurry that, sometime during the years 1317-32, King Robert the Bruce's nephew Thomas Randolph, Earl of Moray, as superior, granted to William de Moravia (Murray), his sister's younger son, all the lands and

tenements of Cumlungan and Ryvel (Ruthwell), together with half the patronage of the church.[6] The castle of Cockpool became William's seat, and it was from it that he and his successors for the next three centuries took their designation 'of Cockpool'.

The relationships of the Murrays of Cockpool during the 14th century are not clear. The third laird appears to have been Sir Adam Murray, who is said to have been prominent during the reigns of Robert II and Robert III.[7] He was succeeded by Patrick Murray, perhaps his son, who may have been the Patrick Murray who was recorded killed at Otterburn in 1388.[8] The next laird was Sir Thomas Murray, Patrick's eldest son. He received a new charter of the lands and 'tenements of Ryvale' from Archibald, Earl of Douglas, in 1411.[9]

Sir Thomas was succeeded by his eldest surviving son, Sir Charles Murray of Cockpool, who had sasine of the lands of Ruthwell in 1438.[10] He went to Rome with the Earl of Douglas in 1450, and two years later was granted a new charter under the Great Seal of 'the tenement of Rewel' and other lands.[11] In 1457 he was appointed a commissioner for the peace with England, and in 1459 he was made Warden of the West March.[12] He died c.1474. It was previously thought that it was he who built the new castle of Comlongon, sometime early in the third quarter of the century, but it is now known to have been the work of his grandson some 50 years later.[13]

Sir Charles was succeeded by his eldest son, Cuthbert, who had sasine of the lands of Ruthwell and others in 1474.[14] Three years later he granted part of the lands of 'Colnlungane (Comlongon) Wode' to Archibald Carruthers of Mouswald.[15] The charter also mentions certain Carruthers lands of Comlongon that had belonged to the late Norman Johnson in Ruthwell; it bears the seal of 'S. CUTHBERTI MURRAY DNI DE COKPOULL'. Cuthbert attended parliament in 1481 and 1487/8 as 'Lord of Cockpool', which was still the family's principal residence,[16] and in 1484 he was one of the commanders of the

Fig. 175 Comlongon Castle: view from S.

army that defeated the rebel Albany and the Earl of Douglas at the battle of the Kirtle after their abortive rising at Lochmaben.[17] Cuthbert died c.1493, and was succeeded by his eldest son, John.

Sir John Murray of Cockpool had sasine of the lands of Ruthwell, Cockpool, Renpatrick and others in 1494.[18] It was he who built the great new tower-castle of Comlongon, following 'a Letter of Licence' granted him by James IV in, or around, May 1501.[19] Under this Licence, 'JOHNNE of MURRAY of Cokpule and his aeris [were authorized] to big a towre and fortalice apone his landis liand in Ananderdale, and to mak apone the sammyn machcoling, corbalsalze, irnezettis and windois, etc., and to ras and big the said towre to quhat hicht he ples, but ony impediment, etc.'[20] It is not known how long the work took, but the castle is first mentioned on 15 February 1507/8, when Sir John, who in the meantime had been knighted, was granted a new crown charter of 'the lands of Cokpule, Ruvale-tenement,

Fig. 176 Comlongon Castle: view from NW.

the tower and fortalice of Cunlungane, Coklakis, Pihyllis, Sclathwait, Ranepatrik, Bridechapell, Preist-dikis [and] Howalside', all of which were 'for special favour' incorporated into 'the one free barony of Cokpule',[21] and it may well be that the request for, and granting of, this new charter coincided with the completion of his new castle. At the same time the 'Town of Ruvale' and the lands of the same in Ruvale-tenement were created a free burgh of barony, now to be called the Burgh of Ruvale (Ruthwell).[22] The charter was confirmed by parliament the following year.[23]

COMLONGON CASTLE is one of the most sophisticated tower-houses of its age, comparable only with Borthwick and Elphinstone, with both of which it has a close affinity of sophistication, despite the much earlier date of Borthwick.[24] Douglas Simpson described it as 'perhaps the ablest thing of its kind in Scotland, and in it the plain rectangular tower-house . . . may be thought to have reached its climax',[25] while Cruden de-

scribed the three as 'pre-eminent among all towers . . . never to be surpassed in scale or strength'.[26] What is perhaps surprizing, though, is that the Murrays of Cockpool, who are not known to have been especially rich or prominent at the time, and who generally kept a low profile, should have commissioned such an outstanding work.

Standing upon a barely perceptible outcrop of rock, and originally surrounded by extensive marshland, this outwardly plain but massive tower dominated the surrounding landscape. Its external appearance gave no hint of the complexity of its interior. Indeed, the walls were so weakened by the veritable warren of mural chambers, especially on the N side, that, but for the protection afforded by the marshes, the tower would have been very vulnerable to bombardment; and in the 1930s it had to be shored up inside just to prevent it from collapsing.[27]

The tower, which is oblong in plan, measures 48ft 7in from E to W by 42ft 7in from N to S, and rises some 59ft to the top of the battlements and a further 10ft to the top of the watch-turrets on the E gable. It is complete apart from the wooden floors, of which only a few isolated joists remain. The main accommodation was provided by a vaulted basement with entresol floor and three upper floors, but this is generously supplemented by the great number of mural chambers, especially on the N side. At the level of the basement the N wall is 13ft 2in thick, the E and W walls 10ft 3in and the S wall 10ft. These are reduced at hall level to 12ft 7in, 9ft 6in, 9ft 2in and 9ft respectively, while higher up the S wall is reduced to about 8ft 3in by a scarcement at second floor level and the N wall to 10ft by a similar inset at third floor level. Like nearby Torthorwald, the tower has a splayed plinth course. The masonry is local sandstone rubble in varying shades of pink, cream and grey, with dressings and mouldings of the rather softer red sandstone. Apart from the ornamental decoration in the great hall, the only mouldings used are a heavy chamfer on the arrises of the doorways and windows.[28]

The entrance doorway, which is about 3ft above ground level, is near the E end of the N wall. It is 7ft 3in high, with a semi-circular head, and is rebated for a wooden door opening outwards and an iron yett opening inwards, a less common arrangement that is also found at Borthwick and Elphinstone.[29] The outer door has long since gone, but the yett, though badly corroded, is still *in situ*; it is hung on two massive hinges, has a single, central bolt, and incorporates on either side a large, elongated, wrought iron ring through which the drawbar passed for added strength.[30] When not in use, the drawbar was housed in a slot 7ft deep in the E jamb. Inside the entrance a vaulted lobby gives access to the basement and, in the NE corner, a wheel-stair, 7ft 6in in diameter, which serves all the floors and terminates in a cap-house at the level of the parapet-walk. Immediately behind the door there is a mural recess, 2ft 9in wide, 4ft deep, 3ft 8in high, and 2ft 1in above the floor, for the use of the porter.

The basement is a simple chamber with an ashlar-lined well in the middle of the floor and a barrel-vault of carefully coursed ashlar, 17ft 6in high. It was formerly divided by an entresol floor supported on scarcements at the springing level, the upper level being reached from a vestibule and doorway, now blocked, off the main stair. It appears to have been designed solely for storage. At each level the only illumination provided is a small slit-window with widely splayed jambs and stepped sills at each end. In addition to the main stair, there is a service stair, 6ft 3in in diameter, in the SW corner, which connects the basement directly to the dais end of the great hall; and there is evidence to suggest that there may originally have been

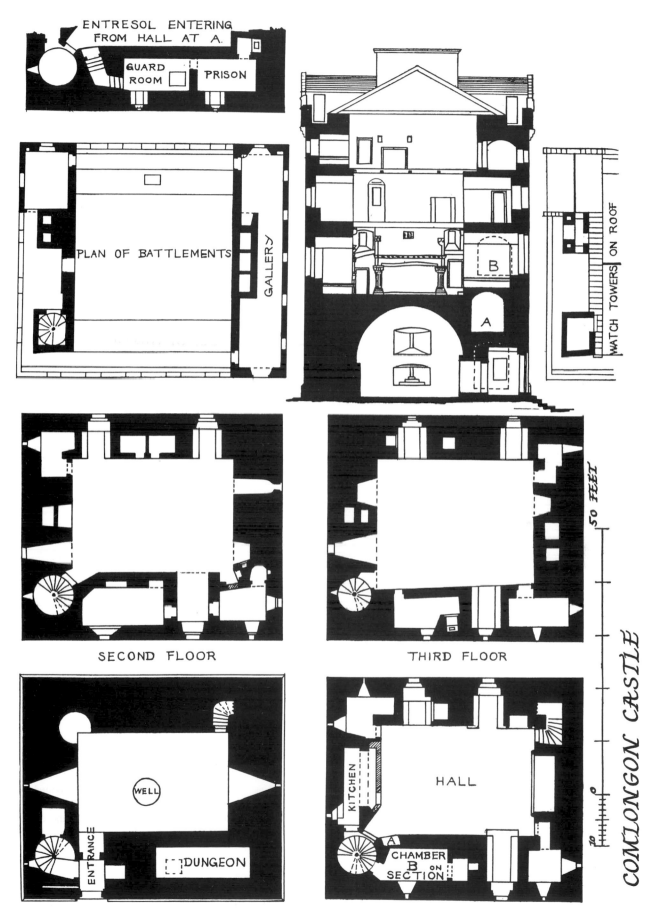

ENTRESOL ENTERING FROM HALL AT A.

GUARD ROOM   PRISON

PLAN OF BATTLEMENTS

GALLERY

WATCH TOWERS ON ROOF

B

A

SECOND FLOOR

THIRD FLOOR

50 FEET

WELL

DUNGEON

KITCHEN

HALL

A

CHAMBER B ON SECTION

COMLONGON CASTLE

Fig. 177 Comlongon Castle: plans and sectional elevation looking west (after MacGibbon & Ross).

Fig. 178 Comlongon: entrance doorway with yett.

Fig. 179 Comlongon: left jamb of great hall fireplace, showing vine scroll moulding on cornice and original damaged jamb. Inside the latter is a 16th century addition supporting a replacement lintel of wood.

a third, service stair between the SE corner of the basement and the hall adjacent to the kitchen.[31]

From the NE corner of the hall, a mural passage and stairs lead down 7ft to a vaulted chamber on the N side of the basement vault. This room, which was lit by a small window with stone seats, was the guardroom for the prison beyond and the pit-prison within the thickness of the N wall immediately below. The upper prison is relatively well-appointed, being provided with a small window with stone seats and a garderobe; it measures 11ft 4in by 6ft 6in and is 7ft 6in high. The pit-prison, on the other hand, although larger – it measures 17ft 6in by 6ft and is some 9ft high –, had neither light nor sanitation, and the only ventilation was provided by a small, dog-legged vent high in the N wall.[32]

The first floor was the Great Hall, a fine chamber despite lacking some of the impressive grandeur created by the high vaulted ceilings found at some of the other tower-castles of the period. Like Threave and Newark, Comlongon has no main vaults above the basement, though here the reason may have been to avoid adding further thrust to the walls, honeycombed as they are with mural chambers. The central feature in the hall is the large fireplace, 10ft 10in wide and 4ft 10in deep, in the middle of the W wall. On each side it has finely moulded pillars and bases with carved capitals, which must originally have supported a huge stone lintel; but at some period the lintel broke and was replaced by a crooked oak beam, the left end of which is now supported by an additional jamb with a 16th-century-style QER moulding.[33] Above this there is a fine stone frieze carved with vine scrolls and human masks.[34] This was reassembled after the lintel broke, and is misaligned. Higher still, there is an armorial panel with an erroneous version of the Scottish royal arms, and on each side of it corbels, possibly lamp brackets, carved with angels bearing shields carved with the Murray arms.[35]

Several of the corbels supporting the floor above are also carved with shields bearing the arms of other families, including those of Johnston and Maxwell.[36] A door on the left of the fireplace gave access to the stair leading directly to the basement, while another on the right admits, via an angled passage, to a square vaulted chamber in the NW corner of the tower. The main illumination for the hall is provided by two large windows in the S wall and one in the N wall, each with stone seats. In addition, the more easterly of the S windows has a large, closed aumbry within its right ingo. Like the other principal windows in the tower, these have iron grilles and were originally glazed in the upper half and provided with shutters below.[37] There is also one

Fig. 180 Comlongon: royal coat of arms over great hall fireplace.

window high above each doorway in the W wall to throw more light into the centre of the hall. At the W end of the S wall there is a magnificent buffet, 3ft 7in wide, 2ft 9in deep and 6ft 2in high, with a projecting sill. It has finely moulded jambs, matching those of the fireplace, capped with tall, crocketted finials on either side of a Gothic cinquefoil arch with decorated cusping and carved foliage. A striking peculiarity of the arch is its unashamed asymmetry, with halves that do not match and cusping whose depth is not even consistent; nor is it properly assembled, leading to a suspicion that the entire surround may, in part or in whole, have been re-used. Originally the buffet had a dividing shelf. In the SE corner of the hall there is a dog-legged mural chamber, where the third stair from the basement was originally designed to emerge. The hall is paved with sandstone slabs, but these are not original and the level has been raised.

As at Elphinstone and several other towers dating from the same general period,[38] the opposite end of the hall from the main fireplace is taken up by the kitchen. This has an arched opening, 11ft 5in wide by 7ft 9in high, built of fine ashlar voussoirs, 1ft 3in deep, with a bold chamfer on the hall side. Beyond is the huge kitchen fireplace, 14ft wide and 3ft 5in deep, which could also be reached through a door leading directly off the main stair. Originally the kitchen would have been separated from the hall by a timber screen, but at some later date this was replaced by a wall with a hatch, built just 1ft 7in out from the arch. This must have been carried out after the kitchen ceased to be used as such, and its chimney was blocked off below the new fireplace inserted on the second floor. A small window to one side of the old fireplace was opened up in the 19th century to form a doorway connecting with the adjacent mansion; it was later closed up again.

A short distance up the stair from the hall, there is another vaulted chamber within the N wall. It is lit by a slit window, and originally had a garderobe with a lamp shelf at its W end. At some later date the garderobe was altered and the flue closed off.[39]

The second floor was originally a single room with a large fireplace in the middle of the S wall. When the room was later divided in two, the old fireplace was converted into two cupboards or close garderobes, one for each room, and new fireplaces were inserted in the end walls, the one at the E end, which intruded into the former kitchen chimney, having a QERH moulding on the surround, while the one at the W end was provided with a salt box. Most unusually, the moulding around the former fireplace also continues along the base of the hearth. The eastern chamber was the 'lairds chalmer'. The partition, like the floor, has now gone. There are two large window recesses in the S wall and one in the N wall, the former having stone seats, while further illumination is provided by one smaller window at each end. Within the SE corner there is a dog-legged mural chamber, similar to the one in the hall below. Another mural chamber with a garderobe, which occupies the NW corner, was originally entered directly from the main chamber, via a short passage with an aumbry in its wall; but at some later date a new doorway was formed to give access from the N window recess. This room is believed to have been the 'scholehous chalmer', referred to in an inventory of the castle's contents in 1624.[40] Another door in the opposite ingo of the N window admits to a large vaulted chamber, 15ft 6in long by 7ft wide, within the thickness of the N wall. This served as 'the chappell'.[41] It has a window in the N wall and, on the other side, two mural recesses, referred to in the inventory as 'twa locket chalmers'.

The third floor was always two chambers, known, no doubt from their draughty disposition, as the 'outer windiehall' and the 'inner windiehall'.[42] The former, which is at the E end, has a window recess with stone seats and an aumbry in the S wall and a smaller window recess and fireplace in the E wall, while the N wall is occupied by a mural chamber with a small window and garderobe. At the other end, the 'inner windiehall' has a window recess with stone seats in both the N and S walls and a smaller fireplace at the W end. In addition, it has a large mural chamber with two slit windows in the NW corner and another, much smaller chamber with one slit window in the SW corner. The latter chamber has a very odd shape, which cannot be readily explained.

Fig. 181 Comlongon: detail of corbelling and covered gallery in SW corner.

Above this level, the parapet-walk runs unbroken around the wall-head. It was from this walk, with its crenellated parapet carried on bold, 3-stage corbels, that the principal defence of the tower was carried out. This is how the tower is portrayed in the English survey of 1547.[43] In addition, the wall-head was splayed back between each corbel to accommodate machicolations – a reminder of why corbels were originally used. When the parapet-walk was later modified, probably late in the 16th century, an enclosed gallery was formed over the W walk utilizing the former embrasures as windows, and the SE corner was also enclosed; both have pitched roofs with crow-stepped gables.[44] The gallery was also provided with a lamp recess and slop-sink. At the same time the machicolations were closed off. The small fireplace incorporated into the chimney stack on the W side was probably added at this time. Within the parapet walk was the attic, which, because of the roof's unusually low profile and absence of any windows, could only have served as a very restricted storage space. It was entered from a doorway leading directly off the parapet walk. Above this, and sitting astride the E gable, are two look-out platforms, one on top of the cap-house at the head of the stair and the other combined with a cluster of chimneys. They were reached by way of the crow-stepped gable on the N side, the steps themselves being made 2ft 6in wide for this purpose. When the new fireplaces were added on the second floor, the former chimney on the S side was closed off and the stacks in the gables were modified to accommodate the new flues.

There is no visible evidence of either the barmkin, which must have existed on the N side of the tower, and which is shown on the 'Platte of Castlemilk' in 1547,[45] or of other works on the site, but various foundations have recently been detected in the ground to the S. In the inventory of 1624, mention is made of three locked stables and an 'utter [outer] yett' with 'a strong lock and key'. Cardonnel's view of the castle in 1788 shows a single storey building with thatched roof and two chimney stacks, one not central, to the S of the tower and a substantial, two-storeyed house immediately E of the tower.[46] The latter building was the mansion added by the 5th Viscount Stormont early in the 18th century.[47] It was replaced by the modern mansion in 1900-2.[48]

Like other important strongholds, Comlongon also had a large deer park, known as 'Koig pool park', which is shown on Pont's map of Annandale c.1595.[49]

The next laird of Comlongon was Cuthbert Murray, who succeeded his father c.1527. He had sasine in 1529,[50] and died c.1540. His eldest son, Sir Charles Murray, 10th of Cockpool, was laird for more than sixty years, but as he was still a minor when he succeeded, James V granted the ward of his estate to Robert, Master of Maxwell.[51] He eventually had sasine in 1547.[52] In the same year, his uncle and tutor, Patrick Murray, whilst a prisoner of the English, discussed terms for the surrender of Comlongon, and by November the tower was in the hands of an English garrison.[53] For his treachery, Patrick was subsequently charged with 'tressonabill byding with the Inglismen' and giving them 'the hous of Cokpule', and forfeit all his property.[54] It was at this time that Lord Wharton reported to Somerset that he had 'despatched the surveyor into Scotland' to view various houses, including 'Cockpool', and that 'the Surveyor of Calais, Mr. Petit, will bring you a plan of the tower'.[55] This appears to have been the 'Platte of Castlemilk', which includes a thumbnail sketch of Comlongon.[56] A few months later, when the tide turned in the Scots favour, 'Cokpule' (i.e. Comlongon) was one of the strongholds recovered by the Master of Maxwell.[57]

After peace was concluded with England in 1550, Sir Charles was appointed one of the Conservators of the Truce.[58] Five years later, he received the gift of the non-entries of his estates, including the lands of Cockpool, Ruthwell-tenement and 'the toure and fortalice of Cumlingane'.[59] Despite the truce, however, the English kept a wary eye on Scottish affairs, and c.1564-5 undertook a new military survey of the West March. This noted that, 'there is other pretie howses within Annerdale, suche as Cokpule xiiij foote thik of the wall, stonding vpoun roke, . . . [which] was in the warres of Edward the six in Yngles posession, witht a garisone of Fyftie horsmen under the Lorde Wharton'.[60] In 1570, Lord Scrope, the English Warden, invaded the West March. As his forces made their way along the coast to Dumfries, they met a Scots force under Lord Maxwell at Old Cockpool, and in the skirmish that followed – as Scrope later reported – the Lords Maxwell, Carlisle, Johnston, and others, 'escaped by the strength of the laird of Cockpole's house, and a great wood, and a 'marris' [morass] there adjoining'.[61] Four years later, Sir Charles was one of those appointed by parliament with responsibility for holding 'wapinschaws' in the Stewartry of Annandale,[62] and in 1585 he was one of the lairds

ordered by the Privy Council to do as he was directed 'for the weill and quietnes of the cuntrey'.[63] 'Cumlonge castel' is shown on Aglionby's platte in 1590,[64] and 'Kumlingan Cast.' on Pont's survey c.1595.[65]

Sir Charles was succeeded by his eldest surviving son, Sir James Murray, who was served heir in 1605.[66] Four years later, parliament ratified his infeftment in the barony of Cockpool and the burgh of Ruthwell.[67] In 1613 he was appointed a Commissioner of Justiciary.[68] On his death in 1620, without male issue, the estate was claimed by Sir Charles's next surviving son, Sir Richard Murray, but this was contested by Sir James's three daughters. It was finally agreed to refer the matter for arbitration by Sir Charles's youngest son, Sir John Murray of Lochmaben (infra), who upheld Sir Richard's claim as the heir male.[69] But Sir Richard, who also had estates in England and Ireland, continued to live in London, while Comlongon was left in the care of a chamberlain. A surviving Inventory of the castle's contents, made when Andrew Murray of Moriquhat took over this office in 1624, is of special interest for its record of the castle at that time.[70] In the same year, the lands and barony of Cockpool, 'with the tower called Camlungane', manor-places, etc., were apprised for debt, and granted to Sir William Grierson of Lag.[71] The following year, Sir Richard was made a Baronet of Nova Scotia.[72]

Sir Richard was succeeded in 1636 by his youngest brother, Sir John Murray of Lochmaben, who was served heir the following year.[73] Sir John had a distinguished career as Gentleman of the Bedchamber, Master of the Horse and personal adviser to James VI, as well as holding the offices of Commendator of Dundrennan Abbey, Provost of Lincluden and Steward of Annandale.[74] In 1622 he was created Viscount Annan and Lord Murray of Lochmaben, and in 1624 Earl of Annandale.[75] It was as such that he attended parliament in 1630, 1633 and 1639.[76] In 1627 he was appointed with the laird of Amisfield to inspect the highways between Dumfries and Carlisle.[77] He died in 1640.

The second Earl was a regular attender of parliament from 1641 until 1645.[78] He was a member of the Covenanting War Committee for Dumfriesshire, and was with Montrose when he crossed the Border and raised the royal standard in Dumfries in 1644.[79] The following year he was given the commission of Lieutenant-Colonel for Dumfriesshire by the Committee of Estates.[80] In 1642 he succeeded a distant cousin as 3rd Viscount Stormont. Nine years later, he was a Commissioner to the Committee of Estates;[81] but by this time he was seriously in debt, and in 1655 the lands of Cockpool and Ruthwell, together with 'the manor-place and fortalice of Comlonghame', were apprised under reversion.[82] He died three years later without issue, whereupon the Earldom became extinct, while Comlongon and the Viscounty of Stormont passed to another distant cousin, David Murray, 2nd Lord Balvaird.[83]

As the apprised lands had not been redeemed within the prescribed term, Dame Elizabeth Wardlaw and her husband, Sir Henry Wardlaw of Pitreavie, were, in 1663, granted a crown charter of them;[84] but by 1666 the 4th Viscount Stormont had evidently recovered the lands, for in that year he received a new crown charter of the superiority of his vast estates, including the lands of Cockpool and Ruthwell and 'the tenement, tower and fortalice of Cumlonghame', all of which were erected anew into the Viscounty of Stormont and Lordship of Balvaird, Cockpool and Lochmaben.[85] Lord Stormont married Lady Jean Carnegie, the widow of his predecessor, the 2nd Earl of Annandale, but evidently chose to live at Scone. He attended parliament regularly from 1661 to 1667,[86] and in the former year was also appointed to the Commission for the Plantation of Kirks and the Valuation of Teinds.[87] He died in 1668, and was succeeded by his son David, 5th Viscount Stormont.

Thereafter, Comlongon remained with the Viscounts Stormont, later Earls of Mansfield, until it was finally sold in 1979. But although Comlongon continued to be used by the family from time to time, and was sometimes the home of the eldest son, Scone was to become their principal residence. The 5th Viscount was an exception; he added 'sundry buildings', including a new mansion, at Comlongon early in the 18th century,[88] lived here for many years, and also died here in 1731.[89] It was, however, at Scone that he entertained Prince James in 1715, for which he was later fined and imprisoned.[90] He was a regular attender of parliament from 1703 to 1707,[91] voting against the Act ratifying the Treaty of Union in the latter year.[92] He was appointed a Commissioner for the Borders in 1683/4,[93] and in 1704 he was a Commissioner of Supply for Nithsdale and Dumfriesshire;[94] but most of his duties related to Perthshire and Fife.

Lord Stormont was succeeded by his eldest son, David, 6th Viscount Stormont, who, like his father, was fined and imprisoned for joining the Jacobites in the 1715 rebellion.[95] Thirty years later he also entertained Prince Charles at Scone.[96] He died in 1748. His eldest son, David, 7th Viscount Stormont, succeeded to the Earldom of Mansfield on the death of his uncle, William, 1st Earl of Mansfield, in 1793. He became a Privy Councillor, a Knight of the Thistle and a Representative Peer for Scotland, as well as holding many high offices of state,[97] and his descendants have likewise served their country with distinction; but none of these appointments have related specially to Dumfriesshire or the Borders.

Cardonnel's view of Comlongon in 1788 shows the 5th Viscount's new house (supra) close to the tower.[98] Four years later, it is recorded that Comlongon was occupied by the 7th Viscount's factor, and that 'the hall and larger rooms [of the tower] are still occupied, as the roof is standing'.[99] Meanwhile, the earlier stronghold at Cockpool had long since been abandonned, but 'the remains' could still be seen in 1845.[100] The family still held more than 14,000 acres in the county in 1883.[101]

In 1900-2, three years after he succeeded his father, the 5th Earl of Mansfield demolished the 18th century house at Comlongon and in its stead built the present baronial mansion. It was here that the Earl died in 1906.[102] The family finally sold the castle in 1979.[103]

---

1 Bain I, No.1681. R. C. Reid, in 'The Site of Cokpule' (TDGAS, 3rd Ser., XXXII, 191), points ou that the date assigned in Bain is incorrect, and should read c.1370.
2 See also Reid, R.C., op. cit., 190-2.
3 Reid, R.C., op. cit., 191. Mottes without baileys are quite common in SW Scotland, but this example is larger than most.
4 Remains of the old castle could still be seen in 1792 (Stat Acct X, 226).
5 It has been suggested that the gift of 'half the patronage' of Ruthwell church could well imply that Thomas de Duncurry left two daughters, who were co-heiresses (Reid, R.C., op. cit., 191).
6 Scots Peerage I, 215. William's father was Sir William Murray, who is said to have been descended from the Murrays of Duffus.
7 Ibid, 216.
8 Ibid.
9 Ibid, 217.
10 Ibid, 218.
11 RMS II, No.546.
12 Scots Peerage I, 219.
13 Maxwell-Irving 1997, 871-9.
14 Scots Peerage I, 219.
15 Buccleuch MSS, 58 (No.114).
16 Scots Peerage I, 220; APS II, 175, 180.

17 Ridpath 447.
18 ERS X, 770.
19 RSS I, No.692. Although the Licence is not dated, it can be placed fairly accurately in sequence from the other information available. See also Maxwell-Irving 1997, 877, Note 5.
20 'A Letter of Licence granted to John Murray of Cockpool and his heirs to build a tower and fortalice upon his lands lying in Annandale, and to include in the construction machicolations, corbelling, iron yetts and windows, etc., and to raise and build the said tower to whatever height he pleases, without impediment, etc.'
21 RMS II, No.3194. The cost of the charter was £100 (ALHT IV, 5).
22 See Pryde, G.S. 'The Burghs of Dumfriesshire and Galloway: Their Origin and Status', TDGAS, 3rd Ser., XXIX, 100.
23 APS II, 274.
24 It is interesting to note a connection between Comlongon and Elphinstone. Elphinstone was built by a branch of the Johnstons, cadets of the Johnstons of that Ilk in Annandale. They inherited Elphinstone in 1436 through the marriage of Gilbert Johnston to Agnes, daughter and heiress of Sir Alexander Elphinstone of that Ilk. Not only did Gilbert retain his family connections with Annandale, but in 1472 he received a crown charter of the lands of Dumgree there (RMS II, No.1058).
25 Douglas Simpson, W. 'Comlongon Castle', TDGAS, 3rd Ser., XXIII, 20.
26 Cruden 1960, 144.
27 Elphinstone fared even worse; it became so unsafe, albeit aggravated by subsidence, that in 1955 it had to be demolished down to the level of the basement walls.
28 One mason's mark is found in a number of places, especially in the great hall, while another appears just inside the entrance. A third is questionable.
29 It has been suggested that there was a second wooden door inside the yett, but this would seem to be a misinterpretation of a further, partial rebate there (See also Christison, D 'On the Grated Iron Doors of Scottish Castles and Towers', PSAS, XVII, 111).
30 See Christison, op. cit., 109-111.
31 Part of the stair-well survives at ground level.
32 Details of the vent are given by Christison, D., op. cit., 110. It has since been blocked.
33 The additional jamb, which replaces the right half of the original pillar, is not shown by MacGibbon & Ross. They show the original left column complete, so it would seem that the new jamb was only added in recent times. It has been suggested that the oak beam was originally coated in plaster (Simpson, W.D., op. cit., 24).
34 The presence of vines in the decoration suggests that the masons may have been of continental origin, though vines were a popular decoration throughout the Middle Ages.
35 The arms on the left show Murray impaled with another, unknown coat. The wives of the lairds around this time are not recorded.
36 Another shield bears three spears or arrows paly, with the points uppermost. This has not been identified.
37 It has been observed (Simpson, op. cit., 21) that the grille of the N window has at some time been violently torn out and then replaced. This occurred in the 20th century when heavy timber had to be brought into the hall to shore up the inner face of the N wall.
38 Little Cumbrae (?c.1537), Law, Fairlie and Skelmorlie (c.1502) in Ayrshire and Saddell (c.1508-12) in Kintyre (See MacGibbon & Ross, III, 173-83, 197-200).
39 It has been suggested that this was the muniment room (Simpson, op. cit., 25); but this assumption seems to be based on the premise that the inner chamber was a safe for the family silver, overlooking its original use as a garderobe, the flue for which still exists.
40 See Appendix (2).
41 Ibid.
42 Ibid
43 Merriman, M. 'The Platte of Castlemilk, 1547', TDGAS, 3rd Ser., XLIV, Plate XV.
44 Some of the original drainage arrangements for the parapet-walk may still be seen within the W gallery.
45 Merriman, op. cit., 181.
46 Cardonnel, 'Comlongon'.
47 Stat Acct X, 226.
48 It was designed by the Dumfries architect, James Barbour (Wolffe, A. 'James Barbour', TDGAS, 3rd Ser., LXXI, 157).
49 Blaeu, 57, 'THE STEWARTRIE OF ANNANDAIL'.
50 Scots Peerage I, 223.
51 RSS II, No.3800.
52 Scots Peerage I, 223
53 Merriman, op. cit., 177. Sir Charles was, evidently, also a prisoner for a while (Scots Peerage I, 224).
54 RSS III, No.2933 (see also No.2714). Patrick's lands were later granted to Lord Somerville, the father-in-law of his nephew, Sir Charles Murray.
55 Merriman, op. cit., 177.
56 Ibid, 181.

57   Fraser 1873, I, 501.
58   Scots Peerage I, 224.
59   RSS IV, No.3109.
60   Armstrong 1883, cxiii.
61   Scottish Papers III, No.188.
62   APS III, 91.
63   RPC III, 735.
64   Hyslop, 320.
65   Blaeu, 57, *op. cit.*
66   Scots Peerage I, 226.
67   APS IV, 431.
68   Scots Peerage I, 226.
69   Ibid.
70   R. C. Reid, 'The Furnishings of Comlongon, 1624', *TDGAS*, 3rd Ser., XXXII, 180-5. See Appendix A.
71   RMS VIII, No.597.
72   Scots Peerage I, 227; RMS VIII, No.831.
73   Scots Peerage I, 227.
74   Ibid.
75   Ibid., 228; Complete Peerage I, 165; APS V, 69.
76   APS V, 8, 208, 251.
77   RPC, 2nd Ser., I, 615.
78   APS V, 331, 426; VI, Part I, *passim.*
79   Maxwell 1900, 251.
80   APS VI, Part I, 468.
81   Ibid, Part II, 679.
82   RMS X, Nos.339, 418, 465.
83   Complete Peerage I, 399; XII (Part 1), 292-4.
84   RMS XI, No.460.
85   Ibid., No.965.
86   APS VII, *passim.*
87   Ibid, 48.
88   Stat Acct X, 226.
89   Complete Peerage XII (Part I), 295.
90   Scots Peerage VIII, 204.
91   APS XI, *passim.*
92   Ibid, 404.
93   RPC, 3rd Ser., VIII, 682.
94   APS XI, 142.
95   Scots Peerage VIII, 207.
96   Moncrieffe, Sir I. *Scone Palace* Guide, 28.
97   Scots Peerage VIII, 208.
98   Cardonnel, 'Comlongon'.
99   Stat Acct X, 226.
100 NSA IV, 229.
101 Complete Peerage VIII, 394; Return of Landowners, 57.
102 Complete Peerage VIII, 393.
103 Murray, 69.

20.   CORNAL TOWER
(1¾ m ESE Moffat)   (NT112044)

The lands of Cornal, or more correctly Polcornal, formed the northernmost part of the ancient 'tenement of Logan', which was held by the Carruthers at least as early as the beginning of the 15th century. In 1411, Archibald, 4th Earl of Douglas, granted a new charter of the lands to Simon Carruthers of Mouswald, his 'shield-bearer',[1] and the lands remained in the family until after the death of Simon Carruthers, 10th of Mouswald, in 1548. Simon left two daughters, Janet and Marion, his co-heiresses, who were made wards of Sir James Douglas of Drumlanrig.[2] In 1562/63, Janet, sold her share of the family estates to Sir James,[3] and, after the tragic death of Marion in 1570, the other half of the estates were granted by the Crown to Sir James's eldest son, Sir William Douglas of Hawick.[4] Sir William died two years later, whereupon his estates passed to his father, who granted them to his only grandson, Sir William's son, Sir James Douglas.[5] The latter Sir James succeeded his father in 1578. In 1588 he resigned all his lands to the Crown,[6] and in 1590/91 he obtained a new charter of the barony of Drumlanrig, including the £20 lands of Logan-tenement.[7] This was further confirmed by another crown charter in 1609.[8]

Fig. 182 Cornal Tower: remaining section
of walling seen from the W.

But although the Carruthers of Mouswald owned the lands, it was the powerful local Johnstons who came to occupy them. In 1504 Sir Adam Johnston of that Ilk and his wife, Marion Scott, widow of the late Archibald Carruthers, 7th of Mouswald, were challenged by officers of the crown for wrongfully labouring the lands of Polcornal and others, to which Marion laid claim, during the minority of Simon Carruthers.[9] This Simon died in 1531, and in August 1532 it is recorded that his son and heir Simon, 9th of Mouswald, then a minor, appeared with John Johnston of that Ilk, his guardian, before Mark Carruthers, notary public in Dumfries, and was formally asked by Johnston if he was willing 'to pay and refund all the expenses that Adam Johnston of Corrie [his brother] had incurred in building and constructing the place and tower of Polcornar from that time until the entrance thereto of the said Simon'.[10] This document is of special significance because it puts a precise date on the building of the present tower.

Simon Carruthers agreed to Johnston's request, but entry was not so easily obtained, and in 1535 he had to warn Adam Johnston of Corrie formally to remove himself and his belongings and desist from further occupation of the 'lands of Polcornar, Logan-tenement, together with the tower . . . of Polcornar'.[11] Nevertheless, by the middle of the century James Johnston (d.a.1561), a younger son of James Johnston of that Ilk, had become lawful feuar of the lands of Polcornal. In 1548 'James Johnstoun of Pocornwell' was granted a remission for pledging his services to the English,[12] when they overran Dumfriesshire the previous year, and the following year he was granted a charter under the Great Seal confirming his purchase of the lands and lordship of Wamphray from Adam Scott, younger of Wamphray.[13] Wamphray subsequently became the family's principal residence.[14]

The **TOWER** is strategically situated on a small plateau on the left bank of the Cornal Burn, a short distance before it joins the Moffat Water. From there it had a commanding view up the valley of the Moffat Water to the NE and across Annandale to the W. The plateau measures approximately 95ft from N to S and 55ft from E to W. It is protected on the E side by the ravine through which the burn flows and on the other three sides by steep, natural escarpments averaging some 15ft in height. On the W side, there are traces of a barmkin wall, 2ft thick, which, with the buildings, presumably surrounded the summit. The tower itself stood near the SE corner of the site. Only a vestige now remains, comprising the foundations of an oblong tower-house and a section of its E wall near the SE corner. The latter is 13ft 3in high, 10ft long and 4ft 11in thick. The tower is said to have measured 37ft from N to S by 21ft from E to W,[15] over walls varying in thickness from 4ft 8in to 5ft. The masonry is local greywacke rubble. At the N end of the site there are the remains of an outbuilding of indeterminate date. It appears to measure 39ft 10in from E to W by 21ft 10in from N to S over walls averaging 3ft 6in in thickness.[16] There are also indications that there was a mill beside the burn.[17]

Following the death of James Johnston, 1st of Wamphray, it appears that Cornal was to have become the dower house for his widow, Margaret McClellan; but she was unable to obtain possession, because John Johnston of Selcoth had forcibly taken 'occupatioun', and was 'lawbouring, manuring and withhalding fra the said Margaret of the tour and fortalice of Polcornar with the tuenty mark land, mylnis, woddis [woods] and pertinentis thairof'. Margaret accordingly had recourse to the law, and had Johnston of Selcoth declared a rebel; and in 1566 her son, James Johnston of Wamphray, obtained from the Crown the forfeiture of Selcoth's goods, etc.[18]

'Pocornel' tower is shown on Aglionby's Platte of 1590. It is not certain who was then in possession, but early in the

following century the lands were held by Captain James Johnston of Lochhouse, a younger son of John Johnston of that Ilk.[19] He died between 1621 and 1632 leaving no lawful issue.[20] By this time the tower may already have been abandoned.

1 Carruthers 1934, 51.
2 For Drumlanrig's connection with the Carruthers' heiresses, see 'Mouswald Tower'.
3 RMS IV, No.1440.
4 Carruthers 1934, 72.
5 RSS VI, Nos.1914, 2365, 2733.
6 Carruthers 1934, 72-3.
7 RMS V, No.2034.
8 RMS VII, No.53.
9 Fraser 1894, I, xxvii.
10 MS Protocol Book of Mark Carruthers in Drumlanrig Charter Chest, cited in Carruthers 1934, 65.
11 Carruthers 1934, 66.
12 RSS III, No.3042.
13 RMS IV, No.404; Fraser 1894, I, xxxi. In 1542/3 'John Johnston in Pocorner' was appointed by the Crown to act as an attorney for the said James Johnston (Fraser 1894, I, lxiii).
14 See Fraser 1894, I, cccxxiv.
15 RCAHMS 1920, No.476. Foundations currently traceable suggest that the width of the tower may in fact have been 26ft 3in.
16 The RCAHMS recorded the length as 46ft 6in, but this would seem to be in error.
17 RCAHMS 1997, 215.
18 RSS V, No.2914.
19 Fraser 1894, I, lxii.
20 See 'Lochhouse Tower'.

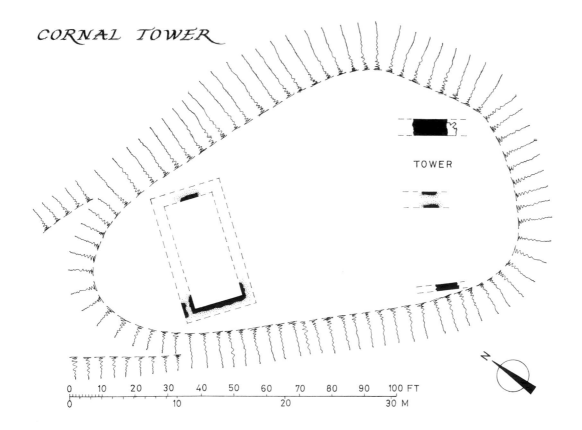

Fig. 183 Cornal Tower: site plan.

21.   CORRA CASTLE
(¹/₂ m S Kirkgunzeon)   (NX867662)

The lands of 'Kircwinnyn' (meaning the church of St. Winning), or Kirkgunzeon, on which the remains of Corra Castle stand, were at first leased to the monks of Holm Cultram Abbey in Cumbria *c*.1170 by Uchtred, Lord of Galloway.[1] Later, the lease was converted to a feu by Uchtred's son Roland,[2] and this was confirmed by the bishop of Glasgow in 1190 and Pope Innocent III in 1207.[3] Thereafter, the monks continued to pay their dues, first to the Lords of Galloway, and then, after the death of Alan, the last Lord of Galloway, to the Balliols, who inherited that part of Galloway through Alan's daughter and co-heiress Dervorguilla.[4] But with the onset of the War of Independence, this simple arrangement was thrown into confusion while the Balliols' lands repeatedly changed hands,[5] and during this period there is no evidence that any feus were paid. For a time Edward Balliol was in possession of his father's patrimony, but in 1334 he resigned much of Galloway in favour of Edward III, retaining for himself, so it is said, only the castles of Buittle, Kirkgunzeon and Kenmure.[6] This is the first, albeit highly questionable, suggestion that there may have been a castle at Kirkgunzeon this early. Balliol finally renounced his rights to these lands in 1356.

One of the foremost followers of the Douglases, when they brought Galloway firmly under the control of the Scottish Crown again in 1353, was Sir John Heryz, whose family were first recorded in Dumfriesshire the previous century.[7] After his release by the English in 1357, David II rewarded Sir John 'for his services' with a grant of the lands of Terregles, and ten years later, in 1367, he also granted him the lands of 'Kirkgunyane' that 'formerly belonged to the monks, abbot and monastery of Holme'.[8] It was a condition of the latter grant that Sir John should compensate the monks for any losses they should sustain as a result. These two properties then became the principal seats of the Herries family.

It is not clear who built the original stronghold on the site, nor when it was begun. If there was indeed a stronghold at Kirkgunzeon in the time of Edward Balliol, it could have been the work of either Edward or his father, if its origins were not even earlier. There is no evidence of a motte, but neither is there

any trace now of the moat that surrounded the old castle, and which could still be traced as recently as 1845.[9] The earliest definite reference to the stronghold is in a crown charter granted to Andrew, 2nd Lord Herries, in 1510. This confirms his possession of various lands in Galloway, Dumfriesshire and Roxburghshire, including the lands and barony of Terregles, and the lands and barony of Kirkgunzeon, with the tower and fortalice, which were now incorporated into the free barony of Herys.[10] Although a manor-house is mentioned at Terregles (q.v.) in 1484, it is perhaps worthy of note that the charter of 1510 mentions a tower and fortalice at Kirkgunzeon, but makes no mention of one at Terregles.

After the death of the 3rd Lord Herries in 1543, the Herries estates were divided between his three daughters. In 1549/50, the eldest daughter, Agnes, and her husband John, Master of Maxwell, later 4th Lord Herries, were granted their third of the lands, including one third of Kirkgunzeon.[11] Sir John finally acquired the shares of the other two heiresses in 1561,[12] and in 1566 he was recognized, jure uxoris, as 4th Lord Herries.[13] In the same year, in recognition of his outstanding service in 'quieting the Borders' during some twenty two years service as Warden and Justiciar of the West March, Queen Mary granted him a new crown charter of the lands and barony of Terregles, with the tower and fortalice, and the lands and barony of Kirkgunzeon, with the tower and fortalice;[14] and this was confirmed by parliament in 1567.[15] According to the old family records, he also built 'the house of Kirkgunzeon' to replace the older castle.[16] Nothing is known of this edifice, which was also apparently known for the first time as 'Corra',[17] but it was an important residence of the Lords Herries until well into the following century. This work may have been carried out in 1566, the same year in which he built Hoddom Castle (q.v.) and Repentance Tower as well as becoming Lord Herries. It has been said that Queen Mary spent a night here in 1568, whilst fleeing south to Dundrennan after her defeat at Langside.[18]

The site chosen for the **CASTLE** was a low outcrop of rock surrounded by a small area of marshland in a gently undulating landscape. It was not a place of great natural strength, but it was close to the main road between Dumfries and Buittle and the Solway coast beyond. Because of extensive development of the farmyard and buildings that now occupy the site, there is no longer any visible trace of either the early castle or its moat

Fig. 184 Corra Castle: view from the E.

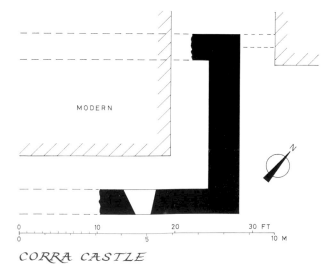

CORRA CASTLE

Fig. 185 Corra Castle: plan of surviving NE end.

(*supra*), or of the 16th century buildings erected by the 4th Lord Herries.

All that remains is one end of a small **HOUSE** that appears to date from the 17th century: the rest has been removed. It was oblong in plan, and measured 23ft 3in from NW to SE by about 53ft[19] from NE to SW over walls averaging 3ft 3in in thickness along the sides and 4ft at the gable ends. It comprised two storeys and possibly an attic. It was not vaulted. The masonry is local rubble with roughly-dressed granite quoins and sandstone mouldings. Only the NE gable wall and an adjacent section of the SE wall, some 18ft long and 17ft 6in high to the wall-head, survive. These were pointed early in the 20th century to prevent further decay, but most of the features have been lost. There is a window recess in the SE wall at ground floor level, and another above it on the first floor; both have lost their window surrounds and other features, so it is no longer possible to be sure of their original size. The only complete window is a small one in the gable at first floor level; this has rounded arrises on all four sides, glazing grooves and sockets for one vertical bar. Adjacent to it, In the middle of the gable, there is a recess for a fireplace. The only other feature is a moulded skewput at the N corner. A sketch of the ruins in 1878 shows that they were much more extensive at that time, including a section of the NW side wall adjacent to the surviving gable, the chimney stack on that gable, and another substantial section of the SE side wall towards the S corner.[20]

Both the 5th and 6th Lords Herries appear to have resided at Kirkgunzeon for some of the time, although Terregles was their principal seat. In 1583, the year after his father's death, the 5th Lord Herries erected a dovecot at Kirkgunzeon;[21] and in both 1609 and 1627 the 6th Lord Herries dated letters there.[22] By the last date, however, Lord Herries had had to mortgage Kirkgunzeon as surety for his increasing debts.[23] Then, in 1633, on the resignation of Lord Herries, Sir Richard Murray of Cockpool, baronet, received a crown charter of the lands and barony of Kirkgunzeon, with the towers, and various other lands, all of which were incorporated into the barony of Hutton;[24] and ten years later his nephew, the 2nd Earl of Annandale, received a new grant confirming these and other lands.[25] The 7th Lord Herries was again in possession in 1662, when, still burdened by financial losses incurred under the Commonwealth, his lands were apprised for debt and granted to George Seton, 4th Earl of Winton.[26] Some time later, Lord Herries recovered the lands. In 1667 he succeeded as 3rd Earl of Nithsdale, and in 1669 his eldest son, Robert, was married. As part of the marriage contract, Lord Nithsdale bound himself to infeft Robert and his spouse, Lucie Douglas, in the lands and barony of Kirkgunzeon, with the castle, etc.[27] If it is correct that the Maxwells of nearby Breconside occupied the castle at some time during this century,[28] it was presumably as feuars or tenants.

At that time the castle was still usually known by the same name as the lands, 'Kirkgunzeon'. The name 'Corra', although reputedly used as early as the 16th century, did not come into common usage until about 1791, when the Statistical Account relates that 'The Corrah ... has been both a large building and a place of considerable strength'.[29] By then, however, the major part of the old stronghold had been demolished, and the masonry used to build new houses, while the remaining part was used as a farm-house.[30] Early in the 19th century, the house was occupied by a farm tenant.[31] Later, a new farm-house was built on the site, and it was presumably then that the older house was abandonned.

1 Reid, R.C. 'The Early Ecclesiastical History of Kirkgunzean', *TDGAS*, 3rd Ser., XIV, 202; Gillespie, J.E. 'Notes on the Parish of Kirkgunzeon', *TDGAS*, 2nd Ser., XXIV, 177; Barrow 1971, Nos.88, 540.
2 Reid, *op. cit.*, 202.
3 Gillespie, *op. cit.*, 177. Part of the original grant to Holm Cultram was later revoked by Uchtred, and the lands given to Walter de Berkeley, Chamberlain of Scotland, who had built his caput on the adjoining lands of Urr; but Berkeley gave Holm Cultram a new charter of the lands, which was confirmed by William the Lion, and by 1190 the abbey was again in possession (Tabraham, C.J. 'Norman Settlement in Galloway: Recent Fieldwork in the Stewartry', in *Scot. Antiq.*, 109; Scott, J. G. 'Galloway in the 1100s', *TDGAS*, 3rd Ser., LXVIII, 133; Barrow 1971, No.256).
4 Reid, *op. cit.*, 211.
5 See 'Buittle Castle' for the fluctuating possession of the Balliols' lands.
6 Cardonnel, 'Buitle: Plate I'.
7 Bain I, No.1680.
8 RMS I, No.282 & Appendix II, No.1574.
9 NSA IV, 220
10 RMS II, No.3446.
11 RMS IV, No.405.
12 See Scots Peerage, IV, 410, for details.
13 Scots Peerage IV, 410.
14 RMS IV, No.1728.
15 APS II, 558-9.
16 Fraser 1873, I, 568.
17 Mackenzie & Nicholson 1841, 507.
18 Ibid; McDowall 1986, 265. cf.Fraser 1873, I, 523.
19 At the time of the RCAHMS report of 1914, the extension of the SE wall and S corner were still clearly traceable (RCAHMS 1914, No.275).
20 M'Kerlie IV, 223.
21 Stat Acct VII, 192; Gillespie, *op. cit.*, 148.
22 Fraser 1894, II, 276; Fraser 1873, II, 106.
23 RMS VIII, Nos.705, 1403; IX, No.397.
24 RMS VIII, No.2121.
25 RMS IX, No.1450.
26 RMS XI, No.251.
27 Fraser 1873, I, 397.
28 Stat Acct VII, 192.
29 Ibid. Lady Winifred Maxwell, granddaughter and heiress of the 5th and last Earl of Nithsdale, was owner of 'Corra' c.1770 - Directory of Landownership, 196.
30 Ibid, 193.
31 Gillespie, *op. cit.*, 148.

22. CRAWFORDTON TOWER

(2½ m ESE Moniaive) (NX816889)

The Crichtons first acquired an interest in the extensive lands and barony of Sanquhar early in the 14th century, when Isobel Ross, younger of the co-heiresses of Sanquhar, married William Crichton, younger brother of Sir John de Crichton of that Ilk (d.ante 1357).[1] William thus acquired half the barony of Sanquhar,[2] and not long afterwards his successors purchased the other half from the Edgars. It is not clear whether the lands of Crawfordton formed part of the estate at this time, but they were part of the estate in 1466, when Sir Robert Crichton of Sanquhar (d.1478-79) granted them to his younger son, Alexander.[3] Sir Robert, however, retained the superiority.[4] He was succeeded in 1478 or 1479 by his eldest son, Robert, who, in 1487/8, was created Lord Crichton of Sanquhar; and Lord Crichton was in turn succeeded in 1494 by his grandson and heir, Robert, 2nd Lord Crichton of Sanquhar, who had sasine of Sanquhar, Eliock and Crawfordton later that year.[5] Then, in 1506/7, Robert, 2nd Lord Crichton, received a new crown charter of the lands and barony of Crawfurdstoun, 'now also called Balmakane'.[6] This states that the 8 merk lands of Crawfordton and 6 merk lands of Stewarton were at that time occupied by Cuthbert Crichton, presumably a descendant of Alexander. The 2nd Lord Crichton died in 1513, possibly killed at Flodden, and was succeeded by his son Robert, who had sasine of 'Crawfurdston' in the same

Fig. 186 Crawfordton Tower: ruins seen from NW, with later house on left.

year.[7] Then in 1522, for reasons not specified, the ward of the lands and barony of Crawfordston were granted as a 'royal gift' to Robert Lord Maxwell.[8]

There is mention of Andrew Crichton of Crawfordton in 1560,[9] and of two incidents 'in Crawfordstoun' in 1579 and 1580. The first incident concerned the theft of 18 head of nolt by Johnston of Rowantreeknowes,[10] and the second a charge of treasonable fireraising by one Patrick McCrerik.[11] By 1587 Crawfordton was in the possession of 'John Creichtoun of Crawfurdstoun',[12] probably a son; but there is no indication as to which Crichton built the present tower, which appears to date from sometime in the second half of the 16th century. It is first recorded as 'Krafurdton'[13] on Pont's survey of Nithsdale c.1595, where it is shown as a substantial tower-house, larger than 'Iarbrugh' nearby, but not as large as 'Glen-kairn Cast[le]' immediately across the valley.[14] The tower stands on rising ground on the SW side of the Cairn valley, whence it looks across the valley to the NE to Maxwelton House, the more modern successor to the castle of Glencairn, part of which is reputedly incorporated in it.[15]

The **TOWER** is trapezoidal in plan, with a width of 19ft 6in and a mean length of 32ft 9in over walls that vary in thickness from 2ft on the N side to 5ft at each end. Such a large discrepancy is not readily explainable, and, as only the basement has survived, nothing is known about the upper floors that might help in understanding the unusual layout, which includes solitary slit-windows, with rounded arrises, in the S and E walls, but none in either the W wall or, more surprizingly, adjacent to the entrance on the N side.[16] The masonry is greywacke rubble, with sandstone dressings and mouldings. The entrance, which has a QER moulding on the jambs, is near the middle of the N wall. It opened on to a mural passage leading to a wheel-stair, 6ft 6in in diameter, in the NW corner, while doorways opposite admitted to two chambers, each with a barrel vault running N-S. All three doorways are now blocked by fallen masonry, preventing access, but the inside of the chambers was recorded by the RCAHMS in 1912.[17] The rest of the passage and stair are now open to the sky. The only features are a lamp-shelf in the W chamber and another at the foot of the stair. The courtyard to the N is cobbled.

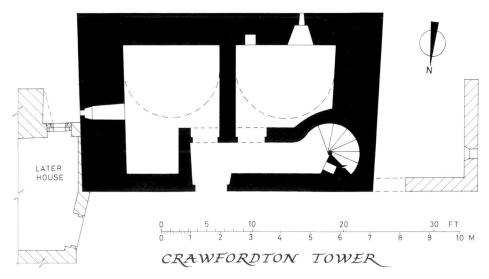

Fig. 187 Crawfordton Tower: plan of basement.

Adjoining the NW corner of the tower is a wall, 1ft 6in thick, which extends W past a passage doorway for 11ft 7in and then turns S for a further 12ft 4in. The latter section includes a small window, now blocked, showing that the wall is a remnant of a later extension or building. No date can be assigned to this work. More recently, two further walls have been added to form a shed.

On the other side of the tower, at the NE corner, there are further additions, which represent more than one later building phase. Whatever the earlier one comprised, all but the SW corner was swept away when the present **L**–plan house was built adjoining the tower in the late 17th or early 18th centuries. The SW corner, however, which in part is orientated at an angle to both the tower and later house, is a relic of an earlier 17th century addition, which encroached upon the NE corner of the tower. It includes a S-facing entrance doorway, partly built of re-used dressed stone and with a new, enhanced, roll-and-hollow moulding on the surround. This doorway was later blocked and converted to a window.

In 1609, the 8th Lord Crichton of Sanquhar was granted a new charter of the lordship of Sanquhar, including the lands and barony of Crawfurdstoun.[18] He was succeeded by his cousin, William, 9th Lord Crichton of Sanquhar, who received a new charter in 1619.[19] Two and a half years later, William was made Viscount of Air, and in 1633 Earl of Dumfries. Soon afterwards, he got into financial difficulties, and in 1637 he was compelled to sell the estate of Sanquhar to the 1st Earl of Queensberry,[20] whose son, William Douglas, Lord Drumlanrig, received a grant of the lands and barony of Sanquhar in 1664.[21] This grant also included the lands and barony of Crawfordton, which, together with the baronies of Sanquhar and Glencairn, were erected into a free regality within the Earldom of Queensberry; and this was confirmed by parliament five years later.[22]

Meanwhile, the Crichtons continued to occupy Crawfordton. John Crichton of Crawfordton was appointed a Commissioner of War in 1643, 1644 and 1645,[23] and a Commissioner of Supply in 1643, 1648, 1650, 1655, 1656 and 1659.[24] He was also a Lieutenant-Colonel of Foot under Colonel Douglas of Dornock in 1650.[25] Having no son or male heir, he made an entail of the estate in 1647, wherein he named his three daughters.[26] Eight years later his daughter Agnes was contracted to marry John Brown, who was to take the name and arms of Crichton;[27] and in 1657, by which time he had five daughters, John Crichton made a new entail of the estate.[28] But although he had secured the succession of the name, it is not known whether he was the father of William Crichton, who subsequently succeeded to Crawfordton.

William Crichton of Crawfordton took the Test in 1683,[29] and the following year became Captain of the 9th Company of the Dumfriesshire Militia.[30] He was appointed a Commissioner of Supply for Nithsdale and Dumfries in 1685, 1689, 1690, 1696 and 1698,[31] and a Captain in the Militia in 1689.[32] He was an additional Commissioner to Parliament in 1690,[33] and represented Dumfriesshire in parliament from 1693 until his death in 1702.[34] In 1696 he was a signatory to the Association for the defence of King William,[35] and in 1701 he was one of those who voted for the foundation of the colony of Caledonia.[36] He was succeeded by his eldest son, John, who was recorded by Nisbet in 1722 as 'the appearing Heir Male of the Family of Crawfoordston', resident in France.[37]

The estate later came into the possession of one John Walker (d.1857),[38] whose eldest son, Colonel Sir George Walker,

commissioned the architects Peddie & Kinnear to design a new, baronial-style mansion for the estate in 1863.[39] This was built on a new site, 1½ miles NW of the old house, and assumed the name of 'Crawfordton', while the old house henceforth became known as 'Old Crawfordton'. The Walkers finally sold the old house and tower in 1926,[40] and the new mansion and the rest of the estate about a year later.[41]

1   Scots Peerage III, 56; Nisbet I, 285.
2   RMS I, No.27 and App.1, No.56.
3   Scots Peerage III, 221.
4   Robert Crichton had sasine of Sanquhar, Eliock, Crawfordton, etc., in 1494 (ERS X, 768), and his son Robert in 1513 (ERS XIV, 523).
5   ERS X, 768.
6   RMS II, No.3025.
7   ERS XIV, 523.
8   Hamilton-Grierson, Sir P. 'The Craigdarroch Papers', *TDGAS*, 3rd Ser., XIV, 82, No.3.
9   RPC XIV, 301.
10 RPC III, 254.
11 Ibid, 634.
12 Hamilton-Grierson, *op. cit.*, 87, No.18.
13 The '-ton' on Pont's original was smudged, and thus got omitted from Blaeu's Atlas, where the name is given as 'Krafurd'.
14 Pont MS. No.35 in National Library of Scotland.
15 See Forman, S. 'Maxwelton', Scottish Field, May 1947 and October 1965.
16 This may be explained by the fact that the western portion of the N wall has clearly been rebuilt at some period. A slit-window is shown in the eastern portion of the same wall on the plan reproduced in RCAHMS 1920, 85, but recent surveys have failed to find it.
17 RCAHMS 1920, No.233.
18 RMS VII, No.124. In 1602 Lord Crichton had granted various lands, including the lands and barony of Crawfordton, to David Crichton of Lugtoun (RMS VI, No.1375).
19 Ibid, No.2061.
20 Complete Peerage IV, 499n.
21 RMS XI, No.546.
22 APS VII, 645.
23 Ibid, VI, Part I, 53, 200, 559.
24 Ibid, 29; Part II, *passim*.
25 Ibid, Part II, 598.
26 Laing Charters, No.2377.
27 Ibid, No.2474.
28 Ibid, No.2499.
29 RPC, 3rd Ser., VIII, 640.
30 Adams 1921, 159.
31 APS VIII, 465; IX, 70, 139; X, 29, 131.
32 Ibid, IX, 26.
33 Parl. of Scot., I, 155.
34 APS IX, 238, 347; X, *passim*.
35 Parl. of Scot., I, 155.
36 Ibid, X, 247.
37 Nisbet I, 285.
38 Burke L.G. 1906, 1736, 'Walker of Crawfordton'.
39 NMRS, Drawings of Crawfordton House, 1863.
40 Reg. Scot., Dumfries, 2nd Series, Nos.4695, 8833.
41 Burke L.G. 1952, 2613, 'Walker of Morrington, formerly of Crawfordton'.

23.   CUMSTOUN CASTLE
(1½ m N Kirkcudbright)   (NX682532)

The earliest reference to Cumstoun appears in 1296, when Walter fitz Walter de Cummstun swore fealty to Edward I.[1] But whilst the neighbouring barony of Twynholm, with which Cumstoun later became amalgamated, and which at the time was possessed by Walter de Twynham,[2] had a motte as its stronghold, there is no clear evidence of one at Cumstoun. There is a small, irregular earthwork on the top of a bank above the confluence of the Tarff Water and a burn some 250 yards NE of the later castle, which may have served as a small motte.[3] On the other hand, Reid has suggested that the rectangular earthwork which surrounds the later castle, and which has an entrance on its N side, could have been the fortified manor of Walter de Cummstun.[4]

Nothing more is heard of Cumstoun or its owners until after the fall of the Douglas Lords of Galloway in 1455.[5] Then, in 1463, John Kennedy of Blairquhan, in Ayrshire, was made Steward of Kirkcudbright.[6] This, together with a grant of the lands of Cumstoun and Twynholm, which he seems to have acquired from the Crown around this time, may have been his reward for services rendered in the suppression of the Douglases. Certainly, it would have been in character, for in 1477 he was rewarded by James III for his part in the 'capture and bringing in of certain rebels'.[7] By 1498, his eldest son and heir, Sir John Kennedy, was designated 'of Cumistoune'.[8] It is likely that it was he who built the present castle, which is first mentioned in 1504/5 (*infra*), as he was the first of a succession of eldest sons of the family for whom Cumstoun (or 'Twynholm', the name of the barony)[9] both became the residence[10] and gave them their designation. Indeed, Sir John Kennedy was still styled 'of Twinam' for a while after his father's death early in 1501, before he took formal possession of Blairquhan.[11] He is last mentioned in 1508, when he founded and endowed a chapel in honour of St. Ninian in the barony of Myretoun.[12]

The present castle, which stands on an outcrop on rising ground above the confluence of the River Dee and Tarff Water, has a commanding view over the beginning of the Dee estuary and the river crossing at Tongland. It has already been suggested that the rectangular enclosure, within which it stands, may belong to an earlier stronghold on the site; but without excavation this cannot be established, nor whether it was used to form any part of the later barmkin.

Only the SW half of the **CASTLE** survives, the NE end having fallen long ago. It is oblong in plan, measures 37ft 6in by 27ft 8in over walls 5ft 9in thick, and comprised four storeys and presumably an attic. Nothing survives of the NE end, apart from the overgrown foundations, and there is no evidence of either an entrance or a stair, which must have been somewhere in the missing portion, with the entrance possibly at first floor level. None of the floors was vaulted, the socket holes for the floor joists being clearly visible in the surviving section of the NW wall. The masonry is local Silurian rubble, with sandstone quoins and dressings. The arrises of the original windows are boldly chamfered – a feature that would tend to confirm a date generally *c*.1500 – and are provided with socket holes for iron grilles, now missing.

In the surviving portions of the basement walls, there is one ruinous slit window in the SW wall and another, restored one in the SE wall. Both have steps in their sills. There are no gun-loops. On the floor above, which was presumably the great hall, there is a large window at the S end of the SW wall and another in the SE wall. The former, which has splayed ingos, is original, while the latter has at some period been widened.

The second floor has a fireplace in the middle of the SW wall, with a small window high up on either side. The fireplace itself is missing. There is also a larger window in the SE wall, which has parallel-sided ingos and a segmental scoinson arch, all of well cut ashlar, and a matching window opposite in the NW wall.

All that survives on the third floor is one large window, now blocked, at the N end of the SW wall. There was presumably a corbelled-out parapet above, but nothing of this has survived.

In 1504/5, Sir John Kennedy of Blairquhan gave the lands and barony of Twyname, with the castle and fortalice, the lands of Blairquhan and many other lands to his eldest son, Sir Gavin Kennedy.[13] Sir John reserved the free tenement of these lands for himself and a third share for his spouse, except for the lands of Cumystoun and the third share of the castle of Cumystoun, together with the £10 lands of Over and Nether Cumystoun and the £10 lands of Camplew and Glengap, all in the barony of Twyname, which he gave unreservedly to his son for his upkeep. Sir Gavin was succeeded in 1522 by his brother James, who was eventually succeeded by his grandson John. But al-

Fig. 188 Cumstoun Castle: view from the W.

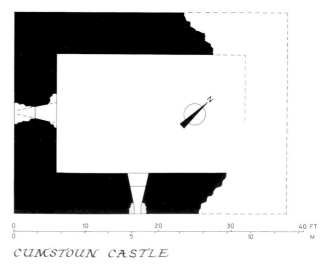

CUMSTOUN CASTLE

Fig. 189 Cumstoun Castle: plan of surviving SW end.

though it is probable that John's father, Gilbert Kennedy, apparent of Blairquhan, also had possession of Cumstoun up to the time of his death, sometime after 1542, no confirmation of this has been found.

John Kennedy had a Crown charter of his grandfather's estates, including the lands and barony of Twyname, with the castle, all of which were erected into the barony of Blairquhan, in 1550/1, whilst reserving the free tenement to his grandfather;[14] but it was not until a few weeks before his grandfather's death in 1553 that he was infeft in 'the lands and barony of Twynem', 'at the principal messuage of the barony called Comstoune'.[15] At that time he was still a minor.[16] John eventually married Margaret Keith, daughter of William, Earl Marischal, to whom in 1569, as part of the marriage contract, he granted a liferent of the lands of the manor of Cumstoun, with the tower and fortalice, and various other lands in the barony of Twynholm.[17] Four years later Kennedy unlawfully appropriated the teinds due to the abbey of Holyroodhouse from the lands and parish of Twynholm. As there were no movable crops that could be apprized in compensation, the Crown, in 1575, granted to Adam Bothwell, Bishop of Orkney and Commendator of Holyroodhouse, an annualrent of £19:12s from the lands of Cumstoun.[18] Then, in 1588/9, Kennedy gave the barony of Twynholm to William Maclellan of Gelston in exchange for the barony of Remiston in Wigtownshire.[19] Maclellan did not live in the castle himself, and for some years it was leased to the Scottish poet laureate, Alexander Montgomerie. It is said to have been here, c.1595, that Montgomerie composed his celebrated poem 'The Cherrie and the Slae'.[20] 'Kumstoun' is shown on Pont's map around that time.[21]

On the death of William Maclellan without issue in 1605, his estates passed to his uncle, Sir Thomas Maclellan,[22] who the following year received a new Crown charter of the lands and barony of Gelston, with 'the castle of Compstoun as the principal messuage'.[23] Then in 1607 Sir Thomas disponed the estates to Sir William Maclellan of Auchlane, whilst reserving for himself the liferent.[24] Sir William, however, seems to have got into financial difficulties, for, instead of retaining the '£50 lands and barony of Twynham, with the castle', in 1608 he granted them in feu-ferme to John Hay, Clerk Depute of Edinburgh;[25] and four years later Hay received a Crown charter of the lands.[26]

There is no evidence that Hay ever held Twynholm other than as payment for outstanding debts, and in 1614 he sold the barony to Sir Robert Maclellan of Bombie, who received a Crown charter of the lands, incorporating them into the barony of Twynholm, with the castle of Cumstoun as the principal messuage.[27] The property then remained with Sir Robert until 1624, when, having got himself seriously into debt, he wadset the estates of Bombie, Twynholm, Cumstoun and others to John Henryson, son and heir of Sir Robert Henryson of Tunygask.[28] He subsequently spent most of his time in Ireland, where he possessed several estates and assisted the Crown in the 'plantation' of Ulster. He was ultimately rewarded in 1633 by being raised to the peerage as 1st Baron Kirkcudbright.[29] He died in 1639.

Sir Robert was succeeded by his nephew, Thomas Maclellan, who became 2nd Lord Kirkcudbright. Thomas succeeded in paying off many of the estate's debts, and in 1642 received a new Crown charter of the lands and barony of Twynholm, *alias* Campstoun, with the castle of Twynholm, *alias* Campstoun, the lands and barony of Bombie, and various other lands.[30] These lands were now incorporated into the barony and lordship of Kirkcudbright, for which the castle of Kirkcudbright was to be the principal messuage.

Thomas died without issue in 1647, when the title and estates passed to his cousin John Maclellan, who became 3rd Lord Kirkcudbright. Like his uncle the 1st Lord, he was soon in financial difficulties, so that once again the estates had to be mortgaged. There was a whole succession of wadsets from 1653 to 1656,[31] and when he died in 1665 his creditors seized the whole property, leaving his son, the young 4th Lord Kirkcudbright, with nothing.

The barony of Twynholm and Cumstoun Castle thus passed to Sir David Dunbar of Baldoon, who had been granted a wadset of the estates in 1655.[32] He was created a baronet in 1664.[33] Dying without surviving male issue, he was succeeded in 1686 by his granddaughter, Mary, who five years later married Lord Basil Hamilton, brother of the 4th Duke of Hamilton; and in 1695 Lord Basil had sasine of Baldoon and the other estates.[34] On his death in 1701, he was succeeded by his son Basil, who took part in the 1715 Jacobite rebellion, was taken prisoner and sentenced to death, with the forfeiture of his estates. He was later reprieved, and the forfeiture rescinded, and subsequently he served as Provost of Kirkcudbright and Member of Parliament for the Stewartry.[35] Meanwhile, in 1725, to save the estates for the family, his mother, Lady Mary Hamilton, claimed her late grandfather's estates of Baldoon, Cumstoun and Lochfergus, and in 1725 succeeded in obtaining possession.[36] Basil died in 1742, and was succeeded by his eldest son, Dunbar Hamilton.

Two years later, Dunbar succeeded his great-uncle as 4th Earl of Selkirk and took the surname of Douglas; but it was not until after the death of his grandmother, Lady Mary, in 1760, that he formally succeeded to the estates of Baldoon and Cumstoun. He later served as Lord Lieutenant of the Stewartry and as a Representative Peer for Scotland. On his death in 1799, he was succeeded by his youngest, but only surviving son, Thomas, who became 5th Earl of Selkirk. Thomas decided not to keep the estate of Cumstoun, and in 1802 sold it to Adam Maitland of Dundrennan.[37]

Maitland subsequently employed Thomas Hamilton, a noted Edinburgh architect, to design a new mansion-house at Cumstoun, just below the old castle. It was completed in 1828,[38] and has been the home of the Maitlands ever since. The house was modified and enlarged by the architects Kinnear and Peddie in 1890 and 1896.[39]

It is not known when the old castle was abandonned as a residence. In 1794 it was described as 'the remains of an old building'.[40] If the NE end had not already fallen, it certainly had by the time the New Statistical Account was published in 1845,[41] and it has remained very much the same ever since. It is known to have been occupied by a tenant – Alexander Montgomerie – as early as c.1590, and is unlikely ever again to have been occupied by one of its lairds.

1   Bain II, No.810.
2   Ibid, No.823, p.198.
3   RCAHMS 1914, No.469.
4   Reid, R. C. 'Cumstoun Castle', *TDGAS*, 3rd Ser., XVIII, 416.
5   The Twynholms of that Ilk are on record until c.1340, when they too disappeared (Reid, *op. cit.*, 411).
6   ERS VII, 312.
7   RMS II, No.1336.
8   Ibid, No.2433. Reid, *op. cit.*, says he was so designated in 1488 (p.413), but this has not been confirmed.
9   Sir John apparently only held the southern portion of the barony of Twynholm, while the Crown retained the rest (See ERS XII, 654).
10   He bought meal from Senwick mill, further down the Dee estuary, in 1486 (ERS IX, 382), and later took a lease on the mill (ERS XI, 454).
11   ERS XI, 339*; RSS I, No.685. He did not, in fact, get sasine of Twynam until 1502 (ERS XII, 711), but was styled 'of Twynane' as early as 1500 (ERS XI, 454).

12   RMS II, No.3245.
13   Ibid, No.2829.
14   Laing Charters, Nos.574, 575; RMS IV, No.580.
15   Laing Charters, No.609.
16   RSS IV, No.2069. After his grandfather's death the right of his marriage was
     given to the Earl of Argyle.
17   RMS IV, No.1900.
18   Ibid, No.2418.
19   RMS V, No.1636. The contract was apparently drawn up in 1584 (Torrance,
     206).
20   DNB, 1404; Ordnance Gazetteer, 282.
21   Blaeu, 66, 'The Steuartrie of Kircubright, The most easterlie part of Gallo-
     way'.
22   Torrance, 207.
23   RMS VI, No.1693.
24   Ibid, No.1914.
25   Ibid, No.2169.
26   RMS VII, No.707.
27   Ibid, No.1059. A Crown charter granted to Josias Stewart of Bonnyton in
     1618 mistakenly still includes the lands of Twynholm and the castle of
     Cumstoun in the estates of the Kennedys of Blairquhan (RMS VII, No.1758).
28   RMS VIII, No.660. There was a further wadset of the barony of Twynholm
     in 1635 (RMS IX, No.336).
29   Scots PeerageV, 266.
30   RMS IX, No.1049.
31   RMS X, Nos. 178, 300, 380, 469.
32   Ibid, No.380.
33   RMS XI, No.672.
34   M'Kerlie I, 388.
35   Ibid, 388-9; Burke Peerage 1959, 1035, 'Hamilton & Brandon'.
36   Scots Peerage VII, 520; M'Kerlie I, 389.
37   Maitland titles.
38   Maitland family archives.
39   Ibid; Gifford, 206.
40   Stat Acct XV, 89.
41   NSA IV, 40.

Fig. 190 Dalswinton Tower: NW corner tower, showing entrance
doorway and gun-loops.

24.   DALSWINTON TOWER
(5m NNW Dumfries)   (NX945840)

The Romans were the first to appreciate the strategic
importance of Dalswinton, when, c.82 AD, Agricola built a major fort here from which to direct his campaigns up Nithsdale
and into SW Scotland.[1] This was later enlarged, before being
abandonned c.105 AD; and there were no less than five other
forts and marching-camps, of varying size and date, constructed
adjacent to this site before the Romans finally left Scotland and
retreated south.[2]

After the Dark Ages, Dalswinton again rose to prominence, and by the middle of the 13th century the lands were held
by Sir John Comyn.[3] It may well have been he who founded the
castle that subsequently played an important part in the War of
Independence. Nothing is known of its layout, but it stood on an
outcrop of rock washed by the river Nith on the W side[4] and
further defended by a marsh to the N, while strong earthworks
completed the outer defences on the other sides. In 1291/2 Henry
de Boyville was paid for keeping the castles of Dumfries,
Wigtown, Kirkcudbright and Dalswinton,[5] and in 1302 the garrison included four men-at-arms of Sir John de Botetourte.[6] In
1309 Lord Clifford, Warden of the Scottish Marches, was commanded to furnish the castles of Caerlaverock, Dumfries,
Dalswinton and Tibbers with men and provisions,[7] and two years
later there is an account for provisions paid for by the King's
receiver in Carlisle while Thomas Gerard was constable.[8] c.1313
the castle was taken and burnt by Bruce,[9] and, having been forfeited by the Comyns, was later granted by him to Sir Walter
Stewart, fourth son of Sir John Stewart of Bonkyl.[10] Meanwhile,
in 1319, the English again supplied provisions to Sir John Comyn
for 'his castle of Dalswynton'.[11] The castle was in the hands of

the English again in 1335,[12] and was repaired by them in 1348.[13]
In 1356 Roger Kirkpatrick took it again by storm.[14] After this it
may never have been fully repaired.

Sir Walter Stewart of Dalswinton left an only daughter
and heiress, Marion, who in 1396 had married her cousin Sir
John Stewart, elder son and heir of Sir William Stewart, a younger
son of Sir Alexander Stewart of Darnley.[15] Their common ancestor Alexander, 4th High Steward of Scotland, had been granted
the lands of Garlies, in Galloway, by Alexander III in 1263,[16]
and Garlies had passed by descent to Sir Walter.[17] But while Sir
Walter at first appears to have looked upon Dalswinton as his
principal residence, he was the last to do so. With Dalswinton
largely in ruins after the English depredations, either Sir Walter
or his son-in-law decided sometime c.1400 to move their principal residence to Garlies.[18] Later references to Dalswinton refer
only to its former strength.

The last of the family to reside at Dalswinton was John
Stewart (fl.1477), eldest son of Sir Alexander Stewart, 6th of
Garlies and Dalswinton, who died in his father's lifetime.[19] Al-
though the castle at Dalswinton appears on Pont's map of
Nithsdale c.1595,[20] it had long since ceased to be of importance.
It played no part in the battle of Dalswinton, fought between the
Scots and English 'near to the old castell of Dauswinton' in
1548,[21] and in an English military survey c.1564-5, the emphasis is very much in the past tense: 'The Oulde Castell of
Dawsynton . . . It haitht been in oulde tymes a notable strength'.[22]
The last vestiges of the castle were still standing in 1792, and
are illustrated by Cardonnel. The etching shows massive pieces
of broken walling, which were elsewhere recorded as having
been 12ft thick, and in one place 14ft thick, with 'bits of burnt
wood' still clinging to them.[23]

It is possible that a new fortalice was built at Dalswinton
during the closing decades of the 16th century, before the present

'tower' was built, although there is no tangible evidence of one.[24] It would, however, be surprising if the Stewarts of Garlies did not have a residence of some sort on such an important estate at a time when tower-houses were becoming commonplace for even the smallest laird; and the records of the time, although arguably using fairly standard forms of legal terminology, persist in referring to the 'tower', 'fortalice', and 'manor-place'. To what were they referring? In 1575, for example, the Crown gifted the nonentry of the lands and barony of Dalswinton ('that is, the lands of Dalswintoun, with tower, fortalice, manor-place', etc.) to Sir James Douglas of Drumlanrig until the entry of the heir.[25] Then in 1617, Sir Alexander Stewart, Lord Garlies, sold half the lands and barony of Dalswinton (later called 'Mains of Dalswinton'), with 'the castle, tower and fortalice', under reversion to Francis Irving, member of parliament for, and merchant burgess of, Dumfries.[26] In 1624 Sir Alexander, now Earl of Galloway, sold his superior's right in the reversion to John Rome, merchant burgess of Dumfries, who received a crown charter incorporating his lands of 'Maynes of Dalswinton', with the castle, etc., into the new barony of Dalswinton-Rome.[27] Shortly afterwards, he gave Francis Irving, now Provost of Dumfries, a new title to his reversion,[28] but nine months later, in November 1625, he redeemed it to acquire full possession of the property.[29]

It was apparently soon after this that John Rome built Dalswinton Tower, or the 'Old House' as it was often later known. A stone bearing the date 1626 and the initials IR and EM, for John Rome and his spouse Elizabeth Maxwell, is believed to have come from it.[30] Defence being no longer a prime consideration, the new tower was built on a more convenient site, on low ground some 150 yards E of the castle.

The '**TOWER**' was a transitional building, combining the defensive characteristics of a late **Z**–plan structure, with the comforts of a more modern central block. Built of roughly squared and coursed red sandstone rubble, the main building measured 38ft 3in from E to W by 25ft from N to S, over walls 4ft 3in thick, and comprised a vaulted, subterranean basement, two full storeys above the ground, and apparently a garret with

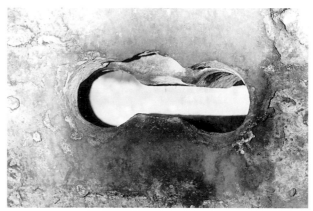

Fig. 192 Dalswinton: inside of dumb-bell gun-loop. (See Fig. 32).

dormer windows.[31] Only the basement has survived; it was the kitchen. The only part of the building to have survived above the ground is the NW corner tower, which houses the wheel-stair that served all the floors. It is 15ft 2in in diameter overall, with walls averaging 2ft 6in in thickness. It also contains the entrance to the building, with its finely moulded surround of a QER with cavetto and quirked-outer-bead and, on the inside, the customary double rebate for two doors. But unlike the doors of earlier towers, the outer one at Dalswinton is on record as having been 'of wrought iron' and the inner one 'traced with broad iron bars fastened with iron rivets'.[32] On either side of the entrance, and also on the S side of the tower, are well moulded, horizontal, dumb-bell gun-loops; and there was no doubt a fourth one on the W side, where there is now a later window. These were not just ornamental, as they were clearly intended for use if the need arose, giving cover to the adjacent walls of the main block and much of the ground beyond. Above the entrance, there is a moulded drip-stone.

At first floor level, the stair tower has a small window with an elaborately moulded surround facing NW, and opposite to it two adjacent doorways. The more northerly of these, which

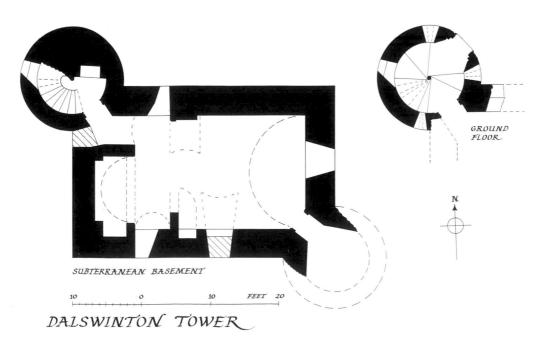

SUBTERRANEAN BASEMENT

GROUND FLOOR

N

10   0   10   FEET 20

DALSWINTON TOWER

Fig. 191 Dalswinton Tower: plan of subterranean basement and ground floor entrance and stair tower.

is only 1ft 10½in wide and now blocked, apparently gave access to a mural cupboard or passage within the thickness of the main block's N wall, while the other doorway, which is 3ft 3in wide, led directly into the main block. Higher up the outside wall, at the level of the second floor, a moulded string-course encircles the tower, and some two feet above this there is a continuous corbel-course, which appears to have been the wall-head.

Descending the stair to the basement, there is a large recess, 2ft 11in wide, 2ft 10in high and 1ft 8in deep, below the stair itself. It is only 1ft 8in above the ground. Such recesses are believed to have served as seats. From here, a short passage with a doorway led into the kitchen at the W end of the basement. This was equipped with a vast fireplace, 9ft 9in wide and 4ft 7in deep, against the W wall, which was separated from the rest of this part of the kitchen by a finely wrought arch of ashlar voussoirs.[33] This end of the kitchen was separated from the larger, E end of the basement by a dividing wall, with a door at the N end.[34] On both sides of this division there was generous provision for light and ventilation, quite unlike earlier towers. However, because the kitchen was below ground level, the splayed window recesses had to be angled steeply upwards towards the outside. Another doorway in the SE corner of the basement gave access to the other corner tower; but what is left of this has caved in, and its circular shape can only be deduced at present from an old plan of the house.[35]

At some later date, an oblong addition was built running N from the W side of the stair tower. It does not appear to have connected directly with the older building, and there is evidence that it was only one storey high. Another, larger building stood to the N of this.[36] It may have served as stables.

Following the death of John Rome in 1637, his son and heir, John, granted the lands of Dalswinton-Rome, as it was now known, to Archibald Douglas, a younger son of the Earl of Queensberry, and in 1642 this grant was assigned to James Douglas of Mouswald.[37] Ten years later the lands passed to John Maxwell, advocate.[38] He was succeeded by Hugh Maxwell, probably a son, who was a Commissioner of Supply for Nithsdale and Dumfries in 1689 and 1690.[39] In 1689, he was also one of the commissioners appointed to oversee burgh elections in the county of Dumfries.[40] He may have been the 'Laird of Dalswinton' who was a Commissioner of Supply in 1696 and 1698,[41] as it is not known precisely when he died.[42] He was succeeded by George Maxwell of Dalswinton, who was a Commissioner of Supply in 1704.[43] The Maxwells remained in possession of the estate until 1785, when it was bought by Patrick Miller.[44] However, Sir Robert Dalzell of Glenae evidently had some feudal claim on Dalswinton in 1670, for in that year he was granted a 'charter of recognition' of the barony.[45]

Patrick Miller cleared part of the old castle site and there built the present mansion. He also built a new village on the public road to the N to serve the estate. It is said that it was he who demolished most of Dalswinton Tower,[46] possibly to supply materials for the buildings. His son sold Dalswinton c.1830.

The new owner of the estate, James Macalpine-Leny, served as Convenor of Dumfries County Council and a Justice of the Peace for the county.[47] He died in 1867, and was succeeded by his eldest surviving son, William, who had served as a Captain in the 15th Hussars and was later a Justice of the Peace and Deputy-Lieutenant for Dumfriesshire.[48] His eldest son, Robert, who succeeded in 1905, served in both the South African War and World War I, rising to the rank of Lieutenant-Colo-

nel and being awarded the DSO in 1918.[49] The following year he sold the Dalswinton estate to David Landale,[50] whose family have held it ever since.

1 Frere, 127, 136, 143, Plate 1b.
2 Maxwell, 51-3, 69-70, 81, 127.
3 NSA IV, 56.
4 The river has since changed course, and is now some 700 yards to the W.
5 Bain II, No.580. Henry was probably the son of Sir William de Boyville, who was the previous Keeper of Dumfries, Wigtown and Kirkcudbright, and who died in 1291.
6 Ibid, No.1324. Sir John de Botetourte had been at the siege of Caerlaverock in 1300 (Nicolas, 32-3), and was later keeper of Dumfries and Lochmaben castles.
7 Nicolas, xvi.
8 Bain, III, No.278.
9 Fraser 1885, II, 603.
10 RMS I, App.2, No.323; Burke Peerage 1959, 910, 'Galloway, Earl of'.
11 Bain III, No.646.
12 Smith, A.C. 'The Estate of Dalswinton', TDGAS, IX, 215.
13 Webster, B. 'The English Occupations of Dumfriesshire in the fourteenth Century', TDGAS, XXXV, 74.
14 Fraser 1885, I, 221; Cardonnel: 'Dalswinton Castle'.
15 Scots Peerage IV, 145, 149.
16 M'Kerlie IV, 362, 375.
17 RMS I, App.2, No.1260.
18 Sir Walter Stewart, 1st of Dalswinton, was granted the lands of Garlies by his nephew, the Earl of Moray, early in the 14th century (RMS I, App.2, No.1260).
19 Burke Peerage 1959, 910, 'Galloway, Earl of'.
20 Pont MS. No.35 in National Library of Scotland.
21 Irving 1907, 34.
22 Armstrong 1883, cx.
23 NSA IV, 59.
24 A fortalice is said to have been recorded here in 1542 (Gifford, 216).
25 RSS VII, No.288.
26 GRS XVII, 93.
27 RMS VIII, No.703.
28 PRS Dumfries II, 143.
29 GRS XVIII, 247.
30 Smith, TDGAS, IX, op. cit., 218. John Rome and Elizabeth Maxwell were married in 1622.
31 A thumbnail sketch was shown on a painting by Alexander Nasmyth (1758-1840) (Smith, A.C. 'Dalswinton before Patrick Miller', TDGAS, XVIII, 188).
32 Smith, TDGAS, XVIII, op. cit., 187.
33 Dalswinton is credited with a total of 11 fireplaces in 1690 (Adamson, D. 'The Hearth Tax', TDGAS, 3rd Ser., XLVIII, 143).
34 The RCAHMS report refers to a double wall, but this may be a mis-interpretation (RCAHMS 1920, No.338).
35 Smith, TDGAS, XVIII, op. cit., 187-8. Although the surviving walling might suggest a square tower at this corner, old plans show it to have been round like the one at the NW corner.
36 Ibid.
37 RMS IX, No.1202. The superiority of the rest of the Dalswinton estate evidently rested with the Earl of Queensberry. In 1681 parliament granted the 3rd Earl a ratification of the Earldom, Lordship and Regality of Drumlanrig, which included the lands and barony of Dalswinton and Conheath (excepting so much thereof as was sold by the late Earl of Galloway to the late James Rome) now to be known as the free barony of Dalswinton (APS VIII, 372).
38 PRS Dumfries I, 140.
39 APS IX, 70, 139.
40 Ibid, 51.
41 Ibid, X, 29, 131.
42 He appears to have been alive in January 1696 (PRS Dumfries II (1672-1702), Index, 259).
43 APS XI, 142.
44 Smith, TDGAS, IX, op. cit., 219.
45 Scots Peerage II, 409.
46 Smith, TDGAS, XVIII, op. cit., 187.
47 Burke L. G. 1972, 266, 'Macalpine-Downie of Appin'.
48 Ibid.
49 Ibid.
50 Gifford, 216.

25.   DRUMCOLTRAN TOWER
(8m SW Dumfries)   (NX869682)

Drumcoltran originally formed part of the lands of Kirkgunzeon, granted by Uchtred, Lord of Galloway, to the monks of Holm Cultram Abbey in Cumbria c.1170.[1] A little over a century later, with the onset of the War of Independence, the abbey forfeit its lands north of the Border for siding against the Scots. Kirkgunzeon thus passed to the crown, and in 1367 David II granted it to Sir John Heryz of Terregles as a further reward for past services.[2] Thereafter, Terregles and Kirkgunzeon became the principal seats of the Herries family.

The lands of Drumcoltran first appear as a separate entity in 1501, when Andrew, 2nd Lord Herries, sold the 3 merk land of Duncowterane, in the barony of Kirkgonzeane, to Robert Vaus, burgess of Edinburgh, to be held of him in albe-ferme.[3] This was confirmed by crown charter in 1529.[4] The superiority remained with the Lords Herries until 1550, when it passed by marriage to Sir John Maxwell, Master of Maxwell and later, jure uxoris, 4th Lord Herries.[5] It was sometime before 1547 that Drumcoltran came into the possession of Edward Maxwell, second son of Edward Maxwell, 1st of Hills,[6] for in 1548 'Eduerdi Maxwell de Drymcoltrane' was included in the list of those granted remission for having assisted the English the previous year.[7] Nothing more is heard of him until October 1574, when he witnessed a charter granting certain lands and fishings in Annandale to Lord Maxwell.[8] The following month, he was one of those named by Lord Maxwell to resolve disputes with Johnston of that Ilk; and he also stood surety, with Robert Maxwell of Cowhill, that none of Johnston's friends or servants attending the Stewart Court of Annandale would come to any harm.[9] It was apparently Edward who built the tower. Standing on a south-facing slope of gently rising ground, it was not a position of any natural strength, but, like Hills and Kirkgunzeon,[10] it lay along the strategically important route from Dumfries to Dalbeattie.

Contrary to some accounts,[11] which suggest that the **TOWER** was originally a simple oblong block to which a wing was later added, there is no doubt that Drumcoltran has always been an **L**–plan tower-house. In this, it has certain affinities with the Maxwells' tower at Kirkconnell;[12] and although Drumcoltran has also undergone various changes over the centuries, the original layout is still clearly discernible. The tower is complete apart from the upper floors, which, having become rotten, were removed early in the 20th century. It comprises a main block of three storeys and a garret, aligned NE-SW, with a parapet-walk around the wall-head, and a stair wing with the re-entrant angle facing N: the former measures 34ft 3in by 26ft 10in over walls 5ft thick, while the wing, which has a width of 15ft 2in, extends 8ft 4in towards the NW. The masonry consists of small pieces of granite and Silurian rubble with simple gritstone and sandstone dressings. The corners of the tower are unique; at basement level they are rounded off with a small radius, while for the upper floors they are constructed as a clean-cut chamfer built up from small slices of Silurian rubble. No trace of the original barmkin now survives, but there is one jamb of a doorway, some 7ft high, built into the NE wall of the main block, which may date from that period.

The entrance to the tower is in the re-entrant angle of the wing. It has simple, rounded arrises, and on the inside is provided with the usual double rebate for a wooden door and inner yett, reinforced with an iron drawbar.[13] Above the entrance there is an empty armorial panel and, immediately above that, a stone bearing the inscription 'CELA SECRETA LOQVERE PAVCA: VERAX ESTO A VINO: CAVE: MEME[N]TO: MORI: MISERICORS: ESTO'.[14] The entrance admits to a vestibule, which leads to the wheel-stair, 8ft 8in in diameter, in the wing and the vaulted basement of the main block. The vestibule is provided with a small, splayed gun-loop on the NW side, while beneath the stair may still be seen some of the original flagstones. The basement itself has been greatly altered: large windows have been inserted in the SE and NW walls;[15] a window at

Fig. 193 Drumcoltran Tower: view from SE, before the later house (left) was partly demolished.

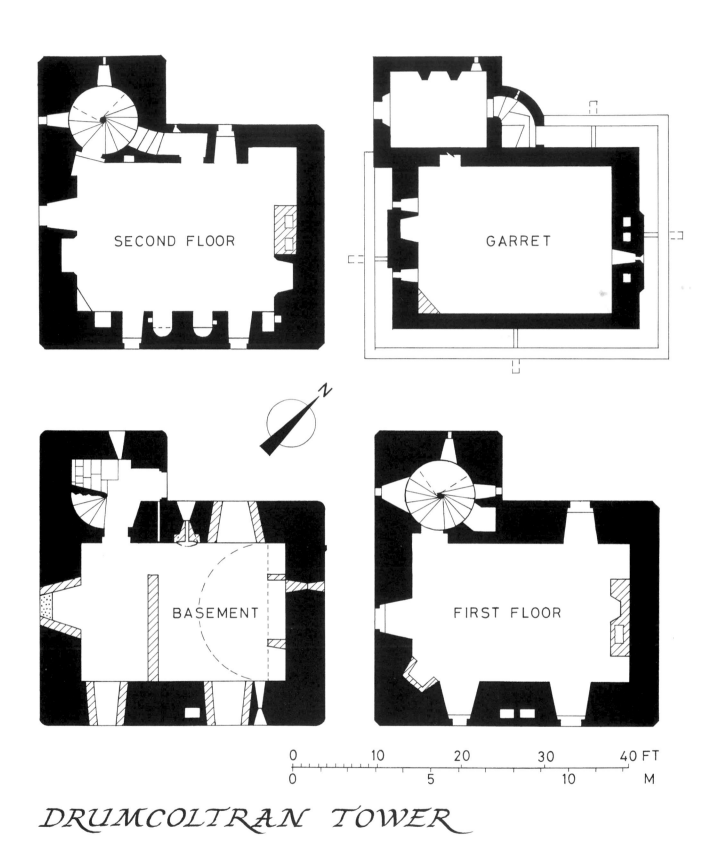

SECOND FLOOR

GARRET

BASEMENT

FIRST FLOOR

0   10   20   30   40 FT

0   5   10   M

DRUMCOLTRAN TOWER

Fig. 194 Drumcoltran Tower: plans.

Fig. 195 Drumcoltran: empty armorial panel with quotation above.

Fig. 196 Drumcoltran: mural passage leading to
E chamber on the second floor.

the SW end has been opened out and converted into a doorway,
now blocked, to connect with the adjacent, later house; and the
chamber itself has at some time been partitioned to form two
rooms. At the NE end there is a large fireplace, 7ft 4in wide, and
in the NW wall a slop-sink, which discharges through a small,
splayed gun-loop – similar to the one in the wing – that originally covered the entrance. The fireplace has a small
roll-and-hollow moulding on the jambs and a straight lintel.
These features date from when the basement was used as a
kitchen, and form part of a 17th or 18th century conversion. The
only original feature surviving in the basement is a small
gun-loop, or ventilation slit, at the E end of the SE wall; but
another blocked gun-loop is discernible in the outside wall behind the fireplace, and no doubt at least some of the later windows and doors occupy the positions of others.

The first floor was originally a single chamber, serving
as the hall. It has two large windows on the SE side and one
each on the NW and SW sides, all of which were fitted with iron
grilles. The only window that was originally smaller is the W
window on the SE side. The remaining end accommodated a
large fireplace between two arched recesses. When the basement was later converted into a kitchen, the fireplace on this
floor was greatly reduced in size to make room for the kitchen
chimney;[16] and in the 19th century, when this room was subdivided into three,[17] a second, smaller fireplace was inserted across
the S corner. Just outside the doorway to this chamber there is a
large mural recess in the NW wall; it measures 2ft 10in wide, 2ft
9in deep and 3ft 7in high. Although there is a similar recess at
Kirkconnell, their precise purpose is still uncertain.

The second floor was always divided into two rooms,
each of which was provided with a fireplace in its gable wall,
two windows and a garderobe on the SE side. The fireplace at
the NE end retains the original QER-moulding on its surround.
The garderobes shared a common drain, discharging at ground
level. Access to the SW room was directly from the wheel-stair,
while the other chamber was reached by way of a straight stair

and passage within the NW wall.[18] Each room also had a large
open-aumbry, or recess, in the SE wall. In addition, the one in
the NE chamber had a further, inner aumbry, or cupboard, within
its left jamb. Another feature of the NE chamber is a large mural recess within the NE and NW walls in the N corner.[19] This
was provided with a lamp-shelf but no window, which suggests
it may have served as part of an inner, more private room for the
owner.

The wheel-stair rises as far as the garret. This is a simple chamber that is largely contained within the roof of the main
block, but has no direct access to the parapet-walk outside. It
has a fireplace at the SW end and two small windows high up in
the gable on either side, while in the opposite gable there is a
third window. The gables are now capped with straight skews
in place of the usual crow-steps. The roof rises to a maximum
height of 50ft above the ground.

The arrangement at the head of the wheel-stair is reminiscent of Kirkconnell, except that, instead of separate stairs to
the parapet and watch-chamber, there is a single stair that rises
straight up the NW wall to the parapet. Access to the chamber
above is then gained via a stair-turret continuing within the
re-entrant angle. This turret, which formerly had a conical roof,[20]
is not supported in the usual way on corbel courses, but on a
continuously moulded projection of rubble.[21] The parapet-walk
extends around the main block on all sides, except where it abuts
the wing. It is paved with sandstone flags, while the parapet
itself, which is supported on individual, single-stage corbels, is
made of rubble and capped with a plain sandstone coping. The
top of the parapet is 42ft above the ground. The watch-chamber
at the top of the wing is entered on the NE side. It measures 11ft
8in by 9ft 6in internally, and is provided with a small fire and a
slit-window on the NW side and another window, which was
later enlarged, on the SW side. The room has a wooden floor.

sage. The builder is not known. Sadly, most of it was demolished in 1990, and the remainder incorporated, almost unrecognizably, in a new cattle court.

Drumcoltran is said to have remained in the possession of the Irvings until 1799, when it was acquired by John Hynd.[36] In 1819 it was bought by James Heron of Duncow, and in 1875 Alfred Constable-Maxwell of Terregles bought it back for his family after a lapse of almost 200 years.[37] By then, both the tower and adjoining house had long been in use, first as a farm-house, and then to accommodate farm labourers. It was finally abandoned as a residence c.1900, probably after the present farm-house was built in 1899. Later, the tower was used as a farm store for a while, before being taken into care by the State in 1951. It is now under the custodianship of Historic Scotland.

Fig. 197 Drumcoltran Tower: view from the N.

Edward Maxwell's son and heir, George, appears to have succeeded his father before 1598, when he was a cautioner for Lord Maxwell, but it was not until 1609 that he was formally infeft in Drumcoltran.[22] The Maxwells continued to live here until 1679, when Joanna and Mariota, daughters and co-heiresses of John Maxwell, 4th of Drumcoltran, were served heirs portioners to their father.[23]

Drumcoltran subsequently passed to John Irving, senior, a merchant burgess and later bailie of Dumfries.[24] In 1668 he and his wife, Agnes Carlyle, were granted an annualrent of 160 merks out of the 40 shilling lands of Drumcoltran by Agnes, Margaret and Janet Carlyle, heirs portioners of William Carlyle, late bailie in Dumfries.[25] The following year Lord Maxwell had sasine as superior of the lands and barony of Kirkgunzeon.[26] According to M'Kerlie, the foresaid John Irving had principal sasine of Drumcoltran in 1675, following an apprizing of the lands, and this was confirmed in 1676 and 1678.[27] It was not, however, until 1690 that John was first styled 'of Drumcoltran', when he was appointed a Commissioner of Supply for the Stewartry of Kirkcudbright.[28] He must then have acquired outright possession, taken up residence, and soon after retired from business, as the following year he is described as 'formerly merchant'.[29] His sons George and Robert had sasine in 1691, but it was his eldest son, John, who succeeded him in 1705.[30] The latter John died without issue, when Drumcoltran passed to Christopher Irving, son of the late Thomas Irving, chirurgeon in Dublin.[31] Christopher had sasine in 1713.[32] Three years later, Christopher's brother Thomas had sasine;[33] and in 1750 Thomas was succeeded by his sister Agnes, who married Captain John Maxwell, younger of Cardoness.[34] Captain Maxwell inherited Cardoness from his father two years later.

It was around this time that a new house was built on the site, immediately W of the old tower. It was a simple dwelling of two storeys with gabled roof.[35] The two buildings stood only 4ft 8in apart, and were connected at ground level by a short pas-

1   M'Kerlie IV, 229; Gillespie, J.E. 'Notes on the parish of Kirkgunzeon', TDGAS, 2nd Ser., XXIV, 177.
2   RMS I, No.282 & Appendix II, No.1574.
3   RMS III, No.834.
4   Ibid.
5   Stell 1986, 97.
6   Ibid.
7   RSS III, 430.
8   RMS IV, No.2311.
9   RPC II, 422-3.
10 See 'Corra Castle'.
11 RCAHMS 1914, No.276; Stell 1986, 97.
12 Drumcoltran has been compared with Carsluith Castle, further west, but Carsluith is different in that its original plan was a simple oblong, to which a wing was later added.
13 Unusually, the drawbar can only have been of iron, as its slot is a mere 3½in wide by 2½in high. It is 4ft 10in deep. Iron bars were also used at Isle (q.v.).
14 Keep secrets, speak little, be truthful, avoid wine, remember death, be merciful'. This stone was built into the farmhouse in 1887 (MacGibbon & Ross, II, 85), and only returned to the tower in the 20th century.
15 The latter window was opened up to form a second doorway early in the 20th century, but it has now been restored as a window again.
16 The original relieving arch, spanning the whole chimney, is still visible.
17 The arrangement is shown in RCAHMS 1914, Fig.111.
18 It has been suggested that this mural passage started life as a mural chamber, which was later converted. This is not so. Apart from other considerations, the stairs have massive treads that are built into the original structure (c.f. Kirkconnell).
19 Kirkconnell has a similar arrangement.
20 MacGibbon & Ross II, Fig.550.
21 This is a form of construction commonly used for vaults in Ireland.
22 M'Kerlie IV, 231.
23 Ibid, 232.
24 It has not been established whether Irving of Drumcoltran was directly related to the family of Provost Francis Irving of Dumfries and his descendants, the Irvings of Gribton (See Maxwell-Irving 1968 (III)).
25 GRS XVIII, 308. It is not clear whether the two Agnes Carlyles referred to were the same person.
26 M'Kerlie IV, 232.
27 Ibid.
28 APS IX, 144. When he was elected bailie in 1688, he was designated 'at the Vennelheid' in Dumfries, presumably his town-house (Reid Notes, 'Kennan Notes', 144).
29 PRS Kirkcudbright IV, 711.
30 M'Kerlie IV, 232-3; GRS, LXXXVIII, 62.
31 M'Kerlie IV, 233. Thomas is said to have been a grandson of John Irving, 1st of Drumcoltran, but the relationship is not certain. The said John also had a grandson Alexander Irving, writer in Dumfries, who was served heir to his grandfather in 1717 (Dumfries Burgh Papers, 'Dumfries Burgh Documents, 1710-19', Nos.650, 652).
32 Ibid; PRS Kirkcudbright IX, 28.
33 M'Kerlie IV, 233.
34 Ibid.
35 Stell 1986, 97; M'Kerlie IV, 233.
36 M'Kerlie IV, 233.
37 Ibid.

26.   DUNDEUGH CASTLE
(4m SE Carsphairn)   (NX601880)

The precise location, and identity, of Dundeugh Castle has been a matter of contention. According to the Ordnance Survey, it stood at the confluence of the Water of Deugh and the Polmaddy Burn, where the remains of an L-plan tower, probably dating from the second half of the 16th century, may still be seen; but Pont calls this 'Kars' and shows 'Dungeugh' a little further to the NE, on the slopes of Dundeugh Hill nearer the Water of Ken.[1] M'Kerlie also refers to 'Kars' on the former site, and states that the farmhouse of Dundeugh stood on the site of the castle, where 'a number of hewn stones' were found when the house was built.[2]

Late in the 12th century, the lands of 'Kar', or 'Keresban', which comprised a quarter of the lands of Dalmellington, were leased by Thomas Colville to the abbey of Melrose.[3] The attraction in this remote spot may have been the rich mineral deposits in the surrounding hills, which, like those at Wanlockhead and Leadhills, are believed to have been first worked at an early date.[4] Later, Alan, Lord of Galloway, exchanged Kar with the monks for his lands in the Lammermuirs.[5] Kar was then let to the abbey of Vaudey, in Lincolnshire, another Cistercian house,[6] but in 1223 Vaudey gave the lands back to Melrose on a perpetual lease.[7] Kars subsequently faded into obscurity; apart from the reference on Pont's map, there appears to be no other mention of it in the later Middle Ages.

The lands of Dundeugh are first mentioned in 1492, when 'John Maknacht of Drumgeoucht' sold a quarter of his lands of Clouburn, in Lanarkshire, to Hugh Were, one of his tenants there.[8] The MacNaughts had, however, already been in Galloway for many generations, Gilbert Makenaght having sworn fealty to Edward I in 1296.[9] Then, c.1504, Matthew Maknacht of Dungcich forfeited his goods and was declared a fugitive.[10] He was later pardonned, and in 1515 was granted a respite for his part in the murder of John Dunbar of Mochrum.[11] The MacNaughts continued to reside at Dundeugh until the death of John MacNaught in 1572, when Robert Cannan was granted the non-entry of the 2½ merk lands of Dungeyth, with the walk-mill, and the 20 shilling lands of Mardrochwood, in the barony of Earlstoun, until the entry of John MakNauchtane, younger of Dundeugh.[12] John had succeeded to Dundeugh by 1587, when he sat on an assize,[13] and five years later he is on record as one of the feudal vassals of the lands and barony of Earlstoun, held of Francis the forfeited Earl of Bothwell.[14] In 1597 he was bound over not to harm Lord Ochiltree.[15]

By this time the tower-house already referred to beside the Water of Deugh had been built, and, on both the architectural and historical evidence, there can be little doubt that it was the castle of the MacNaughts of Dundeugh. Not only are the ruins those of a typical 16th century tower-house and not those of an early monastic building, but there is no record of a second stronghold in the area. Perhaps Pont got the names transposed, as he occasionally did elsewhere,[16] and M'Kerlie perpetuated the error, or did the MacNaughts of Dundeugh build their castle at the place traditionally called 'Kars'?

The **CASTLE**, which was built on the L-plan, was protected by the river to the W and by marshland on the other three sides. It comprised a main block measuring 26ft 8in from N to S by 17ft 2in from E to W, with a stair wing 12ft 7in in width projecting from the N end of the W side for some 7ft. Now enclosed by a forestry plantation, it is very ruinous, the best pre-

served section of walling being on the E side, where it reaches a height of about 6ft. The masonry is greywacke rubble. Without excavation the precise thickness of the walls cannot be established.[17] Although there is no longer any evidence of vaulting in the basement, M'Kerlie refers to a surviving 'arch' and adds that c.1825 a second arch could still be seen.[18] These may have been sections of vaulting.

There was also a secondary building to the SW of the castle, which measured 35ft by 21ft 8in and had walls averaging 3ft 3in in thickness.[19]

Roger MacNaught of Dungeuch is recorded in 1630,[20] and in the same year his son John had sasine of the 3 merkland of Dingewche.[21] Then sometime c.1651, when he resigned some other lands,[22] John disposed of the lands of Dundeugh to one William Gordon, who was in residence by 1655.[23] Gordon was a descendant of the Gordons of Lochinvar, and subsequently registered arms recording this fact.[24] It is not clear, however, whether the William who had sasine of Dundeugh in 1674 was the first Gordon of Dundeugh or his son.[25] William fought for the Covenanters at Bothwell Bridge in 1679, for which he was sentenced to forfeiture of life and lands.[26] His lands were subsequently given to Lord Livingstone for disposal,[27] while William disappeared from the scene. A census of the parish of Carsphairn in 1684 gives those living at Dundeugh as Bessie Gordon, Jane Gordon and seven others,[28] while a list of 'disorderly persons' in the parish in the same year includes Bessie Gordon 'of Dindeugh' and her family.[29] Eventually, in 1690, an Act was passed rescinding the forfeiture,[30] and in 1696, the 'Laird [Gordon] of Dundeugh' was appointed a Commissioner of Supply for the Stewartry of Kirkcudbright.[31] By this time, however, the laird – whose name is not given – may no longer have been resident, and the castle may already have been abandonned.

The Gordons of Dundeugh are later found living in Edinburgh, where they may have been for some time. Eventually they got into financial difficulties, and in 1740 the lands were wadset to William Hamilton, late bailie of Edinburgh.[32] The Gordons continued in nominal possession for a while, and in 1751 James Gordon in Edinburgh had sasine;[33] but Hamilton must have obtained possession very soon after, for his son-in-law John West, Clerk to the Secretary of the Board of Customs in Scotland, had sasine the following year, and his son John had sasine in 1771.[34]

By the end of the century, Dundeugh was in the possession of Alexander Birtwhistle.[35] Later in the 19th century the property passed into the hands of William Alexander of Glenhowl, who was still in possession in 1877.[36] He had no issue.[37] The property now belongs to the Forestry Commission.

---

1   Blaeu, 66, 'The Steuartrie of Kircubright, The most easterlie part of Galloway'.
2   M'Kerlie III, 282.
3   Brooke, D 'The Glenkens, 1275-1456', *TDGAS*, 3rd Ser., LIX, 52.
4   Greig 1971, 105; Stat Acct VII, 514. The mines were revived in the 19th century (Sassoon, J 'Lead-Mining at Woodhead, Carsphairn', *TDGAS*, 3rd Ser., XLVI, 170-7).
5   Brooke, *op. cit.*, 52; Easson 1957, 194.
6   Brooke, *op. cit.*, 52. In 1220/1, Henry III ordered the Justiciar of Ireland to allow the monks at Kar, in Galloway, to buy corn, meal and other victuals in Ireland (Bain I, No.795).
7   Easson 1957, 194. For details of Vaudey Abbey, see Victoria County History: Lincoln, 143.
8   RMS II, No.2114.
9   Bain II, 210 (references to Nithsdale and Eastern Galloway were often confused in early records). Gilbert must have been a man of some substance, as he had his own seal (Bain II, 531).

10   ALHT II, 169.
11   RSS I, No.2626.
12   RSS VI, No. 1757.
13   RMS V, No.1472, 1474.
14   Ibid, No.2223.
15   RPC V, 686.
16   As for example at Bogrie and Sundaywell, just over the hills to the east, and
     at Bonshaw and Bonshawside in Annandale.
17   The RCAHMS estimated the thickness to average about 3ft (RCAHMS 1914,
     No.86).
18   M'Kerlie III, 282.
19   RCAHMS, *op. cit.*
20   PRS Dumfries I (1617-71), Index, 245.
21   M'Kerlie III, 312.
22   RMS IX, No.334.
23   PRS Dumfries I (1617-71), Index, 120.
24   Nisbet I, 319.
25   M'Kerlie III, 312.
26   RPC, 3rd Ser., VII, 217.
27   Ibid, 488.
28   Ibid, IX, 576.
29   Ibid, 574.
30   APS IX, 164.
31   Ibid, X, 30.
32   M'Kerlie III, 312.
33   Ibid.
34   Ibid., 313.
35   Ibid., 313, 472.
36   Ibid.
37   Ibid., V, 387.

Fig. 198 Earlstoun Castle: view from SE.

27.   EARLSTOUN CASTLE
(1¾ m NNW Dalry)   (NX614841)

Like the neighbouring lands of Lochinvar (q.v.), the lands of Earlstoun formed part of the Glenkens, a vast tract of the Upper Ken valley that was included within the ancient Lordship of Galloway. From Alan, the last of the ancient Lords, the Glenkens passed by descent to the 7th Earl of Buchan, who soon after 1290 granted half of the territory to John Maxwell, younger of Caerlaverock, who in turn granted it in feu to Sir Adam Gordon, progenitor of the Gordons of Lochinvar.[1] But whilst Lochinvar was included in this grant, there is no evidence that it also included Earlstoun; nor is it known whether 'Earl's toun' derived its name from the Earls of Buchan or the Earls of Douglas,[2] who acquired the superiority of the Glenkens when Archibald, later 3rd Earl of Douglas, was granted the Lordship of Galloway in 1369.[3]

The earliest stronghold at Earlstoun was a motte, which probably dated from the late 12th or early 13th century, though there is no record of who built it, or who lived here that early. And although there are frequent references to the 'Mote of Earlstoun' in the 15th and 16th centuries,[4] it had by then become no more than a convenient name for a particular portion of the lands of Earlstoun. The motte in question was evidently the one that still stands beside the river in St. John's Town of Dalry, 1¾ miles to the S; it has an average height of about 20ft and a diameter at the summit of 107ft.[5] It first comes on record in the Exchequer Rolls for 1457, when the fermes (or annualrent) for the land of 'le Mote de Erelistoun' was 6s. 8d.[6] Thereafter the Mote of Earlstoun appears in the rolls regularly until 1588.[7] Sometimes the name of the tenant is given, as in 1488 when it was let to one John M'Mulane (McMillan);[8] and it was in the same year that Hutcheon Wallace of Smithstoun was granted a remission for his part in the plunder of certain goods of the McMillans 'oute of the barony of Erlistoun'.[9]

Some time in the 15th century the lands of Earlstoun came into the possession of the Hepburns of Hailes, presumably by grant from the Earls of Douglas.[10] Then *c.*1472 Sir Patrick Hepburn, 1st Lord Hailes, is said to have sold Earlstoun to John Sinclair of Herdmanston, who gave it to one of his younger sons, the name of whom has not been established.[11] The Hepburns, however, retained the superiority, and in 1511 Adam Hepburn, Earl of Bothwell, received a new crown charter confirming his possession of the lordship and barony of Hailes and many other lands, including 'the lands and barony of Erlistoun now called Glenken';[12] and the following day certain of the lands, including the lands and barony of Earlstoun, were granted to his spouse, Agnes Stewart, daughter of the Earl of Buchan, for her maintenance for life.[13]

The earliest Sinclair on record at Earlstoun was David, who in 1536, along with his son John and James Gordon of Lochinvar, was granted a respite against prosecution whilst absent in the King's service.[14] David may have died shortly afterwards, as he does not appear again, and in 1541 and again in 1542 his son John 'in Eirlistoun' was a witness to charters.[15] John married Janet, daughter of Roger Gordon of Troquhain,[16] and they had a son John, who eventually succeeded to Earlstoun after the murder of his father in, or shortly before, 1583. It was in 1583 that the Crown issued a commission for the apprehension of the father's murderer.[17] However, surprisingly little is known about the Sinclairs of Earlstoun, who ultimately failed in the male line on the death of the latter John at the end of the 16th century.

Meanwhile, on the forfeiture of the 4th Earl of Bothwell in 1567, the Regent Moray granted the superiority of his estates, including the lands and barony of Earlstoun, to Francis Stewart, Commendator of Kelso;[18] and in 1581 Francis was raised to the peerage as 5th Earl of Bothwell. Ten years later he too suffered forfeiture, whereupon the lordship and barony of Hailes, including the lordship and barony of Earlstoun, were granted to the Duke of Lennox.[19] Three years later Lennox resigned these estates, which James VI then granted to Sir Walter Scott of Branxholm.[20]

It was the Sinclairs who originally built the castle some time during the second half of the 16th century. It appears on Pont's map as 'Erystou' *c*.1595.[21] Clearly defence was not a major consideration, for, not only are there no gunloops, but the site itself, which is on the edge of a low bank on open ground between Earlstoun Wood to the NE and the River Ken to the W, provides no natural protection.

The **CASTLE**, which is built on the **L**–plan, is unusually squat in only having three storeys, but as the roof has been rebuilt at least once, one cannot be certain that it was not originally taller. Built of local greywacke rubble with sandstone dressings, it measures 34ft 4in from E to W by 21ft 10in from N to S over walls 3ft 10in thick, with the wing, which is 13ft 8in wide and projects 11ft 7in, at the W end of the S side. It was originally harled. As well as the roof having been reconstructed, there have been a number of other structural changes, including the complete removal of the original chimney stack for the great hall, a rebuilt entrance doorway, and enlarged windows on the upper floors of the main block.

The entrance is in the re-entrant angle of the wing, where it admits to a spacious vestibule leading to the basement and a wheel-stair, 9ft 6in in diameter, serving the first floor. The doorway itself has been rebuilt; it has rolled arrises and a segmental arch, and the jambs are of gritstone.[22] Originally, there appears only to have been a wooden door, as the position of the drawbar tunnel, now blocked at its outer end, did not leave room for a yett as well, unless it was behind the drawbar, which is unlikely. The basement of the main block is vaulted. It has a small slit-window and an open aumbry at each end, and in addition the E end had a mural recess in the SE corner, which was converted into a doorway in 1655 to give direct access to the wing added at that date. A small rectangular opening in the S wall covered the approach on that side, though, surprizingly, it is not adjacent to the entrance itself. The partition across the basement is of later date.

The first floor was the hall. It has walls about 3ft 8in thick at each end, 4ft thick on the S side, where the original hall fireplace was accommodated, and only 2ft 9in on the N side. The original fireplace, which was 7ft 8in wide, was adjacent to the stair turret, and was of generous proportions, with bold QERH

mouldings on the jambs. The jambs have survived, built into the wall, but the fireplace itself was partly filled in and partly converted to a second window embrasure on this side before the hall was panelled, apparently sometime late in the 17th century: in its place, there is now a small fireplace, 4ft wide, at the E end. There is a second, original, window embrasure at the E end of the S wall, two more window embrasures on the N side and another at the W end. All the windows have been enlarged,[23] but not seemingly at the same date, as those on the S and W sides have QER surrounds, while those on the N side have inset edge-rolls. Indeed, the N windows may be a later addition. A further peculiarity is that the more westerly of these embrasures has had its left jamb reduced by 7in, for no apparent reason. All the surrounds are backset to accommodate the harling. All these changes seem to have been carried out over a relatively short period of time, before the hall was fitted throughout with fine Renaissance panelling, including fluted pilasters, moulded panel-surrounds and dentilated cornices, all now sadly decayed and largely missing. The new fireplace presumably also had a Renaissance surround, which is also missing. When the tower was extended in 1655, a doorway was cut through the N end of the E wall to communicate with the garret of the new wing. From this level, the second floor of the main block and the two upper floors in the wing are reached by a corbelled-out stair-turret in the rentrant angle, the stair of which is 6ft 2in in diameter. This turret is unusual in having an offset course at the level of the second floor.

The second floor of the main block was divided into two rooms, each with a small fireplace in the end wall and a single window on the S side; but it is not clear whether the second, W window on the S side was inserted where the flue for the original hall chimney had been, as on the floor below, or whether the flue had risen between the windows. The windows on this floor have also been enlarged, though the arrises only have simple roll-mouldings. There was a small window, now blocked, high in the E wall, but none at the W end. These rooms were also panelled late in the 17th century.

At this level the wing contains a small chamber, and above it there was a garret. The lower room has a small fireplace in its S wall and a large window, probably enlarged, in the E wall, while the garret had an even smaller fireplace in the S

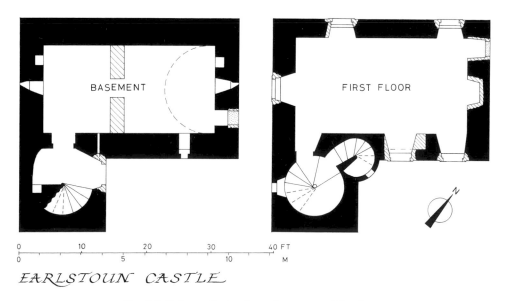

Fig. 199 Earlstoun Castle: plans of basement and first floor.

gable and a window to one side above it. The floors of both chambers are now missing.

There is no evidence that the castle ever had either a parapet or corner turrets. The former is most unlikely in view of the position of the original hall chimney-stack and relatively thin walls, and the rebuilding of the roof, and possible lowering of the wall-head, would have obliterated any trace of turrets. The gable-heads now have plain coping.

There used to be a well in the courtyard.[24]

On his death c.1600, John Sinclair of Earlstoun was succeeded by his two daughters,[25] Margaret and Rosina, the elder of whom, Margaret, had in 1582 married John Gordon of Airds.[26] John Gordon thus acquired Earlstoun, and went to live there,[27] though it was not until the two sisters renounced their rights in 1615 that he obtained formal possession.[28] By Margaret, John had an only daughter, Margaret, who had no issue. After his wife's death, he married Mary Chalmers, by whom he had three sons, the eldest of whom, Alexander, succeeded to Earlstoun.[29] In 1601, Lord Ochiltree, who had meanwhile acquired an interest in Earlstoun,[30] sold the merkland of Earlstoun, with the fortalice, and other lands in the lordship of Earlstoun to John Gordon of Earlstoun.[31] This is the first direct mention of the castle. Then, in 1615, being heavily in debt, Ochiltree sold his superiority of the £40 lands and barony of Earlstoun, with the castles and manor-places, to his cousin, Sir James Stewart of Killeith;[32] and five years later this superiority was incorporated into the free barony of Earlstoun and granted by the Crown to Sir Robert Gordon of Lochinvar.[33] It was a part of this barony, extending to 52 acres, that was chosen in 1629 as the site of the new burgh of Galloway, before there was a change of mind in favour of another site nearer to Kenmure (q.v.).[34] In the same year, Alexander Gordon had retour of Earlstoun and other lands.[35]

Alexander was appointed a Justice of the Peace in 1634,[36] and represented the Stewartry in parliament in 1641.[37] In the latter year, he was also appointed a Commissioner for Regulating the Common Burdens, for receiving Brotherly Assistance from the English Parliament, and for the Plantation of Kirks and Valuation of Teinds;[38] and in 1643 he was appointed a Commissioner of Supply.[39] He was on the Committee for War with his eldest son John in 1643, 1644 and 1645, and with his second son, William, after John's death in 1646.[40] As a young man, he was a zealous Covenanter, but later he changed his allegiance and became an Episcopalian. He attended the General Assembly of the Church of Scotland in 1638 and 1639.[41] He subsequently had a serious disagreement with the Bishop of Galloway over the minister nominated for Dalry, which led to him being fined.[42] He died in 1653 or 1654.

Alexander was succeeded by his eldest surviving son, William, who had sasine in 1655.[43] As well as having been a Commissioner of War with his father in 1646, he had again been appointed a Commissioner in 1648 and 1649.[44] During the Civil War, William held a command at first under General Leslie, and later under Lord Glencairn;[45] but in 1654 he subscribed to Cromwell's act of indemnity and returned home.[46]

Soon after succeeding to Earlstoun, William set about modernizing the castle, adding a new wing at the E end. This extension, which increased the length of the castle by 22ft 6in, apparently comprised a single storey and a garret – though the earliest record of it was not made until it was in an advanced state of ruin.[47] It included a new kitchen, and it connected with the older building at both floor levels. All that now survives is the base of the walls. Some of the outbuildings around the court-

yard, although later modified, may also date from this period. The work was commemorated by a stone bearing the date '1655' and the initials 'W G' and 'M H' for William and his wife, Mary, daughter of Sir John Hope of Craighall.[48]

Two years later, Cromwell granted William a new charter of the lands and barony of Earlstoun.[49] This records the interest in the estate of Viscount Kenmure, Rosina Sinclair, Margaret Gordon (daughter and heir of Margaret Sinclair) and James Gordon of Strangassell,[50] all of whom resigned their respective interests in William's favour. William was a Commissioner for Raising Taxation for Cromwell in the Stewartry in 1656 and again in 1659,[51] and he was a Commissioner of Supply for Charles II in 1661.[52]

William's adherence to presbyterianism, and his refusal to present an episcopal curate to the church of Dalry against the people's wishes, ultimately led, in 1663, to his banishment from Scotland.[53] But eventually, in 1668, on the petition of his wife, the Crown permitted him to return 'to order his affairs'.[54] When his eldest son, Alexander, married in 1676, William gave him the estate, which by this time extended to more than fifty properties, whilst retaining an annualrent for himself.[55] The following year, William was appointed one of the Commissioners for Excise, Supply and Militia for the Stewartry,[56] and in 1678 he was again a Commissioner of Supply.[57] Then, in 1679, William and his son Alexander again took up arms on behalf of the Covenanters, but they were defeated at Bothwell Bridge; and although William did not take part in the actual engagement, he was killed nearby immediately afterwards.[58] Alexander subsequently fled to Holland, was declared a traitor, and in 1680 sentenced to death with forfeiture of his estates.[59] Earlstoun subsequently became a barracks for the Crown's forces; and it is again recorded in use as a barracks in 1683 and 1684, the garrison on the latter occasion being transferred from Barscobe.[60]

Alexander later returned to the United Kingdom, and in 1683 was taken prisoner; but instead of being put to death, he was tortured and kept in prison.[61] Two years later parliament passed an Act of Forfeiture against Alexander and his late father for treason, annexing his lands to the Crown.[62] After the Revolution in 1689, he was released and appointed a Commissioner of Supply for the Stewartry and a Commissioner for ordering the Militia;[63] and he was re-appointed a Commissioner of Supply the following year, and again in 1704.[64] Nevertheless, he had difficulty in recovering legal title to Earlstoun. He eventually took possession in 1690, and the following year, with the assistance of his cousin Charles Hope, later 1st Earl of Hopetoun, he recovered possession of the Wood of Earlstoun.[65]

Alexander also had a younger brother, William Gordon of Afton, who had been an active supporter of King William and in 1706 was rewarded for his services by being created a baronet, with special remainder. It was Sir William who eventually succeeded in recovering formal title to the estate of Earlstoun, and in 1712 he had sasine.[66] On his death in 1718, he was succeeded in the baronetcy and his estates by his brother Alexander. The following year Sir Alexander gave Earlstoun to his eldest son, Thomas.[67] As well as having at last recovered possession of Earlstoun, Sir Alexander had also recovered Airds, and it was there that he died in 1726.[68]

Sir Alexander was succeeded by his son Thomas, who became the 3rd Baronet. During the Jacobite rebellion of 1715, Thomas had served as a Deputy-Lieutenant under the Marquess of Annandale.[69] The estate that Sir Thomas inherited was seriously in debt; and despite the temporary relief afforded by the dowry of his wife, Ann, eldest daughter and coheiress of William

Boick, a prosperous merchant burgess in Edinburgh and Glasgow, his liabilities still exceeded his income.[70] Matters could only get worse. When his eldest son, Thomas, was married in 1737, Sir Thomas gave him the estate;[71] but it was a meaningless gesture. The estate was mortgaged to the hilt, and eventually Sir Thomas had to give up the struggle. In 1743 he disponed both Earlstoun and Afton to Daniel Campbell of Shawfield, and the following year Mains of Earlstoun to William Newall of Barskeoch, who subsequently acquired the whole estate.[72] In 1745 Sir Thomas finally left Earlstoun and retired to Cumbria.[73]

In 1746 William Newall sold the Earlstoun estate to Alexander Murray of Broughton;[74] and in 1785 Alexander's son, James Murray of Cally, sold it to William Forbes of Callendar.[75] William Forbes was a younger son of William Forbes in Aberdeen, who had amassed a considerable fortune in business in London. The Forbes have held Earlstoun ever since. In 1872 the estate comprised 40,445 acres in Galloway.[76]

No laird ever lived in the castle after the Gordons, and by 1845 it had evidently lain uninhabited for some time. In that year the *New Statistical Account* reported that 'With some repair it might be made habitable'.[77] Presumably some repairs were subsequently carried out, as MacGibbon and Ross recorded in 1889 that there were 'people not yet old, who were born in the house'.[78] By then, however, it had again fallen into a state of decay, and, although the roof has been maintained, it is now only used as a farm store. A new house, Earlstoun Lodge, was built nearby in the middle of the 19th century.

---

1 Fraser 1873, I, 92; Scots Peerage V, 99.
2 According to the Statistical Account (VIII, 55), Earlstoun Wood was named after the Earls of Bothwell, but in fact the name pre-dates the grant of that earldom.
3 Fraser 1885, I, 328. The lands on which Dalry stands were that part of the barony of Earlstoun that had originally been intended as the site for the new burgh of Galloway in 1628 (RMS VIII, No.1346).
4 ERS VI, 345, 569, 643; VII, 9, 115, 605; etc.
5 RCAHMS 1914, No.157.
6 ERS VI, 345. The previous year the rent for the 'lands of Erlistone' was £10 (ERS VI, 192).
7 Ibid., XXI, 355.
8 Ibid., X, 658.
9 RSS I, No.1.
10 The Hepburns received at least one other grant from the Earls of Douglas: Dunsyre in Lanarkshire (RMS II, No.557).
11 Nisbet I, 318. M'Kerlie (III, 414) disagrees with Nisbet, and suggests that the Sinclairs of Earlstoun were descended from the Sinclairs of Longformacus, but his argument lacks details and is unconvincing.
12 RMS II, No.3635.
13 Ibid., No.3637.
14 RSS II, No.2155.
15 RMS III, Nos.2405, 2729.
16 Adams 1921, 137.
17 ERS XXI, 492.
18 RSS VI, No.97; RMS V, No.218.
19 RMS V, No.1888.
20 RMS VI, No.166n; Fraser 1878, I, 173-4.
21 Blaeu, 66, 'The Steuartrie of Kircubright, The most easterlie part of Galloway'.
22 M'Kerlie (III, 435) relates a story that originally there was a panel bearing the Sinclair arms over the entrance, and that this was later replaced by the arms of Gordon. Now there is not even an empty panel.
23 The recesses themselves may also have been enlarged, as the lintels are all of timber.
24 MacGibbon & Ross III, 521.
25 His son George (RPC IV, 548) had evidently predeceased him.
26 Burke Peerage 1959, 954, 'Gordon of Earlston'.
27 He was 'in Erlistoun' in 1600 (RPC VI, 637) but still designated 'of Airdis' in 1604 (RPC VII, 589).
28 M'Kerlie III, 414.
29 Burke Peerage, op. cit.
30 Lord Ochiltree's interest was apparently a mid-superiority under the Scotts of Branxholm, who retained overall superiority under the Crown.
31 RMS VI, No.1317. It is by no means clear how Ochiltree could 'sell' to Gordon lands that were still the property of Gordon's wife and her sister.
32 RMS VII, No.1248.
33 RMS VIII, No.67.
34 Ibid., No.1346.
35 M'Kerlie III, 414.
36 RPC, 2nd Ser., V, 381.
37 APS V, 331.
38 Ibid, 392, 395, 400.
39 Ibid, VI, Part I, 29.
40 Ibid, 53, 199, 559.
41 M'Kerlie III, 415.
42 Ibid.
43 Ibid.
44 APS VI, Part II, 35, 493.
45 M'Kerlie III, 415-6.
46 DNB, 810.
47 MacGibbon & Ross III, 522-3.
48 This stone was originally incorporated in the wing (MacGibbon & Ross III, 523), but sometime after 1890 it was moved to the fabric of the original castle to preserve it.
49 RMS X, No.609.
50 James Gordon's connection with Earlstoun is not known. The Gordons of Strangassell were a branch of the Gordons of Lochinvar.
51 APS VI, Part II, 851, 884.
52 Ibid, VII, 92.
53 RPS, 3rd Ser., I, 520; II, 396.
54 Ibid., 396, 418.
55 M'Kerlie III, 417.
56 RPS, 3rd Ser., VIII, 205.
57 APS VIII, 228.
58 M'Kerlie III, 418; DNB, 810.
59 RPS, 3rd Ser., VII, 217; M'Kerlie III, 419.
60 RPS, 3rd Ser., VIII, 254, 523.
61 Ibid, IX, 99, 141, 178; X, 56, 100; XIII, xxxvi; M'Kerlie III, 420.
62 APS VIII, 490.
63 Ibid, IX, 28, 74.
64 Ibid, IX, 144; XI, 150.
65 M'Kerlie III, 421.
66 Ibid.
67 Ibid, 423.
68 Ibid.
69 Ibid, 424.
70 Ibid.
71 Ibid, 425.
72 Ibid, 426.
73 Ibid, 426-7.
74 Ibid, 428.
75 Callendar Estate Records. The price was £20,677.
76 Return of Landowners, 117.
77 NSA IV, 371.
78 MacGibbon & Ross III, 522.

---

28. EDINGHAM CASTLE
(1m NE Dalbeattie)   (NX839628)

'Edyngaheym' first appears on record c.1120, when it was the site of an early church belonging at that time to the diocese of Glasgow.[1] Shortly afterwards it was relegated to the status of a chapel and passed into the possession of Fergus, Lord of Galloway, while a new parish church was established at Urr; and c.1164 Fergus's son Uchtred granted both church and chapel, together with a ploughgate of land, to the abbey of Holyrood.[2]

By 1465 the lands of Edingham were in the possession of Sir George Campbell, son and heir of Sir George Campbell of Loudoun. In that year Sir George agreed with Alexander Livingstone of Duchray to exchange the lands of Eddingham and Cowlach (Culloch) for Alexander's lands of Duchray in Ayrshire.[3] Early in the following century, the £5 lands of 'Edinghame' are found in the possession of Alexander Levingstoun of Little Airds, whose relationship is not known.[4] In 1529 he gave Edingham, together with other lands, in liferent

Fig. 200 Edingham Castle: view from S.

to his wife Elizabeth, daughter of Sir Robert Gordon of Glen, and two years later this was confirmed by crown charter.[5] The Livingston family relationships are by no means clear, but Alexander appears to have been succeeded by John Livingston, who was in turn succeeded in 1553 by another Alexander Livingston of Little Airds.[6] The following year the latter Alexander transferred ownership of various lands under entail,[7] including the £10 lands of Edingham and Culloch, with the mills, woods, tow-

ers and fishings, to his younger brother Robert.[8] Then in 1576 Alexander Livingston of Little Airds was given principal sasine of the lands of Edingham and Culloch,[9] and three years later he granted his wife, Margaret Charteris, a liferent from these and other lands.[10]

Alexander's debts were, however, causing him increasing embarrassment, and soon after he had to mortgage part of his estates.[11] Around the same time, the £5 lands of Edingham

Fig. 201 Edingham Castle: view from N.

were apprised for debts owing to John Moresoun, son of John Moresoun in Grange, and Robert Livingston, son of Hector Livingston in Donance. Robert assigned his interest in the debts to John Morison, who, in 1588, purchased the £5 lands of Edingham and was granted a crown charter of the same.[12] It was a condition of the charter that Alexander Livingston and his heirs could recover the property if they paid off the debts within seven years. At that time Edingham was occupied by an Edward Moresoun. His relationship is not stated; but the Morisons continued in occupation, and when, in 1591, Alexander Livingston of Little Airds – who had meantime apparently recovered Edingham – sold the superiority of the lands of the barony of Levingstoun, including the £10 lands of Edingham and Culloch, with the castles, etc., to William M'Clellane of Crofts, John

Fig. 202 Edingham: NW corner of basement,
with entrance doorway beyond.

Moresoun in Edingham was a witness.[13] A week later, M'Clellane sold the same lands to Alexander M'Ghie of Balmaghie,[14] who, in 1606, was granted a new crown charter of the lands.[15]

It is not known for certain when the castle was built, nor by whom, though it clearly dates from some time in the 16th century, and is thought to have been built, either by the Morisons themselves, or on their behalf by one of their landlords. The tower-house of 'Edinghaim' is included in Pont's survey of Galloway c.1595. It does not occupy a position of natural strength, being situated on a gentle slope on low ground, facing SW; and apart from traces of what may have been an outer ditch, noted by the RCAHMS in 1911,[16] there is no evidence of any special provision for defence.

The **TOWER**, which is oblong in plan, measures 28ft from N to S by 20ft 3in from E to W over walls averaging 3ft 6in in thickness. The masonry is granite boulders with rubble pinnings, while the dressings are of gritstone with rounded arrises, except for the slit windows which have margins of the local granite. Only the first two storeys and part of the S wall of the second floor have survived.

The entrance is in the W wall, where it is provided with the usual double rebate for an outer, wooden door and an inner, iron yett. It admits to a vaulted vestibule, which gives access to the wheel-stair, 6ft 6in in diameter, in the NW corner and two doorways leading to separate chambers in the basement. This is a rare arrangement in the Borders, which is found elsewhere only at Crawfordton. Although the doorways are clearly original, the basement has been constructed as a single, vaulted chamber with a partition, which was later removed. The N end is provided with a single slit window, a fairly large recess under the stair and an open aumbry, 1ft 9in by 1ft 5in by 1ft 8in high,

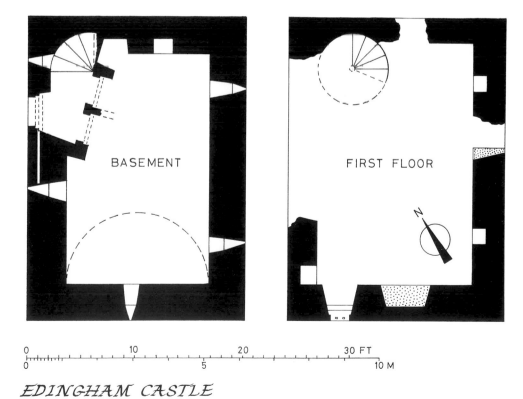

BASEMENT

FIRST FLOOR

0   10   20   30 FT
0   5   10 M

EDINGHAM CASTLE

Fig. 203 Edingham Castle: plans of basement and first floor.

in the end wall, while the larger S end is provided only with three slit-windows.

The first floor had a fireplace in the middle of the S gable, which is now built up. To the right of this there is a small window that was originally provided with an iron grille,[17] and in the side walls on either side at this end there are lamp-shelves. There is another lamp-shelf towards the N end of the E wall, and to the right of this there is a window recess that has been altered and partly blocked at some period. There were also window recesses in the N and W walls, but most of these have now gone, together with the adjacent walling to the N and W and most of the NW corner at this level.

On the second floor, all that remains are some of the corbels that supported the floor itself and a small window, with one vertical bar, in the S gable wall. This may not be original, as, by the time MacGibbon and Ross recorded the castle in 1889, it had already been converted into a two-storeyed house with an attic illuminated by this window, and had subsequently fallen into ruin.[18]

John Morison was succeeded in Edingham by Edward Morison, whose son John had retour in 1612.[19] The latter John is mentioned again in 1626.[20] He was eventually succeeded by his son Edward, who, in 1642, granted John M'Clene, merchant burgess of Dumfries, a charter of half the £5 lands of Edingham, with the oat mills, manor-place, etc., which were to be held of Edward in feu farm under reversion.[21] In 1659 Edward's son John had retour of Edingham,[22] and in 1666 another son, Henry, had sasine of Meikle Culloch.[23] John Morison later resigned Edingham in favour of Robert Affleck of Little Culme, who took the designation 'of Edingham', and as such was granted a crown charter of Edingham in 1663.[24] His son Robert Affleck, or Auchinleck, had principal sasine in 1677.[25] As 'Robert Auchinleck of Edinghame', he took the Test in 1683.[26]

The Afflecks remained in possession until some time between 1799 and 1819, when Edingham was acquired by William Maitland of Auchlane and Gelston.[27] He was succeeded by his daughter Matilda, who married Charles Kirwan of Dalgin Park, Co. Mayo, and subsequently of Gelston.[28] It is likely that the conversion of the tower into the more modern dwelling already mentioned took place prior to this, while the rest of the property became a modern farm with a new farmhouse and farm buildings across the road, a short distance to the NW. The tower was later abandonned, and by the time the property was purchased by John Hutchison, the son of a Glasgow merchant, in 1872,[29] it had become a roofless ruin.[30]

1   Brooke, D. 'The Deanery of Desnes Cro and the Church of Edingham', *TDGAS*, 3rd Ser., LXII, 49-53.
2   Ibid, 53.
3   RMS II, Nos.841, 842.
4   The Livingstons gave their own name to the property of Little Airds, but it continued to be known by both names long after they lost it, and is now known only as Livingston.
5   RMS III, No.1078.
6   M'Kerlie V, 294.
7   The entail shows a connection with the Lords Livingston and Livingstons of Dunipace, Kilsyth, Castle Cary and Terrentera (Glentirran) in Stirlingshire, but it does not explain it.
8   RMS IV, No.934.
9   Exchequer Rolls XX, 501.
10   RSS VII, No.1852.
11   RMS V, No.1474.
12   Ibid, No.1523.
13   Ibid, No.1849.
14   Ibid, No.1865.
15   RMS VI, No.1745.
16   RCAHMS 1914, No.488.
17   There are sockets for 3 hortizontal and 2 vertical bars.
18   MacGibbon & Ross III, 398.
19   M'Kerlie V, 294.
20   PRS Dumfries I (1617-71), Index, 295.
21   RMS IX, No.1142.
22   M'Kerlie V, 295.
23   Ibid.
24   RMS XI, No.436.
25   M'Kerlie V, 295.
26   RPC, 3rd Ser., VIII, 640.
27   M'Kerlie V, 295.
28   M'Kerlie IV, 113; V, 295; Burke L.G.1906, 955, 'Maitland-Kirwan of Gelston Castle'.
29   M'Kerlie III, 113; V, 296.
30   Ibid, V, 296; MacGibbon & Ross III, 398.

---

29.   ELIOCK CASTLE
(1¹/₂ m SE Sanquhar)   (NS797075)

The lands of Eliock formed part of the ancient Celtic lordship of Nithsdale, which in the time of David I was held by Dunegal of Stranit.[1] From Dunegal the lands passed first to his younger son, Duvenald, whose share of his father's lands included Sanquhar, Eliock and Dunscore, and then to Duvenald's son Edgar, whose descendants took the surname of Edgar.[2] It was not, however, until the time of King Robert the Bruce that Eliock first appears in the records, when Bruce granted Richard Edger a new charter of 'the lower pennyworth land of Elyoc' and certain other lands in Upper Nithsdale.[3]

The lands of Eliock subsequently came into the possession of Sir William de Dalzell of that Ilk, who, in 1388 and again in 1400, is designated lord 'of Elliok'.[4] But whilst the Dalzells retained a share of Eliock for the next two centuries, the superiority of their portion was evidently acquired by the Douglases of Drumlanrig. What is not clear, though, is how the other portion of Eliock came into the possession of the Charteris of Amisfield. The earliest reference to their possession is in 1434, when the lands of 'Aymisfelde, Trailflat and Elyok' were in the king's hands by reason of ward, while Robert, son and heir of Roger Charteris, was under age.[5] Then in 1456 the fermes of Eliok were again held in ward by the Crown, as sasine had been taken by Robert Charteris 'in error';[6] but by 1461 the matter had been resolved, for in that year Robert Charteris of Amisfield had lawful sasine of the lands of Amisfield, Charteris and 'Elyot';[7]

Fig. 204 Eliock House: NW corner. The old tower stood behind the farthest angle.

and two years later he exchanged the lands of Eliock and certain lands in Moray with Sir Robert Crichton of Sanquhar for his lands of Longniddry in East Lothian and an annualrent of £20 from the lands of Sanquhar.[8] At that time the lands of Eliock were described as being in the barony of Sanquhar.

From Sir William de Dalzell, the Dalzell family's share of Eliock passed down through successive generations of the Dalzells of that Ilk, though, as they continued to live at Dalzell, Eliock rarely gets a mention.[9] In 1494 Sir William's great-grandson, William Dalzell of that Ilk, had sasine of Eliock from Sir William Douglas of Drumlanrig as heir to his father,[10] and the following year it was as William Dalzell of Eliock that he was appointed a Lord of Council.[11] William was killed in a fray in 1508,[12] and was succeeded first by his grandson, Robert Dalzell of that Ilk, and then, in 1549, by Robert's eldest son, also Robert. When the latter Robert married his second wife, Cristine Dundas, two years later, the marriage contract included provision for her out of the lands of Eliock, and Cristine's terce as a widow was reiterated in charters of 1574 and 1596 to his grandson and eventual heir, Sir Robert Dalzell of that Ilk.[13]

Further light is shed on the Dalzell's 'tenandry' of Eliock by a contract concluded between Sir James Douglas of Drumlanrig and Robert Dalzell of that Ilk in 1572/3. This followed the murder in 1555 of William Dalzell, Robert's uncle, by John Douglas of Erschemorton, natural son of Douglas of Drumlanrig, and was designed to settle the dispute between the two families. In the meantime, some time before 1563, Robert Dalzell had died and been succeeded by his elder son, also Robert.[14] The contract decreed that Drumlanrig give to Robert Dalzell, eldest son and heir of Robert Dalzell of that Ilk, a charter granting him the 26 merk land of Eliock, in the barony of Drumlanrig, whilst reserving to the laird of Dalzell his liferent

Fig. 205 Eliock Castle: ruins of NW corner of old tower showing gun-loop.

and to his wife her terce of the lands, and to Drumlanrig his superiority.[15]

Meanwhile, in 1479, Sir Robert Crichton of Sanquhar (and Eliock) was succeeded by his eldest son, Robert, who, in 1487/88 was created Lord Crichton of Sanquhar. Lord Crichton died in 1494, and in the same year his grandson and heir, Robert, 2nd Lord Crichton of Sanquhar, had sasine of Sanquhar, Eliock, Crawfordstoun and other lands.[16] Robert died sometime in 1513, probably killed at Flodden, and later that year his only son, Robert, succeeded and had sasine of the lands of Eliock.[17] He sat in the General Council in November 1513, when the question of the Regency was discussed,[18] and attended parliament again in 1516.[19] On his death some four years later, the ward of the lands of Eliock passed to the Crown, and possession was not taken up until 1533, when Robert Crichton had sasine.[20] This was probably the 4th Lord Crichton, though he never in fact took formal entry to his principal estate of Sanquhar before his early death c.1535. The ward then reverted to the Crown, until his brother William, 5th Lord Crichton, took possession in 1538/9.[21] He, however, was killed in a fray in 1550, when once again the ward reverted to the Crown.

The following year, one Robert Crichton, who is said to have been a cadet of Sanquhar, was granted a Letter of Tack of the 3 merk 40d land of Eliock and the 3 merk land of Zochane (Euchan), in the barony of Sanquhar.[22] Robert became a distinguished lawyer, who, in 1559-60, was appointed Lord Advocate jointly with John Spens of Condie.[23] Later that year his eldest son, James, the renowned 'Admirable Crichton', was born at Eliock.[24] In 1562 Robert was granted the estate of Clunie in Perthshire by his kinsman Robert Crichton, Bishop of Dunkeld,[25] and this was confirmed by charter three years later.[26] In the latter year he also received from Lord Crichton of Sanquhar a feu-charter of the 40s 40d lands of Eliock and the 40s lands of Euchan, of which he had previously only been a tenant.[27] A loyal supporter of Queen Mary, Robert took her side at the battle of Langside in 1568, and for his part was sentenced to forfeiture of his goods;[28] but soon afterwards he submitted to James VI, and resumed office as King's Advocate, being so designated only four months later.[29] After the death of Spens in 1573, Robert was Lord Advocate jointly with David Borthwick. In 1579 he was appointed Administrator of Beauly Priory.[30] A month later his appointment as King's Advocate was confirmed,[31] and he continued as Joint Advocate with Borthwick until Borthwick's death in 1581, when he became sole Advocate and a Senator of the College of Justice.[32] He retired the following year,[33] and died shortly before 1586.[34]

It must have been this Robert Crichton who built the 'castle' at Eliock, probably soon after he was granted the feu of the lands in 1565. The site is a natural platform on the lower slopes of the Nith valley, beside the Garpal Burn and about $1/2$ mile S of the river, from where it had a good view across the valley, N to Ryehill motte and NW to Sanquhar Castle.

It is not known whether the **CASTLE** was oblong in plan or had a stair wing, as the E end, which contained the stair, was demolished when a new geometric stair and E wing were added in the late 18th, or early 19th, century. What remains is the W end of the original tower-house and adjacent sections of the N and S walls, extending for 20ft 6in and 19ft respectively. The tower was 21ft 3in wide, with walls 3ft 6in thick on each side and 4ft 6in at the W end. It probably comprised three storeys and a garret, but was subsequently reduced to three storeys, with a plain pitched roof. For that reason, one cannot now tell

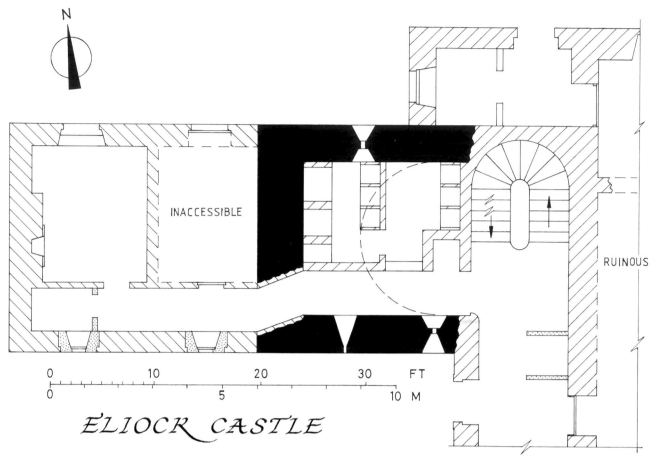

N

INACCESSIBLE

RUINOUS

| 0 | 10 | 20 | 30 | FT |

| 0 | 5 | 10 | M |

ELIOCK CASTLE

Fig. 206 Eliock Castle: plan of west end of basement and later adjoining works.

whether there was originally a parapet – as one would expect at that period – or turrets. The masonry is greywacke and sandstone rubble, with quoins and margins of dressed sandstone; it was harled.

The basement, which is vaulted, is provided with a single splayed gun-loop, with a rectangular opening and circular throat 4in in diameter, in each of the N and S walls. The only other feature at this level is a slit-window near the W end of the S wall. When the 2-storey extension was later added at the W end, the W wall was breached to form a connecting passage. The removal of the E end, however, was part of a major programme of reconstruction, which included the addition of the oval geometric stair in its place and a new wing with a subterranean cellar to the E, while at the same time the adjacent wing to the S, which was first added in 1658, appears to have been at least partly rebuilt.

The upper floors are now ruinous and inaccessible following a disastrous fire *c.*1940 (*infra*), but appear to retain no features of interest. The windows at both first and second floor levels are modern, having been enlarged and replaced when the E end was rebuilt. A smaller window of the same period at the W end of the N wall at first floor level may, however, be associated with a mural chamber in that corner.

'Eliock Cast.' is shown as an important building on Pont's map *c.*1595.[35]

Robert Crichton, the King's Advocate, was succeeded by his eldest surviving son, Sir Robert Crichton of Eliock and Clunie, a wild and extravagant young man, who was soon in

financial difficulties. In 1593 he sold his 40s 40d lands of Eliock, with the castle and manor-place, and also the estate of Clunie, from which he now took his designation, to his brother-in-law, Sir James Stewart of Sticks and Ballechin.[36] Three years later, with the consent of Sir James, he transferred the sale of his share of Eliock to his other brother-in-law, Robert Dalzell, younger of that Ilk,[37] who was already in possession of the 26 merk lands of Eliock, which he had obtained from his father. Dalzell had been granted a charter of the latter lands by Sir James Douglas of Drumlanrig in 1572/3 (*supra*),[38] and he had also had another charter from his father eighteen months later,[39] the latter charter being confirmed by James Douglas, grandson and heir of Drumlanrig.[40] Thus, after more than two centuries, the two halves of the lands of Eliock were once again united, and this was confirmed by crown charter in 1596.[41] The superiority, however, apparently remained divided between the Crichtons of Sanquhar and the Douglases of Drumlanrig.

Sir Robert Dalzell of Eliock appears to have succeeded his father in 1607, the same year in which he became Provost of Sanquhar.[42] Three years later he was reported to the Privy Council, together with his son, Robert Dalzell of that Ilk,[43] and Sir Robert Crichton of Clunie, for taking James Donaldson, son of the late James Donaldson, Advocate, from Edinburgh by force and taking him 'to the place of Eliok, quhair they yit keep and detene [me] in strait presone and captivitie' with the intention of forcing him, a minor, to hand over various deeds relating to his lands 'to the undoing of me and my poore estait'.[44] But despite this act of lawlessness, Sir Robert was made a Justice of the Peace for Dumfriesshire later that year.[45] He was raised to the peerage as Lord Dalzell in 1628,[46] and attended parliament as such five years later.[47] In 1638 he was admitted to the King's Council.[48] He died the following year, when he was succeeded by his eldest son, Sir Robert Dalzell of that Ilk, 2nd Lord Dalzell.

In the same year that he succeeded his father, Sir Robert, 2nd Lord Dalzell was made Earl of Carnwath.[49] Two years later he was appointed to the Privy Council.[50] He attended parliament in 1643 and 1645,[51] but later that year he fell out with parliament, was found guilty of treason, and sentenced to death, while the earldom and his estates were given to his eldest son, Gavin.[52] Being absent in England, he survived the sentence, fighting for Charles I at Naseby in 1645 and Charles II at Worcester in 1651, where he was taken prisoner. He was subsequently sent to the Tower, and languished there for ten months.[53] Meanwhile, earlier in 1651, he had had his earldom restored.[54] His

Fig. 207 Eliock Castle: gun-loop on S side.

name was then added to the Committee for revising Acts of the Committee of Estates.[55] It is not clear who was living at Eliock during the Civil War, but Cromwell's forces used both Sanquhar and Eliock for quarters during their frequent visits to Upper Nithsdale.[56] The Earl died in 1654.

Gavin, 2nd Earl of Carnwath, attended parliament regularly from 1646 to 1648, and, after the Restoration, from 1661 until his death twelve years later.[57] He was also appointed a Commissioner of War for Dumfriesshire in 1644, 1645 and 1648.[58] In 1647 he sold Dalzell to meet debts arising from his father's forfeiture, and the following year he received a new grant of the lands, lordship, earldom and barony of Carnwath.[59] He fought alongside his father at Worcester in 1651, where he too was taken prisoner.[60] It is not certain when he was released, but he was back at Eliock by 1658, when he built an extension to the castle. This took the form of a central wing to the S, giving the building a 'T' plan, and abutting the SW corner of this wing was a circular stair-tower, which also incorporated a new entrance. The doorway of this entrance has a bolection-moulded surround and bears the date 'MDCLVIII' on the lintel. Above this, there is an empty armorial panel. No other details from this period survive, as the whole wing was extensively altered, if not rebuilt, when the E end of the original castle was rebuilt in the late 18th, or early 19th, century. Gavin was a Commissioner of Supply in 1661 and 1667,[61] and with his eldest son, James, was appointed a Justice of the Peace for Dumfriesshire in 1663.[62] He died in 1673, being succeeded by his son James, who became 3rd Earl of Carnwath.

The 3rd Earl had a new crown charter of the lordship and barony of Carnwath in 1675, but, being increasingly bur-

dened by debt, had to sell that estate in 1684.[63] He was appointed a Commissioner of Supply for Dumfriesshire in 1685,[64] and attended parliament in 1685 and 1686.[65] He died two years later, when he was succeeded by his brother John, 4th Earl of Carnwath. John took the Oath of Allegiance in 1690,[66] and was a regular attender at Parliament from 1690 to 1700.[67] He was appointed a Commissioner of Supply for Dumfriesshire in 1696 and 1698.[68] In 1701 he voted in favour of the colony of Caledonia.[69] He died unmarried the following year, when the earldom and estate of Eliock passed to Sir Robert Dalzell, 3rd Baronet of Glenae, the great-grandson of Sir John Dalzell of Glenae (q.v.), younger brother of the 1st Earl of Carnwath.

Sir Robert, who became 5th Earl of Carnwath, never lived at Eliock, preferring the family home at Kirkmichael. In 1706 he was appointed a Commissioner of Supply for Dumfriesshire.[70] He subsequently joined the Jacobite cause, and was at Preston in 1715, where he was taken prisoner. Being found guilty of treason, he was sentenced to death, with forfeiture of all his honours and estates; but this was later commuted, and he was eventually pardonned.[71] Meanwhile, Eliock had reverted to the superior, Douglas of Drumlanrig, now Duke of Queensberry, who in 1720 undertook to convey it to Alexander Urquhart of Newhall, to whose daughter Carnwath was about to be married.[72] However, it is not certain that Urquhart ever got possession, and in 1723 Eliock was purchased by William Veitch of Boigend, WS, Carnwath's lawyer.[73]

William Veitch was a younger son of Alexander Veitch of Hall Lyne and grandson of Alexander Veitch of Hall Lyne and Manor, a cadet of the Veitches of Dawyck.[74] William was succeeded in 1747 by his son James, a distinguished lawyer, who in the same year was appointed Sheriff-Depute for the county of Peebles.[75] He was said to have been 'one of the most accomplished scholars of his time'.[76] Subsequently moving his home to Eliock, he served as Member of Parliament for Dumfriesshire from 1755 to 1760.[77] The following year he was made a Lord of Session, taking the title Lord Eliock.[78] He greatly increased the house at Eliock c.1770 by dispensing with the former chapel,[79] extending the wing of 1658 further to the S, and adding a fine new block at its S end to give the house an H–plan.[80] Being unmarried, he drew up an entail of his estates in 1790,[81] whereby, on his death in 1793, he was succeeded by his kinsman, Henry Veitch, great-grandson of William Veitch in Redpath, elder brother of Alexander Veitch of Hall Lyne.[82]

Henry was Lieutenant-Colonel of the 98th Regiment of Foot and one of the Commissioners of Customs for Scotland.[83] He was served heir to Lord Eliock in 1796, and the following year had a crown charter of his estates.[84] It was probably he who rebuilt the NE corner of the house and remodelled the adjacent wing immediately to the S (supra). He later got into financial difficulties, which may be the reason why, in 1820, he resigned his lands in favour of his eldest son, James, keeping only the liferent for himself.[85] After his death in 1838, the Peeblesshire estates were sold to pay off his debts.[86]

James Veitch was Sheriff-Substitute for the county of Lanark, and a Justice of the Peace and Deputy-Lieutenant for Dumfriesshire.[87] In 1872 the estate comprised 5163 acres.[88] On James's death without male issue in 1873, Eliock passed to his brother, William, who had been a vicar in Paddington.[89] William died in 1884. Eliock subsequently passed, first to his son, Henry (d.1903), who was a vicar in Somerset, and, on his death in 1903, to Henry's son, George.[90] George was called to the Scottish Bar in 1899.[91] On inheriting Eliock in 1910, he sold the house and estate to a Mr. M'Connel and moved to Eliock Grange.[92]

M'Connel filled in the E side of the '**H**' with a new entrance front, and he also raised the height of the NW corner to three full storeys and a garret to match the adjacent tower-house and later extensions to the S.

In 1927 the estate was purchased by George Greenshields, a former tea planter in Ceylon, and it has remained in his family ever since. It was, however, requisitioned for Polish troops during the Second World War, and it was they who, in 1940, set the N wing on fire. It has never been restored, and for many years the house lay empty before the Greenshields again took up residence.

Up till Mr. M'Connel took over in 1910, one of the rooms in the N wing had been 'carefully preserved' by successive owners reputedly just as it was when The Admirable Crichton was born there.[93]

---

1   Scots Peerage VI, 286.
2   Ibid, 286-7; McDowall 1986, 17 (McDowall incorrectly gives Duvenald as the grandson of Dunegal).
3   RMS I, App.2, No.317; Robertson's Index, 13.88 ('To Richard Edzear, of the land of Elietis, &c, &c.').
4   Scots Peerage II, 397.
5   ERS IV, 562, 600.
6   Ibid, VI, 167-8.
7   Ibid, IX, 668.
8   RMS II, No.815-6; Scots Peerage III, 221.
9   Scots Peerage III, 398-405.
10 Ibid, 402.
11 Ibid.
12 Scots Peerage II, 402.
13 RMS VI, No.483.
14 It is unfortunate that so many, successive generations of the Dalzells of that Ilk all had the Christian name Robert.
15 Adams 1921, App.A, No.28. See also RPC I, 300.
16 ERS X, 768. As he is only referred to as 'Robert Creichtoun' in the records, his father was presumably still alive at the time.
17 ERS XIV, 523. He paid 2d silver as double alba-ferme.
18 APS II, 281.
19 Ibid, .
20 ERS XVI, 573.
21 ERS XVII, 763.
22 RSS IV, No.1525.
23 Brit, Chron. 1961, 196; DNB, 467. His salary was £40 per annum.
24 James was a prodigy, who travelled widely in Europe and became renowned for his scholarship. In 1582 he entered the service of the Duke of Mantua, but shortly afterwards was murdered in a fit of jealousy by Prinze Vincenzo Gonzaga, the Duke's eldest son and heir. He was only 22. (Crichton, D. 'The Circumstances relating to the death of James (The Admirable) Crichton in Mantua, on 3rd July 1582', *PSAS*, XLIII (1909), 296-308; DNB, 467).
25 DNB, 467; Wilson & McMillan, 48.
26 RSS V, No.2005. His eldest son, James, 'The Admirable Crichton', had a further charter from the Bishop of Dunkeld in 1579 (RMS IV, No.2871).
27 Ibid, No.2040.
28 Ibid, VI, No.301.
29 RPC I, 642.
30 RSS VII, No.2133.
31 Ibid, No.2185.
32 Brit. Chron. 1961, 196; DNB, 467.
33 Ibid.
34 DNB, 467.
35 Pont MS. No.35 in National Library of Scotland.
36 RMS VI, No.18.
37 Ibid, No.483. Sir Robert Dalzell married Margaret, eldest daughter of Robert Crichton of Eliock (RMS V, No.14), while Sir James Stewart married her younger sister, Mary (RMS VI, No.435).
38 Adams 1921, App.A, No.28.
39 RMS VI, No.483.
40 Ibid.
41 Ibid.
42 Wilson & McMillan, 329. It is there suggested that he may also have been Provost of Sanquhar in 1602.
43 Sir Robert Dalzell senior chose to live at Eliock, while handing over the Dalzell estates to his son. His son had a crown charter of Carnwath in 1634 and Dalzell in 1635 (RMS IX, Nos.129, 342).
44 RPC VIII, 841-2.
45 Ibid, IX, 77.
46 Scots Peerage II, 407.
47 RPC, 2nd Ser., II, 483.
48 Scots Peerage II, 408.
49 Complete Peerage III, 49, Note (b). In the Scots Peerage, the earldom is erroneously credited to his father (Scots Peerage II, 408).
50 APS V, 675.
51 APS VI, Part I, 3, 440, 474.
52 Scots Peerage II, 412; APS VI, Part I, 345, 392.
53 Scots Peerage II, 412.
54 APS VI, Part II, 678..
55 Ibid.
56 Wilson & McMillan, 108.
57 APS VI, Part I, 612; Part II, 3; VII, *passim*; VIII, *passim*.
58 Ibid, VI, Part I, 200, 559; Part II, 32.
59 RMS IX, No.1992; APS VI, Part II, 117.
60 Complete Peerage III, 50.
61 APS VII, 91, 544.
62 Ibid, 505.
63 Scots Peerage II, 414.
64 APS VIII, 465.
65 Ibid, 451, 576.
66 Ibid, IX, 110.
67 Ibid, IX, X, *passim*.
68 Ibid, X, 29, 131.
69 Ibid, 247.
70 Ibid, XI, 318.
71 Scots Peerage II, 415.
72 Ibid, 416.
73 Burke L.G. 1906, 1721, 'Veitch of Eliock'.
74 Ibid.
75 DNB, 2148.
76 Ibid.
77 Ibid.
78 Ibid.
79 Wilson & McMillan, 40.
80 RCAHMS 1920, No.552; Gifford, 303.
81 Buchan & Paton III, 53.
82 Burke, *op. cit.*
83 Ibid.
84 Buchan & Paton III, 53.
85 Ibid.
86 Ibid.
87 Burke, *op. cit.*
88 Return of Landowners, 59.
89 Burke, *op. cit.*
90 Ibid.
91 Ibid.
92 County Directory 1912, 193.
93 NSA IV, 306; Imperial Gazetteer I, 608; Gray 1894, 29; Wilson & McMillan, 48.

---

30.   ELSHIESHIELDS TOWER

(1½ m NW Lochmaben)   (NY069850)

Elshieshields first comes on record, albeit fleetingly, c.1245, when Humphrey de Boys granted 'Elsyscales', in the county of Dumfries, to Robert de Brus, Lord of Annandale.[1] It then seems to have disappeared from the records for nearly two centuries, before re-emerging early in the 15th century in the possession of Gavin Johnestoun, commonly called 'Gawen of the Wood', who is reputed to have been a son of Johnston of Lochwood.[2] It is not known when, or from whom, he obtained Elshieshields and the adjoining property of Esbie, though it is said that it was early in the century when he obtained permission from Roger de Ross to bring water from the river Ae.[3] In 1485/6, Gavin Johnston, now designated 'of Esby', having outlived his eldest son, granted the 12 merk lands of Esby and the 1 merk lands of Elcheschelis to his grandson Gawin Johnestoun, reserving free tenement for himself and a third share for his wife, Mary Scott.[4] This was done at the 'manerium de Elcheschelis'.[5]

Fig. 208 Elshieshields Tower: view from SE.

Wilkin was granted remission for various offences committed by himself, his four sons, his brother Robert and his nephew John.[16] Wilkin was Provost of Lochmaben in 1617, and it was in that year, when various Border lairds subscribed a band to uphold the laws of the realm, that Wilkin had to sign both for himself and for the burgh.[17]

It is impossible to be certain when the oldest part of the present tower at Elshieshields was built. It could date from the time of the first laird, but it is more likely that it was built to replace an earlier dwelling, probably of timber, sometime during either the closing years of the 15th century or the first half of the 16th century. The stair wing was added later, perhaps in 1567 (*infra*), and the tower finally completed in its present form by Wilkin Johnston, reputedly *c.*1590. It stands on a cliff on the right bank of the Water of Ae, from where it had an extensive view over the flat lands of the Ae and Kinnel valleys. Despite the close bond that existed between the Johnstons of Elshieshields and their chiefs at Lochwood, the proximity of Elshieshields to the territory of the Maxwells, and the wild life led by some of the family, the tower itself seems to have had a fairly quiet history.[18] It was well away from the main English invasion routes, and had the added advantage of natural defences provided by marshes on three sides.

There is evidence that the present, **L–plan TOWER** started life as a simple, rectangular fortalice with the entrance at first floor level and wooden stairs or ladders between the floors. A stair-wing with a new entrance was subsequently added, and later

The younger Gavin was succeeded by his son William in 1520, and he in turn by his eldest son John, following William's death 'in Elsoschelis' in 1535 or 1536.[6] It appears, however, that John did not receive formal sasine until shortly before his death in 1574.[7] It was during the 'Rough Wooing' by England in 1547 that the tower achieved a rare mention, when John Jardine of Applegarth held Alexander Baillie in Little Gill 'in firm custody in the places of Spadlinggis and Elcheschelis and other places in Annandale' for 6 months before handing him over to the English Warden.[8] In 1560 John was called upon to assist his chief in keeping order in the Borders.[9]

John was succeeded by his eldest son, Wilkin, who was laird of Elshieshields for over 50 years, and died *c.*1628 'at a great age'.[10] Wilkin features in numerous records. Although he did not take part himself in the great clan battle fought between the Johnstons and Maxwells at Dryfesands in 1593, three of his brothers were present.[11] Two years later Johnston of that Ilk had to name pledges for the good rule of various 'gangs' of Johnstons, including 'the gang of Brumel and Elscheschelis'.[12] Then, in 1597, Wilkin himself had to stand surety that he and his men would keep good rule.[13] In an age when lawlessness was a part of everyday life in the Borders, Wilkin and his family would seem to have been an especially wild lot. Trouble flared up again in 1610, when there were various reports of Wilkin and his sons carrying hagbuts and pistolets, and even of one son, Archibald, using them against anyone with whom he had a quarrel.[14] Eventually, the lairds of Amisfield and Kirkmichael had to stand surety that Wilkin and another son, James, would keep the peace and not carry hagbuts or pistolets again.[15] The next day

Fig. 209 Elshieshields Tower: view from NW.

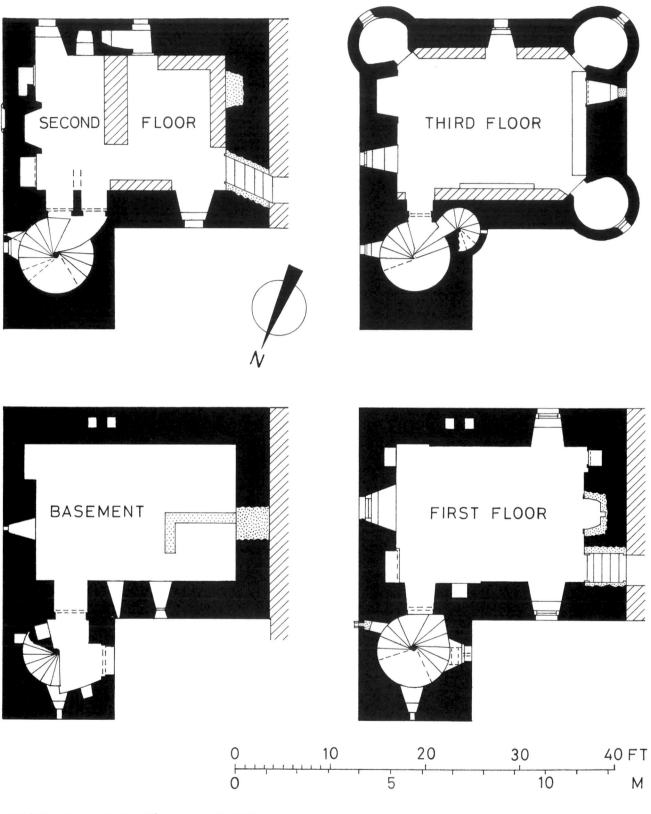

ELSHIESHIELDS TOWER

Fig. 210 Elshieshields Tower: plans.

still the upper works, which have a close affinity with the work carried out at Amisfield in 1600. There is a tradition that the latter work was added *c*.1590. When Sir Steven Runciman carried out a major restoration of the tower in 1966-7, many early features and structural changes were revealed. An early history of the Johnstons of Elshieshields[19] included the statement 'Building of Tower 1567', but this is unconfirmed and there is insufficient evidence to say what part may have been built at that time, or to what period the oldest part of the present main block should be assigned. The absence of gun-loops would suggest an earlier date for the basement than might be inferred from the thickness of the walls.

The main block measures 28ft 2in by 22ft 4in over walls varying in thickness from 3ft 9in to 4ft, while the wing at the E end of the N wall is 13ft wide and projects 10ft 7in. The masonry is local rubble with sandstone dressings; the walls are harled. At the lower levels the mouldings are a simple roll or QER, but just above the main wall-head the wing has a cable moulded string-course and, at its own wall-head, a billet- or chequer-moulded course that continues across the wing's gables. All the gables are crow-stepped.

The entrance, which is in the re-entrant angle, gives direct access to the stair and to the basement. Above it there is a short drip-stone and an empty armorial panel with a dog-tooth surround, while the doorway itself is provided with a double-rebate for an outer wooden door and an inner yett, now gone. Inside, at the foot of the stair, there is an open aumbry and behind the door a small lamp-shelf. Surprizingly, the basement is not vaulted. It had a small window at each end and a third one on the N side, where there is also a squint or shot-hole, presumably a later insertion, covering the entrance. There is also a recess for a press in the SE corner. The clearance beneath the beams supporting the floor above is only 6ft 1in.

The first floor was the hall. It had a fireplace at the W end[20] and one window in each of the other three walls, though the windows have at some period been greatly enlarged. When the tower was restored in 1966, the E window was found to have been inserted in the doorway of the original first floor entrance, the threshold stone for which was still *in situ*. In the wall outside, and immediately above, there is a heraldic panel with a bold QER surround bearing the arms of Johnston of Elshieshields. The original fireplace was also revealed, badly decayed, beneath

Fig. 212 Elshieshields: slop sink in stair-well.

the bolection-moulded surround of the smaller, 17th century fireplace that superseded it. There are two small buffets, each with QER mouldings on the jambs and lintel; that in the E wall has a rectangular surround, while the one in the middle of the N wall terminates on the lintel in two semi-circles that meet at a central boss, now broken off.[21] On the left of the fireplace is a closed aumbry, probably intended as a salt-box. Between this floor and the next there are two slop-sinks in the stair-wing. One of these discharged through the E wall, while the other, now blocked, discharged over the entrance like the one at Fourmerkland.

The second floor was originally divided into two chambers, each with its own doorway off the stair; but whilst the rooms in such an arrangement were often similar in size and layout, here they were quite different. The smaller room to the E had a surprizingly large fireplace for its size and, on the S side, a solitary window and a small garderobe recess, the latter feature having neither a lamp shelf nor a window. The fireplace is 4ft 5in wide, with a QER moulding on its surround,[22] and to the right of it there is an aumbry, which returns towards the fire at the rear to keep salt or other items dry. The other room was much larger. It originally had at least two windows, though only one, on the N

Fig. 211 Elshieshields Tower: open aumbry in great hall.

Fig. 213 Elshieshields: fireplace on second floor.

side, has survived: the one to the W was converted into a doorway when the adjoining house was added. As on the first floor,
all these windows would originally have been protected by iron
grilles, some of the sockets for which have survived, showing
that the sills have at some time been lowered. The fireplace in
this room was destroyed in Victorian times when a smaller one
was inserted in its place; that too has now been filled in. This
room also had a garderobe, but unlike the one in the adjacent
room it was provided with its own door and small window.[23]
The shafts from both garderobes, though now blocked, were
found to discharge into a common drain below ground level.

The third floor – which is part of the works added c.1590
– consists of a single room, partly contained within the
steeply-pitched roof. It is provided with a window in each gable
and a dormer window in the middle of the S side, the latter having an elaborate QERH moulding on its jambs, which continues
up the pediment in a most unusual manner and terminates in a
finial. At the SE, SW and NW corners there are corbelled-out
corner-turrets of a unique type; each has one small window at
normal level, 4ft 4in above the floor, while at a height of 6ft 7in
there are three, small, square openings, or shot-holes, covering
every angle. Access to these would have been by means of removable platforms, but the reason for this apparently-unnecessary
complication is a mystery. At the E end there is a large fireplace
with a corbelled-out lintel and multiple QER-type surround; it is
of a more elaborate and later type than those on the floors below. From the form of the old beams supporting the roof, it is
evident that the ceiling of this room has always taken the form
of a segmental vault. The main stair ends at this level, access to
the higher floors in the wing being by means of a stair-turret
corbelled-out in the re-entrant angle.

The two further floors in the wing each comprise a single, small chamber. The lower one has a fireplace in the N wall
and small windows, with QER surrounds, on three sides. Beneath the N window is a lamp-shelf. The top floor is a garret.
High in its S wall is a hatch, reached by ladder, that gave access
to the open watch-turret on the gable head. The latter feature is
elaborately corbelled-out and provided with one small shot-hole,
angled downwards, on each side immediately below the coping.
Both the head of the watch-turret and the chimney-stack on the
N gable carry a billet moulding.

In 1617 John Murray of Lochmaben was granted a crown
charter of the superiority of various lands, including the lands of
Elshieshields and Esbie, 'with the manor-places',[24] and this was
confirmed by a further charter in 1625, after he was created Earl
of Annandale.[25] That title became extinct on the death of the
2nd Earl in 1658. Three years later James Johnston, 2nd Earl of
Hartfell, was made Earl of Annandale, and the following year
he received a crown charter of many lands, including the lands
of Elshieshields and Esbie, all of which were now erected into
the free barony, lordship and earldom of Annandale.[26]

Meanwhile, in 1625, Wilkin Johnston died and was succeeded, first by his eldest son James, and then, in 1629, by his
second son, Archibald. It was from Archibald that the owners of
Elshieshields for the next three centuries were descended.[27]
Archibald was succeeded in 1647 by his son John. John was
appointed a Justice of the Peace for Dumfriesshire in 1663.[28]
Two years later, he represented the burgh of Lochmaben at the
Convention of Estates;[29] and he was present at the Convention
again in 1667 and 1678,[30] as well as representing Lochmaben in
parliament from 1669 to 1674, and again in 1681.[31] He was
appointed a Commissioner of Supply in 1667 and 1678.[32] He

was also a Captain of Foot in the militia in 1668,[33] a Commis-
sioner of Excise in 1675,[34] and Provost of Lochmaben in 1681.[35]
In the last year, parliament granted him a ratification under the
Great Seal of the 12 merkland of Esbie and the merkland of
Elshieshields, with the manor-place, houses, etc.[36] He took the
Test in 1683.[37] He was succeded by his elder son Alexander.[38]

Alexander Johnston, who was retoured heir in 1688,[39]
was appointed a Commissioner of Supply for Dumfriesshire in
1691, 1696 and 1698,[40] and represented Nithsdale and the
Stewartry of Annandale in parliament from 1693 until 1701.[41]
His daughter Marion married Robert Edgar, burgess of Dumfries,[42] and they had an only son, Theodore, who practised for a
while as a chirurgeon in London. On Alexander's death in 1738,
there arose a dispute over the succession between Marion and
James Maxwell of Barncleugh, to whom Marion's half-brother
Alexander Johnston (by Alexander's second marriage) had conveyed his interest in Elshieshields. This led to litigation, which
was eventually resolved in 1744 by Maxwell selling Elshieshields
to Theodore.[43] It was presumably Theodore who built the
two-storeyed house that was added at the W end of the tower
around this time.

After Theodore Edgar's death in 1784, Elshieshields
passed to his niece Marion Edgar. She married one John Dickson,
and had two sons and a daughter. Neither of the sons married,
and only the younger one, John, survived his parents; it was he
who eventually succeeded to Elshieshields. He added a second
floor to the house during the 1830's and a kitchen wing in 1848.[44]
On his death in 1858, Elshieshields passed to his sister, Marion,
and her husband, William Byrne. They made various additions
and alterations to the house, and further changes were made by
their descendants early in the 20th century.[45]

Elshieshields was finally sold by Colonel Byrne c.1945,
after the property had been in the same family for 500 years.[46] It
was ultimately purchased in 1966 by the Hon. Sir Steven
Runciman, the distinguished Byzantine scholar, who undertook
a complete restoration of the tower and house.

---

1   Bain V, No.14.
2   Edgar, 91. His designation 'of the Wood' may well allude to Lochwood.
3   Forman, S. 'Elshieshields', *Scottish Field*, January 1948.
4   Both Gavin and his wife must have lived to a great age, as, according to one
     account, they are first mentioned as husband and wife in 1419 (Edgar, 91).
5   RMS II, No.1661.
6   RSS II, No.1993; ERS XIV, 635. William was still alive in 1535.
7   RMS IV, No.451.
8   RMS IV, No.451.
9   Edgar, 93.
10   Edgar, 95; Forman, *op. cit.*
11   Fraser 1873, II, 497-8.
12   RPC V, 739.
13   Ibid, 744.
14   RPC IX, 301.
15   Ibid, 655.
16   Edgar, 95.
17   RPC XI, 226.
18   According to one account, the tower was attacked and burned by William
     Maxwell of Kirkhouse in 1602 (Johnstone 1889, 145); but this appears to be
     confused with the raid made on nearby Dalfibble at that time, when Lord
     Maxwell burned Dalfibble and murdered its occupant, William Johnston, a
     younger brother of Elshieshields (RPC VIII, 767, 805; Fraser 1894, I, cxliii).
19   Written by one of the Edgar descendants, and at one time loaned to the Hon.
     Sir Steven Runciman of Elshieshields.
20   In the Hearth Tax returns c.1690, Elshieshields is credited with a total of 9
     fireplaces – Adamson, D. 'The Hearth Tax', *TDGAS*, 3rd Ser., XLIX, 73.
21   This type of moulding, comprising two semi-circular arches meeting at a
     central boss, is also found at Fairgirth House, in the Stewartry, where it also
     appears over an aumbry (Gifford, 307), and Hoddom, where it is found on the
     lintel of the wing's fourth floor fireplace (q.v.).

22 The size of the fireplace is hard to explain. Had it survived from an original arrangement when the room was not divided, there would not have been two drains down to ground level for the gardrobes.

23 Sir Steven Runciman has suggested that the E room was for the use of the gentlemen and the W room for the ladies.

24 RMS VII, No.1600.

25 RMS VIII, No.826.

26 RMS XI, No.230.

27 Edgar, 95-98 and Pedigree of Johnston of Elshieshields.

28 APS VII, 505.

29 Ibid, 526.

30 Ibid, 536; VIII, 213.

31 Ibid, VII, 548; VIII, *passim*.

32 Ibid, VII, 544; VIII, 225.

33 RPC, 3rd Ser., II, 542.

34 Ibid, IV, 474.

35 Parl. of Scot., I, 380.

36 APS VIII, 401.

37 RPC, 3rd Ser., VIII, 640.

38 Edgar, Pedigree of 'Johnston of Elshieshields'.

39 Ibid, 97.

40 RPC, 3rd Ser., XVI, 232; APS X, 29, 131.

41 APS IX, 238, 347; X, *passim*.

42 It was this Robert Edgar who, *c*.1746, wrote the well-known *Introduction to A History of Dumfries*, which, with copious notes by the celebrated scholar Dr. R. C. Reid, was published by the Dumfriesshire & Galloway Natural History & Antiquarian Society in 1915. It was to have been part of a much more comprehensive history of the burgh, which was never completed.

43 The conflict arose from the terms of Alexander Johnston's first marriage settlement (Edgar, 97). Another claimant to the estate was one James Johnstone, described as 'now of Elshieshields'.

44 Notes of Sir Steven Runciman.

45 Ibid.

46 Forman, S., *op. cit.*

31.   FOURMERKLAND TOWER

(4¹/₂ m NW Dumfries)   (NX908808)

Fourmerkland is a classic, small tower-house of the late 16th century. It was built in 1590 by Robert Maxwell on lands that had formerly belonged to the abbey of Holywood, but nothing seems to be known about either Robert or his family. His initials, together with those of his wife 'I.G.', the date and his

Fig. 214 Fourmerkland Tower: view from SE.

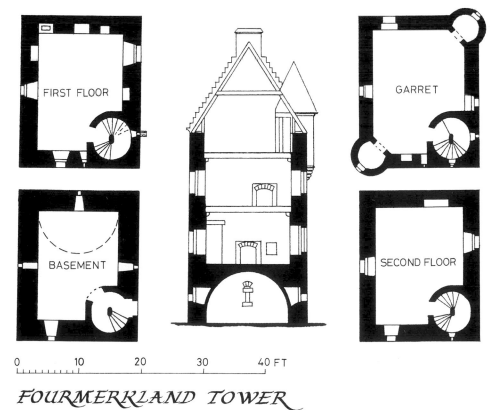

FIRST FLOOR

BASEMENT

GARRET

SECOND FLOOR

0   10   20   30   40 FT

FOURMERKLAND TOWER

Fig. 215 Fourmerkland Tower: plans and sectional elevation (after MacGibbon & Ross).

'arms'[1] appear on the armorial panel over the entrance.[2] Nothing now remains of the barmkin, outbuildings or later works that presumably once existed, while the marsh that originally provided a strong natural defence for the site has long since been drained. 'Fourmarkland' is shown on Pont's survey of Nithsdale c.1595.[3]

The **TOWER**, which is oblong in plan, measures 24ft 2in by 19ft 6in over walls 3ft thick at basement level and progressively less higher up, and rises through four storeys to the steeply pitched roof, whose apex is some 44ft above the ground. Corbelled-out from the E and W corners are diagonally opposed corner-turrets, the upper halves of which have been rebuilt. A dormer-window on the SE side, the upper half of which has also been rebuilt, is a very early example, but the one on the NW side is a modern addition. The masonry is local rubble, mainly red sandstone, with ashlar dressings and mouldings. For the main features, such as the entrance doorway and hall fireplace, QER mouldings have been employed. The windows were protected with iron grilles.

The entrance admits directly to the foot of the wheel-stair and the vaulted basement, a low chamber only 7ft 11in high. This chamber has a slit-window in each wall, and is floored with a mixture of rubble and flags. There was a hatch to the floor above. The stair is unusual in being slightly oval in plan, with a minimum diameter of 6ft. Between the first and second floors there is a 'slop-sink' that discharged over the entrance.[4] Several of the higher slit-windows illuminating the stair have a lancet shape.

The first floor was the hall. It has a fireplace, 5ft 2in wide, at the NE end, with an aumbry on its right that was probably intended as a salt-box. There are also open-aumbries in the

Fig. 216 Fourmerkland: restored corner turret.

NW and SE walls. The latter one, which is close to the stair, is unusually large and seems to have served as a simple, unadorned buffet; it measures 2ft 4in wide, 3ft 2in high and 1ft deep. In the N corner there is a garderobe. Because of the relative thinness of the walls (2ft 8in), this encroached upon the hall, but was presumably partitioned off. The window on the SE side has been greatly enlarged in modern times.

On the second floor the corresponding window has also been enlarged. Other features on this floor are a small fireplace, 3ft 9in wide, at the NE end; an aumbry, which opens out by about 3in behind each jamb; and a shot-hole at the S end of the NW wall. 6½in in diameter at the outer wall-face, and widely splayed on the inside, this shot-hole is reminiscent of the one covering the entrance from first floor level at Lochar Tower.

The third floor, which has a small fireplace at the SW end, gave access to the corner turrets. Each turret is carried on three, continuous corbel-courses and has one small window looking straight out from the angle; but there is no evidence of any shot-holes. In the roof above this floor, there is in each gable a most unusual, horizontal opening, resembling a splayed gun-loop.

In 1618 the superiority of the lands of Fourmerkland and many other properties that had formerly belonged to the abbey of Holywood were granted by the crown to John Murray of Lochmaben.[5]

Mungo (also known as Quintigern) Maxwell of Fourmerkland is on record in 1630, when he granted his wife, Margaret, daughter of John Wilson of Croglin, a liferent in the property;[6] and their son Robert is on record in 1660.[7] Robert was evidently succeeded by his daughter Agnes. She married James Ferguson, who in 1696 is designated 'of Fourmerkland'.[8] He was appointed a Commissioner of Supply for Nithsdale and Dumfries in 1704.[9] The next laird appears to have been Robert Fergusson, presumably the son, who purchased the patronage of the parish of Holywood and was living at Fourmerkland in 1720,[10] having married Jean, daughter of Alexander Fergusson of Isle, the previous year.[11]

Later, Fourmerkland came into the possession of Robert Beveridge 'of Fourmerkland', who was proprietor of the estate and patron of the living until his death c.1790.[12] He evidently had no issue, being succeeded by his sisters, the eldest of whom married James McMillan, minister of Torthorwald.[13]

The tower continued to be inhabited until 1896,[14] and, although without modern facilities, is still maintained in excellent repair.

1   A saltire, in chief a holly leaf and in base a stag's head in pale between in fesse, dexter a mullet and sinister ? (worn away). These arms are 'unofficial', being both unrecorded at the Lyon Court and an unrecognized 'difference'.
2   Despite this information, and all that is known of Maxwell family genealogies, neither the builder's wife nor family have been identified.
3   Pont MS. No.35 in National Library of Scotland.
4   The positioning of slop-sinks directly over the entrance is not uncommon, and suggests an intended secondary use against unwelcome visitors.
5   RMS, VII, No.1817.
6   PRS Dumfries, III, 68.
7   PRS Dumfries I (1617-71), Index, 284.
8   Ibid, II (1672-1702), Index, 94, 247.
9   APS XI, 142.
10   Tranter 1965, III, 83.
11   Burke L.G. 1906, 579, 'Gillon-Fergusson of Isle'.
12   Stat Acct I, 25.
13   Ibid.
14   NSA IV, 559; RCAHMS 1920, No.280.

32. FRENCHLAND TOWER
(1m E Moffat)   (NT102054)

The lands of Frenchland take their name from the Norman family of French, who are first recorded in the Moffat district late in the 12th century. At that time William Franciscus (French) held two oxgangs of land at Moffat in farm of Sir Robert de Brus, Lord of Annandale.[1] Sometime around the middle of the following century, William's son Roger resigned a similar area of land that he held of de Brus at Warmanbie, near Annan, in exchange for his father's former holding at Moffat.[2] This was presumably the original land of Frenchland. Despite the apparently small extent of the property involved, Roger must have been a man of some substance – he appended his seal to the deed –, who would have required a strong house for his protection. This may well have been one of the mottes or moated sites whose earthworks still abound in the area, but none can be ascribed to the Frenches with any certainty.[3]

Fig. 217 Frenchland Tower: view from SW, with later stair wing on the right.

The Frenches subsequently disappear from local records for more than two centuries, until, some time c.1500, a branch of the Frenches of Thornydykes acquired the barony of Cuthberts from the Knights Templar.[4] This barony comprised Chapel and other lands immediately west and NW of Moffat. It is not clear whether the Frenches had continued to hold Frenchland during the intervening years, though the circumstantial evidence would suggest that they did. In a charter of 1527, it is stated that the Frenches held the lands of Frenchland of the king for service of ward.[5] Ten years later, on the death of Adam French of Frenchland, his son and heir, Robert French of Gilbertrig,[6] together with John French in The Gill-foot, received from the crown the gift of ward of the £5 lands of Frenchland, with the mill and mill land.[7] Robert is also said to have had 'rights' in the adjacent lands of Auldton and Moffat.[8] There is no mention of a 'tower' or 'fortalice' at this date, nor in later records in the century, and it may be significant that no tower of Frenchland appears on Aglionby's Platte c.1590.[9] 'Frenscheland' is, however, included in the 'Roll of landlords . . . dwelling on the Borders . . . where broken men has dwelt and presently dwell' in 1590;[10]

and later the same year Robert French of Frenchland had to find caution for his good behaviour and that of his clan.[11]

After 1600, references to the Frenches of Frenchland become increasingly frequent.[12] In 1611 Robert French of Frenchland and his son William were charged to find lawburrows,[13] and in 1622 the 'Laird of Frenchland' was nominated to assist the Earl of Nithsdale in administering justice in the Borders.[14] It is not, however, until 1629 that the tower is first mentioned. In that year, 'the town and lands of Frenchland, with the tower and manor-place', which had been apprised from William French of Frenchland by William Carnegie for debt, were assigned by Carnegie to John Jonkene, inhabitant of Leith.[15] Perhaps it was the cost of building the tower that proved too much for French. Tower-houses were expensive ventures, and only four years earlier, when the Earl of Annandale received a crown charter erecting all the lands of which he was superior into the Earldom of Annandale, various towers and manor-places were mentioned, but none in association with 'the lands of Frenschland'.[16] – The tower was built on a south-facing hillside, beside the Frenchland Burn, from where it had an excellent view down Annandale and westwards to Moffat and the roads north.

The oldest part of the present building was a simple, oblong **TOWER**, on to which a new stair and accommodation wing was later added, possibly later in the 17th century. At the same time, the floor levels of the tower were altered and the roof-line changed to a simple, pitched roof. The tower measures 21ft 4in from N to S by 26ft 3in from E to W, over walls averaging 3ft 6in in thickness. It is built of local Silurian rubble, with roughly dressed quoins and sandstone mouldings for the windows and aumbries. There is no evidence of vaulting. Most of the side walls collapsed long ago, leaving no record of the features they contained, nor of the later entrance in the re-entrant angle of the wing.[17] The only feature to have survived at basement level is the curved profile of a partly-mural wheel-stair, 6ft in diameter, which rose to serve all floors in the SE corner. There is no evidence of an original entrance at this level, nor is one shown in MacGibbon & Ross's plan of 1889, made when the tower was more complete.[18] On the other hand, although the

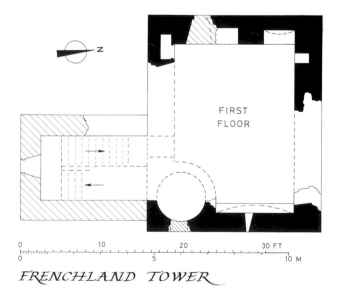

Fig. 218 Frenchland Tower: plan of first floor and later stair-wing.

remains of a doorway giving direct access to the wheel-stair at first floor level may be seen blocked up inside the E wall, it is highly unlikely that a tower of such a late date would have had its entrance at this level. A more likely explanation is that it gave access to an extension, which at one time abutted the N gable.

The first floor seems to have been divided into two chambers, a hall at the W end and a smaller chamber, probably a kitchen, to the E. The latter was partly mural, where a relieving arch, evidently for a large fireplace, spans the width of the E wall. In the back of this recess there is a small slit-window. A similar arrangement may be seen at Timpendean.[19] Immediately adjacent in the N wall, there is the jamb of a recess, which may have been an oven or another slit-window. At the W end of this floor, and above the later floor level, there is a central fireplace. This is flanked by a mural recess in the NW corner and a window recess, now blocked, on the other side. The outer face of this window has sockets for an iron grille. Immediately adjacent in the S wall there is a closed aumbry, which opens out within the corner of the wall, and to the E of it are the remains of a window recess. Opposite, in the N wall, there is a lamp shelf.

The second floor was also divided into two chambers. It had a fireplace adjacent to the stair at the E end and to the left of it, in the NE corner, what appears to have been a partly-mural garderobe, with a small window that still retains the sockets for an iron grille. Another small window at the W end only has sockets for two vertical bars, suggesting a later date.

A little above this level, there appears originally to have been a square corner-turret, which was corbelled out from the SW corner on roughly-cut, individual corbels.[20] Despite later alterations, four of the corbels have survived; each is about 7in wide, and they extend across the W gable for a distance of 5ft 9in. Normally one would expect to find a similar turret at the NE corner, but no evidence of a second turret has survived and it is possible that, being on the uphill side and away from any expected source of attack, there wasn't one. When the tower was later modernized, the turret or turrets were removed and a new, steeply-pitched, slate roof added.[21] This incorporated an additional, high level attic, which was lit by two small windows in the E gable.

The later wing, which is 12ft 11in wide, was added at the E end of the S wall, from where it extends 15ft 6in towards the S. The walls are 2ft 6in thick. This wing contained a new entrance in the re-entrant angle and a generously proportioned scale-and-platt stair that rose to the second floor. Above this level there was one attic room with a large window facing S. This was probably reached from the old wheel-stair.

David French of Frenchland and his son William are on record in 1635.[22] David was apparently the son of Roger French in Moffat, and he too had been living in Moffat in 1618.[23] It is not apparent what their relationship to William French of Frenchland (*supra*) was.

Later, in 1684, Robert French of Frenchland is on record, when those living in the township of 'Frenchland' also included Adam French, Roger French, John French, Marion French, Katherine French, Margaret French and 19 others.[24] The township itself, or fermtoun, lay some 400 yards to the N of the tower, and comprised a group of four buildings, with a fifth building a short distance apart to the SSE. The remains of the buildings and their associated rig-and-furrow fields may still be seen on the hillside above the Frenchland Burn.[25] Robert was still at Frenchland in 1692, when the Hearth Tax lists credit Frenchland

with just two fireplaces;[26] but by 1701 Frenchland was apparently in the possession of one David French, writer in Edinburgh,[27] whose possession of ' all and haill the Toune and Lands of Frenchland, with the tower, fortalice, manner place and milne thereof' was ratified by parliament in 1707.[28] His relationship is not given, but he had obtained Frenchland by the resignation of Rodger French of Frenchland and his brother Robert, and also by an adjudication obtained against Margaret French, daughter of Thomas French and, through Thomas's mother, great-niece and heiress of Adam French of Frenchland.[29]

The Frenches finally sold Frenchland c.1750 to James Veitch of Eliock (d.1793), later Lord Eliock, the eminent lawyer.[30] In 1790 it was purchased by Dr. John Rogerson,[31] formerly first physician to the Empress Catherine of Russia, who subsequently joined it with the nearby estate of Dumcrieff, where he died in 1823. It was then that the tower is said to have fallen into disuse.[32]

---

1   Bain I, No.705.

2   Ibid; Macquarrie, A. 'Notes on some Charters of the Bruces of Annandale', *TDGAS*, 3rd Ser., LVIII, 73.

3   See RCAHMS 1920, Parish of Moffat, pp.170-6. – There is a moated site ½ mile NNW of the tower, beyond the later fermtoun, that could have been the Frenches original home.

4   Moffat, 26. – Thornydykes, in Berwickshire, had been granted to Robert Franche by Robert III c.1400 (RMS I, App.2, No.1921). Thereafter, Thornydykes and Frenchland remained in the same family for more than 200 years.

5   RMS III, No.525.

6   'Gilbertrig' is the same as 'Kirkbertrig' and 'St. Cuthbert's', the 'Chapel' lands of the Knights Templar.

7   RSS II, No.2401.

8   Moffat, 26.

9   Hyslop, 320. Pont's maps do not cover Upper Annandale.

10   RPC IV, 786.

11   Ibid, 790, 808.

12   MacGibbon & Ross III, 552; RMS VII, Nos.270, 1967; Moffat 1908, 26.

13   RPC, 2nd Ser., VIII, 316.

14   RPC XII, 695.

15   RMS VIII, No.1498. For the 'town of Frenchland', see RCAHMS 1920, No.494.

16   Ibid., No.826. – The wording was based on a charter granted to the same John Murray in 1617 (RMS VII, No.1600).

17   The Sketch Books of William L.Ferguson in the NMRS include views of the tower drawn in 1900, together with a measured drawing of a fragment of one of the door jambs (Sketch Book 10). There is no indication as to whether it belonged to the original entrance or the later one, but it has a double rebate (the inner one rather shallow) and a QERH moulding on the surround.

18   Gibbon & Ross III, Fig.496.

19   Here the relieving arch may well have been part of an original kitchen fireplace, which was later modified, whilst at Timpendean the arrangement is clearly that of a small, vaulted room.

20   Another suggestion is that there was a timber parapet, though the use of timber for such a feature would have been rare, if not unique, at such a late date (See RCAHMS 1997, 215-6).

21   It is believed that the original roof was of thatch (RCAHMS 1997, 215).

22   PRS Dumfries I (1617-71), Index, 96.

23   Ibid.

24   RPC, 3rd Ser., IX, 399.

25   See RCAHMS 1997, 233, Figs. 249, 250.

26   Adamson, D 'The Hearth Tax for Dumfriesshire', *TDGAS*, 3rd Ser., XLIX, 82.

27   GRS LXXIX, f.399.

28   APS XI, 467.

29   Adam is described as the son of Robert French of Frenchland, whose father was also Robert French of Frenchland. Thomas's father had been Captain William French, portioner in Moffat.

30   Turnbull 1871, 28.

31   Dr. Rogerson was the son of Samuel Rogerson, who farmed at Lochbrow on the Annandale Estates.

32   Prevost 1954, 19.

33.   FRIARS CARSE
(6m NNW Dumfries)   (NX925850)

The lands of Carse, in Nithsdale, belonged of old to the abbey of Melrose, which established a cell there. By the latter half of the 15th century, however, it had become difficult to maintain this outpost, and with the decline in the abbey's fortunes early in the 16th century, it was decided to feu out various of the abbey's lands to increase its revenue. Accordingly, in 1536,[1] Abbot Andrew granted the £4 land of 'Freirkers', with the mill called the Grange Mill and the restricted multures of the £36 lands of Dalgonar and other lands, to John Kirkpatrick of Ellisland, reputedly a cadet of Closeburn.[2] He was succeeded by his son Thomas Kirkpatrick 'of Freirkers', who, with his wife Janet Gordon, are on record in 1565;[3] and in 1579 John Kirkpatrick of Friars Carse was witness to the registration of a band.[4]

Six years later, in 1585, John Kirkpatrick of Friars Carse, son and heir of Thomas Kirkpatrick of Ellisland, received from the Commendator of Melrose a new charter of the £4 lands of Friars Carse and the mill, and of the restricted multures of the £36 lands of Dalgonar, etc., for the yearly payment of £120 for the lands and multures and 1d for the office of bailie.[5] John succeeded to Ellisland the same year.[6] Evidently Friars Carse had become the home of successive heirs to the family seat. It was the Kirkpatricks who built the tower at Friars Carse – on a rocky promontory in a bend of the river Nith – sometime during the latter half of the 16th century. The tower at 'Freercarss' is shown on Pont's map of Nithsdale c.1595.[7]

Fig. 219 Friars Carse from the SE, c. 1772.

Nothing of that period now remains. Soon after Dr. Robert Riddell, the antiquary, inherited the property from his maternal grandfather in 1771 (infra),[8] he pulled down the, by then ruinous, old buildings to make room for a modern mansion. Among these buildings was the monks' old refectory, of which Grose says that the walls were 8ft thick and the fireplace 12ft wide.[9] Riddell's enthusiasm for antiquity, however, ensured that the old work did not pass unrecorded. Both Cardonnel (1788) and Grose (1789), who was a guest at Friars Carse, included it in their respective 'Antiquities of Scotland'; and despite the fact that some sixteen years had elapsed since the old tower was demolished, their illustrations of the former buildings, viewed respectively from the SE and N, are sufficiently alike to give a fair idea of how the old tower must have appeared.

The illustrations show a range of buildings around three sides of a courtyard, which is open to the N. On the S side is the **TOWER**, a rectangular building, shown relatively small on plan,[10] which rose through three storeys to a garret. The entrance was on the N side. It admitted to the basement and the NW corner, where a wheel-stair rose to parapet level, terminating in a cap-house. The basement, which had no windows at the sides, was probably vaulted. Both pictures show a splayed, rectangular gun-loop at basement level and a corbelled-out parapet, but Cardonnel also shows a splayed plinth course and rounds at the corners of the parapet, details that are missing from Grose's picture. He also shows the parapet supported by broken corbelling, while the corbelling shown by Grose is continuous.

Fig. 220 Friars Carse from the N. 1789.

Adjoining the E side of the tower is a short, two-storey extension, with an armorial panel built into its N wall. The arms shown appear to be a saltire for Maxwell. At its NE corner, this addition abuts a substantial two-storey range, with three chimney stacks and crow-stepped gables, which runs along the E side of the courtyard. As many as five doorways are shown, suggesting that the latter building comprised stables and other offices, as well as accommodation for servants. From the NE corner of this building, a small, single-storey outhouse extends to the E. On the other side of the courtyard, an ornamental, arched gateway is shown flanked by two, single-storey buildings. None of these buildings, however, looks old enough to have been 'the old refectory, or dining room', with 'walls eight feet thick, and the chimney…twelve feet wide', referred to by Grose.[11]

Early in the 17th century, Friars Carse passed briefly to a branch of the Stirlings who ended in an heiress, Jean Stirling, who married John Maxwell of Templand, a cadet of the Maxwells of Tinwald.[12] John Maxwell had a charter of the £4 lands of Friars Carse and the mill from the commendator of Melrose, for the yearly payment of £120, but it is undated.[13] His son Herbert obtained sasine of Friars Carse from his mother, Jean, in 1643;[14] and the lands remained in the possession of his descendants until 1737, when they were sold to Robert Riddell of Glenriddell, the grandfather of the distinguished antiquary. But for a century possession was in dispute.

The problem arose because, some time before 1647 John Irving, merchant burgess and provost of Dumfries, had also obtained possession of Friars Carse. How, and from whom, he acquired the property is not known,[15] but it was later apprised from him by his father-in-law, Stephen Laurie of Maxwelton, who obtained unrestricted possession when the reversion expired.[16] Then, in 1647, Stephen Laurie granted the '£4 lands of Friercarse, with the tower, fortalice and manor place', to his grandson, John Irving, 2nd of Friars Carse, and John's spouse, Elizabeth Crichton, as part of their marriage contract.[17]

After her husband's death, Elizabeth Crichton, having obtained a decreet of adjudication in her favour, granted Friars Carse in 1680 to her daughter Margaret and son-in-law John Maxwell, 2nd of Barncleugh;[18] and the lands remained in their family until 1744, when James Maxwell, 3rd of Barncleugh, and his son agreed to submit all questions regarding the disputed ownership of Friars Carse to arbitration. The final decision was that the Maxwells of Barncleugh were bound to remove from the estate and, in return for £1500 compensation, convey it to Robert Riddell of Glenriddell.[19] Thereafter, Robert lived at Friars Carse until his death in 1771.

Robert's wife was Jean, daughter of Alexander Fergusson of Craigdarroch and Annie Laurie, the famous 'Annie Laurie' of Scottish song; and it was at Friars Carse that Annie died in 1764, aged 81.[20] Robert was succeeded at Friars Carse by his grandson, Dr. Robert Riddell, the antiquary, whose mother, Anne, one of Robert's daughters and co-heiresses, had married Walter Riddell of Newhouse.[21] Dr. Robert Riddell was a neighbour and great friend of Robert Burns, and often entertained him at Friars Carse, and it was for Dr. Riddell's guest, Francis Grose, that Burns composed *Tam O'Shanter* for inclusion in Grose's *Antiquities of Scotland*.[22] Dr. Riddell died in 1794.

Fifteen years later, Friars Carse was bought by Dr. James Crichton, a wealthy physician who had been in the service of the East India Company. It was from his bequest of £100,000 for 'beneficent purposes' that the famous Crichton Royal Institution in Dumfries was founded.[23] It opened in 1839. His widow was still living at Friars Carse in 1850.

The subsequent ownership of Friars Carse has not been fully established by the writer, but the present Scots baronial mansion is evidently the result of a remodelling and additions by James Barbour in 1873 and Barbour and Bowie in 1909.[24] A Mr. C. Dickson lived here in 1912.[25] Friars Carse is now a convalescent home.

---

1   According to McDowall (McDowall 1986, 240), the lands of Friars Carse were first granted to the Kirkpatricks of Ellisland in 1465, but he does not give his source, and as all the names are the same as in the 1536 charter, the date must be questioned.
2   Melrose Regality Records, III, 385.
3   RSS V, No.2172.
4   RPC III, 244.
5   Melrose Regality Records, III, 388, 402.
6   Ibid, 323-4.
7   Pont MS. No.35 in National Library of Scotland.
8   DNB, 1775.
9   Grose I, 149.
10 The fact that each gable had a chimney stack strongly suggests that the tower was, in reality, considerably larger on plan than the illustrations portray.
11 Grose I, 149.
12 Fraser 1873, I, 597.
13 Melrose Regality Records, III, 412.
14 Fraser 1873, I, 598.
15 John Irving was the eldest son of Provost Francis Irving of Dumfries (d.1633). In 1620 he married Janet Laurie. – See Maxwell-Irving 1968 (III), 19-21; Burke L.G. 1968, 337, 'Irving of Dumfries'.
16 PRS Dumfries, XI, 114.
17 Ibid, X, 480; XI, 114.
18 Ibid, XI, 114. She actually 'sold' Barncleugh to her son-in-law, whilst reserving the liferent to him and his wife, Margaret.
19 Fraser 1873, I, 602.
20 Burke Peerage 1959, 1906, 'Riddell of Riddell', 1320, 'Laurie of Bedford Square'; Forman, S, 1967, 22.

21 Burke Peerage 1959, 1906, 'Riddell of Riddell'.
22 Grose II, 31-3.
23 NSA IV, 341; McDowall 1986, 813.
24 Gifford, 308.
25 County Directory 1912, 209.

---

34.   GILLESBIE TOWER
(¹/₂ m NE Boreland)   (NY172919)

A branch of the Grahams of Dalkeith held the lordship of Hutton as early as the reign of William the Lion, and it was there that they erected their first stronghold, the Motte of Hutton.[1] By the middle of the 14th century one branch of this family was in possession of the lands of Mosskeswra, some 3 miles to the NNE.[2] It was from a younger son of Mosskeswra that the Grahams of Gillesbie sprang.[3] The earliest of the family on record is John de Graham of Gillenbie, who in 1474 granted the Earl of Morton a reversion in the lands of Brakinwra.[4] Thereafter the family and their descendants appear regularly in the records for more than three centuries.[5] After William Graham lost possession of Mosskeswra early in the 16th century, the Grahams of Gillesbie seem to have become the acknowledged clan leaders locally, and their position was further enhanced when, c.1540, James Graham of Gillesbie also acquired Mosskeswra. It was as laird of Gillesbie and Mosskeswra that he and 40 of his men attended the wapenschaw held by Lord Maxwell at Burnswark in 1541.[6] Six years later, in 1547, the 'lard of Gyllysbye and those under hym' pledged 72 men to serve the English.[7]

Fig. 221 Gillesbie Tower: remains of tower seen from the south.

The ruins of the tower stand on top of a steep, rocky bank, high above the river Dryfe. This forms a natural defence to the SE, while a substantial rampart and outer ditch surround the site on the other three sides, enclosing an area about 90 feet square. The rampart still survives to a maximum height of 9 feet above the ditch. It is likely that these earthworks date from the earliest period of occupation – evidently in the 15th century[8] –, when the first tower may have been of timber. The present tower was probably built a little later, perhaps early in the following century, though there can be little doubt from its unusually large size and thick walls that it was an important strength, more akin to the smaller towers of the 15th century than those built a century later. Its first appearance on record is on Aglionby's Platte in 1590. Although the site has been disturbed and divided by a modern road, the outline of an outbuilding or inner court may still be discerned immediately NW of the tower.

The **TOWER** is oblong in plan, and measures 40ft 6in by 31ft 6in[9] over walls some 6ft thick, which now reach a maximum height of about 12ft in the S corner. The masonry is greywacke rubble, with extra large slabs being employed at the tower's boldly rounded corners for added strength. There are no visible dressings. What remains of the building is so ruinous and overgrown that, without excavation, the only features visible are a lamp shelf and garderobe flue at first floor level. The former is at the W end of the NW wall, while the flue, which is 9in square, descended in the S corner from an upper floor to emerge through an opening 2ft wide by 1ft 3in deep at ground level, whence it discharged down the cliff. The basement is now full of rubble and inaccessible, but one account states that it was vaulted.[10] No evidence of an entrance survives.

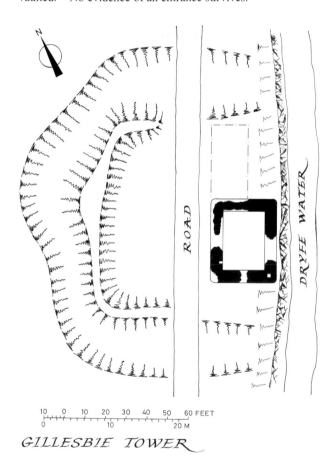

GILLESBIE TOWER

Fig. 222 Gillesbie Tower: site plan.

In 1606 Janet Graham was retoured heir to her grandfather, John Graham of Gillesbie,[11] and in 1624 Robert Graham of Gillesbie was cautioner for a bond.[12] The last Graham on record there was James Graham of Gillesbie, who was a cautioner in 1635. He may have been the last occupant of the old tower, for it is said to have been abandonned in 1641.[13] By 1793 the tower had been reduced to little more than may be seen today.[14]

Later in the 17th century Gillesbie came into the possession of the Scotts, whose male line came to an end in 1712,

when Janet Scott of Gillesbie was served heir to her grandfather, Robert Scott of Gillesbie.[15] Janet subsequently married Thomas Fordyce, a writer in Edinburgh.[16] Thereafter the estate changed hands several times before it was acquired in 1782 by Dr. John Rogerson, formerly first physician to the Empress Catherine of Russia,[17] and the Rogersons remained in possession until well into the present century.[18] William Rogerson of Gillesbie and Wamphray, who was laird in 1845,[19] was succeeded, first by his eldest son James, and then, on James's death without male issue, by his second son, William. William was a Colonel in the 53rd Regiment and a Justice of the Peace for Dumfriesshire.[20]

The modern house of Gillesbie stands some 400 yards SW of the old tower.

1   Reid, R.C. 'The Border Grahams', *TDGAS*, XXXVIII, 87-9. The earliest surviving Gillesbie writ, dated 1567, is a charter to John Graham, son and heir of James Graham of Gillesbie, of lands in Dalkeith (Reid MSS, 'MSS Various III', Calendar of Gillesbie Writs, 147).
2   Reid, 'The Border Grahams', *op. cit.*, 88.
3   Reid, R.C. 'Gillesbie Tower', *TDGAS*, XVIII, 377.
4   Reid, 'The Border Grahams', *op. cit.*, 92.
5   e.g. Hope-Johnstone MSS, Nos.8, 30, 31, 47; Reid, 'The Border Grahams', *op. cit.*, 87-9.
6   Buccleuch MSS, 66 (No.135).
7   Armstrong 1883, lxxvi
8   It has been suggested that, in view of its Anglo-Norman name, the earthworks could possibly be the remains of a small timber castle that existed as early as the 12th century (RCAHMS 1997, 195-6).
9   It is hard to measure the width: the RCAHMS give a dimension of 35ft.
10 Ordnance Gazetteer, 175.
11 Reid MSS, 'MSS Various III', Calendar of Gillesbie Writs, 148.
12 Reid, 'The Border Grahams', *op. cit.*, 93-4.
13 Reid, 'Gillesbie Tower', *op. cit.*, 377.
14 Stat Acct XIII, 578
15 Reid MSS, *op. cit.*, 150.
16 Ibid, 152.
17 Reid, 'Gillesbie Tower', *op. cit.*, 377. See also Frenchland.
18 Reid MSS, *op. cit.*, 159; Burke L.G. 1906, 1437, 'Rogerson of Gillesbie'; County Directory 1912, 218.
19 NSA IV, 538. Samuel Rogerson, who lived at Boreland at that time, was presumably a relative.
20 Burke, *op. cit.*

35.   GLENAE TOWER
($\frac{3}{4}$ m N Ae)   (NX984905)

The 3 merk lands of Neis and Glenaebank were, in 1463/4, granted to Herbert Johnston of Dalebank by the Earl of Crawford in recognition of faithful services rendered;[1] and twenty years later Herbert's son and heir, Herbert, received a crown charter re-affirming the grant.[2] At that time the lands were held by the crown following the forfeiture of Lord Crichton. Glenae subsequently remained with the Johnstons until, on the failure of the male line, they passed to Oliver Dinwoodie 'in Glenae', great-nephew and heir of Herbert Johnston, who was in possession in 1615.[3] It was presumably the Johnstons who built the tower sometime in the 16th century.[4]

The **TOWER** stands on a small outcrop of rock on the steep hillside E of the Water of Ae, from where it had a commanding view of the Upper Ae valley. This was originally open country, but today the site is completely shrouded by a forestry plantation and is hard to find. All that remains of the tower is the ruinous basement, with the walls rising to a maximum height of about 10ft on the S side and in the NW corner. Built of greywacke rubble, the tower measures 19ft from N to S by 24ft

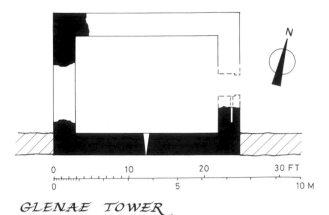

GLENAE TOWER

Fig. 223 Glenae Tower: plan of basement.

10in from E to W over walls 3ft thick. It was not vaulted. The entrance was at the E end, where the remains of the drawbar hole, 6in high by 3½in wide and 3ft 9in deep, survive, though the doorway itself is missing. This is a most unusual position for the entrance, reminiscent of a bastle-house or pele-house, which it may indeed have been. On the S side, there is a small, splayed, ventilation-slit, which is reduced in the outer wall-face to a mere 1¼in wide by 1ft 2in high, making it virtually invisible; and no doubt there would have been at least one other such ventilation-slit in the wall opposite. Above this level all that remains are some of the rough holes that supported the joists for the first floor. – Adjacent to the tower on the S side, there is an irregular enclosure, measuring approximately 50ft from N to S and 80ft from E to W, with an entrance at the SW corner. This is probably a sheep or cattle fold of much later date.

Oliver Dinwoodie resigned the lands of Glenaebank in 1615,[5] but he was still in possession of Over Glenae two years later, when it was specifically excluded from a new charter of lands in the barony of Kirkmichael granted to William Kirkpatrick of Kirkmichael.[6] On the resignation of these lands by Kirkpatrick in 1622, the £10 lands of Kirkmichael, the ½ merkland of Glenae and other lands, together with the towers, etc., were granted to John Charteris of Amisfield,[7] and in 1643 these lands were erected into a new barony of Kirkmichael in favour of James Crichton, a younger son of the Earl of Dumfries.[8]

Six years later Glenae was included in a grant of the lands and barony of Amisfield to Sir John Dalzell of Newton,[9] younger brother of the 1st Earl of Carnwath, who subsequently took the designation 'of Glenae'; and this grant was confirmed in 1666, when he received a charter of novodamus of the same,[10] and ratified by parliament in 1669.[11] Sir John supported the Royalist cause during the Civil War, and was taken prisoner at the battle of Worcester in 1651.[12] He died in 1669, when he was succeeded by his eldest son, Sir Robert, who had been created a baronet by Charles II three years earlier.[13]

Sir Robert Dalzell represented Dumfriesshire in parliament from 1665 to 1674, and again in 1681 and 1685.[14] He was also a Commissioner of Supply for Nithsdale and Dumfries in 1661, 1667, 1675, 1678 and 1685,[15] a Justice of the Peace in 1663,[16] and a Commissioner for the Borders in 1674.[17] A soldier by profession, he was commissioned as a Lieutenant-Colonel in the Dumfries Militia in 1668.[18] He later served as a Captain in General Monro's and the Earl of Mar's Regiments of Foot.[19] In 1682 he was re-appointed Lieutenant-Colonel in the Militia.[20] The following year, he was appointed to administer the Test and

to try recusants.[21] He died in 1685 or 1686, and was succeeded by his eldest son, Sir John Dalzell of Glenae, 2nd Baronet.

Sir John succeeded his father as Captain in the Earl of Mar's Regiment of Foot in 1679.[22] He was appointed a Commissioner of Supply for Nithsdale and Dumfries in 1685,[23] and was elected to represent the county in parliament in 1689,[24] but he died the same month. He was succeeded by his infant son Sir Robert, 3rd Baronet of Glenae. It is not clear where the family was living at this time, but it is almost certain that Glenae Tower had never been occupied by the Dalzells.

Sir Robert succeeded as heir-male of the family in 1702, and thus became 5th Earl of Carnwath.[25] He supported the Jacobites in the rebellion of 1715, was taken prisoner at Preston and sent to the Tower of London, where he was sentenced to death with forfeiture of all his honours and estates.[26] He was later pardonned, and in 1734-5 recovered most of his estates, including Glenae;[27] but it was not until 1826 that the earldom was restored.[28] The family then moved to Kirkmichael House, 3 miles to the SE, and they remained there until 1789, when Sir Robert's grandson, Robert, 6th of Glenae, a distinguished advocate, built the present house of Glenae, 3¾ m south of the old tower.[29] Robert's father was Alexander Dalzell, styled Earl of Carnwath, elder son of Sir Robert, who had been served heir to his father in Glenae, Amisfield and the other family estates in 1737.[30]

On the death of Robert's son, John Dalzell, 7th of Glenae, in 1814, the lands passed to his sister Margaret (d.1847), whose husband, Major Dougall Stewart, took the name and arms of Dalzell of Glenae.[31] The estate was finally sold c.1922 by Violet Dalzell, daughter and co-heiress of Robert Dalzell (d.1906) of Glenae.[32]

1   RMS II, No.786.
2   Ibid, No.1588.
3   Ibid, VII, No.1251.
4   Neither the tower, nor even the Water of Ae, appear on Pont's maps c.1595, as he completely omitted Upper Annandale.
5   RMS VII, No.1251.
6   Ibid, No.1702.
7   Ibid, VIII, No.323.
8   Ibid, IX, No.1406.
9   Ibid, No.2102.
10   Scots Peerage II, 408.
11   APS VII, 643.
12   Scots Peerage II, 408.
13   Ibid, 409; RMS XI, No.905.
14   APS VII, 526, 536, 548; VIII, 3, 55, 208, 231, 451.
15   Ibid, VII, 91, 544; VIII, 225, 465; RPC, 3rd Ser., IV, 474..
16   Ibid, VII, 505.
17   RPC, 3rd Ser., IV, 221.
18   Ibid, II, 554.
19   Parl. of Scot., I, 178.
20   Ibid.
21   RPC, 3rd Ser., VIII, 137.
22   Parl. of Scot., I, 178.
23   APS VIII, 465.
24   APS IX, 3.
25   Scots Peerage II, 415.
26   Ibid.
27   Ibid, 416. The estates had been bought from the Commissioners on forfeited estates in 1723 by William Veitch, WS, the Dalzell family's solicitor, who had advanced the family large sums of money.
28   Scots Peerage II, 417.
29   Dunbar, 86; Forman, S. 'Glenae', Scottish Field, April 1964, 50-2. The house was designed by the Dumfries architect Thomas Boyd (Gifford, 321).
30   Scots Peerage II, 416.
31   Ibid, 417
32   Burke L.G. 1937, 556, 'Dalzell late of Glenae'.

36.   HILLS TOWER
(4m SW Dumfries)   (NX912726)

Apart from a crannog on the loch itself,[1] the earliest stronghold to be erected on the lands of Lochrutton was a motte-and-bailey castle at Auchenfranco, on the SW side of the loch. Little is known about this early work, but it was here that Edward I spent a night in 1300 on his way from Caerlaverock to Kirkcudbright.[2] The castle appears to have been abandoned soon afterwards, and after the forfeiture of the Douglases in 1455, the lands of Auchenfranco and Lochrutton became separated.[3] Auchenfranco was granted to the Herries,[4] while Lochrutton, of which Hills forms a part, came into the possession of the Eccles.

Fig. 224 Hills Tower: view from the NE. The gatehouse can be seen on the right and the later house on the left.

In 1500 John Eclis received a crown charter of the 18 merk lands of Louchrutoun, confirming a previous grant by his father, John Ecclis of that Ilk;[5] and in 1517 he granted these lands, together with the lands and barony of Eccles, to his eldest son, Kentigern.[6] Five years later, the Eccles sold Lochrutton to James Douglas of Drumlanrig,[7] who in turn sold it, in 1527, to Edward Maxwell 'in Brakansyd' for 1400 merks.[8] It was then described as the '18 merk lands of Lochrutoun and Hillis'. Three years later Edward is described in a charter as 'of Lochrutoun'.[9] Edward, a man of considerable wealth and influence, was the son of Herbert Maxwell, who was reputedly a natural son of John, Master of Maxwell.[10] It was Edward (d.1546) who built Hills Tower, standing high on a hillside facing S and with a com-

Fig. 225 Hills: barmkin wall and part-excavated courtyard in 1970.

manding view to the S and westwards towards Lochrutton Loch and the site of Auchenfranco, just over a mile away.

Hills has the rare distinction for a Border stronghold of retaining its barmkin and gatehouse, which, despite some re-building and restoration, give a very good idea of how a Border tower must have appeared in the 16th century. The **BARMKIN** is also of special interest because its measurements are generally similar to those laid down in the Act of 1535 'For building of Strengths on the Borders'.[11] This decreed that barmkins should be 60ft square, 1 ell (3ft 1in) thick and 6 ells (18ft 6in) high. By comparison, the one at Hills measures 65ft by 57ft, and has a wall 3ft thick with a maximum surviving height of about 12ft 6in. The E wall is only 1ft 6in thick, but it has been rebuilt. When Grose recorded Hills in 1789, the N wall was incorporated in a building range.[12] This was later demolished; but excavations in 1970 uncovered the foundations, as well as revealing that the courtyard had been cobbled and provided with drainage channels.

The **GATEHOUSE**, which measures 11ft wide by 5ft 6in on plan, comprises a gateway and pend with a guardroom above.[13] It is of later date than the tower, and according to one account used to incorporate a stone bearing the date '1598', but this has now gone.[14] Built of local rubble with sandstone quoins and mouldings, it is situated in the centre of the W wall of the courtyard, whence it projects 2ft 6in beyond the outer wall-face of the barmkin. This arrangement was apparently designed to provide flanking cover for the gateway, as there are the remains of shot-holes, now blocked, in the N wall of the projection at both ground and guardroom levels. The gateway itself has a semi-circular head with a QERH moulding on the surround and a hood moulding above; it is 6ft wide and has a maximum clear-

Fig. 226 Hills: shot-holes and royal arms over gateway.

ance of 7ft 5in to the top of the arch. The jambs are provided with a double rebate to accommodate an outer door of wood, now missing, and an inner yett, both of which were of the two-leaved variety, closing in the centre; but there was no provision for a drawbar. The present yett is a replacement. The guardroom above, which measures 8ft 10in by 4ft 4in internally with a maximum headroom of about 5ft 6in, projects some 2½in on all sides on a continuous corbel-course, while on the W side there is another corbel-course, with a chequer moulding, at the wall-head. The guardroom has no windows as such: instead, there are two inverted key-hole shot-holes, 5in high, on either side of an armorial panel bearing the royal arms of Scotland, in the W wall and a small, cross-shaped opening facing the court-

Fig. 227 Hills Tower and Gatehouse: view from N.

yard. In addition, there was apparently another shot-hole in the N wall (supra), and it is likely that there was originally a similar one on the S side. The guardroom has a gabled roof, aligned with the barmkin; the slates are modern, and the roof has been restored. Access to the guardroom was by means of an open stair, 2ft wide, leading up from the courtyard. All that remains of it are the top three steps, which turn within the thickness of the barmkin wall to admit to the guardroom on the N side.

The **TOWER**, which is oblong in plan, is situated on the S side of the barmkin, adjacent to the SW corner. It measures 30ft from E to W by 24ft 3in from N to S over walls 4ft 6in thick, and rises some 45ft to the top of the parapet. The masonry is mainly greywacke rubble with quoins and mouldings of sandstone and gritstone. The tower appears to represent two distinct building periods, with the four storeys below the wall-head forming part of the original work carried out by Edward Maxwell c.1530, while the parapet walk and garret were either added, or rebuilt, some time c.1600.[15] Various alterations were subsequently carried out, probably when the adjacent house was added in 1721, and further alterations were undertaken between 1789 and 1889.[16] The tower had long been uninhabited when, c.1930, Nigel Lindsay restored it; and in 1970 James Williams carried out further work.

The entrance to the tower is situated at the E end of the N wall. Above it there is an elaborate armorial panel, which bears the arms and initials of Edward Maxwell and his wife, Janet Corsane, beneath the arms of Lord Maxwell.[17] The doorway has a mason's mark on each jamb and a hollow chamfer on its surround, a rare moulding that also appears around the original doorways and windows on the first and second floors. Another mason's mark has been found on some of the quoins nearby. Although the doorway no longer has a double rebate for a wooden door and yett, it is presumed that originally there was a yett, as the original windows on the floors above still retain sockets for wrought iron grilles. Inside, the doorway gives direct access to the wheel-stair, 6ft 6in in diameter, in the NE corner and a mural passage leading into the vaulted basement. This chamber has a maximum height of 8ft 9in. In each wall there was originally one, crudely-formed slit-window with splayed jambs, but the E one was later replaced by a doorway connecting with the adjacent house.

The first floor has a fireplace, 6ft 8in wide, in the middle of the W wall. It has a QER moulding on the surround,[18] and on either side there are mural recesses, the one on the right being designed for a wall press. Originally, there was one window with stone seats towards the W end of each side wall, and there was probably also a window in the E wall, where a door was later inserted to connect with the adjoining house. Some time before 1789, a second window was added on each side, and then, between 1789 and 1889, all four windows in the N and S walls

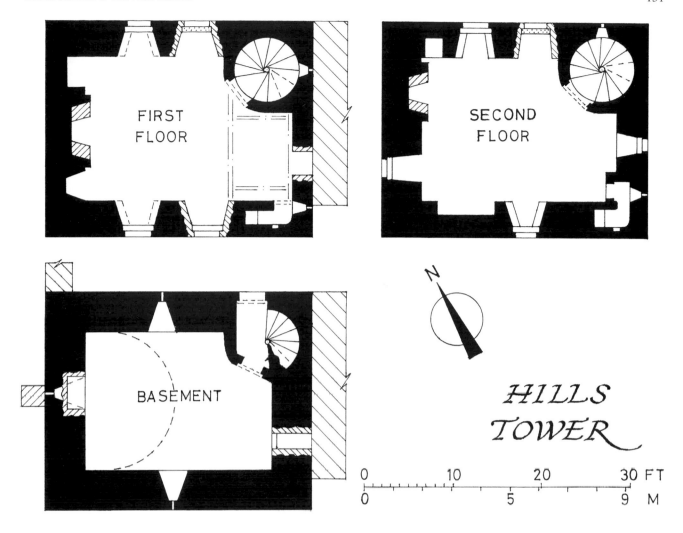

Fig. 228 Hills Tower: plans.

were enlarged. The E window on the N side was later closed up again. A garderobe, with the usual stone seat, lamp recess and slit-window,[19] is situated in the SE corner. It is provided with a drain, which, together with the drains from similar garderobes on the two floors above, discharges into a rock-cut sump under the tower's foundations. This is an unusual arrangement. The walls at this level are 4ft thick, except at the E end where it is only 2ft 6in. It is unlikely that the latter dimension is an original feature, especially as the wall's thickness increases again on the floors above; no doubt it had some connection with the wooden loft that formerly existed at this end of the hall. The latter feature, for which two transverse supporting beams have survived, would seem to have been a later addition; it stretched the full width from the stair-well to the S wall, and projected some 7ft 3in into the room. Its purpose is puzzling. It could not have been a gallery, as there is no provision for access (except by ladder), and it was only about 3ft 6in below the floor above. There is an original slit-window in the E wall at this level.[20]

The second floor is now about 1ft below its original level, which can be seen at the fireplace, window recesses, etc. At the W end there is a fireplace with a QER moulding on its surround and adjacent to it, in the N wall, an aumbry. Opposite this in the S wall there is a large mural recess, 6ft 6in wide. There was originally one window recess with stone seats in each side wall,

as on the floor below, and a smaller window in each of the end walls. The former were later enlarged, sometime before 1789, while on the N side a second window was inserted nearer the stair. The garderobe occupies the SE corner.

The third floor has a fireplace in the W wall and one small window in each of the N, E and S walls, the last being provided with stone seats. The jambs of the fireplace are wrought with a QER moulding: the lintel is a modern replacement. There is also a garderobe in the SE corner, which had long been closed up and forgotten when it was discovered, together with the sump into which all the garderobes drain, c.1970. The floor of the garret above was originally lower, where its supporting corbels may still be seen.

Above this level, and to some extent encroaching upon the third floor, the tower was evidently either rebuilt or modified later in the 16th century. The enriched corbelling of the parapet walk and the cannon-shaped gargoyles are much later than 1530,[21] and the rounded corners of the parapet itself, which are very slightly corbelled-out as if to become rounds, sit uneasily on the squared corners below. The wall itself has been restored, but the irregular crenellations and QER mouldings on the coping appear to be original. The walk, which has a maximum height to the top of the wall of about 5ft 2in, is stepped in the usual manner to drain through the gargoyles. These are made

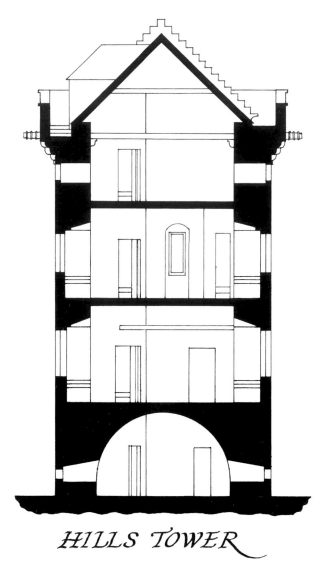

HILLS TOWER

Fig. 229 Hills Tower: sectional elevation looking east.

in two halves, with the lower half of coarse gritstone and the upper half of sandstone. The carvings even include bands to represent the larger cannons of the period. Inside this walk the stair terminates in a cap-house, which admits directly to the walk as well as leaving a clear passage round it, while a separate doorway, with a dripstone above, leads from the walk to the garret.

The garret has been altered several times. The floor was raised as recently as c.1930;[22] the roof has been rebuilt and slated at a lower pitch; and the side walls have been lowered. There is one slit-window in each gable, that at the W end penetrating the huge chimney stack. Both the doors and windows at this level have rounded arrises.

In 1545/46, the Crown gave Andrew Hamilton, captain of the palace of Linlithgow, the relief of the 18 merk lands of Lochrutton and Hills, together with other lands belonging to John Maxwell, 2nd of Hills, which relief was then in the Queen's hands.[23] It was at Hills that the 6th Lord Maxwell was living when he died, aged only 4, in 1554/5.[24] In 1568, when the Regent demanded the submission of the local clans, it was the Goodman of Hillis (John Maxwell) who did so on behalf of the Maxwells.[25] John died not long afterwards, and in 1570/71 his

widow, Katherine Maxwell, 'lady of the Hillis', received the gift of the ward and nonentry of the lands of the Hillis until her son Edward should come of age.[26]

Edward Maxwell, 3rd of Hills, leased additional lands from the crown in 1593.[27] It was he who carried out further works at Hills in 1598 and 1600 (supra); but he was soon in financial difficulties, and in 1610 had to mortgage the lands, including the fortalice and manor-place, to Gordon of Lochinvar and Grierson of Lag.[28] Edward was appointed a Justice of the Peace for the Stewartry in 1625.[29]

Despite the acquisition of additional properties in 1612, on the forfeiture of Lord Maxwell,[30] the family's finances did not improve, and a succession of wadsets and apprisings followed from 1635 to 1658.[31] Nevertheless, the family managed to keep possession of Hills, and at some time additional accommodation must have been added, for it is specifically referred to in the contract for the later, and present, house.

Edward Maxwell, 3rd of Hills, was succeeded by his grandson and heir, Edward, who took the Test in 1683.[32] Six years later he was appointed a Commissioner of Supply for the Stewartry of Kirkcudbright, and this appointment was renewed in 1690.[33] In 1689, he was also appointed a Commissioner for ordering the militia in the Stewartry.[34] Edward was still alive in 1704, when his eldest son, Robert, was made a Commissioner of Supply for the Stewartry,[35] but he died soon after. He was succeeded, first by his son Robert, who died without issue, and then, sometime before 1721, by his second son, Edward.

It was Edward Maxwell, 6th of Hills, who built the new house, which adjoins the tower and opens off the courtyard. It was the work of John Selchrig, mason in Cairn, who was contracted to build 'ane good and sufficient house and join the same to the southeast end of his house of Hills called the Tower'.[36] In addition to details of size, etc., the contract stipulates that he is to 'take down the house, then possessed by the said Edward Maxwell, on the east side of the Close and to fit and prepare the stones, timber and slate thereof for building the foresaid new house so far as they will serve', and Maxwell will provide all other materials required.[37] The house is a simple rectangular block of two storeys, with two apartments on each floor. Because of the position of the much higher tower, the fireplaces and chimney stack for the rooms at the W end are unusually situated in the centre of the building. Above the entrance there is an empty armorial panel, and at the wall-head above this another stone bearing the date 1721 and the initials 'E M J' for Edward Maxwell and his wife Janet (Goldie). Between these

Fig. 230 Hills Tower in 1789.

two panels, and distributed along the wall at first floor level, there are four more armorial panels, which undoubtedly came from one or more earlier buildings. One panel is empty, but the other three bear the arms of: (1) Edward Maxwell (d.*c.*1646), 3rd of Hills, and his wife Agnes Maxwell; (2) John Maxwell, 4th Lord Herries; and (3) ? Lord Maxwell.[38]

Edward Maxwell, 6th of Hills, died the following year, and was succeeded by his daughter Agnes, widow of the Reverend James Elder, who had sasine in 1723.[39] On her death without issue *c.*1730, Hills passed to her nephew Edward M'Culloch of Ardwall; and the M'Cullochs have retained possession ever since, though they have not lived here themselves since at least 1782.[40] By 1789 the house and tower were divided into 'different tenements', associated with the farm.[41] It was still inhabited *c.*1900, but was abandoned soon after and fell into disrepair before being restored by Nigel Lindsay *c.*1930.

1   RCAHMS 1914, No.331.
2   Grose II, 18.
3   Ibid.
4   Auchenfranco was sometimes misleadingly referred to as 'Lochrutton Castle' (See, for example, M'Dowall, 165).
5   ALHT II, 10.
6   RMS III, No.236.
7   M'Culloch, W. 'Hillis Tower', *TDGAS*, 3rd Ser., XIX, 337.
8   RMS III, No.499; M'Culloch, *op. cit.*, 338.
9   RMS III, No.927.
10   Fraser 1873, I, 156. The late Dr. R. C. Reid had another theory about Edward's parentage – See M'Culloch, *op. cit.*, 337.
11   APS II, Cap.22.
12   Grose II, 17.
13   This gatehouse is very similar in design to the later gatehouse at Harthill in Aberdeenshire. See MacGibbon & Ross II, 245; Tranter 1966, IV, 53.
14   Grose II, 18; NSA IV, 288.
15   In addition to the date 1598, formerly on the gatehouse, Grose mentions an escutcheon bearing the date 1600 (Grose II, 18).
16   Changes to the windows are clearly shown in the illustrations of Grose (1789) and MacGibbon & Ross (1889).
17   This is presumed from the undifferenced Maxwell saltire and stag, but the motto is a puzzle and the significance uncertain.
18   The moulding on the lintel itself is a later addition.
19   This slit-window, together with others lighting the stair at this level and the garderobe above, are shaped like a vertical dumb-bell, similar to the one in the hall at Amisfield (q.v.)
20   The window is now blocked by a beam, which helps support the floor above at its new level.
21   Similar corbelling is found at Hoddom (1565) and Hollows (*c.*1600), q.v.
22   The elevation in RCAHMS 1914, 174, shows the floor at its original level.
23   RSS III, No.1501.
24   Fraser 1873, I, 222.
25   CSPS II, No.717.
26   RSS VI, No.1065.
27   RMS V, No.2322.
28   RMS VII, No.320.
29   RPC, 2nd Ser., I, 659.
30   Ibid, 1st Ser., XIV, 616.
30   Fraser 1873, I, 319.
31   RMS IX, Nos.410, 433, 706, 1486, 1649; X, No.649.
32   RPC, 3rd Ser., VIII, 640.
33   APS IX, 74, 144.
34   Ibid, 28.
35   Ibid, XI, 149-50.
36   M'Culloch, op.cit., 344.
37   Re-used timbers are clearly evident in the roof.
38   All the arms at Hills are illustrated in Fraser 1873, I.
39   M'Kerlie IV, 336.
40   M'Culloch, *op. cit.*, 346.
41   Grose II, 18.

37.   HODDOM CASTLE
(2½ m WSW Ecclefechan)   (NY155729)

William, 3rd Lord Herries of Terregles, died in 1543 leaving three daughters, and co-heiresses, who were still minors. Four years later, the eldest daughter, Agnes, Baroness Herries, married Sir John Maxwell of Terregles, Master of Maxwell, who eventually, through his wife, became 4th Lord Herries.[1] It was not, however, until 1548/49 that Lady Agnes formally received her share of her father's vast estates, which included a third part of the £20 lands of Hoddom,[2] and a year later before she and her husband had a crown charter of the same.[3] Meanwhile, in May 1549, Lady Agnes, with the express consent and assent of her husband, granted 'all and haill my twenty pound land of old extent of Hoddom' to Richard Irving, 'called of old Duke Ritchie', as a reward for what must have been very substantial services rendered during the recent troubles with England.[4] The old castle of Hoddom (q.v.) was not included.

Fig. 231 Hoddom Castle: view from N.

The present castle of Hoddom, however, does not stand on the lands of Hoddom, nor even in the parish of that name, but on the lands of Trailtrow on the opposite bank of the river Annan. These lands had of old been granted to the Knights Hospitallers, who founded a hospital there.[5] In 1563, three years after the Reformation, Archibald Menzies, preceptor of Trailtrow, granted a portion of the lands of Trailtrow, amounting to a 40 shilling land of old extent, in feu-ferme to Sir John Maxwell.[6] This became the site of the new castle, which, because it incorporated masonry from the old castle of Hoddom in its construction, subsequently became known as 'Hoddomstanes'.[7] Ten years later, Menzies sold the 10 husbandlands of Trailtrow to Lord Maxwell, 'reserving to John Lord Herries the 40 shilling lands of the same called 'Hodomestanis', with the tower and fortalice'.[8]

The new castle was built by Sir John in 1565. In a letter to Sir William Cecil in May of that year, Thomas Randolph

Fig. 232 Hoddom Castle: view from the S. after the removal of the 19th century wings.
The gable lines on the tower's walls show several periods of additions and alterations.

writes: 'My chief desire in going to Carlisle was to return by the Master of Maxwell's and see the works he has in hand. In Annan town he has builded a fair tower . . . Within two miles of it he 'byldethe' two other forts – the one great – the other a watch tower of great height'.[9] This rare reference to the construction of a castle puts a precise date on these two forts: Hoddom Castle and Repentance Tower.

Hoddom was arguably the largest and strongest tower built in the Borders in the 16th Century, the only other contender being the very different castle built by Sir John Maitland *c*.1590 at Thirlestane, near Lauder. More akin to the great tower-castles of the previous two centuries than to other contemporary tower-houses, Hoddom was built not so much as a home – Sir John's seat was Terregles (q.v.) – , but as a fortress. It was an extension of Lord Herries' avowed policy to enforce law and order upon the Borders, whether the threat came from England or nearer home. Although not always on the right side of the law himself, he was nevertheless a great statesman, diplomat and patriot, and was variously Warden of the West March, Keeper of Liddesdale, and a Commissioner to deal with Border affairs, from 1546 to 1580.[10] He was a close confidant of Mary Queen of Scots, by whom he was, in 1565, specially charged with guarding the Borders,[11] while in 1566 even Queen Elizabeth bore testimony to his efficacy as Warden.[12]

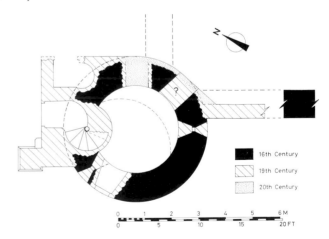

Fig. 233 Hoddom: tower, much modified, at NW corner of barmkin.

The castle comprised a **FORTIFIED ENCLOSURE**, measuring some 115ft from N to S by 92ft from E to W, with a massive, L-plan tower-house at the NE corner and 2-storeyed, round towers at the other three angles. It stood on level ground, in the shadow of the new watch-tower on Trailtrow hill, and was defended on the E side by a steep bank, which dropped some

Fig. 234 Hoddom: entrance doorway with empty armorial panel (later made into a dummy window) above.

46ft to the valley floor, and to the S by an artificially-enlarged gully. Earthworks were no doubt raised to defend the other sides too, but these have long since disappeared. Part of the original barmkin wall survives, much altered, on the W side, where a later gateway has been inserted.[13] It is 3ft 4in thick, about 12ft high and has an offset course on the inner face, probably associ-

ated with a parapet walk.[14] The earliest illustrations (18th cent.) show a crenellated top.[15] The corner towers were 17ft in diameter over walls 3ft 4in thick and had vaulted basements from which three, rectangular, splayed gun-loops covered the adjacent walls and ground beyond. Although 18th century illustrations show the towers with conical roofs, it is more likely that they were originally flat and embattled. Part of the NW tower survives, greatly altered, but the SE tower was removed and the SW one rebuilt c.1830. Within the courtyard there would have been the kitchen, stables and other outbuildings.

The **TOWER** itself consists of a main block, 51ft by 35ft 2in, from the N end of which a wing, 27ft 7in wide, projects 15ft 3in towards the W. The main block rises four storeys to a corbelled-out parapet-walk, 47ft 3in above the ground, above which a gabled roof contains a garret, while the wing continues for a further two storeys before terminating in a flat roof with parapet some 70ft above the ground. Up to third floor level the walls average 8ft 10in in thickness, thereafter being progressively reduced. The masonry is roughly-coursed, red-sandstone rubble, except for the dressings, vaults, turrets and other details, which are of finely-cut ashlar. The majority of the original mouldings are of the QERF type: exceptions are the vast, empty, armorial panel over the entrance, which has a boldly-projecting, heavy roll-moulding on the jambs and lintel; the boldly-rounded arrises of the internal doors of the basement; and the fireplace on the wing's fourth floor (q.v.).

The entrance doorway, which was renewed and enlarged in the 19th century, is in the re-entrant angle of the wing, where it is protected by two, narrowly-splayed gun-loops at the foot of the stair, a large, widely-splayed gun-loop on the W side of the main block and a large, corbelled-out machicolation at fourth floor level. Originally, the door was protected by an iron yett, which was still *in situ* in 1772.[16] The main wheel-stair, 10ft 10in in diameter, occupies the wing as far as the second floor, where a smaller wheel-stair, 8ft in diameter, continues in the re-entrant angle to serve the higher floors. From the entrance a passage leads past a small guardroom on the right and a prison opposite

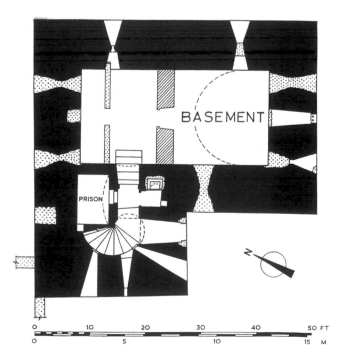

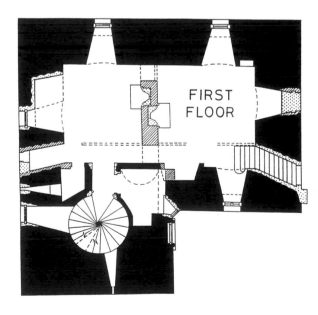

Fig. 235 Hoddom Castle: plans of basement and first floor.

Fig. 236 Hoddom: inside prison showing air vent (top left)
and passage beyond. 1565. The shelves are later.

into the basement of the main block. This was originally a single, barrel-vaulted chamber with two large, widely-splayed, rectangular gun-loops in each of the N, E and S walls and one in the
W wall. Only one loop has been left unfilled. It is of special
interest because its inner sill has been found to retain an original
oak beam, with central, vertical hole, set flush with the sill, that
can slide into the wall on either side to support a small, swivel-
ling cannon. When the upper floors of the tower were later divided in two, sometime in the 18th century, the basement was

Fig. 237 Hoddom: great hall fireplace, showing wall later inserted on
right side when fireplace became redundant and adjacent chamber in
wing was altered.

also divided to support the weight. The prison, which measures
9ft 1in by 5ft 10in and is 7ft 4in high, is built of massive, well-cut
masonry, with floor slabs 9in thick to frustrate any attempt at
escape. The floor is 2ft 5in lower than that of the adjacent passage, from which it is reached through a small door, only 4ft 2in
high by 2ft wide, with massive jambs. The prison is unusual in
having a 'lamp' shelf, while the only ventilation is a small flue
that rises up through the vault.

The first floor of the main block was the great hall. It
had a large fireplace, 7ft 4in wide, in the middle of the W wall, a
garderobe in the NW corner and an aumbry. No other original
features have survived. When the hall was subsequently divided,
new fireplaces were incorporated in the partition wall and the
original fireplace blocked up. Next to the hall, in the re-entrant
angle, is a small chamber with a barrel-vaulted roof, 11ft 9in
high. Its purpose is obscure. Apart from its awkward shape, the
S side of the vault is inexplicably cantilevered 1ft 1in out from
the wall on a continuous course of heavy, squared slabs for its
entire length, while the great-hall fireplace intruded into the
room's SE corner.[17] The only illumination was a small
slit-window, later enlarged.

On the second floor the original fireplace was in the S
wall. Immediately to the right is an aumbry that retains its original surround and panelled door, while in the NW corner there
was another closed-aumbry and in the SE corner a lamp-shelf.
Mural chambers in the NE corner and middle of the E wall were
later altered: the former was in all likelihood a garderobe.

The third floor of the main block was designed to be
first and foremost a high-level gun-battery. Despite considerable, later alterations, it appears that it originally contained two,
splayed gun-loops each on the N, E and S sides and one on the
W side, complementing those in the basement; but unlike the
basement, these loops were only splayed outwards and had a
much shallower angle of fire (15°). In addition, there were two
or three windows for better visibility and, in the NE corner, a
garderobe. Between this room and the wing there is a long,
narrow, mural chamber with a slit-window unusually high up
(7ft 9in). It opens off the barrel-vaulted room in the wing, and
may have served as some form of safe. There is another, unusual storage-space at the N end of the garret, where a small doorway, only 2ft 10in high, gives access to a mural cupboard or
safe, 4ft 7in wide by 2ft 1in deep and 4ft 7in high, within the
thickness of the gable.

The parapet-walk runs around the main block from the
re-entrant angle to the NW corner, where a second doorway, now
blocked, gave direct access to the fourth floor of the wing. The
parapet itself is massive: 5ft high with crenellations, it is carried
on a bold course of enriched corbelling that continues, at a slightly
higher level, around the wing. It incorporates rounds at the NE,
SE and SW corners and projecting machicolations on the N and
E sides. On either side of each round the parapet is pierced by a
small, rectangular shot-hole, while a similar shot-hole, angled
steeply downwards, covers the approach to the entrance from
the re-entrant angle.

At the top of the main block's N gable there is a beacon
or look-out platform, which is reached by way of the 2ft 4½in
wide crow-steps on the W side.[18] This massive platform, which
measures 5ft 6½in by 4ft 1in, oversails the parapet walk on
seven bold courses of enriched corbelling, while a low wall, 2ft
3in high, serves as a counter-weight on the inner side.[19] Originally this must have been the highest point of the castle. The
adjacent roof seems to pre-date the later, central chimney-stack,
and may well be original. It is of double-collar, rafter construc-

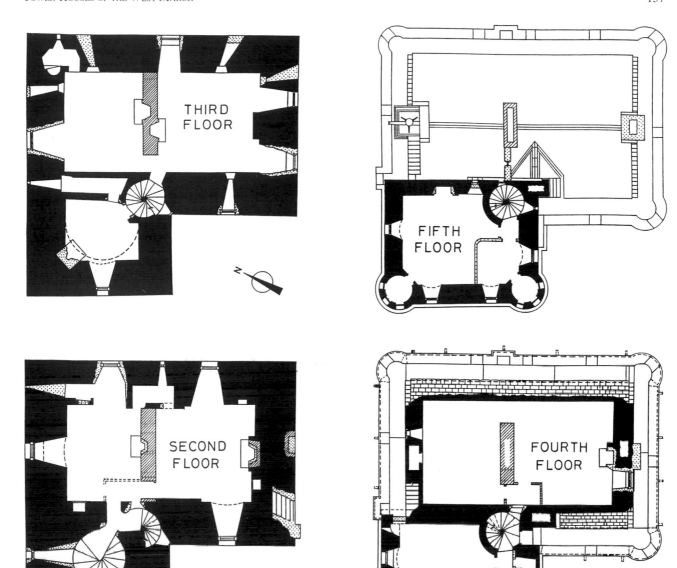

Fig. 238 Hoddom Castle: plans of upper floors.

Fig. 239 Hoddom: inside gun-loop on 3rd floor.

tion, with each principal[20] made from two pieces tenoned into a common purlin that runs the length of the roof. The purlins are made from scarf-jointed sections.

The fourth floor of the wing has turrets at the NW and SW corners and a large fireplace between. The turrets were later continued upwards, when the fifth floor was added, and additional windows were inserted some time after 1789. Unlike the fireplaces in the main block, this one has a bold, roll-and-hollow-moulded surround, which terminates on the lintel as two semi-circles meeting at the centre.[21] The floor of the chamber is of stone. It is supported by the vault below, and was evidently a precaution against fire from boiling liquids being carried to the various machicolations or, possibly, embers to light the beacon.

The fifth floor was probably added by the 1st Earl of Annandale c.1636. Apart from the fireplace being of a later style and on the E side, where there is an additional window, the lay-

Fig. 240 Hoddom Castle: mural chamber on 3rd floor.

Fig. 241 Hoddom: beacon platform on top of north gable.

out is similar to that of the floor below. The roof above was restored *c*.1889 but, with the exception of the larger cap-house at the stair-head, closely follows the earlier design, as portrayed in 18th century illustrations.

Lord Herries' new castle soon established its importance in the West March. Shortly after Queen Mary's defeat at Langside in 1568, the Regent Moray ordered Herries, the Queen's most loyal supporter, to deliver up the principal strongholds held by the Maxwells, including the house of Hoddom.[22] Herries refused, so Moray made an expedition to the West March, and on the 20th June laid siege to Hoddom, camping overnight in 'the warde of Hoddome'. The defending garrison put up a spirited defence: they 'shot heavy ordnance and slew a horse and some men', and then at night, the 'thieves gathered 1000 men' and

harried the Regent's men outside their camp, before the 'Regent's men issued and took 2 or 3'.[23] The following day, the garrison surrendered on condition that their lives were spared 'and na mair – all bag and bagges to remane in it' – though Moray reported that 'thai mycht haif holdin long enewcht, yf thai had bene gud fellows within it'.[24] The castle was then delivered into the safe keeping of Douglas of Drumlanrig's servants. Two years later, in the autumn, the Earl of Sussex marched into Annandale and reported that he 'threw down the castles of Annand and Hodoun'.[25] However, despite Bishop Ross's bitter complaint to Queen Elizabeth about Sussex's 'extreme proceedings in Scotland . . . throwing down ten of the principal castles (two of which are most strong – Annand and Hodoun)',[26] the damage was greatly exaggerated, there being no evidence of damage to the tower itself.

In 1578 Lord Herries, who had been appointed one of James VI's new council of twelve, submitted his proposals for quietening and keeping good order in the West March. These included a recommendation that in times of 'great disobedience' he should remain at Hoddom to assist the warden.[27] The proposals were accepted, and in January 1578/9 he was re-appointed warden and justiciar.[28] The following year he was one of the commissioners sent to quieten the Borders.[29]

Lord Herries died in 1582/3, and was succeeded by his son William, 5th Lord Herries. William was Warden of the West March for four brief terms between 1587 and 1600.[30] On the last occasion, he was appointed in succession to Sir John Carmichael of that Ilk, who had been treacherously murdered by a band of Armstrongs, and was ordered by James VI 'to lie at Hodom'.[31] William also attended the king during two judicial expeditions to Dumfries in 1597.[32] In 1601, he and James Murray of Irnealmerie, Captain of Hoddom, were ordered to appear before the Privy Council to give their 'best advice touching the weal and quietness of the country'.[33]

John, 6th Lord Herries, who succeeded his father in 1603, was, in 1618, appointed a Commissioner for Keeping Order in the Middle Marches.[34] He married his cousin Elizabeth, sister of the 1st Earl of Nithsdale, and their eldest son eventually succeeded, in 1667, to the Earldom of Nithsdale, Lordship of Maxwell and Chiefship of the Maxwells. Meanwhile, in 1627, Lord Herries sold Hoddom to Sir Richard Murray of Cockpool.

It is not clear why Sir Richard bought Hoddom, as he had no issue and continued to live at Comlongon (q.v.), while the keys were kept by Patrick Murray of Brocklerig.[35] However, on his death in 1636, he was succeeded by his youngest, and only surviving, brother, Sir John Murray, 1st Earl of Annandale, who preferred to live at Hoddom, which he 'greatly increased and improved with additional buildings'.[36] His son, the 2nd Earl, who succeeded in 1640, went to live in England during the Civil War. Having no children, he conveyed Hoddom *c*.1653 to his grandfather-in-law, Sir David Carnegie, 1st Earl of Southesk. Hoddom eventually passed to the 4th Earl of Southesk, who was served heir in 1688. Two years later, he sold Hoddom to John Sharpe of Collieston, whose family had been burgesses in Dumfries for generations.

John was Commissary and Sheriff Clerk of Dumfries.[37] He also represented Dumfriesshire in parliament in 1686 and from 1702 to 1707, when he voted against the Treaty of Union.[38] In 1693 he petitioned parliament for a bridge across the Annan.[39] He was appointed a Commissioner of Supply for Dumfriesshire in 1691, 1696, 1698 and 1704, and for the Stewartry of Kirkcudbright in 1702 and 1704.[40] After the Union, he retired from politics. He died in 1715, and was succeeded by his second, but eldest surviving son, George, an advocate.[41] The next laird was Matthew Sharpe, who appears to have been George's next younger brother.[42] The line ended in 1769 with the death of Matthew Sharpe of Hoddom,[43] though it is unlikely that he was the same Matthew.

Matthew Sharpe was succeeded by his nephew Charles, the son of William Kirkpatrick of Ailsland (Ellisland), a younger brother of Sir Thomas Kirkpatrick of Closeburn, who, on inheriting Hoddom, took the name Sharpe. He 'repaired, and much improved, [the castle] by adding several rooms to it'.[44] This may well have been when the main block was sub-divided, though it is evident that many additions and alterations were made, both within the courtyard and to the N of it, during the previous 200 years.

Fig. 242 Hoddom Castle: view from Trailtrow hill in 1789.

Charles Sharpe had four sons, none of whom had issue. The eldest, Lieutenant-General Matthew Sharpe, succeeded him at Hoddom in 1813, and in 1826 commissioned the distinguished architect William Burn to undertake extensive additions and alterations to the castle. He added a great new range on the S side of the tower, heightened and extended an existing range to the W, and added new offices to the NW.[45] General Sharpe represented the Dumfriesshire burghs in parliament from 1833 to 1841.[46] On his death in 1846, the estate was administered by trustees until the death of the third son, Admiral Alexander Sharpe, in 1860, when the only surviving brother, William, registered his sole right to the lands of Hoddom, Ecclefechan, Hoddomstanes and others as heir of General Sharpe,[47] and to Carruthers, Trailtrow and other lands as heir of his second brother, Charles Kirkpatrick Sharpe (d.1851) in Edinburgh, the celebrated antiquary, scholar and artist.[48]

On the failure of the Sharpe family with William's death in 1877, the estate was bought by Edward Brook of Meltham Hall (near Huddersfield),[49] who demolished most of the existing buildings to the N of the castle and in their stead built a vast new range extending for more than 220ft. Edward also bought the nearby estate of Kinmount from the Marquess of Queensberry in 1896. On his death in 1904, he was succeeded at Hoddom by his elder son, Edward, and at Kinmount by his younger son, Lieutenant-Colonel Charles Brook. When Edward died in 1924, Hoddom passed to his brother, but was only occupied by a housekeeper and an assistant until 1935, when it became a Youth Hostel. Lt.-Col. Brook died in 1930, and was succeeded by his only son, Colonel Edward Brook, who served in World War I and later in Egypt.[50] He was also for a time Equerry to HRH the

Duke of Gloucester and a member of the Royal Company of Archers.[51]

At the outbreak of the Second World War, Kinmount was requisitioned as a hospital, while the family moved to Hoddom; but shortly afterwards Hoddom was also requisitioned for the duration of the war. The castle was finally abandoned as a residence in 1947, and in 1953 demolition of the S and W wings began. Since then, all the plasterwork has been removed from the original tower, revealing for the first time all the changes that have taken place over the centuries.

———————————

1   RSS III, No.2674. See also Scots Peerage IV, 409-11.
2   For a more detailed history and description of Hoddom, refer to Maxwell-Irving 1988, 183-217.
3   RMS IV, No.405.
4   Irving 1907, 120-1.
5   According to Bain, the keeping of the Preceptory of Trailtrow and the guarding of the 'Old Kirk Ford' at Hoddom had been entrusted to the Carruthers when the Bruces were still Lords of Annandale (Carruthers 1934, 49). See also Easson 1957, 158.
6   RMS VII, No.295.
7   RMS IV, No.2311; VII, No.295; etc. The new castle appears as 'Ye Cast of Hoddamsteanes' on Aglionby's Platte in 1590 (Hyslop, 320), and as 'Hoddom C.' on Pont's map of Annandale c.1595 (Blaeu, 57, 'THE STEWARTRIE OF ANNANDAIL').
8   Ibid, No.2311.
9   Scottish Papers II, 174; CSPS I, 209.
10 Rae, 240-41, 244, 258-9.
11 Fraser 1873, I, 509.
12 RPC, cited in Fraser 1873, I, 514.
13 This appears to date from the mid to late 17th century.
14 The offset is only 11in, suggesting a timber walk projecting inwards.
15 Illustrations by John Clerk of Eldin, c.1750, and Francis Grose, 1789.
16 Pennant, 92.
17 When the hall fireplace was later blocked up, the corner of the ante-room was finally squared off – into the fireplace.
18 A similar use of extra-wide crow-steps is found at nearby Comlongon.
19 The prime purpose of this wall is uncertain, whether as counter-weight, fire barrier or seat.
20 The principals still bear their assembly reference numbers.
21 This type of moulding, which is also found at nearby Bonshaw, is contemporary with the castle's foundation. The twin semi-circles on the lintel are also found over an aumbry at nearby Elshieshields and over a window at Barholm in Galloway.
22 ALHT XII, 128.
23 Scottish Papers II, Nos.716, 717.
24 Ibid.
25 Ibid., III, No.436.
26 Ibid., No.441.
27 RPC III, 80.
28 Rae, 241.
29 Ibid, 259.
30 Ibid, 243.
31 Scottish Papers XIII, 661.
32 Rae, 268.
33 RPC VI, 301.
34 Scots Peerage IV, 415.
35 Edgar, 120.
36 Stat Acct VII, 310.
37 Parl. of Scot., II, 631; PRS Dumf., XI, f.174.
38 APS VIII, IX, X, XI, passim.
39 Parl. of Scot., II, 631.
40 RPC, 3rd Ser., XVI, 232; APS X, 29, 131; XI, 23, 142, 149.
41 George Sharpe was admitted an advocate in 1712.
42 Parl. of Scot., II, 631; PRS Dumf., VII, f.80; IX, f.269.
43 Anderson 1868, 445.
44 Stat Acct VII, 310.
45 Some of his drawings are preserved in the NMRS. See also Maxwell-Irving 1988, Illus 16 and 17.
46 Johnstone 1889, 199.
47 Reg. Scot. Dumf., 1861, Nos.24, 25.
48 Ibid, Nos.33, 34. See also DNB, 1902, for biography of Charles Kirkpatrick Sharpe.
49 Ibid, 1877, No.814.
50 Burke L.G. 1952, 270, 'Brook of Upperwood House'.
51 Ibid.

38.   HOLLOWS TOWER
(1½ m WNW Canonbie)   (NY382785)

The tower of Hollows, or Holehouse, stands on a steep
bank on the west side of the river Esk. It was on this site that
'Johnnie Armstrong of Gilnockie', as he was popularly known,
a brother of the laird of Mangerton, built himself a strong house
soon after he was granted lands in Eskdale by Lord Maxwell in
1525.[1] However, the house was erected on lands which the English still considered to be part of the 'Debateable Land' between
Scotland and England, wherein no settlement was allowed;[2] and
for this reason, in 1528, Lord Dacre, the English Warden of the
West March, led a force of 2000 men across the Border and burnt
'ane place called the Holehouse' and various other houses as
well as carrying off much livestock and goods.[3] Maxwell lodged
a complaint, but Dacre rejected it, 'because the Holehouse...is
no part of the said lordship of Eskdale, but a parcell of the De-
batable grounde... And as but the burnyng of the said Hoolehouse
the said Lord Dacre grantith the burnyng of the same, whilk he
may lawfully do, because it was beylded and occupied contrary
to the treux taken betwene the princes of both the realmes of
Englond and Scotland'.[4] The subsequent death of Johnnie
Armstrong, in 1529, at the treacherous hands of King James V is
a sad chapter in Scotland's history.[5]

The present tower is of later date, but it is possible that
Hollows was also the site of 'Sande Armestronges new hous',
illustrated on the 'Platte of Castlemilk' in 1547,[6] and that part,
or all, of that tower is retained in the present structure. On the
other hand, it has been suggested that Sandy's tower may have
been of timber, as various towers on both sides of the Border
were still being built in this way at that time.[7] Sandy's tower, a
notable stronghold some four storeys high, with a splayed basement course, was certainly somewhere in this area, although the
exact site has never been confirmed. After the truce of 1550,

Fig. 243 Hollows Tower: view from SW before restoration.

Sandy Armstrong chose to remain allied to the English. This
proved too much for Lord Maxwell and Johnston of that Ilk,
whose hostility Sandy had already incurred in earlier years, and,
gathering a force of 2000 men, they set out with the intention of
destroying his tower with gunpowder. On learning of this, Lord
Dacre immediately went to Sandy's asistance. Reaching the
tower first, he filled it with dry turves and peats, and set it alight.

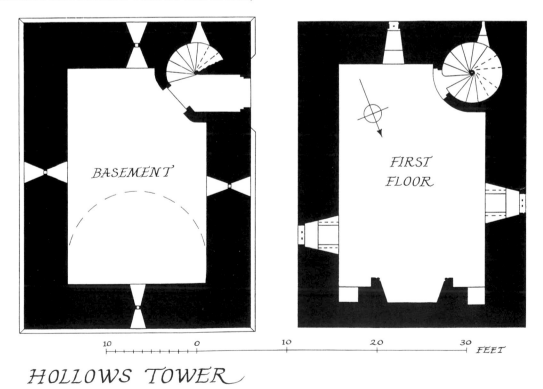

HOLLOWS TOWER

Fig. 244 Hollows Tower: plans of basement and first floor.

The tower was blackened, but otherwise, apparently, none the worse.[8] Dacre was subsequently instructed to defend Sandy should there be any further attacks by the Scots.[9]

Two years later, the Debateable Land was divided by agreement between the two countries along 'a line drawn from the water of Sark to the Esk on a chart. Which line leaves the stone house of Thomas Grem [Graham] on its west side, and leaves the stone house of Alexander [Sandy] Armstrong on the east. And so the land is divided in two parts, by boundary stones, and the west part adjudged to England, and the east part to Scotland'.[10] Thus Sandy Armstrong's tower finally became fixed in Scotland, while Sandy quietly fades from history.

Thereafter, nothing more is heard of Hollows until 1579, when the lands were in the possession of Johnne Armstrong 'of Hoilhous',[11] a son of Christopher Armstrong of Barngleish;[12] and he, or his namesake, was still in possession in 1597.[13] Then in 1605 Johnne Armstrong 'in Hoilhous', perhaps the same person, is on record,[14] and two years later 'Johne Armestrang of Hoilhous' and others were charged with keeping James Maxwell and Robert Douglas, servitors to his Majesty, from the Debateable Lands that had been granted to them.[15] Johnny Armstrong is still on record in 1623,[16] but by 1633 he had been succeeded by Archy Armstrong, 'called Hollas, who duelltt in the Mearburnheid'.[17]

The tower stands back from, and above, the right bank of the river Esk, at a point where the river negotiates a sharp bend, providing the tower with some natural protection on two sides. It is shown as 'Hollas' on Aglionby's Platte in 1590,[18] and as 'Holhouse' on Pont's map of Liddesdale and Lower Eskdale c.1595.[19]

The **TOWER**, which is oblong in plan, measures 33ft 6in by 25ft 4in and rises some 38ft to the parapet walk and a further 16ft to the top of the beacon on the S gable. It comprises four storeys and an attic. Built of cream sandstone rubble with

Fig. 245 Hollows: entrance doorway in 1968.

dressed margins and mouldings, the walls are 5ft thick immediately above the splayed plinth-course and 4ft 8in higher up. The larger windows have QER surrounds and were originally protected by iron grilles, while the entrance doorway has a QER moulding embellished with an additional quirked-bead and fillet on either side. The tower had long been a roofless shell before its recent restoration.

The entrance doorway, which is on the W side, has the usual double-rebate for a wooden door and inner yett, now gone, and also retains the slot for a wooden drawbar. It admits to the wheel-stair, 6ft 8in in diameter, in the SW corner and the basement beyond. At some period the treads of the stair have been renewed. On the other side of the vestibule, an ancient, incised slab has been employed for the sill of the basement doorway.[20] The basement, which is lower than the tower's entrance, has a barrel-vault of well-cut ashlar rising to a height of 10ft 5in; one splayed gun-loop with a rectangular mouth in each wall; and a small, high-level window at the N end. Another recess high up at the S end may originally have been another window, though there is no evidence of this in the outside wall.

Fig. 246 Hollows: gun-loop in basement.

Fig. 247 Hollows: great hall fireplace before restoration.

The first floor was the hall. It has a central fireplace 7ft 4in wide, at the N end, with an open-aumbry or lamp shelf on either side. The jambs of the fireplace carry a QER moulding, but the lintel is missing and has been replaced by a modern relieving arch. On either side of the room there is a single window with stone seats in the recess, and high up at the S end an additional, very small window, only 1ft square, which was reinforced with a single bar each way. The second floor was unusual in that the supporting joists were built into the side walls as well as being supported on moulded corbels. This floor had a small

Fig. 248 Hollows: east window and garderobe on second floor (before restoration).

fireplace at the N end, one window with stone seats in each of the side walls, and a third window, larger than that on the floor below, at the S end. In addition, there was a mural garderobe on the E side. The third floor had similar windows with stone seats in the side walls, but no windows at the ends and no fireplace. Unlike on the floors below, the window recesses at this level, being immediately below the parapet walk, had flat lintels instead of scoinson arches. There is also a broad relieving arch in the S wall immediately below the corbel table. The feature that this served was in all probability removed when the new parapet walk was built. The wheel-stair terminates at the level of the attic, a chamber contained entirely within the roof and lit by one small window in each of the crow-stepped gables. From here a doorway with projecting jambs and lintel in the S gable leads directly on to the parapet walk.

Fig. 249 Hollows: embellished corbelling for corner turret and parapet, and access doorway at head of stair, before restoration.

The corbelling that supported the parapet and projecting rounds at the corners is of a sophisticated type normally associated with the early years of the 17th century. It is quite out of keeping with the quality and style of the work below, and clearly of a later date. The five courses comprise 3-stage, enriched corbelling above a continuous double-roll, with a bold cable moulding on top, while the rounds are supported on a further

two courses of continuous corbelling, each with a double-roll. Instead of following a level contour, the cable moulding is inflected opposite each peak in the stepped parapet-walk. According to the New Statistical Account, the rounds were provided with shot-holes.[21]

At the apex of the S gable there is a rare feature, which is assumed to have been a beacon, though how it was reached, or how any fire was kept from the roof, is no longer apparent. It comprises five stone beams balanced across the gable, which support two stone walls, now only two courses high, with a relatively narrow space between. Although partially restored in the present century, its complete arrangement is not known. Until recently, however, there was a bastel-house at Melkridge, in Tynedale, only 24 miles away, which had a remarkably similar feature, presumed to have been a look-out turret, on its E gable. It also seems to have dated from around the turn of the 17th century.[22]

The tower is believed to have had a barmkin on its E side.

In 1606 the Earl of Home received a crown charter of the superiority of various lands, including those of 'Hoilhous', or Hollows, that had formerly belonged to the priory of Canonbie;[23] and in 1619, on the Earl's resignation, they were granted to Sir John Ker of Jedburgh.[24] Two years later, they were granted to Walter Scott, 1st Earl of Buccleuch.[25] He was succeeded first by his son, Francis, 2nd Earl of Buccleuch, and then by his eldest granddaughter, Lady Mary Scott, who, on the death of her father in 1651, became *suo jure* Countess of Buccleuch . She herself died without issue ten years later, when she was succeeded by her youngest sister, Lady Anne Scott. Lady Anne married Sir James Scott,[26] Duke of Monmouth, an illegitimate son of Charles II, in 1663. To celebrate the occasion, Charles II created the Duke and Countess Anne Duke and Duchess of Buccleuch, Earl and Countess of Dalkeith, and Lord and Lady Scott of Whitchester and Eskdale;[27] and the following year the Duke and Duchess were granted a crown charter, with clause of novodamus, of all their lands, including 'the lands of Hoilhous' and others that had formerly pertained to the priory of Canonbie.[28] These lands continued to be held by their descendants until *c.*1975.

It is not known for certain when the tower was abandonned as a residence, but the Dukes of Buccleuch long maintained it as an empty shell before its restoration in 1978-80.[29]

1   Fraser 1873, II, 461.
2   Armstrong 1883, 231. – The attitude of the Armstrongs to authority at this time did not help either: Thomas Magnus, the English diplomat, complained to James VI that the Armstrongs of Liddesdale had reported that 'they woolde not be ordoured, naither by the king of Scottes, thair soveraine lorde, nor by the king of Einglande, but after suche maner as thaire faders had used afore thayme' (Armstrong 1883, 267).
3   Ibid, xxv.
4   Ibid.
5   Armstrong 1960, 80-4.
6   Merriman, M 'The Platte of Castlemilk, 1547', *TDGAS*, XLIV, 181.
7   RCAHMS 1997, 215.
8   Armstrong 1960, 106-7.
9   Ibid.
10   Scottish Papers I, No.392.
11   RPC III, 169.
12   Christopher Armstrong of Barngleish is said to have been a son of Johnnie Armstrong of Gilnockie (Hyslop, 338, 355).
13   Scottish Papers XIII, No.39.
14   RPC VII, 48.
15   Ibid, 2nd Ser., VIII, 292.
16   Ibid, 1st Ser., XIV, 694.

17 Fraser 1878, II, 354. Muirburnhead was 5m to the NE.
18 Hyslop, 320.
19 Blaeu, 53, 'LIDISDAIL'.
20 RCAHMS 1920, 27.
21 NSA IV, 489.
22 RCHM 1970, Part II, No.53.
23 RMS VI, No.1721. Lord Home obtained another grant of the lands of Hollows in 1624, but this appears only to have been a wadset to help the Earl with a temporary financial embarrassment (RMS VIII, No.581).
24 Ibid, VII, No.290.
25 Ibid, No.2027. As part of her marriage contract in 1663, the Countess of Buccleuch resigned her estates to the king, who then re-granted them to her husband, the Duke of Buccleuch and Monmouth – Fraser 1878, II, 461; RMS XI, No.673.
26 He had taken the surname Scott in anticipation of his marriage (Complete Peerage IX, 60-1).
27 Complete Peerage IX, 61; Fraser 1878, II, 461-482.
28 RMS XI, No.673.
29 AFS 'Ewesdale & Lower Eskdale', No.144; Gifford, 319.

39. ISLE TOWER

(5m NNW Dumfries) (NX935833)

The forty penny land of Isle was originally an island in the middle of the river Nith, and hence the name, but the W channel has long since silted up. It belonged to the monks of the nearby abbey of Holywood, who leased it to the Fergussons of Isle, reputedly a cadet branch of the Fergussons of Craigdarroch, near Moniaive,[1] and even as late as 1600 the Fergussons of Isle were still closely allied to the Craigdarroch family.[2] The Fergussons had been at Craigdarroch at least since 1398, and were in all probability descended from 'Fergus de Glencarn', who is on record early in the previous century.[3]

It is not known when the Fergussons first obtained Isle. The earliest record of their tenure is in 1498/9, when John Rorysone received a remission for the forethought felony done by him upon Donald Fergusson of Yle.[4] Fifty years later, in 1548, John Fergusson, son of the late John Fergusson of Ile, received sasine of the 40 penny land of Ile, in the barony of

Fig. 250 Isle Tower: view from NE.

Dalswinton, on precept from Alexander Stewart of Garlies, the superior.[5] This was done 'at the mansion of Ile', the predecessor of the present tower.

It was not until after the Reformation that the Fergussons gained full possession, when, in 1580, the lands of Isle were formally granted to John Fergusson;[6] and seven years later, in

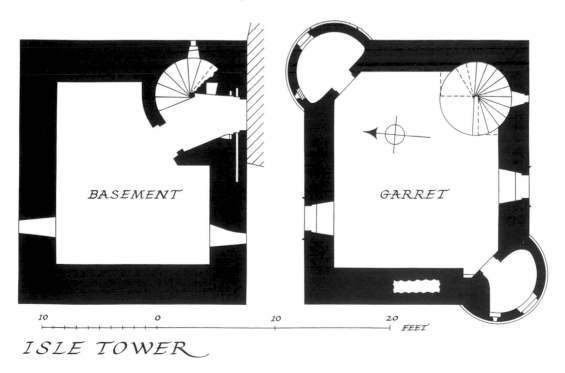

Fig. 251 Isle Tower: plans of basement and garret.

1587, he built the small, squat tower that has stood there ever since. His arms, together with the date and the initials of himself and his wife 'B.R.'[7] appear in the armorial panel over the entrance. The old 'mansion' and any outer works that formerly existed were either swallowed up by the later buildings or, more likely, demolished to make way for them.

The **TOWER**, which is a delightful example of its kind, is oblong in plan, and three storeys and a garret in height, with diagonally-opposed corner-turrets and crow-stepped gables. Measuring 22ft 6in by 19ft 4in, over walls 3ft 6in thick at basement level and 2ft 8in higher up, it is built of local sandstone and whin rubble, with sandstone dressings and mouldings. The mouldings are of the QER type. The entrance, which is on the S side, was defended by a strong wooden door and an iron yett. The latter, which is fastened by a single bolt, is still *in situ*. The door was reinforced with a single wooden drawbar,[8] while the yett was reinforced by two, horizontal iron bars, so designed that they were removable and could be slotted into place.[9] Inside, a mural vestibule gives access to the basement and the wheel-stair, 6ft 4in in diameter, in the SE corner. There is a lamp-shelf at the foot of the stair, and a loop higher up in the S wall to give added protection to the entrance. Beneath the later floor was found the original cobbled surface. The basement was reported to be vaulted at the beginning of the 20th century,[10] but, if correct, the vault has since been removed. It was lit by a slit-window at the E end. The two small windows low down on the N and S sides are later insertions.

The first floor was well appointed, despite its modest size and the intrusion of the stair-well. It had a relatively small fireplace in the middle of the W wall, which was later reduced, and one window in each of the other walls. The windows in the S and E walls were provided with stone seats in the ingos, but the one in the N wall was much smaller and high up, presumably because it was outwith the protection of the barmkin. To the left of the fireplace there is a small, plain buffet; and in each of the other walls a closed-aumbry. The latter have been restored. The aumbry in the E wall is very unusual, in that a small hole in the top gave access to a secret chamber above, where valuables could be secluded.[11] There was also a close-garderobe in the NE corner, which, because of the relative thinness of the walls, intruded slightly into the room. Wooden panelling was added to this room and the floor above in 1891.[12]

The second floor is similarly disposed, with a fireplace at the W end, a small window in each of the other three walls, and two, restored, closed-aumbries, but no garderobe.

The garret on the top floor is provided with one dormer window in each of the N and S sides. Although restored, these appear to be original features. There was no fireplace. It is at this level that small doorways, cutting across the NE and SW corners of the room, give access to the corner turrets. Carried on four courses of continuous corbelling, each turret has a single small window and one shot-hole; but while the windows look straight out from the angle of each corner, both shot-holes point towards the W and NW. This was the direction of approach on the island, and thus the side most vulnerable to attack. Near the top of the E gable, there is a projecting ledge with a small opening above it. This gave access to a small pigeon loft contrived immediately below the roof ridge. The roof itself has at some period been restored and the stone slabs replaced with slates.

The Fergussons lived at 'The Isle', as it was known, for more than three centuries, during which time they led a fairly uneventful life of quiet domesticity. In 1612 the second laird, Alexander, who had succeeded his father c.1603, purchased the adjoining property of Farthingwell. His son, Alexander, was a Commissioner of Supply for Dumfriesshire in 1643,[13] and in 1699 his grandson Alexander, 4th of Isle, further added to the estate.[14] It was evidently the latter laird who added a second building, adjacent to the tower. This was later demolished, but two panels from it are incorporated into a low, two-storeyed building that adjoins the tower to the W.[15] One of these formerly bore the date 1700 with the initials 'A F', 'M' and 'A L', for Alexander Fergusson and his second wife, (?Mistress) Agnes Laurie, daughter of Sir Robert Laurie of Maxwelton and half-sister of the famous 'Annie Laurie'; but it is now almost illegible. Alexander was an advocate. He was appointed a Commissioner of Supply for Dumfriesshire in 1691,[16] and re-appointed in 1696, 1698 and 1704;[17] and at the same time as he was made a burgess of Edinburgh, in 1703, he was appointed one of the city's Assessors.[18] He represented Dumfriesshire in parliament from 1703 to 1707.[19] In 1706 he voted against various clauses in the proposed Treaty of Union,[20] and the following year he voted against the Act ratifying the Treaty.[21]

In 1768 Robert Fergusson, 5th of Isle, entailed the estate. He died without issue later the same year.[22] Four years later his surviving sisters renounced their liferent interest in the property in favour of Captain John Chalmers of Camelon, the only son of their sister Janet and her husband, Captain George Chalmers.[23] John then assumed the surname Fergusson. It was some time around this period that the new mansion-house was built, a modest but fine building, which stands immediately SE of the tower and adjoins it so as to enclose the old entrance. According to one account, Robert Burns stayed in the older portion of the house in 1788, while the farmhouse at Ellisland was being built.[24]

Captain Fergusson was succeeded by his only child, Johanna, whose second husband, Captain Selkirk Stewart, also assumed the surname of Fergusson; but in 1831 Johanna too died without issue.[25] The estate then passed to her cousin, Robert Gillon, who took the additional name of Fergusson.[26] He lived at The Isle for 48 years. On his death in 1879, he was succeeded by his only son, Joseph, who, in 1891, employed the architects Kinnear & Peddie to carry out extensive alterations to the house, including the addition of neo-Jacobean panelling in the tower and dormer-pediments and crow-stepped gables to the house.[27] The estate was eventually sold by his grandson, Robert Gillon-Fergusson c.1912.[28]

1   Burke L.G. 1906, 579, 'Gillon-Fergusson of Isle'; Hamilton-Grierson, Sir P. J., 'The Protocol Book (1541-1550) of Herbert Anderson, Notary in Dumfries', *TDGAS*, 3rd Ser., II, 211.
2   RPC VI, 658, 687.
3   Corrie, 100.
4   RSS I, No.341.
5   Hamilton-Grierson, *op. cit.*, 211 (No.68).
6   Burke, *op. cit.*, 579.
7   Possibly standing for 'B. Rome' – RCAHMS 1920, No.337.
8   The slot measures 3½in high by 2¼in wide.
9   The yett is described in detail in Christison, D. 'On the Grated Iron Doors of Scottish Castles and Towers', *PSAS*, XVII, 107-9.
10 RCAHMS 1920, No.337.
11 This was noted by Christison, *op. cit.*, 109
12 Gifford, 351.

13 APS VI, Part I, 29.
14 Burke, *op. cit.*, 579.
15 This was added in 1806 by John Milligan (Gifford, 351).
16 RPC, 3rd Ser., XVI, 232.
17 APS X, 29, 131; XI, 142.
18 Parl. of Scot., I, 239.
19 APS XI, 29, 113, 205, 300.
20 Ibid, *passim*.
21 Ibid, 404.
22 Burke, *op. cit.*, 579.
23 Ibid.
24 *TDGAS*, 3rd Ser., IX, 211.
25 Burke, *op. cit.*, 579.
26 Ibid.
27 Gifford, 351.
28 County Directory 1912, 270. The writer's grandfather, John Bell Irving of Beanlands, leased the property for a year in 1911. By 1921 it was in the possession of Brigadier-General W. Dickson.

40.   KENMURE CASTLE
(³/₄m S New Galloway)   (NX635764)

Kenmure Castle is situated on an outcrop of rock, some 50ft high, which rises steeply on all sides from the marshy ground at the head of Loch Ken. Such a site was a natural choice for a stronghold, which was further strengthened by a wide moat cut on the W side and a ditch and ramparts to the N. But although it is said to have been occupied by the ancient Lords of Galloway from as early as the 12th century,[1] and to have been a favourite residence of King John Balliol,[2] whose mother, Dervorguilla, was a daughter of Alan, the last Lord of Galloway, there is no evidence to support this assertion. The lands of Kenmure certainly belonged to Balliol, forming part of his barony of Kells, which was forfeited after he surrendered the Crown in 1296. The barony was then granted by Edward I to Sir John de St. John,[3] whose family held it until soon after Edward Balliol's coronation in 1332, when Edward III, who held the lands in ward while Edmond de St. John was a minor, restored them to Edward Balliol.[4] Then in 1352, Balliol granted to Sir William de Aldeburgh, his 'valet', his barony of Kells in Glenken, together

with 'the granter's castle 'in Insula Arsa'',[5] which is not Kenmure, but Burned Island some 2¹/₂ miles further down Loch Ken.[6] And if it was Burned Island that was Edward Balliol's local base, it was almost certainly that of his father and his predecessors too.[7]

Meanwhile, during the War of Independence, the Balliols lands in Galloway had been claimed first by King Robert the Bruce and then by David II, who granted them to Gilbert Carrick (*alias* Kerr).[8] Bruce also established a new forest in the Glenkens, immediately to the N, and in 1358 his grandson Robert, Earl of Strathearn, granted the keeping of this forest to William Gordon of Stitchill.[9] All these lands were subsequently included in the Lordship of Galloway granted to Archibald 'The Grim', later 3rd Earl of Douglas, by David II in 1369. Then in 1403, on precept from the 4th Earl of Douglas, Sir Alexander Gordon of Stitchill was infeft in the lands of Kenmure;[10] and around the same time he also received from the Earl a new charter of the lands, possessions and lordships in the Forest of Glenken.[11]

Sir Alexander was succeeded by his elder son, Roger Gordon of Stitchill, who in turn was succeeded *c*.1442 by his son William. William is said to have been the first of the family to settle in Galloway. He took the designation 'of Lochinvar' (q.v.), which, it is believed, became the family's first residence and principal messuage, and in 1450 was infeft in the lands. In the same year his eldest son, Sir John Gordon, received a charter of the lands of Kenmure from the Earl of Douglas.[12] It was probably Sir John who built the first stronghold at Kenmure, for, although the Gordons continued to be styled 'of Lochinvar' until raised to the peerage in 1633, it is believed that it was Kenmure that very soon became the family's principal residence.[13] Sir John later resigned Kenmure in favour of his eldest son, Sir Alexander Gordon, who in 1487/8 was granted a charter of the lands of Kenmure, Laggan and Balmaclellan, called *Le Park*, which were incorporated into the new barony of Kenmure;[14] and this was confirmed by James IV after his accession the following year.[15] Sir John sat in parliament in 1487 and 1487/8[16] and was sometime Armour-bearer to James IV,[17] while his son was a Gentleman of the Bedchamber to James III.[18] By his second wife, Sir John had a son, Sir Robert Gordon, who married Marion, daughter and heiress of John Acarsane of Glen, and for a while took her family name of Acarsane. In 1494 Sir Robert and Marion had a charter of her father's lands of Glenskyreburn, or Glen, later known as Rusco.[19]

On the death of Sir Alexander Gordon at Flodden in 1513, his estates were claimed by his only daughter, Janet. In 1517 she had sasine of the 19 merk lands of Kenmure and Laggan, 'with the tower and fortalice of Kenmure', and of the lands of Balmaclellan and The Park, whilst reserving the liferent to her grandfather, Sir John Gordon of Lochinvar.[20] Then, in accordance with a prior agreement, by which she had been persuaded[21] to sell these lands to her uncle Sir Robert Gordon of Glen, the heir male of the family,[22] she duly disponed these lands to him the next day, while, by way of compensation, her uncle granted her the liferent of Shirmers (q.v.) and certain other lands in the parishes of Balmaclellan and

Fig. 252 Kenmure Castle, by Alexander Nasmyth.

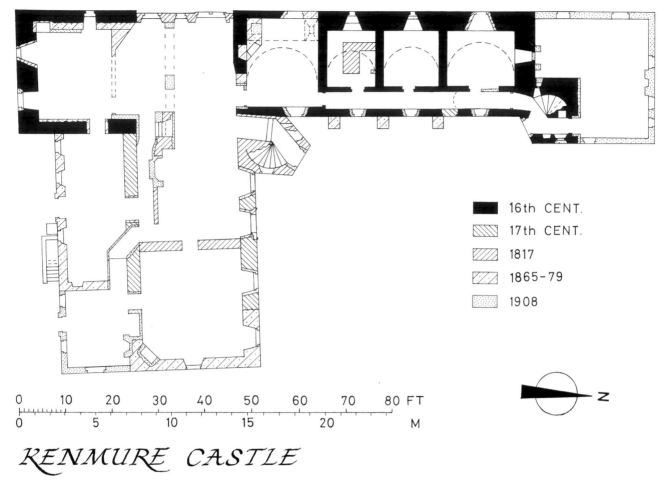

16th CENT.

17th CENT.

1817

1865-79

1908

KENMURE CASTLE

Fig. 253 Kenmure Castle: plan of basement level.

Kells.[23] This was the first formal reference to a stronghold at Kenmure, though two charters had been signed at 'the manor of Kenmore' two years earlier.[24] Sir Robert was succeeded in 1525 by his eldest son, James, who had sasine later that year.[25] In 1528 he was appointed King's Chamberlain for the Lordship of Galloway,[26] and in 1542 and 1546 he sat in parliament.[27] Falling at the battle of Pinkie in 1547, he was succeeded by his son Sir John Gordon.

Sir John was laird of Kenmure for more than fifty years, holding many offices of state and rebuilding the castle after its destruction by the Regent Moray in 1568. In 1555 he was made Justiciar of the Stewartry,[28] and the following year Vice-Admiral for Galloway.[29] Three years later, he granted the barony of Kenmure and many other lands to his brother William, later of Penninghame, whilst reserving for himself and his wife the liferent.[30] This was confirmed in 1563/4,[31] but must later have been rescinded after Sir John had male issue by his second wife, Elizabeth Maxwell, whom he married in 1563. The following year he obtained substantial grants of church lands from the Bishop of Galloway and the abbey of Tongland.[32] Meanwhile, in 1560, Sir John had attended parliament.[33] An English survey *c.*1565 reported that among the 'notable places within the nether part of Gallowaye' was 'Kenmure, pertenyng to the larde of Lowghinwar'.[34]

Sir John was an ardent supporter of Queen Mary. He entertained her at Kenmure in 1563;[35] was the first 'baron' who signed the Bond subscribed by her adherents at Hamilton in 1568;[36] and after her defeat at Langside, refused to join the Re-

gent, despite the Regent's conciliatory overtures. 'The laird of Lowinvar', it was reported, 'utterly refused either to come in or give pledges';[37] and when the Regent arrived at Kenmure two days later, during his progress through the West March, he again 'offered the laird, if he would accompany him 'only this jorney' he would save his house and forget the past';[38] but Sir John was steadfast in his refusal. Consequently, the Regent attacked the castle and destroyed it – so completely, it seems, that one cannot be certain how much of the earlier castle survived. According to *The Diary of the Regentis campe of Scotland*, 'they camped in 'the Kenmwyr in the howme callit Beisk hawcht' underneath the castle, 'swte [?seized] the castell, and haill place wes cassin [cast] downe and brynt [burnt]',[39] while another, contemporary account relates that '60 men appeared on a hillside, but enterprised nothing. The Place of Kenmure was destroyed and cast down, and another "proper place" a friend's of Lochinvar'.[40] Grose records that, during excavations near the foot of the mount, some 48 cannon balls and some six-pounders were found.[41] Some or all of these may date from the later seige of 1650, but there must have been some resistance, as one of those in the Regent's army was later given compensation for the loss of his horse at Kenmure.[42] Later that year Sir John was one of the Commissioners acting for Queen Mary in negotiations concerning her release.[43]

Little is then heard of Sir John – apart from his appointment as a Commissioner for holding wapin-schaws in the Stewartry in 1574[44] – until 1583/4, when he was appointed to the Privy Council.[45] In 1587, he attended parliament,[46] and the following year he was again appointed a Commissioner for proclaiming and holding wapinschaws[47] as well as being appointed a Commissioner responsible for preparations for the expected invasion by the Holy League (the Spanish Armada).[48] Then, in 1589/90, he was appointed to mete out justice to enemies of the 'true religion', in accordance with the new Act of 1587.[49] He was re-appointed to the Privy Council in 1592,[50] and in 1593 was one of the Commissioners appointed to keep peace in the West March.[51] Three years later, he, Lord Sanquhar and Alexander Stewart of Garlies were appointed as joint Wardens of the West March, following a protracted crisis over the office; but they all refused to serve.[52] He also attended parliament that year under the designation 'Lord Lochinvar'.[53] He died in 1604. 'Kenmoir Castle' is shown on Pont's map c.1595.[54]

The **CASTLE** has undergone so many changes since it was rebuilt after the siege of 1568, as well as being besieged by Cromwell's forces in 1650, that it is difficult to be precise as to which works belong to each phase. There has also been considerable re-use of older material and mouldings. However, Grose's two views of the castle, as it was in 1790, give a very good picture of what existed before the major changes of the 19th century.[55] There were two tall towers near the SE and SW corners of the site, both of which were roofless and described as being 'in ruins'. Each appears to have comprised three storeys and a garret. The former had a corbelled-out turret at the SE corner and the latter a corresponding one at the SW corner; and there may also have been turrets at the diagonally opposite corners, which are not shown. To the N of the latter tower there was a large building, three storeys high, running N-S, with a square stair-tower at its NE corner and a small projection beyond. The stair tower evidently had a corbelled-out parapet on the N side,[56] while tusking in the N gable of the main building shows that it had been intended to extend it further north, though more than 100 years were to pass before this was achieved. Another building of two storeys, which we later learn served as 'stables, hay-lofts and other offices',[57] extended across the site immediately N of the two towers; but it is not clear whether it was directly connected to either tower, or, indeed, whether the W range was connected to the SW tower: Grose shows a gap here, and all the present masonry in this space is of 19th century or later date, apart from an unexplained, blocked fireplace with QERF moulded jambs at first floor level. Finally, the courtyard formed to the N and E of the main buildings was enclosed by a high curtain wall, with an arched gateway in the middle of the N wall.

The oldest of the surviving buildings appears to be the W range, the lower two floors of which, although considerably altered, may well belong, in part at least, to the original castle, while the stair tower at the N end dates from the rebuilding carried out after 1568. Measuring 64ft 4in from N to S by 22ft 7in from E to W over walls varying in thickness from 1ft 7in on the courtyard side to 4ft 1in on the W, the basement comprises four vaulted chambers of unequal size and a connecting passage along

Fig. 255 Kenmure: passage in W range.

Fig. 256 Kenmure: one of the basement chambers in W range.

the E side. The most southerly of the chambers was the largest, and served as the kitchen, with a large fireplace, 15ft 2in wide and some 4ft deep, at its W end.[58] Originally, each chamber except the kitchen had one small window high up in its W wall, and there was a corresponding small window in the E wall of the passage opposite each door. Most of these windows have since been enlarged. An additional window in the N wall of the northernmost chamber was blocked when the range was extended to

Fig. 254 Kenmure Castle: view from NW in 1967.

Fig. 257 Kenmure: remains of blocked, "double cross" gun-loop
in N stair tower.

the N in 1908. At the foot of the stair, which is 8ft in diameter, there are two splayed gun-loops, both now blocked on the outside, one facing W and the other E. The latter is unique, and presumably more ornamental than practical, as its throat is cut in the form of a double, horizontal cross.

The entrance at the foot of the stair tower has a QERFH-moulded surround and a cable moulding, which runs round the door and then up and around an empty armorial panel above. The style of this doorway and its associated surround are char-

acteristic of post-Reformation work of the late 16th century,[59] but it is not clear whether it belongs to the reconstruction carried out immediately after 1568, or is part of another, much more ambitious phase of work carried out by Sir John Gordon towards the end of the century. It does, however, seem to have been carried out at the same time as the W range had its second floor added. Indeed, the stair tower also served that floor. The original entrance, now blocked, was nearer the middle of the building, and led directly from the courtyard into the passage; and there was almost certainly another entrance admitting directly to the kitchen at the S end of this range. Some of the walling on the first floor and a small window on the W side appear to date from the earliest period of construction, but the rest of the windows were apparently either enlarged or added later, when they and the second floor windows were fitted with cage-type iron grilles,[60] the sockets for which may still be seen. The E wall on the first floor can also be clearly seen to have been increased in thickness from 1ft 4in to 3ft at this time to carry the weight of the extra floor above.

The same cable moulding that adorns the doorway of the stair tower was also added on the courtyard side of the main block and stair tower as a string course at both first and second floor levels. It is situated at the level of the window sills, and rises up to surround each window frame. In addition, at what was the central window on the second floor,[61] the moulding is carried under the sill in an inverted ogee arch. There is also a cornice of diminutive, enriched corbelling at the wall-head, which continues around the S, E and N sides of the taller stair-tower at the same level.

The earlier work at Kenmure employs both QER and QERF mouldings, both of which are commonly found from the 1560s onwards – as, for example, at Hoddom and Abbot's (q.v.). They are thus no help in trying to establish a firm date. All the early masonry was of local greywacke rubble, with sandstone dressings and mouldings; it was harled.

The lower part of the SW tower probably dates from c.1570 too, though it has been so greatly altered that only the recesses for the W window and the more easterly of the S windows in the basement are original. While the latter window has been enlarged and its QERF surround is modern, the W window, with its QERF moulding and bar sockets for iron grilles, would seem to be original. The basement was originally vaulted, but both the vault and large sections of the walls' thickness were torn out when it was converted to a kitchen in 1817.[62] This tower is 26ft 11in wide from E to W, and has walls averaging 4ft 4in in

Fig. 258 Kenmure Castle: entrance to NW stair tower.

Fig. 259 Kenmure Castle: view from the NE in 1790.

thickness: its original length cannot now be determined. As shown by Grose, it was three storeys and a garret in height, and had a corbelled-out turret at its SW corner, which, like its 19th century replacement, may well have been supported on embellished corbelling. Indeed, the corbelling itself may be original, as may be the shot-hole at the turret's NW corner.

The SE tower may also have dated from the 16th century, though it is more likely that it belonged to the following century. It was demolished in the 19th century, and the only record of it is that shown by Grose and other illustrators around that period.[63] The curtain walls and former entrance gateway were removed in 1817 (*infra*).

Sir John Gordon, 4th of Kenmure, was succeeded by his eldest son, Sir Robert Gordon of Glen, a Gentleman of the Bedchamber to James VI.[64] In 1609 he was appointed one of His Majesty's Justices for the Middle Shires,[65] an appointment that was confirmed the following year,[66] and two years later he represented the Stewartry in parliament.[67] In 1617 he was made Provost of Lincluden.[68] He also claimed the office of Admiral on the South-West Coast, a claim, however, that did not go unchallenged.[69] He added many lands to the family estates, and in 1621 received from James VI a grant of the barony of Crossmichael, including the lands and manor-place of Greenlaw, which thereafter became his principal residence.[70] One of the first to become interested in the colonization of North America, he obtained a charter of the 'barony of Galloway' in Nova Scotia later in 1621;[71] and in 1626 he was created a Baronet of Nova Scotia.[72] In the latter year he had his earlier appointment as a Commissioner for the Middle Shires renewed,[73] and was made a member of the Council of War for Scotland.[74]

Fig. 260 Kenmure Castle: S elevation.

Sir Robert was succeeded in 1628 by his eldest son, Sir John Gordon of Lochinvar, 6th of Kenmure. Sir John had a tragically short life, but in that brief span achieved a great deal. In 1629 he was granted a crown charter for the establishment of a new burgh, to be called the Burgh of Galloway, on that part of the barony of Earlstoun (now St. John's Town of Dalry) that his father had purchased in 1605.[75] However, before this could be implemented, a new charter was issued establishing the burgh on a different site, in the barony of Kenmure.[76] This became the royal burgh of 'Newton of Galloway', now New Galloway. In 1633 he was raised to the peerage as Viscount Kenmure and Lord Lochinvar.[77] Although Sir John spent much of his time in England, and like his father made Greenlaw his principal residence, he 'brought Kenmure to the perfection of a complete fabric as it was never before'.[78]

The 6th laird's work at Kenmure included the rebuilding of the central block of stables and offices, though this building was so greatly altered in 1817 and subsequently that little more of his work is left than the core of the walls. A later doorway in the N front of this block has the same mouldings as the one in the north stair-tower, and clearly belongs to the same period. More will be said of this later.

John, 2nd Viscount Kenmure, succeeded his father in 1634, while he was still a minor. The estate was by then heavily in debt, and in 1635 the baronies of Kenmure and Earlstoun, with their respective castles, were apprized by Robert McBrair of Almagill.[79] A further mortgage was raised two years later.[80] Lord Kenmure died in 1639, and was succeeded by his father's cousin, John Gordon of Barncrosh, who succeeded as the 3rd Viscount. He attended parliament regularly from 1640, when he was still under age, until his death three years later.[81] He was also appointed to the Committee of War for the Stewartry in 1643, but may never have served.[82]

The 3rd Viscount was succeeded by his brother Robert, 4th Viscount Kenmure. Robert was a regular attender of parliament from 1644 to 1648, and again, after the Restoration, from 1661 until his death.[83] He was also on the Committee for the South in 1644,[84] and a Commissioner of War for the Stewartry from 1645 to 1648.[85] In the latter year he was appointed Colonel in charge of 80 horse from Wigtownshire and the Stewartry.[86] During the Civil War, he supported the Crown. When Cromwell's forces marched across the Border in 1650, he garrisoned Kenmure Castle against them, and for a while held out; but eventually he was compelled to surrender. Lord Kenmure then undertook to deliver up 'his Castle of Kenmore, with all the armes and ammunition for the use of His Excellency, the Lord Cromwell'.[87] But he still continued to support Charles II, and in 1651 fought for him at Worcester, where he was taken prisoner.[88] Two years later, he again took up arms, this time to join in Glencairn's rising, and he remained a constant thorn in the English side, until, in 1654, he eventually gave himself up to General Monck on terms that secured his estates.[89] The following year he had to raise a further mortgage against the barony of Kenmure.[90] In 1659 he was imprisoned in Edinburgh Castle, but escaped. After the Restoration he retired to Greenlaw,[91] but he still attended parliament, and in 1661 was appointed a Commissioner of Supply for the Stewartry.[92] He died two years later.

Lord Kenmure was succeeded by a distant cousin, Alexander Gordon of Penninghame, who became 5th Viscount Kenmure. Alexander's succession to the family estates was, however, contested by Robert Maxwell, Master of Herries, who claimed them as 'heir of line', his mother having been the sister of the 1st Viscount, and it was some years before the matter was finally resolved.[93] At this time the estates were still heavily encumbered, and in the same year that Alexander succeeded, David McBrair granted his wadset of the Kenmure estates to William Gordon of Earlstoun.[94] Alexander was a regular attender of parliament from the time he succeeded in 1663 until his last appearance in 1696, just two years before he died.[95] He was appointed a Justice of the Peace for the Stewartry in 1663,[96] and served as a Commissioner of Supply for the Stewartry from 1667 until 1685.[97] It was also in 1667 that the Crown approved a commission empowering him to hold courts in the royal forest of Buchan, in Galloway, of which his predecessor had been 'forester'.[98] Eventually, in 1676, Alexander obtained a new charter of the lands and barony of Kenmure, having presumably settled his debts;[99] and in the same year he was appointed Captain of the troop of horse for Wigtownshire and the Stewartry.[100]

Following an uprising by the Covenanters in 1679, Lord Kenmure was, in 1680, ordered to prepare Kenmure to receive a garrison, 'as being more fitt for the Kings service and convenient for your Lordship' than Greenlaw, which had previously been suggested.[101] This was approved by the King in person.[102] Nevertheless, the garrison did not materialize until after Graham of Claverhouse took over command in the SW in 1682, and proposed to use Kenmure as his headquarters. Claverhouse then wrote to the Marquess of Queensberry that there should be 'a fixt garison in Kenmur . . . a mighty strong pleace and propre above all ever I sau for this use'.[103] He also reported that, if the king should 'bestou two or three hondred pounds to repair the house', Lady Kenmure 'would be very well pleased his souldiers came to lieve in it'. This suggests that, with the ongoing indebtedness of the estate, the damage sustained during the 1650 siege may never have been fully made good. The following year Lord Kenmure was appointed one of the Commissioners for the Revaluation of the Stewartry,[104] and in 1684 one of the Justices for Proceeding against Recusants.[105] In 1685 he was Convenor of the Justices for the Stewartry and Wigtown.[106] But it was a turbulent time to be involved in politics, and later that year he fell from grace and forfeited the lands and barony of Kenmure for treason.[107] He subsequently served with his regiment in Central Scotland, before holding a command under General Mackay at the battle of Killiecrankie in 1689.[108] Alexander's forfeiture having been rescinded following the deposition of James VII, he was again appointed a Commissioner of Supply for the Stewartry.[109] He was also re-appointed, first Captain of a troop of the militia, and then Colonel of the regiment of foot for Wigtownshire and the Stewartry,[110] a commission that was confirmed by the Crown the following year.[111] In 1690 he was again made a Justice of the Peace for Kirkcudbright,[112] and in 1691 he was Convenor of the Commissioners of Supply for the county.[113] He died in 1698.

Lord Kenmure was succeeded by his only son, William, 6th Viscount Kenmure, who was appointed a Commissioner of Supply for the Stewartry of Kirkcudbright in 1704.[114] At the outset of the Jacobite rebellion of 1715, William joined the prince's party, and was declared a rebel.[115] He was subsequently given the chief Jacobite command in the south of Scotland, and was active in the Border counties, where he proclaimed the Old Chevalier as King James VIII, before marching south to Preston.[116] There he was captured, taken prisoner to the Tower of London, found guilty of high treason, and, in February 1716, executed, with the forfeiture of all his honours and estates.[117] It was an ignominious end to what he believed a noble cause.

Lady Kenmure then actively campaigned for the restoration of the family estates to her son, Robert, claiming that they had been held in trust for him. In this she was eventually successful, the estates being adjudged in Robert's favour in 1722.[118] They were, however, still heavily in debt, wadsets being granted in 1719 and 1724,[119] and it was not until 1737 that Robert had sasine of the baronies and lands of Kenmure, Crossmichael and Gordonstoun.[120] By then the castle is said to have been almost in ruins.[121] Robert died in 1741, unmarried, when the estates passed to his uncle, John Gordon.

John immediately set about clearing the estate's debts and restoring the castle. He sold the lands of Tongland[122] and the barony of Crossmichael,[123] where the new house of Greenlaw started by his nephew was still incomplete. When Prince Charles Edward came to Scotland in 1745, he wrote to 'Lord Kenmure' requesting his support; but although John attended the Prince at

Holyrood House, wiser counsels prevailed, and he declined the offer.[124] He died in 1769, and was succeeded by his eldest son, William, a captain in the Royal Scots Regiment of Foot.[125] William died unmarried in 1772, and was succeeded by his brother John.

John also served in the army, and in 1780 was elected Member of Parliament for the Stewartry.[126] Despite his father's endeavours to clear the estate's debts, there was still money owing, so in order to pay off his creditors he sold more of the estate, including the family's original lands of Lochinvar.[127] Fortunately his mother, Lady Frances Mackenzie, was able to assist his finances, when she inherited some of her father's estates in England.[128] In 1793 John entertained Robert Burns at Kenmure: Burns referred to him in one of his ballads as 'Kenmure sae gen'rous'.[129] John was appointed Vice-Lieutenant of the Stewartry in 1822, and two years later had the honour, dignity and titles of (7th) Viscount Kenmure and Lord Lochinvar restored.[130] He died without issue in 1840, when the titles and estates passed to his nephew, Adam Gordon.

Lord Kenmure had started a major programme of changes at Kenmure in 1817. Advised by one Mr. Carruthers, a Catholic priest,[131] and possibly using William McCandlish, a local architect and contractor who was working in the area around that time, and who is known to have been employed at Kenmure in the 1840s,[132] he swept away the old courtyard wall and entrance; landscaped the mound such that the old earthworks were largely destroyed and a new drive formed up to the summit; and demolished 'with gunpowder' the SE tower.[133] He greatly changed the character of the various surviving buildings, including the SW tower, which for many years had been a roofless ruin,[134] modernizing their internal arrangement and adding the new stair tower in the NE re-entrant angle. The changes are too numerous to detail; but the kitchen in the old W range was replaced by a new one in the basement of the restored SW tower, after the vaulting and large sections of the side walls had been removed; the cellar next to the old kitchen had a massive stone pillar inserted in its centre, which was necessary to carry a new transverse wall and fireplaces on the floor above; and the whole area between this range and the SW tower was rebuilt, and provided with a further staircase to serve the upper floors. In the new arrangement, the entrance doorway and hall were situated in the E wing. The door surround itself is 17th century work, which was taken from elsewhere on the site, but with a new lintel to provide a wider entrance.[135]

Adam Gordon was the 8th and last Viscount Kenmure; when he died in 1872, without issue, the title became dormant, and so it has remained ever since. Adam served in the navy, and as a young cadet was present at the battle of Trafalgar in 1805.[136] He was invalided out of the service while a lieutenant in 1818.[137] It was apparently Adam who, in 1865, had the buttresses added on the E side of the W range to stabilize that wall.[138]

From Adam the estate, which at that time extended to 14,000 acres,[139] passed to his sister Louisa, who in 1843 had been accorded the title of a Viscount's daughter. She had married Charles Bellamy (d.1823-4) of the Honourable East India Company, and on succeeding to Kenmure took the name and designation Bellamy-Gordon (or sometimes Gordon-Bellamy) of Kenmure. In 1879 she commissioned the architects M. E. Hadfield and Son[140] to undertake an extensive programme of alterations to the castle, including the extension of the E wing[141] and the addition of a secondary building in the SE re-entrant angle – though it is often difficult to be sure precisely when the various changes took place. The Hon. Louisa Bellamy-Gordon died in 1886, and was succeeded by her eldest daughter, Louisa, who in 1837 had married the Reverend James Maitland of Fairgirth. On succeeding to Kenmure, she took the name Maitland-Gordon.[142] It is doubtful whether she ever lived at Kenmure; she was already a widow when she inherited the estate, and went to live at Overton, on the other side of New Galloway, while the castle was let, and none of the family was ever to live there again. After her death in 1899, Kenmure passed to her eldest surviving son, James.

It was while James was laird, in 1908, that an American tenant made the last additions to the castle. These comprised the extension of the W range to the N, the addition of a secondary building in the SE re-entrant angle, and the removal of the main entrance from the E range to the foot of the main stair tower. This work was designed by the architect Christian Eliot.[143] James died in 1915, and his son John sold Kenmure in 1935.[144]

During the Second World War the castle was leased by a General MacEwan. It subsequently served as an hotel for a short while, but did not pay. Towards the end of the 1950s the roof was taken off to save rates, after which a demolition contractor stripped it of every feature that could be sold. Contrary to popular belief it was not burned down. By the time Graeme Gordon, a scion of the Gordons of Lochinvar, bought it in 1961/2, it was no more than an empty shell, and so it remains.

---

1 Stat Acct IX, 637; Grose II, 21; M'Kerlie IV, 39.
2 Ibid; Imperial Gazetteer II, 180.
3 Bain III, No.69.
4 Ibid, IV, No.54.
5 Ibid, III, No.1578.
6 According to M'Kerlie, in 1359 David II permitted Balliol to exercise free jurisdiction in the lands of Buittle, Kenmure and Kirkandrews, but the source is not given (M'Kerlie IV, 40).
7 Burned Island probably started life as a crannog, to which a timber stronghold was later added; but it has never been properly investigated.
8 RMS I, App.2, Nos.831, 894, 1100; Robertson's Index, 40-29, 46-5, 56-9.
9 Scots Peerage V, 99.
10 Ibid, 100.
11 Fraser 1885, III, 405-6. See also 'Lochinvar Castle' for further details of the various grants and offices concerning The Glenkens and the new forest.
12 Scots Peerage V, 102.
13 Ibid, 101.
14 RMS II, No.1722.
15 Ibid, No.1883.
16 APS II, 175, 180.
17 RMS II, No.2100.
18 Ibid, No.1722.
19 Ibid, No.2204. It is believed that Sir Robert either built or greatly enlarged the present castle there (Scots Peerage V, 106).
20 ERS XIV, 592; Scots Peerage V, 103.
21 Probably by her grandfather, Sir John Gordon, who was still alive.
22 RMS III, No.163.
23 Scots Peerage V, 104; Affleck, J 'Kenmure Castle', TDGAS, 2nd Ser., XXIII, 183.
24 RMS III, No.51.
25 ERS XV, 636.
26 Scots Peerage V, 107.
27 APS II, 425, 468.
28 Scots Peerage, 110. He apparently also held this office in Wigtown, so was probably effectively Justiciar of all Galloway.
29 Affleck, op. cit., 186.
30 RMS III, No.1369.
31 Ibid, No.1492: RSS V, No.1515.
32 RMS III, Nos.1719, 1743.
33 APS II, 525.
34 Armstrong 1883, cviii.
35 Scots Peerage V, 110.
36 Scottish Papers II, No.650. Other signatories in the West March included the Lords Herries, Maxwell, Carlyle and Sanquhar; the abbots of Holywood, New Abbey, Dundrennan and Glenluce; the bishop of Galloway; and the lairds of Johnston, Closeburn, Comlongon, Bombie and Ryehill.

37 Ibid, No.717.
38 Ibid, No.706.
39 Ibid, No.716.
40 Ibid, No.717. The 'proper place' was probably Shirmers Castle (q.v.).
41 Grose II, 22.
42 ALHT XII, 151.
43 Scottish Papers III, 452.
44 APS III, 91.
45 Scottish Papers VII, No.36.
46 Ibid, IX, 452. In the same year he was included in a list of those who had harboured 'broken' men (APS III, 465).
47 RPC IV, 302.
48 Ibid, 308.
49 Ibid, 465.
50 Ibid, 750.
51 Ibid, V, 113.
52 Rae, 243.
53 APS IV, 104, 106.
54 Blaeu, 66, 'The Steuartrie of Kircubright, The most easterlie part of Galloway'.
55 Grose II, 21-2, Plates I and II.
56 An etching dating from c.1810 in the NMRS shows the parapet more clearly.
57 MacGibbon & Ross IV, 258.
58 The later work in the SW corner of the kitchen includes a blocked brick arch that may have been an oven.
59 Mackechnie, A. 'Design Approaches in Early Post-Reformation Scots Houses', in Gow & Rowan 1998, 17-18.
60 Cage-type grilles were rare in the south, and were usually only employed where part, or all, of a window frame already existed, such that a conventional grille could not be fitted without a complete rebuild of the masonry. Presumably cage-type grilles were also used on the second floor for symmetry.
61 The E front of this building was originally symmetrical, with five windows on each of the two upper floors; but the most southerly windows were lost when the stair-tower was added in the re-entrant angle in 1817.
62 MacGibbon & Ross IV, 259.
63 Ibid, 258.
64 Scots Peerage V, 113.
65 RPC VIII, 814.
66 RPC IX, 77.
67 APS IV, 466.
68 RPC, 2nd Ser., I, cxlvii.
69 Ibid, 557; Scots Peerage V, 113.
70 RMS VIII, No.176.
71 Scots Peerage V, 115.
72 Ibid; RPC, 2nd Ser., I, ciii.
73 RPC, 2nd Ser., I, 193, 373.
74 Ibid, 337-8.
75 RMS VIII, No.1346.
76 Ibid, No.1667.
77 Scots Peerage V, 119.
78 Ibid.
79 RMS IX, No.442.
80 Ibid, No.661.
81 APS V, 258, 308, 331, 426; VI, Part I, 3.
82 Ibid, VI, Part I, 51.
83 Ibid, 95, 474, 612; Part II, 3; VII, passim.
84 Ibid, VI, Part I, 91.
85 Ibid, 204, 559; Part II, 35.
86 Ibid, Part II, 30, 56.
87 Scots Peerage V, 121. The full terms of the surrender are given by Affleck (op. cit., 189-190).
88 Ibid.
89 Ibid, 122.
90 RMS X, No.507.
91 M'Kerlie IV, 60.
92 APS VII, 92.
93 RPC, 3rd Ser., I, 347; II, 11, 98, 124, 160.
94 RMS XI, No.520.
95 APS VII-X, passim.
96 Ibid, VII, 505.
97 Ibid, 544; VIII, 228, 469.
98 RPC, 3rd Ser., II, 255.
99 M'Kerlie IV, 62.
100 RPC, 3rd Ser., IV, 588.
101 Ibid, VI, 605.
102 'We have seen a list of houses proposed as most convenient for having garrisons put in them, [including] the houses of Balgregan and Kenmuire in Galloway, . . . all of which we approve' (State Papers, Domestic, 1680-1681, 70).
103 Buccleuch MSS, 265.
104 RPC, 3rd Ser., VIII, 207.

105 Ibid, X, 87.
106 Ibid, 140.
107 APS VIII, 490.
108 Scots Peerage V, 124.
109 APS IX, 74, 144.
110 Ibid, 26, 56.
111 State Papers, Domestic (1689-1690), 430; RPC, 3rd Ser., XVI, 291.
112 RPC, 3rd Ser., XV, 541.
113 Ibid, XVI, 289.
114 APS XI, 149.
115 Scots Peerage V, 126.
116 Ibid, 127-8.
117 Ibid, 128-9.
118 Ibid, 130.
119 M'Kerlie IV, 95. His mother is said to have cleared the debts, but when he
     came of age his extravagance soon had him in financial difficulties again
     (Affleck, op. cit., 193).
120 M'Kerlie IV, 95.
121 Ibid.
122 Scots Peerage V, 131.
123 Ibid; M'Kerlie III, 365-7.
124 Scots Peerage V, 131.
125 Ibid, 133.
126 Ibid.
127 Ibid, 134.
128 Ibid; M'Kerlie IV, 67.
129 Scots Peerage V, 134.
130 Ibid.
131 MacGibbon & Ross IV, 256.
132 Gifford, 354.
133 MacGibbon & Ross IV, 258.
134 Various engravings of the castle early in the 19th century clearly show the
     state of the SW tower at that time.
135 It has been suggested that this doorway was originally in the W range
     (MacGibbon & Ross IV, 260).
136 Scots Peerage V, 135.
137 Affleck, op. cit., 194.
138 Gifford, 355. They were the work of Hugh Maclure.
139 Return of Landowners, 117.
140 Gifford, 354.
141 MacGibbon & Ross IV, 259.
142 Burke L. G. 1937, 919, 'Maitland-Gordon, late of Kenmure'.
143 Gifford, 354.
144 Burke L. G. 1937, op. cit., 919.

41. KINNELHEAD BASTLE-HOUSE
(3¼ m W Beattock)   (NT028016)

Situated on the western extremity of Annandale, at an altitude of 850ft and with little beyond to the west but a vast wilderness, Kinnelhead was always a remote outpost near the head waters of the Kinnel. It is a naturally rocky site, where the rock formation has been used to advantage, both as a foundation for the buildings and to provide building material of Cyclopean proportions.

Kinnelhead first comes on record in 1529, when Janet Scrymgeour, widow of James, 3rd Lord Carlyle, was granted a liferent interest in half the Carlyle family estates.[1] These included the £42 lands of Roklenheid, 'Kindalheid' (Kinnelhead), Holmshaw and Cogrie. Later, Kinnelhead and Holmshaw came into the possession of John Johnston of that Ilk, who, in 1568, granted occupation of them, 'without conditions', to John Johnston in Glenkill in exchange for the lands of Armynnie, in the Stewartry of Kirkcudbright.[2]

The Carlyles, however, still retained the superiority, for on the death of the 4th Lord Carlyle in 1575 the Crown granted the ward and nonentry of the Carlyle estates, including the £42 lands of Reklehead, 'Kindalheid', Holmshaw and Cogrie, to George Douglas of Parkhead until the entry of the heir.[3] Four years later, Elizabeth Carlyle, daughter of William, Master of Carlyle, and granddaughter of the 4th Lord Carlyle, was served heir to her grandfather; but she was not infeft in her patrimony until 1587.[4] Meanwhile, in 1584, Douglas had suffered forfeiture for rebellion, and the ward of the estates had been granted to Thomas Cranstoun of Remilton.[5] In 1612, Dame Elizabeth Carlyle[6] assigned her liferent interest in the lands of Kinnelhead to Robert Johnston of Raecleugh.[7]

Another portion of Kinnelhead lay in the parish of Dumgree, and formed a part of the barony of Amisfield that was held by the Charteris at the turn of the 17th century.[8] It was on this part of Kinnelhead that one Andro Johnston, grandson and heir of Andro Johnston, called 'Marjoribanks', and his uncle David Johnston in Kinnelhead were tenants when John Charteris of Amisfield tried to evict them in 1608.[9] The family appears to

Fig. 261 Kinnelhead Bastle-House: remains of bastle-house (left) and outbuilding (far right) with courtyard between, seen from the NE.

have acquired the tenancy some time during the second half of the 16th century, and it may well have been they who built the earliest surviving buildings on the site.

It is unlikely that there was ever a Tower as such, for, although 'towers' are vaguely alluded to in the Earl of Annandale's title to 'Kinleheid' and other lands in 1662 and 'Kinnelhead Tower' is marked on the earliest, large-scale, Ordnance Survey map of the area, the proportions of the surviving buildings are more reminiscent of the long, vaulted outbuildings found at such sites as Tushielaw and Holydean than of a typical, compact tower-house. One has also to consider whether a tower would have been appropriate at such a remote, windswept site. While the majority of towers were in valleys, where their height served as a look-out and means of communication from one tower to the next, no such advantage could be claimed for a tower at Kinnelhead.[10] Indeed, the site was so well camouflaged by the surrounding rocky eminences and hillside that a low profile could have been a distinct advantage. What is most likely is that the principal building at Kinnelhead was in fact a bastle-house, of the type recently excavated in nearby Upper Clydesdale,[11] and similar to those commonly found on the English side of the Border.[12]

The **PRINCIPAL STRUCTURE** is oblong in plan and measures about 49ft 5in from NE to SW by 23ft from NW to SE, over walls which average 4ft thick at the sides and 4ft 6in at the gable ends. The masonry is local rubble, bonded with lime mortar. Throughout most of its length the basement has been cut out of a cleft in the living rock. This rises to a height of over 7ft on the NW side, above which a barrel-vault rose to a maximum height of more than 16ft to contain an entresol floor. What remains of the basement is largely concealed beneath a vast mass of rubble, but due to the nature of the site there cannot have been any openings at this level except at the NE end, where the wall

is missing. This is where the entrance to the basement must have been located, unless the basement was reached from the floor above. At the other end, there is an intriguing recess, $6\frac{1}{2}$ in wide and $12\frac{1}{2}$ in deep, near the middle of the wall and roughly at the level of the entresol floor. If this were the socket for a longitudinal joist, it would have been a most unusual arrangement: it is more likely that the floor above was supported on strong, vertical posts.

What is unique about this building, however, is the existence of an entresol floor beneath the vault, a feature found in no other bastle-house on either side of the Border. This arrangement was no doubt dictated largely by the site, the nature of which enabled the entresol floor to be provided with a separate entrance in the middle of the NW side without the need for an outside stair. The threshold for this entrance is cut through the living rock, while the doorway itself is provided with two drawbar holes in the S jamb. These holes are not aligned vertically in the usual manner, but are staggered in each plane, the inner one (which is 4in wide by 6in high and about 5ft deep) being $6\frac{1}{2}$in further in and 18in lower than the outer one (which is $3\frac{3}{4}$in wide by 5in high and only about 4ft 4in deep). As they are both contemporary within the same structure, it must be assumed that one was to reinforce an outer door, while the other provided separate reinforcement for an inner door or yett. At the S corner of this floor there are the remains of a splayed ventilation-slit. Nothing survives above this level, though if one assumes that 'the bastle-house' was the model for this building, in all probability there was nothing above the vault but the roof.

34ft 6in W of this building, and parallel with it, was another building, which measured approximately 46ft 8in from NE to SW by 23ft 6in from NW to SE over walls which vary in thickness from 4ft 6in to 5ft. It abuts another rock face in the W corner. The masonry of these walls is of truly massive, drystone construction, with some of the stones weighing as much as $1\frac{1}{2}$

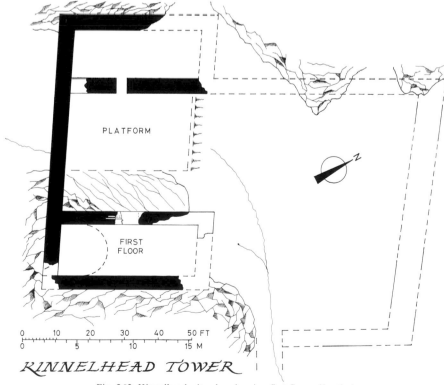

Fig. 262 Kinnelhead: site plan showing first floor of bastle-house.

tons. Apart from the remains of a crude doorway in the middle of the SE wall, no features survive, while at the NE end all but the outline of the building has gone.

Between these two buildings – whose SW gables are aligned –, and extending beyond them to the NE and E, was an L-shaped, paved courtyard designed to fit the site. This measured approximately 104ft from NE to SW by 74ft 6in from NW to SE overall, and was enclosed by a drystone wall that varied in thickness from 4ft 6in between the buildings to, apparently, about 7ft 6in (at least at foundation level) on the NE side, suggesting an affinity with the equally massive and unusual barmkin wall at Blacklaw (q.v.). It was entered through a gateway on the SE side. Between the two buildings, the courtyard has been built up to provide a level platform, 22ft 6in wide and 36ft long. A crude stone culvert under the platform carries a small rill from the hill behind, but it is not clear whether this arrangement was primarily to keep the platform dry, or to convey water into the courtyard.

Although David Johnston was only a tenant in Kinnelhead, the records of the time abound with the wealth of his dealings both as a farmer and as a merchant.[13] He died in 1612, and was succeeded in Kinnelhead by his eldest son, Samuel, who is last mentioned in 1629.[14] Another son, William, was murdered by William Johnstone of Kellobank in 1619.[15] David also had three natural sons, Thomas and James, who are on record in 1611, when, with various other local Johnstons, they and their father were charged by Neil Ewart of Bodesbeck with 'continually molesting us, our men, tenants', etc.,[16] and David in Broomhills.[17] Thomas, 'called of Kindilhead', was in trouble again in 1618, when, with others, he was accused of breaking the law by carrying hagbuts and pistols.[18]

Samuel Johnston was probably the last to live in the old house. Shortly afterwards Easter Kinnelhead was acquired by Thomas Johnston of Bearholm, from whom, in 1632, it passed to James Johnston of that Ilk (later 1st Earl of Hartfell),[19] while in 1649 Sir John Charteris of Amisfield disponed Wester Kinnelhead in favour of Sir John Dalzell of Newton.[20] The two properties were finally united in 1662, when James, Earl of Annandale, received a crown charter erecting all his lands, including Kinleheid, etc, 'with the towers, mills, etc.', and Kindleheid, 'with the mosses, etc.', into the Earldom of Annandale and Hartfell;[21] and it remained with his descendants until 1965. — In 1845 the New Statistical Account recorded that there was 'lately one vaulted ruin at Kinnelhead'.[22] The vault has since collapsed.

Not least among the remarkable features at Kinnelhead is the existence of at least three crosses cut in the living rock, one immediately outside the entresol doorway of the main building and two on the rocks above and beyond the W corner of the site. The first of these is a finely cut 'Calvary crucifix' (i.e. a crucifix with the figure of Christ on a stepped plinth), while the others comprise a plain Calvary cross and a Greek cross with splayed arms. It is difficult to date these crosses, or explain their significance, but it is thought most likely that they are of late mediaeval date.[23] One cannot, however, rule out the possibility that they may belong to the time of the Covenanters.

1   RMS III, No. 868.
2   Fraser 1894, I, lxvi.
3   RSS VII, No.263. There was a long legal dispute over the succession between Elizabeth, the heir general, and her uncle Michael Carlyle, the heir male.
4   Scots Peerage II, 392.
5   RSS VIII, No.2313.
6   Elizabeth was suo jure 5th Baroness Carlyle of Torthorwald.
7   Reid, R.C. 'Johnstone of Kinnelhead', *TDGAS*, XIII, 194. – Johnston of Raecleugh was 1st cousin of the John Johnston of that Ilk who received title in 1568.
8   The early history of Dumgree is summarised under 'Boreland Tower', q.v.
9   Acts & Decreets, Vol.228 (Scott), 294.
10   J. T. Johnstone notes that two of the beacons set up by Statute in 1448, on The Blaze hill (near Wamphray) and Gallowhill (Moffat), could be seen from Kinnelhead ('Kinnelhead Tower', *TDGAS*, 2nd Series, XVII (Part 5), 421).
11   Discovery & Excavation in Scotland 1990, 37, 38; 1991; 69; 1992, 66; etc.
12   RCHM 1970, 61-95.
13   Register of Deeds, Vol.292 (or ?202), cited in Reid, 'Johnstone of Kinnelhead', *op. cit.*, 195-6.
14   Reid, R.C. 'The Border Grahams', *TDGAS*, XXXVIII, 103.
15   Reid, 'Johnstone of Kinnelhead', *op. cit.*, 197.
16   RPC, 2nd Ser., VIII, 316.
17   Reid, 'Johnstone of Kinnelhead', *op. cit.*, 197, 199.
18   RPC XI, 476.
19   Fraser 1894, I, ccviii.
20   RMS IX, No.2102. – There is some confusion over which lands constituted Easter Kinnelhead and which Wester Kinnelhead.
21   RMS XI, No.230.
22   NSA IV, 127.
23   Crosses with Calvary bases at Hoddom, however, are attributed to the 10th-12th centuries (RCAHMS 1997, 257).

Fig. 263 Kinnelhead Bastle-House: Calvary crucifix cut in rock.

42.   KIRKCONNEL TOWER
(¹/₂ m NW Ecclefechan)   (NY187753)

When the Irvings finally lost possession of the old tower of Kirkconnel to the Maxwells early in the 17th century, they transferred the name 'Kirkconnel' to another of their towers at Ecclefechan. This has led to considerable confusion ever since, especially during the transitional period when it sometimes appears as if there were two towers called Kirkconnel, with the same families laying claim to both.

The **OLD TOWER** stood some 4 miles to the east, on the left bank of the Kirtle Water, close to the mediaeval village of Kirkconnel and some 200 yards W of Springkell House. Only the site remains, much overgrown.[1] The earliest record of the lands appears to be in 1347, when an inquisition at Lochmaben declared that 'the dominical lands of Kyrkconwelle' belonged to the 'lord of Luse' (Luce), William de Carlyle (son of the deceased John de Carlyle), nephew and heir of William de Carlyle of Luce.[2] The lands subsequently came into the possession of John de Carruthers, 'bastard', on whose death without lawful issue they passed to the overlord, Archibald, Earl of Douglas and Lord of Annandale.[3] Then in 1426, Archibald granted the lands of 'Kircconveth', otherwise called 'the Flemynglands', to one William Bell as a reward for his services.[4] They were to be held in feu from the 'lord of the lands of Luce', Sir John Carlyle of Torthorwald. This grant was confirmed by crown charter the same year.[5] The reference in the charter to the 'Fleming lands' must refer to their earlier possession by the Fleming family, whose holdings in this part of Dumfriesshire were at one time quite extensive, and gave their name to the later, combined parish of Kirkpatrick-Fleming, of which Kirkconnel forms a part.[6]

According to the Bell family records, it was William Bell who erected the first stronghold at Kirkconnel.[7] It subsequently became known as 'Bell's Tower', and is on record as such ('Bellis tour') in 1481, when parliament decreed that in time of war the laird of Amisfield, Sir Robert Charteris, and two deputies were to be based at Castlemilk, Annan and Bell's Tower, with one in charge of each.[8] Bell's Tower was to have a garrison of 20 men, no mean force. Thomas Bell was laird at the time. He had been a loyal adherent of the Douglases, and had accompanied the Earl of Douglas when he visited the English court in 1451.[9] Three years later, in 1484, the Duke of Albany and Earl of Douglas are said to have spent a night at 'Bell's Castle, close to Kirkconnel' on the way to their ill-fated uprising and defeat at Lochmaben.[10]

Some time around 1500, Thomas Bell of Kirkconnel was summoned, with others, to appear at the Justice Ayre in Dumfries, though for what offence is not clear. Bell failed to appear, so, in 1502, John Carruthers of Holmains, who had stood surety, was duly fined.[11] As he could not raise the money himself, he apprised lands to the required value from the accused, and assigned them to the Crown; and they were still in the Crown's possession in 1515, when James V granted them, including 'the four merkland of Kirkconell which pertained to Thom Bell', to Sir Alexander Jardine of Applegarth.[12]

Throughout this time the superiority of the lands had remained with the Carlyles of Torthorwald. In 1529 Michael, 4th Lord Carlyle, was granted a crown charter of the superiority of the lands and barony of Carlyle, formerly Torthorwald, reserving to his brother James's widow her liferent of half the lands.[13] These included the £20 lands of Kirkconnel.

Kirkconnel passed to the Irvings of Bonshaw some time before 1542, when one William Irving was in possession.[14] Bells did, however, continue to live on the lands as tenants. In a list of Scots who swore allegiance to England in 1547, there were 312 Bells of 'Tofteyeates, Kyrkconwell land, Mydlebye, and the Kyrk'.[15]

In 1573, Lord Carlyle sold most of his estate to his eldest surviving son, Michael,[16] although the Crown clearly considered that it should have gone to his granddaughter Elizabeth, daughter and heir of his eldest son, William (d.1572). Accordingly, in 1575, the Regent Morton gifted the ward and nonentry of the lands and barony of Carlile, including the £20 land of Kirkconnel and the patronage of the kirk of Kirkconnel, to George Douglas of Parkhead until Elizabeth should come of age.[17] This led to a bitter and protracted dispute between Elizabeth and her uncle, which was not finally resolved until 1587.[18]

Meanwhile, in 1581, Michael sold many of the lands, including Kirkconnel, to his father-in-law, Lord Maxwell.[19] But Maxwell, who was created Earl of Morton later that year, wanted more than just the title to the lands; he wanted actual possession. Considering the feud that was then raging between the Johnston-Irving Alliance and the Maxwells, that was a recipe for trouble; and as William Irving of Kirkconnel is referred to as a 'tenant' of Johnston of that Ilk a few years later,[20] that may well have been a further cause of contention. In 1585, Lord Scrope reported that 'thErle of Morton with his forcies came to a stone howse of his owne called Kirkonell, inhabited by one Willye Irwyn sonne to Edward of Boneshawe . . . And lyeing abowt the same xxiiij houres, with the losse of two of his men being slayne, and three horses, he retyred . . . to Annande'.[21] Two months later he again 'placed his forces about Kyrkkonnell and the house of Bonshawe, and is determined on some further enterprise',[22] The outcome of this confrontation is not clear. The Irvings certainly kept Bonshaw (q.v.), but some time later they evidently lost Kirkconnel and retired to their other tower at Ecclefechan. The former tower is shown as 'Kirkconnall' on Aglionby's Platte in 1590[23] and as 'Kirkonnell' on Pont's map of Lower Annandale c.1595.[24]

The Irvings were still not prepared to give up Kirkconnel without a struggle. In 1608 John Maxwell of Conheath complained to the Privy Council that 'although he had been in peaceable possession of the lands of Kirkconnell with the castle thereof till January last, William Irwing, sometime of Kirkconnell, now in Auchilfechen, . . . came then to the said place of Kirkconnell, surprised the same, and furnished it with men, victual and armour of purpose to detain the place'.[25] The Irvings contested the claim, and lost; but whether they were ousted at this time is not clear.

The dispute flared up again in 1622/3, when William Irving of Kirkconnel and his son William complained to the Privy Council that, in January of that year, they had been forcibly ejected from their lands of Kirkconnel by the Earl of Nithsdale, who had sent forty 'speciall gentlemen', all armed with hagbuts, under the command of the Earl's brother, James Maxwell.[26] It was stated that they had 'invyroned [the tower of Kirkconnel] on all pairtis and hes plantit thame selffis in the laich houssis and otheris pairtis of saulftie aboute the tour, and thay ly aboute the house day and night, asseidging the same with all kynd of hostilitie', and that neither people nor victuals were allowed in or out. The Maxwells were prosecuted and fined for carrying pistols, but were absolved from the rest of the complaint.[27] Thus the Irvings finally lost Kirkconnel.

The old tower is mentioned again in 1645, when James Hay of Mains received a Crown Charter of the '30 merk lands of Kirkconnel, with the castle, . . . in the parish of Kirkconnel'.[28] It is said to have been finally demolished in 1734, when the new mansion of Springkell was built some 200 yards east of 'the old mansion-house and town of Kirkconnell'.[29] This was not, however, the first house called Springkell, for in 1662 William Maxwell 'of Springkell', advocate, is on record as holding part of the £20 lands of Kirkconnel from the Earl of Nithsdale, and it may well be that the tower was abandonned at this time.[30]

Fig. 264 Kirkconnel New Tower: remains of N wall.

The **NEW TOWER** of Kirkconnel, the remains of which still stand adjacent to Kirkconnell Hall at Ecclefechan, presents something of an enigma. Its few surviving features, including the great thickness of its walls, are immediately reminiscent of nearby Bonshaw, and would likewise appear to belong to the third quarter of the 16th century, yet it must be significant that it does not appear on either Aglionby's Platte of 1590 or Pont's map of c.1595 (supra).[31] It would thus seem likely that, like Robgill (q.v.), it was not built until later, whilst copying the general design and layout of the Irvings' much earlier stronghold at Bonshaw.

The earliest reference to the Irvings holding land at Ecclefechan was in 1506, when William Irving of Bonshaw was infeft in the £3 lands of Ecclefechan by Andrew Lord Herries.[32] These appear to be the same £3 lands that Irving of Bonshaw held of the Master of Maxwell (later 4th Lord Herries), together

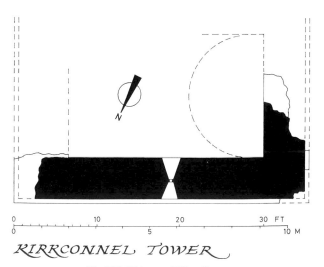

Fig. 265 Kirkconnell New Tower:
plan of surviving fragment of basement.

with an adjacent £3 lands in Ecclefechan held of the laird of Knock and 40 shilling lands held of the laird of Holmains, in 1566.[33] Eight years later Lord Herries went to law to try and recover the lands, but all he received was the right to one penny Scots annually.[34] In 1610 William Irving of Kirkconnel was granted numerous Templelands in and around Ecclefechan.[35]

There is no mention of a tower as such in history, and it is not until 1622/3, when the Maxwells came in force to take possession of Kirkconnel (supra), that any form of dwelling is mentioned. It was then that William Irving of Kirkconnel complained to the Lords of Council and Session that, on 25 January, James Maxwell and others came armed 'to the complainers house in Egilfachine, entered the house violently with drawn swords and bended pistollets in search of [the] complainer with intent to kill him, and in his absence broke down and destroyed the greater part of his timber work and plenishing in the house'.[36] The Maxwells claimed to be pursuing a horning against the Irvings of Kirkconnel, and to be unaware of a judicial suspension at the time. Apart from being fined for the illegal carrying of pistols, no further action was taken. It was evidently after this that, having finally lost their cause and the original Kirkconnel Tower, they transferred the name to their stronghold at Ecclefechan. No doubt it was as much a challenge to the Maxwells, as a matter of pride, still to call themselves 'Irvings of Kirkconnel'.

All that remains of the **TOWER** – which is believed to have been oblong in plan – are the N wall of the basement and part of the W wall adjacent to the NW corner, where the ruins reach a maximum height of about 18ft. These show that the tower was about 34ft 5in long from E to W,[37] with a 6in wide, splayed plinth course and vaulted basement, while from the curvature of the vault it can be deduced that the width of the basement was 14ft 8in internally. The masonry is roughly squared blocks of local sandstone, which are laid in courses that vary in height between 13 and 16 inches. On the N side the wall is 5ft thick and at the W end 5ft 6in. One would expect the corresponding S and E walls to be similar, but the surviving foundations at the E end suggest that the thickness of the E wall was in fact 6ft 6in. Near the middle of the basement's N wall is a widely-splayed, rectangular gun-loop, with a circular throat, and this would undoubtedly have been matched by similar gun-loops on the other three sides. The only other feature to survive is part of the right jamb of the hall fireplace on the first floor. This is in the surviving fragment of the W wall. Although nothing survives of the entrance or stair, it would appear that they were in the SE corner, similar to the arrangement at nearby Bonshaw.[38]

The Irvings of Kirkconnel (now at Ecclefechan) were all called William at this time, so it is difficult to differentiate between generations. One died in 1642, and his eldest son died in 1680. In the same year, the next laird, also called William, was granted a tack of half the £10 lands of Ecclefechan by John Carruthers of Holmains,[39] and in 1681 he obtained sasine.[40] Having no surviving male issue, he made over Kirkconnel to his brother, Herbert Irving of Woolcoats, who was subsequently 'called of Kirkconnel'.[41] According to one account,[42] Herbert, having no issue, made over Kirkconnel in 1709 to John Irving of Luce; but c.1718 Sarah Irving, 'daughter and heiress of Herbert and Janet Irving of Kirkconnel' married Dr. William Knox of Moffat, and they came to live at Kirkconnel.[43]

To the E of the tower there is a small, single-storey house, which is believed to have been built by Dr. Knox after his marriage. He and his wife are commemorated on the lintel above the entrance doorway and on the sills of two windows, which bear the inscriptions 'MDCC WK SJ XXXV', 'JJ WK SJ 1724' and 'WK SI 1738' respectively, while a skewput on the N gable bears the arms of 'Irving of Bonshaw'. Their only daughter and heiress, Janet, married George Arnott, son of George Arnott, younger of Woodmylne, in Fife;[44] and it was their descendants who built the present hall, now a hotel, sometime during the 19th century. The family continued to live here until c.1910.

---

1   See Mercer 1997, 22, 97.
2   Bain III, No.1499.
3   RMS II, No.85. Archibald had been given the Lordship of Annandale in 1409.
4   Ibid.
5   Ibid.
6   The Flemings were witnessing Bruce charters in Annandale as early as the 12th century (Buccleuch MSS, 38-9 (Nos.66, 67)). An old gravestone in Kirkconnel churchyard bearing the crude inscription 'Hi[c] jacet Adam Flemeng' belongs to a much later period. It is said to be that of Fair Helen Irving's lover in the famous ballad. – See RCAHMS 1920, No.373; Irving 1907, 60-3.
7   Steuart 1932, 15.
8   APS II, 140.
9   Steuart 1932, 15.
10 Ibid, 16.
11 Carruthers 1934, 82-3.
12 Ibid; RSS I, No.2660.
13 RMS III, Nos.868, 871.
14 Irving 1907, 57.
15 Armstrong 1883, lxxvi.
16 RMS V, No.134.
17 RSS VII, No.263. In 1584, the gift of the ward and nonentry were transferred to Thomas Cranston of Remilton (RSS VIII, No.2313).
18 See Torthorwald Castle for details of the dispute.
19 RMS V, No.136.
20 RPC IV, 250.
21 Border Papers, I, No.312.
22 Ibid, No.327.
23 Hyslop, 320.
24 Blaeu, 57, 'THE STEWARTRIE OF ANNANDAIL'. Aglionby shows Kirkconnel on the right bank of the Kirtle Water, while Pont shows it on the left bank.
25 RPC VIII, 120.
26 RPC XI, 644.
27 Ibid, 645.
28 RMS IX, No.1598.
29 Stat Acct, X, 455. – The site of the old 'town' was excavated in 1968, and amongst other things found was the ground plan of a large timber hall, 55ft by 20ft, of a type dating from the 7th or 8th century ('Excavations at Kirkconnel, 1968', TDGAS, 3rd Ser., XLVI, 128-39.
30 RPC, 3rd Series, 181, 192.
31 Neither Aglionby nor Pont are completely reliable in respect of towers, such as Ecclefechan, which were not located beside a watercourse.
32 Lag Charters, No.54. These were presumably the same lands that had been held by Adam Moffat in the middle of the previous century, and whose son Thomas had sasine in 1457 (ERS VI, 333).
33 Irving 1907, 38.
34 Ibid, 37.
35 Reid, R.C., 'Miscellaneous MSS - I', 96.
36 RPC XII, 645. The case was minuted as: 'Ryott and wearing pistollis: Irwing of Kirkonell against the Earle of Nithisdale' (Ibid, 665).
37 It can be deduced that the width of the tower was probably 24ft 8in, but it can no longer be measured.
38 In 'The Old Hall of Ecclefechan', TDGAS, Series II, XV (1898-9), 16, G. Irving recorded that, at that time, the remains of the E wall still extended for about 16ft from the NE corner, while in the NW corner there were 'signs' of a wheel-stair. Now that all the ivy has been cleared away, the latter suggestion has been found to be incorrect. He also hoped that the S wall would still be found beneath the lawn, but when the house was extended into this area c.1980 no further remains were found.
39 Carruthers 1934, 111.
40 Irving 1907, 57-8.
41 William Irving was 'called of Kirkconnel' in 1684 (RPC, 3rd Ser., IX, 595).
42 Irving 1907, 58.
43 Ibid, 228.
44 Ibid. See also RCAHMS 1933, No.3.

43.   KIRKCONNELL TOWER
(1½ m NE New Abbey)   (NX979680)

The earliest family on record at Kirkconnell is said to have settled there in the time of Malcolm Canmore.[1] They took their name from the place, which in turn was presumably named after an early church dedicated to St. Congal.[2] The following century, John de Kirkconnell is said to have founded the Abbey of Holywood, or Dercongal, some 7½ miles to the north,[3] and during the 13th century the family made several grants of land at Kirkconnell to the monks of Holm Cultram Abbey in Cumbria.[4] In 1296 Thomas de Kirkconnell swore fealty to Edward I,[5] following which the sheriff of Dumfries was ordered to restore to him his lands.[6] Eight years later, he sat on a jury enquiring into the privileges claimed by Robert de Brus, Earl of Carrick, in Annandale.[7]

The male line came to an end early in the 15th century, when Janet de Kirkconnell succeeded to the property. She married Aymer de Maxwell, second son of Sir Herbert Maxwell of Carlaverock and brother of Herbert, 1st Lord Maxwell, some time c.1430,[8] but it is not until 1448 that Aymer first appears on record as lord of Kirkconnell.[9] Eight years later, in 1456, James II granted him and his wife a new charter of the lands of Kirkconnell, 'just as the foresaid lands had been held by Janet and her predecessors'.[10] There is no mention of a tower or manor-place. The next laird, Herbert, was succeeded by his granddaughter Elizabeth, who was infeft in Kirkconnell in 1492;[11] and three years later she was succeeded by her nephew Herbert Maxwell, son of her sister Agnes and Thomas Maxwell, son of Robert, 2nd Lord Maxwell. Herbert had sasine in 1495.[12] He was succeeded by his grandson, Herbert, who was infeft in the lands of Kirkconnell in 1548.[13]

It appears to have been around this time that the present tower of Kirkconnell was built, possibly the work of the last-named Herbert. It is situated on low ground close to the Nith estuary, on the other side of which, and only three miles away, lay Caerlaverock, the seat of the Lords Maxwell. There is no trace of the earlier dwellings that must have existed on or near the site.[14]

The **TOWER** is built on the **L**–plan, with the re-entrant angle facing NE. It comprises a main block of three storeys and a garret, with a parapet walk on all sides, and a stair wing that terminates in a small watch-chamber at the same level as the main roof. The main block measures 33ft 2in from E to W by 25ft 1in from N to S over walls 4ft 7in in thickness, and rises about 38ft to the top of the parapet, while the wing, which is 13ft 9in wide, extends 11ft 3in towards the N. The masonry is local granite rubble with dressings and mouldings of red sandstone. The entrance, which is in the re-entrant angle of the wing, is now reached from the 18th century house that abuts the tower on the N side. It admits to a small vestibule, on the right of which is an equally small room, approximately 3ft 6in square, which served as a guardroom; its only feature is a 'crosslet' shot-hole in the N wall, similar to those in the basement (infra). On the other side of the vestibule, a mural passage leads to the basement, a vaulted chamber, 7ft 11in high, with a floor of stone flags. This is provided on the N, S and W sides with a 'crosslet' shot-hole, a rare feature dating from the middle of the 16th century and, as far as is known, found elsewhere only in Aberdeenshire.[15] It is in the form of a Latin cross with a slight enlargement, or roundel, at the base, and has a total height of 1ft 9in. Unlike the more common gun-loops of the period, the throat is

Fig. 266 Kirkconnell Tower: view from SE. The blocked-up original windows are clearly visible.

situated close to the outer wall-face with all the splay on the inside. Originally, there would also have been one in the E wall, but this was destroyed when a doorway was later inserted to give direct access to the basement. This doorway, which has a wooden lintel, was later built up again. There was also one small window high up at each end of the basement, but these too have been closed up.

The first floor was a single chamber, which served as the usual hall. It was provided with a large fireplace at the E end, one window each in the N and W walls and two windows in the S wall, the more westerly of which was both smaller and much higher than the others. But although the surrounds of the latter three windows can still be clearly seen with their QER mouldings in the walls outside, they were all closed up in the 18th century, and in their place a single, large window, with a central mullion, was inserted in the middle of the S wall. It was probably at the same time that the N window was closed up and a second doorway inserted adjacent to it to connect with the later house. The fireplace now has a smaller, 18th century surround, but the original jambs, with their bold QERH mouldings, have been found behind the plaster.

The second floor was originally divided into two rooms, each with its own entrance off the stair. This was achieved by incorporating a mural passage in the N wall to give direct access

to the E room – an arrangement also found at nearby Drumcoltran. The passage, which is three steps up from the stair, is roofed with large stone slabs, and has a doorway with boldly chamfered arrises at its inner end. In order to give the passage sufficient width, its inside wall is partly corbelled-out from the wall below. The E chamber had a fireplace with a bold, QER-moulded surround in its E wall, a large mural recess below a segmental arch in the SE corner, and windows in the N and S walls, the former of which was blocked up when the Georgian house was added. The W chamber had windows in the S and W walls, and probably had a fireplace in its W wall, though the present one, with its bolection-moulded surround, only dates from the late 17th century.[16] At some period, the level of this floor was raised, which is why the entrance doorway to the W chamber has a second rebate on the outer side of the jambs. This was probably done in the middle of the 18th century, when the partition was removed and the two windows in the S wall filled in (at the same time as those on the floor below) and replaced by a new, double window in the centre.

The wheel-stair, which is 8ft 8in in diameter, continues to the level of the garret, where it also gives access to the parapet-walk and to a smaller wheel-stair, 5ft 8in in diameter, leading to the watch-chamber above. The position of this latter stair is unusual: because the stair to the parapet walk rises straight

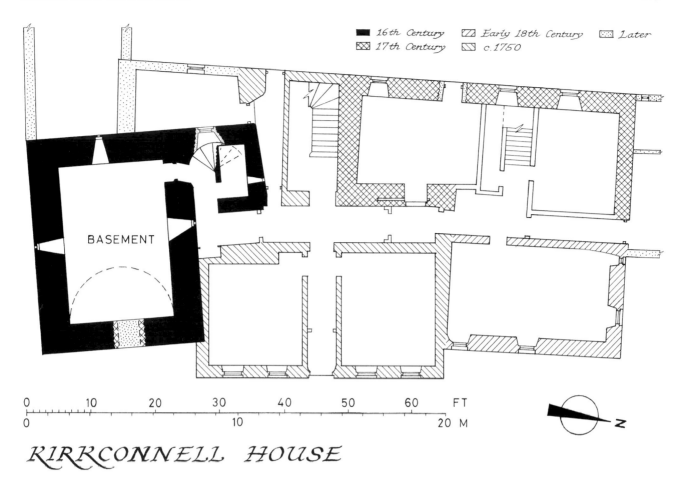

16th Century   Early 18th Century   Later
17th Century   c.1750

BASEMENT

0   10   20   30   40   50   60   FT
0   10   20 M

N

KIRKCONNELL HOUSE

Fig. 267 Kirkconnell Tower and House: plan of basement level.

Fig. 268 Kirkconnell: crosslet gun-loop in basement.

up the re-entrant angle on the N side, the wheel-stair has been built on the opposite side, necessitating a continuation of the parapet's corbelling along the W wall to help provide support.

The garret is a simple chamber with a fireplace at the W end and three slit-windows, with sills some 8ft above the floor, piercing the gables to the side of the chimney stacks. This room was later divided by a central partition, now removed. The roof was completely renewed in 1961, when a programme of restoration was carried out. Surrounding the wall-head at this level, except at the wing, is a parapet-walk, supported on two-stage, individual corbels above a continuous corbel-course. It was originally stepped to assist drainage, but both the walk and the parapet itself have at some time been modified. In the original arrangement, the parapet was crenellated on all sides: on the N side it still retains two deep embrasures; but on the other sides all the merlons in the central sections of the walls have been removed, and the coping, which has a QER moulding along the projecting outer edge, modified to suit. Some of the timbers around the doorway leading on to the parapet-walk show fire damage.

The watch-chamber at the top of the wing has a wooden floor, a small fireplace in the S wall, slit-windows in the E and W walls, and a larger window facing N. All these windows have QER surrounds. The roof, which is aligned N-S, has crow-stepped gables, and on the skewput at the NE corner there is a carved head. Before the main roof was rebuilt, there was an additional section of roofing bridging the gap between the two roofs, but at a slightly lower level. The top of the roof is about 48ft above the ground.

To the north of the tower, and separated from it by only about 15 feet, is an early 17th century house, which has subse-

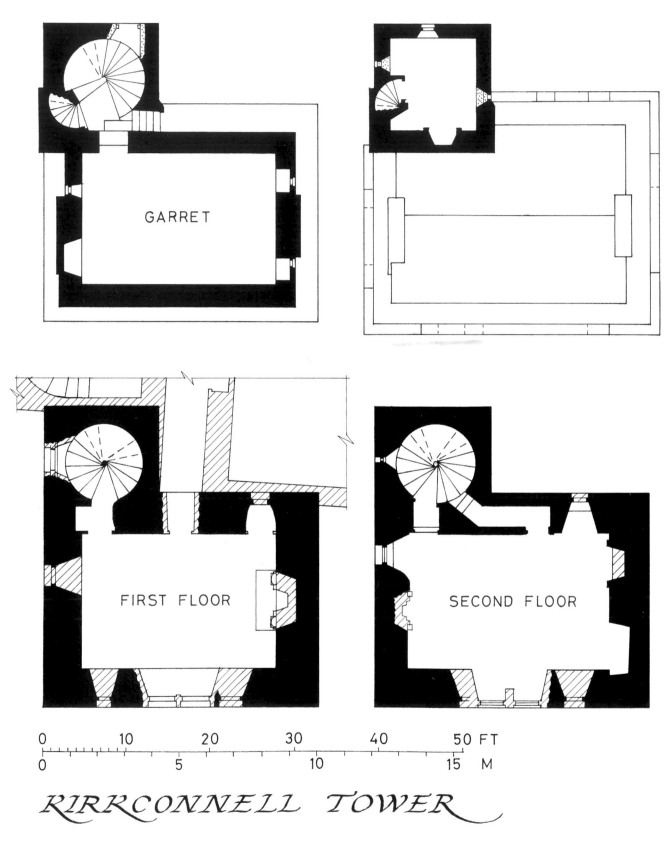

Fig. 269 Kirkconnell Tower: plans of upper floors.

Fig. 270 Kirkconnell Tower: view from NW.

quently been modified to accommodate the complex of later buildings and extensions to the E and S of it. It is basically a two-storey building, aligned N-S, with walls 3ft thick and an entrance doorway that still retains its slot for a draw-bar. The builder has not been established. To the E of this, and incorporating the modified N end of the earlier building, is the so-called 'Queen Anne' house, a 2-storeyed building standing at right angles to the earlier house. This was added by the 15th Maxwell laird early in the 18th century; and it was his son, James Maxwell, 16th of Kirkconnell, who closed the gap between the tower and later buildings with a Georgian mansion c.1750. This last house, which is built with bricks made on the estate, is symmetrically disposed about a central entrance doorway, facing E. It is three storeys in height.

Herbert Maxwell was succeeded in 1561 by his son Bernard, sometimes called Barnabas, but as he was still a minor the ward of the lands was granted by the Crown to Sir John Maxwell of Terregles until he should come of age.[17] Then, in 1573, with consent of his curators, Bernard granted the 20 merk land of Kirkconnell and the 12 merk land of Kelton to his uncle, John Maxwell, whilst reserving the liferent for himself;[18] and he was still at Kirkconnell in 1580, when he gave the relief of the lands of Kirkconnell to his late uncle's son and heir, John Maxwell 'of Kirkconnell'.[19]

John Maxwell of Kirkconnell was included in a list of 'Landit Men' in 1590,[20] and not long afterwards the tower was illustrated on Pont's map of Nithsdale.[21] His son Herbert received a charter of novodamus of the lands of Kirkconnell, with the fortalice and manor-place, in 1616.[22] These lands were held of the crown in feu-farm. The next laird, John Maxwell, 12th of Kirkconnell, who succeeded his father in 1637, was appointed a

Commissioner of War for the Stewartry of Kirkcudbright in 1648.[23] He soon got into financial difficulties, and in 1658 had to mortgage the estate.[24] Later, the lands were apprised from his son James, the 13th laird; but although James had to raise another mortgage in 1665,[25] he eventually cleared the debts. He was appointed an additional Commissioner of Supply for the Stewartry in 1686,[26] and two years later was appointed one of the two General Receivers of the Revenue for the Crown.[27] He died in, or before, 1699, and was succeeded, first by his eldest son, James, who was served heir-general to his father in that year,[28] and then, in 1705, by his second son, William. William, the 15th laird, was granted a new charter and entail of the lands by Queen Anne in 1708.[29] It was he who built the 'Queen Anne' house. He died in 1746.

William was succeeded by his eldest son James, who was infeft in Kirkconnell in 1734, and received a crown charter of the lands in 1738,[30] during his father's lifetime. He joined the Jacobites in the rebellion of 1745, and after Culloden fled to France, where he wrote a Narrative of the rebellion.[31] Returning home in 1750, he set about modernizing the accommodation by adding the Georgian house, which was the last major addition and ever since has remained the central feature.[32] It was also around this time that the new, larger windows were inserted in the S wall of the tower. James died in 1762, and was succeeded by his eldest son, James.

James, the 17th laird, was only three when he succeeded. He was served heir to his father in 1764, and the following year was infeft in the estate.[33] In 1823 he added a chapel to the N of the house,[34] and this was still in regular use until the middle of the 20th century. On James's death in 1827, the estate passed to his daughter, Dorothy, who later married her cousin Robert Witham, DL, JP.[35] He took the surname Maxwell-Witham.

Dorothy died in 1903, when she was succeeded by her second son, Colonel James Kirkconnell Maxwell-Witham, CMG, DL, JP, who served with distinction with the 3rd Battalion, Kings Own Scottish Borderers in the South African War.[36] He died without issue in 1938, leaving Kirkconnell to a collateral branch of the family, the Maxwells of Breoch, who still live there.[37] At first they took the surname Maxwell-Witham, but later they dropped the second name.

1   Gray 1894, 100.
2   There are four other places called Kirkconnell in the area – near Eaglesfield (see Kirkconnel Tower); near Ringford; near Moniaive; and in Upper Nithsdale.
3   Dugdale, Sir W. Monasticon Anglicanum, II, 1057, cited in McDowall 1986, 39. See also Buccleuch MSS, 70; Easson 1957, 87, 147.
4   William, son of Michael de Kirkeconeuel, made a grant c.1235-53 (Reg. Holm Cultram, No.116); his grandson Andrew made a small grant c.1270-80 (Ibid, No.119); and Andrew's son, Thomas, made a further grant c.1280-90 (Ibid, No.117).
5   Bain II, 198 (No.823).
6   Ibid, No.832.
7   Ibid, No.1588.
8   Fraser 1873, I, 600. Amer de Maxuel is first mentioned in a charter in 1424 (RMS II, No.15).
9   Fraser 1873, II, 431.
10 Ibid, 434
11 Ibid, I, 600.
12 Ibid.
13 Ibid.
14 It has been suggested that the main block of the tower could date from the time the Maxwells became lairds in the 15th century, with the gun-loops and wing added later, but this is not borne out by the structural evidence.
15 Maxwell-Irving 1974 (II), 216
16 There is said to be another fire surround, now hidden, outside the bolection moulding.
17 RSS V, No.867.

18   RSS VI, No.1946.
19   RSS VII, No.2625.
20   RPC IV, 786.
21   Pont MS. No.35 in National Library of Scotland.
22   RMS VII, No.1515; Laing Charters Nos.1755, 1758.
23   APS VI, Part II, 35.
24   Fraser 1873, I, 600; RMS X, No.668.
25   RMS XI, No.740.
26   APS VIII, 610.
27   Ibid, IX, 19; Fraser 1873, I, 601.
28   Fraser 1873, I, 601.
29   Laing Charters, No.3320.
30   Fraser 1873, I, No.601.
31   Ibid.
32   Ibid.
33   Ibid.
34   Ordnance Gazetteer, 978.
35   Burke L.G. 1937, 2475, 'Maxwell-Witham of Kirkconnell'.
36   Ibid.
37   See Fraser 1873, I, 592-3.

44.   LAG TOWER
(1½ m NE. Dunscore)   (NX881862)

The first of the name of Grierson was apparently one Gilbert Grersoun, described as 'son of Duncan', who rapidly rose to prominence around the turn of the 15th century, when he acquired extensive lands in Dumfriesshire and Galloway.[1] He received a grant of the lands and barony of Aird from the Earl of March in 1400,[2] and a few years later, as 'Gilbert Grersoun of Ardis', purchased the lands of Lag and Bardonan from 'his kinsman' John McRath of Lacht.[3] The latter purchase was confirmed in 1408 by 'his kinsman' Henry Sinclair, 2nd Earl of Orkney, for the payment of a pair of gilt spurs yearly in Dumfries.[4] Gilbert was for a time armour-bearer to Archibald, Earl of Douglas, and is so described in a charter by that Earl in 1410.[5]

Gilbert was succeeded by his eldest son, Gilbert, 2nd of Lag, who married Isabel, daughter and co-heiress of Sir Duncan Kirkpatrick of Torthorwald. It was through this marriage that Gilbert acquired the lands of Rockhall and Collin, the history of which thereafter became inextricably linked with that of Lag. It was apparently Gilbert who built the 'mansion of Rokell' (Rockhall, q.v.). He died c.1444, and was succeeded by his eldest son, Vedast, 3rd of Lag, who is said to have built a tower at Lag in 1460.[6] Vedast was granted a new charter of the lands of Rockhall by the Duke of Albany in 1473,[7] and in the same year his eldest son, Roger, received a crown charter of the lands of Lag on the occasion of his marriage.[8] Roger was killed at Sauchieburn in 1488, and was succeeded by his eldest son, Cuthbert, who had sasine of Lag in 1492[9] and of Rockhall in 1504.[10]

On the death of Cuthbert Grierson, 5th of Lag, without issue in 1513, Lag passed to Cuthbert's nephew Sir John Grierson, who was but an infant at the time, his father having been killed at Flodden.[11] Sir John had sasine of Lag and Rockhall in 1514,[12] and was laird for almost half a century. In 1515/16 a disposition in favour of his mother was signed 'at the hall of the manor of Lag'.[13] In 1526 Sir John received a new crown charter of the lands of Lag, 'with the tower and fortalice', and various other lands, all of which were incorporated into the free barony of Lag;[14] and this was subsequently confirmed by parliament in respect of Sir John's 'lands of ye Lag, mylne toure and fortalice thereof . . . [and] the lands of Rokkell and collyn and mylne thereof'.[15] Three years later, the Crown issued a decree that his infeftment was to be accepted in all the courts, notwithstanding the fact that he was still a minor.[16] It was this laird, Sir John Grierson (d.c.1559), who evidently either restored or rebuilt the present tower. His armorial panel formerly stood over the tower's entrance gateway.[17] In 1547 he pledged more than 200 men to the service of England,[18] and the following year was included in the general remission for those who had done so.[19]

The tower of Lag stands in ruins on a rocky knoll on the NW slope of Crawston hill, some 350ft above sea level. On the top of the hill, at an elevation of 700ft, is the site of Crawston Beacon, one of the chain of beacons set up by parliament in 1448 to warn of an English invasion.[20] 'Lagg' is shown as a substantial stronghold on Pont's survey c.1595.[21]

Fig. 271 Lag Tower: view from S.

The **TOWER** is rectangular on plan, and measures 29ft 6in from N to S by 25ft from E to W over walls averaging 5ft 9in in thickness. It is built of sandstone, a very hard gritstone and whin rubble, with dressings of gritstone and some sandstone. None of the floors was vaulted. The SE corner has completely fallen, but elsewhere the ruinous walls still rise to the level of the third floor, whilst old prints show the walls rising higher, but with no evidence of the wall-head or a parapet.[22] There is, however, one sketch by James Skene, which would appear to show the remains of a turret at the NW corner.[23]

The entrance was in the middle of the S wall, where the jambs are rebated for an outer wooden door opening outwards and an inner iron yett opening inwards. This admitted to the wheel-stair, some 6ft 9in in diameter, in the SE corner and,

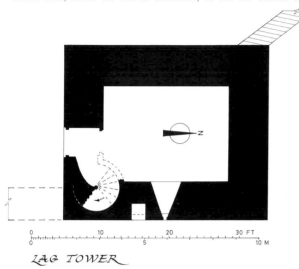

LAG TOWER

Fig. 272 Lag Tower: plan of basement.

through an inner door, to the basement beyond. The only illumination at this level was a small slit-window, reinforced with a single vertical bar, on the E side. Above this level the walls were reduced in thickness to 4ft 4in, except on the N side. At first floor level there was a fireplace in the N wall and a deeply-splayed slit-window, with a pointed scoinson-arch, in each of the E and W walls. The W jamb of a third window also survives on the S side, where the wall has fallen. The second floor had a fireplace in the N wall, larger windows in the E and W walls, and presumably a third window in the missing S wall. On the W side of the fireplace there was a garderobe with a small window and corbelled-out flue discharging at this level.[24] Another, substantial flue discharges from the E wall at ground level near the SE corner. It served a second garderobe, now gone, presumably at third floor level.

From the NW corner of the tower a **BARMKIN** wall, 2ft 9in thick, ran some 38ft to the NW and then 27ft to the SW, where it joined an arched gateway, 5ft 10in wide with walls 3ft 6in thick.[25] Although long ruinous, old prints give a better idea of its original form.[26] Until recently traces of outbuildings could be discerned within the wall. The foundations of further stretches of barmkin wall can be traced in the adjacent field. They run S from the tower's SE corner for about 87ft, then SW for about 60ft, before turning back NW. This mortar-bonded wall, which in places measures 4ft 8in thick, has had a secondary, apparently-later wall, 2ft 6in thick, built flush with its inner face. Grose shows the ruins of an outbuilding in this area.[27]

Fig. 273 Lag Tower: view of entrance gateway
and tower from NW in 1790.

Sir John Grierson was succeeded at Lag by his eldest son, William, who had sasine of Lag in 1549,[28] during his father's lifetime, while Rockhall passed to Roger, Sir John's eldest son by his second marriage. However, the two properties were not destined to remain separate for long, for when William died in 1562, apparently without surviving issue,[29] Lag passed to his half-brother, Roger Grierson of Rockhall, who in 1565, in anticipation of his marriage, granted a liferent in Lag to Helen, daughter of Sir James Douglas of Drumlanrig.[30] From this time on Rockhall seems to have been the Griersons' preferred residence, though they still retained the designation 'of Lag'. They also had a 'town residence' in Dumfries, though how early this was established is not known.

The next laird was Roger's son, Sir William Grierson, 9th of Lag, who had sasine of Lag in 1593 'at the tower and fortalice of Lag'.[31] Three months later he succeeded his father. During a long and distinguished career Sir William held many judicial and administrative offices in the West March. In 1593 he was appointed a Commissioner for keeping peace and good rule in the West March,[32] and this post was confirmed again in respect of the Middle Shires, as the Borders became known after the Union, in 1609, 1618 and 1622.[33] He was also one of those who, in 1600, was commanded to give advice to the King and Privy Council regarding the suppression of outlaws in the Borders,[34] a request that was repeated again in 1606.[35] He was appointed a Justice of the Peace for Dumfriesshire in 1610,[36] and was Sheriff of Dumfries in 1615, 1617 and 1621.[37] Sir William represented Dumfriesshire in parliament in 1617, 1621 and 1625.[38] He was also a Commissioner for [the standardization of] Weights and Measures in 1617;[39] Keeper of the Rolls in 1623;[40] and a Commissioner for the Coin in 1625.[41] Sir William died in 1629.

Lag now appears to have been finally abandonned by the Griersons in favour of Rockhall (q.v.), which Sir William had 'laitlie constructit' as a modern residence shortly before 1610. Although it has been said that the last laird to live in the tower was Sir Robert Grierson of Lag (1655-1738), 'Auld Lag', the 1st Baronet,[42] Rockhall was in fact his home, and it is unlikely that he ever resided at Lag.

By 1789 Lag was already in an advanced state of decay.[43]

1   Lag Charters, 3.
2   Ibid.

3   Lag Charters, 9 (No.1 – undated). The lands are described as 'lying in broken
     barony' among the lands of the monks of Melrose.
4   Ibid., No.2.
5   Burke Peerage 1959, 1006, 'Grierson'.
6   Ibid.
7   Ibid.
8   Ibid.
9   ERS X, 764.
10   Ibid, XII, 715.
11   Burke, op. cit., 1006.
12   ERS XIV, 566.
13   Lag Charters, No.78.
14   RMS III, No.395.
15   APS II, 310.
16   RSS II, No.421.
17   Grose, I, 156. The panel was later moved to Friars Carse, and subsequently
     built into a memorial to Sir Robert Grierson (d.1733), 'Auld Lag', in Dunscore
     churchyard.
18   According to one contemporary account he pledged 370 men (Armstrong
     1883, lxxvi), while another states that he pledged 202 men (Scottish Papers I,
     No.396).
19   RSS III, No.2698.
20   APS, I, 716.
21   Pont MS. No.35 in National Library of Scotland.
22   Grose, I, 155; Cardonnel: 'Lagg'.
23   Gray 1894, 35. Skene's sketch is unlikely to be earlier than those of Grose
     and Cardonnel (he was only 14 in 1789), unless copied from an earlier work.
     His friend Sir Walter Scott described him as 'the best draughtsman I ever
     saw'.
24   That the flue does not pass down within the thickness of the wall, unlike the
     one on the E side, may indicate that this garderobe was added as part of a
     rebuilding of the upper floors.
25   The remains of the gateway disappeared sometime after 1968.
26   Grose, I, 155-6; Cardonnel: 'Lagg'.
27   Grose, I, 156, Plate 2.
28   Burke, op. cit.
29   William's only son, John, who had no issue, appears to have predeceased his
     father.
30   RSS V, No.2200.
31   Lag Charters, No.150.
32   RPC V, 113.
33   Ibid, VIII, 814; XI, 345, 446; XII, 650.
34   Ibid, VI, 137.
35   Ibid, VII, 271.
36   Ibid, IX, 77.
37   Lag Charters, 4; RPC X, 382-3.
38   APS IV, 524, 581, 593; V, 166.
39   Ibid, IV, 538.
40   DNB, 846.
41   APS V, 184, 187.
42   Gray 1894, 35; Ordnance Gazetteer, 446.
43   Cardonnel, op. cit.

45.   LANGHOLM CASTLE
(¹/₄ m NNW Langholm)   (NY361849)

Situated where the rivers Esk and Ewes meet, and only
a short distance from their confluence with the Wauchope Water, Langholm Castle became the focal point for control of
Eskdale in the 16th century. It was never intended as a personal
stronghold, but was from the outset designed as a military base
to house a small garrison and its captain, who would assist the
Warden of the West March in maintaining law and order. The
captain was also sometimes referred to as 'the keeper of
Annandale'.[1]

In or before 1266, the lands on which the castle stood
were granted by Sir William de Coninburcht to Herbert de
Maxwell, younger of Carlaverock.[2] They were subsequently
resigned in favour of Sir John de Lyndsay, and later came into
the possession of the Earls of Douglas and then, after the battle
of Arkinholm in 1455, the Earls of Angus, before once again
returning to the Maxwells.[3] When Lord Dacre raided the West

Fig. 274 Langholm Castle: view from SW.

March in 1516, Langholm was one of the many places he destroyed.[4] Then in 1525, Robert, 5th Lord Maxwell, granted the
lands of Langholm to Johnnie Armstrong of Gilnockie, who held
them for three years before resigning them again in Maxwell's
favour.[5]

It was evidently this Lord Maxwell (d.1546) who built
the castle.[6] In April 1544, the Earl of Hertford instructed Lord
Wharton[7] and Sir Robert Bowes to send 'Patie Grayme' or some
other trusted man to ascertain the strength and situation of the
castles of Lochmaben, Caerlaverock and 'Langhole', which were
then in the custody of Robert, Master of Maxwell, who had recently been released from custody by the English.[8] The following October, Wharton reported that 'certen of the Armestrangs
of Lyddesdaill wan and spoyled the tower of Langhope, brought
away all the goods in the same, and 4 prisoners';[9] and shortly
afterwards he took possession of the tower himself, garrisoning
it with a considerable number of foot-soldiers, whom he intended
to reinforce with about fifty horse.[10] This was presumably the
occasion subsequently alluded to in 1546, when it was reported
to the Scots parliament that 'ane tower called Langhope pertaining to umquhile Robert Lord Maxwell wes thiftuislie takin be
ane Scottis tratour quhilk wt his craft drew in Inglismen for
proffitt And put in yair hands', while Lord Maxwell was a prisoner in England.[11] Lord Maxwell was released in October 1545.

Two years later the castle was besieged by a Scots force
for several days without success, while the English garrison,
which consisted of a captain and sixteen men, destroyed the lower
part of the tower and carried on the defence from the highest
floor.[12] The recovery of the castle was, however, considered to
be a matter of such importance that, in June 1547, the Regent
Arran sent messengers throughout the kingdom charging 'all
maner of men' to meet him at Peebles the following month, before marching against 'the Langhope' and the rebels. It was to
be a military expedition on the grand scale, backed up by artillery, including two double-falcons, a single falcon and a me-
dium culverine, munitions, pavilions, etc., the cost of which is
recorded in minute detail.[13] This force duly laid siege to the
castle, but after seven shots had been fired the garrison surrendered.[14] Those who did not turn up for the expedition, of whom
there is a long list, were declared traitors and forfeit all their
goods.[15]

An impression of how the castle looked at that time is
illustrated on 'The Platte of Castlemilk', prepared for Lord
Wharton shortly afterwards. It shows a stocky, tower-like building of two storeys surmounted by a turret or cap-house.[16]

What remains of the castle is a fragment of the S end of a strong **TOWER**, which survives to a maximum height of about 20ft. Its date is not certain, though it was presumably built after the siege of 1547 when the lower part of the original tower was reportedly destroyed. It is 30ft 1in wide from E to W over walls 5ft 3in thick, and appears to have been about 41ft long. Of the E and W walls, only about 9ft 9in and 15ft 8in respectively survive at their southern ends. The masonry is grey sandstone rubble with ashlar dressings. The only features left are in the S wall. These comprise: at basement level, a splayed plinth course, 3½in broad, and a splayed, rectangular gun-loop, with a round throat 6in in diameter; at first floor, or perhaps upper basement

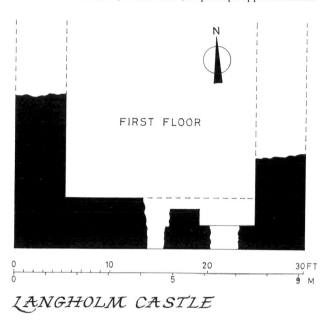

LANGHOLM CASTLE

Fig. 275 Langholm Castle: plan of remains of first floor.

level, a small, splayed window-recess on the W side and another opening, perhaps a second window, on the E side; and at second floor level, a window recess, once arched, on the E side and the remains of an aumbry on the W side.[17]

Evidence of other walls and outbuildings may still be seen on the N, E and W sides of the tower, but without excavation nothing can be said of their date or purpose. Some idea of the castle's overall extent, however, can be gleaned from the fact that in 1557 six hundred Gascoigne soldiers were divided between Langholm and Annan.[18] Some earthworks to the SW may be the remains of a moat that took its water directly from the adjacent River Esk.

Early in the 20th century some of the masonry missing from the two surviving corners was replaced and the ruinous openings tidied up, so one cannot be certain to what extent the plan given by Hyslop in 1912[19] represents original details.

In 1550, the 5th Lord Maxwell received from the crown a gift of the nonentries of many lands, including the £5 land of Langholm, which had formerly belonged to his father.[20] Nothing more is then heard of the castle until 1562, when Christie Armstrong of Barngleish, also known as 'John's Christie', was granted 'the use and keiping of the hous and place of Langholme' by Sir John Maxwell of Terregles, tutor to Lord Maxwell, for a yearly payment of £40 in time of peace, and for what should be thought reasonable in time of war.[21] Christie entrusted the task

to two of his sons, Robert and Archie, who were allowed twenty-four men for policing the Borders.[22] Later, however, after Lord Maxwell came of age and took control of his own estates, the Armstrongs evidently lost possession.

When the question of keeping good order in the West March was discussed by the Privy Council in 1578, Lord Herries was invited to submit his own proposals. These included a recommendation that Lord Maxwell should remain at Langholm himself, or, if he were warden, appoint a deputy as captain.[23] However, although Herries' proposals were generally accepted, when John Johnston of that Ilk was made Warden the following year, the custody of Langholm was taken from Maxwell and given to Johnston. This angered Maxwell, and a year later he petitioned the Privy Council for repossession on the grounds that Johnston had left it uninhabited and a ready prey for thieves.[24] Maxwell reported that 'the said hous servis nathing to his [Johnston's] use, . . . and the key thairof cassin only in ane byre to the said Lordis awin servandis that duellis in the laich houssis besyde the same; quhom . . . the said Lord will not permit to enter in at the yett thairof'. The Privy Council accordingly agreed that Maxwell should be allowed to keep the castle, on condition that it be made available to the Warden when required.[25] Maxwell duly took possession, and put in a small garrison under a captain.

In April 1581, Lord Maxwell was again appointed Warden. The following September, Christie Armstrong of Barngleish, who had meanwhile fallen out with him, and a band of Scots fugitives from across the Border, attacked the castle, burnt all the furnishings,[26] and took the captain, Herbert Maxwell, prisoner.[27] This 'verie much offended' the king and Privy Council, who lodged a complaint with the English commissioner.[28] It was also reported that Maxwell was threatening to retaliate by embarking upon a similar raid into England.[29]

In the same year, the Earl of Angus suffered forfeiture for his support for the late Regent, Morton, and fled to England. He already had an intense hatred of Lord Maxwell, who had previously (in 1578) ousted him as Warden of the West March, but, in addition, they were both now claimants to the vacant Earldom of Morton. So when, in October 1581, James VI granted the earldom to Lord Maxwell, Angus could not contain his wrath. Early in 1582, he crossed the Border into Eskdale, laid waste Maxwell's lands, and attacked the castle at Langholm, but failed to take it.[30]

Before long, Johnston of that Ilk and Christie Armstrong again conspired to take possession of Langholm, and evidently succeeded, for in an English report about 'The Armestronges of the Langholme and theire allyes with England' in 1583, Christie is once again referred to as 'the goodman of the Langholme castell'.[31] But although Johnston was by now again Warden, his action was not supported by the Privy Council, who, in September 1583, ordered 'Johnneston of that Ilk and Cristie Armistrang of Barngleis, called Johnnis Cristie, to deliver the place and fortalice of Langholme to Johnne, Earl of Mortoun, within forty-eight hours after being charged'.[32] It is presumed that Maxwell regained possession at this time; but two years later Langholm was again 'in the keaping of . . . Johns Christie'. Lord Scrope reported that Maxwell then 'toke the howse of Langholme . . . and hath placed theirin gunners and men of his owen',[33] and a month later Maxwell was again planning to 'plante some forces of footemen' in the castle.[34]

Maxwell and Johnston were by now engaged in a deadly feud that was to involve the whole of the West March. At the same time, however, Maxwell was also becoming increasingly involved in the Catholic plot for a Spanish invasion of England through Scotland, and in 1587 he went on a mission to Spain to further that cause. This presented a real danger to King James, so as soon as Maxwell returned, James marched against him, burned the castles of Langholm, Castlemilk and Morton, secured other Maxwell strongholds, and took Lord Maxwell prisoner.[35] He was released in 1589 against a bond of £100,000, and in 1592 was again made Warden. The following year the feud between the Maxwells and Johnstons reached a climax at Dryfesands, the last clan battle fought in the Borders, where Lord Maxwell was killed. Four years later, in 1597, Langholm is described as one of his Majesty's 'oun houses',[36] which the Privy Council ordered to be made available to Lord Ochiltree, the new Lieutenant and Warden of the West March.[37] The castle appears on both Agionby's Platte of 1590, as 'Ye Langhame',[38] and Pont's maps of Liddesdale ('Langhoom C.') and Eskdale ('Cast. of Langhoome') c.1595.[39]

For services rendered in pacifying 'the lait Borderris', the newly created Lord Cranstoun was, in 1610, granted the lands of Langholm, with the fortalice, manor, etc., all of which were erected into a free barony.[40] This was acquired by the Earl of Nithsdale in 1616,[41] and confirmed by crown charter five years later.[42] Then in 1643, after Nithsdale had fled the country, the barony was purchased by the Earl of Buccleuch.[43] The transaction was confirmed by crown charter the same year,[44] and reaffirmed in favour of his son-in-law and successor, the Duke of Buccleuch and Monmouth, in 1664.[45] In the Hearth Tax lists for Staplegordon parish c.1670, reference is made to 'the Dutches [Duchess's] house in Langholm castle'.[46]

During the rebellion of 1715, the castle was occupied briefly by the Jacobites.[47] It is last mentioned as a residence in 1726, when the Duke of Buccleuch's local chamberlain was living there and his daughter was married in the castle.[48] Soon afterwards it was largely dismantled to provide materials for the Duke's new house within the burgh itself.[49]

1   Border Papers I, 393.
2   Fraser 1873, I, 81.
3   Hyslop, 204-5.
4   RCAHMS 1997, 240.
5   Armstrong 1883, 228-9.
6   It has been suggested that the castle was originally built by the Armstrongs following Maxwell's grant in 1525 (Armstrong 1883, 229; Hyslop, 332), but there is no mention of a castle here this early and the present remains are certainly of later date.
7   The letter is addressed to 'Sir Thomas Wharton', although he had in fact been made Lord Wharton the previous month (See Complete Peerage XII/2, 596).
8   Salisbury MSS, 35 (No.144); Fraser 1873, I, 211-12.
9   Armstrong 1883, lxix.
10   Hyslop, 331.
11   APS II, 473.
12   Fraser 1878, I, lxi. Those who were summoned to join the Scots force but did not attend suffered forfeiture (RSS III, No.2342, et al.).
13   Armstrong 1883, lxxvii-lxxxv.
14   Hyslop, 337.
15   RSS III, Nos. 2342, 2344, 2360, 2398, 2420, 2514, 2570, 2677, 2863; IV, Nos.1550-1.
16   Merriman, M 'The Platte of Castlemilk, 1547', TDGAS, XLIV, 175-181.
17   These features were noted by the author in 1968, but the castle is now much more ruinous.
18   Hyslop, 331.
19   Ibid, 330. A photograph taken by the author's grandfather c.1902 shows several quoins from the SE corner and the whole of the lower part of the SW corner missing.
20   RSS IV, No.622.
21   Fraser 1873, II, 480.
22   Hyslop, 339.
23   Fraser 1873, II, 485.
24   RPC III, 304-5.
25   Ibid.
26   The furnishings belonged to Herbert Maxwell of Cavens, so when Cavens sued for redress in 1605, Johnston, who had stood surety for Armstrong's good behaviour, was fined 1000 merks (Fraser 1894, I, cxlvi).
27   Border Papers I, No.110. Earlier that year the captain of the garrison had been one Robert Maxwell (RPC III, 416)
28   Ibid, No.111.
29   Ibid.
30   Fraser 1873, I, 254.
31   Ibid, II, 485.
32   RPC III, 598.
33   Border Papers I, No.321.
34   Ibid, No.334.
35   RCAHMS 1920, xliii.
36   Hyslop, 343.
37   RPC V, 425.
38   Hyslop, 320.
39   Blaeu, 53, 'LIDISDAIL'; 55, 'EVSDAIL et ESKDAIL'.
40   RMS VII, No.214.
41   Fraser 1878, I, 252.
42   RMS VIII, No.228.
43   Fraser 1878, I, 252.
44   RMS IX, No.1341.
45   RMS XI, No.673; Fraser 1878, II, 473, 476. There had arisen a protracted dispute with the Earl of Nithsdale over ownership of Langholm. This was not finally resolved until 1666, when the curators of the Duke of Buccleuch and Monmouth purchased any remaining right which Nithsdale might pretend to the barony. - Fraser 1878, II, 394.
46   Adamson, D. 'The Hearth Tax', TDGAS, 3rd Ser., XLVIII, 141.
47   Hope-Johnstone MSS, 131 (No.97).
48   Hyslop, 344.
49   Fraser 1878, I, lxii.

46.   LOCHAR TOWER
(5¹⁄₂ m SSE Dumfries)   (NY028690)

Known variously as Lochar, The Isle and Bankend, there has been a defensive tower on this site since early in the second half of the 16th century, and there is good reason to believe that the main block of the present tower dates from this time. Its purpose was to guard the vital ford across the Lochar Water at the southern end of Lochar Moss, a vast, almost impenetrable morass stretching inland for some seven miles, and thus to control the eastern approach to Caerlaverock Castle and an important alternative route into Dumfries from the south. The site was originally an island, but the W channel has since been drained.

The earliest reference to the site is c.1563, when an English military report proposed that 'THE BANK ENDE . . . , upoun the west syde of Lowghare watter, may be well fortifyed upoun a convenient place aboute that hill, or elles in the vale besyde Lowghare watter foorde'. The report goes on to suggest that 'a garrison assistant' might be stationed at Caerlaverock, and 'yf stones were requyred to your fort at the bankende Carlaweroke wolde wele serve for the same'.[1] There is no suggestion of any fortification already in existence at the ford at that date, but a few years later, in 1568, Sir James Douglas of Drumlanrig became surety that William Maxwell 'of the Ile' would truly serve the King's Majesty and assist Sir James as Warden of the West March.[2] Lord Scrope burned the 'Town of Lowgher' in 1570.[3] William was succeeded by Edward Maxwell of the Yle, who was declared a rebel and put to the horn in 1585.[4] Later that year he was included in the general amnesty for those charged with rebellion.[5] He appears frequently in the records of the 1590s.[6] 'Yl [Isle] of Locchyir' tower was recorded by Timothy Pont c.1595-6.[7]

Fig. 276 Lochar Tower: view from N in 1963. The entrance can be seen in the re-entrant angle.

The **TOWER** was originally rectangular in plan, and measured 29ft 9in from NE to SW by 22ft from SE to NW, over walls averaging 3ft 2in in thickness. Built of roughly-coursed, sandstone rubble, with dressed margins and simple mouldings, the tower was three storeys and a garret in height, and there is evidence that it originally had a parapet walk. Because of the nature of the site, the basement was not vaulted:[8] instead, all the floors were supported on massive beams, which, to help distribute the weight of the floors above, were arranged alternately, those for the first and third floors running NE-SW, and those for the second floor SE-NW. There is no trace of the original stair, which was probably also of timber.

The entrance was evidently in the middle of the NW side, where the wing was later added; but because of the alterations carried out at that time, no details have survived. The tower's importance as guardian of a vital ford dictated the need for strong defences. These were provided within the tower itself by an array of splayed, oval gun-loops at the basement and second floor levels of the main block, very much in the manner of the defences at Hoddom, which no doubt served as the model. Within the basement there were two gun-loops in each of the SE and NW walls and one at the SW end, and there was probably also one at the NE end, where a small window was later inserted. The two slit-windows on the SE side may have been original.

By the end of the 19th century, the SW end of the tower had largely fallen, despite an attempt to buttress the W corner, and there is no record of its features above basement level.[9] The NE end, however, has survived. At first floor level it has a generous window in the end wall, and adjacent to it a shallow, mural garderobe, with rebates for a wooden door and a small window, now filled, while on the SE side there is the jamb of another window. The second floor also retains the jamb of a former window on the SE side, while at the NE end there is a small window recess and a small, central fireplace. In addition, both the NE and NW walls have small, square recesses serving the gun-loops on those sides. All the windows originally had iron grilles. Above the second floor level there are the remains of a continuous, moulded corbel-course, which may have been added when the attic floor was rebuilt, or which may be a survival from the original parapet.

Nothing is known of any outer works, apart from the reference by MacGibbon & Ross to 'traces of building on each bank of the Lochar'.[10] It is, however, likely that there was originally an enclosing wall, which the second floor gun-loops would have been intended to fire over, as at Hoddom.

The tower underwent major alterations in 1622, when a new stair wing and entrance were added in the middle of the NW side; at the same time, a new top floor was added to the main block in place of the former parapet-walk and attic. The

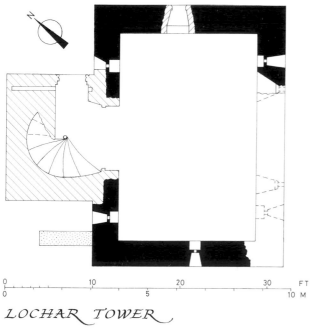

LOCHAR TOWER

Fig. 277 Lochar Tower: plan of basement.

Fig. 278 Lochar Tower: view from S after collapse of the stair wing in 1969.

wing was 14ft 3in wide and extended 9ft 7in, with walls averaging 2ft 6in in thickness. The new entrance was situated in the N re-entrant angle, and admitted directly to the wing. Above it there was an armorial panel bearing the date 1622 and the initials of Edward Maxwell of Isle and his wife Helen Douglas, together with various heraldic devices of their families.[11] The doorway itself, which had a QER moulding on its surround, was provided with a double rebate for an outer wooden door and inner iron yett, reinforced with a strong drawbar.[12] Inside, a large wheel-stair, 8ft 8in in diameter, with curved treads rose to serve the first two floors. Above this, the old stair, of which no trace survives, was presumably used to reach the third floor, as at this level the wing was occupied by a small chamber with a fireplace, the chimney stack for which was illustrated by MacGibbon & Ross.[13] Defence, however, was still clearly a priority, as this chamber also served a large machicolation, heavily corbelled-out on two pairs of 3-stage corbels immediately over the entrance, while an additional opening (shot-hole? or spy-hole?), 8in in diameter, was inserted in the first floor of the main block to overlook the entrance.

A most unusual feature between the new wing and basement was the vast doorway, which presumably replaced the original entrance. It was 6ft 10in in width, and was rebated for single or double doors on the basement side, but without any provision for a drawbar. No other details of the modifications carried out to the main block survive, apart from the remains of a dormer window with moulded surround at third floor level at the NE end. This gives some idea of how the new top storey was arranged. MacGibbon & Ross also show part of a crow-stepped gable at the E corner.[14]

After the dismantling of Caerlaverock Castle in 1640, the tower of Lochar, then known as 'Isle of Caerlaverock', became the home of the 2nd Earl of Nithsdale, and it was here that he died in 1667.[15] Some of his correspondence during this period (addressed to or from 'The Isle') is quoted by Fraser.[16] It was soon after the Earl's death, with his immediate family's fortunes at a very low ebb, that the tower appears to have been abandonned.

Because of the nature of the site, the ground is inherently unstable, and, despite the lack of vaulting and relatively thin walls to reduce the load, the present ruins have continued to suffer from subsidence and progressive collapse. The wing itself finally fell in 1969.

Fig. 279 Lochar: gun-loop on first floor covering entrance in wing.

1   Armstrong 1883, cix.
2   RPC I, 631.
3   McDowall 1986, 270.
4   RPC III, 735.
5   APS III, 388.
6   RPC V, 280, 543, 587, 744.
7   Blaeu, 57, 'THE STEWARTRIE OF ANNANDAIL'.
8   The reference to vaulting in RCAHMS 1920, No.34, is in error.
9   The basement was evidently still complete when recorded by MacGibbon & Ross in 1892.
10   MacGibbon & Ross V, 234.
11   See MacGibbon & Ross V, Fig.1342, and Fraser 1873, I, 621.
12   The slot was $5^{1}/_{2}$ in square and 5ft deep.
13   MacGibbon & Ross V, Fig.1342.
14   Ibid.

15   Fraser 1873, I, 382; Scots Peerage VI, 487.
16   Ibid, II, 143-159.

47.   LOCHHOUSE TOWER
(1¼ m SSW Moffat)   (NT082033)

Strategically situated where the valleys of the Evan, Annan and Moffat waters converge at the head of Annandale proper, Lochhouse was a stronghold of the Johnstons of that Ilk and at one time second only to Lochwood in importance. It stood on a slight eminence at the northern end of a loch, now drained, from which it took its name and whose waters provided a natural defence to the SE and SW. Lochhouse appears to have been built soon after the English occupation of Lochwood ended in 1550. It is not mentioned at that time, but was firmly established when the important marriage contract between Margaret, daughter of John Johnston of that Ilk, and Christopher, eldest son and heir of Edward Irving of Bonshaw, the Irving Chief, was drawn up 'at the Lochhouse' in 1566.[1] Johnston died the following year, and in the inventory attached to his will reference is made to oats and beir stored at his place of Lochhouse, and also to a 'hoard of gold and silver in a coffer in Lochhouse'.[2] A year later, in 1568, when the Regent Moray made a progress through the West March to enforce obedience to James VI, following Queen Mary's defeat at Langside, Johnston's grandson and heir, Sir John Johnston of that Ilk, who was still a minor, handed his places of 'Lokat' and 'Lowchthous' to the Regent, and promised submission. In recognition of this, the towers were not cast down.[3]

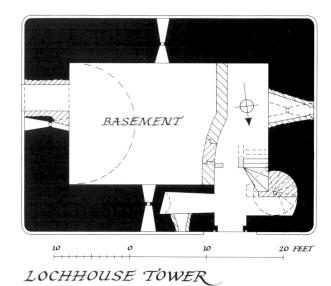

Fig. 281 Lochhouse Tower: plan of basement in 1969.

The **TOWER** is oblong in plan, with rounded corners, and comprises three storeys and an attic. On the outside there is the familiar plinth course, some 3ft above the ground, but a second offset course higher up, at the level of the second floor window-sills, is very unusual. It may represent a later phase of building, though this seems unlikely; both offsets are similar and of the same width. The tower measures 37ft 11in by 27ft 10in over walls 6ft thick. It is built of local rubble, mainly a

Fig. 280 Lochhouse Tower: view from NW in 1968, before the gabled roof was restored.

black greywacke, with red sandstone dressings. Around the entrance doorway, which is at ground level on the N side, the jambs and lintel carry a roll-and-hollow moulding.[4] Immediately inside, a mural recess on the left served as a guard chamber, while to the right, in the NW corner, lay the wheel-stair, 5ft 8in in diameter. The guard chamber measures on average 6ft 8in long by 2ft 9in wide, and is roofed with a segmental vault; it has one small window, now enlarged, high up. The basement beyond is vaulted. It has a maximum height above the cobbled floor of 8ft 9in, and was lit by a single window high up at the E end. In each wall there was one, narrowly-splayed, gun-loop, which emerged through an oval opening in the outer wall-face. When the tower was restored c.1900, the wheel-stair was superseded by a straight wooden stair rising up the W wall to the first floor, while the basement was partitioned off to serve as a separate store, with its own, new entrance at the E end.

The first floor had a fireplace at the E end and one window in each wall, that to the E being on the right of the fire. On the other side of the fireplace, in the NE corner, both walls are reduced in thickness, indicating that there was originally an additional feature here, the purpose of which is now lost. Both this floor and the floor above were greatly altered as the tower was successively restored. The second floor had a garderobe on the N side, but no window at the E end. All the windows had iron grilles, which were still in place in 1887;[5] they were only removed at the time of the first restoration.

Above the second floor, a parapet walk ran around the wall-head on all sides. The parapet itself has long since gone, but the disproportionately-narrow corbels that supported it have survived. The roof and W gable had also gone, leaving only a ruinous gable and chimney stack at the E end. The roof has recently been restored.

Two years after the death of John Johnston of that Ilk in 1567, the young laird of Johnston agreed to lease from his grandfather's widow, Nicola Douglas, her interest in the lands of Johnstoneholm and other lands for a period of nine years.[6] After that, Nicola was to have 'the use of her house of Lochhouse'.[7] But when the lease expired, in 1578, she could not get possession; and in 1582, Robert Johnston of Greenlands, in Nithsdale,[8] was charged with withholding 'of the hous of Lochous with the haill plenissing being thairintill' from her, and put to the horn.[9] It is presumed that Nicola subsequently got possession. Both her sons by Johnston of that Ilk, John and James, later became 'of Lochhouse'.[10]

The elder son, John, who became lay parson of Johnston, was executed for robbery and murder in 1603.[11] It was, however, James, later known as 'Captain James Johnston', who was designated 'of Lochhouse' in 1597, when John Maitland of Auchengassel gave surety for the good behaviour of the two brothers,[12] and James continued to live there until his death in 1632.

It was around this time that a dispute arose between James Johnston of that Ilk and William Douglas, Viscount Drumlanrig, concerning the superiority of the lands of Lochhouse and Thornick, which both claimed. The matter was eventually referred to the Privy Council, who decided in favour of Drumlanrig, and the property remained in his family until it was finally sold by the Duke of Buccleuch in the 19th century.[13]

In 1609, Drumlanrig gave surety that Captain James Johnston of Lochhouse would keep good rule in the country,[14] and in 1612 James himself was made a Justice of the Peace for Annandale.[15] The following year James had to find surety that

he would give Robert Graham of Thornick 'possession of the dwelling house of Lochhouse and those lands, to restore the iron gate to the house, and not to harm Robert'.[16] – Lochhouse lay within the old barony of Thornick, which the Grahams had held since the 15th century, and which, with other lands, they had been selling off to the Johnstons piecemeal for many years.[17] Whatever subsequently transpired, the matter seems to have been resolved and the Captain retained possession. Five years later, he was put to the horn for not producing the titles to certain other lands, and in 1619 the Captain of the Guard was ordered to 'apprehend the defender, seize his houses, and inventory his goods'.[18] It is presumed that this matter was also resolved, as the next year James was one of those directed to oversee the repair of Dumfries bridge.[19]

Captain James Johnston of Lochhouse died in 1632, leaving only an illegitimate son, James Johnston of Corehead.[20] In the same year James received letters of legitimation, and was infeft in the 25 merk lands of Lochhouse and Thornick,[21] while his uncle John Johnston's only son, James Johnston, who settled at Neiss in Moffatdale, renounced all claims he had to the family estates in return for an annuity.[22] James subsequently held many high appointments in the county. He was appointed a Justice of the Peace in 1634,[23] and Steward of Annandale in 1637.[24] Five years later he was made a Commissioner to apprehend Papists,[25] and later that year an Assessor for the trial of Border rebels,[26] while the following year he was appointed a Commissioner of Supply for Dumfriesshire.[27] He represented Dumfriesshire in the parliament held under Cromwell in 1652,[28] and was re-appointed a Commissioner of Supply in 1655, 1656 and 1659.[29] In 1655 he was put into serious financial difficulties by the debts of the Earl of Hartfell, for whom he had stood surety.[30] Following a petition to parliament by the Earl of Queensberry and Lord Drumlanrig seeking compensation for losses sustained under the Commonwealth, James was one of the Commissioners appointed in 1661 to obtain restitution from those concerned.[31] In later years he seems to have made Corehead his principal residence. He survived his son James, and died in, or soon after, 1693.[32]

In 1657, his eldest son, James, younger of Lochhouse, married Janet, daughter of James Douglas of Morton. In the

Fig. 282 Lochhouse Tower: view from SW after the roof was restored. The parapet walk still lacks its parapet.

marriage contract James Johnston of Corehead bound himself to infeft his son in the 25 merk lands of Lochhouse and Thornick, 'to sit in his maynes of Lochhouse with the pertinents presently possessed by James Symingtoun', and in various other lands and 'his myln belonging to the Lochhouse', whilst reserving to himself and his wife their liferents.[33] In 1687, Janet was infeft in the lands in liferent, and seven years later she was infeft in fee.[34] The younger James also held high public office during his father's lifetime, which has led to some confusion. He was appointed a Justice of the Peace in 1663 and again in 1688,[35] and he was a Captain of Foot in the Militia in both 1668[36] and 1689.[37] He was also a Commissioner of Supply in 1661, 1667, 1678, 1685, 1689 and 1690;[38] a Commissioner for the Borders in 1684;[39] and a Member of Parliament for Dumfriesshire in 1690.[40] He took the Test in 1683.[41] He predeceased his father, leaving an only son, William.

William Johnston of Corehead and Lochhouse succeeded his grandfather in the family estates, though he was not formally served heir until 1714.[42] In 1704 he was appointed a Commissioner of Supply for Dumfriesshire.[43] He was also a Deputy Lieutenant for the county, and in 1715 he assisted in the defence of Dumfries against the Jacobites.[44] He died in 1743, leaving two sons, William and James, and a daughter, Sophia, each of whom in turn succeeded to the family estates.[45] By this time Corehead had become the established family seat, while Lochhouse had ceased to be of importance, and was eventually abandonned. Sophia, who had married George Milligan, a surgeon in Moffat, was served heir of provision to her brother James in 1770. She inherited the family estates, and took the surname Milligan Johnstone.[46]

After the death of Sophia in 1785, Corehead and Lochhouse passed, first to her elder son, Dr. George Milligan Johnstone, who made a supplementary deed of entail, and then to her younger daughter, Elizabeth, who was infeft in 1799.[47] Elizabeth married Lieutenant-General William Johnstone, and made a new entail under which the estates passed, in 1816, to the General's niece, Isabella Johnstone Munro. Isabella married the Honourable Henry Butler, and had a son, Henry Milligan Butler Johnstone, M.P. for Canterbury, who, in 1879, sold Corehead and Lochhouse to William Younger of Auchen Castle.[48] William also purchased the superiority from the Duke of Buccleuch.[49]

It was William's son, Sir William Younger, 1st Baronet of Auchen Castle, who partially restored the roofless shell of Lochhouse Tower c.1900. At that time the first two floors were modernized and covered with a flat roof, while the basement was made into a separate store. The tower was eventually sold off as a separate house c.1978. The new owner replaced the roof and carried out further restoration work, revealing a number of original features that had long been covered over.

1 Irving 1907, 38-39, where the whole contract is quoted.
2 Fraser 1894, I, lix.
3 Scottish Papers, II, Nos.716, 717.
4 The roll-and-hollow moulding was common in the West March at this period (e.g.Bonshaw and Hoddom, q.v.).
5 MacGibbon & Ross, II, Fig.506.
6 Nicola Douglas was the second wife of John Johnston of that Ilk (1507-67).
7 Fraser 1984, I, lxv.
8 Possibly her step-son, Robert, the second son of John Johnston of that Ilk by his first wife, who subsequently lived at Carnsalloch, and died there in 1592.
9 RSS VIII, Nos.815, 903.
10 Fraser 1894, I, lxii.
11 Adams 1921, 116; Fraser 1894, I, lxvi, cccxxv.
12 RPC V, 679.
13 Fraser 1894, I, ccviii.
14 Adams 1921, 119.
15 RPC, IX, 355.
16 Adams 1921, 119.
17 RMS IV, Nos.428, 1552. Robert Graham's mother was also an illegitimate daughter of Johnston of that Ilk (Fraser 1894, I, lxii; Adams 1921, 118-9).
18 RPC XI, 587.
19 Ibid, XII, 251.
20 See Adams 1921, 121-2, for details of how James acquired Corehead. Ibid, XIV, 677.
21 Adams 1921, 121.
22 Ibid, 122, where full details are given.
23 RPC, 2nd Ser., V, 381.
24 Ibid, VI, 523.
25 Ibid, VII, 290.
26 Ibid, 354.
27 APS, VI, Part I, 29.
28 Ibid, Part II, 794.
29 Ibid, 839, 851, 881.
30 Adams 1921, 124.
31 APS VII, 96.
32 Adams 1921, 125.
33 Ibid, 90.
34 Ibid, 91-2.
35 APS VII, 505; RPC, 3rd Ser., XIII, 342.
36 RPC, 3rd Ser., II, 542.
37 APS IX, 26.
38 Ibid, VII, 91, 544; VIII, 225, 465; IX, 70, 139.
39 RPC, 3rd Ser., VIII, 682.
40 APS IX, 106, 109.
41 RPC, 3rd Ser., VIII, 640.
42 Adams 1921, 126.
43 Ibid, XI, 142.
44 McDowall 1986, 525.
45 Adams 1921, 127.
46 Ibid, 128.
47 Ibid.
48 Ibid, 129.
49 Fraser 1894, I, ccviii.

48. LOCHWOOD CASTLE
(3½ m S Beattock)   (NY084968)

The first of the Johnstons of Annandale was evidently one John, to whom Robert de Brus, Lord of Annandale, granted a tract of land on the west side of Upper Annandale c.1170-90.[1] This became the lands, and later parish, of 'John's Toun', or Johnston, and it was here, on a naturally strong site with a commanding view of the Annan valley, that John built his small motte-and-bailey castle.[2] Known at first as Johnston, and later as Lochwood,[3] this castle was rebuilt and extended several times until it became one of the most important strongholds in the West March. For more than five centuries it was the principal residence of the Johnston chiefs, later Earls and Marquesses of Annandale, who in the 16th century were to vie with the Maxwells for supremacy in the West March.

As all the family papers were destroyed in 1585 (infra), little is known of the castle and its lairds before that date, except what can be gleaned from official records and the titles of other families to which they were party or witnesses. Virtually nothing is known about the original John, but his son Gilbert was a frequent witness to Bruce charters as 'Gilbert son of John', and later 'Gilbert de Jonestone, knight' between c.1190 and c.1240.[4] In 1218 he was one of those who stood surety for Robert de Brus himself.[5] For their first three hundred years at Lochwood, however, the Johnstons remained a fairly small, albeit noble, family unit. Both the fourth laird, Sir John Johnston, and his son Gilbert de Johnston, later fifth laird, swore fealty to Edward I in 1296.[6]

Fig. 283 Lochwood Castle: view S from motte over castle ruins in 1969. In the foreground is the courtyard surrounded by
building ranges and the barmkin, with the ruinous tower beyond.

It was probably during the 13th or 14th centuries – family tradition relates the latter[7] – that the old motte was succeeded
by a new castle of stone. Certainly the family had attained a
leading position in Border affairs before 1380, and would by
then have required something more substantial for their protection. The new castle is presumed to have been built on the site
of the original bailey, immediately south of the motte where the
present ruins stand. Whether any of the visible remains date
from this period has not been established, but some of the mouldings found re-used in the present tower (and in some instances
used merely as rubble infill for the walls), almost certainly do.[8]

Gilbert de Johnston evidently had two sons, John and
Gilbert, both of whom appear to have succeeded in turn, but it is
not clear whether the next recorded laird, Sir John Johnston, 8th
of that Ilk, was the son or grandson of Gilbert.[9] Sir John was the
first of the family to hold public office. He was Warden of the
West March,[10] and in 1398 a Conservator of the Truce on the
Borders.[11] He was renowned for his many successes, and it may
well have been he who built the new castle. Sir John's son,
Adam, took part in the battle of the Sark in 1448 and, when
peace was restored, was also a Conservator of the Peace.[12] He
died c.1454-5.

John Johnston of that Ilk, 10th laird, supported his King
against the Douglases at both Arkinholm and Threave in 1455
and again at Lochmaben in 1484.[13] For this, he and his family
were richly rewarded with grants of forfeited lands,[14] and in the
latter year his grandson John received a new charter of the lands
of Johnston, whilst apparently reserving the liferent to his grandfather.[15] This seems to have been the turning point in the
Johnstons' fortunes, for it greatly increased their territorial influence at the same time as the power of the Douglases and their
allies was eclipsed. John attended parliament in 1469 and 1471,[16]
and died in, or soon after, 1493, when he was succeeded by his
younger grandson, Sir Adam Johnston.

Sir Adam succeeded his elder brother, John, in the lands
of Johnston, Kirkpatrick-Fleming and Cavartsholm in 1488,[17]

but did not succeed his grandfather until 1493, or soon after. It
was during his lairdship, in 1496, that there is the earliest reference to 'a place callit Lochwood in Annandaill'.[18] After Sir
Adam's death in 1509, his eldest son, James, the 13th laird, received a new crown charter of 'the lands of Johnestoun, with the
tower, fortalice, manor and place of the same'; the £20 lands of
Kirkpatrick-Fleming, including the lands of Dunskellie (Cove);
the £10 lands of Cavartsholm in tenandry; and the 10 merk lands
of Wamfray.[19] James was one of the keepers of the West Marches
in 1523, evidently as a deputy to the Warden.[20] He died the
following year.

James was succeeded by his eldest son, John, who was
Deputy Warden in 1531 and again in 1542.[21] In the latter year
he was effectively Warden following Lord Maxwell's capture at
Solway Moss. Later, in 1542/3, John had a new crown charter
of 'the lands of Johnstoun, with the tower, fortalice and
manor-place', and other lands, including Kirkpatrick,
Cavartsholm, Wamphray and Polmoodie, all of which were incorporated into 'the free Barony of Johnstoun'.[22] He attended
parliament in 1545.[23] It was during John's lairdship that the feud
with the Maxwells started, fomented by the conniving Lord
Wharton, the English Warden, who was tireless in his efforts to
stir up dissention in the Scottish camp.

It was during the wars with England that Lochwood first
came into prominence as a stronghold of national importance,
when, in 1547, the English chose it as their base in Upper
Annandale. The story of its capture by Sir Thomas Carleton and
subsequent role is recorded in considerable detail, though the
English and Scots versions of events disagree in emphasis. At
the time Johnston was a prisoner in England, so Lochwood was
only lightly guarded. Carleton described Lochwood as 'a fair
large tower, able to lodge all our company safely, with a
barnekin-hall, kitchen, and stables all within the barnekin'.[24]
Arriving secretly by night, about a dozen men climbed the
barmkin wall, and 'stole close into the house within the barnekin
and took the wenches and kept them secure in the house till day-

light'. The next morning, when one of the men in the tower had gone to the tower head and checked that nothing stirred about, he called on the wench below to open the door and 'call up them that lay beneath'. This she did, 'opening the iron door and a wood door without it'; but Carleton's men broke too soon, so that the wench leaped back into the tower and almost succeeded in closing the door again, 'but we got hold of it that she could not get it close to. So the skirmish rose, and we over the barnekin and broke open the wood door; and she being troubled with the wood door left the iron one open; and so we entered and won the Loghwood'.[25] Carleton was appointed keeper, and there he remained 'very quietly . . . as if we had been at home in our own houses', adding that 'every man within Annerdale being within twelve or sixteen miles of the Loughwood would have resorted to me to seek reformation for any injury committed or done'.[26] Johnston, on the other hand, complained of Carleton's rough-handedness, that he 'enterit in my said hous and brint and distroyit the samin', and of the heavy losses sustained by his tenants.[27]

Shortly afterwards Lord Wharton arranged for a survey of the West March of Scotland, which was to include Lochwood,

his most recent capture. The result was the 'Platte of Castlemilk', a pictorial map that included thumbnail sketches of all the principal strongholds, including Lochwood.[28] For the next three years Carleton used the castle as his base.

The major part of the present ruins pre-dates this period, being the remains of the stronghold depicted on the Platte. It comprises two, adjacent, quadrilateral enclosures, with an overall measurement averaging 150ft from N to S by 95ft from E to W, while at the SE corner of the site was the tower itself. Around these enclosures ran the barnekin. Varying in thickness from 4ft to 4ft 6in, with boldly rounded corners, it was built of local Silurian rubble. The only entrance to either enclosure appears to have been on the S side, adjacent to the tower, where the outline of another structure, possibly a gatehouse, could, until recently, still be traced.[29]

The **NORTHERN ENCLOSURE** is the earlier of the two, and may represent a much-altered vestige of the first stone castle. It measures on average 81ft from N to S and 95ft from E to W. Along the N wall are the remains of a building range with walls 4ft 6in thick and an internal width of 13ft. A section of

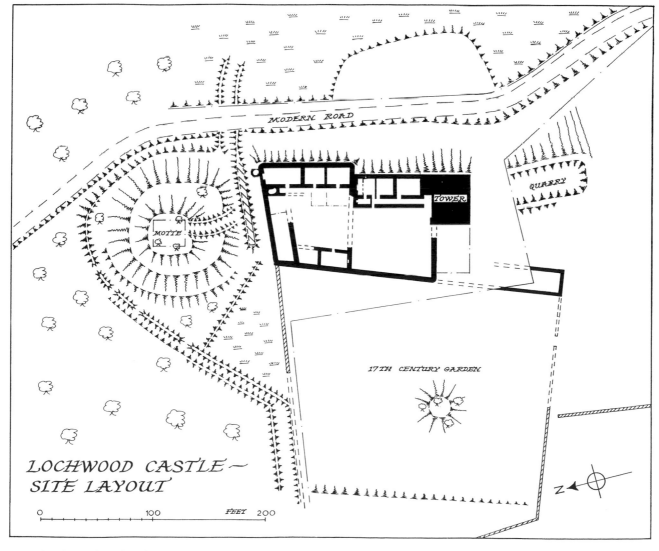

Fig. 284 Lochwood Castle: site layout. In the lower part of the plan is the 17th century, formal garden with central mount, now removed.

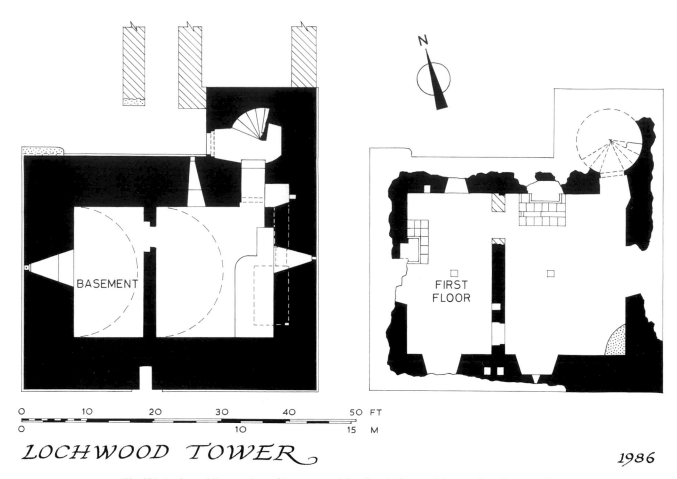

LOCHWOOD TOWER

1986

Fig. 285 Lochwood Tower: plans of basement and first floor before partial restoration of upper walls.

walling entrapped by tree roots suggests it was at least two storeys high. Another range, which was excavated in 1982, extended the whole length of the E wall. It comprised three chambers, each with an internal width of 15ft and inner walls averaging 3ft in thickness, which were reached from a common passage along the W side. The most northerly chamber was a kitchen
or bakehouse with a relatively small fireplace, 4ft 10in, in
the N wall. Immediately outside at this point (and outside the
barmkin), is a large, circular oven, some 5ft 4in in diameter.
The remains of another, larger oven, 7ft 2in in diameter, were
found at ground level in the NW corner of this building, but
without any obvious means of access, suggesting it had been
abandoned and closed off. The remains of a third range on the
W side of the courtyard were partly excavated in 1968.[30] This
revealed a room measuring 24ft by 13ft internally, with a fireplace at the S end, a central doorway and inner walls 2ft 9in
thick. It was a 17th century addition. The continuation of this
enclosure's outer wall right across the S side – apart from a gateway, now gone – effectively segregated the two courtyards.

The **SOUTHERN COURTYARD** was much more
open, the only known buildings being the large E range, 60ft 6in
long and 29ft 6in wide, inserted between the tower and the earlier courtyard. At basement level this range comprised a fine
kitchen and two vaulted cellars, connected on the W side by a
common service passage, while to the N of the passage, and
entered directly from the kitchen, there was another, smaller
chamber – probably a store room – with an aumbry. The kitchen
was at the N end of this range, with its great fireplace, 14ft 3in
wide and 4ft 6in deep, separated from the rest of the room by a

fine, semi-circular arch, some 8ft 6in wide, with finely-wrought,
ashlar voussoirs and rounded arrises. Only the W end of this
arch survives. The only other feature in the kitchen is a slop-sink,
which discharged outside the barmkin on the E side.[31] The masonry of this range is local rubble with sandstone dressings, and
the walls are 3ft 6in thick. In all probability this range was the
'barnekin-hall' mentioned by Carleton, the first floor of which
would have been the great hall of the castle.[32]

The **TOWER** itself appears to date from late in the 15th
century, or, just possibly, early in the 16th century. The thickness of the walls – 7ft 8in at basement level and 5ft 6in at the
first floor – and the lack of any provision for firearms virtually
precludes a later date, while the widespread re-use of older, probably 14th century mouldings makes an earlier date unlikely. The
tower is built on the **L**-plan, and has a main block measuring
43ft 8in by 34ft 6in, from the N end of which a stair wing, 17ft
6in wide, projects 10ft 5in to the N. There is a splayed plinth
course. The masonry is local rubble with red sandstone mouldings. Apart from a QER moulding around the entrance, all the
margins have rounded or chamfered arrises.

The entrance, which is at ground level in the re-entrant
angle, was protected by the usual wooden door and iron yett.[33]
This admitted directly to the unusually large wheel-stair, 10ft in
diameter, and a mural passage leading to the basement. A low
doorway, only 3ft 6in high, on the E side of this passage leads
down to a second mural passage serving the prison. The latter
passage, which is only 5ft high, is roofed throughout its length
with large, dressed, sandstone slabs, all of which have come from
an earlier work. Two of the slabs are inverted drainage gulleys,

Fig. 286 Lochwood: detail of fastening for yett from the tower
(it is standing upside down).

tion for the prison or its passage, and the only ventilation is provided by a vent, 8in square, at the N end of the passage and another, only 7in by 4in, at the S end of the prison,[36] both of which rise up within the E wall.

The basement is barrel-vaulted and subdivided into two unequal chambers by a cross wall supporting a similar partition on the floor above. Each chamber has a hatch in the vault. The only illumination at this level is provided by three slit-windows, one at each end with widely splayed jambs and a third covering the entrance.

The first floor is noteworthy for the fact that, contrary to usual practice, it was not the hall, which, as already explained was probably in the adjacent range to the N. Instead, this floor was always divided into two small chambers. The E chamber, which was entered directly from the stair, had a small fireplace in the N wall and window recesses in the E and S walls, the latter incorporating a slop-sink below the sill. The smaller western chamber was reached through doorways at either end of the dividing wall. The N doorway was later altered. In each of the outside walls there was one window, the S and W ones being recessed. This room also had a small fireplace beside the W window and two aumbries.

Nothing survives above this level; but two flues, which emerge from a common outlet at ground level near the middle of the S wall, indicate the former existence of at least two levels of garderobes above the first floor. The only other clues to the upper works were to be found amongst the fallen masonry cleared from the first floor. These included small corbels with carved heads; pieces of billet- or chequer-corbelling; the pediment from a dormer window bearing the initials 'S I [I]' and 'D S M', for Sir James Johnston (d.1608) and Dame Sarah Maxwell (d.1636)(daughter of the 4th Lord Herries); and a stone bearing the date '1603'.[37] All but the corbels have clearly come from alterations to, or a reconstruction of, the upper works carried out in 1603.

perhaps from a parapet walk, while a third has a raised edge on either side. Two thirds of the way down this passage is the doorway guarding the prison.[34] The prison itself measures 8ft 9in by 5ft 4in and has a barrel-vaulted roof 5ft 7in high.[35] The lower half is subterranean, while the upper part is contained partly within the thickness of the wall and partly by a stone platform intruding upon the E end of the basement. There is no illumina-

John Johnston of that Ilk regained his freedom around the same time that peace was concluded in 1550. Two years later, he was one of the Commissioners for settling the bounda-

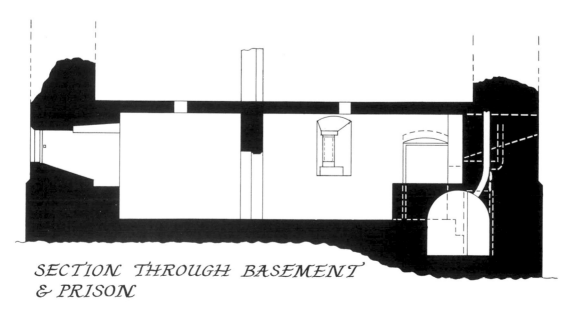

SECTION THROUGH BASEMENT
& PRISON

Fig. 287 Lochwood Tower: sectional elevation through prison and basement looking north, before partial restoration of upper walls.

Fig. 288 Lochwood Tower: W window of basement (partly ruinous).

ries of the Debateable Land,[38] and in 1560 he attended parliament.[39] He died in 1567, and was succeeded by his eldest grandson, John Johnston, who was still a minor.

The following year John subscribed to the Bond of support for Queen Mary at Hamilton,[40] but after her defeat at Langside he changed his allegiance. Thus, when the Regent

Moray made his military progress through SW Scotland, he received Johnston's houses of Lochwood and Lochhouse and 'cast them not down', as John had promised to submit and give surety.[41] John also submitted to the new Regent, the Earl of Lennox, in 1570;[42] but when Morton was Regent in 1574, he had Johnston warded for four months for unpaid fines.[43] In 1577-78, John was made Deputy-Warden of the West March, and in 1579 Warden.[44] Two years later, however, he was accused of laxity in his duty, and removed from office. He came into special favour with James VI following the Raid of Ruthven in 1582, being re-appointed Warden in that year and evidently remaining in office until his death in 1587, though for a while in 1585 he was a prisoner of Lord Maxwell.[45] When he was knighted in 1584, instead of recognizing his seat at Lochwood, he was styled 'Sir John Johnston of Dunskellie', after a lesser property he had at Cove, in the parish of Kirkpatrick Fleming;[46] and he and his successors continued to use that designation until raised to the peerage.

It was while the Johnston-Maxwell feud was at its height in 1585, and Johnston himself absent, that Robert Maxwell of Cowhill and about 120 English and Scots rebels attacked Lochwood and 'brint the place, mantioun, and haill houss thairof, with the haill insycht thairin, bedding, plenesching, and brint and distroyit my chartour kist with my haill evedentis and wreittis besyd uther jowellis'.[47] The loss of the charters was a great loss to both the family and history, but no time would have been wasted in repairing the castle, and later, in both 1592 and 1602, James VI spent a night there during military expeditions to quieten the Borders.[48] Sir John died in 1587 and was succeeded by his only son, Sir James.

The feud between the Johnstons and Maxwells flared up again in 1593, when, following a bloody raid by the Johnstons of Wamphray against the Crichtons, Lord Maxwell was given a special commission to apprehend Sir James Johnston of Dunskellie, who, although not personally involved, was held responsible for his clan. The two clans met at Dryfesands, near Lockerbie, where Lord Maxwell was killed.[49] It was the last great clan battle ever to be fought in the Borders. The following year Johnston received a remission for his offences,[50] and in 1596 was appointed Warden of the West March, but a year later he was dismissed for breaking his pledge and warded in Edinburgh Castle.[51] He was put to the horn again in 1598 and 'all His Majesty's subjects [ordered] to have no dealings with him';[52] but the following year he bound himself to observe the King's peace,[53] and in 1600 was re-appointed Warden.[54] Eight years later, a meeting was arranged between Sir James and the 8th Lord Maxwell to settle their differences, but it ended with the murder of Sir James, the last tragic act in the families' long-standing feud.

Either at the same time as the tower was modified in 1603, or later in the century, various other works were carried out at Lochwood. These included the addition of a new range, 111ft long and 22ft 6in wide, running S from the SW corner of the southern courtyard and the laying out of a formal, walled gar-

Fig. 289 Lochwood Castle: ruins of tower and E range after excavation and consolidation, seen from the motte.

den, with a central 'mount', on the W side. The garden measured some 235ft by 190ft.[55] When the Hearth Tax was introduced in 1690, the Roll listed 14 fireplaces 'in Lochwood'.[56]

Sir James was succeeded by his only son, James, who was laird for forty-five years. During this time James purchased Moffatdale and Evandale and many other lands to become one of the greatest landowners in the south,[57] thereby greatly increasing his power and influence. In 1622 he was appointed a Commissioner for the Middle Shires,[58] and in 1633 was raised to the peerage as Lord Johnston of Lochwood.[59] Two years later he was appointed a Commissioner for keeping good order in the Borders.[60] Lord Johnston joined the Covenanters in 1637,[61] but with the onset of the King's dispute with both the Covenanters and parliament in 1639, Johnston was appointed colonel of the King's forces within the Stewartry of Annandale, with special orders to preserve the peace.[62] He was a regular attender of parliament from 1639 to 1641,[63] and in the latter year was appointed to the committee for scrutinizing all bills and supplications.[64] At the same time he himself had to petition parliament for the officers of his regiment to be paid.[65] In 1643 James was raised to the dignity of Earl of Hartfell and Lord Johnston of Lochwood, Moffatdale and Evandale.[66] The following year he again attended parliament,[67] being appointed to the Committee for the South,[68] and he was made a Commissioner of War for Dumfriesshire;[69] but his support for Montrose brought him into conflict with the Committee of Estates, and he was arrested and imprisoned.[70] Free once more in 1645, he fought at Philiphaugh, where he was again taken prisoner; he was sentenced to death, but was later pardonned.[71] Three years later he was appointed Lieutenant-Colonel on behalf of the Committee of Estates in Dumfriesshire,[72] and in 1651, when he again attended parliament, he was one of parliament's commissioners to the Committee.[73] It was during the Earl's time that Lochwood came increasingly to be subordinated to Newbie Castle, near Annan, as the family's principal residence in the Borders.

The Earl died in 1653, 'probably at Newbie',[74] and was succeeded by his elder son, James, 2nd Earl of Hartfell. James was appointed a Commissioner of Supply for Dumfriesshire in 1655 and again in 1659.[75] After the Restoration, he became a regular attender of parliament until 1670[76] and sat on various of its committees. In 1661 he was appointed a Lord of the Articles and Processes,[77] a Commissioner for the Plantation of Kirks and Valuation of Teinds,[78] and a Commissioner for agreeing the losses sustained by the Earl of Queensberry during the recent troubles.[79] He was also re-appointed a Commissioner of Supply.[80] It is worthy of note that, when all James's losses under the Commonwealth were assessed, prominence was given to the plundering of Newbie, but nothing was said of Lochwood.[81]

As the Earl's marriage seemed at first unable to produce a son and heir, and his only brother had died unmarried in 1657, the Earl feared for the succession. In order, therefore, to secure the interest of his daughters and their children, he resigned his peerage and in 1661 received a new creation as Earl of Annandale and Hartfell, Viscount of Annan, Lord Johnston of Lochwood, Lochmaben, Moffatdale and Evandale, with special remainder.[82] The following year he received a new charter erecting all his estates into the free barony, lordship, earldom, regality and justiciary of the Earldom of Annandale and Hartfell and the Lordship of Johnston, with the 'tower of Johnston, otherwise called Lochwood, or Newbie,' as the principal messuage, and further erecting the town of Moffat into a free burgh of barony and regality;[83] and this was all ratified by parliament in 1669.[84] The

Earl was also made hereditary keeper of Lochmaben Castle,[85] a Privy Councillor and principal Steward of the Stewartry of Annandale.[86] Meanwhile he continued to pursue his parliamentary duties, again being appointed a Lord of the Articles and a Commissioner for the Plantation of Kirks and Valuation of Teinds in 1663,[87] and to the committee for Inbringing of the Taxation two years later.[88] In 1667 he was given the commission of Captain of a troop of horse in Lieutenant-General Drummond's regiment.[89] He died in 1672.

The 2nd Earl of Annandale was only eight when he succeeded, and sixteen when he was served heir to his father.[90] Two years later he married Sophia Fairholm of Craigiehall, after which Newbie became the favoured summer residence of the young couple.[91] During a long and distinguished career in public service, the Earl held some of the highest offices of state. He attended parliament regularly from 1685,[92] was Lord President of the Privy Council in 1695 and again in 1704,[93] Lord Privy Seal in 1702,[94] and one of His Majesty's Principal Secretaries of State in 1705.[95] He was also commissioned as Captain of a troop of horse under Claverhouse in 1688[96] and, after the Revolution in 1689, under Major-General Mackay,[97] and was a Commissioner of Supply for Dumfriesshire in 1685, 1689, 1690, 1696 and 1704.[98] Although he became involved in what was known as 'Montgomerie's Plot' in 1689, he quickly recanted and was forgiven.[99] For a while afterwards he lived at Lochwood, where he kept a low profile.[100] In 1693 he was made an Extraordinary Lord of Session,[101] and eight years later he was appointed Lord High Commissioner to the General Assembly of the Church of Scotland, a post he held again in 1705 and 1711.[102]

In recognition of his services, the Earl was in 1701 raised to the dignity of Marquess of Annandale,[103] and in 1704 Queen Anne made him a Knight of the Thistle.[104] The following year he and his lady moved from Lochwood to the latter's family home at Craigiehall, near Edinburgh.[105] Lochwood was now virtually abandonned: it is said to have been destroyed by fire c.1710,[106] although sasine was still recorded 'at the mansion house of Lochwood' in 1719.[107] Lord Annandale subsequently took an active part in the debates concerning the proposed Treaty of Union and voted against the final Act ratifying the Treaty in 1707.[108] However, once the Treaty had been signed, he worked hard to make it a success. At the outbreak of the Jacobite rebellion in 1715, Lord Annandale was made Lord Lieutenant and Commander-in-Chief over the shires of Dumfries, Kirkcudbright and Peebles.[109] He died in 1721.

A survey of the estate in 1759 shows the castle layout at that time.[110] The feature of greatest interest is an enclosure on the E side of the castle, where the present road runs. All trace of this has since disappeared. The site was finally abandoned c.1773,[111] some eleven years after the 2nd Earl of Hopetoun, as curator for his maternal uncle the 3rd and last Marquess of Annandale, had a new residence, Moffat House, built in Moffat. Later, in 1786, the Earl had another mansion built at Raehills, two miles to the SW, and this is still the family's principal residence.

Lochwood Castle remains the property and seat of the Hope-Johnstones, the lineal descendants of the Marquesses of Annandale, who established their right to the dormant Earldom of Annandale & Hartfell in 1985.[112] A survey of the site and limited excavations were carried out by the writer in 1967-8, and in 1982-86 Lord Annandale undertook a full excavation of the tower and east ranges.[113]

1   Fraser 1894, I, i-iii.
2   RCAHMS 1920, No.316; Maxwell-Irving 1974 (I), 18-22. The intermediate terrace around the motte may be original, though it is now thought more likely that it was 'landscaped' in the 17th century (RCAHMS 1997, 195). Terraced mottes are certainly unusual, but there are two others in the same region: at Garpol, 5 miles to the NNW, and at Lincluden, near Dumfries.
3   The name 'Lochwood' is taken from the ancient wood of oaks immediately north of the site and adjacent to a vast area of bog that was formerly a loch. Some of the trees are of a venerable age and among the oldest surviving in Scotland, while the wood itself may well pre-date the motte.
4   Buccleuch MSS, 39-40 (Nos.67-70); Bain I, No.705; Fraser 1894, I, iii-vi.
5   Bain I, No.700.
6   Ibid, II, Nos.810, 823. They both appended their seals, but, although incomplete, they are quite different from one another and from the later arms of Johnston of that Ilk.
7   Fraser 1894, I, xxix.
8   Maxwell-Irving 1968 (II), 188-9. During the excavation of the tower in 1986, a considerable number of early-type sandstone mouldings were exposed within the core of the walls before the walls were 'restored'.
9   An Adam Johnston is recorded around this time, who may have been the father of Sir John (Scots Peerage I, 234).
10 Fraser 1894, I, ix.
11 Ibid, cccxxiii.
12 Ibid, xiv. John, the 10th laird's only son, James, died some time before 1484.
13 Ibid, xix; Scots Peerage I, 237.
14 Fraser 1894, I, xix, xxix.
15 Ibid, xxiv.
16 APS II, 93, 98.
17 Fraser 1894, I, xxv-xxvi.
18 Ibid, xv.
19 RMS II, No.3382.
20 Rae, 240.
21 Ibid.
22 RMS II, No.2874.
23 Scots Peerage I, 244.
24 Memoirs of Sir Thomas Carleton, formerly at Carleton Hall, cited in Irving 1907, 33-4.
25 Ibid; Mackenzie 1927, 94; Fraser 1984, I, xliv..
26 Fraser 1894, I, xlv.
27 Ibid, xlviii-xlix.
28 Merriman, M 'The Platte of Castlemilk, 1547', TDGAS, XLIV, 175-181.
29 This area has now disappeared under a vast heap of rubble from the excavated tower.
30 Maxwell-Irving 1974 (I), 37-46.
31 Another gully now near the SE corner was 'rebuilt' into the wall in error where it was found in 1983 – a lesson in not making assumptions, for some 15 years earlier it had been put there by the writer for safety!
32 Ritchie and Harman 1985, 74. There is a somewhat similar arrangement between the tower-house and adjacent range at Carnasserie Castle in Mid Argyll, except that there the two buildings are of the same date.
33 This was found still in situ when the rubble was cleared in 1986. The yett is now at Raehills. There was no evidence of provision for a drawbar. See Maxwell-Irving 1994, 443-6.
34 The supposition in the RCAHMS Report (RCAHMS 1920, 116) that the door 'folded vertically in leaves' was due to a misinterpretation of the inverted drainage gulley immediately above it. An almost identical drainage gully is still in situ for its correct purpose at Kilchurn Castle in Argyll.
35 This prison can be compared with those at Hoddom and Bonshaw, q.v.
36 The prison vents are similar to those at Comlongon, Hoddom and Bonshaw.
37 These stones are now preserved at Raehills.
38 Fraser 1894, I, l.
39 APS II, 525.
40 Scottish Papers II, 403.
41 Ibid, Nos. 716-7.
42 Scots Peerage I, 249.
43 Ibid, 250.
44 Hope-Johnstone MSS, 27 (No.46); Rae, 241.
45 RPC III, 531; Rae, 241.
46 Fraser 1894, I, xcii.
47 Hope-Johnstone MSS, 32 (No.64); Warrender Papers I, 182.
48 Border Papers, I, No.780; Scottish Papers XIII, No.778.
49 Fraser 1894, I, cxix-cxxiii.
50 Scots Peerage I, 253.
51 Hope-Johnstone MSS, 37 (No.76); Rae, 243. Although Johnston was warded in July, he was not officially removed from office until his successor, Lord Ochiltree, was appointed in November 1597.
52 APS IV, 166; RPC V, 456.
53 Hope-Johnstone MSS, 38-9 (No.82).
54 RPC VI, 155.
55 The form of this garden was perhaps inspired by the 'King's Knot' garden laid out at Stirling Castle in 1627. It has been suggested that it was at this

time that the motte was terraced (RCAHMS 1997, 195). Regrettably, the central mount of the garden was levelled by the tenant farmer some time during the 1970s or 1980s.
56 Adamson, D 'The Hearth Tax for Dumfriesshire', TDGAS, XLIX, 78.
57 Fraser 1894, I, clxxv, ccvi-ccix.
58 RPC XII, 650.
59 Hope-Johnstone MSS, 43 (No.97).
60 Fraser 1894, I, clxxviii.
61 Scots Peerage I, 255.
62 Fraser 1894, I, cxcii.
63 APS V, 251, 258, 301, 308, 331, 426.
64 Ibid, 318.
65 Ibid, 681, 704.
66 Hope-Johnstone MSS, 43 (No.97); Fraser 1894, I, cxc.
67 Scots Peerage I, 256.
68 APS VI, Part I, 91.
69 Ibid, 200.
70 Fraser 1894, I, cxcii-cxcv.
71 Ibid, cxcvii-cc.
72 APS VI, Part I, 468.
73 Ibid, Part II, 679.
74 Scots Peerage I, 258.
75 APS VI, Part II, 839, 881.
76 Ibid, VII, 3, 368, 446, 526, 536, 548; VIII, 3.
77 Ibid, 8.
78 Ibid, 48.
79 Ibid, 96.
80 Ibid, 91.
81 Fraser 1894, I, cc, ccxxxvii.
82 RMS XI, No.39. The Murray Earldom of Annandale had become extinct in 1658.
83 RMS XI, No.230.
84 APS VII, 641.
85 RMS XI, No.230.
86 Fraser 1894, I, ccxxxvii; APS VII, 442.
87 Ibid, 449, 474.
88 Ibid, 529.
89 Fraser 1894, I, 94 (No.93).
90 Fraser 1894, I, cclv.
91 Ibid, cclvi.
92 APS VIII, 451, 576; IX, passim; X, 113, 183, 196; XI, passim.
93 Ibid, IX, 350; XI, 29, 34, 113.
94 Ibid, XI, 3, 6.
95 Ibid, 205, 210.
96 Scots Peerage I, 265.
97 APS IX, 54.
98 Ibid, VIII, 465; IX, 70, 139; X, 29, 131; XI, 142.
99 Fraser 1894, I, ccl; Scots Peerage I, 266.
100 Scots Peerage I, 266.
101 Ibid.
102 Ibid, 266-7; Fraser 1894, I, ccci.
103 Hope-Johnstone MSS, 44 (No.101)
104 Fraser 1894, I, ccc.
105 Ibid, cccvii.
106 Ibid, cccxxxiv.
107 Ibid, cccxxi.
108 APS XI, passim, 404.
109 Fraser 1894, I, cccxvi
110 Maxwell-Irving 1974 (I), 13-16.
111 Ibid, 3.
112 Debrett's Peerage 1990, Annandale & Hartfell, Earl of.
113 Maxwell-Irving 1990, 93-99.

---

49. LOCKERBIE TOWER
(Lockerbie)   (NY136814)

The lands of Lockerbie – of old 'Locardebi', meaning 'the farm of Locard' – take their name from the Norman family of Locard (later Lockhart), who were supporters of the Bruces and a family of some consequence. In 1166 Simon Locard witnessed a charter of William the Lion confirming to Robert de Brus his lands in Annandale,[1] and c.1200 Malcolm Loccard witnessed a resignation of lands in Warmanbie and Annan in favour of William de Brus.[2] The family's connection with Lockerbie, however, is somewhat obscure, as there is no direct reference to their tenure. The lands formed part of David I's original grant of Annandale to Robert de Brus *c*.1124,[3] and it seems likely that the Locards acquired the lands from the Bruces soon after. Later, probably during the third quarter of the century, the lands were granted by Bruce's son to Robert de Karleol (Carlyle). This is recorded in a charter *c*.1198, when, following a dispute over possession between Adam Carlyle, Robert's son, and William de Brus, the granter's son, an agreement was reached in the King's Court at Westminster whereby Adam de Karleolo quitclaimed his whole right to the 8 carucates of land in 'Locardebi' to William

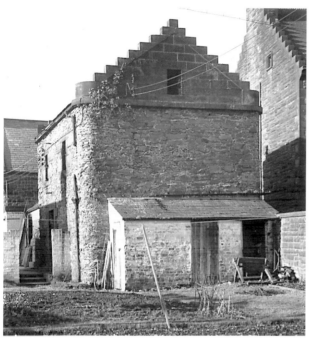

Fig. 290 Lockerbie Tower: view from E.
(Crown copyright: RCAHMS.)

in exchange for 7 carucates of land in and around Kinemunt (Kinmount) and a mill.[4] It would thus seem that the Locards did not hold the lands for long, but gave them up when they acquired the lands and barony of Symington, in Clydesdale, reputedly early in the reign of William the Lion.[5]

The Bruces continued to hold the lands of Lockerbie as part of the Lordship of Annandale until 1306, when, following the murder of the 'Red Comyn', Edward I escheated Annandale from Bruce and granted it to Humphrey de Bohun, Earl of Hereford.[6] Bohun then granted 40 merks worth of his newly acquired lands, comprising the lands of 'Hotone (Hutton) and Lokardebi', to Sir Bartholomew Denefeud for life in return for his services.[7] How long Sir Bartholomew held the lands is not known, but it was not until 1384 that the English were finally compelled to relinquish Lochmaben, the principal stronghold in the area.

Meanwhile, with the coronation of Bruce in 1306 – challenging King Edward's claims to the kingdom –, the Lordship of Annandale became vested in the Scots Crown, and in 1316 Bruce granted it to his nephew Thomas Randolph, Earl of Moray.[8] It subsequently passed by marriage to the Earls of March, who held it until 1409, when the 9th Earl was compelled to resign it in favour of the Earl of Douglas.[9] On the forfeiture of the 6th Earl of Douglas in 1440, Annandale reverted to the Crown,[10] and in 1455 James II granted it to his infant son the Duke of

Albany; but when, in 1483, Albany too was found guilty of high treason, it was once again annexed by the Crown.[11]

At some stage during this chronicle of events the lands of Lockerbie had evidently come into the possession of the Herries of Terregles, for in 1486 Andrew Herries, son and heir of Herbert Herries of Terregles received a crown charter of many lands, including 'Lokartby' and other lands in Annandale, on the resignation of his father.[12] The lands continued in the family until the death of the 3rd Lord Herries, when they were divided between his three daughters. Two portions were later granted by the crown to John Hamilton, son of the Duke of Chatelherault,[13] while the third portion was retained by the eldest daughter, Agnes, and her husband, John, Master of Maxwell.[14] Then, in 1561, Hamilton sold his share in the £20 lands of Lockerbie to John Maxwell, now of Terregles (later 4th Lord Herries of Terregles).[15] Half a century later, in 1613, the lands were apprized from the 6th Lord Herries for debt and granted with other lands in Annandale to Thomas Johnston of Castlemilk as security;[16] and in 1629 the crown granted these lands in special warrant, under reversion, to James Johnston of that Ilk.[17] Four years later, on the resignation of Lord Herries, the lands were incorporated into the barony of Hutton and granted to Sir Richard Murray of Cockpool.[18] After the Restoration, the lands of Lockerbie were included in the vast estates that were erected into the Earldom of Annandale and Hartfell and granted to James, Earl of Annandale, in 1662.[19]

In the meantime, a cadet branch of the Johnstons of that Ilk had become feuars of the lands, and it was evidently they who built Lockerbie Tower – later known as 'The Mains' or 'Mains Tower' –, probably around the middle of the 16th century. There is a reference to the Johnstons of Lockerbie in 1534,[20] and in 1548 Cuthbert Johnston of Lockerbie was cited to be tried for treason.[21] The site chosen for their stronghold was a narrow ridge of land between, and almost surrounded by, two lochs that have since been drained. On the east side was the Flosh Loch and to the west the Quaas Loch. A close kinsman of Cuthbert Johnston built another tower just a quarter of a mile further south, at Nether Place, and several other Johnston towers are later recorded in the same vicinity.[22]

The **TOWER** was oblong in plan, and measured 25ft from E to W by 20ft from N to S over walls which measured about 3ft 2in in thickness.[23] The masonry was local whinstone rubble, with rounded corners, similar to those at Lochhouse. But by the time the tower was finally demolished in 1967, it had been so altered that little original work survived, apart from the lowest two storeys of the outer walls and two vaulted chambers in the basement. Nothing was left of any stair, and the dressings of the doorways and windows, the crow-stepped gables and the roof were all modern.

The entrance was at the S end of the W wall, where it admitted to a small lobby. This is where any stair would presumably have been located, but by 1868 there was no trace of a stair, and it is hard to see how one could have been accommodated. It is possible, therefore, that there was a separate entrance to the first floor, with no more than a hatch between the two, if there was any internal communication at all. From the lobby, a door on the N side admitted to a small vaulted chamber in the NW corner, while a door at the end gave access to a large vaulted chamber which occupied the whole of the E half of the basement. The two vaults ran at right angles to one another. Some time after 1868 another entrance was inserted on the S side of the lobby.[24]

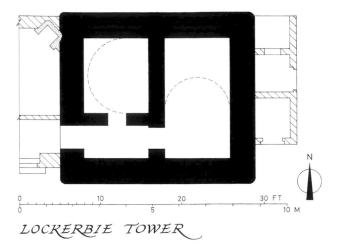

LOCKERBIE TOWER

Fig. 291 Lockerbie Tower: plan of basement
in 1868 (after Alexander Fraser, architect).

Nothing is known about the first floor, except that at the time the tower was demolished there were two windows with modern surrounds on the S side.

Immediately above the W entrance, at first floor level, there were four, large, 3-stage corbels, which appeared to have been later insertions. Their purpose in that position is not known.

During the closing decades of the 16th century, the Johnstons of Lockerbie were very much involved in the clan's increasing feud with the Maxwells, and twice this led to their towers being besieged or threatened. Following a raid by the Johnstons on Nithsdale early in May 1585, John Lord Maxwell, Earl of Morton, marched against the lands of the Johnstons and their allies. After a sortie in Lower Annandale, he moved north to Lockerbie. Lord Scrope, the English Warden, recorded the proceedings as they unfolded: 'the said Erle ... and his said forcies have comme to Lockerbye and beseiged two stone houses of two of the principalles of the Johnstons, wherein were certein persons which kept the same, and stoode at their defence and killed one of thErles gooniers; but in thend therle having woonne the said howses by force, dyd furthwith hang foure of them being Johnstons, over the walles of the said howses'.[25] Eight years later, in 1593, following further depredations by the Johnstons, Lord Maxwell, now Warden of the West March, was ordered to force obedience upon them.[26] Lord Scrope reported that 'the Lorde Maxwell with a great force of his frendes, did assemble them selves together, and assaye the dimolishing and casting downe of one Mongo Johnston his howse at Lockerbye'.[27] But before Maxwell could reach his objective, he was met by Johnston of that Ilk at Dryfesands, a short distance to the NW, and in the ensuing battle Maxwell was killed and his force routed. It was the last clan battle to be fought in the Borders. The tower was again mentioned in 1600, when, as part of measures to maintain order in the Borders, Lord Herries was ordered to reside either at Hoddom or Lockerbie.[28]

By the beginning of the 17th century, Mungo Johnston of Lockerbie was an old man 'outwith thre scoir yeris', who had at least three sons, William (known as 'The Constable'),[29] Francis and Archibald, the last a mere 'boy within xv yeir'.[30] Mungo must have died soon after. Another of the family who first appears around this time was Andrew Johnston of Lockerbie, whose relationship is not stated.[31] What is evident, however, from the continued use of the two names in the two branches of the fam-

ily, is that Andrew represented the branch of the family who lived at The Mains, while Mungo represented the branch who lived at Nether Place, both of whom were designated 'of Lockerbie'.[32] When, in 1508, a meeting was arranged between Sir James Johnston of that Ilk and Lord Maxwell to try and settle their differences, it was William Johnston of Lockerbie (Mungo's son) who was chosen to accompany Sir James.[33] The meeting had tragic results, as it ended with Sir James's murder. The following year, William was summoned to appear before the Privy Council concerning the murder.[34] William and his brother Archibald were put to the horn in 1615 for occupying certain lands, and they were still at the horn four years later,[35] but by 1623 William was free to serve as a juror.[36] Two years later, mention is made of a feud between the Johnstons of Lockerbie and the Maxwells of Castlemilk, the former being represented by Mungo, son of William Johnston, 'called of Lockerbie', and John, son of the 'late Francis Johnston of Lockerbie'.[37] Andrew Johnston of Lockerbie was appointed both a Commissioner of Supply and a Commissioner of War for Dumfriesshire in 1643,[38] and a Commissioner of War again the following year.[39] This may have been the same Andrew who was designated 'elder of Lockerbie' in 1663,[40] and who took the Test in 1683,[41] although there could have been another generation. What is certain is that it was Andrew Johnston of Lockerbie to whom parliament granted the right to hold two annual fairs and a weekly market in Lockerbie in 1672,[42] and Andrew Johnston, 'younger of Lockerbie', who was appointed a Commissioner of Supply for Nithsdale and Dumfries in 1689, and again in 1690.[43] It was also Andrew Johnston, 'younger of Lockerbie', who, in 1689, was appointed a Commissioner for ordering the militia in Dumfriesshire,[44] a post that required a man of some maturity. He died the following year, whereupon his widow, Margaret Johnston, who resided at 'the maynes', was infeft under the great seal in the £20 lands of Lockerbie and the £20 lands of Turnmuir and Mantuarig.[45] However, Andrew Johnston, 'elder of Lockerbie', was still alive, and, with his son James, did all in his power to frustrate Margaret's legal rights.[46] In 1696 the 'laird of Lockerbie' was again appointed a Commissioner of Supply,[47] but it is not clear who this was, as there is no mention of a son of Margaret and her husband, the younger Andrew.

The last laird to live in Mains Tower was William Johnston of Lockerbie, who died in 1772.[48] The tower was then abandonned as a residence, and subsequently fell into ruin. It was described as ruinous c.1831, when the ground floor's vaulted chambers were converted for use as the local prison.[49] The walls, however, were evidently still complete, for it was reported in 1856 that 'the entire walls of the original structure yet remain and now form the eastern portion of the county police station'.[50] At this time the tower was known as 'The Mains'.[51] Some time later the walls were reduced to two storeys and a new roof was built. The tower continued to be associated with the police station until 1967, when the site was cleared to make way for the present police station. Sadly, no one thought to make measured drawings of the tower before it was demolished.

1   Bain I, No.105.

2   Fraser 1894, I, 3.

3   Gladstone, R. 'The Early Annandale Charters and their strange resting place', *TDGAS*, 3rd Ser., VI, 145-6, where the charter is reproduced.

4   Bain I, No.2666; Fraser 1894, I, 1 (the charter is reproduced facing page XXXI).

5   Simon Locard is said to have acquired the lands of Symington, or 'Simon's toun', early in the reign of William the Lion (Fraser 1885, II, 578). A Symon

Locard, son of Malcolm, who was either the same Simon or perhaps a grandson, confirmed the church of Symondeston to the abbey of Kelso c.1180 (Black
1946, 436). The barony of Symington subsequently remained with the family until it was granted by Robert the Bruce to Thomas, son of Richard, early
in the 14th century (RMS I, No.78). Although it seems likely that Simon
Locard obtained the lands of Symington in exchange for, or in place of,
Lockerbie, no original charters for these properties have survived.

6   Complete Peerage VI, 468.
7   Bain II, No.1899.
8   Complete Peerage IX, 168.
9   Ibid IV, 508-9.
10   Ibid, 435.
11   Ibid I, 80.
12   RMS II, No.1654.
13   RMS IV, Nos.562, 695.
14   Ibid, No.405.
15   Ibid, No.1393.
16   RMS VII, No.827.
17   RMS VIII, No.1459.
18   Ibid, No.2121.
19   RMS XI, No.230.
20   Henderson, T 'Lockerbie Tower', TDGAS, 3rd Ser., XIV, 180.
21   APS XI, 480.
22   Stat Acct, IX, 424.
23   The details are largely taken from RCAHMS 1920, No.111, drawings by Al-
     exander Fraser, architect, in 1868, and photographs in the National Monu-
     ments Record. Fraser scaled the walls' thickness at 3ft 2in, while the RCAHMS
     report states it was 3ft 9in at the W entrance.
24   Further alterations were carried out to the police station and tower in 1881
     and 1903 (Wolffe, A. 'James Barbour', TDGAS, 3rd Ser., LXXI, 158, and
     archives of Sutherland, Dickie and Copland, architects).
25   Border Papers I, No.312.
26   Fraser 1873, I, 289.
27   Border Papers I, No.918.
28   Fraser 1894, I, cxxxix.
29   Hope-Johnstone MSS, 37 (No.78).
30   RPC VI, 115, 842.
31   Ibid VII, 639.
32   Among the heretors in Annandale in 1684 were Andrew Johnston of Lockerbie
     and Mungo Johnston of Netherplace (RPC, 3rd Ser., IX, 628).
33   RPC VIII, 70n.
34   Ibid, 300.
35   Ibid, XII, 70.
36   Ibid, XIV, 709.
37   Ibid, 2nd Ser., I, 108, 129.
38   APS VI, Part I, 29, 53.
39   Ibid, 199.
40   RPC, 3rd Ser., I, 448.
41   Ibid, VIII, 640. There was also an Andrew Johnston at Nether Place at this
     time.
42   Ibid, Appendix, 23.
43   APS IX, 70, 139.
44   Ibid, 28.
45   RPC, 3rd Ser., XV, 230.
46   Ibid, 368.
47   APS X, 29.
48   Henderson, 'Lockerbie Tower', op. cit., 180. One of William's daughters
     married Sir William Douglas of Kelhead and built Lockerbie House some
     time before 1812.
49   RCAHMS 1996, 214, No.101.
50   O.S.Name Books, Parish of Dryfesdale, 92.
51   Ibid.

50.   TOWER OF LUN, or CORRIE
(3¹/₂m E Lockerbie)   (NY197824)

The Corrie family first appears in Annandale late in the
12th century, when they settled on the lands from which they
took their name.[1] Their principal residence was the castle of
Corrie, a motte-and-bailey stronghold which is believed to have
stood on the site now occupied by the remains of the later Tower
of Lun.[2] Indeed, it is suggested that the earthworks upon which
the ruins stand are not natural, but the levelled base of the original motte.

The earliest identifiable member of the family was Hugh
de Corri, who witnessed a number of Bruce charters
c.1190-1218.[3] He was later succeeded by Walter de Corri, probably a son or grandson, who married Agnes de Levington; and it
was through Agnes that Walter's son and heir, Sir Walter de Corri,
eventually came into possession of some of the Levingtons' extensive estates in Cumbria.[4] For a while in 1291, and again in
1292, Sir Walter was governor of the castles of Dumfries,
Kirkcudbright and Wigtown.[5] Sir Walter died in 1303, and was
suceeded by his son, also Sir Walter, who took the Scottish side
in the War of Independence.[6] For this he eventually forfeited his
English estates.[7] Later, his Scottish estates were divided between his son and heir, John Corrie of that Ilk, and Robert Corrie
of Newbie, who is thought to have been another son.[8]

The Corries of that Ilk remained an important and powerful family in the West March until 1484, when, having sided
with the Douglases in their rebellion, they too forfeit all their
lands.[9] The lands of Corrie, together with the patronage of the
church of St. Mary of Corry, were then granted to Thomas
Carruthers, a younger son of the laird of Holmains, for his part
in putting down the rebellion;[10] but whether he ever got possession is not clear, as George Corrie was still designated 'lord of
the whole tenement of Corri' in 1498[11] and 'lord of Corri' in
1506 and 1509.[12] The lands were briefly in the possession of
Lord Maxwell – having been apprised to the King[13] –, upon whose
resignation in 1516 the '40 shilling lands of Lund' were granted
to James Johnston of that Ilk,[14] who bestowed them on his second son, Adam.[15] There is a tradition that the Bells of
Blackethouse burned the tower of Lun about this time.[16] It is
likely, therefore, that the present tower was built by the Johnstons
soon afterwards to replace it.[17] On the death of Adam in 1544,
the Crown granted the ward of 'all the lands of Corre, with the
maner-place', together with the gift of marriage of Adam's son
and heir, James, to Adam's eldest brother, John Johnston of that
Ilk, until James should succeed to his inheritance.[18] James, however, must have had other ideas about his marriage, for in 1550
he was granted a respite for having married in England without
the Crown's permission.[19] In 1565 James Johnston 'of Corre',
together with Johnston of that Ilk and certain other lairds, bound
himself to 'trewlie serve the King and Quenis Majesteis our
Soveranis', and whosoever their Highnesses should appoint as
Lieutenant or Warden, to pursue rebels or defend the country
against invasion by England.[20]

Whereas the majority of towers are found on naturally
strong sites, with a commanding view of the neighbouring countryside, the site of Corrie and Lun is very different. It is at the
bottom of a steep-sided, secluded valley, in a bend of the Water
of Milk, which for most of the year can hardly be described as
more than a large stream, and it has no prospect. Its sole strength
lay in its ramparts and walls, of which very little now remains.

The **TOWER** was oblong in plan, with the long axis
running from N to S; but without excavation its overall size cannot be determined. The masonry is local rubble. By 1793 it was
very ruinous, although part of the walls were 'still of a considerable height',[21] and in 1894 part of the S gable was still some 30ft
high.[22] When the RCAHMS visited it in 1912, this fragment of
wall was 25ft high, 20ft long and 3ft 8in thick; it also showed a
'trace of vaulting interiorly'.[23] By 1934 this had collapsed, and
now only a heap of rubble survives, about 6ft high, with no more
than a fragment of the S wall face, with part of a ventilation-slit
or slit-window, visible. About 35ft E of the tower, and following the edge of an earth bank, may be seen the foundations of

Fig. 292 Tower of Lun: view of remains from S.

Fig. 293 MacLellan's Castle: view from the NW in 1790.

the E side of the barmkin wall. This terminated at its S end in a round tower, very approximately 12ft in diameter, before turning W to follow another earth bank.

'Ye tower of ye Lunne: Corries house' is shown on Aglionby's Platte of 1590.[24] The Johnstons of Corrie continued to live here until 1623, when George Johnston resigned his rights in the property to Sir James Johnston of that Ilk in exchange for the lands of Girthhead,[25] to which he removed.[26] It was probably at this time that the tower was abandonned, at least as a laird's house, and it soon fell into disrepair.

1   Fraser 1894, I, cccxli.
2   Reid, R.C. 'Corrie Castle', *TDGAS*, 3rd Ser., XVIII, 385ff.
3   Buccleuch MSS, 38 (No.66), 39 (No.67), 40 (Nos.68-9).
4   Johnston, C 'The Early History of the Corries of Annandale', *TDGAS*, 3rd Ser., I, 87-8.
5   McDowall 1986, 51-3.
6   Johnston, C., *op. cit.*, 88.
7   Ibid, 89.
8   Ibid, 90.
9   RCAHMS 1920, xxviii; Reid, R.C. 'The Bonshaw Titles', *TDGAS*, 3rd Ser., XXXVII, 48.
10 RMS II, No.1590; Carruthers 1934, 81.
11 Buccleuch MSS, 58 (No.113).
12 Johnston, C., *op. cit.*, 93.
13 Ibid.
14 RMS III, 99.
15 Fraser 1894, xxx.
16 Ibid, cccxli.
17 It was the same Adam Johnston of Corrie who built Cornal Tower (q.v.).
18 RSS III, No.925.
19 RSS IV, No.723.
20 RPC I, 378.
21 Stat Acct XIII, 578.
22 Fraser 1894, I, cccxli.
23 RCAHMS 1920, No.288.
24 Hyslop, 320.
25 6m SSE Beattock.
26 Fraser 1894, xxxi.

51.   MACLELLAN'S CASTLE
   (Kirkcudbright)   (NX683511)

One of the earliest references to the MacLellans is in 1304/5, when Patrick, son of Gilbert McLolan, was one of those who took the castle of Dumfries from Robert the Bruce's men;[1] and there are further references to Gilbert, son of Gilbert,[2] and other members of the family in Galloway later in the century.[3] If they were not already settled near Kirkcudbright at that time,[4] they were certainly there early in the following century. John

MacLellan was one of the custumars for the burgh and port of Kirkcudbright in 1434,[5] and William MacLellan of Bombie was Provost of the burgh in 1466.[6] Bombie was an early stronghold, situated just 1½ miles ESE of Kirkcudbright,[7] and, whether by family seniority or pre-eminence in local affairs, it was the MacLellans of Bombie who came to be recognized as the senior branch of the family.

The MacLellans of Bombie continued to be active in the affairs of the burgh of Kirkcudbright, and in 1565 Sir Thomas MacLellan of Bombie was elected Provost.[8] Four years later, on 6 December, Sir Thomas received from the Regent Moray a grant of 'all and whole the site, foundation and place, upon which the place and church of the Friars of Kirkcudbright were originally constructed and built, together with all the remaining stones, with the orchards, gardens and pendicles.'[9] This was the site of the old Friary, which is believed to have been originally founded by James II *c.*1455,[10] and which had been destroyed by the populace at the time of the Reformation. Sir Thomas subsequently sold the Greyfriars church to the town to serve as the parish church,[11] whilst keeping the major part of the site for his future town-house, the present castle, and using the stones from the conventual buildings for its construction.

MacLellan's Castle stands on the left bank of the river Dee, some 500 yards upstream from the old royal castle of Kirkcudbright[12] and close to the centre of the town. When the castle was built, the ground immediately to the E of the site used to be flooded at high tide.[13] However, as defence was not a primary concern, the site was chosen more for pomp and show within the burgh itself than for any strategic reasons. There must, nevertheless, have been an enclosing wall, and Grose mentions the former existence of a 'handsome gate'.[14] Building work started early in 1581, and the main structural work was evidently completed the following year, the date appearing on the heraldic stone, though it has always been asserted that the upper floors, although roofed, were never completely finished.[15] Sir Thomas's first wife, Helen Gordon, died in June 1581, while the work was in progress, and from the evidence of her testament one learns the names of the masons and the outstanding payments due[16]:-

   To Robert Couper, mason, in Kirkcudbright, and Alexander Couper, his brother, masons there, 'for the work and labour in biging the hous in Kirkcudbright for the space of five months up to the lady's decease' £1000
   To John Williamsone in Nynbellie for lime and lime stanes .... 300 merks

Fig. 294 MacLellan's Castle: view from SE.

To Adam Merschell there and John Merschell there for the
    same .... 400 merks
To John Law, Archibald Law and Mathew Law,
    brothers, for carrying the white stanes, free stanes and
    timber .... 400 merks

The **CASTLE** is built on an extended L–plan, with the
almost unique feature of a double projection in the re-entrant
angle, where the entrance is situated, and a projecting, rectangular corner-tower at the SE angle. The main block measures 72ft
8in from E to W by 28ft 4in from N to S, over walls varying in
thickness from 4ft 4in to 5ft 9in, and comprises three storeys
and a garret with corbelled-out turrets at the NW and SW corners, while the wing, which is 25ft 6in wide, extends for 42ft 8in
at the E end of the N wall. The wing also has three storeys and
a garret, with matching turrets at the NE and NW corners; but
the SE tower, which measures 21ft 4in from N to S by 31ft 6in
from E to W, is one storey higher and terminated in an even
higher cap-house, now ruinous, near its SW corner. This tower
projects beyond the main building on both the adjacent sides,
and has a service entrance in the SW re-entrant angle thus formed.
The projections in the main re-entrant angle were used to accommodate the main stair to the first floor, one of the service
stairs, the passage connecting the cellars in the main block and
additional accommodation on the upper floors, before terminating in a short parapet over the main entrance. In the garden,
near the entrance, there is a fine, stone-lined well.

The castle's masonry is greywacke and coarse gritstone
rubble, with quoins and mouldings of coarse gritstone. The
moulding around the main entrance doorway is an embellished
form of QER, while the moulding used for all the principal fire
surrounds is of the QERH form. Above the entrance there is a
magnificent armorial panel with an elaborate Renaissance surround and open-bed pediment on top, and echoing this there is
another elaborate surround, with nail-head moulding and similar pediment, around the adjacent window in the wing.[17] The
armorial panel, which is now badly weathered, contains a large
upper panel above two smaller panels. The upper panel has a
border of thistles and roses on either side of what was probably
the royal coat of arms, while the lower panels bear, on the left,

the armorial bearings of Sir Thomas MacLellan[18] and, on the
right, the arms of Sir John Maxwell, 4th Lord Herries.[19] Above
the last shield are the initials 'G M', for Grissell Maxwell, and
the date 1582, and below it the motto 'DONS (DOMINUS)
DEDIT', under which on a separate panel is the additional inscription 'THE HOWS OF HERR[EI]S'. It was Sir John's
daughter, Grissell, who became Sir Thomas MacLellan's second wife in 1582, although the formal contract was not in fact
drawn up until she came of age two years later.[20]

Immediately inside the main entrance a straight stair, 4ft
11in wide, leads up to the first floor. At the foot of the stair, a
gun-loop on the left covers the wing, while a doorway on the
right admits to a passage serving the cellars in the main block.
There are three of these cellars, all of which are vaulted. The E
cellar has an open-aumbry in its N wall, and the middle one a
gun-loop under the sill of its window in the S wall. The one at
the W end, which had a lower floor, is said to have been an ice-
house, but this attribution is questionable, as there are two gun-
loops in the NW corner and an open-aumbry in the N wall, all of
which would have been inaccessible if the chamber had contained ice. Where the main passage connects to this chamber,
via a short dog-legged passage, a wheel-stair starts 5ft above the
floor and rises to serve the upper floors. This cannot be the
original arrangement, and can only be explained as a later alteration.[21] A small window on the N side of the passage overlooks the entrance, which is also covered by a gun-loop in the
wing. At its E end, this passage joins another passage connecting the wing with the SE corner tower. Where the two passages
meet, the N corner is partly cut away and then supported by a
corner pillar, whose purpose has never been satisfactorily explained.

The wing contains the vaulted kitchen. It has a huge
fireplace at the N end, with a hearth 14ft wide, a domed oven in
its left jamb and a small window high up on the right. In front of
it, to support the chimney above, there is a great arch of finely
cut voussoirs 12ft 4in wide. The kitchen itself has the usual
slop-sink in the E wall and a window and the gun-loop already
referred to in the W wall, while on the S side there is an open-
aumbry and, adjacent to the doorway, a service hatch.

MACLELLAN'S
CASTLE
~ BASEMENT

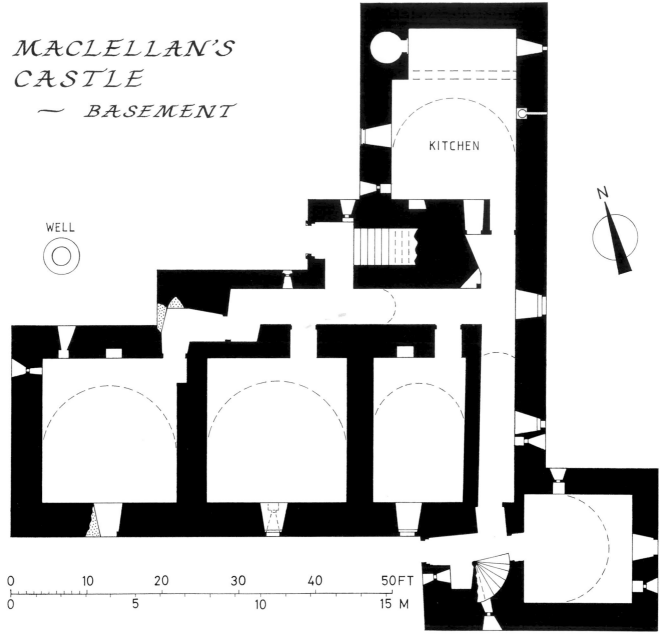

WELL

KITCHEN

N

0   10   20   30   40   50FT
0   5   10   15 M

Fig. 295 MacLellan's Castle, Kirkcudbright: plan of basement.

The SE corner tower has a single chamber on each floor. The lowest one is vaulted and has gun-loops on the N and E sides, while each of the upper floors is provided with a fireplace and a close-garderobe. These rooms are all served by a wheel-stair, which rises from the service entrance in the SW re-entrant angle, and which also connects with the basement passage and, on the upper floors, the adjacent rooms of the main block. At the foot of the stair, there is a small recess with a gun-loop to cover the service entrance, and a few steps up there is another gun-loop covering the tower's S side.

The principal chamber on the first floor is the great hall, which occupies the E end of the main block; it measures 42ft 6in by 19ft. It has a vast fireplace, 10ft 7in wide, with a single massive lintel in the middle of the N wall, and large windows on the N, E and S sides. Like all the other fireplaces on this floor, the surround carries a QERH moulding. In the back of the fireplace there is a small rectangular aperture, which connects with a small

room, or 'laird's lug', contained within the thickness of the wall behind. This room is reached from the spacious landing, or entrance hall, at the top of the stairs. Beyond the great hall, at the W end of the main block, there is a smaller hall for the private use of the family. This is provided with a fireplace in the W wall and windows in the N and S walls. A salt box in the right jamb of the fireplace has a rebate for a second door, which was reached from a recess in the NW corner of the room; but this was later filled in. It has now been partly re-opened to reveal the original arrangement. Leading off the left jamb of the S window, there is a small close-garderobe contained within the thickness of the wall. As well as connecting directly with the great hall, this chamber could also be reached from the service stair in its NE corner. It is a feature of the overall design of this castle that all the upper rooms could be reached, either directly from one of the three wheel-stairs, or from the adjoining room, thus dispensing with the need for passages.

Fig. 296 MacLellan's Castle: kitchen fireplace.

The first floor of the wing was a private family room, perhaps a bedroom. Apart from having a fireplace in the W wall, it would also have been heated by the huge kitchen chimney passing up just behind the N wall. It was provided with windows in the E and W walls. Two small closets lead off from the NE and NW corners. The former was probably a close-garderobe, but the purpose of the other, which is provided with small windows in both its N and W walls, can only be surmised.

Across the passage from the head of the main stair, there is a wheel-stair, partly corbelled-out from the wall below, which continues the ascent to the upper floors. It leads to a room in the wing that is very similar to the one below, including the two closets, and to a larger room above the main staircase and landing. The latter room is provided with a small fireplace in its S wall, windows in the E and W walls, and a small closet in the SW corner, above the 'laird's lug'. At the W end of the room, there is also a slit-window, which overlooks the wing, and above

MACLELLAN'S
CASTLE
~ FIRST FLOOR

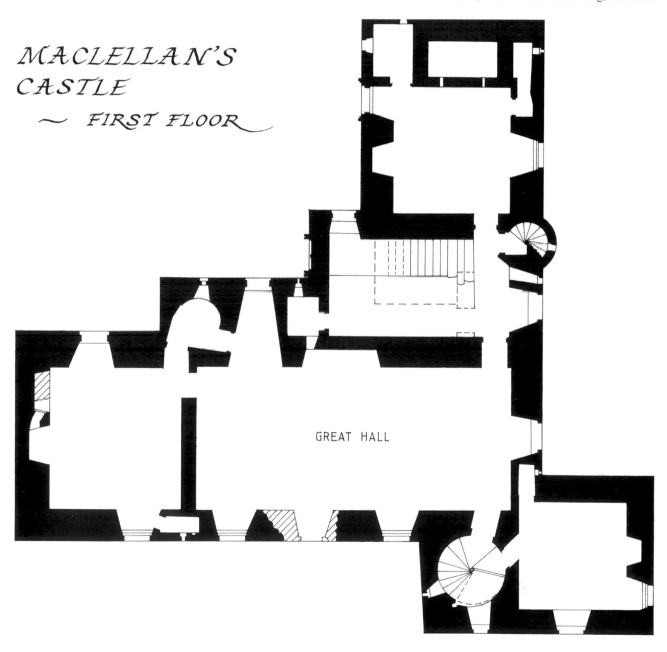

GREAT HALL

Fig. 297 MacLellan's Castle, Kirkcudbright: plan of first floor.

Fig. 298 MacLellan's Castle: N wing.

this a section of barrel-vaulting that supports the doorways and floors of the two 'chambers' above.[22] From this room a doorway leads into a large upper hall or withdrawing room over the great hall, and of similar proportions. But despite the size of this chamber, the only means of heating it was a relatively small fireplace in the S wall and any benefit it could derive from the chimney rising up the opposite wall from the hall below. The lintel of this fireplace comprises a flat arch of six joggled stones, while the surround carries a QERH moulding. This room has windows on the N, E and S sides, that on the N side having an especially deep embrasure, some 12ft deep overall, with stone seats on either side. To the W of this chamber, there is a smaller room with a fireplace in its W wall and windows in the N, S and W walls. Like the room below, it has a small close-garderobe within the wall in the SE corner, though this one is entered directly from the room, instead of from the window recess.

The third floor is incomplete, but it was generally similar in layout to the floor below, except that, apart from the SE tower, which is a storey higher, it was partly contained within the roof and thus had dormer windows. The largest room, over the withdrawing room, had a small fireplace in the S wall and windows in the N, E and S sides, that on the N side again having an especially deep embrasure. To the W of this was a smaller chamber, with a fireplace in the W wall and windows on the N and S sides. On either side of the fireplace there is a doorway, which admits to the turrets in the NW and SW corners. These turrets are corbelled-out with the embellished corbelling typical

of the period, and each is provided with one small window and shot-holes angled down to cover the adjacent walls. There is a similar room in the wing, which has a fireplace in the S wall and windows in the E and W walls, while small recesses in the NE and NW corners lead to doorways admitting to the NE and NW corner turrets. These turrets are similar to those already described. Between this chamber and the larger room in the main block, there is another room, which has a small fireplace in its S wall and a single window in its E wall. Leading off this room at the W end, there are two doorways which admitted to a small closet in the SW corner and the small 'parapet walk' over the entrance. Both these features are now largely ruinous.[23]

Fig. 299 MacLellan's Castle: view from the south in 1789.

The fourth floor of the SE tower is also partly ruinous. The main wheel-stair in this corner appears to have stopped at the third floor, while a smaller wheel-stair, partially corbelled-out from the S wall, continued the ascent to the garret on the fourth floor and the small cap-house, or look-out turret, near the SW corner. The fourth floor has a small fireplace in its N wall, and had one window in the E gable and a dormer on the the S side. Above this level, only a small part of the turret now survives, on its E side, though rather more was shown by Grose in 1789.[24]

In 1580 Sir Thomas MacLellan was appointed a Gentleman of the King's Chamber.[25] Then in 1591/2 he received a crown charter of various church lands, which were to be held of the Commendator of the Priory of St. Mary's Isle and of the Commendator of Dundrennan; and at the same time, as he and his predecessors had for many years been bailies of the lands and barony of Kirkcryst,[26] which had now come into the hands of the King from the bishopric of Galloway, the King appointed Thomas and his heirs hereditary justiciars and bailies of the said lands and barony, with the power to hold 'wapenshawings'.[27] Five years later, just before he died, Sir Thomas handed over his estates to his eldest son, Robert, whilst reserving the liferent for himself.[28] He died in 1597.

Shortly after receiving his father's estates, Sir Robert was granted a charter of novodamus of the £10 lands of Bombie, the castle and manor lately built by Sir Thomas in the burgh of Kirkcudbright, and many other lands, all of which were now incorporated in the free barony of Bombie.[29] Sir Robert was elected Provost of Kirkcudbright in 1607,[30] and in 1621 he represented Wigtownshire in parliament.[31] Two years later he was appointed a Justice of the Peace for Kirkcudbright and Wigtown,[32] and in 1625 and 1626 a Commissioner for the Middle Shires.[33] He was also a Gentleman of the Bedchamber to both James VI and Charles I.[34] By this time, however, his wild early life and subsequent extravagance had left him in financial difficulties, and in both 1624 and again in 1625 he had to wadset his estates,[35] while a further wadset was arranged with his former enemy, Gordon of Lochinvar, in 1631.[36]

Sir Robert had been one of the leading Scottish proponents for the Plantation of Ulster, having been granted lands in Donegal as early as 1610.[37] He sold these six years later, and leased lands in County Londonderry, while he himself settled in County Down.[38] He also acquired the castle at Ballycastle in County Antrim.[39] In 1625 he was given a commission to raise forces for His Majesty's service in Ireland,[40] and by 1628 he was reported to have been living in Ireland 'this long tyme bygane'.[41] It is believed to have been for services rendered in that country that he was made a baronet c.1631,[42] and raised to the peerage as Lord Kirkcudbright in 1633.[43] He died in 1638/39, when he was succeeded by his nephew, Thomas MacLellan of Glenshinnoch.[44]

Thomas, 2nd Lord Kirkcudbright, was an active supporter of the Covenanters, serving under General Leslie at Duns Law in 1639 and later in England as Colonel of the South Regiment of Cavalry.[45] As a lord, he attended parliament regularly from 1639 until shortly before his death.[46] In 1643, and again in 1645, he was appointed a Commissioner of War for the Stewartry of Kirkcudbright,[47] and he was also on the committee for the defence of the true Protestant religion in 1643,[48] and on the commission to the Committee of Estates two years later.[49] In 1644 he was appointed Steward of the Stewartry of Kirkcudbright.[50] The following year he fought at Philiphaugh, where he commanded a regiment raised in Galloway at his own expense.[51] Thomas recovered many of his uncle's mortgaged lands, and in 1642 was granted a new crown charter of these lands, including the lands and barony of Bombie and the castle and manor-place built by Sir Thomas MacLellan in the burgh of Kirkcudbright, all of which were now incorporated in the free barony and lordship of Kirkcudbright.[52] Thomas died in Ireland in 1647, when he was succeeded by his cousin, John, son of John MacLellan of Borgue, who became 3rd Lord Kirkcudbright.[53]

Like his predecessor, the 3rd Lord Kirkcudbright was a zealous Presbyterian, but he was also a strong supporter of the Crown. He attended parliament regularly from 1648 to 1650,[54] and again, after the Restoration, in 1661.[55] He was a Commissioner of War for the Stewartry of Kirkcudbright in 1648 and 1649,[56] and in the latter year was appointed Colonel of Foot for Wigtownshire and Kirkcudbright.[57] Later that year he served in Ulster.[58] It was also in 1649 that he was appointed to the Committee for the Common Burthens and the Commission for the Plantation of Kirks. The following year he bore Charles II's train at his coronation.[59] His loyalty, however, cost him dearly. In 1653 the barony of Kirkcudbright was apprised for debt,[60] and further wadsets followed in the ensuing years.[61] The year after the Restoration, Lord Kirkcudbright was appointed a Commissioner of Supply for the Stewartry,[62] and two years later he was made a Justice of the Peace. In 1663 he opposed the introduction of an Episcopalian minister in Kirkcudbright, which led to rioting and his subsequent imprisonment and a fine in Edinburgh.[63] He died in 1665, and was succeeded by his only surviving son, William, who was still a minor.

After the death of Lord Kirkcudbright, his estate was seized by creditors, from whom it was obtained first by one George Henderson, and then by Sir David Dunbar of Baldoon,

who permitted 'the goods, geir, plenishings and prices' to be retained by Lady Kirkcudbright for the benefit of her son.[64] The young Lord Kirkcudbright, however, died only three years after his father.

MacLellan's Castle subsequently passed into the possession of the Maxwells of Orchardton,[65] while the peerage passed to another branch of the family.[66] In 1752, Sir Thomas Maxwell, 6th Baronet of Orchardton, took the roof off, and stripped the castle of its contents.[67] It has lain empty ever since. Then, in 1782, his cousin, Sir Robert Maxwell, 7th Baronet, sold the ruin to the Earl of Selkirk,[68] whose family had acquired the adjacent estate of St. Mary's Isle, and it has remained with his descendants ever since. In 1912 the Guardianship of the building was entrusted to the State by Sir Charles Hope-Dunbar, 6th Baronet.[69]

---

1   Bain IV, 389.
2   The Gilbert who was a witness to letters of Simon, Bishop of Whithorn, in 1347 (Scots Peerage V, 256) may have been the son of the Gilbert Maclelan of Galloway who was elected Bishop of Man and the Isles c.1321 and died c.1327 (Brit. Chron., 294; M'Kerlie IV, 194).
3   Scots Peerage V, 256.
4   There is said to have been a 'MacClellan of Bondeby' who received a grant of land from the monks of New Abbey in 1135 (Torrance, 2), but the 'New Abbey' was not founded until c.1270.
5   ERS IV, 606.
6   Scots Peerage V, 258.
7   It is not certain exactly where the Maclellans' caput was situated, as there are two possible sites at Bombie, one of which supported an early timber castle, while the other, a short distance to the SW, was occupied by a later moated manor. It may be that by the early 16th century they had moved to nearby Loch Fergus, an ancient stronghold of the Lords of Galloway, where the MacLellans also had a stronghold. In a sasine of their lands in 1548, it is only the 'fortalice' at Loch Fergus that is mentioned (Torrance, 123).
8   ERS XIX, 300.
9   Grose II, 20.
10 Easson 1957, 107.
11 NSA IV, 21.
12 Sir Thomas also purchased the lands of Castledykes, where the royal castle had stood, in 1577. It is believed that the principal reason for this was so that he could have the masonry from the ruins to provide additional building material.
13 RCAHMS 1914, No.218.
14 Grose II, 20.
15 MacGibbon & Ross I, 153.
16 Reid, R. C. 'The Building Date of M'Clellan's Castle', TDGAS, 3rd Ser., XXX, 196-7. Reid suggests that she may have supervised the work while her husband was absent in France during that summer, just as Grierson of Lag's wife supervised the building of Rockhall (q.v.).
17 See MacGibbon & Ross II, 154.
18 Or, two chevronels sable. The crest is a naked arm supporting on the point of a sword a man's head; the Motto, 'Think On'; and the supporters, dexter, a man armed at all points holding a baton, and, sinister, a horse furnished.
19 Quarterly: 1st and 3rd, argent a saltire sable, with a label of three points in chief gules (for Maxwell); 2nd and 3rd, argent, three urcheons sable (for Herries). See Fraser 1878, I, 515, and Nisbet, I, 343.
20 As Grissell Maxwell was not yet 14 years of age in May 1582 (Fraser 1873, II, 492), the formal marriage contract, which was ante nuptial, had to wait until January 1584/5, after she came of age (Reid, op. cit., 196-7). Grissel's father died in January 1582/3.
21 MacGibbon & Ross show a different arrangement at this point, but their plans of this castle are unreliable.
22 Presumably the vaulting was required because the northern 'chamber' was in fact a short, open, parapet walk subject to the vagaries of the weather.
23 They were little more complete in Grose's day (Grose II, 20, Pl.2).
24 Grose II, 19, Pl.1.
25 RPC III, 323.
26 These lands lay just across the river Dee from Kirkcudbright.
27 RMS V, No.2050.
28 RMS VI, No.566.
29 Ibid.
30 RPC VIII, 50.
31 Parl. of Scot., II, 446.
32 RPC XIII, 344.
33 RPC, 2nd Ser., I, 193, 373.

34 Complete Peerage VII, 333.
35 RMS VIII, Nos.660, 863. See also Scots Peerage V, pp.265-6.
36 RMS VIII, No.1775.
37 Scots Peerage V, 266.
38 Ibid; Bell 1988, 142.
39 Bell 1988, 142.
40 RPC, 2nd Ser., I, 196-7.
41 Ibid, II, 254.
42 Complete Peerage VII, 333.
43 Scots Peerage V, 267.
44 Ibid.
45 Ibid, 268.
46 APS V, *passim*; VI, Part I, *passim*.
47 Ibid, VI, Part I, 51, 559.
48 Ibid, 57.
49 Ibid, 380.
50 Ibid, 210.
51 Ibid, 687.
52 RMS IX, No.1049.
53 Scots Peerage V, 268.
54 APS VI, Part II, 3, 124, 377, 555.
55 Ibid, VII, 3.
56 Ibid, VI, Part II, 35, 493.
57 Ibid, 219, 598.
58 Scots Peerage V, 268.
59 Ibid.
60 RMS X, Nos.178
61 Ibid, Nos.274, 300, 380, 469.
62 RPC, 3rd Ser., V, 160; APS VII, 92.
63 Grose II, 20; NSA IV, 15.
64 Torrance, 140; Scots Peerage V, 269.
65 Grose II, 20; M'Kerlie IV, 168.
66 Scots Peerage V, 269.
67 M'Kerlie IV, 168.
68 Ibid, 169.
69 Archives of Historic Scotland.

Fig. 300 Mellingshaw Tower: stair wing.

52.   MELLINGSHAW TOWER
(3³/₄ m NW Moffat)   (NT037088)

The lands of Mellingshaw[1] are first mentioned at a justice-ayre in Dumfries in 1507/8, when, in satisfaction for a debt of £380 owing to the Crown, various lands, including 'the 5 merk lands of Graskin and Madingschaw' were apprised from Andrew, 2nd Lord Herries.[2] The following year, at the special request of 'our dearest cousin the Queen of France', whom Lord Herries was then visiting, James IV agreed to relieve Lord Herries of all his debts to the Crown.[3] It would appear, however, that Lord Herries soon incurred further debts, and again had the lands apprised, for only two years later, in return for 'great sums of money', the Crown sold the 4 (sic) merk lands of 'Greskyn and Malingschaw' under reversion to John, 3rd Lord Maxwell, who assigned them to his eldest son, Sir Robert Maxwell.[4] The lands were subsequently redeemed by Lord Herries, and in 1527/8 Archibald Johnston, son of Gavin Johnston of Elshieshields, sold the 5 merkland of 'Graskyne and Malynschaw . . . pertenand to my Lord Heres heritabill' to 'my cheyf', John Johnston of that Ilk.[5]

The relationship of the Johnstons of Mellingshaw is not known, but clearly they became a family of some consequence. In 1547 they pledged 65 men to the service of the English king;[6] and in the English military report prepared c.1563, Johne Johneston of Malingshaw is credited with having ten horsemen, which compares favourably with the Chief of the Jardines, who had nine, and the town of Lochmaben, which had twelve.[7] It was this family that built the present tower some time in the 16th century. It is said to have formed part of the estate of Blacklaw.[8] Situated on high ground on the W side of the Evan

valley, and defended by the Mellingshaw Burn and a lesser tributary on two sides, the tower had a commanding view down the valley towards Annandale.

All that remains of the **TOWER** is part of the stair wing. This contained the entrance on its N side, and extended east-

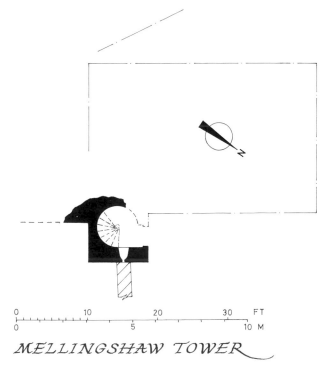

MELLINGSHAW TOWER

Fig. 301 Mellingshaw Tower:
site plan showing remains of stair tower.

wards from the main block for about 7ft. It is 8ft 6in wide. The masonry is local Silurian rubble with roughly dressed quoins, but the entrance doorway – of which only the E jamb survives – and two windows in the E wall have surrounds of dressed, red sandstone, with a plain chamfer on the arrises. The lower window is a mere slit, $4\frac{1}{2}$ in wide and 16in high, but the upper window, which measures 1ft $8\frac{1}{2}$ in wide by 2ft high, retains the sockets for an original iron grille. In the surviving jamb of the entrance doorway, there is a slot 4in square and 9in deep for fastening the drawbar. The wheel-stair, which was about 4ft 6in in diameter, was contained within walls that varied in thickness from 2ft on the S side to 2ft 4in on the E side and 2ft 8in at the entrance.

Without excavation it is impossible to be certain of the precise size or shape of the complete building. The position of the entrance and rubble remains suggest that the main block was about 20ft wide and extended northwards beyond the wing for about 24ft, such that the entrance was in the re-entrant angle of an L–plan tower-house.[9] There is, however, clear evidence of another re-entrant angle on the S side of the wing, only 5ft 9in from its SE corner, which would suggest that the tower did at some period have a T–plan, perhaps after the addition of a later wing or other structure at this point. There are also the remains of various outbuildings and enclosures, of indeterminate date, on the N, E and S sides of the building.[10]

In 1662 James Johnston, 1st Earl of Annandale, received a crown charter of the lands of Greskine and Mellingshaw, with many others, erecting the said lands into a free barony, etc., to be called the Earldom of Annandale and Hartfell;[11] and these lands remained part of the Johnston's Annandale Estates until they were sold c.1965.

---

1   It has been suggested that the name means 'Melville's Wood' (Johnson-Ferguson 1935, 99).
2   RSS I, No.1778; RMS II, No.3522.
3   RSS I, No.1778.
4   RMS II, No.3522; Fraser 1873, I, 166-7.
5   Fraser 1894, I, 16.
6   Armstrong 1883, lxxiv.
7   Ibid, cxiv.
8   RCAHMS 1997, 215.
9   Such a building would have measured approximately 27ft by 32ft 6in overall.
10 The walls of the enclosures are about 2ft 6in thick.
11 RMS XI, No.230.

---

53.   MOUSWALD CASTLE

(5$\frac{1}{2}$ m ESE Dumfries)   (NY062739)

The earliest reference to Mouswald is found c.1270, when Richard de Bancori quitclaimed to his lord Robert de Brus the whole land of Locherwood, with a certain common pasture in the fee of Comlongon, which the said Robert's men of 'Musfaud' (Mouswald) were wont to have from the granter in farm, for 1 merk yearly.[1] It next appears in 1303, in the accounts of James de Dalilegh, Edward I's escheator, where the rental for the provostry of 'Mosefald' is given as 3s. 6d., plus a supplementary payment of $13\frac{1}{2}$ qrs. of oatmeal.[2]

Then, c.1320, King Robert the Bruce granted the lands of 'Muswald' and 'Appiltretwayt' to 'Thomas the Clerk', son of John de Carutherys, for services rendered.[3] Thomas's son or heir, William de Carruthers 'of Mosswald', received a charter of

the lands of Middlebie from David II in 1351,[4] and ten years later John de Carrotheris, who is presumed to have been his son, received from the same king, personally at Mouswald, a charter of half the lands in the tenement of Mousfald that had formerly belonged to John de Rafhols.[5] These and other grants were subsequently confirmed by Archibald, Earl of Douglas, in a number of charters after he became Lord of Annandale. The first of these, dated 1411, re-granted to Simon de Carruthers, 4th of Mouswald, who is described as the Earl's 'esquire' or 'shield-bearer', 'his tenement of Mouswald and his lands of Appultrethwate'.[6] Then, in 1452, King James II gave John Carruthers, 6th of Mouswald, a new charter erecting all his lands into 'one free barony to be called the barony of Carutheris',[7] – no doubt partly in recognition of his services as Captain of Lochmaben Castle, an office he held from 1446 to 1454.

Sir Simon Carruthers, the 8th laird, had sasine of the lands of Mouswald, Logan-tenement, Rafflesgill, Hetlandhill, Middlebie, Dornock and others in 1492.[8] Six years later, he was tragically murdered in a local dispute, while his elder son, Simon, was still a minor.[9] After Simon came of age in, or shortly before, 1512, James IV granted him a new charter, 'for good service to the king', of 'the 20 merk lands of the dominical lands of Mouswald', with the mills of the same, and also the lands of Howthat, Hetlandhill, Dornock, Pennersax, Middlebie, Logan-tenement and West Scales.[10]

Simon Carruthers, 9th of Mouswald, was himself only about forty when he died, once again leaving a minor, his eldest son, Simon, 10th of Carruthers, to succeed under the guardianship of John Johnston of that Ilk.[11] This Simon received a new crown charter in 1544, erecting all his father's lands, and others, into the free barony of Mouswald, with an entailed succession.[12] By this time the family's estates were extensive, comprising the '£20 lands of old extent of Mouswald, Howthat and Hetlandhill, with the tower, fortalice, mills [and] advowson (patronage) of the church of Mouswald', the £20 lands of Logane tenement, Dornock, Cummertrees, Pennersax, Middlebie and West Scales, and a considerable number of lesser properties.[13] In 1547 'Simon Carrudders' pledged 71 men to the service of England,[14] but a year later he was tragically killed in a Border raid by the 'Thevis of the Marche'.[15]

Simon died without male issue, leaving two young daughters and co-heiresses, Janet and Marion, the ward and marriage of whom was now granted by Queen Mary to Sir James Douglas of Drumlanrig.[16] It was an arrangement that met with considerable opposition, the repercussions from which were to last for more than half a century. Lord Maxwell promptly took possession of 'the house and place of Mowswald', and refused to deliver them up to Sir James, while John Carruthers of Woodfoot, the next brother of Simon, raised an action to claim his rights under the entail. Eventually Drumlanrig agreed a financial settlement with Carruthers, and had the entail set aside;[17] but Maxwell refused to hand over Mouswald until he was ordered to do so by the Regent Arran and Privy Council nearly two years later.[18]

Janet was married in 1560, and in 1562/3 she assigned her half of the barony of Mouswald, with the tower and fortalice, to Drumlanrig.[19] At that time the property was in fairly poor shape following the recent English incursions; Drumlanrig described it as for 'the maist part . . . ewthir [be]reft and withhaldin fra him [her father] or laid waist'.[20] Finding a husband that met with Marion's approval proved much harder, and a long dispute between her and her guardian over the selected spouse ended with her tragic death at Comlongon Castle in 1570.[21] But for the

Fig. 302 Mouswald Tower: ruins viewed from the SW.

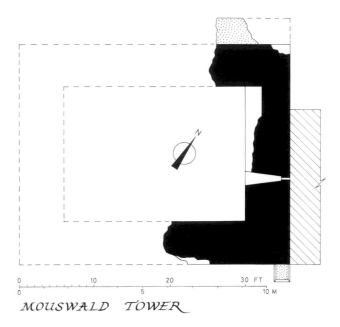

MOUSWALD TOWER

Fig. 303 Mouswald Tower: plan of basement,
showing remains of NE end.

fact that Marion had sold her half of the Mouswald estates to Charles Murray of Cockpool in 1564,[22] Janet would now have succeeded to her sister's share of the barony; but the crown now laid claim on the grounds that Marion had committed suicide,[23] and granted an escheat to Drumlanrig's only son, Sir William Douglas of Hawick.[24] He died two years later, so that when Sir James Douglas of Drumlanrig died in 1578, Mouswald passed to Sir James's grandson, also Sir James, 7th of Drumlanrig.[25] Earlier that year, Lord Herries had submitted his report to James VI and the Privy Council on the keeping of good order in the West March. This included the proposal that in times of trouble the laird of Drumlanrig should remain with an honest household either in Mouswald or Ros.[26]

The present tower at Mouswald is on record as having been 'reformit' by Sir James Douglas (d.1578), 6th of Drumlanrig, probably not long after 1562.[27] It stands on rising ground, close to the road from Annan to Dumfries and overlooking the vast expanse of Lochar Moss to the SW.

The **TOWER**, which was oblong in plan, measured 36ft from E to W by 29ft 1in from N to S over walls which are 5ft 8in thick at the sides and 6ft thick at the ends. It was evidently three storeys and a garret in height. When the RCAHMS published their report in 1920,[28] all but the N wall was still standing to a height of some 30ft, but since then the whole of the W end has been removed to permit an extension to the nearby house. All that now remains is the E wall and adjoining sections of the N and S walls, the two surviving corners having been buttressed early in the century. The masonry is Silurian rubble with dressed quoins and simple mouldings. The E wall has a slit window at basement level and a solitary stone, with QER moulding, remaining from the right jamb of a fireplace at second floor level. The centre section of the E wall has been partially restored at the higher levels. When the RCAHMS surveyed the ruins, the gun-loops were still in situ, but nothing of these now remains, though the base of the E wall is inaccessible. The basement was apparently not vaulted.

In 1588 Sir James Douglas, 7th of Drumlanrig, resigned all the lands of Carruthers, Mouswald and Logan-tenement into the king's hands, and in 1591/2 was granted a new charter of these lands under the Great Seal.[29] This was further ratified by parliament in 1594.[30] However, despite the escheat granted to

his father by James VI in 1570, there must have been grave doubts as to its legality and thus whether all the barony was his to resign, for in 1604 he ultimately purchased the other half from Janet for 'grete soumes of money'.[31] Three years later he was finally granted a crown charter of the second part of the barony in free tenantry.[32]

Because of the run-down state of the property after the English incursions of the 1540s and the subsequent conflicts over possession, Mouswald appears to have had only token occupation during much of the latter half of the 16th century. Yet Lord Maxwell clearly considered it worth taking in 1548, and Pont portrayed 'Mousel Cast.' as a substantial and important fortalice when he surveyed the area c.1595, some 30 years after the tower was rebuilt.[33] In 1596/7 Mouswald again came into prominence. At that time the feud between Lord Maxwell and Sir James Johnston of that Ilk was extremely bitter, and Maxwell had once again taken possession of Mouswald. Johnston had been made Warden of the West March in 1596, and it was apparently in support of his Warden that James VI demanded that Maxwell surrender the castles of Caerlaverock, Mouswald and Torthorwald. When Maxwell refused, James resolved to march there in person on the 20th March and, if necessary, lay siege.[34] Fourteen days later it was reported that the castles had been delivered to the king, and that Mouswald had been committed to the care of Drumlanrig.[35]

Sir James Douglas of Drumlanrig, having finally obtained the second half of the Mouswald estates in 1607, granted it in feu the following year to his second son, Sir James, 1st of Mouswald.[36] It was to held in free tenantry, to be called the Tenantry of Mouswald, which could be redeemed by Drumlanrig for 5 merks. A year later, Drumlanrig received a new charter under the Great Seal of the superiority of all his estates, including the £20 lands of Mouswald.[37] But once again there must have been a problem with the Mouswald titles, for in 1613 his eldest son, William, later 1st Earl of Queensberry, obtained a new charter of the superiority of the second half of the Mouswald estates, subject to a seven-year reversion in favour of Janet Carruthers.[38]

In 1627, Sir James Douglas of Mouswald granted his son, James, and James's espoused wife, Agnes Rome, the £20 land of Mouswald, Howthat and Hetlandhill, with the tower, fortalice and manor-place of Mouswald, together with the 20 shilling land of Raffles, whilst reserving various lands to himself in liferent.[39] Sir James was succeeded by his son James sometime before 1641, the year in which James, now 'of Mouswald', was given his first appointment, as a Commissioner for Keeping the Peace in the Borders.[40] Two years later, he was made a Commissioner of Supply[41] and a Commissioner of War for Dumfriesshire,[42] and a Commissioner for the Loan and Tax;[43] and the following year he was elected to parliament for the first time, being re-elected again in 1649.[44] He was also re-appointed to the Committee of War in 1644, 1645 and 1648.[45] He was Colonel of a regiment of foot in the Dumfries Militia in 1648,[46] and was Sheriff of Dumfries the following year.[47] Two years later, he was appointed to the Committee for revising Acts of the Committee of Estates.[48] His eldest son, James, having pre-deceased him without issue, he was succeeded, first c.1657 by his second son, William, and then, on William's death without issue in 1670, by his third son, John. Little is known about William, except that he was appointed a Justice of the Peace for Dumfriesshire in 1663.[49]

John Douglas, 4th of Mouswald, had sasine of Mouswald and his father's other estates in 1670, on precept from the Earl of Queensberry, the superior.[50] The estates were, however, by now heavily encumbered, and in 1674 he was compelled to resign all his lands in favour of the Earl, who was also the principal creditor.[51] John continued to live at Mouswald, but died without issue. He was succeeded by his niece Elizabeth, the daughter of his brother Robert, who obtained a decreet of adjudication in her favour in 1691.[52] The following year she was also served heir to her uncles George and Archibald, the other two brothers.[53] In 1695 the Earl of Queensberry granted Elizabeth and her three Douglas aunts, Nicolas, Jean and Agnes, a new charter and sasine of Mouswald;[54] but evidently none of them chose to reside there.

Mouswald was then abandonned and, with the permission of the Duke of Queensberry, 'stripped of its coping and corner stones'.[55] The Duke also let Grierson of Lag have the old entrance gateway, as Lag wanted it for his stables,[56] while a stone that once stood 'over the arch of the drawbridge gate' is built into the later house at Mouswald.[57] By the end of the 18th century the tower was a ruin.[58]

The present house on the site, Mouswald Place,[59] was built sometime in the middle of the 19th century, probably by Sir James Reid, formerly Chief Justice of the Ionian Islands, who acquired Mouswald around this time. He was succeeded by his second son, Sir Robert Reid, a distinguished lawyer and politician, who became member of parliament for Dumfries in 1886, being re-elected in 1895 and 1900.[60] He became successively Solicitor-General and Attorney-General in 1894, and in 1905 was raised to the peerage and made Lord Chancellor, taking the title Baron Loreburn of Dumfries.[61] In 1911 he was given an earldom, as Earl Loreburn of Dumfries, and the following year he retired to Dover, where he died in 1923.[62] He was twice married, but had no issue. By this time he had given up Mouswald, which in 1912 was occupied by Isabella, Lady Woodburn.[63]

1   Bain I, No.1684. See also Macquarrie, A. 'Notes on some Charters of the Bruces of Annandale, 1215-1295', TDGAS, 3rd Ser., LVIII, 74.
2   Bain II, No.1608.
3   RMS I, No.92. During the previous century Thomas's forebears had been stewards of Annandale under the Bruces.
4   Holmains MSS, 709.
5   Ibid, 709 (No.1).
6   Fraser 1885, III, 409-10.
7   Carruthers & Reid, 53.
8   ERS X, 764.
9   Carruthers & Reid, 62.
10 RSS I, No.2420.
11 Carruthers & Reid, 65.
12 RMS III, No.3041.
13 Carruthers & Reid, 66-7.
14 Armstrong 1883, lxxiv. At the Weapon-show held by Lord Maxwell at Burnswark in 1541, Carruthers of Mouswald attended with four score men.
15 Reid, J. J. 'The Barony of Mouswald and its Barons: A page of Border History', PSAS, New Ser., XI, 51.
16 RSS III, No.2904.
17 Carruthers & Reid, 68.
18 RPC I, 96.
19 RMS IV, No.1440.
20 Fraser 1894, I, XXX.
21 Carruthers & Reid, 70-2.
22 RMS IV, No.1537.
23 Despite the official account of what happened, there has always been a suspicion that Marion was in fact murdered (See Carruthers & Reid, 72).
24 Carruthers & Reid, 72; Maxwell 1902, II, 253-4.
25 See RSS VI, Nos.1914, 2365, 2733.
26 Fraser 1894, II, 485. Ros was another tower built by Sir James Douglas (Buccleuch MSS, 5).
27 Buccleuch MSS, 5.
28 RCAHMS 1920, No.515.
29 RMS V, No.2034.
30 APS IV.
31 Carruthers & Reid, 73.
32 RMS VI, No.1968.
33 Blaeu, 57, 'THE STEWARTRIE OF ANNANDAIL'. The tower is also shown on Aglionby's Platte of 1590, which shows the strongholds in the West March at that time.
34 Scottish Papers XII, No.390; Border Papers II, No.548.
35 Scottish Papers XII, No.405.
36 Carruthers & Reid, 73.
37 RMS VII, No.53
38 Ibid, No.911.
39 PRS Dumfries, II, f.233-6.
40 APS V, 685.
41 Ibid, VI, Part I, 29.
42 Ibid, 53.
43 Ibid.
44 Ibid, VI, Part I, 95; Part II, 124, 377.
45 Ibid, 200, 559; Part II, 32.
46 APS VI, Part II, 30, 219.
47 Parl. of Scot., I, 197.
48 Ibid, 643.
49 Ibid, VII, 505.
50 Reid, J.J. 'The Barony of Mouswald and its Barons: A Page of Border History', PSAS, 73.
51 Ibid, 75.
52 Ibid, 76.
53 Ibid.
54 Ibid.
55 Ibid, 23, 77.
56 Ibid.
57 Ibid.
58 Stat Acct VII, 298.
59 See Gifford, 454.
60 DNB, 2854.
61 Ibid.
62 Ibid.
63 County Directory 1912, 347.

54.   ORCHARDTON TOWER
(4m SSW Dalbeattie)   (NX817551)

The lands of Orchardton, also known of old as 'Irisbuitle',[1] came into the possession of the Cairns family sometime before 1456, possibly through Alexander de Carnys, who was Provost of Lincluden *c.*1408-*c.*1422.[2] Alexander also held various offices under the crown, and during his time in office acquired many lands in Galloway and elsewhere. Several of these properties he resigned in favour of his nephew John, son of William de Carnys, during his lifetime,[3] and the rest he apparently bequeathed to him on his death.[4] John also had an eventful career. Succeeding his uncle John de Carnys in 1401 as Collector of Customs at Linlithgow, he subsequently became armour-bearer to the Earl of Douglas, and served him until the Earl's death at Verneuil in 1424.[5] John de Carnys was succeeded in office at Linlithgow by his son, also John, who eventually resigned in 1456 and retired to his estates in Galloway. In the same year, he was granted sasine of the lands of Irisbuitle 'by sealed mandate of the king', who remitted to him two years' crown charges due on the property.[6] It was this latter John who built the tower.[7]

Situated on a gentle hillside, in a small valley only half a mile from the Urr estuary, Orchardton has the unique distinction of being the only round tower-house in Scotland. There are, however, a considerable number of circular tower-houses, as well as circular keeps such as Dundrum, in Ireland, so it is a matter of conjecture whether the choice of shape at Orchardton derives from Galloway's proximity to Ireland or from the Cairns family's own, considerable experience of military architecture, or both.[8]

The **TOWER**, which is structurally complete apart from the upper floors and roof, had a vaulted basement and three further storeys below the parapet walk, but no attic above. At ground level, it is about 29ft in diameter over walls that vary in thickness from an average of 6ft at the ends of the vault to about 9ft at the centre of each side. As one goes higher, however, the walls have a pronounced entasis – like a Greek column –, such that the diameter at the wall-head is reduced to about 27ft 6in over

walls averaging only 5ft in thickness. The masonry is granite, with rubble boulders for the walls and simple, chamfered dressings at the margins. The basement is entered through a doorway on the SW side. This has a bold chamfer on the arrises and a semi-circular head, cut from two stones that meet at the apex. Inside, the floor is cut from the living rock. The only other openings are three 'slit-windows' with a very narrow splay; these provide ventilation, but negligible light. There is no communication with the floor above.

Access to the first floor was originally by means of a doorway, similar to the one below, on the E side; but instead of being reached by ladder or fore-stair, it appears to have been reached by some form of retractable bridge from the adjacent range of outbuildings. Unlike the doorway below, this one has provision for two drawbars, one above the other. It led directly into the hall, a circular chamber, averaging 17ft in diameter, which was provided with a small fireplace and two window recesses. One of the recesses has stone seats, and the other was probably similar before it was converted into the new entrance in more recent centuries. To the right of the fireplace there is a beautifully moulded piscina, now considerably damaged, which has a triangular arch-head infilled with a drop-arch and trefoil cusping. Although the sill has the usual hole for a drain, there is no provision for the drain in the adjacent wall. This would seem to confirm the belief that the piscina has been re-used. It probably came from some religious establishment, and there is a tradition that it did in fact come from the ancient chapel of Kirkmirren, a mile further west.[9] Another doorway at this level gives access to a mural vestibule, leading to a small, irregularly-shaped garderobe[10] and the mural wheel-stair, only 4ft 8in in diameter, which serves the upper floors and parapet. Built into the left jamb of this doorway, there is a moulded lamp-bracket, which, like the piscina, appears to have been re-used and may well have come from the same source. The step at the garderobe doorway has also been re-used, having started life as either the sill or lintel of a window.

The second floor is similarly furnished, with a small fireplace, two window recesses with stone seats, a garderobe and an aumbry. The lintel of the fireplace is made in three pieces, with a wide keystone in the centre, while the doorway to the stair,

Fig. 304   Orchardton Tower: view from S.

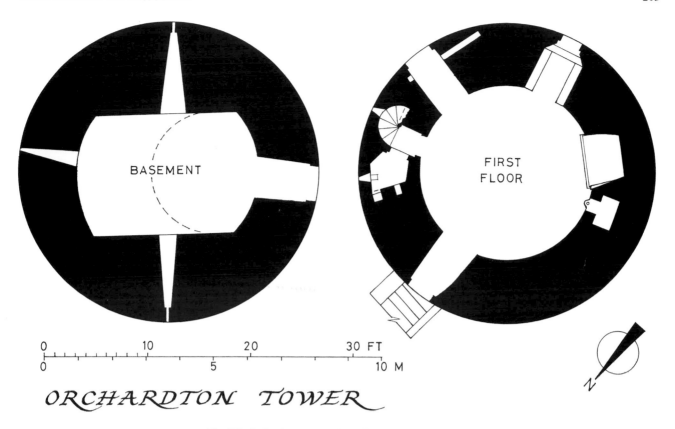

ORCHARDTON TOWER

Fig. 305 Orchardton Tower: plans of basement and first floor.

unlike the other internal doorways, has a pointed arch-head. In this instance, the garderobe is not entered from the stair passage, but has a separate doorway to give the family more privacy. Both the aumbry on this floor, and the one on the floor below, open out behind the jambs to almost three times the width to provide greater storage capacity. At this level the internal wall-face has an offset course to support the floor joists.

The third floor is very much more spartan, having but one window facing NE and a simple fireplace and aumbry. Above

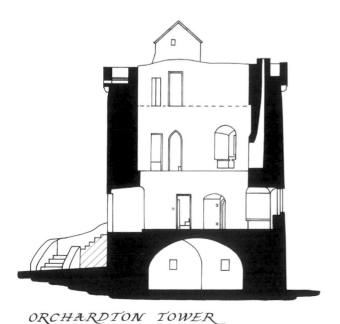

ORCHARDTON TOWER

Fig. 306 Orchardton Tower: sectional elevation looking east.

this was the roof, which, from the surviving evidence at the wall-head, is seen to have been of extremely shallow, pitched construction, covered with stone slabs.

The stair terminates above this level in a simple, rectangular cap-house, which leads directly on to the parapet-walk. The roof of the cap-house is also pitched and covered with stone slabs, but one cannot be sure to what extent it has been restored; it has plain coping on the gables. The walk itself averages about 2ft 8in in width. It is irregularly stepped, and is contained between an inner wall, which supported the roof and incorporated the chimneys from the various fireplaces below, and an outer wall that was carried on crude, single-stage corbels. Some of the corbels bear crudely carved faces.

Adjacent to the tower on the E side are the remains of a range of roughly rectangular outbuildings. Little more than the base of some of the walls has survived, except in the NE corner, where there is a vaulted basement below the general ground level, but it is clear that these buildings were at least two storeys high, and probably included a great hall. There is also, on the W side, the first few steps of a simple wheel-stair. The purpose of these rooms, and an explanation for the irregularities in the arrangement and thickness of the walls, can now only be surmised; but it is believed that they are contemporary with the tower, and were all originally contained within the barmkin, the overall extent of which has yet to be excavated.[11]

The Cairns of Orchardton frequently appear on record thereafter for more than a century.[12] William Cairns had sasine of Orchardton and Dalbeattie in 1499.[13] By 1547 the 'Lard of Orchaldton', William Cairns, was able to pledge 102 men to the service of Lord Wharton.[14] Three years later, his eldest son, William Cairns 'of Dalbeattie', received a gift of the nonentries of the 9 merk land of Orchardton;[15] but he evidently died before

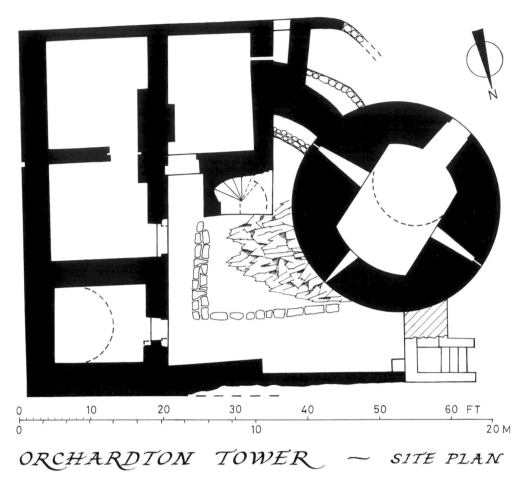

ORCHARDTON TOWER — SITE PLAN

Fig. 307 Orchardton Tower: site plan, showing tower, outbuildings and courtyard.

his father,[16] for, when the elder William died in 1555, the lands of Orchardton passed into the custody of the Crown,[17] while another son, John, remained at Cults in Wigtownshire, which he had bought from his father in 1548.[18] William Cairns of Dalbeattie left only three daughters, Margaret, Elizabeth and Janet, who became co-heiresses when, in 1560, the estate was finally divided into three equal portions. The Crown then granted sasine of one part each to Elizabeth and Janet.[19] In the meantime, in 1558/9, David Kennedy of Knockdaw was granted the nonentries of the lands of Orchardton and the marriages of Janet and Elizabeth Cairns.[20] The remaining portion of the estate presumably went to the eldest daughter, Margaret, though no record of this has been found.[21] Margaret married William Kirkpatrick of Kirkmichael, Elizabeth married a Kennedy,[22] and Janet married George Maxwell of Drumcoltran.

Elizabeth Cairns died before 1570, when her daughter, Janet Kennedy, had sasine of her mother's share of the estate.[23] Two years later, the Crown granted the ward and nonentry of Elizabeth's third of the Orchardton estates to Edward Maxwell, eldest son of George Maxwell, younger of Drumcoltran, together with the marriage of her daughter.[24] However, such was the management of the fragmented estate at this time that the estate got into debt, and in 1582 Sir Robert Maxwell of Spottes, a younger son of the 4th Lord Herries, obtained a wadset of Orchardton.[25] The following year, Margaret Cairns confirmed an earlier disposition of her share of the estate to Roger Kirkpatrick of Closeburn, since deceased.[26] Then, apparently, c.1600, Sir Robert Maxwell of Spottes purchased from Edward

Maxwell of Drumcoltran the share of Orchardton that his mother had inherited.[27]

Sir Robert's eldest son, also Robert, succeeded his father in Spottes in 1615,[28] and the following year he purchased the principal share of Orchardton, which included the tower, from Alexander Kirkpatrick of Kirkmichael.[29] Following this transaction, Robert, 'now of Orcheartoun', was granted a new crown charter of the 9 merk lands of Orchardton, with the fortalice and manor-place, which were to be held of the crown in alba-ferme.[30] However, Robert had to wadset Orchardton c.1625,[31] and during the Civil War he suffered heavy losses in the Royalist cause, such that when, in 1660, the Earl of Nithsdale petitioned Charles II concerning his own losses, he also mentioned various kinsmen, including the laird of Orchardton, who had been 'totally ruined in their estates'.[32] Robert was appointed a Commissioner of War for the Stewartry of Kirkcudbright in 1645 and 1648,[33] and a Commissioner of Supply for the Stewartry in 1656 and 1659.[34] He also represented the Stewartry in parliament in 1669 and 1670, shortly before his death.[35] He was created a baronet in 1663.[36]

Sir Robert died in 1671 or 1672, and was succeeded by his son, Sir Robert, 2nd Baronet. Sir Robert represented the Stewartry in parliament in 1672 and 1681,[37] and was a Commissioner of Supply for the Stewartry in 1678, 1685 and 1690.[38] He was also recommended for the heritable jurisdiction of the Stewartry of Kirkcudbright in 1682,[39] and later that year he was appointed to administer the Test.[40]

Sir George Maxwell of Orchardton, 3rd Baronet, who

succeeded his father in 1693, was appointed a Commissioner of Supply for the Stewartry in 1704.[41] On his death without issue in 1719, Orchardton passed to his first cousin, Robert Maxwell of Gelston, only son of Thomas of Gelston, younger brother of Sir Robert Maxwell, 2nd Baronet of Orchardton.[42] Sir Robert died in 1729, but instead of leaving Orchardton to his eldest son, George, who succeeded as the 5th baronet, he left it to his eldest son by his second marriage, Mungo.[43] Mungo, however, agreed to resign Orchardton in favour of Sir George, whilst retaining Glenshinnoch and Potterland for himself.[44] Orchardton subsequently passed to Sir George's only son, Sir Thomas, on whose death without issue in 1761, both Orchardton and the baronetcy passed to Mungo's only son, Robert, who became the 7th Baronet.[45]

Up till this time, the Maxwells of Orchardton had continued to live in the old tower and its associated complex of buildings. Sir Robert, however, decided it was time for a change, and sometime c.1765 started work on a new mansion, two miles SSW of the old tower.[46] Sadly, the cost of the work, together with other financial difficulties, proved too much for Sir Robert's resources, and he was compelled to mortgage the estate to the Bank of Scotland for £25,000.[47] Then in 1785, the year before he died, he sold it to James Douglas, a merchant in Liverpool.[48]

Douglas was succeeded by his daughter Sara, who married Lieutenant-Colonel Christopher Maxwell, a younger son of David Maxwell of Cardoness.[49] On her death in 1874, the estate passed to her nephew, the Reverend George Robinson of Almorness, who took the surname Robinson-Douglas.[50] He was succeeded in 1878 by his eldest son, William, who, three years later, demolished most of the old house and replaced it with a large, baronial mansion.[51] William died in 1921. His widow, Constance, subsequently married William Herries Maxwell of Munches; but she retained for herself the name Douglas, and after Maxwell died in 1933 she returned to Orchardton, where she was still living in 1937.[52]

1 The link between Irisbuitle and Orchardton was confirmed in 1614, when there is reference to 'Orchardton, otherwise called Irisbuitle' (Lawlor 1906, 58,59). M'Kerlie (V, 83) states that another old name for the property was Glenshinnock. There was another, better known Irisbutil, or Arsbutil, at Burned Island, 3 miles NW of Parton (Brooke, D. 'The Northumbrian Settlements in Galloway & Carrick', PSAS, CXXI, 302).
2 Lawlor 1906, 48; M'Dowall 1886, 71.
3 RMS II, No.255.
4 Lawlor 1906, 48.
5 Ibid, 50.
6 Ibid, 58.
7 The crest of the Cairns family was a round tower with a martlet on top.
8 Alexander de Carnys' brothers John and William both worked on the new stronghold of David's Tower at Edinburgh Castle, 1375-9 (RCAHMS 1951, 3, 15; ERS II, 520, 526, 551, etc). William was also Constable of Edinburgh Castle.
9 'Orchardton', TDGAS, 2nd Ser., XIX, 190.
10 The present sill of the garderobe doorway is a re-used window sill or lintel, incorporating a central socket for an iron bar.
11 The tower is shown within an enclosure on Pont's map (Blaeu, 66, 'The Steuartrie of Kircudbright, The most easterlie part of Galloway').
12 e.g. RMS II, Nos.976, 1702, 2638; RMS III, Nos.501; RMS IV, Nos.240, 676; ALHT I, 272; etc.
13 ERS XI, 462.
14 Armstrong 1883, lxxiv.
15 RSS IV, No.743.
16 He was certainly dead by 1558 (RSS V, No.576).
17 ERS XIX, 456.
18 RMS IV, No.240. Cults (Qwiltis) is 2 miles NNE Whithorn. John had two more brothers, Peter and Henry.
19 ERS XIX, 456.
20 RSS V, No.576.
21 Gourlay, W.R. 'Orchardton Tower', TDGAS, 3rd Ser., XV, 150.
22 The relationships of the Kennedys has not been established.
23 ERS XX, 412.
24 RSS VI, No.1510.
25 Fraser 1873, I, 590.
26 RSS VIII, No.1451.
27 Gourlay, op. cit., 150.
28 Ibid.
29 Gourlay, op. cit., 150, according to whom, Maxwell did not purchase the last third of the property until 1640.
30 RMS VII, No.1363.
31 RMS VIII, No.873.
32 Fraser 1873, I, 379.
33 APS VI, Part I, 559; Part II, 35.
34 Ibid, VI, Part II, 851, 884.
35 Ibid, VII, 548; VIII, 3. If Sir Robert did not die until at least April 1671, it must have been he who attended parliament as 'Sir Robert Maxwell of Orchardton' in 1669 and 1670 (cf. Parl. of Scot., II, 480).
36 Fraser 1873, I, 590.
37 APS VIII, 55, 231.
38 Ibid, 228, 469; IX, 144.
39 RPC, 3rd Ser., VII, 306.
40 Ibid, 808.
41 APS XI, 149.
42 Fraser 1873, I, 590.
43 Ibid.
44 Ibid.
45 Ibid, 591.
46 Gourlay, op. cit., 154.
47 M'Kerlie V, 91.
48 'Orchardton', TDGAS, 2nd Ser., XIX, 184.
49 M'Kerlie V, 92; Fraser 1873, I, 604.
50 M'Kerlie V, 92
51 Gifford, 483-4.
52 Burke L.G. 1937, 635, 'Robinson Douglas of Orchardton'.

55. RAECLEUGH TOWER
(5m NW Moffat)   (NT038118)

At the beginning of the 16th century the £4 lands of 'Racleugh' formed part of the barony of Craufurd-Lindesay. In 1510, Gilbert Weir 'of the Raclucht' was one of the free tenants of Crawford-muir who petitioned James IV to infeft the Earl of Angus in the lordship of Crawford-Lindsay, while John Weir, 'chaplain', was one of the witnesses.[1] Later that year, the Crown granted the lordship to George Douglas, eldest son of the 5th Earl of Angus, as part of the new barony of Crawford-Douglas;[2] and in 1516 George's eldest son, Archibald, 6th Earl of Angus, gave a new grant of the £5 (sic) lands of Raecleugh to Adam Weir.[3] In 1540, following the 6th Earl's forfeiture, the crown annexed these lands,[4] and two years later leased the 7½ merkland of 'Racleugh' to John Johnston of that Ilk.[5] Shortly afterwards James V died, and Angus returned to power; and in 1546 Angus gave to Adam Weir, son and heir of Adam Weir of Raecleugh, a new charter and sasine of the 'said lands of Racleugh'.[6]

Johnston, however, either retained or recovered possession, for in 1558 he paid the Crown the due fee of £50 'for his [formal] entry of the lands of Racleuch',[7] which he then gave to his second son, Robert. Robert was subsequently designated 'of Raecleugh'.[8] This was confirmed in Johnston's will, dated 1562, wherein he also gave Robert the parsonage of Lochmaben.[9] But Johnston's right to the lands was challenged by 'John Douglas of Racleugh', at whose instance, in 1564, Johnston was denounced a rebel and put to the horn for debt and for 'not desisting and ceasing from the lands of Raecleugh'.[10] He was later released on bail. Some agreement must eventually have been reached, for, although Robert died at Carnsalloch, in Nithsdale,[11]

Raecleugh remained in the possession of his family until well into the next century.

It is not possible to be certain who built the tower, but the likelihood is that it was built by the Johnstons. Raecleugh was the northernmost of the towers in the Evan valley. Tucked into the hillside on the right bank beside a tributary stream, it had little prospect to the S, but an extensive view towards

Fig. 308 Raecleugh Bastle-House: remains of tower in the foreground, looking NW.

Howcleugh[12] and the summit of Beattock to the NW. Although the site is now largely buried beneath modern farm buildings, and the tower is little more than a heap of rubble, 'the ruins of the former house of Raecleugh' were described in 1894 as 'conspicuous'.[13]

All that can now be discerned of the **TOWER**[14] is the S end of a vaulted basement, 21ft 8in wide over walls 4ft thick, with the E jamb of the entrance doorway admitting to an adjacent wing on the W side. The wing itself has been removed, but the proximity of the re-entrant angle – which faced SW – to the S end of the main block suggests the possibility that the tower was built on the unusual **T**–plan. Certainly the keying of the door jamb into the wall of the main block appears to be original, and not a later addition. According to the survey of the RCAHMS in 1912,[15] the overall length of the main block was about 36ft, with walls varying in thickness from 3 to 5ft; thus the surviving internal length of about 29ft 6in would seem to represent the total. The masonry was local Silurian rubble with dressings of red sandstone. The latter may be seen at the entrance, where the external arris is rounded, and also amongst the fallen rubble. Among local towers, the size of the main block is almost identical to Breconside and Cornal.

By the beginning of the 17th century the ownership of Raecleugh seems to have been resolved, with the Douglases receiving crown charters of the superiority of the lands in 1602[16] and 1631[17], while the Johnstons remained in possession, presumably as feuars. Robert Johnston of Raecleugh is on record in 1601 and 1602.[18] This was presumably the same Robert, 2nd of Raecleugh, who, by 1610, had become a Justice of the Peace for Dumfriesshire and tutor of James Johnston, son and heir of Sir James Johnston of Dunskellie (Johnston of that Ilk).[19] He is mentioned again the next year, when he was at the horn for not paying a debt,[20] and in 1616 he had certain lands in and around Moffat apprised for debt.[21] The following year, he and Sir James

Murray of Cockpool were charged with supervising the conveyance of James VI's carriage from Dumfries to Carlisle at the end of His Majesty's State Visit.[22] He also signed a band, on behalf of both himself and his charge, James Johnston of that Ilk, to uphold the laws of the realm.[23] He was elected Provost of Annan in 1618,[24] and two years later he was one of those delegated to arrange the repair of the bridge at Dumfries.[25] Then, in 1622, he was one of those appointed to assist the Earl of Nithsdale in administering justice in the late Borders.[26]

The family's finances did not improve, and in 1634 his son Robert Johnston, 3rd of Raecleugh, had the lands of Raecleugh itself apprised, whereupon they were bought by James Johnston of that Ilk, later 1st Earl of Hartfell.[27] Robert moved to Stapleton (q.v.), near Annan, while Raecleugh passed into the possession of Francis Scott of Carterton, who, in 1636, assigned them to Alexander Johnstone, Advocate.[28]

Raecleugh was not included amongst the many lands that were erected into the Earldom of Annandale in 1662,[29] but later it is again found included among the Johnstones' Annandale estates, and so it remained until finally sold *c*.1965.

1   Fraser
2   RMS II, No.3532.
3   RMS III, No.3246.
4   Ibid, No.2233; APS II, 405.
5   RSS III, No.27; Fraser 1894, I, lvi.
6   RSS III, No.1670; RMS III, No.3246.
7   ERS XIX, 77.
8   Fraser (1894, I, lvi) says Johnston assigned Raecleugh to his natural son John in 1543, but does not include such a son among the natural sons listed elsewhere (pp. lxii.n and cccxxv).
9   Fraser 1894, I, lix.
10   Ibid, liii; Johnstone 1889, 116 (inaccurate quote).
11   Fraser 1894, I, cccxxv. Robert's wife, Marion Maxwell, was the widow of George Maxwell (d.1566), 3rd of Carnsalloch, and mother of William Maxwell, 4th of Carnsalloch.
12   Howcleugh was acquired by Mungo Johnston, younger brother of Robert Johnston, 2nd of Raecleugh.
13   Fraser 1894, lxi.
14   Some scholars now think it more likely that the remains represent a bastle-house, like Kinnelhead (q.v.) or the bastle-houses that have recently come to light in Upper Clydesdale, rather than a 'tower', but without detailed excavation this cannot be resolved.
15   RCAHMS 1920, No.478.
16   RMS VI, No.1283.
17   RMS VIII, No.1750.
18   RPC VI, 710, 719.
19   Ibid, VIII, 402; IX, 77.
20   Ibid, IX, 295.
21   RMS VII, No.1805.
22   RPC XI, 200.
23   Ibid, 226.
24   Johnstone 1889, 202.
25   RPC XII, 251.
26   Ibid, 694.
27   Fraser 1894, I, ccix.
28   Adams 1921, 117.
29   RMS XI, No.230.

56.   REPENTANCE TOWER
(4¼ m NW Annan)   (NY155722)

Known as 'Repentance' after the inscription over the entrance doorway, this watch-tower was built in 1565 by Sir John Maxwell, Master of Maxwell, later 4th Lord Herries.[1] It was intended both as an outpost for his new castle at Hoddom, which was being built at the same time, and to augment the role of the adjacent beacon. From its position on the summit of Trailtrow hill, it had a commanding prospect over much of Lower Annandale and the Solway plain, including the two principal invasion routes into SW Scotland.

Fig. 309 Repentance Tower: view from SE.

The site, which is a very ancient one, and which had connections with the earliest church of St. Kentigern when he established his episcopal see at Hoddom,[2] was first formally recorded as a look-out post at a meeting convened in 1448, following the sack of Dumfries by the English.[3] Referring to the practices of the March in times of warfare in the days of Archibald Douglas, 'The Grim', and his successors, it was confirmed that 'a bail be burned on Trailtrow Hill', which would be the outpost for chains of beacons running up Annandale, Nithsdale and into Galloway. After Repentance was built, a new 'Order to be observed in the Stewart Court of Annandale' decreed that 'the [keeper of Hoddom] assuredly take heed, that the Watch-house of Trailtrow be keeped be the Watch thereof: And in the time of Warfare, the Beaken, as is devised, that is ever in Weir and in Peace, the Watch to be keeped on the House-head; and in the Weir the Beaken in the Fire-pan to be keeped, and never faill burning, so long as the Englishmen remain in Scotland; and with ane Bell to be on the Head of the Fire-pan, which shall ring whenever the Fray is, or that the Watchman seing the Thieves disobedient come over the Water of Annand, or thereabout, and knowes them to be Enemies; And whosoever bydes fra the Fray, or turns again so long as the Beaken burns, or the Bell rings, shall be holden as Partakers to the Enemies, and used as Traitors…'[4]

Despite its diminutive size, the **TOWER** was well-suited to its purpose, strongly defended and virtually inaccessible to enemy artillery. Built of local sandstone rubble, roughly coursed,

with dressed margins and plain, roll mouldings, it measures 23ft 8in by 21ft 4in, over walls averaging 5ft 6in thick, and originally rose – the adjacent ground was about 3ft lower then – some 30ft to the parapet walk, which surmounts the wall-head on all sides. Within this a hipped roof of large, overlapping, sandstone flags, supported by a barrel vault, rises to a central, stone 'beacon'. The tower was originally divided into four storeys; but the top floor was later removed and much of the work above the wall-head 'restored' during the 19th century.[5] Most of the original masonry is reputed to have come from the old church of Trailtrow, which stood on the site and which was demolished at that time.[6]

The tower's entrance is on the first floor, some 6ft above the old ground level. It was protected by strong inner and outer

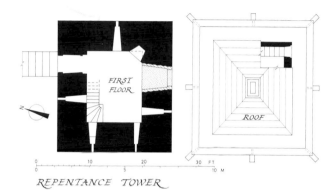

Fig. 310 Repentance Tower: plans of first floor and parapet levels.

Fig. 311 Repentance: entrance doorway showing 'REPENTANCE' inscription above. 1565.

doors, and was originally reached by a removable, wooden ladder. From this level a second wooden ladder inside led down to the unvaulted basement. This chamber has no features save two narrow gun-loops in each wall, some of which are now blocked.[7] These have openings averaging 10in wide by 6½ in high on the outer wall-face, and are angled slightly outwards, perhaps to give the impression of providing a wider angle of cover than was in fact the case: in practice they would have been of very limited use, as the absence of any splay limited them to firing in one direction only; but no assailant could have known that. The only features on the first floor are a stone seat, or recess, built into the SE corner, opposite the entrance, two slit-windows in the W wall and one slit-window on each of the other sides. During the 19th century a large window was inserted in the S wall to give some light to the interior, but this has been filled in again so that only the outline remains. It is interesting to note that there was no fireplace in the tower, no doubt to avoid the possibility that any smoke seen might give a false alarm.

From the first floor, a further wooden ladder – more recently replaced by a stone stair, cantilevered out from the wall – gave access to the next floor. This was probably little more than a landing, which could be used as sleeping accommodation for those keeping the beacon when required. It has one very small, almost square opening on each side. In more recent times it has been used as a pigeon loft. Above this level, a stone stair rises steeply in two, straight flights past the third floor to the parapet walk. The third floor was supported on scarcements, and provided a large storage attic rising up 10ft to the top of the vault supporting the roof.

The original bell would need to have been of a substantial size if the sound was to carry any distance; but in mistakenly replacing it with the modern 'beacon' – the original beacon was

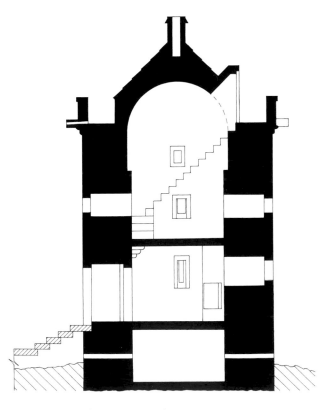

REPENTANCE TOWER

Fig. 312 Repentance Tower: Sectional elevation looking east.

beside the tower –, the 19th century restorers swept away any vestige of how and where it was mounted.

It is not known for certain why the motto 'Repentance' is carved over the tower's entrance, but the most likely explanation concerns an incident that occurred in 1547. At the time, the Master of Maxwell was desirous of marrying the young Agnes, Baroness Herries, while her guardian, the Earl of Arran, Regent of Scotland, intended her for his own son. The West March was at that time under English domination, and Maxwell, like most of the local clan leaders, had been forced to pledge his clan's support for the English cause and to lodge a number of his kinsmen at Carlisle as surety.[8] But he did more. Furious at being crossed by Arran in his suit for Lady Agnes, he also promised to meet the Earl of Lennox and his English allies at Dumfries with a large body of reinforcements. So great was the threat posed by Maxwell, that Arran felt compelled to give up his own ambitions and offer him Lady Agnes in marriage, if he would change sides. Maxwell accepted. Thus, when Lennox arrived in Nithsdale, instead of finding the expected reinforcements, he found that Maxwell had changed sides and joined Douglas of Drumlanrig and the Earl of Angus against him. It was to be the turning point for English fortunes in the SW of Scotland, and in revenge they hanged Maxwell's pledges.[9]

Another tradition relates that, by demolishing the ancient chapel on Trailtrow hill to provide the building material, the Master of Maxwell earned from the powerful Archbishop of Glasgow[10] the strongest censure for desecrating the one-time seat of his hallowed predecessor, St. Kentigern.

Whatever the true reason, Maxwell purged his sin by building the new watch-tower to guard the kingdom, with its reminder of his 'Repentance'. The tower is not shown on Aglionby's Platte in 1590,[11] but it does appear as the 'Tour of Repentãce' on Pont's map of Annandale.[12]

1   Scottish Papers II, 155.
2   Maxwell-Irving 1989, 185.
3   McDowall 1886, 190-5. See also APS, I, 716.
4   Border Laws, 197.
5   See RCAHMS 1920, No.89.
6   RCAHMS 1997, 246.
7   Those in the E and W walls have been blocked at the outer end, while the two in the S wall and one in the N wall have had grilles fitted to keep vermin out. The remaining one in the N wall has now been blocked by the modern steps leading up to the entrance.
8   Maxwell was acting chief of his clan, while his elder brother, Lord Maxwell, was held captive by the English.
9   Fraser 1873, I, 499; Scots Peerage IV, 409-10. The Maxwell Memoirs refer to fourteen hostages having been taken, but only four are known to have been hanged.
10   James Beaton II, who was archbishop from 1552-70 and again from 1598-1603 (Brit Chron 1961, 293). This tradition is most unlikely, as Repentance and Hoddom are now known to have been built at the same time.
11   Hyslop, 320.
12   Blaeu, 57, 'THE STEWARTRIE OF ANNANDAIL'.

57.   ROBGILL TOWER
(1m SE Kirtlebridge)   (NY248717)

The lands of Robgill are first mentioned in the 14th century, when the Corries obtained them from the Carlyles by marriage.[1] In 1517, the '40 shilling lands of Robgill' were sold, along with the Barony of Newby and various other lands, to another branch of the family, the Corries of Kelwood;[2] and in

1529 all these lands were incorporated into the new Barony of Kelwood.[3] Seven years later, following a protracted dispute with the Johnstons of Gretna over ownership of Newby, George Corrie of Kelwood sold the lands of Newby, Robgill, Stapleton and others to William Johnston of Gretna.[4] This was confirmed by crown charter in 1541/2.[5] In the same year, the 'Laird of Robgill' and twenty of his men attended a Weaponshow held by Lord Maxwell upon Burnswark hill.[6]

Three years later, during a raid upon the West March, Lord Wharton 'burnt Bonshaw, Robgyll and all the houses, peills, steds, and corn in their way'.[7] After another invasion by Wharton in 1547, 'Cuthbert Urwen of Robbgill' pledged 34 'assured' Scots to the service of England.[8] This is the first record of the Irvings as occupiers of Robgill, though it may well have been the Irvings who were there earlier as feuars of the Corries.

Cuthbert Irving of Robgill apparently had a son David, who succeeded to Robgill.[9] He is mentioned in 1563 for having taken part in an attack on Roger Kirkpatrick of Closeburn.[10] Then by 1585 there was a Walter Irving of Robgill, who was included in a list of those who had 'intercommuned' with the Earl of Morton,[11] and he was presumably the Watt Irving of Robgill who was declared a rebel ten years later for pillaging the home of John Grier of Rigsyde.[12] There was also around this time a Christopher Irving of Robgill, who is said to have died in 1604.[13]

It was the Irvings who built the present tower – which has a close affinity with its neighbours at Bonshaw and Woodhouse –, though its date would seem to be later than it appears. Although its design is very similar to that of Bonshaw, and is clearly based upon it, the evidence would suggest that it was not built until considerably later, for it does not appear on either Aglionby's Platte in 1590[14] or Pont's survey of Lower

Annandale c.1595,[15] both of which are fairly detailed. While Pont shows an important tower and enclosed 'park' at Bonshaw, all that is shown at Robgill is an ordinary 'settlement' or 'fermtoun'. The tower stands on a cliff on the right bank of the Kirtle Water, almost opposite to Woodhouse and just below a ravine cut by a tributary burn, which provides a natural defence on two sides.

All that remains of the **TOWER** is the basement and the shell of the upper walls, which have been incorporated into the modern house, but it is clear from the surviving evidence that its design had much in common with its earlier neighbour at Bonshaw. The tower is oblong in plan and measures 34ft 2in from E to W by 23ft 9in from N to S above the splayed plinth course, which projects a further 6in on all sides. Made of roughly coursed, pink sandstone rubble, with dressed quoins and margins, the original walls, which average 5ft in thickness immediately above the plinth, survive to half the height of the present second floor windows on the N side and higher in the E gable: the other sides are obscured by later additions. Above this, the walls have been rebuilt with roughly coursed, dressed sandstone

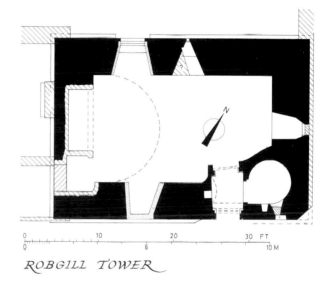

ROBGILL TOWER

Fig. 314 Robgill Tower: plan of basement.

to the level of the modern roof. It was presumably at this time that the parapet walk was removed. Sometime later in the 19th century, new, large windows have been inserted on the N side at both first and second floor levels. The entrance to the tower, which is on the S side, is now reached from the basement of the later house. Its surround has a roll-and-hollow moulding similar to that at Bonshaw, but with the addition of a quirk on either side. To the right of this, there was formerly a small gun-loop, which has been filled in,[16] and above this a small window, now also closed up, was inserted at a later date.

The entrance was protected by the usual wooden door and yett, neither of which has survived. It admits to a mural vestibule with a cross-vaulted roof, from the centre of which hangs an octagonal, pendant boss bearing the sacred monogram 'IHS'. This is similar to the one at Bonshaw, but much cruder, and may be a later insertion. It has been suggested that it may occupy the position of a former hatch from the floor above, but there is no architectural evidence for this.[17] The vestibule is also provided with a lamp shelf, so positioned that it is protected from draughts by the outer door. On the right of the vestibule, in

Fig. 313 Robgill Tower: view from NW. The rebuilt wall-head and modern windows are clearly visible.

220

Fig. 315 Robgill: pendant boss with IHS monogram
in vault of entrance vestibule (*cf.* Bonshaw Tower, Fig. 17).

the SE corner, is the old stair-well, some 6ft in diameter and
now without its steps, while straight ahead is the vaulted basement. The latter chamber has been greatly altered. Contrary to
some accounts,[18] the large kitchen fireplace at the W end is not
original, but was incorporated into the W wall when this was
partially rebuilt, presumably for that purpose.[19] The date of this
work is uncertain, though it was probably part of the initial restoration *c*.1800. The fireplace is 8ft 1in wide, and has a fine
segmental arch of dressed, chamfered and backset[20] voussoirs.
To the left of this, there is a large mural recess with a doorway,
now blocked, which formerly led into the extension to the W.
Originally there was presumably a gun-loop in this wall, and the
slit-windows in the other two walls have probably also taken the
place of gun-loops. The vault is 9ft high. During the 19th century the basement was sub-divided into two cellars, and a second doorway inserted in the S wall in place of the original
gun-loop. Opposite this in the N wall, a large window was also
inserted, while the slit-window on that side became partly blocked
by the partition. In 1990 the partition was removed and the second doorway closed up again.

The floors above were completely modernized internally
when the tower was restored, but blocked windows may still be
seen on the outside of the E wall at each level. At first floor
level there was a small central window with a QER surround,

Fig. 316 Robgill: west end of basement with later, inserted fireplace.

and to the N of this a much larger window of later date; while on
the second floor there was one small window near the NE corner. It is also apparent from the remodelling of the upper windows on the N side that the height of the first floor, and thus the
level of the second floor, was raised as part of the alterations
carried out in the 19th century.

A stone-lined well, 3ft in diameter, was found close to
the tower in 1993.[21] It could be contemporary with the tower.

The Irvings continued to occupy Robgill until 1622, when
Jeffray Irving of Robgill, a younger son of William Irving of
Bonshaw, was declared a fugitive and outlaw and sentenced to
death, before fleeing to Ireland.[22] The following year his son
Christopher, 'called of Robgill', attended trial and was dismissed;[23] but neither he, nor his brother William, appear to have
resided there.

Robgill subsequently passed to Jeffray's brother William
Irving of Rockhillhead, the eldest son of Bonshaw by his second
wife, who, in 1627/8, was granted a charter of the 40 shilling
lands of Robgill, with fishings in the parish of Dornock, by James
Johnston of that Ilk, later 1st Earl of Hartfell.[24] This was in
implementation of a marriage contract drawn up between
Johnston and William of Rockhillhead, and for the sum of 2000
merks paid to Johnston by William of Bonshaw. Three years
later Bonshaw gave his son William, now of Robgill, the lands
of Woodhouse, which thereafter became his home. William
Irving of Woodhouse had three sons, but as the first two had no
issue, his estates eventually passed to his youngest son, John
Irving of Woodhouse, who received sasine of Robgill and various other lands in 1661.[25] John died eight years later, leaving an
eldest son, William of Woodhouse, who eventually, in 1696, succeeded in establishing his claim to be heir-male of the family
and his right to Bonshaw (q.v.).

Meanwhile, Robgill almost disappears from the records
until the end of the following century, though John Edgar is
mentioned as the feuar of Robgill in 1713, 1720 and 1729[26] and
again later.[27] Robgill is not listed in the Hearth Tax returns *c*.1690,
but neither is Bonshaw.[28]

Throughout this period the Johnstons were the feudal
superiors. In 1609, James Johnston of that Ilk received a new
crown charter of various lands, including the 40 shilling lands
of Robgill, all of which were incorporated into the barony of
Newbie, with the castle of Newbie as the principal messuage.[29]
Then, in 1662, these and many other lands were erected into the
Earldom of Annandale and Hartfell in favour of James Johnston
of that Ilk, 1st Earl of Annandale and Hartfell,[30] and this was
confirmed by parliament in 1669.[31] The Marquess of Annandale
was superior in 1770,[32] and his heirs, the Hope-Johnstones of
Annandale continued to hold the superiority until it was finally
sold *c*.1932.[33]

The lands of Robgill came into the possession of Paulus
Aemilius Irving some time *c*.1795. Like his father, Colonel
Aemilius Irving of Woodhouse, Paulus had had a distinguished
military career, and returned from active service in the West Indies
in 1795. On his father's death the following year, he inherited
Woodhouse (q.v.), but whether Robgill was also inherited is not
known, as there is a suggestion that either he or his father purchased the property in 1792.

It seems to have been Paulus who first repaired the old
tower, and it was certainly he who added the adjacent block to
the S of it, together with the semi-circular extension overlooking the Kirtle.[34] It was this house that appears in a painting by
Sam Bough in 1841.[35] Paulus was made a Baronet in 1809 and

a General in 1812. But despite his achievements he got badly in debt, and in 1818 was forced to sell the estates of 'Robgill Tower and Woodhouse'. The advertisement for the sale gives some idea of how Sir Paulus had developed the house: 'Robgill Tower . . . an ancient structure, placed upon a fine rampart . . . contains every accommodation for a large family, with offices, gardens, and pleasure grounds'.[36] The whole property extended to some 1200 acres.

In 1826 Robgill was mortgaged to one William Smail, who lived there until it was bought by Frederick McConnel c.1853. McConnel added a new west front in 1854;[37] but later he sold Robgill to a Mr. Paterson, and moved next door to Blackyett. Paterson made further additions and alterations to the house, and his descendants remained in possession until 1983.

1   Johnstone 1889, 6.
2   RMS, III, No.145.
3   Ibid., No.815.
4   Ibid., No.1598.
5   Ibid., No.2570.
6   Buccleuch MSS, I, 66 (No.135).
7   Armstrong 1883, lxvi; L & P, XIX, Nos.191, 625.
8   Armstrong 1883, lxxiv.
9   Irving 1907, 36 (Table).
10 Ibid, 36.
11 APS III, 389.
12 RPC V, 380.
13 According to one account, he was the son of David, while others say he was 'Black Christie', a younger son of Christopher Irving of Bonshaw and ancestor of the Irvines of Castle Irvine, County Fermanagh, in Ireland (Irving 1907, 35, 36 (Table), 198; Irvine MS 1678).
14 Hyslop, 320.
15 Blaeu, 57, 'THE STEWARTRIE OF ANNANDAIL'.
16 The outline of this gun-loop was still clearly discernible in 1969, but it has since been plastered over.
17 Hatches over vestibules are almost unknown at this period. Where they do appear in earlier works, they are almost invariably served from above by a mural chamber, and there is no evidence for such a chamber at Robgill.
18 MacGibbon & Ross, III, 401; RCAHMS 1920, No.107.
19 It is inconceivable that the fireplace is an original feature. Apart from the practical difficulties in having a kitchen fire in the basement of such a tower, in this instance it reduces the thickness of the wall to only 2ft on a side vulnerable to attack, and deprives it of a gun-loop for its defence (cf. Drumcoltran).
20 The backset may date from the time when the fireplace surround was tiled in the 19th century.
21 Discovery & Excavation in Scotland 1993, 18.
22 RPC XII, 282, 626; XIV, 670, 677; Irving 1907, 64-5.
23 RPC XIV, 698, 710.
24 Bonshaw Charters, No.14.
25 Irving 1907, 74.
26 PRS Dumfries III (1703-32), Index, 90; GRS Index (1701-20), 274.
27 PRS Dumfries IV (1733-60), Index, 40; V (1761-80), Index, 46. The sale particulars for Robgill in 1983 also mentions George Bell of Conheath as the owner in 1749, but this has not been confirmed (Savills, Estate Agents, Edinburgh).
28 Adamson, D. 'The Hearth Tax', TDGAS, 3rd Ser., XLVII-XLIX.
29 RMS VII, No.76.
30 RMS XI, No.230.
31 APS VII, 641.
32 Directory of Landownership, 99.
33 Feu Register of Annandale Estates. The exact date of sale is not recorded.
34 McConnel, F.R. 'Irving Towers', TDGAS, 3rd Ser., XX, 145.
35 Irving 1907, facing 87.
36 Newcastle Chronicle, 11th April 1818, cited in Irving 1907, 88.
37 McConnel, F.R., op. cit., 145.

58.   ROCKHALL
   (5m E Dumfries)   (NX056755)

'Rochel' is first mentioned as a place c.1200,[1] the earliest stronghold being the motte three quarters of a mile N of the present house. This was presumably 'the moite of Rockell' where

an attempted ambush was reported in 1592.[2] In 1412, by the marriage of Gilbert Grierson, younger of Lag, to Isabel, daughter and co-heiress of Sir Duncan Kirkpatrick of Torthorwald, the lands of Rockhall and Collin passed to the Griersons.[3] There was no mention of a stronghold then, but when Gilbert's son and heir, Vedast, 3rd of Lag, received a charter of the lands from the Duke of Albany in 1473, sasine was taken 'at the mansion of Rokell'.[4] It seems likely, therefore, that 'the mansion' referred to was built by the Griersons soon after they acquired the property.

Vedast was succeeded first by his eldest son, Roger, and then, after Roger's death at Sauchieburn in 1488, by Roger's eldest son, Cuthbert, 5th of Lag, who had sasine of Rockhall in 1504.[5] Throughout this period the history of Rockhall is inextricably linked to that of Lag (q.v.). Cuthbert died in 1513, and was succeeded by his nephew Sir John Grierson, 6th of Lag, who had sasine of Rockhall the following year, his father Roger having been killed at Flodden.[6] At this time Sir John was still only an infant.[7] Sir John had a crown charter of Lag, Rockhall, Collin and other lands in 1526,[8] and this was confirmed by parliament later that year.[9] By his first wife Sir John had a son, William, who succeeded to Lag, while his next son, Roger, inherited Rockhall; but the separation of the two properties did not last long, for when William's only son died without issue, Roger also succeeded to Lag.[10] It was while Roger was laird, in 1578, that Lord Herries submitted to James VI his 'Advice for good order to be observed in the West Marches'. This included the proposal that the laird of Lag should assist the warden and, in times of great disobedience, remain with an honest household 'in Rockell'.[11] Nothing is known of the size or form of the stronghold at this time, but it must have been substantial. No doubt the oldest part of the present house formed a part of it.[12]

Roger was succeeded by his only son, Sir William Grierson, 9th of Lag, who was granted a charter of confirmation of the lands of Lag and Rockhall in 1593.[13] By the end of the century, the Privy Council was becoming so concerned about the increasing lawlessness of the 'broken' men, especially in the West March, that in 1600 they decided further measures should be taken. Following the advice of the late Lord Herries, their proposals included a decree that the barons and landed men should dwell in 'sic houssis of strenth and utheris places as ar maist ewest [close to] the saidis thevis themselffis': Sir William was to stay in either 'Rochell or Mouswell'.[14] It was sometime during the next ten years that he rebuilt and modernized the old stronghold. This is recorded in a charter of 1610, by which Sir William granted his wife, Dame Nicolas Maxwell, 'the mansion and mains of Rockell in liferent' . . . calling to remembrance the care and trouble taken by her 'upoun my directioun in the edifeing and bigging of the place of Rockell laitlie constructit be me'.[15] In a further charter, which formed part of the marriage contract between his eldest son, Robert, and Margaret Murray in 1622, Sir William granted Margaret the lands of Rockhall and others in liferent, reserving to himself 'his principal tower and manor-place of Rokkell within the "iron yett"'.[16]

Rockhall stands at an elevation of 250ft on the western slopes of the hills that divide Nithsdale from Annandale, from where it overlooks the vast panorama of the Lochar Moss and the road into Dumfries. On the same slopes to the NW lies Torthorwald and to the SE Mouswald.

Rockhall, as seen today, is an L-plan mansion of three storeys, with a stair-tower in the re-entrant angle and a modern gabled roof. There is little evidence of the former mediaeval

Fig. 317 Rockhall: view from the south.

stronghold, which has undergone so many changes during the course of its transformation that even the precise sequence of construction and alteration is not always clear. The masonry is Silurian rubble with red sandstone dressings.

The oldest part of the house is the N wing. This measures 24ft 6in from N to S by 50ft from E to W, and at basement level originally comprised three chambers connected by a common passage on the S side. The chamber at the W end is much the smaller. It has a barrel-vault, 8ft 5in high, and walls 4ft 6in thick, the only openings being two, very small slit-windows. This is the earliest surviving work. The other two chambers, which are 10ft high, were not vaulted (contrary to the impres-

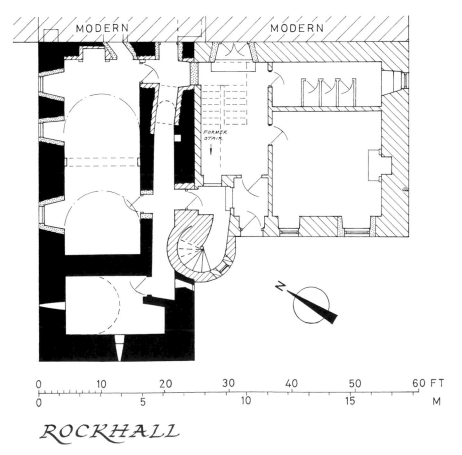

ROCKHALL

Fig. 318 Rockhall: plan of basement.

sion given by the modern lath-and-plaster vault),[17] and long ago the dividing wall between them was removed and modern windows and doorways inserted. The walls here are 4ft thick, except at the E end, where the wall, which is 3ft thick, appears to have been rebuilt when the S wing was added. The bolection-moulded fireplace at this end also belongs to the latter period. The passage connecting the chambers has undergone several changes, including the intrusion of the later stair-well and a later, vaulted section towards the E end. Although the whole of this basement may be contemporaneous, the various changes in the structure suggest that the W end is older than the rest.[18] There is no evidence of where the original stair was located.

Whilst the first floor has been completely modernised internally, the thickness of the walls (4ft) suggests that this part of the building is contemporary with the E portion of the basement. The windows on both this floor and the floor above have all been enlarged. This appears to have been carried out when the S wing was added, except for the windows of the W room on

Fig. 319 Rockhall: vaulted basement chamber at W end.

this floor, which are larger still and thus probably of later date. The astragals in all the windows have only recently been restored.[19] An earlier window for the E room can be seen blocked up in the N wall. On the second floor the thickness of the walls is reduced to 2ft, except for the dividing wall with the S wing, which is 3ft 9in thick; it incorporates a chimney stack from the old block.

The stair-tower that serves the upper floors appears to be contemporary with the present second floor, and is probably part of the work undertaken by Sir William Grierson c.1610. It intrudes clumsily into the old basement passage, without admitting directly to it, and originally incorporated a new entrance doorway with a QER surround. The tower is 10ft 8in in diameter with a wall 1ft 6in thick. Unless the basement had a separate entrance there must have been a further addition on the E side, similar to the present interconnecting passage, to give covered access to it. Some time after the S wing was added, the doorway in the tower was blocked up and converted into a window, but there is some uncertainty as to when this first happened.[20] Indeed, the surviving masonry shows that the opening has been altered more than once.

The S wing was added in the 18th century, possibly in two phases,[21] to provide more spacious accommodation with a central hall and new staircase. It measures 30ft 6in from E to W

and extends 34ft towards the S; the side walls are 3ft thick and the gable wall 4ft.[22] There is also believed to have been a new entrance, though, because of later changes, it is not certain where this was first located. The present entrance dates only from c.1915, when it superseded another entrance, now a window, that existed from c.1880-1915 at the SW corner.[23] Above the entrance there is a modern armorial panel bearing the arms of Grierson of Lag. The staircase between the ground and first floors was later removed, so that the stair-tower once again became the only means of access to the upper floors.

The smaller, two-storeyed house standing only 15ft away to the NE was built in the 18th century for the coachman. It was subsequently enlarged by the addition of an E wing, and has since been joined to the main house.

During a long and distinguished career, Sir William Grierson of Lag held many judicial and administrative offices in the West March, details of which are given under Lag (q.v.). It was Rockhall, however, that became his principal residence. On his death in 1629 he was succeeded by his eldest son, Sir Robert Grierson, 10th of Lag.

Sir Robert also had an outstanding career in public service. He first represented Dumfriesshire in parliament in 1628,[24] during his father's lifetime, and he attended parliament again in 1633 and from 1639 to 1648,[25] when he was one of the eight Commissioners elected to represent the barons.[26] He was appointed Sheriff of Dumfries in 1629,[27] and the following year a Commissioner for maintaining law and order in the Middle Shires[28] and Steward of Annandale.[29] He was also a Commissioner for the Surrender and Teinds in 1633,[30] and Convener of the Justices of the Peace in Dumfriesshire a year later.[31] In 1638 he was appointed to superintend the subscribing of the King's Covenant at Dumfries.[32] Three years later, his services being increasingly in demand, he was appointed to the Committee for the Incendiaries,[33] as well as being on the Commissions for Regulating the Common Burdens,[34] for Receiving Brotherly assistance from the Parliament of England,[35] for the Plantation of Kirks and the Valuation of Teinds,[36] and for Conserving the Articles of Treaty;[37] and In 1643 he was also on the Committee for Furnishing the Army in Ireland,[38] the Commission for proportioning of the Loan,[39] the Committee anent the Annuity,[40] and the Committee for the Defence of the True Protestant Religion.[41] In the same year he was appointed a Commissioner of Supply for Dumfriesshire.[42] In addition, he was on the Committee of War from 1643 to 1648,[43] and the Committee of Estates from 1643 to 1645, and again in 1651.[44] He also served as a Lieutenant-Colonel of Foot in the Dumfriesshire militia in 1645,[45] and three years later both he and his eldest son were commissioned as Colonels.[46] Sir Robert died in, or shortly after, 1651, and was succeeded, first by his eldest son, Sir John Grierson, 11th of Lag, and then by his grandson, Robert. As well as being a Colonel of Foot, Sir John was appointed a Commissioner of Supply for Dumfriesshire in 1655 and 1656.[47] He was also named as a Commissioner again in 1659,[48] though this was an error, as he had died the previous year.[49]

Robert Grierson, 12th of Lag, was served heir to his father and given sasine of the estate in 1658, on a commission from Oliver Cromwell.[50] At this time he was very young, and he was still a minor when he died eight years later.

Robert was succeeded by his cousin Sir Robert Grierson, son of William Grierson of Barquhar (second son of Sir Robert Grierson of Lag), who became 13th of Lag and was served heir in 1669.[51] It was this laird, known as 'Auld Lag', who achieved notoriety for his ruthless persecution of the Covenanters, some of whom he is said to have hanged at Rockhall.[52] In 1672, parliament ratified the lands and barony of Lag in his favour, with sasine to be taken 'at the maner place of Lagg'.[53] Sir Robert represented Dumfriesshire in parliament in 1678,[54] the same year in which he joined Claverhouse's campaign against the Covenanters in the SW,[55] and he attended parliament again in 1681, 1685 and 1686.[56] He was appointed a Commissioner of Supply for Dumfriesshire in 1678[57] and for both Dumfriesshire and the Stewartry of Kirkcudbright in 1685 and 1704,[58] while his eldest son, William, was also a Commissioner in 1698, 1702 and 1704.[59] On the establishment of military courts to deal with the Covenanters in the SW in 1681, Sir Robert was appointed to preside over the one held in Kirkcudbright.[60] He took the Test in 1683,[61] and the following year he was appointed Steward of Kirkcudbright.[62] Later that year, following the issue of the 'Sanquhar Declaration' by the Covenanters, he was one of the Commissioners specially appointed to prevent conventicles and punish those attending them.[63] At the accession of James II in 1685, he was created a Baronet of Nova Scotia,[64] and appointed one of the Lords Justices of Wigtownshire,[65] in which capacity he presided over the trial of the 'Wigtown Martyrs'.[66] In the same year he was also made a Justice of the Peace for Nithsdale and Annandale.[67]

After the Revolution in 1689, Sir Robert incurred the full wrath of the Covenanters, who were now in the ascendant, and was repeatedly fined and imprisoned on various pretexts. In the Hearth Tax returns for 1690, Rockhall is credited with a total of nine fireplaces.[68] Two of Sir Robert's sons, William and Gilbert, subsequently took part in the Jacobite rebellion of 1715, which led to the family's estates being forfeited; but Sir Robert succeeded in getting the sentence reversed.[69] He died in 1733, when he was succeeded first by his eldest son, William, 2nd Baronet, who died without issue in 1760; then by his second son James's only son, Robert, 3rd Baronet, who died unmarried five years later; and then by his third son, Gilbert, who became the 4th Baronet. Thereafter, the Griersons continued to live at Rockhall, with successive generations progressively enlarging and modernizing the house.

Sir Alexander Grierson, 9th Baronet, who succeeded his uncle in 1879, was a Justice of the Peace for Dumfriesshire and a Major and honorary Colonel of the 3rd Battalion, King's Own Scottish Borderers.[70] He served in the South African War, 1899-1902.[71] He was succeeded in 1912 by his eldest son, Sir Robert Grierson, 10th Baronet, who served as a Major with the King's Own Scottish Borderers in World War I.[72] Sir Robert died in 1957, and was succeeded by his only son, Sir Richard Grierson, 11th Baronet. Sir Richard finally sold Rockhall in the late 1950s to a Brigadier Russell-Morgan, who sold it again in 1963, after which it was converted into a hotel.

---

1   Fraser 1894, I, 2.
2   Border Papers, I, 422.
3   Lag Charters, 3.
4   Ibid., No.19; Burke Peerage 1959, 1006, 'Grierson'.
5   ERS XII, 715.
6   Burke, op. cit.
7   When John received a new infeftment of the lands in 1529, James V emphasized that this had been granted notwithstanding the fact that John was still a minor. (RSS II, No.421).
8   RMS III, No.395.
9   APS II, 310.
10 Burke, op. cit.
11 Fraser 1873, II, 485.
12 It is inconceivable that a substantial stronghold would have been totally demolished and rebuilt from scratch as early as 1610.
13 RMS V, No.2321.
14 RPC VI, 154.
15 Lag Charters, No.171. Dame Nicolas was the daughter of the 4th Lord Herries.
16 Ibid, No.200; RMS VIII, No.994.
17 The 'vaulting' is said to have been added when the enlarged room was used as a chapel.
18 One is reminded of the oldest work at Traquair. See RCAHMS 1967, II, Fig.296. There is said to have been a cellar under the E end, entered via an outside stair, which was only closed up in the 1950s.
19 See illustration in Stell 1986, 93. The astragals have only been restored since the house became a hotel.
20 See Stell, op. cit., 93.
21 Externally there are suggestions that the wing was built in two stages, but examination of the interior has been unable to confirm this.
22 At first floor level the side walls are reduced to 2ft.
23 See Stell, op. cit., 93. James Barbour, the Dumfries architect, was employed at Rockhall in 1880 (Wolffe, A. 'James Barbour', TDGAS, LXXI, 156.
24 APS V, 3.
25 Ibid, passim.
26 Ibid, 10, 12.
27 RPC, 2nd Ser., III, 274.
28 Ibid, IV, 13.
29 Ibid, 48.
30 Ibid, V, 124.
31 Ibid, 380.
32 Ibid, VII, 76.
33 APS V, 319.
34 Ibid, 392.
35 Ibid, 395.
36 Ibid, 400.
37 Ibid, 404.
38 Ibid, VI, Part I, 7.
39 Ibid, 19.
40 Ibid, 20.
41 Ibid, 57.
42 Ibid, 29.
43 Ibid, 53, 199, 559; Part II, 32, 35.
44 Ibid, Part I, 57, 380, 616; Part II, 679, 684.
45 Ibid, Part I, 468.
46 Ibid, Part II, 30.
47 Ibid, 839, 851.
48 Ibid, 881.
49 Burke Peerage 1959, 1006, 'Grierson of Lag'.
50 Ibid.
51 Ibid.
52 DNB, 846. 'Auld Lag', as he was known, was the archetype for Sir Robert Redgauntlet in 'Wandering Willie's Tale' in Sir Walter Scott's novel Redgauntlet, part of which was set at Rockhall.
53 APS VIII, 159.
54 Ibid, 213
55 DNB, 846.
56 APS VIII, 231, 451, 576.
57 Ibid, 225.
58 Ibid, 465, 469; XI, 142, 149.
59 APS X, 131; XI, 22, 142.
60 DNB, 846.
61 RPC, 3rd Ser., VIII, 640.
62 RPC, 3rd Ser., X, et seq.
63 Fraser, 1894, I, cclvii.
64 Burke, op. cit., 1006.
65 DNB, 846.
66 Margaret MacLachlan and Margaret Wilson.
67 APS VIII, 575.
68 Adamson, D. 'The Hearth Tax', TDGAS, 3rd Ser., XLVIII, 136.
69 DNB, 846.
70 Burke, op. cit., 1006.
71 Ibid.
72 Ibid; Who's Who 1941.

59. SANQUHAR CASTLE
(Sanquhar)   (NS786092)

Sanquhar, or *Sean-caer* meaning 'old fort', where the upper reaches of the Nith valley broaden out as they pass through the Southern Uplands and are joined by two significant tributaries, has been a place of strategic importance at least since the Romans built a fortlet here in the first century AD.[1] The lands of Sanquhar later formed part of the Celtic lordship of Nithsdale, which in the time of David I was held by Dunegal of Stranit.[2] From Dunegal the lands passed first to his younger son, Duvenald, whose share of his father's lands included Sanquhar, Eliock and Dunscore, and then to Duvenald's son Edgar, whose descendants took the surname of Edgar.[3]

Fig. 320 Sanquhar Castle: SW corner tower seen from NW.
Note 14th century window on the right.

Edgar may still have been alive in 1191, when Robert de Ros of Helmsley (Co. York) and Wark (Northumberland) married Isabel, natural daughter of William the Lion, and was granted the barony of Sanquhar as her dowry.[4] How this was arranged with the Edgars is not known, but the Rosses established themselves on the lands and, it is believed, built their stronghold at Ryehill, where the remains of a somewhat diminutive motte may still be seen.[5] But while Ryehill continued to be occupied by the Rosses, a 'New Place of Seneware (Sanquhar)', perhaps built by the English,[6] comes on record in 1296, with William le Taillur as its warden,[7] and it was evidently this New Place, now under the command of William de Beauvair (?Belvoir) with a garrison of 40 men, that was captured from the English by Sir William Douglas the following year.[8] The English rallied and tried to retake the castle, but Sir William Wallace came to Douglas's assistance and drove the English all the way to Dalswinton, inflicting heavy losses.[9] The New Place of Sanquhar was not where the present castle stands, but is believed to have been some 400 yards to the SE, where the farm of Newark perpetuates the name. After Wallace's defeat in 1298, the English retook Sanquhar, and it was here that the Earl of Cornwall entertained Edward II in 1307.[10]

Sir Robert de Ros, who held the barony of Sanquhar at this time, having no male issue, was succeeded by his two daughters, Margaret and Isabella. Margaret was married firstly to John Salveyn, and secondly to Richard Edgar of Wedderbie, a descendant of the Edgars who had formerly held Sanquhar, while Isabella was married firstly to John de Knoches (Knox), and secondly to one William Crichton, who was evidently closely related to the Crichtons of that Ilk.[11] As a result of the two daughters' second marriages, the barony of Sanquhar, which had been recovered from the English by King Robert the Bruce, was divided between Richard Edgar and William Crichton some time before 1329, with Edgar receiving 'the place', or 'principal manor', and half the lands, and Crichton getting the other half; and this was confirmed by crown charter.[12] Edgar, whom Bruce appointed sheriff of Dumfries,[13] subsequently gave his share of the lands to his son Donald,[14] while by 1335/6 Crichton's share, valued at 100 merks, was in the hands of Edward III 'through forfeiture'.[15] It was reported, however, that the lands brought Edward no revenue, as they had been laid waste.[16] Crichton recovered his lands after the English were again driven out, and he also acquired the Edgars' share of the barony by means that are not clear. According to one charter, 'Margaret Saluan (Salveyn)' forfeited her lands to 'Elizabeth Crichton' in the time of David II,[17] while other accounts state that Donald Edgar sold his share of the barony to the Crichtons.[18] Whatever the circumstances, the Crichtons ended up with the whole barony of Sanquhar.

William Crichton of Sanquhar is said to have died c.1360.[19] The next laird on record is Edward Crichton, about whom nothing is known, except that he witnessed a charter by Sir John Crichton of that Ilk sometime between 1368 and 1400, and he appears in a writ of 1412.[20] It was either William or Edward, probably the former, who founded the present castle some time before 1400.

The **CASTLE** is situated on the top of a steep bank, some 50ft high, overlooking the broad plain of the Nith valley, where a large deer park was later enclosed. This bank to the W and an adjacent ravine to the N provided a natural defence on two sides, while the other sides were defended by massive, dry ditches, some 35ft wide and 15ft deep. The S ditch was later filled in. The area thus enclosed was roughly trapezoidal in shape, measuring about 163ft from N to S by 130ft from E to W. Access to the site was gained from the NE, where the abutments, 19ft 8in wide and 10ft 6in apart, of a bridge crossing the E ditch may still be seen, and from here an offset gateway, rebuilt in the 17th century,[21] led into the outer courtyard at the N end of the site.

In the original arrangement there were tall curtain-walls, some 5ft thick, which enclosed the site, and in the SW corner stood a small, but strong, square tower, known as 'Wallace's Tower', which projected to cover the flanks. This enclosure may also have been divided into outer and inner courts, and no doubt there were other buildings on the site, but no evidence of these has survived. The SW tower was largely restored by the 3rd Marquess of Bute after 1894, but, although again suffering from the ravages of vandalism, enough of the original structure survives to provide a fair idea of the original arrangement.

The tower, which is 24ft square, has a vaulted basement and is built of sandstone ashlar with a 3-stage, splayed plinth, which projects 10in on all sides and continues along the curtain walls. The walls vary in thickness from 5ft 9in to about 8ft. The basement was entered on the E side through a doorway which

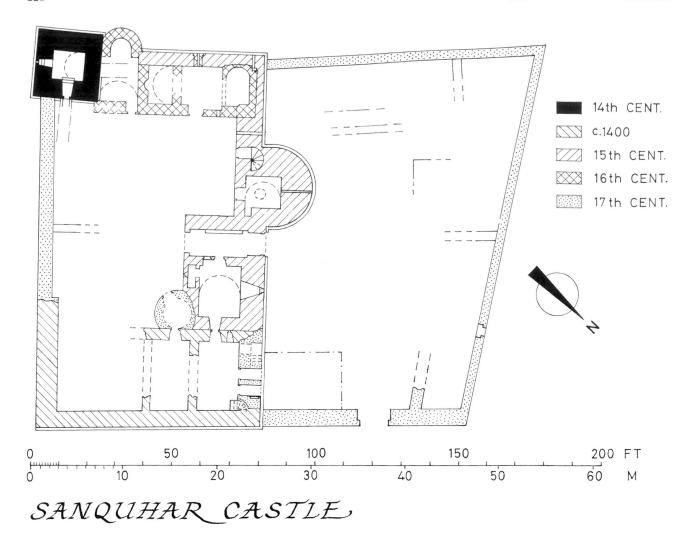

14th CENT.
c.1400
15th CENT.
16th CENT.
17th CENT.

SANQUHAR CASTLE

Fig. 321 Sanquhar Castle: plan of basements and courtyards.

was contained within the thickness of the S curtain. The only other opening is a small slit window in the S wall, which is provided with a stepped sill, the steps of which have chamfered arrises. There was no communication with the floor above.

Access to the first floor was through a second door immediately above the basement entrance, which was also reached from a mural recess within the thickness of the S curtain. From this entrance a mural passage led to a wheel-stair in the NE corner, which rose to serve the upper floors. There appear to have been windows in the N and E walls flanking the outside of the curtain-walls, and another in the S wall, but these were all rebuilt in the 1890s, and the small fireplace in the N wall is also of this date.

The second floor is likewise largely a modern reconstruction, with replacement windows in the N, E and S walls and a fireplace on the E side. The W wall, however, is original, and contains a fine, 14th century window comprising four lights divided by a stone mullion and transom. The lights have a form of QERH moulding across the angle[22] and are grooved for glazing, and the upper two have ogee heads. The scoinson arch had a pointed, segmental head reinforced with three bold, chamfered ribs, two of which have now fallen.

No original details survive on the third floor, but it is known that in the original arrangement there were doorways in the N and E walls which gave direct access to the parapet walks

Fig. 322 Sanquhar Castle: partly restored SW tower, with deer-park beyond on the right, seen from the keep-gatehouse.

on the adjacent curtain-walls. Simpson also records a garderobe
in the W wall, now gone, whose doorway had 'a drop-centred
pointed arch wrought in two stones, with a broad chamfer', which
had 'a notable resemblance to the original entrance of David's
Tower' at Edinburgh Castle.[23] This is shown in a distant view
by Grose,[24] while, in one of his views in 1788, Cardonnel shows
a window in the S wall with a head in the form of two semi-
circles.[25] Above this he shows a decorative quatrefoil, and above
that a smaller, attic window with a round-arched head in a gable
that is a straight continuation of the wall below. Simpson suggests that both this feature and some of the masonry at this level
was 16th century or later work.[26]

One of the great mysteries at Sanquhar is the fate of the
original curtain-walls, for it is clear that they were at least partly
demolished within about half a century of being built, and eventually replaced by new walls at two, quite distinct periods. The
first of these was sometime c.1400, when a large new building
range was added in the SE corner of the site, along the E side of
the inner court. This building, which comprised three or four
unvaulted cellars and one or more floors above, was built of
sandstone rubble with walls varying in thickness from 3ft 8in on
the W side to about 6ft at each end. Little of the building now
remains, but its S and E walls were used to form part of the new
enclosing wall, with the S wall continuing towards the tower
along a new line outside the old curtain.[27] This wall was rebuilt
again at some later date, probably in the 17th century.

The only features of the SE building that have survived
are: a section of walling on the E side; the bottom of a wheel-
stair, with steps some 3ft wide, in the NE corner; remnants of
the N wall, which was rebuilt in the 17th century to accommodate an adjacent building to the N; and a doorway and adjacent
slit-window on the W side of the northernmost cellar. The window was subsequently blocked up when the new keep-gatehouse
was built against it later in the 15th century.

The next laird after Edward Crichton, was Sir Robert
Crichton, probably his son, who is first recorded as 'Robert de
Crechtoun of Sanchare' in 1439/40.[28] He must have been
knighted soon after, for less than two months later, as 'Sir Robert',
he had a charter of confirmation of the barony of Sanquhar,[29] a
charter that was confirmed again by James III in 1464.[30] Sir
Robert attended the General Council in 1440 and 1441,[31] and

Fig. 323 Sanquhar Castle: view from the north in 1788.
The building in the foreground is the 15th century
keep-gatehouse showing the entrance to the pend.

was often present in parliament.[32] In 1452 James II appointed
him Sheriff of Dumfries, an office that was confirmed and made
hereditary in his family in 1464 by James III;[33] and in 1468/9 he
was appointed Coroner of Nithsdale.[34] It was almost certainly
Sir Robert who built the keep-gatehouse, the great central block
of Sanquhar Castle, and its associated ranges linking up to the
SW tower. He died in 1478 or 1479.

The **KEEP-GATEHOUSE** and adjacent, projecting
DRUM-TOWER occupied the central section of the N side of
the inner court, with the keep-gatehouse abutting the earlier E
range and the drum-tower on the opposite side, at the keep's
NW corner. The design bore a striking affinity with the layout
at Doune Castle.[35] The keep, which measures 39ft 6in from E to
W by 27ft 9in from N to S, appears to have comprised four storeys and an attic, with, on the N side at least, a corbelled-out
parapet walk. The walls vary in thickness from 7ft on the N side
to 4ft 6in at each end. The masonry is sandstone ashlar, though
the sizes of the blocks and thicknesses of the courses vary considerably.[36] Cardonnel shows that by the end of the 18th century
nothing remained above the basement except the N wall,[37] and
by 1820 even this had been reduced to a mere fragment of
corbelling and a solitary chimney-stack.[38] By the time the Marquess of Bute started the restoration of the castle in 1894, the
keep was a sorry sight; the basement and pend vaults had partly
collapsed, and little remained of the hall above.

At ground level, the keep comprises a large vaulted
guard-room with entresol floor and, at the W end, a vaulted pend,
about 14ft 6in high, leading into the inner court.[39] At its outer
end, the pend has a round-arched doorway, 7ft 3in wide and about
10ft high, which is rebated on the outside for a wooden door and
on the inside for an iron yett; and at the inner end there was
another doorway, now rebuilt, which was no doubt provided with

Fig. 324 Sanquhar Castle: basement of keep-gatehouse looking
through to the pend.

further wooden doors. The pend has a stone bench along its W
side, and opposite this a doorway, with adjacent window, which
leads into the guard-room, while another doorway at the opposite end of the guard-room connects directly with the northernmost cellar of the earlier E range. On the S side of the guardroom there is a mural ?garderobe with a slit window, but, apart
from this and the small window into the pend, there was no external illumination. There are, however, two large windows with
widely splayed jambs in the N and S haunches of the entresol
floor above. This floor was supported by two rows of substantial corbels that survive in the N and S walls. There is no trace
now of any stair leading to the entresol floor, so presumably it

Fig. 325 Sanquhar Castle: view from NW.

was reached by either a wooden stair or a ladder within the chamber. The vault was restored in brick in the 1890s.

The first floor was presumably the great hall. According to Simpson,[40] it was vaulted at two levels, but no evidence of this now survives, and neither Cardonnel's nor Grose's views of the ruins are clear on this point.[41] The only features that have survived are in the remaining fragment of the N wall. These comprise a large window recess with stone seats and a pointed scoinson arch; on its left, a restored mural recess, which was presumably an aumbry or buffet; and to the left of this, a mural cupboard with a slop-sink, whose drain, instead of passing straight through the N wall, starts off towards the W, presumably to avoid the pend below.

The **DRUM-TOWER**, which projected from the N wall in a semi-circle with a triple-splayed plinth-course, was about 15ft in radius. It had at least three storeys, but the drum portion had largely collapsed prior to 1788.[42] The basement, however, whose floor is below the level of the adjacent courtyard, has survived. It was the well-room, a high, barrel-vaulted chamber measuring 12ft 3in by 11ft 5in and rising 12ft 6in to the top of the restored vault. It was entered from the inner court through a round-arched doorway with chamfered arrises. Immediately inside the doorway was the well, so inconveniently situated that it must already have existed, presumably from the earliest phase of the castle and possibly within an earlier building. Although now filled in for safety, it is on record as having been 3ft 10in in diameter and 42ft deep, built of 'excellent ashlar, resting at the base on a wooden brander'.[43] When the well was cleaned out in 1876, a bucket was found still suspended in it.[44] The only other features in the basement are a mural recess in the SE corner and a drain that discharges through the N wall. There was no communication between this chamber and the floor above.

A second doorway further W admitted direct from the inner court to a wheel-stair serving the upper floors, though the present doorway and stair are largely a reconstruction of the 1890s. The stair is 7ft 6in in diameter. No details of the upper

floors have survived, beyond the unusual feature that the S wall of each room was inset further at each floor level on two courses of continuous corbelling. The reason for this is not known. It is, however, apparent from the surviving tusking that the rooms on the upper floors were larger than the basement, and it is also likely that the inner face of the walls on the N side followed the curve of the tower.

Fig. 326 Sanquhar Castle: doorway to well room.

Fig. 327 Sanquhar Castle: keep-gatehouse (on right) and
drum-tower (on left) seen from inner courtyard.

To the W of the drum-tower, the original W curtain having been demolished, a new wall was built running W across the
line of the original curtain and then S to join the SW tower at its
NW corner. This also formed part of a new building at the NW
corner of the inner court, where a drain from one or more
garderobes on the upper floors still survives; but apart from this
detail nothing is known of this building, as it was replaced by a
new kitchen range late in the 16th century. There was a new
postern near the middle of the W wall, and a drain connecting
the inner court to the outer court close to the drum-tower.

The one feature that is not apparent in any of the buildings at this time is a prison, yet there must have been one in so
important a castle, and in the following century there are references to some of those held here. One John Crichton 'in the
Bar', for example, was imrisoned at Sanquhar in 1564,[45] and ten
years later William Crichton, tutor of Sanquhar, was charged
with keeping certain persons prisoner without lawful authority.[46]

Sir Robert Crichton was succeeded by his eldest son,
Robert, who in 1479 had sasine of the lands of Sanquhar, Eliock,
Crawfordjohn and Kirkpatrick.[47] Five years later he played an
active role in suppressing the rebellion of Albany and the Earl of
Douglas, and for this he was rewarded with a new charter confirming him in the office of Sheriff of Dumfries and in the barony
of Sanquhar.[48] Then in 1587/8 he was raised to the peerage as
Lord Crichton of Sanquhar.[49] He attended parliament in 1481,
1483, 1487 and 1491.[50] He died in 1494. In recognition of his
new-found dignity, he may well have added to the castle, but it
is no longer possible to identify any work dating from this period.

Sir Robert Crichton, who succeeded his grandfather as
2nd Lord Crichton, was in financial difficulties throughout his
lairdship, and had to mortgage or sell many of his lands to meet
debts.[51] He died in 1513, probably killed at Flodden. He was
succeeded by his only son, Robert, 3rd Lord Crichton, who had
sasine in 1513.[52] Robert attended parliament in the same year
and again three years later,[53] but died in 1520.

Robert Crichton, who succeeded his father as 4th Lord
Crichton, was probably still a minor when he died shortly before 1536. He was succeeded by his brother William, who had
sasine in 1538/9.[54] But although William was subsequently a
regular attender of parliament,[55] his lands were still held in ward,
and so they remained until after his eldest surviving son and
heir, Robert, 6th Lord Crichton of Sanquhar, succeeded and had

sasine in 1557/8.[56] During this time the castle was badly ne-
glected and fell into a state of disrepair.[57]

The 6th Lord Crichton died in 1561, and was succeeded
by his brother Edward. Four years later, Edward was a signatory to a Bond pledging support for Queen Mary and was given
command of a troop of horse in the van of the royal army.[58] He
attended parliament in April 1567, but the following month his
loyalties changed after Mary's marriage to Bothwell, and in July
he attended the coronation of James VI; he also became a member of the Regent Moray's council.[59] After Mary's escape from
Loch Leven, Edward again changed sides. He fought for Mary
at Langside in 1568,[60] and was in attendance upon her at Sanquhar
on the first night of her flight south.[61] Moray followed a month
later and camped beside the castle, but he 'cast not down 'my
lordis place', as he had promised to come in and found surety'.[62]
Edward died the following year. Once again Sanquhar was left
with a son and heir, Robert, 8th Lord Crichton, who was under
age, while Moray wasted no time in granting the ward and non-
entry of the barony of Sanquhar, and of the offices of sheriff and
coroner of Dumfries, to his daughter Annabel Stewart.[63]

Robert, 8th Lord Crichton of Sanquhar, who was served
heir to his father in 1589,[64] attended parliament in 1585, 1587
and 1596,[65] and was also a member of the Privy Council.[66] In
1596 he was directed to levy horsemen to attend upon King
James,[67] and in the same year was also appointed Joint-Warden
and Justice of the West March with Gordon of Lochinvar and
Stewart of Garlies, although they all refused to take up the appointment.[68] Robert was subsequently employed by James VI
as a 'secret political agent' on the Continent,[69] and was much in
favour with the king. However, for reasons unknown, he resigned his lands and barony of Sanquhar, together with the
fortalices, etc., and many other lands, in 1602 in favour of David
Crichton of Lugton,[70] who held them until 1609. Robert then
recovered his estates, and obtained a charter of novodamus of
the same.[71] But his loyal service did not save him when, having
lost an eye in a friendly contest with a fencing-master named
Turner, he was found guilty of plotting Turner's murder in revenge and hanged at Westminster in 1612.[72]

It was during the latter half of the 16th century that a
new kitchen range was built on the W side of the inner court. It
utilized the existing walls on the N and W sides, blocking up the
former postern, and comprised a range of three chambers, the
most northerly of which served as the new kitchen, with a large
fireplace at its N end. The kitchen has a small opening, of unknown purpose, low down beside the doorway to the courtyard
and a slop-sink inserted in the former postern on the other side.
The fireplace, which was about 13ft wide and 9ft deep, was
fronted by a large arch, some 8ft wide, of well cut voussoirs
with a QER moulding on the outer edge.[73] The two chambers to
the S were vaulted at right angles to one another, and at the back
of the more southerly one a large oven was pushed through the
former enclosing wall. The adjacent chamber had a small fireplace in its S wall, but there is no evidence of any window in
either chamber, nor of a second storey above.

Another feature first recorded on Pont's map[74] around
this time is the large deer park situated on the low ground to the
N and W of the castle. Of unknown antiquity and extending to
some 70 acres, the park was enclosed by a 6ft high, drystone
wall of carefully coursed rubble, much of which still survives.
It is tapered in section, measuring 2ft wide at the top and about
3ft at the base, and has an 'embattled' top made up of dressed,
oblong stones laid across the wall at regular intervals.

Robert had an illegitimate son, William, known as Lord Crichton, who was legitimated in 1609; but two years after his father's death, James VI declared William's claims invalid and ordered that he give up all claim to the barony of Sanquhar,[75] whereupon his father's cousin, William Crichton of Ryehill, was formally recognised as 9th Lord Crichton of Sanquhar.[76] It was not, however, until 1618 that Lord Crichton obtained undisputed possession of the lands, and the following year before he obtained a crown charter erecting all his lands, including the barony of Glencairn, into the new barony of Sanquhar.[77] Lord Crichton was a member of the Court of High Commission in 1615,[78] and sat in parliament in 1617 and 1621.[79] In 1618 he was appointed to the Commission for Preserving Peace in the Middle Shires[80] and admitted to the Privy Council.[81] During James VI's state visit to Scotland in 1617, Lord Crichton had the honour of entertaining him at Sanquhar,[82] and in 1633 he attended Charles I during his visit to the country.[83] For these and other services, William was created Viscount Air in 1622 and Earl of Dumfries in 1633.[84] By the latter date, however, he was heavily in debt, and in 1638 he was compelled to sell the entire estate to William Douglas, 1st Earl of Queensberry.[85] He died four years later.

The 1st Earl of Queensberry died only two years after acquiring Sanquhar, and there is no evidence that his son James, the 2nd Earl, ever lived there either, Drumlanrig (q.v.) being their principal residence. However, the 2nd Earl's widow, Margaret Stewart, made her will at Sanquhar in 1673,[86] so she may have lived there with her eldest son after her husband's death in 1671. During the Civil War, the castle was twice requisitioned. In 1650 the English 'put ane garrisone of Dragouns' in it, who caused so much damage that it 'cost the said Earle in repaireing thairof four thousand punds' and, moreover, 'the saids English dragouns did exact aff the barronie of Sanquhar belonging to the Earle more then their due proportion the sume of four hundreth punds weeklie',[87] and three years later, after two troops of parliamentarian forces had mistakenly attacked each other at Sanquhar tolbooth, the castle was used as a hospital for the wounded.[88]

The 2nd Earl's eldest son, William, Lord Drumlanrig, set up house at Sanquhar during his father's lifetime. In 1664 he was granted a crown charter of the lands, lordship and barony of Sanquhar, including the tower and fortalice, and many other lands, including the lands and baronies of Crawfordston and Glencairn, all of which were erected into a free regality, within the earldom of Queensberry and regality of Drumlanrig, to be held in blench-ferme.[89] This was ratified under the Great Seal the following year, and by parliament in 1669.[90] William was also, in 1667, granted the offices of Sheriff and Coroner of Dumfriesshire that had formerly been held by the Crichtons.[91] In addition, he held many high offices of state, details of which are given under Drumlanrig (q.v.). After his father's death in 1671, when he succeeded to the earldom, he decided to remain at 'The Sanquhar', as it was then known, until he had rebuilt Drumlanrig. It was an undertaking that almost ruined him. He eventually moved to Drumlanrig c.1690, but stayed only one night before returning again to Sanquhar, where he spent the rest of his days. Meanwhile, in 1682, he had been made Marquess of Queensberry and two years later Duke of Queensberry, before falling from favour in 1685. He died ten years later.

It was presumably the 3rd Earl who carried out most, if not all, the works undertaken at Sanquhar during the 17th century. These included a new enclosing wall for the outer court; a new building in the SE corner of this court, which connected with the adjacent range in the inner court; the reconstruction of part of the S wall of the inner court adjacent to the SW tower, together with a spur running N, which may have formed part of an outbuilding; and a circular stair-tower in the NE corner of this court, which served both the gatehouse and adjacent range, as well as incorporating a new entrance. Above this entrance, there was an armorial panel. Although both these features are illustrated by Grose,[92] the position in which they are shown amongst the ruins is a little disoriented. The stair itself was about 9ft in diameter.

It was probably also the Earl who laid out the avenue of ash trees along the drive from the NE and the formal garden, complete with fish-pond and island, that formerly existed in the deer park immediately to the W of the castle.[93] He may also have been responsible for the bowling green that existed on the S side of the castle.[94]

After the death of the 1st Duke, Sanquhar Castle was apparently abandonned by the family, when the 2nd Duke went to live at Drumlanrig. Then, in 1714, the castle was let to Archibald Douglas,[95] who moved here from Morton Castle. He died at Sanquhar four years later. The castle was subsequently occupied by William Menzies, brother of James Menzies of Enoch, and John Menzies, the town clerk of Sanquhar, who died in 1727.[96] It was then abandonned, although a servant woman 'persisted in remaining there to the end of her days'.[97] The castle was already ruinous when, in 1735, the Duke of Queensberry allowed 'stones to be led from the castle' to assist in the construction of the new town-house in Sanquhar.[98] These are said to have been used for the vaulted rooms on the ground floor.[99] The lead was also stripped from the roof, and further stones were later plundered for houses in Sanquhar.[100]

Fig. 328 Sanquhar Castle: view from the east in 1790.

By the time the castle was recorded by Cardonnel in 1788[101] and Grose in 1790,[102] it was in an advanced stage of decay; and so it remained until both the castle and deer park were purchased by the 3rd Marquess of Bute, the direct descendant and representative of the Earls of Dumfries and Lords Crichton of Sanquhar, in 1894.

Lord Bute set about the complete restoration of the castle, and had almost finished the SW tower,[103] when he died in 1900. He had also restored the vaults in both the keep-gatehouse and the well room, the S end of the pend, and the lower part of the outer wall of the drum-tower and the stair serving it. After his death, all work stopped, and once again the castle is a sad and rapidly crumbling ruin, a prey to constant vandalism.

1   Stell 1986, 117; Maxwell 1989, 177.

2   Scots Peerage VI, 286.

3   Ibid, 286-7; McDowall 1986, 17 (McDowall incorrectly gives Duvenald as the grandson of Dunegal).

4   Reid, R. C. 'Sanquhar Castle', *TDGAS*, 3rd Ser., XIV, 335.

5   RCAHMS 1920, No.556. Helmsley remained the principal seat of the family, and Wark the home of Robert's second son, Robert, and his descendants until forfeited in the time of Edward I (See Burke Peerage 1959, 'Baron de Ros'), so presumably it was a cadet branch of the family who settled at Sanquhar.

6   The New Place may have been built by the English as a smaller version of the new castle built by them at Lochmaben.

7   Bain II, 206.

8   Simpson, W. 'Sanquhar Castle', *TDGAS*, 3rd Ser., XXI, 260. According to Simpson, De Beauvair was related to the de Ros family (Robert de Ros of Helmsley, who was made Baron de Ros in 1264, married Isabel, daughter and heiress of William de Albini, Lord of Belvoir), and was given New Place by Edward I. Henry de Percy and Robert de Clifford wrote to Edward from Sanquhar on 30th June (Bain II, No.902), but the dates of Douglas's venture, as recorded by Blind Harry, are not known.

9   Fraser 1885, I, 95.

10 Bain V, No.521. Edward stayed at Sanquhar again on his return journey ten days later (Bain III, No.13; V, No.497).

11 Wilson & McMillan, 21. It has been suggested that William was either a son of Thomas de Crichton or Alexander de Crichton, both of whom swore fealty to Edward I in 1296 (Bain II, 206, 213; Grose I, 151; Scots Peerage III, 219). That the Crichtons of that Ilk and the Crichtons of Sanquhar were closely related is shown by two crown charters granted to Sir William Crichton of that Ilk in 1440 and 1441. These entailed the lands of Crichton and others in Annandale such that, in the event of Sir William having no surviving heirs male, the lands were to pass to Sir Robert Crichton of Sanquhar and his heirs male (RMS II, Nos.234, 791).

12 Robertson's Index, 5.27, 12.70, 21.34; RMS I, No.27; App.2, Nos.141, 298, 531.

13 ERS I, 123.

14 RMS I, App.1, No.56.

15 Bain III, 318.

16 Ibid.

17 RMS I, App.2, No.1231.

18 Wilson & McMillan, 19, 22.

19 Grose I, 151.

20 Scots Peerage III, 220.

21 The N jamb of the gateway and the springing for the arched head was still *in situ* early in the 20th century, but now only the rybats survive.

22 See MacGibbon & Ross, I, Fig.360.

23 Simpson, *op. cit.*, 264. See also Tabraham 1995, 24. This type of lintel formed from two stones is also found at Cockburnspath and at The Vicar's Pele (*c*.1300) in Corbridge, Northumberland.

24 Grose I, 150, Plate 1.

25 This arrangement is found on the lintel of the fourth floor fireplace in the wing at Hoddom and over one of the first floor aumbries at Elshieshields.

26 Simpson, *op. cit.*, 263-4.

27 It is quite likely that the E wall, which is 5ft thick and has a triple-splayed plinth course, like the original curtains in the SW corner, was built on the foundations of the original curtain-wall. The N wall may also incorporate a section of an original cross-wall dividing the inner court from the outer court.

28 RMS II, No.227.

29 Ibid, No.233.

30 Ibid, No.789.

31 APS II, 55, 56.

32 Ibid, *passim*.

33 RMS II, No.790.

34 Ibid, No.974.

35 See MacGibbon & Ross I, 418-29.

36 MacGibbon & Ross's assertion that the masonry is 'of the finest kind' is hard to justify.

37 Cardonnel, 'Sanquhar: Plate I'.

38 Drawing in NMRS.

39 A new block added at Crichton Castle, in Midlothian, in the 15th century also had a vaulted pend providing a new entrance into the inner courtyard (RCAHMS 1929, 46, 48; Lewis, J 'Excavations at Crichton Castle, Midlothian', *PSAS*, 127 (1997), 698-9).

40 Simpson, *op. cit.*, 266.

41 Cardonnel, 'Sanquhar: Plate II'; Grose I, 151, Plate 2. A corbelled-out projection shown by Grose may have been intended to represent the springing for a vault, though Grose's drawings are usually more accurate.

42 Cardonnel, 'Sanquhar: Plate I'.

43 Simpson, *op. cit.*, 266-7.

44 Ordnance Gazetteer, 1449.

45 RSS V, No.1766.

46 RPC II, 437.

47 ERS IX, 679.

48 RMS II, No.1597.

49 APS II, 181.

50 Ibid, 134, 136, 153, 175, 229.

51 RMS II, Nos. 2288, 3380, 3584, 3585, 3653, 3657, 3785.

52 ERS XIV, 523.

53 APS II, 281.

54 ERS XVII, 763.

55 APS II, *passim*.

56 ERS XIX, 419.

57 Reid, R. C. 'A Sanquhar Castle Document', *TDGAS*, 3rd Ser., XVI, 57-9.

58 Scots Peerage III, 229.

59 Ibid; RPC XIV, 22.

60 Wilson & McMillan, 46.

61 Fraser 1873, I, 523.

62 Scottish Papers II, Nos.716, 717. It was said that 'Sanquhar's house' was spared 'at the suit of Drumlanrig, his father-in-law' (Scottish Papers II, No.703).

63 RSS VI, No.639.

64 Scots Peerage III, 230.

65 APS III, 374, 427, 429; IV, 104, 106, 109.

66 RPC V, *passim*.

67 Scottish Papers XII, 408.

68 RPC V, 292; Rae, 243.

69 Scots Peerage III, 230.

70 RMS VI, No.1375.

71 Ibid, VII, No. 124.

72 RPC IX, 371; Scots Peerage, 230-1.

73 Simpson, *op. cit.*, 265.

74 Pont MS. No.35 in National Library of Scotland. The 'Park of Sanquhar' is mentioned in a charter of 1611 (RMS VII, No.479).

75 Scots Peerage III, 232.

76 Ibid, 233.

77 RMS VII, No.2061.

78 RPC X, 435-7.

79 APS IV, 524, 581, 593.

80 RPC XI, 345.

81 Ibid, 362.

82 Ibid, XI, 207.

83 Scots Peerage III, 234.

84 RMS VIII, Nos.264, 2170.

85 Ibid, IX, No.791.

86 Scots Peerage VII, 135. Margaret had been granted the castle and manor-place of Sanquhar, together with the 'Froy Park' and other lands, in liferent by her husband in 1656 (RMS X, No.521).

87 APS VII, 285.

88 Simpson, *op. cit.*, 261.

89 RMS XI, No.546.

90 APS VII, 645.

91 Ibid.

92 Grose I, 151, Plate 2.

93 Ibid, 150; NSA IV, 305.

94 Grose I, 150.

95 Adams 1921, 262; Wilson, T. 'Sanquhar Castle', *TDGAS*, 3rd Ser., XIV, 340.

96 Wilson, T. 'Sanquhar Castle', *op. cit.*, 340.

97 Adams 1921, 264.

98 Wilson & McMillan, 165-6.

99 RCAHMS 1996, 181.

100 Grose I, 151.

101 Cardonnel, 'Sanquhar: Plates I and II'.

102 Grose I, 150-1, Plates 1 and 2.

103 Some of the 'restoration' in the SW tower is a little fanciful, but the new work is clearly defined by the insertion of red tiles.

60.   SHIRMERS CASTLE

(2½m SE New Galloway)   (NX656743)

The lands of Shirmers lie on the E side of Loch Ken, not far from the head of the loch. They first come on record in 1408, when Archibald, Earl of Douglas and Lord of Galloway, granted the lands of Schyirnes, le Park, le Contrefe, Erncanny and others in the barony of Balmaclellan to Sir Alexander de Gordoun, to be held 'in fee and heritage for ever for rendering a suit of court at the head plea to be held in the barony of

Balmaclelane, next after the feast of Easter'.[1] This Sir Alexander was presumably the same Sir Alexander Gordon of Stitchel, Co. Berwick, who had been granted the neighbouring lands of Kenmure by the Earl of Douglas in 1403[2] and also the lands of the Forest of Glenkens at about the same date.[3]

Nothing more is heard of Shirmers until 1517, when Janet, daughter and heiress of Sir Alexander Gordon, younger of Lochinvar, was granted the liferent of Shirmers and certain other lands in the parishes of Balmaclellan and Kells in compensation for her renunciation of the estates of Lochinvar and Kenmure (q.v.) to her uncle, Sir Robert Gordon of Glen.[4] Two years later Janet married Lachlan Mackintosh of Dunachtan, Chief of the Clan Mackintosh.[5]

Shirmers next comes on record in 1527, when Alexander Gordon 'in Scheirmaris' (presumably a relative)[6] and his wife Marion Livingstone were granted a Precept for a Charter of the lands of Ardmannoch and Finniness, which were resigned in their favour by Alexander Livingstone of Little Airds and Gilbert Grierson of Dalton.[7] Four years later they also purchased the lands of Over and Nether Dullarg and another small property in the neighbouring parish of Parton.[8] Witnesses to this transaction included James Gordon of Lochinvar and John Gordon in Park. In the same year Alexander took over the lease of the lands of Knocksheen and Barskeoch, WNW of Dalry;[9] and three years later, Alexander renewed the lease of Barskeoch in the name of himself and his son William, while he and his son John also took on the lease of the lands of Arnlosk (?Ironlosh), near Balmaclellan.[10]

Alexander Gordon 'in the Schirmars' and other Gordons, including James Gordon of Lochinvar, were 'absent in the King's service' in 1536.[11] Alexander was still alive in 1548, when he witnessed a charter, but was dead by 1565, when Alexander Gordon 'youngar, sone to umquhile Alexander Gordoun of Schirmes', was granted a Letter of Tack for the lease of the lands of Barskeoch and Drumboy, presently occupied by him.[12] On the same day, another son, Roger, styled 'in Schermes', received

Fig. 329 Shirmers Castle: remains of SE corner of tower.

a Letter of Tack of the lands of Arnlosk, Cubbies and Dalquharnawhan.[13] But although Roger was styled 'in Schermes', and was still being so designated as late as 1593,[14] it was his brother Alexander who had succeeded to the property and had the distinctive title 'of Schirmes'.[15]

It is not known when the present castle was built, and there are no features left that might give an indication. Many

tower-houses were built after the Reformation in 1560, and it may be that the present castle was built by the younger Alexander Gordon during that period of building activity. On the other hand, there is a tradition that the castle was burned by the Regent Moray when he marched against the Gordons and 'cast down and burnt' Kenmure in 1568.[16] Depending upon the extent of the damage, the present ruins at Shirmers may date from a rebuilding at that time. 'Chirmers' is shown on Pont's map c.1595.[17] It stands on the high, right bank of a small burn that flows through the old Shirmers Wood into Loch Ken some 400 yards to the W.

Only the SE end of the **CASTLE** survives, the rest having been demolished when the present farm steading was extended in the 19th century. It is 21ft 3in wide, and now extends for 15ft 6in and 12ft along the NE and SW walls respectively. There is no evidence to show whether it was oblong in plan or had a wing. The walls, which are built of greywacke rubble with roughly shaped quoins, reach a maximum height of 9ft at the S corner. They are 3ft 6in thick. The interior is no longer accessible, having been filled in to form a rock garden, but it is on record that the basement was not vaulted.[18] No other features survive. There is, however, a skewput with a carved human head built into the wall above the doorway of the modern farmhouse, which is believed to have come from the castle.

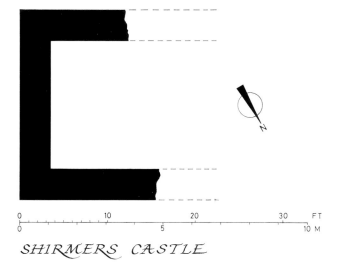

SHIRMERS CASTLE

Fig. 330 Shirmers Castle: plan of remains of basement.

Alexander Gordon of Shirmers evidently died without issue. He was succeeded by his nephew Gilbert, son of Roger Gordon in Shirmers,[19] who is described in 1594 as 'apparent of Schirmers', when, as Commendator of Sweetheart Abbey, he leased certain lands in New Abbey to John Brown of Lands.[20] The lease is dated at 'the Scheirmeris'. After the Union of the Crowns, Gilbert served as a 'Commissioner for conserving His Majesty's peace' in the Stewartry of Kirkcudbright and Wigtownshire.[21]

A later member of the family was William Gordon of Shirmers, who was a Commissioner of War for the Stewartry of Kirkcudbright in 1648 and 1649,[22] and either he, or a son of the same name, was a Commissioner of Supply for the Stewartry in 1656, 1659 and 1661.[23] The following year William was fined for his adherence to the Presbyterian Church.[24] He was appointed a Justice of the Peace for the Stewartry in 1663,[25] and in 1683

'William Gordon of Shirmers elder' subscribed to the Test.[26] His son Robert took the Test a year later.[27] In 1686, both William and Robert were Commissioners of Supply for the Stewartry.[28] William died shortly afterwards, sometime before July 1686.[29]

Robert, who succeeded his father, was a Commissioner of Supply again in 1690,[30] and in the same year he was appointed a Justice of the Peace for the Stewartry.[31] After his death in 1692, his widow, Agnes Laurie, failed to be paid the annuity of 800 merks due to her from the Shirmers estate. She accordingly, in 1706, obtained a Decreet of Poinding against her brother-in-law, William Gordon, who had succeeded to Shirmers, and her (?step-) daughters, Margaret and Agnes Gordon, daughters and co-heiresses of Robert.[32] William was a Commissioner of Supply for the Stewartry in 1695 and 1704,[33] and he was presumably also the 'William Gordon of Shirmers' who was a Commissioner in 1689, when his brother was still alive.[34] William was succeeded by Alexander Gordon, who died in 1735, aged 41, leaving no surviving male issue.[35]

According to some accounts, Thomas Gordon (d.1750), the celebrated editor and publisher in 1719 of a tract called the *Independent Whig*, was born at Shirmers; but others say he was a cadet of the Gordons of Kenmure.[36] He is believed to have become an advocate in 1716, and travelled to London shortly afterwards. The *Independent Whig* was eventually extended to four volumes. Thomas also produced a 'standard' translation of Tacitus, as well as being the author of various other works.[37] Under Walpole's premiership, he became First Commissioner of the Wine Licences.

The next laird of Shirmers was Robert Gordon, whose relationship to Alexander is not known. He was in possession in 1746.[38] He also died without male issue, and was succeeded by his daughter Jean, who in 1792 was styled 'of Shirmers'.[39] In, or shortly before, 1749 she married Alexander Spalding, a wealthy Dumfries merchant who had purchased the nearby estate of Holm. The estates of Holm and Shirmers were thus united.[40] For a while Alexander adopted the surname of Gordon, but later reverted to that of Spalding.[41] In 1792, as 'Alexander Gordon of Shirmers', he was sheriff-depute of Wigtown.[42] Then in 1799, Samuel Spalding, a doctor at Devizes in Wiltshire and close relative of Alexander,[43] obtained possession of Holm and was granted a Crown charter of the property.[44] The reason for this change of ownership is not known, but subsequently Alexander's youngest son, John, who had meanwhile made a very successful career for himself as a merchant in London, bought back the whole estate.[45] John was member of parliament for the county of Wigtown from 1795-1806.[46] He died in 1815, and was succeeded by his only son.

John Eden Spalding of The Holm and Shirmers was a Justice of the Peace. He married the Hon. Mary Upton, daughter of Viscount Templetown, and had an only son, Augustus Spalding, DL, JP, who succeeded his father in 1869 and died unmarried in 1911. On his death the estate passed to his cousin, the Hon. Augustus Upton, who was still in possession of The Holme and Shirmers in 1937.[47]

1   Fraser 1885, III, 405.
2   Scots Peerage V, 100.
3   Ibid. See 'Lochinvar Castle'.
4   Scots Peerage V, 104; Affleck, J 'Kenmure Castle', *TDGAS*, 2nd Ser., XXIII, 183.
5   Ibid; RMS III, Nos.163, 285.
6   Alexander is a common name in the family of Gordon of Lochinvar. Although Gordon of Shirmers does not appear in the Lochinvar family tree, he may have been a natural son, or descended from a natural son, of the family.

Sir Robert Gordon of Lochinvar's daughter Elizabeth married Alexander Livingstone of Little Airds.
7   RSS I, No.3706.
8   RMS III, No.1021; ALHT V, 397.
9   ERS XVI, 487.
10 Ibid, 509.
11 RSS II, No.2155.
12 RSS V, No.2159.
13 Ibid, No.2161.
14 RMS V, Nos. 59, 2190, 2277.
15 Ibid, Nos. 1474, 1523.
16 Ibid; M'Kerlie III, 83.
17 Blaeu, 66, 'The Steuartrie of Kircubright, The most easterlie part of Galloway'.
18 RCAHMS 1914, No.36.
19 RMS VI, No.187.
20 Laing Charters, No.1288.
21 RPC IX, 77, 451.
22 APS VI, Part II, 35, 493.
23 Ibid, 851, 884; VII, 92.
24 M'Kerlie III, 81.
25 APS VII, 504-8.
26 RPC, 3rd Ser., VIII, 640.
27 Ibid, X, 227.
28 APS VIII, 469.
29 PRS Dumfries II (1672-1702), Index, 122.
30 APS IX, 144.
31 RPC, 3rd Ser., XV, 541.
32 Adams 1921, Appendix A, No.94.
33 APS IX, 375; XI, 150.
34 Ibid, IX, 74.
35 M'Kerlie III, 82.
36 Stat Acct VII, 229; Ordnance Gazetteer, 115. He is not included in the genealogy of the Gordons of Kenmure given in the *Scots Peerage*.
37 DNB, 810.
38 M'Kerlie III, 82.
39 Ibid, 83.
40 Ibid.
41 Ibid, 79.
42 Stat Acct VII, 227.
43 It is not clear whether he was a brother or nephew.
44 M'Kerlie III, 79.
45 Ibid.
46 Burke L. G. 1937, 2098, 'Spalding (now Upton) of Holme'.
47 Ibid.

61.   SPEDLINS TOWER
(3m NNE Lochmaben)   (NY098876)

Spedlins Tower was built by the Jardines of Applegarth (or Applegirth), a Norman Family who took their designation from the lands of Applegarth, two miles to the SSE, where the remains of a substantial motte-and-bailey castle may still be seen on the left bank of the river Annan, close to its confluence with the Kinnel Water.[1] It is not known for certain who built this castle. Although the family of Applegarth took their name from the property – William Applegarth witnessed a charter to Cambuskenneth Abbey c.1190,[2] and in 1340 Richard de Applegarth was in the garrison at Roxburgh Castle[3] –, the lands themselves appear to have been part of the original knight's fee[4] granted to one Ingebald by Robert de Brus some time in the 12th century, and restored to his son Hugh c.1215.[5] It seems probable, therefore, that it was Ingebald who built the original motte;[6] and it was from his son that the property subsequently passed, possibly by marriage, to one William de Gardino (or Jardine).[7]

The Jardines were prominent in Annandale as early as the 12th century, where they were close allies of the Bruces. Indeed, it was from the Bruce's 'arms' that their own were derived.[8] A Humphrey de Jardin, or Gardine, witnessed a number of Bruce charters c.1180-1214,[9] and he or his son may have been

Fig. 331 Spedlins: view from SW in 1902.
(Photograph by the author's grandfather,
John Bell Irving of Beanlands.)

the Sir Humphrey de Gardino who witnessed a resignation of lands in Annandale sometime before 1245.[10] In 1298 William de Jardine, 'Scotsman', forfeited lands in Cumbria.[11] The following year Sir Humphrey de Jardine received payment from Edward I for duty in Annandale.[12] Five years later William du Gardyn petitioned Edward for the return of some land in Cumberland that Edward had confiscated.[13] William was also a witness *c*.1329 to several charters by Bruce's nephew, Thomas Randolph, Earl of Moray.[14] Nowhere, however, is a place of residence mentioned. It was not until 1476 that any of the family used the designation 'of Applegarth',[15] when 'John Jardin of Appilgarth' granted a charter of the lands of Jardinfield in Berwickshire to George Hume of Wedderburn.[16] Thereafter the Jardines were always styled 'of Applegarth'. By this time the stronghold on the motte would have been enlarged and strengthened, and the ruined vault, referred to in the New Statistical Account in 1834 as having 'stood till lately' on the motte, was probably a survival of this period.[17]

It was around this time, however, late in the 15th century, that Spedlins appears to have been built as the new family seat. The site of the old motte at Applegarth being wholly unsuitable for a massive tower-castle, a new site was found further north on the top of a steep bank above the river Annan, where natural protection was afforded on two sides by a bend in the river and on the other sides by extensive marshland. From the top of the tower there was a clear view along the valley.

The outward appearance of the tower is misleading, as, despite its apparent, massive simplicity, only the two lower sto-

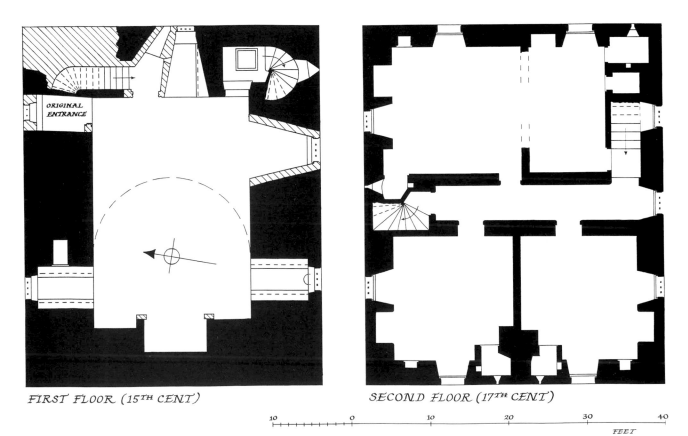

FIRST FLOOR (15TH CENT)   SECOND FLOOR (17TH CENT)

SPEDLINS TOWER

Fig. 332 Spedlins Tower: plans of first and second floors in 1968, before restoration.

reys date from the 15th century. The entire upper half, with its generous supply of windows, corner turrets and twin gabled roof, was not added until 1605, when the upper floors were entirely rebuilt.

In addition to the tower, there was a variety of courtyards and outbuildings on the site, but of these only the earth-covered foundations remained until finally swept away when the tower was restored and the site landscaped in the 1980s. They gave no evidence as to date. One courtyard, measuring approximately 90ft by 60ft, occupied all the ground as far as the cliff to the N. This may have been the original barmkin, though the situation is confused by the fact that terraced gardens are believed to have been laid out on the site sometime in the 17th century.[18] From the remains it appeared that it incorporated a round tower, about 10ft in diameter, towards the western end of its N wall, though this may have been later work. Further enclosures and outbuildings of various dates lay to the S and W of the tower, occupying an area of about 85ft by 75ft, while further S, where there is least natural protection, there was evidence of additional, defensive outworks.

The **TOWER**, which is almost square in plan, measures 38ft 2in from N to S by 45ft 6in from E to W, and rises 48ft 6in to the wall-head. The two lower storeys, both of which are vaulted, have walls averaging 9ft in thickness, while the walls of the later, upper floors are reduced to 3ft 2in. They are all built of red sandstone rubble, with dressed quoins and margins. The only moulding found on the original work is a heavy chamfer on the arrises of the doors and windows.

The original entrance was at first floor level, at the E end of the N wall, and would have been reached by a retractable wooden ladder. It gave direct access to the hall. Sometime in the 16th century this entrance was superseded by a new one at ground level immediately below.[19] At the same time the original entrance and lobby were converted into a window recess,[20] leaving only the dripstone in the wall above, while the N jamb of the window recess at the E end of the hall was either rebuilt, or modified, to incorporate a squint, or shot-hole, covering the new approach up the stair. It is presumed that there was already a service stair at this point connecting the hall to the basement. Early illustrations of the new entrance show a round arch-head and a splayed oval gun-loop on either side,[21] and these were still in place as recently as 1835.[22] The latter features disappeared when this corner of the tower was partially rebuilt later in the 19th century.[23] All the 16th century work is characterised by bold QER mouldings.

The basement is a simple cellar, the floor of which appears to be founded on living rock, a few feet below the level of the ground outside, while the maximum height of the barrel-vault is only 9ft. The only openings are two, strong, defensive arrow-slits, one in each gable-end. They measure 2ft 8in high by 3¼in wide on the outside, and open out on the inside to 5ft 9in high by 3ft 6in wide, with stepped sills. Within these recesses a defender could get within 2ft of the outside wall, but his vision and effective working arc would be severely restricted. The only other original feature in this chamber is a slop-sink at the E end of the S wall. At a much later date a partition wall with two doorways and a hatch, or lamp-shelf, was added along the length of the basement.[24]

The first floor was the great hall, a large chamber 28ft by 20ft and rising 18ft to the top of the barrel-vault. It has a large fireplace, 8ft wide, in the middle of the W wall, but at some period the original surround has been replaced by a new one in early Renaissance style. This was probably in 1605. Its

Fig. 333 Spedlins: great hall fireplace. 1605.

huge lintel has a moulded cornice and a frieze enriched with fluted consoles, while the jambs also comprise fluted consoles with moulded caps and bases. This surround is almost identical to the one in the hall at Newark Castle, Renfrewshire, and is presumably by the same hand.[25] Facing one another in the side walls at this end of the hall are two large, squared, window recesses with stone seats, both of which are one step up from the hall. The one to the N has a large close-aumbry in the right jamb, while the other has a slop-sink cut in the floor below the window and draining to the outside. Both windows retain their iron grilles and, like the other windows on both this floor and the floors above, were originally half-glazed and fitted with shutters. At the E end of the S wall there is another, larger window with a splayed recess, which has either been inserted or modi-

Fig. 334 Spedlins: window with stone seats on N side of great hall.

fied at a later date; it too has an iron grille. The window at the E end, which is also one step up from the hall, has a splayed recess with a stone seat on its right side, while the left jamb has either been reconstructed or substantially modified in the 16th century, as already noted. It was at this time that the two doorways with bold QER surrounds were inserted in this corner of the hall, one at the top of the stair and the other converting the original entrance vestibule into a mural chamber. Above the E window there is a second, high window, with widely splayed jambs and sill, to throw more light into the centre of the hall. There is no evidence of a gallery. The floor of the hall is covered with stone flags.

Leading off the SE corner of the hall, through a doorway which retains its original chamfered surround, there is a mural lobby. This leads to the wheel-stair serving the upper floors, while a hatch in the floor is the only means of access, and ventilation, for a pit-prison contained within the thickness of the wall below. The prison measures 10ft by 3ft 9in, with tapering sides, and has a maximum height of 8ft, except at the hatch. There is an ancient tradition that a man called Porteous perished in this prison in tragic circumstances in the 17th century, when the laird was unexpectedly called away to Edinburgh on business, taking the key with him. By the time he remembered about his prisoner, the man had died of starvation.[26]

The layout of the second and third floors is very similar. Each is divided into four rooms with a central corridor running N to S, and each is provided with two windows with iron grilles, a fireplace, a closed garderobe with a lamp-shelf and slit-window, and an aumbry. The sole exception is the SE room on the second floor, where, because of the intrusion of the upper section of the stair, there is only one window and a much larger aumbry, 3ft 6in by 2ft 8in and 2ft 7in high. The design of the corridor walls is ingenious. To keep their weight and that of the upper floors from overloading the vault below, massive relieving arches, extending across the full width of the vault, have been incorporated within the thickness of the walls themselves. In addition to the features already described, the third floor is also provided with a corbelled-out turret at each corner, reached from the adjoining room. These turrets have a single, central window and two, low shot-holes so contrived that they gave cover to the adjacent walls below. The latter features are devoid of all ornament and almost invisible from the ground. Communication between the second and third floors is provided by a square wheel-stair, with bottle-nosed treads, at the N end of the corridor. There was no parapet walk.

To cover the wide expanse above there were twin pitched roofs with crow-stepped gables and a central drainage valley with cannon-shaped gargoyles. The S gables have a human head and double-billet carved respectively on the E and W outer skewputs. Immediately below the central valley there are small windows with entablatures in the Renaissance style, and below the window at the N end there is an heraldic panel, now barely discernible, which bore the arms of Jardine and Johnston and the date 1605.[27] This panel was originally above the window, as shown in early illustrations,[28] and was surmounted by a classical pediment. Within the roofs there are two attics, lit by slit-windows in the gables.

There is little mention of Spedlins in history, despite its situation in the heart of Annandale. In 1505 Sir Alexander Jardine, grandson and heir of John Jardine of Applegarth, received a crown charter of the £10 lands of Applegarth called 'Murhous' and other lands, which had been held of the king by his grandfather by service of ward.[29] Sir Alexander was knighted

SPEDLINS TOWER

Fig. 335 Spedlins Tower: sectional elevation looking east, before restoration.

Fig. 336 Spedlins Tower in 1788.

c.1504, and from 1525 until his death c.1529 he held the important office of Master of the King's Artillery.[30]

For a while in 1547 John Jardine of Applegarth held Alexander Baillie in Little Gill prisoner in Spedlins.[31] This was during the 'Rough Wooing', when Applegarth pledged 233 men to the service of England.[32] It is, however, a little surprizing that Spedlins was not included in the Platte of Castlemilk, a military survey of the West March prepared in the same year for the Protector Somerset;[33] and 'Speldinges' only achieved a passing mention in the more detailed English report drawn up c.1564-5.[34] Clearly its passive strength was not considered of military significance. On the latter occasion, Applegarth was credited with 9 horsemen.[35] After escaping unscathed from the two devastating raids made on the West March by the English in 1570, Applegarth's lands were laid waste the following year by John Graham, known as 'Prior's John', and a band of broken men;[36] and they were raided again in 1586, this time by Sir John Johnston of that Ilk.[37] Meanwhile, in 1574, Alexander Jardine of Applegarth had been appointed one of the Commissioners for holding wapinschaws in the Stewartry of Annandale.[38] Then, in 1583, he was charged with treason and put to the horn;[39] but two years later he was one of those included in the general amnesty for rebels.[40] 'Ye Spadlins' is shown on Aglionby's Platte of 1590.[41] Pont, however, does not show Spedlins. For some unknown reason he did not travel this far north when he surveyed 'The Stewartrie of Annandail' some five years later.[42]

In 1578 Lord Herries presented James VI with his 'Advice' for keeping good order in the West March.[43] Among his proposals was one that the laird of Apilgirth (Sir Alexander Jardine) should remain with a household of true and honest friends 'at his hous of the Spedlingis', whence he could best assist the Warden. Similarly, when, in 1600, there was renewed trouble locally from 'broken men', the barons and landed men were instructed to dwell in their houses of strength and other places closest to the thieves themselves.[44] This included Alexander Jardine of Applegarth, who was to stay in the 'hous of Speldingis'. Six years later he was one of the barons summoned to give further advice on keeping good order.[45]

The family later got into financial difficulties, and in 1636 the £10 lands of Spedlins and the £80 lands and barony of Applegarth were apprised from John Jardine of Applegarth for debt.[46] In 1641 John was appointed a Commissioner for Keeping the Peace in the Borders,[47] and in 1643 a Commissioner for War for Dumfriesshire.[48] He died later that year, and was succeeded by his son Alexander. The legal title to Applegarth subsequently passed from one family to another until 1644, when it was assigned back to Alexander Jardine of Applegarth by the 1st Earl of Hartfell.[49] Alexander was then granted a new crown charter of all the lands.[50]

Alexander was a Commissioner for the apprehension of Papists in 1642,[51] and a Commissioner for War for Dumfriesshire in 1644, 1645 and 1648.[52] He also represented Dumfriesshire in parliament in 1645.[53] He was elected to represent the county again in 1660, but was prevented from taking his seat by the preference for another Commissioner.[54] Many years earlier, in 1639, Alexander had been employed to purchase arms and ammunition for the Stewartry of Annandale, and had given a bond for 1200 merks to cover the cost. When the arms were subsequently lost in the country's service, and he was unable to honour the bond, the Stewartry apprised his lands and put him to the horn. Alexander considered this most unjust. He accordingly petitioned the Crown to be relieved of his bond, and in 1662, on the advice of the Estates of Parliament, King Charles agreed.[55] The following year, Alexander was appointed a Justice of the Peace for Dumfriesshire.[56] He died some time before 1671, and was succeeded by his only son, Alexander.

Alexander was created a Baronet of Nova Scotia in 1672.[57] Six years later, he was appointed a Commissioner of Supply for Dumfriesshire.[58] The exact date of his death is not known, but he was succeeded first by his eldest son, Sir Alexander, 2nd Baronet, who was a Commissioner of Supply in 1696

and 1698,[59] and then by his second son, Sir John Jardine, 3rd Baronet, who served as a Commissioner of Supply in 1702 and 1704.[60]

The tower continued as the residence of the Jardines until the 18th century, when it was abandonned in favour of a new house they built just across the river.[61] The tower was later inhabited by an old woman, who was there when Cardonnel visited it in 1788, and Grose the following year; but by then it was already falling into ruin and soon became roofless.[62] The new house stood where the gardens were later laid out.

Shortly after Sir Alexander Jardine, 6th Baronet, succeeded to the estate in 1807, he decided to build an even more magnificent, classical mansion, Jardine Hall, close by.[63] This was completed about 1814.[64] The hall remained the family's home until after the death of Sir Alexander Jardine, 8th Baronet, DL, JP, in 1893. The estate was then acquired by David Jardine Jardine, a barrister-at-law and nephew of Sir Robert Jardine, 1st Baronet of Castlemilk.[65] He restored the shell of the old tower, but left the roofs off. He also increased the size of Jardine Hall threefold, to the designs of Edward May,[66] but in so doing he made it too large to survive as a family home in the modern world. After his death the house was sold, and for a while it served as a school; but the cost of upkeep proved too much, and it was finally demolished in 1964.

The old tower was eventually restored between 1982 and 1989 by Nicholas Gray, and is once again a family home.

---

1 The motte is some 29ft high and has a diameter at the summit of about 110ft. The bailey, much altered, extends towards the N. See RCAHMS 1920, No.13.
2 Black 1946, 26.
3 Bain III, No.1382.
4 There were 10 knight's fees in Annandale.
5 Bain I, No.635.
6 The site had at one time been occupied by a minor Celtic monastery, dependent upon Hoddom (Reid, R.C. 'The Monastery at Applegarth', TDGAS, 3rd Ser., XXXV, 14-19).
7 Reid, R.C., op. cit., 15.
8 A saltire and chief differenced. The Johntons and Kirkpatricks have similar arms, which were also derived from those of the Bruces.
9 Buccleuch MSS, 38-9; Black 1946, 382.
10 Black 1946, 382.
11 Bain II, No.1042.
12 Ibid, No.1115. – Applegarth was one of the churches in which Edward I offered prayers while on his way to the siege of Caerlaverock (McDowall 1986, 80; ASH, 88).
13 Bain II, No.1634.
14 Fraser 1894, I, 9-10.
15 There has been confusion between the lands of Appletreethwaite, which Bruce granted to Thomas de Carruthers of Mouswald c.1320 (RMS I, No.92), and the lands of Applegarth (e.g. RCAHMS 1920, xxix). According to Johnson-Ferguson, Appletreethwaite was in Dalton parish, where the Carruthers are known to have had lands. In 1449 the rents from the lands of Apilgarth were held in ward by the king (Exchequer Rolls V, 357).
16 Wedderburn MSS, 23 (No.14).
17 NSA IV, 183.
18 Scot Antiq, 283.
19 There may already have been an entrance at this level serving the basement, as at Closeburn.
20 The present simple window is a 19th century replacement.
21 Cardonnel, 'Spedling's Castle'; Adams 1802, XIII, No.3.
22 NSA IV, 385.
23 Only the lower courses of the original door jambs survive. It is not clear whether the reconstruction was necessary for structural reasons, or whether it was to provide a wider stairway to the first floor. The outer wall of the stair, the treads and the corner of the tower itself to a height of some 14ft were all rebuilt in ashlar at this time.
24 This is said to have been added to provide a wine cellar.
25 MacGibbon & Ross II, 430. It was built by Patrick Maxwell of Newark c.1597.
26 Grose I, 146.
27 RCAHMS 1920, No.446.
28 Grose I, 145; Cardonnel 'Spedling's Castle'.
29 RMS II, No.2844.

30 ALHT V, 258, 322, 329, 346, 389.
31 RMS IV, No.451.
32 Armstrong 1883, lxxvi. At an Annandale Weapon-show in 1541, Applegarth
    attended with 200 men (Buccleuch MSS, 66 (No.135).
33 Merriman, M. 'The Platte of Castlemilk, 1547', TDGAS, XLIV, 175-181.
34 Armstrong 1883, cxii.
35 Ibid, cxiv.
36 RPC II, 95.
37 Border Papers I, No.419.
38 APS III, 91.
39 Ibid, 289.
40 Ibid, 388.
41 Hyslop, 320.
42 Blaeu, 57, 'THE STEWARTRIE OF ANNANDAIL'.
43 Fraser 1873, II, 485.
44 RPC VI, 155.
45 RPC VII, 271, 721.
46 RMS IX, No.521.
47 APS V, 685.
48 Ibid, VI, Part I, 53
49 RMS IX, No.1537.
50 Ibid.
51 RPC, 2nd Ser., VII, 290.
52 APS VI, Part I, 199, 559; Part II, 32.
53 Ibid, Part I, 284, 474, 863.
54 Parl. of Scot., 378.
55 APS VII, 413.
56 Ibid, 505.
57 Burke Peerage 1959, 1222, 'Jardine of Applegirth'.
58 APS VIII, 225; X, 29, 131.
59 Ibid, X, 29, 131.
60 Ibid, XI, 22, 142.
61 Grose I, 145; 'Jardine Hall, Spedlins and Corncockle', TDGAS, 2nd Ser.,
    XIX, 195-202.
62 Cardonnel, op.cit.; Grose, op. cit. It is puzzling that Cardonnel shows the
    tower roofless, while Grose, who did not visit Spedlins until the following
    year, and whose work is noted for its accuracy, shows the roofs intact.
63 Ordnance Gazetteer, 888; 'Jardine Hall, Spedlins and Corncockle', op. cit.,
    196.
64 Gifford, 351.
65 Burke Peerage 1959, 1224, 'Buchanan-Jardine'.
66 Gifford, 351.

---

62. STAPLETON TOWER

(2³/₄ m ENE Annan)   (NY234688)

The earliest reference to Stapleton is early in the 13th century, when Robert de Brus granted to Robert de Crosby a right of commonty in the wood of Stableton, with permission to create within the same a free [deer] park.[1] This is the earliest such park on record.[2] Crosby was a follower of de Brus, who held a large tract of land in the area roughly encompassing the later parish of Dornock.[3]

Early in the following century, Robert the Bruce granted the lands of Newbie to Sir William Carlyle,[4] and it was from the Carlyles that a cadet branch of the Corries acquired them shortly afterwards.[5] It has been suggested that the lands of Stapleton were included in this grant,[6] but the earliest certain reference to the Corrie's possession of Stapleton is not until 1489, when Herbert Corrie, son and heir of Thomas Corrie of Newbie, and his spouse, Esote Murray, daughter of Cuthbert Murray of Cockpool, received from the Crown a charter of confirmation of the £5 lands of Prestonside and the £5 lands of 'Stapiltoun', which had been resigned by Thomas.[7]

The township of Stapleton was one of those destroyed by Lord Dacre in 1514, during one of his relentless raids upon the West March after the Scots defeat at Flodden.[8] Three years later, Herbert Corrie of Newbie sold the £10 lands of Stapleton, and other lands, together with the fishings of Stapleton, to 'his kinsman' Thomas Corrie of Kelwood, to be held of the king as

Fig. 337 Stapleton Tower: view from S.

Lord of Annandale.[9] Then in 1529, Thomas resigned all his lands in favour of his son and heir, George, who received a new crown charter incorporating them into the free barony of Kelwood.[10]

The Corries finally parted with Stapleton in 1535/6, when George Corry of Newbie, with consent of his father, sold the lordship of Newbie, including the £10 lands of Stapleton and the fishings of Stapleton, to William Johnston of Gretna;[11] and this was confirmed by a further charter under the Great Seal in 1541/2.[12] Shortly afterwards, in November 1536, Johnston alienated 'the lands of Stabiltoun' to Christopher Irving of Bonshaw.[13]

Thirty years later, in 1566, Christopher Irving, eldest son and heir of Edward Irving of Bonshaw, married Margaret, daughter of John Johnston of that Ilk, and as part of the marriage contract Edward undertook to infeft the said Christopher and Margaret in various lands, including 'the ten pound land of Stabletoun holden of the Laird of Newby'.[14] The Edward Irving who was later designated 'of Stapleton' is believed to have been one of their younger sons.[15] It has also been said that it was he who built the tower. If both these premises are correct, and the tower is indeed that late, it must have been built around the time of the Irvings' local war with the Maxwells in 1585-6, or even later.[16] It is not shown on Aglionby's Platte in 1590,[17] but it does appear on Pont's map of Annandale c.1595.[18]

Situated on gently rising ground overlooking the Solway, the tower was not provided with any natural defences, whilst any surviving trace of the barmkin was swept away when the modern mansion was built.

The **TOWER** itself is oblong in plan, and measures 36ft 9in by 27ft 3in over walls averaging 5ft 9in in thickness at ground level and 5ft higher up. It comprised three storeys and a garret, but is once again a ruinous shell, with all the wooden floors gone, as well as the pitched roof and crow-stepped gables. A remnant of the original NE gable is shown in the sketch of Stapleton drawn by William Graham of Mossknowe in 1823. The masonry is roughly-coursed sandstone rubble, variable in colour, with dressed margins and unusually refined mouldings of late 16th century date. Around the larger windows and the empty armorial panel above the entrance, the mouldings comprise a nail-head ornament within a double roll, while around

Fig. 338 Stapleton Tower in 1823,
by William Graham of Mossknowe.

Fig. 339 Stapleton: entrance with shot-hole
and empty armorial panel.

the entrance doorway the jambs and segmental arch-head are embellished with a QERH moulding, the hollow of which carries a stylized leaf-and-stalk enrichment in relief.[19] The tower has a splayed plinth course.

Inside the entrance there is a mural lobby that leads to the vaulted basement and to the wheel-stair, 7ft in diameter, in the E corner. The main defence at this level was provided by one splayed, rectangular gun-loop in each wall of the basement. Only those on the NE and SE sides have survived, the former

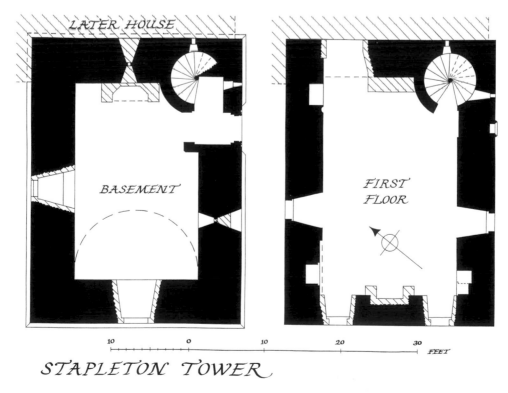

Fig. 340 Stapleton Tower: plans of basement and first floor.

now blocked; the others disappeared when large, modern windows were inserted in their place, one in the mid 19th century and the other early in the 20th century.[20] It is likely that the basement also had the usual high window at the SW end, which disappeared at the same time; but this is not clear from Graham's sketch. As at nearby Bonshaw and Robgill, a small gun-loop at the foot of the stair gave added protection to the entrance.

The first floor hall had a small, central fireplace at the SW end, on either side of which is a large, modern window. At least one of these windows replaced a smaller one, dating from the 16th century,[21] and there was probably another at the opposite end, where a door was inserted in the 19th century to communicate with the new mansion. The large windows on either side of the hall, however, are original; so too are the aumbries adjacent to them in the S and W corners and the large open-aumbry, or buffet, in the N corner. The aumbry in the S corner has, however, been enlarged at some later date, while that in the W corner is in a section of the NW wall which is set back 3in below a continuous moulded corbel-course that restores the wall to its normal thickness. The latter feature appears to be original, but its purpose is not known. The increased thickness of the NE wall, adjacent to the stair, was apparently an early addition, put in to support a new fireplace on the floor above. The date of this work is not known, but another fireplace at the SW end of the second floor was inserted in the mid 19th century. Originally, the second floor had one window on either side and a smaller one at the NE end. The last was blocked when the mansion was built, and additional windows added in the NW and SW walls. High up near the W corner there is a small aumbry.

The main stair ended at the level of the garret, a chamber whose only surviving feature is a very small window at the NE end. From this level a quarter-turn stair in the middle of the SE wall rose to the parapet-walk.[22] This ran around the entire wall-head, supported by three-stage, enriched corbelling above a continuous course, and incorporated machicolations over the entrance. It was unusual amongst local towers in having rounds at the corners. The parapet itself, with its stylized merlons and embrasures, is a 19th century restoration.

Edward Irving was still in possession of Stapleton in 1618, when mention is made of him and his son Christopher, or 'Christie';[23] but not long after Edward's death, c.1622, Stapleton was acquired by Fergus Graham of Blawatwood.[24] This was fiercely contested by Edward's sons, Christie and John Irving, who, in January 1626, 'surprisit and tane the house of Stabiltoun . . . and fortified the said house with men, vittaill, and armour'.[25] This led to a notable and protracted siege. When the Privy Council learned of the tower's capture, they directed Sir John Charteris of Amisfield, one of the Commissioners of the Middle Shires,[26] to recover Stapleton and return it to Graham.[27] This he singularly failed to do, so on the 21 April the Council issued a further commission, addressed to Sir John Charteris of Amisfield, Sir William Greir of Lag and James Maxwell of Kirkconnell, charging them, 'by force, if necessary, [to] retake the house of Stabletoun and to restore it to Fergus Grahame of Blaetwoode'.[28] In the meantime, it was reported that Christie Irving had 'of new fortified the said house with men and victuallis, and keipis the same house as an housse of weare, [and] grantis ressett thairin to the fugitive lymmaris of the late Bordouris'. By the end of May, the commissioners once again had to concede defeat, 'finding it was impossibill without ane long and continueand siege to recover the samyn'.[29] For two months there was silence. Then, on

the 29 July, the Privy Council, having decided upon drastic action, commanded the Earls of Nithsdale, Roxburgh, Buccleuch and Annandale, two lords and ten knights, with all their forces, to march against Christie Irving and recover the tower.[30] This time they seem to have succeeded, for nothing more is heard of the matter. However, if Graham recovered possession, his success would seem to have been short lived, for less than five months later James Johnston of that Ilk, as superior, granted the lands of Stapleton to William Irving of Bonshaw, 'as grandson and heir of the late Edward Irving of Bonschaw';[31] but what William subsequently did with the lands is not known.

In, or shortly before, 1636, Stapleton was acquired by Robert Johnston of Raecleugh, who had lost Raecleugh and his other lands for debt.[32] He was succeeded by his daughter and heiress, Mary, and it may have been as her tenants that the Irvings again came into possession. By a marriage contract of 1676, Mary undertook to provide a dowry for Margaret, daughter of John Irving in Stableton, in return for a liferent from her future husband, George Irving of Stank.[33] One of the witnesses to the subsequent sasine was Herbert Irving in Stapleton.[34] Soon afterwards, John would seem to have acquired outright possession, as in 1684 it was as 'John Irving of Stabletoun' that his advice was sought regarding the trade in 'linning cloth';[35] and five years later [John] Irving of Stapleton was committed to Edinburgh Tolbooth for 'owning the late King James', although he claimed he did not know it was an offence.[36] He continued to protest his innocence, and was eventually released, after swearing and signing an oath of allegiance.[37]

The following year, Stapleton was assessed for the Hearth Tax.[38] At that time it was credited with a total of nine fireplaces, but as the tower at no time had more than five, it is evident that there must have been a number of associated dwellings in the 'fermtoun'. The feudal superior at this time was James Johnston, Earl of Annandale and Hartfell, who had had his earldom, including the superiority of the £10 lands of Stapleton, formally ratified by parliament in 1669.[39]

Not long afterwards, the Irvings either lost or gave up Stapleton. Perhaps it was forfeited, for in 1695 Irving of Stapleton was included in a list of rebels in France who were indicted for high treason.[40] Stapleton then passed into the hands of the superior, now Marquess of Annandale, who, in 1702, granted it to his brother John.[41] When John died leaving no issue, Stapleton reverted to the Marquess; and it was still with his descendants c.1770.[42]

By the beginning of the 19th century, Stapleton had been abandonned as a residence and was becoming ruinous. Thus it was when William Graham of Mossknowe recorded it in 1823. Some years later it was acquired by the Critchley family, who restored the tower and incorporated it in a vast new, baronial-style mansion that they built to the north and east of it.[43] Stapleton remained the home of the Critchleys until the end of the Second World War, when, having become too large for modern needs, it was abandoned and all but the tower demolished.

1   Buccleuch MSS, 40 (No.70); Fraser 1894, I, 5-6.
2   RCAHMS 1997, 216.
3   It is suggested that Woodhall, 1 mile SSE of Stapleton, was probably the 'hall' of the park (RCAHMS 1997, 216).
4   Scots Peerage II, 378.
5   Johnston, C 'The Early History of the Corries of Annandale', TDGAS, 3rd Ser., I, 94. Robert de Corry, Lord of Newbie, was a witness in 1361. Robert married Susannah, daughter of Thomas Carlyle of Torthorwald.
6   Johnstone 1889, 6.
7   RMS II, No.1909.

8   L & P, I, No.2913.
9   RMS III, No.145.
10   Ibid., No.815.
11   Ibid., No.1598.
12   Ibid., No.2570.
13   Hope-Johnstone MSS, 16 (No.19).
14   Irving 1907, 38.
15   Ibid., 36. Another account says Edward was Christopher's younger brother, not his son (Ibid, 54). He witnessed a sasine in 1607 (Laing Charters, No.1522).
16   The thickness of the walls and the open parapet walk suggest a date some 20 years earlier, but the mouldings tend to confirm a later date.
17   Hyslop, 320.
18   Blaeu, 57, 'THE STEWARTRIE OF ANNANDAIL'.
19   A similar leaf moulding was found on the site of Maxwell's Castle, Dumfries (Barbour, J 'The House of the Maxwells of Nithsdale at Dumfries', *TDGAS*, 2nd Ser., VI, facing p.190).
20   The NW gun-loop was still in existence when the RCAHMS visited the tower in 1912 (RCAHMS 1920, 44).
21   Graham's sketch shows a slit-window and another 'feature' approximately at this level, but is too crude for a precise interpretation.
22   This is presumably a 19th century alteration.
23   PRS Dumfries I (1617-71), Index, 169.
24   Christopher Irving was still designated 'in Stabletoune' in February 1623, when he asked the sheriff court at Jedburgh to free him from a caution (RPC XIV, 695). It is not known how Graham got possession, but the legality of it was attested by the Privy Council (RPC, 2nd Ser., I, 226).
25   RPC, 2nd Ser., I, 286-7.
26   The Borders were known as 'the Middle Shires' after the Union of the Crowns.
27   RPC, 2nd Ser., I, 226.
28   Ibid., 286-7
29   Ibid., 667.
30   Ibid., 378.
31   GRS, XX, 302.
32   Adams 1921, 117.
33   PRS Dumfries, Vol. 2, f.101.
34   Ibid.
35   RPC, 3rd Ser., X, 44.
36   APS IX, Appendix, 21; Irving 1907, 50.
37   RPC, 3rd Ser., XIII, 464; XIV, 230-1, 236.
38   Adamson, D. 'The Hearth Tax', *TDGAS*, 3rd Ser., XLIX, 76.
39   APS VII, 641.
40   Ibid, IX, Appendix, 115.
41   Fraser 1894, cccxxvi.
42   Directory of Landownership, 99.
43   Two views of it photographed by the writer's grandfather, John Bell Irving of Beanlands, in 1902, are reproduced in Irving 1907, p.56.

---

63.   SUNDAYWELL TOWER

(3½ m W Dunscore)   (NX811844)

The lands of 'Soundevell', or Sundaywell, first appear on record in 1511, when, together with the lands of Glenesslin, they formed part of the tenanted lands of the earldom and barony of Glencairn. In that year, the Earl of Glencairn received a new crown charter of the lands, in liferent for himself and his wife and in feu for his eldest son and heir, William.[1] There is, however, no indication as to who held the tenancy at that time.

The family of Kirkhaugh,[2] who subsequently feued the lands, are first recorded in Glenesslin during the 15th century;[3] but it was not until a century later that their name is found in association with the adjoining lands of Sundaywell and Bogrie. In 1548/49 Amer Kirkhauch of Soundayvell is mentioned in a sasine in favour of Grierson of Lag's son and heir,[4] and in 1563 John Kirkhauch of Bogrie received a charter of certain lands purchased from Thomas Maxwell, burgess in Dumfries.[5] The relationship of these two members of the Kirkhaugh family is not known, but there can be little doubt that both were descended from the original family of Glenesslin (later known as 'of Chapel'). In due course the family name was condensed to 'Kirko', and ultimately to 'Kirk'.

Fig. 341 Sundaywell Tower: view from S.

John Kirkhaugh of Sundaywell witnessed a charter in 1565,[6] and again in 1580/81.[7] Thereafter there are frequent references to him until 1590,[8] after which he was succeeded by Gilbert Kirko, who is on record in 1591.[9] It was presumably John who built the tower. Meanwhile the Kirkhaughs of Bogrie were likewise flourishing; and the towers of the two families are clearly represented – although the names were inadvertently transposed – on Pont's manuscript survey of Nithsdale *c.*1595.[10] Bogrie (q.v.) stood on the north side of the valley, at an elevation of about 100ft, from where it had a commanding view down Glenesslin to the Cairn valley, while Sundaywell stood below, on the left bank of the burn.

The **TOWER** is oblong in plan, and measures 26ft 8in from NW to SE by 20ft 10in from NE to SW. It was three storeys high, and there is evidence on the top floor that it was originally provided with a single turret, corbelled-out at the N corner.[11] The walls, which are harled, vary in thickness from about 3ft on either side to about 4ft at the ends. Where some of the harling has come away, it can be seen that the masonry is local rubble, with roughly dressed quoins. Some of the stones are

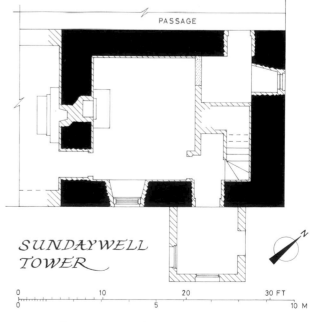

Fig. 342 Sundaywell Tower: plan of basement.

unusually large. Otherwise, the tower was so completely modernized in the 19th century that any other original features have either been covered up or destroyed. Not one of the windows is original, nor is the hipped roof. There is, however, a small window in the W wall at first floor level, which can be seen blocked up in the adjacent barn. The original roof would have been of the usual gabled form. And although the present front door is presumed to occupy the original position, this cannot be confirmed, as anything that remains of the original door frame, or adjacent stair, is concealed behind the present plasterwork. In the Hearth Tax returns *c*.1690, Sundaywell is credited with 3 fireplaces.[12]

Immediately to the S and W of the tower, there are the remains of a small field and irrigation system that is presumed to be contemporary with the tower, and certainly pre-dates the agricultural improvements of the late 18th century.[13]

The Kirko family continued to hold Sundaywell throughout the 17th century. In 1645, James Kirkco of Sundaywell was appointed a Commissioner of War for Dumfriesshire and Annandale.[14] An armorial panel, dated 1651, and bearing his initials and those of his wife, 'S.W.',[15] is now incorporated in the modern porch. This presumably related to some addition or alteration carried out in that year, but, although subsequent events make it clear that there must have been fairly extensive secondary buildings on the site at this period, none of this work appears to have survived the subsequent modernization. Later James Kirko became a strong supporter of the Covenanters, and Sundaywell became one of their favourite haunts. In 1660 Kirko was taken prisoner for threatening the peace, held in Edinburgh Castle for three months, and then fined.[16] Six years later the government billeted both horse and foot soldiers about the house. It was 'sest [taxed] a long tyme with eght suldiers'. Kirko was again fined, and he had to pay 'what cess mouny the suldiers got, and the destructione they mad about his hous'.[17] Ultimately he was forced to leave the country for three years.

James Kirko was succeeded in Sundaywell by his niece, Elizabeth, daughter of Lancelot Kirko, who in 1672 married James MacLellan, a younger son of William MacLellan of Barscobe.[18] James had sasine of Sundaywell three years later.[19] The MacLellans were actively sympathetic to the Covenanting cause, which led to James being frequently in trouble with the authorities.[20] In 1680 he had to wadset the estate to enable him to pay his fines.[21] He took the Test in 1683 (for the second time),[22] but it still did not stop the Dragoons from plundering Sundaywell two years later.[23]

James MacLellan was succeeded by his only son, Samuel, who had a disposition of the 2 merkland of Sundaywell, the merkland of Brockloch and other lands from his mother in 1717.[24] He had sasine of the 7 merklands of Sundaywell in 1720, and again in 1738.[25] He was succeeded by his only son, James, who in 1739 disponed the 7 merklands of Sundaywell to Alexander Moffat of Lochurr.[26] The last of this family was Agnes Moffat, who died unmarried *c*.1832.

The property then passed to Agnes's cousin, Alexander Logan, who henceforth assumed the name of Moffat.[27] His son, also called Alexander, sold Sundaywell and emigrated to Australia *c*.1860.[28]

It is not known which of the Moffats modernized the tower, nor who built the two-storey extension to the south or the adjoining farm steading to the west. The house is believed to date from late in the 18th century. Some of the steading presumably dates from the same period, while the rest belongs to the 19th century and later.

1   RMS II, No.3594.
2   The family of Kirkhauch is on record in Cumbria in the 13th century, where they occupied lands of the same name (Black 1946, 406).
3   Hamilton-Grierson, Sir P.J. 'The Kirkos of Glenesland, Bogrie, Chapel and Sundaywell', *TDGAS*, 3rd Ser., III, 223.
4   Ibid, 233.
5   RMS IV, No.1483.
6   RMS V, No.1721.
7   Ibid, No.104.
8   Ibid, No.1721. The laird of 'Sundeywall' was included in a list of 'Landit Men' in 1590 - RPC IV, 786.
9   Hamilton-Grierson, *op. cit.*, 234.
10 Pont MS. No.35 in National Library of Scotland.
11 A wall survives cutting diagonally across the inside corner, a common feature asociated with a corner turret. – This also corresponds with the conjectural reconstruction drawing illustrated in Moffat, R.M., 1908.
12 Adamson, D. 'The Hearth Tax', *TDGAS*, 3rd Ser., XLVII, 167, 169.
13 See Gough-Cooper, H. and L., and Crowe, C. 'Sundaywell Farm, Dunscore: Field Survey and Excavation of Hitherto Unrecorded Sites, 1988-91, *TDGAS*, 3rd Ser., LXVIII, 87-9.
14 APS VI, Part I, 559.
15 It has been said that his wife was a Welsh of nearby Colliston (RCAHMS 1920, No.137).
16 Hamilton-Grierson, *op. cit.*, 238.
17 Ibid, 240.
18 Torrance, 263.
19 PRS Dumfries, I, f.337.
20 Torrance, 263-4.
21 PRS Dumfries, III, f.202.
22 RPC, 3rd Ser., VIII, 640.
23 Torrance, 264.
24 Ibid, 265.
25 PRS Dumfries, IX, f.248; XIII, f.78.
26 Moffat 1908, 34.
27 Ibid, 35.
28 Ibid, 36.

64.   TERREGLES CASTLE
(2¹/₂ m WNW Dumfries)   (NX934778)

The name 'Terregles', of old 'Trevereglis', which means 'house', or perhaps 'farm', 'by the church', possibly alludes to the ancient 'Ladye Chapel', the site of which is recorded here. The lands adjoin those of Troqueer, which had been part of the vast domain of Uchtred, son of Fergus, Lord of Galloway.[1] Troqueer is next mentioned in the reign of Alexander II, when Thomas of 'Treveg^c r' witnessed a charter of Africa, daughter of Edgar.[2] This may well have been the Thomas who was an illegitimate son of Uchtred, and, if so, he was probably also in possession of Terregles. Later that century Terregles itself appears for the first time, when there are references to Uchtred of 'Toreglis' or 'Travereglis' and his son Malcolm,[3] perhaps descendants of Thomas; and in 1304 there is mention of one Matthew of Terregles.[4]

Terregles subsequently came into the possession of Sir Archibald Douglas (d.1333)[5] and his son William, Lord of Douglas (later Earl of Douglas), who in 1353 received a charter of confirmation of the barony of 'Tarruglis', together with many other lands.[6] Neither of the charters mentions a castle at Terregles, although the earlier charter specifically mentions a number of castles elsewhere. Then in 1357/8, David II granted the barony of 'Trauereglys' to Sir John Heryz 'on the resignation of Thomas, Earl of Mar';[7] and in 1366 he erected these lands into a regality.[8]

The Herries family, which had its origins in France,[9] first came to Scotland in the 12th century, apparently in the train of the Bruces, and settled in Dumfriesshire. Their first home seems to have been in Annandale, though there is no record of the lands

Fig. 343 Terregles Castle, showing the ruins of Moscrope's (or Mosstroops) Tower on the right (after a late 18th century water-colour).

they actually held. The first of the family on record is William de Heriz, who witnessed a gift to the abbey of Holm Cultram by Prince Henry c.1150.[10] Another William de Heriz, believed to be a son,[11] witnessed several charters by the Bruces c.1194-1218,[12] while a Sir Robert de Heris, seneschal of Annandale, was witness to charters by Robert de Brus c.1215-45.[13] Sir William de Heriz swore fealty to Edward I in 1296.[14] Five years later he held Lochmaben Castle for Edward,[15] and c.1304 he granted an acre of land and some fishings near Dornock to Sir William Carlyle.[16] Sir William was succeeded by his son Robert, whom Bruce designated 'Lord of Nithsdale' in a charter of 1323.[17] He is believed to have been the father of Sir John Herries, the 1st of Terregles.

It was evidently Sir John who built the original castle at Terregles, which, after 1365, became the family's principal seat and residence, although it is not until 1484 that the 'mancriem de Terreglis' first appears in a sasine.[18] Sir John attended parliament in 1359,[19] and died sometime after 1382, when he was succeeded by his son, Sir John Herries, 2nd of Terregles. The latter Sir John (d.1420) went to England three times as a hostage for the Earl of Douglas,[20] and in 1423 his son and heir, Sir Herbert Herries, 3rd of Terregles, also went to England as a hostage, this time for the release of King James I.[21]

Sir David Herries, 5th of Terregles, sat in parliament in 1471/2.[22] In 1486 he resigned Terregles in favour of his eldest son, Sir Herbert, but he was still alive in 1495.[23] Meanwhile, in 1489/90, Sir Herbert had been created a Lord of Parliament as Lord Herries of Terregles, and sat in parliament as such in the same year, and again in 1491/2.[24] Lord Herries died c.1502.

While his father was still alive in 1499/1500, but in the care of curators, Andrew, later 2nd Lord Herries, received a crown charter of his father's estates, which then comprised the lands and barony of Terregles and Kirkgunzeon, the lands of half the barony of Ur, the lands of Hoddom and Lockerbie, and many other lesser properties.[25] This was on the resignation of Janet Douglas, daughter of Archibald, Earl of Angus, who had been granted the lands by deceit in 1495, while Andrew was under age.[26] Andrew sat in parliament in 1505/6,[27] and in Council in 1512.[28] In 1510 he received a new crown charter erecting the lands and baronies of Terregles, Kirkgunzeon, and others, into the new free barony of 'Herys', but, surprizingly, although the tower and fortalice of Kirkgunzeon is mentioned, there is again no mention of the castle at Terregles.[29] This charter also made the town of Terregles, 'already called Herys', a free burgh of

barony.[30] Andrew fell at Flodden in 1513.

William, 3rd Lord Herries of Terregles, attended parliament in 1531 and 1540,[31] and was an Extraordinary Lord of Session in 1532.[32] In 1542/3 he was one of the seven lords who proclaimed the Earl of Arran as Regent.[33] On his death in 1543, the title passed to his eldest daughter, Lady Agnes Herries,[34] and in 1566, jure uxoris, also to her husband, Sir John Maxwell, Master of Maxwell, who became 4th Lord Herries.[35] In 1549/50 Lady Agnes and Sir John received a Crown charter of a one third share in the lands and barony of Herries, which included a third of the lands of Terregles, 'with the tower and fortalice',[36] while the other two-thirds of the barony passed to Agnes's sisters, Katherine and Janet. The sisters later resigned their shares in favour of John Hamilton, a younger son of the Earl of Arran, from whom Sir John Herries purchased them in 1561 to reunite the estate.[37] Five years later, in recognition of Lord Herries' outstanding service in quieting the Borders as Warden and Justiciar of the West March, Queen Mary granted Sir John, now Lord Herries, and Lady Agnes a new infeftment in the lands and barony of Terregles, with the tower, fortalice, etc., and the lands and barony of Kirkgunzeon, with the tower and fortalice, etc., in free blench-ferme,[38] and this was confirmed by parliament in 1567.[39] Sir John was Warden of the West March for a total of some twenty-one years between 1546 and 1579;[40] he was a Commissioner for the Borders in 1553,[41] 1557, 1561, 1563 and 1580;[42] and he attended parliament as Sir John Maxwell in 1560 and as Lord Herries in 1567, 1578, 1579 and 1581.[43] He was also one of the Commissioners appointed to hold wapinschaws in Dumfriesshire in 1574.[44]

After Queen Mary's disastrous defeat at Langside in 1568, Lord Herries entertained her at Terregles during her flight south. Two weeks later he was ordered to surrender Terregles to the Regent Moray,[45] but failed to do so. The following month, during a military progress through SW Scotland, Moray 'threw down' a number of castles, including Herries' new castle at Hoddom (q.v.). He also gave orders for 'The Lord Herreis' house of Terreglis' to be thrown down; but on being told he would only be doing Herries a favour, as Herries intended to pull it down himself and build it in another place, the order was rescinded.[46] It was presumably after this date that Lord Herries added the great keep-like tower, known as Mosstroops (or Moscrope's) Tower, which stood at the NE corner and became the castle's principal feature.[47] He also built the 'Queir' of the neighbouring church at Terregles, although it was not completed until after his death in January 1582/3. It is an unusual, post-Reformation building in a late Gothic style, with a pre-Reformation layout.

Lord Herries was succeeded by his eldest son, William, 5th Lord Herries. William sat in parliament as Master of Herries in 1572 and as Lord Herries in 1584.[48] He was made a Gentleman of the King's Chamber in 1580, and a Privy Councillor immediately after his father's death.[49] He subsequently served as Warden of the West March for four terms between 1587 and 1600,[50] as well as being appointed a Commissioner for the Borders in 1585[51] and a Commissioner for Keeping the Peace in the Marches in 1589.[52] In 1601 he carried out some work on the castle, though the extent of this is not known. All that survives is a beautifully carved oak door, now at Traquair, which bears the date '1601'.[53] William died in 1603, and was succeeded by his eldest son, John, who became 6th Lord Herries.

While he was Master of Herries, in 1602, John Maxwell was elected Provost of Dumfries.[54] Three years later, after succeeding to the peerage, he attended his first Privy Council meeting,[55] and in 1618 he was made a Commissioner for the Middle Shires.[56] Like his forebears, he was a staunch Roman Catholic, and for his adherence to the faith was excommunicated by the local minister in 1628, a censure which he 'proudlie and contempnandlie' ignored.[57] He died in 1631.

The following year, Lord Herries' eldest son and heir, John, 7th Lord Herries, became bound to infeft his spouse in 'the tower and manor-place of Terregles'.[58] This was necessary to secure the liferent promised in her marriage contract. Seven years later, during the Civil War, the Covenanters broke open the gates of Terregles and looted the house,[59] and in 1644 Baillie of Lamington was quartered there with his forces.[60] Later that year Lord Herries joined Montrose. For this he was sentenced to forfeiture in 1645 by the Committee of Estates; but two years later this was rescinded on payment of a large fine.[61] Later, he suffered further losses in the cause of Charles II,[62] including the billeting of a whole succession of detachments of troops at Terregles in 1651.[63] After the Restoration, he sat in the first parliament of Charles II in 1661,[64] and he was a member of the Convention of Estates four years later.[65] In 1663, he was appointed a Justice of the Peace for the Stewartry.[66] On the death of his cousin Robert Maxwell, 2nd Earl of Nithsdale, in 1667, he succeeded to both the Earldom of Nithsdale and the Lordship of Maxwell, as well as the Maxwell estates, as heir male of the Maxwell family;[67] he also succeeded as heritable Steward of the Stewartry of Kirkcudbright.[68] However, he continued to live at Terregles. He sat in parliament as Earl of Nithsdale in 1670,[69] and the following year was appointed to oversee the repair of highways and bridges in the Stewartry.[70] He died in 1677, and was succeeded by his eldest son, Robert, 4th Earl of Nithsdale.

By this time the **CASTLE** probably had the general appearance shown in the only two illustrations of it known to have survived. These both show the same elevation of the castle, apparently as seen from the E, one being a stylized line drawing of early date[71] and the other a late 18th century watercolour, made shortly before the castle was demolished.[72]

The central feature is a large block with two principal storeys and an attic floor generously provided with half-dormer windows. There is also a corbelled-out turret at the SE corner, but no parapet. No doubt this building represented many generations of construction and alteration, but would appear to owe its final form to remodelling in the 17th century.

At the NE corner is 'Mosstroops' tower, the substantial tower-house added by the 4th Lord Herries. In the earlier draw-

Fig. 344 Terregles Castle: sketch on an old estate plan.

ing this is shown four storeys high, with a pitched roof, dormer window for the attic and a corbelled-out corner turret at the NE corner; but by the time of the later painting it had become ruinous and only three storeys remained.

Beyond the main block, a high curtain wall (shown in the earlier drawing with two levels of windows but no visible roof) extended S to meet another, later building aligned E-W. This was two storeys high and had a pitched roof with crow-stepped gables and dormer windows.

Robert, 4th Earl of Nithsdale, was a Lieutenant in the Earl of Annandale's troop of horse in 1667.[73] In 1672 he was appointed President of a Commission for the Suppression of Conventicles, and he was re-appointed five years later.[74] In the latter year, on the resignation of his father, he had a crown charter of the lands and lordships of the earldom of Nithsdale.[75] He was a member of the Convention of Estates in 1678,[76] and died in 1683.

Robert's only son, William, 5th and last Earl of Nithsdale, was retoured heir to his father in 1696.[77] He too was a staunch Catholic, and it was on the pretext of searching for priests and Jesuits that, in 1703, an armed mob of local ministers and other fanatics broke into Terregles and ransacked the place.[78] William later joined the Jacobites, but, in anticipation that his sympathies might adversely affect the family, took the precaution in 1712 of disponing in tailzie the lands and earldom of Nithsdale and the lordship of Terregles, etc., with the dignities and titles of Earl of Nithsdale, Lord Maxwell, Herries, Eskdale, and Carlyle, to his son William, Lord Maxwell, reserving only the liferent to himself and his wife.[79] By this time he was also heavily in debt. In 1715 he joined Viscount Kenmure in the uprising and marched south, but was taken prisoner at Preston.[80] Sent to the Tower, he was found guilty of treason and sentenced to death, with forfeiture of all his lands and dignities.[81] However, on the night before his execution, Lady Nithsdale daringly effected his escape, and he fled to Rome, where he died in 1744.[82]

Lord Nithsdale's entail in favour of his son, William, Lord Maxwell, was finally accepted by the House of Lords in 1723,[83] thereby securing the family's estates for the future; and this was confirmed by crown charter in 1741.[84] However, this did not include the honours. When the Jacobites rose in rebellion again in 1745, William was tempted to join the cause, but wiser counsels prevailed, and he stayed at home.[85] He died at Terregles in 1776.

William was succeeded by his only surviving daughter, Winifred, who, in the same year, was served heir to her father in the Nithsdale estates, including the baronies of Caerlaverock and Terregles.[86] Winifred had married William Haggerston-Constable of Everingham, Co. York, in 1758, the marriage contract decreeing that, should she inherit the Nithsdale estates, her husband would take the name of Maxwell and bear the 'proper arms' of the two families of Maxwell and Herries.[87] This he now did, taking the name 'Maxwell Constable'. It was also decided that the old castle at Terregles be demolished and replaced by a fine Palladian mansion, with Italianate gardens, as their principal residence. The new house was completed in 1789.[88] To celebrate the occasion, Robert Burns wrote the song *Nithsdale's Welcome Hame*.[89]

On Winifred's death in 1801, the Nithsdale and Herries estates passed to her eldest son, Marmaduke Constable-Maxwell, who, considering the estates large enough to be divided, disponed the Herries properties to his second son, Marmaduke.[90] It was presumably the younger Marmaduke, who took up residence at Terregles, who enlarged the house in 1830-32.[91] He died without issue in 1872. Terregles then passed to his nephew, Frederick Constable-Maxwell of Terregles, eldest son of his younger brother Peter.[92]

During the 20th century, Terregles came into the possession of the Clanachan family, but its maintenance became too much of a burden, and after the second World War it was abandonned. It was eventually blown up by a company of the Territorial Army in 1961.

---

1   Bain II, No.1606 (6); Scots Peerage IV, 137.
2   M'Kerlie V, 141.
3   Edgar, 222; McDowall 1986, DUM 7.
4   Bain II, No.1526.
5   Fraser 1873, II, 410.
6   RMS I, App.1, No.123.
7   Ibid, App.2, No.1501; Fraser 1873, II, 410. The Earl of Mar's connection with Terregles has not been established.
8   Fraser 1873, II, 414.
9   They are said to have come from Vendôme (Nisbet I, 343).
10 Fraser 1873, I, 586.
11 Sir William Fraser attempted an early family tree (Fraser 1873, I, 586).
12 Bain I, Nos.606, 607, 700; Buccleuch MSS, 39 (No.67), 40 (No.69).
13 Bain I, Nos.1680, 1683.
14 Bain II, No.810.
15 Fraser 1873, I, 586.
16 Buccleuch MSS, 41 (Nos.72, 73).
17 Fraser 1873, I, 586.
18 Ibid, II, 442.
19 APS I, 525.
20 Bain IV, Nos.707, 729, 736.
21 Fraser 1973, I, 586.
22 Scots Peerage IV, 403.
23 Ibid.
24 Ibid, 404; Complete Peerage VI, 494
25 RMS II, No.2526.
26 RMS II, No.2294; Scots Peerage IV, 406.
27 APS II, 262.
28 Scots Peerage IV, 405.
29 RMS II, No.3446.
30 The 'town', of which no trace survives, lay 1 mile SE of the castle.
31 APS II, 332, 355, 368.
32 Scots Peerage IV, 408.
33 APS II, 413.
34 Complete Peerage VI, 495
35 Scots Peerage IV, 410.
36 RMS IV, No.405. See also RSS IV, No.1170.
37 RSS V, No.837; RMS IV, No.1393.
38 RMS IV, No.1728.
39 APS II, 558-9.
40 Rae, 240-3.
41 RPC I, 150.
42 Rae, 258-9.
43 APS II, 525; III, 3, 115, 127, 129, 187, 195.
44 Ibid, III, 91.
45 ATS XII, 128.
46 Fraser 1873, I, 530.
47 Ibid. 568; Gray, 48.
48 APS III, 77, 290, 292, 326, 330, 335. On one occasion in 1584 William is referred to as 'John' Lord Herries, but this is an error.
49 Scots Peerage IV, 414.
50 Rae, 243.
51 Ibid, 259.
52 RPC IV, 426.
53 It is clearly by the same hand as the door from Amisfield, dated 1600, which is now in the Royal Scottish Museum, Edinburgh.
54 RPC VI, 478-9.
55 Ibid, VII, 128.
56 Scots Peerage IV, 415.
57 Ibid, 416.
58 Fraser 1873, I, 384.
59 Ibid, 385.
60 Ibid. Although referred to in the parliamentary report as 'Laird of Lamyngtoun', it is presumed that the gentleman in question was Sir William Baillie of Lamington's illegitimate son, William 'of Letham', who was a lieutenant-general of foot in the Covenanters' army.
61 Scots Peerage IV, 417; VI, 487. After the Restoration, Charles II declared that the forfeiture was 'null and void' (APS VII, 204).
62 APS VII, 344.
63 Scots Peerage VI, 487; Fraser 1873, I, 387.
64 Fraser 1873, I, 388.
65 Ibid, 389.
66 APS VII, 504-8.
67 Scots Peerage IV, 487.
68 Fraser 1873, I, 390.
69 Ibid.
70 Ibid, 392.
71 Fraser 1873, I, 530.
72 This painting was last recorded in the possession of Miss Clenaghan at Terregles. She retired to Edinburgh, but what happened to the painting after her death is not known. The NMRS have a photographic copy.
73 Fraser 1873, I, 397.
74 Ibid, 398-400.
75 Ibid, 400.
76 Ibid, 401.
77 Ibid, 415.
78 Ibid, 418.
79 Ibid, 422.
80 Ibid, 426.
81 Ibid, 430-33.
82 Ibid, 436-45, 453-63.
83 Ibid, 484.
84 Scots Peerage VI, 490.
85 Fraser 1873, I, 485.
86 Ibid, 490.
87 Ibid, 489
88 Gifford, 540. While the work was in progress, Winifred and her husband lived at Tinwald.
89 Fraser 1873, I, 490.
90 Ibid, 494.
91 Gifford, 540.
92 Fraser 1873, I, 585.

---

65.   THREAVE CASTLE
(1½ m W Castle Douglas)   (NX739622)

Threave Castle is situated on an island in the river Dee, at a point where the river meanders through a flat and marshy landscape. It is a site of great natural strength, with the island itself, which is about 21 acres in extent, accessible only by a ford at its southern tip or by boat. The early form of its name, 'Le Treffe', 'Treve', etc., is derived from the old Welsh 'Tref', meaning 'homestead'. This implies that the site was occupied by Britons before the 7th century AD, although the earliest dateable artefacts so far recovered only date from early in the 12th century,[1] when Fergus, Lord of Galloway, is said to have built a new stronghold here.[2] Nothing, however, is known of either that stronghold, or earlier works, beyond traces of one or more early structures of uncertain date encountered, but not fully investigated, when the site was excavated in 1974-78.[3]

The men of Galloway had long posed a threat to Scottish sovereignty in the area, when, in 1353, William Douglas, later 1st Earl of Douglas, compelled them to renounce all allegiance to England and swear fealty to David II.[4] Eleven years later, William's cousin Sir Archibald Douglas, 'The Grim', a natural son of 'the Good Sir James' Douglas, was made Warden of the West March.[5] It is he who is credited with revising and extending the original 'Laws of the Marches'.[6] Then, in 1369, for his 'diligent labour and grateful service', Archibald was granted 'all our lands of Galloway between the Water of Cree and the Water of Nith'.[7] He was charged with bringing the unruly Gallovidians to order, and so effectively did he achieve this, with firm but fair government, that the loyalty of Galloway was never again called into question. The Earl of Wigtown, however, was not so fortunate. He was having so much trouble maintaining order in the western part of Galloway, that, in 1371/2, 'in his urgent necessity', he sold his earldom to Archibald;[8] and later that year Archibald received a new charter from Robert II confirming the sale and the new extent of his Lordship.[9]

It is generally believed that Archibald started the construction of Threave Castle, his stronghold in Galloway, almost immediately, and that, while the work was in progress, he made his local base at Loch Fergus, near Kirkcudbright.[10]

Threave was one of the earliest, and one of the most important, tower-houses, or 'tower-castles', to be built after the War of Independence, and as such exhibits a number of features of particular interest. It evidently stands on the same site as the earlier stronghold. Apart from the tower itself, the original works appear to have comprised a harbour, between the tower and the deep water channel of the Dee on its W side, and two large outbuildings to the east of the tower. There were also some lesser works of uncertain date and unknown extent to the SE, and there is evidence of palisades and earthworks enclosing the whole.[11]

The **HARBOUR** was used to shelter boats from the fast flowing river. It was cut out of the living rock, and measured approximately 35ft from N to S by 20ft from E to W, with a sloping ramp at its southern end to facilitate unloading. At first, there was no harbour wall, just wattle-and-daub fencing. With some 5000 tons of rock needed for the construction of the tower alone, it is likely that most of the material needed was brought by boat when the river was high and across the ford during the drier summer months.

The **TOWER** itself, which is oblong in plan, measures 61ft from N to S by 39ft 6in from E to W over walls some 7ft 9in thick, and rises sheer 73ft 9in to the top of the surviving wall-head. The masonry is local greywacke rubble with sandstone dressings and mouldings. There are, however, two quite distinct types of sandstone, relating to two or more different building periods. One of these was the reconstruction of the NW corner. Associated with these periods, there are no less than eleven different masons' marks.[12] Unlike most other towers, there was no corbelled-out parapet: instead, there was a permanent timber hoarding, or 'bretasche', which projected beyond the wall-head and was supported on putlogs. Although the timber has long since gone, the three rows of openings for the putlogs are still clearly visible.[13] The only entrance to the tower was some 12ft above the ground, at the level of the entresol floor, where it was reached by a removable wooden ladder. The corbels that supported this ladder may still be seen, although the projecting portions have since been cut off. The doorway was originally higher, and had a high, pointed arch; but it was altered early in the 19th century, when the tower was converted to hold Napoleonic prisoners.[14] Behind the door there is a drawbar slot. From this level, the basement was reached by an internal ladder or stair, while access to the upper floors was provided by a wheel-stair, 6ft in diameter and partly corbelled-out from the internal wall, in the NW corner.[15] This, however, may not have been the original arrangement, as it has been established that the entire NW corner of the tower, including the corbelled projection, has at some time been rebuilt.[16]

The basement comprises a large, barrel vaulted chamber, 25ft high, with an entresol floor (long since removed) supported by a scarcement on each side. The lower level was little more than a storage cellar, with a rock-cut well, originally lined with oak planks, in the SW corner. Its floor is bedrock, and the only illumination was provided by two slit windows with deeply stepped sills high up in the W wall. Between these windows

Fig. 345 Threave Castle: view from S.

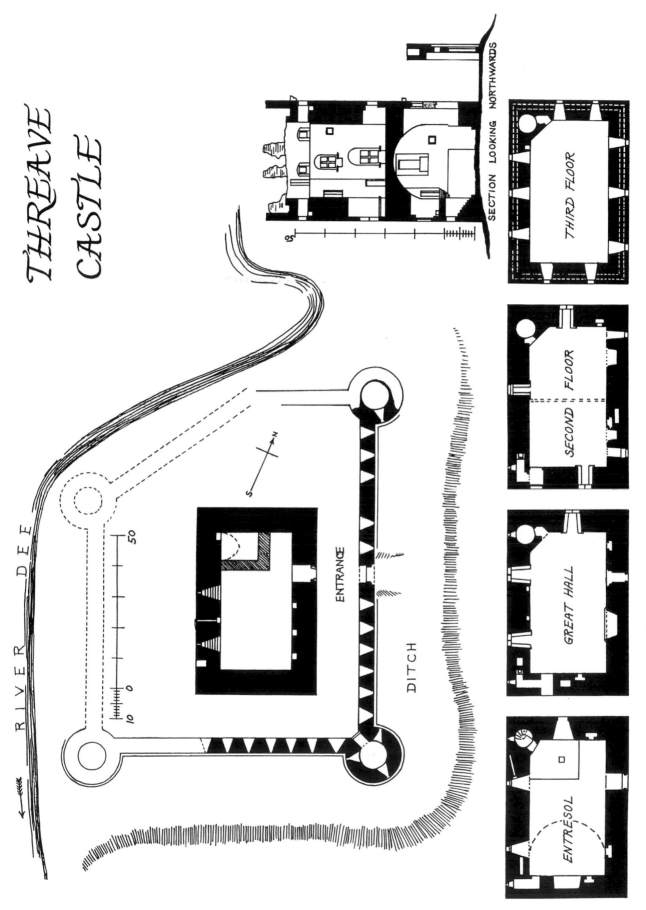

Fig. 346 Threave Castle: plans and sectional elevation (after MacGibbon & Ross).

Fig. 347 Threave Castle: view from N.

there is a slop-sink. The prison in the NW corner was added later.[17] It measures 12ft 6in by 8ft 6in, has a pointed barrel-vault, and is reached through a hatch from the floor above. It is also provided with a garderobe in the W wall, but the only ventilation is a small flue high up in the NW corner of the tower. The entresol floor, like the floors above the hall, was reinforced with a unique arrangement of massive timber struts set into sockets in the side walls below. Four of these sockets, each 20in square, may still be seen in the E wall, but the corresponding ones in the W wall have at some period been filled in.

In later tower-castles, the entresol floor was usually no more than a storage loft, but at Threave this huge chamber, some 16ft high, served two important functions. As well as being the entry level to the tower, it was subdivided such that the N end served as an entrance hall, while the S end was a kitchen. The latter room has a large fireplace, 10ft wide, in its S wall and, adjacent to it, a closed aumbry for the storage of salt. Another aumbry in the E wall opens out behind the jambs to provide a wide cupboard (in this instance some 5ft wide), a characteristic feature of all the aumbries at Threave. This room was lit by one small window with widely splayed jambs in the W wall and, at a higher level, two windows in the S wall, one either side of the chimney. In the SW corner there is a garderobe. The entrance hall at the other end has an aumbry in the N wall, and was lit by one small window with widely splayed jambs in the W wall and another, higher window in the middle of the N wall. The former window has a slop-sink in its right ingo.

The first floor was the great hall, a fine chamber 46ft 3in long and 25ft 5in wide, with a large fireplace, 9ft wide, in the E wall.[18] The main illumination was provided by two large window recesses in the W wall and one in the N wall, each with splayed jambs, stone window seats and a high, round-arched head of well cut ashlar, while the windows themselves were divided into four, glazed lights by finely cut stone mullions and transoms, now missing. All the window arrises on this and the upper floors have a hollow chamfer. Unlike later towers, there were no iron grilles and no half shutters. A smaller window recess in the S wall has a mural passage leading off its right jamb to a garderobe in the SW corner. Another small window in the E wall was formerly a doorway, but whether it was an original feature, or was created in the 1450s to communicate with the top level of the new gatehouse, is not known.[19] Below it, there were two stone corbels, now broken off, which must have served some purpose in connection with a removable wooden ladder to one of the entrances or a bridge to the top of the gatehouse. There are aumbries in the E and S walls.

The second floor was divided across the middle to form two private rooms for the Earl and his family. The S room has a fireplace in the E wall with a finely-cut, joggled lintel and a moulded cornice beneath a springing arch of ashlar;[20] and it is presumed that the corresponding fireplace in the N room was originally similar. Unlike the windows, the arrises have a giblet-check. Beside each fireplace there is a small window recess, and there is another with stone window seats in the W wall of the N room. The principal illumination for the two rooms, however, was provided by larger windows similar to those on the floor below, each divided into four, glazed lights by a mullion and transom, and set in a splayed recess with a high, round-arched head and stone window seats. There is one such window in each end wall. The S room also has a garderobe in the SW corner, the drain from which, like the one in the hall below, discharges through a chute just above ground level.[21] Each room originally had an aumbry, but the one in the S room disappeared when the wall to the left of the fireplace was restored early in the 20th century.[22] The N room has a slop-sink adjacent to the doorway off the stair.

Above this level the tower was dedicated to defence. The third floor was a single chamber with nine very low win-

Fig. 348 Threave: second floor fireplace with joggled lintel
and chases on either side for struts supporting the roof.

dow recesses with segmental-arched heads and a doorway to the
outer wall-face near the SE corner. There were three of these
windows in the W wall and two on each of the other three sides.
It has been reasonably suggested that the doorway, which takes
the place of a window in the SE corner, was to facilitate the
handling of siege engines and other large or heavy items raised
by pulley from below.[23] The only feature in the room itself is a
lamp-shelf in the NW corner. An unusual, if not unique, feature
of the construction at this level, however, was a complete circuit
of heavy timbers built into the walls just below the windows to
tie the walls strongly together, and to take the shock of any siege
engines mounted on the roof above.[24] The heavy struts reinforcing the floors below may also have helped in this respect.

Above the third floor was the bretasche, the put-logs for
which were on the same level as the third floor windows, and
the roof supporting whatever siege engines were available. From
the bretasche, some 65ft above the ground, archers could benefit from a much greater range than their adversaries and a much
clearer view of their targets. The bretasche, however, only extended along the N, S and W sides of the tower. Presumably
because of the nature of the terrain, there was no hoarding on
the E side, just a heavy machicolation over the entrance.

The **PRINCIPAL OUTBUILDING** to the E of the
tower was oblong in plan, and measured 73ft 6in from E to W
by 39ft 4in from N to S over walls 5ft 3in thick, except on the E
side where the wall was 7ft 10in thick.[25] The building is believed to have been at least two storeys high, with the extra thickness of the E wall indicating the position of a mural stair. However, only the foundations survive. The ground floor is thought
to have been used for stabling, excavations having revealed the
post holes for wooden stalls,[26] while the first floor was probably
a hall for the garrison. Both this building and the adjacent one
were demolished c.1450, when the new artillery defences were
built.

The **SECOND OUTBUILDING** lay adjacent to the first
and at right angles to it, with its N gable almost abutting the E
end of the latter's S wall.[27] It too was oblong in plan, and meas-

ured 70ft 10in from N to S by 22ft from E to W over walls some
3ft 3in in thickness. Unlike the first building, which was built of
rubble[28] bonded with shell mortar, the surviving foundations of
this building were only bonded with silt, suggesting that it was
probably only one storey high. It was subdivided with cross
walls into three rooms, the most southerly of which had small
extensions to both the E and W, possibly for food storage and an
oven.[29] The last room may thus have been a kitchen.

During the excavations of 1974-78, traces of at least two
other outbuildings were revealed to the S of the tower; but the
excavations were not completed and insufficient evidence was
found to provide either a precise date or purpose.[30] It was thought
that these buildings may have been half-timbered. Evidence was
also found to the E of the principal outbuilding of a contemporary lead smelting area. No doubt the Douglases made sure that
they were self-sufficient, with trades on the island and food from
their nearby farms at Threave Grange and Kelton.

Archibald Douglas, 'The Grim', succeeded as 3rd Earl
of Douglas in 1388, and two years later he was appointed a Conservator of the Truce with England.[31] On his death in 1400, he
was succeeded by his elder son, Archibald, who became 4th Earl
and Warden of the Marches.[32] The 4th Earl commanded the Scots
at Homildon Hill in 1402, but was defeated and taken prisoner.
He finally returned to Scotland in 1408, and the following year
was granted the Lordship of Annandale.[33] Later, he saw service
in France, became Lieutenant-General of the French forces, and,
shortly before his death in 1424, was made Duke of Touraine.
Although he can rarely have been at Threave himself, his wife,
Lady Margaret Stewart, daughter of Robert III, had a liferent of
the Lordship of Galloway, and in her widowhood, having been
granted the Lordship of Galloway and Annandale by her brother,
James I, in 1426, lived at Threave until her death c.1450.[34]

The 4th Earl was succeeded by his son Archibald, 5th
Earl of Douglas, who, in 1424, was one of the ambassadors sent
to England to negotiate the release of James I. In 1437 he became one of the Council of Regency, and, in 1438,
Lieutenant-General of Scotland. He died in 1439.

William, 6th Earl of Douglas, was still a minor when he
succeeded his father; but the immense power that the earldom
brought engendered a bitter jealousy in his rivals, especially
Chancellor Crichton, and they wasted no time in plotting the
young Earl's downfall. The following year, William and his
brother were invited to Edinburgh Castle, seized, and executed
for high treason. On his death, the Lordship of Annandale reverted to the Crown.

William was succeeded by his great-uncle James,
younger son of the 3rd Earl of Douglas, who, in 1437, had been
created Earl of Avondale. He had been Warden of the Marches
since 1409.[35] On his death in 1442/3, James was succeeded by
his eldest son, William, who became 8th Earl of Douglas.

William added greatly to his estates by his marriage, in
1444, to Margaret, the 'Fair Maid of Galloway', sister of the 6th
Earl of Douglas. He was also high in favour with James II, who
appointed him Lieutenant-General of the Kingdom and, in 1450,
Warden of the Marches.[36] The following year he received new
crown charters of all his estates, including the lands and castle
of Threave.[37] But William had many enemies at court, and when
it was learned that he had formed an alliance with the Earl of
Crawford, his enemies exploited the situation to the full, foment-
ing suspicion in the King's mind. Determined to put an end to
the supposed threat, James II 'invited' William to meet him at
Stirling, and, when William refused to terminate the liaison,

murdered him. The Earl's brothers, the eldest of whom, James, now succeeded as 9th Earl of Douglas, sought revenge, openly challenging the King's authority and refusing to obey his laws.

It was probably at this time that the new artillery defences at Threave went ahead in earnest, although it has been shown that some of the work associated with strengthening the defences had started as early as 1447, during the time of the 8th Earl, for in that year a new gate was built across the harbour mouth and other work carried out W of the tower.[38] It was the 9th Earl, however, who was eventually charged with treason for building new fortifications at Threave.[39] These fortifications, which were probably the earliest of their kind in Scotland, were evidently the work of Sir John Dunbar, who worked for the last Earls of Dunbar before he became master gunsmith to James II after the fall of Threave in 1455.[40]

The new **ARTILLERY DEFENCES** were designed to cater for, and to combat, the new weapons now available. As well as providing the base of the tower's walls with additional protection from the relentless pounding of cannon, they also provided greatly increased facilities for the defending garrison to fight back using the new firearms; and the effectiveness of these measures was amply demonstrated in the subsequent siege of 1455.

The principal defences were on the S and E sides of the tower, which were the only sides from which any serious attack with heavy weapons could be mounted. They comprised a new outer wall on each of these sides, 14ft 6in out from the tower, with a round tower where the two walls met and a further round tower at the other two extremities, and, immediately beyond, there was a rock-cut moat, 26ft wide by 6ft 6in deep, fed by the river. To provide masonry for the new works, as well as to give a clear field of fire, the two principal outbuildings were demolished.

The new walls were 5ft thick and about 19ft high, with a pronounced batter at the base, presumably to help deflect cannonballs. Throughout their length, at approximately 7ft 6in intervals, they were penetrated by widely-splayed arrow-slits so designed that they could be used with either bows or handguns,[41] while along the wall-head there was a parapet-walk which connected with the corner towers. Between these two levels on the S side, a pitched roof was carried across to the main tower. This may have been nothing more than a large, dry, working area, but it is quite possible that it provided some of the accommodation and facilities lost by the demolition of the outbuildings, as the

Fig. 349 Threave: S wall of artillery defences, seen from inside.

substantial garrison had to live somewhere.

The corner towers measured about 19ft in diameter over walls 4ft 6in thick, and were three storeys high, with the top storey an open crenellated platform. Only the SE tower now survives, though a major part of the other two was still standing when recorded by Grose in 1789.[42] In the lowest storey there are three, vertical, 'dumb-bell' gun-loops, while in the middle storey there are three more gun-loops of the 'inverted key-hole' type. All are splayed to the rear, and had transverse slots in their sills to accommodate the timber beams on which the guns – small cannon – were mounted.[43] A characteristic of the two outer towers is that, unlike the middle tower, neither had a ground floor entrance.

In the middle of the E wall there was a gatehouse with a drawbridge across the moat. It was about 26ft high and, like the corner towers, three storeys in height, with the bridge being operated from the middle level. There was no portcullis. The gateway itself was 4ft 3in wide and 8ft high, enough to allow a horseman to pass, but no more; and there are rebates for two doors, the inner of which was probably a yett.

Although these strong defences did not extend around

Fig. 350 Threave: dumb-bell gun-loop inside SE tower.

the N and W sides of the tower, a smaller wall was built along the riverbank to the W of the tower. It was 3ft 9in thick and evidently about 7ft 6in high, bonded with clay-mortar, and it extended from the SW corner tower to the harbour mouth, and then from the other side of the harbour mouth up to the NW corner of the main tower, while another section of walling followed the inner edge of the harbour. There was no wall to the N of the tower, just a turf bank.

In answer to the 9th Earl's challenge to his authority, James II made an expedition into Douglas territory, whereupon the Earl duly repented and pledged allegiance. For the next two years nothing more is heard of rebellion. But early in 1455, for reasons that are not entirely clear, James again marched against the Douglases. He took first one stronghold and then another, and in June arrived at Threave, shortly after parliament had passed an act of forfeiture upon the Earl for procuring munitions and fortifications for the tower and fortalice of Threave and other Douglas strongholds.[44] In the absence of her husband, Lady Margaret, the 'Fair Maid of Galloway',[45] refused to deliver up the castle, so James laid siege. The Earl, in a desperate attempt to save his property, now granted the castle to King Henry VI of England in return for 400 merks for the 'succour, victualling, relief and rescue' of the castle.[46] The siege lasted for more than three months, during which time a great bombard was brought with some difficulty all the way from Linlithgow;[47] but the castle was eventually won by treachery, not force, when the garrison were bribed into surrender.[48] The Douglas titles and estates, including 'ye haill lordschipe of galloway . . . wt ye castell of ye treife', were forfeited,[49] and Threave became a royal fortress, with a garrison under the command of Sir Alexander Boyd of Drumcoll.[50]

Thereafter, Threave had a succession of keepers.[51] In 1458 the keeper, William de Edmonston, was paid for having the arsenal repaired.[52] Two years later James II made another visit;[53] and in 1473 James III granted the Lordship of Galloway, with the castle of Threave, to his queen, Margaret of Denmark.[54] Then in 1483, the Earl of Angus, who by now was Steward of the Stewartry of Kirkcudbright and Keeper of Threave, forfeited these and other offices for allying himself with the rebel Duke of Albany,[55] and five years later they were granted to the Earl of Bothwell.[56] James IV visited the castle in 1501; and after a further visit the following year, he ordered that payment be made to the 'ald lutair' (lute player) in 'the Treif'.[57] With the expectation of war with England in 1512, ten carts were sent to Threave to bring two great guns back to Edinburgh,[58] and later that year one John, a quarrier, was paid for providing gun-stones for another gun there.[59]

After the battle of Flodden in 1513, where the keeper, Sir James Dunbar of Blackcrag, was killed, Lord Maxwell was appointed Steward of the Stewartry of Kirkcudbright and Captain and Keeper of the Castle of Threave.[60] It was reported at the time that the castle was 'falty, ruinois and fallin doun in divers partis', and Maxwell was ordered to repair it.[61] Then, in 1524, the offices of Steward of Kirkcudbright and Keeper of Threave were made hereditary in the Lords Maxwell.[62] This was formally confirmed two years later,[63] and reaffirmed in 1537[64] and again in 1540/1.[65]

Although Threave was never again to be as important as it had been under the Douglases, it was still one of the great strongholds of the West March – with Caerlaverock, Lochmaben and, to a lesser extent, Langholm –, and a place whose possession was considered essential for control of the region. In 1544 Henry VIII ordered a survey of the castle.[66] The following year, despite a pledge by the Master of Maxwell to 'lelely [loyally] and trewlie kepe the houssis of Carlaverok, Lochmaben, and the Treve...fra our auld inymyis of Ingland',[67] the Maxwells, under duress, let the English have possession.[68] But the English did not enjoy Threave for long, as the Regent Arran laid siege, and after only a few days the castle surrendered, and Sir Alexander Stewart of Garlies was appointed the captain.[69]

When the English made a survey of the West March c.1564-5, 'Trave' was listed as one of the 'notable places within the nether part of Gallowaye'.[70] Throughout the rest of the century, the Maxwells were intimately involved in every aspect of both local and national affairs, and especially in defence of the Catholic faith. This led to repeated demands by the Crown for

Threave and other Maxwell strongholds to be delivered up or made available. In 1565, in anticipation of an expedition to the West March, Queen Mary ordered Sir John Maxwell of Terregles, the Master of Maxwell, to deliver 'the Castellis of Lochmaben and Traif . . . witht the haill munitioune and artailzerie',[71] and shortly after Mary's defeat at Langside, three years later, the Regent Moray did likewise.[72] During this time the Master of Maxwell was curator of the young Lord Maxwell, who was still a minor.

Lord Maxwell was only twenty when, in 1573, he was first made Warden of the West March.[73] The rest of his career was one long history of controversy, and conflict, in an area where lawlessness and clan rivalries abounded. In 1584/5, having earlier been dismissed as Warden, he was declared a rebel, and ordered to deliver up 'the Traif' and other castles in his possession.[74] He was, however, quite unrepentant, and shortly afterwards it was reported that he was planning to put more forces in Threave, under the command of George Carruthers of Holmains, one of his most trusted supporters.[75]

After the execution of Mary Queen of Scots in 1586/7, Maxwell became one of the principal protagonists in the plot to restore the Catholic faith. To this end he visited Spain in 1587; but when he returned the following spring, and started garrisoning 'certain royal castles', including Threave, and raising companies of horse and foot, he was again declared a rebel, and ordered to surrender the castles on pain of treason.[76] Threave was subsequently placed in the keeping of Sir John Gordon of Lochinvar, but in 1589 he too was ordered to surrender it.[77] Later, in 1597, when Lord Ochiltree was appointed Lieutenant and Warden of the West March, he was given full authority to order the keepers of 'his Majesty's own houses of Annand, Lochmaben, Langholme and Treiff' to make the castles freely available to assist him in his duties.[78]

In 1608, in revenge for his father's death fifteen years earlier, the 8th Lord Maxwell murdered Sir James Johnston of that Ilk. He then fled the country. For this crime, he was declared guilty of treason and forfeited all his lands. Two years later, the lands were granted to Sir Robert Ker, together with the 'hereditary office of Keeper of the Castle of Treif';[79] but in 1621 the grant was rescinded in favour of Maxwell's brother and heir, the 1st Earl of Nithsdale.[80] Nithsdale, however, was in serious financial difficulties at this time, and it was no doubt to help alleviate his situation that he granted, or wadset, substantial portions of his estates. One of these grants, confirmed by the Crown in 1624, gave various lands, and 'the office of keeper of the castle of Treaff', to the Earl of Abercorn and John Maxwell of Nether Pollok, to be shared equally between them.[81]

When civil war between Charles I and the Covenanters seemed imminent in 1638/9, Nithsdale garrisoned Threave on the king's behalf with 70 men, munitions and sufficient provisions for a lengthy siege.[82] Lord Herries contributed 20 double muskets.[83] It was around this time that the great earthen rampart surrounding the outer enclosure to the E of the tower is believed to have been constructed; the moat was also re-cut.[84] However, the siege did not materialize, and for a while there was a truce. But when, early in 1640, Charles I warned Nithsdale that hostilities were about to resume, the Earl again garrisoned the castle, this time with 100 men and provisions for a year.[85] This time the Covenanting forces, under Lieutenant-Colonel Home, did attack; but although they brought heavy artillery to bear, the siege continued for thirteen weeks without result. Eventually, in September, Charles instructed the Earl that, 'in case they should vrge the surrendry of our Castle of Treeue, (which hitherto you haue soe well defended, . . .) our gratious pleasure is, that you rather quitt the same vnto them . . . rather then hazard the safety of your owne person, and those with you'.[86] Nithsdale duly capitulated. It was evidently during this siege that the outbuildings to the SE of the tower were destroyed.[87]

For a while the Covenanters occupied the castle themselves, but later it was decided to dismantle it, so that it might never again hold out against them.[88] The War Committee ordered that 'the said hows of the Thrieve to be plighted by the laird of Balmaghie [John M'Ghie]. . . that the sklait roofe of the hows and battlement thairof be taken downe, with the lofting thairof, dores and windows of the samen, and to tak out the haill iron worke of the samen, and to stop the vault of the said hows, and with power to the said laird of Balmaghie to use and dispose upon the tymber, stanes, iron work, to the use of the publict'.[89] William Maclellan of Barscobe was then given permission 'to tak as manie of the foirsaid friestane of the said hows, as will serve for his use',[90] – that use being the new tower-house which he was building, or proposing to build, at Barscobe.[91]

After the Restoration in 1660, the Earl of Nithsdale petitioned the Crown for compensation for the losses his father had sustained at Caerlaverock and Threave in garrisoning and provisioning the castles 'seuerall times', and for the subsequent plundering of the castles by the besiegers 'contrary to the capitulation, after the surrander of the sayds garrisons';[92] but to no avail. Threave was not repaired, and continued to decay.

In 1704 the 5th Earl of Nithsdale was relieved of the hereditary office of Steward-Principal of the Stewartry of Kirkcudbright, in favour of the Duke of Queensberry.[93] In the same year, he sold the Threave estate, apart from the castle itself and the island.[94] The office of Keeper of the castle finally reverted to the Crown in 1747.[95]

At the beginning of the 19th century, some minor works were carried out to make the castle suitable for detaining French prisoners during the Napoleonic Wars.[96] But nothing more was done until 1913, when the castle was placed in the care of His Majesty's Office of Works (now Historic Scotland), and an extensive programme of restoration and preservation begun.[97] Extensive excavations were also carried out on the site in the 1920s and again in 1974-78.[98]

---

1   Good & Tabraham 1981, 99, 105-6, 136.
2   M'Kerlie III, 114. Good & Tabraham, *op. cit.*, 92.
3   Good & Tabraham, *op. cit.*, 103 (Fig.7), 136. Traces of walling, some 5ft thick, found beneath the Second Outbuilding suggest a large building of earlier date, which may have been a castle of the Lords of Galloway.
4   Scots Peerage III, 148.
5   Ibid, 158.
6   Cruden 1960, 116. See also Border Laws.
7   RMS I, No.329.
8   Scots Peerage III, 159.
9   RMS I, No.507
10   Maxwell 1902, 119. Loch Fergus is said to have been one of the strongholds built by Fergus, Lord of Galloway (RCAHMS 1914, xxiii, No.263).
11   Good & Tabraham, *op. cit.*, 96, 99, 103-5.
12   See Tabraham, C. 'The Masons Marks at Threave Castle, Stewartry: A Riddle', *TDGAS*, LVII, 87-8
13   There was a similar bretasche at Hermitage later.
14   Grose illustrates it before it was altered (Grose II, 5)
15   The present steps are modern. MacGibbon & Ross record that there were no steps left in 1887 (MacGibbon & Ross I, 163).
16   See Tabraham, C. 'The Masons Marks at Threave Castle', *op. cit.* There can be no doubt that the present wheel-stair is not original, but whether it replaces an earlier wheel-stair or straight, internal, wooden stairs has not been established.
17   The date of the prison is not known, although it was clearly added after the wheel-stair, hence the need for corbelling.
18   All the dressed stone except the lowest courses of the jambs was removed in 1640.
19   Surprisingly little is known about the system of removable ladders used, bearing in mind that they had to be accessible to all members of the family, regardless of age or sex. Simplistic mediaeval pictures of simple ladders (e.g. See Castlemilk) are not wholly convincing.
20   The lintel was found in pieces in the basement, and has been restored.
21   Although the garderobe off the kitchen shows no evidence of a drain, there can be little doubt that it was originally a garderobe of some sort.
22   See MacGibbon & Ross I, Figs.126A, 130.
23   Tabraham 1988, 14.
24   The absence of these timbers in the NW corner, and the cutting of the circuit by the stair-well, is further evidence that the NW corner has at some time been rebuilt.
25   Good & Tabraham, *op. cit.*, 99-101.
26   Ibid, 100-1.
27   Ibid, 101-2, Fig.6.
28   The foundation stones of the first building were rounded, water-worn boulders, whereas those of the second building were greywacke rubble.
29   Good & Tabraham, *op. cit.*, 102.
30   Ibid, 103-4.
31   Complete Peerage IV, 433.
32   Ibid.
33   Ibid, 434.
34   Ibid; RMS II, No.47.
35   Scots Peerage III, 173.
36   Complete Peerage, 436.
37   APS II, 67-73; RMS II, No.467; Scots Peerage III, 177.
38   Tabraham, C. J. & Good, G. L. 'The Artillery Fortification at Threave Castle, Galloway', in Caldwell 1981, 68.
39   APS II, 76.
40   Tabraham & Good 1981, *op. cit.*, 70-1.
41   For some unexplained reason, the splayed recesses adjacent to the corner towers were larger than the others. It is probable that these arrow-slits, unlike the loops in the corner towers, were only intended for use with long-bows or cross-bows, as smaller handguns are unlikely to have been available in Scotland this early.
42   Grose II, 5.
43   At least one of the basement gun-loops at Hoddom was similarly provided.
44   APS II, 76.
45   After the 8th Earl's death, the 9th Earl obtained special dispensation to marry his sister-in-law and thus secure her Galloway estates.
46   Bain IV, No.1272.
47   ALHT I, ccxxi-ii, ccxcix; ERS VI, 161, 200, 456.
48   ERS VI, 199, 203-4. James II, who was present for the latter part of the siege, made his base at Tongland Abbey, but he also had a tent for use on the field (Fraser 1885, II, 608).
49   APS II, 42.
50   ERS VI, 208.
51   Ibid, 203, 208; RMS II, No.1322, 1799; etc.
52   ERS VI, 456.
53   Tabraham 1988, 7.
54   RMS II, No.1143; APS II, 189, 192.
55   Nicholson 1978, 513; Fraser 1885, II, 77.
56   Nicholson 1978, 536.
57   ALHT II, 29, 61, 157-8.
58   ALHT IV, lxxiii, 350.
59   Ibid, 460.
60   Fraser 1873, 174.
61   Good & Tabraham, *op. cit.*, 94.
62   RSS I, No.3277.
63   Ibid, No.3396; RMS III, No.391.
64   RMS III, No.1692, 1694.
65   RSS II, No.3939.
66   Fraser 1873, I, 56.
67   RPC I, 9.
68   Fraser 1873, I, 57, 202.
69   Ibid. It cannot have been force of arms that made it surrender, as its ability to withstand siege was amply demonstrated in both 1455 and 1640.
70   Armstrong 1883, cviii.
71   ALHT XI, 416.
72   Ibid, XII, 128.
73   Rae 241.
74   RPC III, 725.
75   Fraser 1894, I, xcvi; Border Papers I, No.334.
76   RPC IV, 286.
77   Fraser 1873, II, 495.
78   RPC V, 425.
79   RMS VII, No.217.
80   Ibid, VIII, No.228.
81   Ibid, Nos.633, 773.
82   Fraser 1873, I, 354.

83 Ibid, 385.
84 Good & Tabraham, *op. cit.*, 104-5.
85 Fraser 1873, I, 354.
86 Ibid, II, 17.
87 Good & Tabraham, *op. cit.*, 104.
88 Fraser 1873, I, 359.
89 M'Kerlie 1877, III, 145.
90 Ibid.
91 Good & Tabraham, *op. cit.*, 95. The date over the doorway at Barscobe is 1648.
92 Fraser 1873, I, 378.
93 Ibid, 422.
94 Grose II, 7.
95 NSA IV, 181.
96 Ibid,159; Stell 1986, 104-6; Good & Tabraham, *op. cit.*, 95.
97 Good & Tabraham, *op. cit.*, 90.
98 Ibid, 90-140.

---

66. TORTHORWALD CASTLE

(Torthorwald)   (NY033782)

The earliest known possessors of the lands of Torthorwald were the family of 'de Torthorwald', who took their name from the place. They were evidently a family of some consequence, and it was presumably they who raised the first, motte-and-bailey castle on the site some time during the 12th century. It was clearly an important timber castle, and it is from this period that the extensive earthworks surrounding the site would seem largely to date, although the name Torthorwald, meaning 'hill of Thorold',[1] suggests that they may well incorporate earthworks of an even earlier, pre-mediaeval settlement.

David de Torthorwald was witness to a Bruce charter *c*.1250;[2] and around the same date Bruce confirmed to David that no fine for straying animals would be exacted within the barony of Annandale and the tenement of Torthorwald except 1d for 10 cattle, 1d for 10 sheep, etc.[3] Some of the family later

supported the English during the War of Independence, and forfeited their lands.[4] It was presumably then that Bruce granted the barony of Torthorwald to Sir John de Soulis; but he did not enjoy it long, as he was killed in Ireland in 1318, leaving no issue.[5] Another of the family was Sir David de Torthorwald, who swore fealty to Edward I in 1291.[6] On his death in 1296, he was succeeded by his only daughter, Isobel, who, according to some accounts, is said to have married Humphrey de Kirkpatrick, eldest son and heir of Sir Roger Kirkpatrick of that Ilk.[7] It was to this Humphrey in 1321 that Bruce granted the whole lands and town of Torthorwald, with the 3 husbandland of Roucan, in free warren as a reward for his services and in part compensation for the destruction of Auchencass, the family's former stronghold.[8] This grant was confirmed in 1326,[9] and it may well have been Humphrey who started construction of the present tower-house.[10] Thereafter Humphrey and his successors were designated 'of Torthorwald', which presumably became their new seat.

When Edward Balliol invaded Scotland in 1332, Humphrey and his wife fled with his parents to England.[11] They returned some time later, but in 1357 Humphrey returned to England again as a hostage for the release of David II, and there he died. He was succeeded in Torthorwald by Roger Kirkpatrick, who is thought to have been his younger brother.[12] Roger's tenure was very brief, for after taking Caerlaverock Castle and being appointed its captain, he was murdered there later the same year.[13] The next laird was Roger's son, Sir Duncan Kirkpatrick, who was granted a new infeftment in the barony of Torthorwald in 1398.[14] Leaving no male issue, his estates devolved upon his three daughters, the eldest of whom, Elizabeth, inherited Torthorwald, while the next daughter, Janet, received part of the lands of Kirkpatrick with Auchencass.[15]

Elizabeth Kirkpatrick married William Carlyle, son and heir of Sir John Carlyle, the representative of the ancient family of Carlyle from the city of that name.[16] Elizabeth's father died before June 1425, after which time William is designated 'of

Fig. 351 Torthorwald Castle: east elevation before the north end collapsed.
The original first floor entrance can be seen blocked-up just to the left of centre.

Torthorwald'.[17] In 1436 he agreed with Thomas Graham of Auchencass to exchange that part of the lands of Kirkpatrick that he had inherited through his late wife for half the lands of Roucan, in the barony of Torthorwald, which Graham had inherited through his late wife, Janet Kirkpatrick, Elizabeth's sister.[18] By 1443 William had also acquired the lands of Kinmount.[19] He died in 1463.

By this time the present castle of Torthorwald had been built, though whether it was the work of the first Humphrey de Kirkpatrick in 1321, or a later generation, is not certain. As the ruins now stand, they represent no less than four phases of building, the earliest of which undoubtedly dates from the 14th century. Cruden has suggested a date early in the century, pointing out that the masonry incorporates checked or rebated joints, a rare feature found elsewhere in SW Scotland at the castles of Lochmaben and Loch Doon,[20] while Stell is inclined to a date somewhat later.[21] A further problem is that the rebated joints referred to by Cruden belong, not to the first, but to the second phase of building. It is not until much later that the castle itself is first mentioned. Standing on a rocky outcrop, some 250ft up the western slopes of the hills that divide Nithsdale from Annandale, it had a commanding view over the Lochar Moss and Lower Nithsdale to the S and W.

The site of the tower is a platform, now roughly **L**–shaped and measuring some 185ft by 130ft, with the two arms extending to the S and W, but no doubt the missing re-entrant angle was originally complete and formed part of the motte. Beyond this to the N and E are elaborate earthworks, with high ramparts and wet and dry ditches up to 20ft deep; and although the earthworks on the other sides have largely been levelled by modern cultivation, the outline of an outer bailey can still be traced in the adjacent field to the S and W.[22] This bailey measured about 450ft from N to S by 580ft from E to W, and it appears that at some period it was subdivided.[23] Occupying the W arm of the platform is the outline of an irregular, quadrangular enclosure, averaging about 60ft by 50ft, while the tower itself stood in the re-entrant angle. From the SW corner of the tower an enclosing wall ran S to the SW corner of the site, where there is evidence of a circular corner tower.[24] The wall then continued E and N around the edge of the platform to the NE corner, where there appears to have been a second corner tower, before continuing W to the NE corner of the quadrangular enclosure. A further section of the curtain, now no longer traceable, completed the enclosure on the W side, though the tusking, 2ft 6in

wide, that may still be seen in the tower's W wall is not now thought to have formed part of it.[25] Immediately S of the NE corner tower, and abutting the E curtain, there was a range of outbuildings whose foundations can still be traced; they were approximately 13ft wide inside walls 3ft thick. Access to the platform was from the outer bailey to the S, while on the E side the site of a later bridge across the wet ditch is marked by traces of the abutments.

The **TOWER** itself, which is oblong in plan, is very ruinous, the whole of the NW corner and most of the vaulting having fallen prior to 1788.[26] It is only because of an extensive programme of propping and stabilization in the 19th century that the rest survived so well until early in 1993, when the whole NE corner finally collapsed. It remains an impressive edifice, rising to a height of some 60ft.[27] Originally, the tower measured about 47ft from N to S by 39ft 3in from E to W over walls varying in thickness from 7ft on each side to about 9ft 6in at the ends. It was built of Silurian rubble with quoins and margins of dressed red sandstone, all bonded by a very strong mortar of shell lime. There was a splayed plinth course, now almost entirely below ground level, but there was evidently no vaulting. The basement presumably included the two slit-windows in the E wall, parts of which still exist, but the slit-window on the W side bears evidence, in the S jamb, of even earlier work; perhaps it was originally a secondary entrance to the basement. The large recess in the middle of the S wall is now so ruinous that its purpose is uncertain.

The original entrance to the tower was in the middle of the E wall at first floor level, where the dressed jambs and round-arched head of the doorway may still be seen partially built up in the outside wall. Adjacent to this on the S side there was a wheel-stair leading to the basement. This was later filled in, and its existence only came to light recently when fallen masonry exposed parts of it in the body of the wall.[28] A small window in the middle of the W wall at this level also appears to be an original feature. Although its recess has been altered on the inside, the external surround is original and the only one in the castle to survive intact; it has a hollow chamfer on the arrises – a feature also found at Threave –, and originally held an iron grille comprising one vertical and three horizontal bars. The only features in the S wall are two doorways: one at the E end, which is now blocked, probably gave access to a mural chamber in the SE corner, while the other admitted to a straight stair that rose within the thickness of the wall from this floor to the SW corner of the second floor.

At some later date the inside of the tower was transformed, and the floor levels changed, by the introduction of two vaults and the provision of a new entrance at ground level. At the same time the upper floors were largely reconstructed. This work, which brought the tower more into line with the tower-castles of the 15th century, is clearly distinguished from the earlier work by the well cut, sandstone ashlar used throughout most of its construction. It also necessitated an additional 2ft 6in thickness of walling inside the old side walls to support the vaults. The new basement thus formed beneath the lower barrel vault occupied the whole of the original two, lowest storeys. It appears to have been a single chamber, 15ft high, with no entresol floor.[29] As the vaulting and its supporting wall on the E side cut right across the former doorway in the SE corner, this had to be closed up, while the old entrance in the E wall was partly filled up and converted into a window, which, together with the one opposite to it in the W wall, were carried through the upper part of the vault to provide additional illumination for

Fig. 352 Torthorwald Castle in 1789.

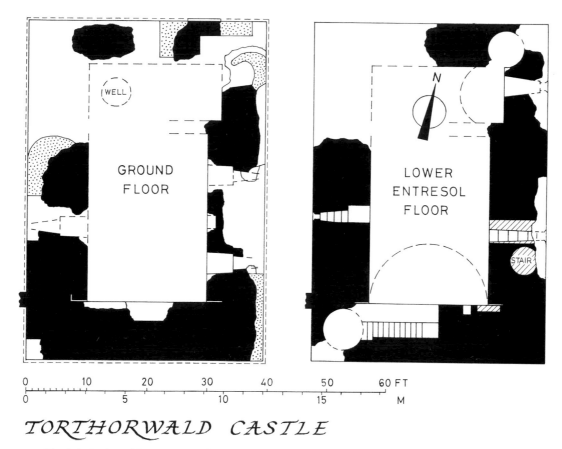

TORTHORWALD CASTLE

Fig. 353 Torthorwald Castle: plans of ground and lower entresol floors in 1992, before the north end collapsed.

the basement. It was at this time that the wheel-stair adjacent to the original entrance was filled in. It was probably also at this time that the suggested early entrance to the basement was converted into a window recess.

Beneath the upper vault was the great hall, a vast chamber that apparently rose straight up to the pointed barrel vault some 25ft above. Again, there is no evidence of an entresol floor.[30] All that remains within the hall is one large window recess in each of the side walls at the S end and a fragment of another window recess further N in the W wall. From this level a wheel-stair, also built of ashlar, rose within the SW corner to serve the upper floors. No details of these floors remain, and the solitary pillar of rubble masonry that rises another 15ft at the SE corner is all that now remains of a still later period of construction.

The N end of the tower was a later addition. It appeared to have been contemporary with the second building phase, but not to have been added until after the upper vault was finished. The builder then seems to have decided that the tower was not large enough for his needs after all, so the N wall was removed in its entirety and an extension added to increase the overall length of the tower to 56ft 6in. However, the new walls, which were of coursed sandstone ashlar, were not so massive, those on the N and E sides averaging only 7ft 3in in thickness. The additional accommodation thus provided was not integrated with the older work, from which it was separated by a new partition wall 2ft 4in thick, and the floor levels themselves were also different, the second floor of the extension being several feet above the level of the hall. It was not until one reached the upper vault that the building lines coincided, with the southern portion of

Fig. 354 Torthorwald Castle: view from NW in 1987, before the north end collapsed.

the vault continuing into the extension, but not before a sharp dividing line, now collapsed, cut right across the vault to show where the old N wall was removed and the extension added. Below this level the extension's layout was much the same as if it were a wing to provide separate family accommodation, as at Cessford or Neidpath but on a smaller scale. There were four storeys below the upper vault. Over the lower two of these there was a segmental barrel-vault built transversely across the width of the tower. In the basement floor near the NW corner there is said to have been a well, while in the NE corner a mural stair rose to the third floor. No details of these chambers remained, except for one small window in the E wall at first floor level, a window recess in the E wall and a mural recess off the stair at second floor level, and the splayed right jamb of another window recess in the N wall at third floor level. Regrettably, these all disappeared in 1993.

William Carlyle was succeeded at Torthorwald by his eldest son, John, who had a distinguished career in the service of the crown. Among the many offices he held at various times were those of Keeper of Threave and Lochmaben castles and Justiciary of Annandale.[31] He was created Lord Carlyle of Torthorwald in 1473.[32] In the same year he changed the name of the castle to 'Carlyle', and received a crown charter erecting the town of Torthorwald into a free burgh of barony, to be called the 'town of Cairleill'.[33] He was a regular attender of parliament from 1478 until 1489.[34] Just before his death in 1500/1, his grandson and heir, Sir William Carlyle, received a crown charter of the lands and barony of Carlyle, with the castle and fortalice, and other lands.[35] Thereafter the fortunes of the Carlyles went into decline.

In 1525 James, 3rd Lord Carlyle, had sasine of the barony of Carlyle as heir to his father, but he died the next year.[36] Three years later, in 1529, his widow, Janet, was granted a crown charter of a liferent from the estate,[37] while James's brother Michael, 4th Lord Carlyle, received a charter of all the lands and barony.[38] This led to a fierce argument years later, in 1544, when Lord Carlyle 'violently evicted' Janet from 'the place of Torthorwald', and the Crown had to intervene to resolve the issue.[39]

In 1547 Lord Carlyle pledged 206 men to the service of England.[40] In the same year he surrendered the castle to the English, but it was recovered the following year by the Master of Maxwell.[41] Meanwhile Lord Carlyle's finances continued to deteriorate, so that by the time the English made a survey of the West March c.1564-5, he was reported to have only 10 horsemen left in his service.[42] Eventually, in 1573, he was forced to sell the lands and castle to his third, but eldest surviving son, Michael, reserving only free tenement to himself and an annualrent from the town of Torthorwald for his wife.[43]

Following the death of the 4th Lord Carlyle two years later, the succession to the peerage, the lands and castle of Torthorwald and other family estates was bitterly contested between his eldest surviving son, Michael, and his second son's daughter, Elizabeth, the heir general. To further confuse matters, the changing fortunes of the Regency of the Kingdom came to have a direct bearing on the fortunes of Torthorwald itself. In 1575 the Regent Morton granted the ward of the lands and barony of Carlyle, including the castle of Torthorwald, to his half-brother, George Douglas of Parkhead, completely disregarding Michael Carlyle's purchase of the lands two years earlier.[44] Not surprisingly, Michael refused to vacate the lands, and in 1578 was put to the horn.[45]

But with the fall of the Earl of Morton in 1580, Douglas of Parkhead lost his support. Michael Carlyle now sold most of the estate, except the lands and castle of Torthorwald, to Lord Maxwell, and this was confirmed by crown charter.[46] Douglas, however, would not surrender the 'toure, fortalice and castell of Torthorall', and so was put to the horn.[47] If Carlyle had found favour again, it was short lived, for in 1583 James Douglas, apparent of Parkhead, was granted the mails and other dues of Torthorwald and other lands belonging to Michael Carlyle, 'callit of Torthorwald', while his brother George was granted the escheat of Michael Carlyle's goods.[48] Later that year James VI

revoked his previous gifts to Douglas of Parkhead, which had been made 'against his highness own good will, liking and intention', and granted the mails, farms, profits and duties of Torthorwald and all the other lands of Michael Carlyle to John Johnston of that Ilk and his spouse for the lifetime of the said Michael.[49] A month later he confirmed that the safe keeping of 'the hous, manis and landis of Torthorw[ald]' should be held by Sir John Johnston of that Ilk, Warden of the West March, and 'remane in your handes for the better sa[fetie] of the cuntrie in cais of ony incursionis be innemyis or thevis'.[50]

The next year Johnston imprisoned one Richard Graham, 'callit Hutschoneis Reche', within 'the towr and fortalice of Terthorwall'. The incident is of interest because, to allow himself a certain amount of freedom, Graham was allowed to give Johnston a bond that he would 'remain within the said fortalice and yards'.[51] In 1585 Lord Maxwell took Johnston prisoner. It was probably then that he took possession of Torthorwald, for only days later Lord Scrope reported that Maxwell was planning to put forces of footmen in Caerlaverock, Threave, Lochmaben, Langholm and 'Tortarrell' with a special person of trust at each as captain.[52]

The dispute within the Carlyle family was not finally resolved until 1587, when, following protracted litigation, Elizabeth was finally infeft in the lands and barony of Carlyle, with the castle, and many other of the family's lands.[53] Later that year she married Sir James Douglas of Parkhead, eldest son of Sir George Douglas of Parkhead, after which Sir James was recognized as Lord Carlyle of Torthorwald.[54] However, despite Elizabeth's infeftment in 1587, the lands of Torthorwald seem to have remained in the possession of Michael's family, and in 1592 his son John was infeft in Torthorwald as his heir.[55]

In 1593/4 the Crown granted the lands and barony of Carlyle, with the castle of Torthorwald, to George Douglas, Lord Carlyle's younger brother.[56] It is not known whether he ever took possession of the castle,[57] but by 1596/7 it was again in the possession of the Maxwells and, together with Caerlaverock and Mouswald, held against the Crown. James VI demanded their delivery, failing which he would lay siege.[58] Against such odds Lord Maxwell capitulated, and Torthorwald was handed over first to Lord Sanquhar,[59] and later that year to Lord Ochiltree, Warden and Lieutenant of the West March.[60] Five years later, in 1602, the keeping of the castle was handed to Sir James Johnston of that Ilk, who was commanded not to 'reset therein James Dowglas of Torthorwald under pain of perjury and defamation'.[61]

In 1606, following the resignation by George Douglas of the lands and barony of Carlyle, with the castle, in favour of William Cunningham of Dolphinton, Cunningham received a crown charter of the lands,[62] but three years later he resigned them again in favour of James, 6th Lord Carlyle. This was confirmed by crown charter the same year.[63] Lord Carlyle attended parliament as 'Lord Torthorwald' in 1612.[64] He was, however, no better at managing his affairs than his Carlyle forebears, and the following year he sold Sir Robert Douglas an annualrent from the lands,[65] and in 1617 granted him the lands, lordship and barony as well.[66] A few years later he sold or mortgaged all his estates, including Torthorwald, to Sir William Douglas of Drumlanrig, later 1st Earl of Queensberry, who, in 1622, received a crown charter granting him in liferent and his eldest son and heir, James, the lands, lordship and barony of Torthorwald, comprising the lands and barony of Carlyle, with the castle, and other lands.[67]

It is said that the castle was last repaired as a residence

in 1630.[68] If this is correct, it must have been the work of James Douglas, who did not succeed to Drumlanrig until 1640. The last inhabitant is said to have been one of his younger brothers, Archibald Douglas, 1st of Dornock.[69] Some time after that the castle was abandoned and fell into ruin. It does not feature in the Hearth Tax returns for 1690,[70] but at that time it must still have had a roof, as Grose mentions an old man alive in 1789 who remembered the roof being taken off for use elsewhere.[71] By 1788 it was very much as it remained until the NE corner collapsed in 1993.[72]

The castle was retained by the Douglases until c.1890, when it was sold by the 9th Marquess of Queensberry to James Jardine of Dryfeholm, brother of Sir Robert Jardine, 1st Baronet of Castle Milk.[73] It was apparently he who carried out the various works that have since helped to preserve the ruin.[74]

Fig. 356 Torthorwald: N end after 1993 collapse.

1   Johnson-Ferguson 1935, 120.
2   Bain I, No.706; Macquarrie, A. 'Notes on some Charters of the Bruces of Annandale', *TDGAS*, 3rd Ser., LVIII, 74-6.
3   Bain I, No.1683; Macquarrie, 'Notes', *op. cit.*, 74-6.
4   Bain II, No.1437; IV, 386; RCAHMS 1920, xxvi. In 1330/1 Edward III granted a pension to John de Torthorwald, as his father had lost his lands in Scotland for supporting Edward II (Bain III, No.1020).
5   RMS I, App.2, No.143; M'Michael, T. 'The Feudal Family of de Soulis', *TDGAS*, 3rd Ser., XXVI, 186-7.
6   Black 1946, 776.
7   Black 1946, 776; Grose I, 154. In 1332, Humphrey's wife is on record as 'Idonia', who may be the same lady or a later wife (Bain III, No.1067). Other accounts say Isobel married Duncan Kirkpatrick, a younger son of Sir Stephen Kirkpatrick of Closeburn.

Fig. 355 Torthorwald Castle: NE corner after collapse in 1993.

8   Buccleuch MSS, 42 (No.75); RMS I, App.1, No.58 and App.2, Nos.305, 354; Reid, R. C. 'The Early Kirkpatricks', *TDGAS*, 3rd Ser., XXX, 71-2. Auchencass had been destroyed by Bruce while occupied by an English garrison. It was later repaired, and again destroyed c.1332. See also 'Closeburn Castle'. Some lands adjoining Torthorwald were granted by David II to the daughter and heiress of Thomas de Torthorwald (RCAHMS 1920, xxvii).
9   Ramage, 389.
10 See RCAHMS 1997, 201.
11 Reid, *op. cit.*, 71.
12 Ibid, 72.
13 Ibid, 73-5.
14 Ibid, 76; RMS I, App.2, No. 1764.
15 Reid, *op. cit.*, 76-7.
16 Scots Peerage II, 369-80.
17 Ibid, 380.
18 Ibid, 381.
19 Ibid. See also 'Lockerbie Tower' (c.1198).
20 Cruden 1960, 52.
21 Stell 1986, 92.

22 It shows up as a distinct crop mark in aerial photographs, and could still be deverned on the ground within living memory.
23 See RCAHMS 1997, 190, 200.
24 RCAHMS 1920, 201.
25 RCAHMS 1997, 201. It is suggested that the tusking may have formed part of a forestair to a first floor entrance.
26 Cardonnel, 'Torthorwald'; Grose I, 147.
27 MacGibbon & Ross compared it with the massive character of Dundonald, but on a smaller scale.
28 This stair is not mentioned by either MacGibbon & Ross or the RCAHMS.
29 MacGibbon & Ross believed there was an entresol floor, unless they were referring solely to the extension.
30 The great hall at Borthwick, which is also 15th century work, is 29ft high.
31 Scots Peerage II, 383.
32 Ibid.
33 Ibid.
34 APS II, *passim*.
35 RMS II, No.2564.
36 Ibid, III, No.868.
37 'Lord Carlyle' attended parliament in June 1526 (APS II, 300), but as James was dead by 16 June, it was probably Michael, 4th Lord Carlyle, who attended..
38 RMS III, No.871.
39 RMS IV, No.75.
40 Armstrong 1883, lxxiv.
41 Fraser 1894, I, lxiv; Fraser 1873, I, 501.
42 Armstrong 1883, cxi.
43 RMS V, No.134.
44 RSS VII, No.263. George Douglas of Parkhead was the natural son of Sir George Douglas of Pittendreich, and thus a half brother of Morton.
45 RSS VIII, Nos.1346, 1508.
46 RMS V, Nos.134, 136.
47 RSS VIII, No.340. It is not clear to whom Douglas should have surrendered the property.
48 Ibid., Nos.1346, 1357.
49 Ibid., No.1508.
50 Fraser 1894, II, 9.
51 Ibid., I, 47; Hope-Johnstone MSS, 31 (No.57).
52 Border Papers I, No.334.
53 Scots Peerage II, 392.
54 Ibid.

55 Ibid.
56 RMS VI, No.70.
57 The castle is shown on both Aglionby's platte of 1590 (Hyslop, 320) and Pont's map of Annandale c.1595 (Blaeu, 57, 'THE STEWARTRIE OF ANNANDAIL').
58 Border Papers II, No.548; Scottish Papers XII, No.390.
59 Scottish Papers XII, No.405.
60 Border Papers II, No.864.
61 RPC VI, 358.
62 RMS VI, No.1718.
63 RMS VII, No.48.
64 APS IV, 466.
65 RMS VII, No.847.
66 Ibid, No.1687.
67 RMS VIII, No.252.
68 'Torthorwald', TDGAS, 2nd Ser., XIX, 182.
69 Grose I, 147.
70 Adamson, D. 'Hearth Tax of Dumfriesshire', TDGAS, 3rd Ser., XLVIII, 137.
71 Grose I, 147.
72 Cardonnel, 'Torthorwald'; Grose I, 147.
73 'Torthorwald', TDGAS, 2nd Ser., XIX, 183; Complete Peerage X, 708.
74 Ibid., 182.

Fig. 357 Woodhouse Tower in 1902: view from SE.
(Photograph by the writer's grandfather,
John Bell Irving of Beanlands.)

67.   WOODHOUSE TOWER

(1m SE Kirtlebridge)   (NY251715)

The earliest tower at Woodhouse may well have been of timber construction, as many in the Borders were before the second half of the 16th century. However, it is more likely that the name derived from 'the house in the wood', the name 'Wodhouse' being found as early as 1347, when an inquisition regarding the ownership of the lands of Kirkconnel stated that William de Carlyle, nephew of William de Carlyle of Luce, was heir to the latter William's lands of Luce, Annan, Woodhouse and others.[1]

Woodhouse next comes on record in 1456, when the fermes due to the Crown for the lands were £10:13s:4d;[2] but because the lands of Woodhouse and others in the neighbourhood had been 'laid waste', presumably by the recent English incursions, the rent was remitted.[3] In the same year, John de Dennon, or Denholm, was given sasine in alba-ferme.[4] Prior to that, the lands had been in the King's hands for four years.[5] The Denholms, however, did not reside at Woodhouse, but at Creakane (Crichen) in the parish of Glencairn. In 1506, Peter Denholm had sasine of the lands of Glencorse and 'Wodhowis'.[6] Five years later he was granted a licence to sell his lands of Glencorse to Sir William Douglas of Drumlanrig;[7] but there is no further mention of his family's possession of Woodhouse, nor is it clear what the connection was between the Denholms and the Glencorses of that Ilk, both of whom had an interest in both Woodhouse and Glencorse around this time.[8]

Meanwhile, in 1475/6, John de Glencorse of that Ilk wadset the '4 merksworth of his lands of Wodhous . . . lying beside the Water of Kirtyll', under reversion, to one John Johnston.[9] It is unlikely that Glencorse exercised the reversion, for the next time these lands are mentioned the Johnstons are still found in possession. Meanwhile, the other 4½ merks worth of the lands of 'Wodhous' were retained by the Glencorse family, and after the death of John Glencorse in, or shortly before, 1543, they passed to Thomas Glencorse of that Ilk.[10] Later that year, Thomas was murdered, and his titles burned, by William Kirkpatrick of Kirkmichael.[11] Thomas was succeeded by his eldest son, Alexander, who, in 1564, received a new crown charter of the lands.[12]

The portion of the lands of Woodhouse acquired by the Johnstons later became known as Woodhouse-Johnston. In 1551,

following the death of Laurence Johnston of Woodhouse, John Johnston of that Ilk was gifted the ward and nonentries of 'the five mark land of auld extent of Wodhous' until the heir should come of age.[13] Nevertheless the lands continued to be held by the Crown until 1574, when John Johnston of Wodhous finally took sasine of that half of the lands of Woodhouse called 'Wodhous Johnnestoun', extending to 33s:4d of old extent;[14] and later that year Johnston sold these lands to Edward Irving of Bonshaw.[15]

The Irvings had already been occupying part of the lands of Woodhouse for many years. In 1542/43 Christopher Irving of Bonshaw and his son Edward were reported to have violently evicted one David Irwyn from his mailing of the lands of Bonshaw and Woodhouse,[16] and later there are several references to Jeffrey Irwen, 'called of Woodhouse', a younger son of Bonshaw. Jeffrey must have been a man of some substance, as in 1547 he pledged 93 men to the service of England.[17]

Woodhouse Tower stands on the edge of a cliff on the left bank of the Kirtle Water, almost opposite to Robgill and in full view of Bonshaw and Wyseby, only three quarters of a mile upstream. Both the tower and outbuildings were enclosed by a barmkin to the S and E, and there were also outer earthworks. The remains of the earthworks were finally levelled early this century, but the outline of various enclosing walls can still be traced. A short distance to the N stands the fine, 15th century Merkland Cross,[18] which is said to have been erected by Lord Maxwell to mark the spot where his son, the Master of Maxwell, fell at the battle of the Kirtle in 1484.

What remains of the **TOWER** is partly original ruin and partly a 'romantic' reconstruction carried out in 1877. According to one account at the time,[19] the restoration was carried out immediately after a large section of walling collapsed. If this was the case, it must have been a second fall, presumably of the NE corner, as in 1834 the New Statistical Account recorded that the tower had been 'unroofed and greatly rent for many a year', and in the winter of 1830-31 its 'south side fell down, during a stormy night, with a dreadful crash'.[20] Only the northern half of the tower was restored, but it included a completely new wheel-stair in the NE corner, just 4ft in diameter, which was designed to give direct access to the parapet walk, without any openings at the intermediate floors.[21] There is, however, no evidence to suggest that this was the original arrangement.

The tower dates from the third quarter of the 16th century, and in all likelihood immediately after the Irvings' purchase of the property in 1574. Built of pink sandstone rubble, with QER mouldings, it comprises three storeys and a garret, and was clearly very similar in design to Bonshaw, except that there is no plinth course. It measured 31ft 6in by 23ft 3in over walls varying in thickness from 4ft 7in to 5ft 8in at ground level. All that remains is the N side, substantial sections of the adjacent walling at each end, both of which, including the NE corner, have been heavily restored, and overgrown foundations. Originally, one would have expected both the entrance and stair to have been in the SE corner, as at the other Irving towers, and this is where MacGibbon and Ross show the entrance;[22] but there was a later entrance in the SW corner, at the W end of the S wall, which they do not show, and this is hard to explain. Only the lowest course of the masonry for this survives, but the jambs have an elaborate bolection moulding of 17th century type.[23]

The basement was vaulted, and was lit by a slit-window,

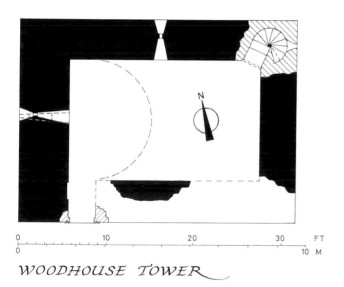

Fig. 358 Woodhouse Tower: plan of basement.

with stepped sill, high up at the W end. In the N and W walls there is a splayed gun-loop, with a circular throat and rectangular mouth, and one presumes there were similar loops on the other sides, as well as an additional one at the foot of the stair, as in the other Irving towers. It is surprising, though, that the splay of these gun-loops is much narrower (29° and 21°) than those found in other local towers.[24]

On the first floor, there was a large fireplace at the W end, one jamb of which survives. This carries a bold, QER moulding and also includes on its inner side, 4ft 2in above the hearth, a small recess 9in wide by 7in high. There were formerly similar holes on either side of the fireplace at Bonshaw,[25] and these are believed to have been for the support of some form of spit. To the right of the fireplace there is a large open-aumbry, and in the N wall a large window recess with stone seats and, in

its left ingo, a closed-aumbry. Originally, the window was fitted with an iron grille, now missing.

Both the second floor and garret were supported on moulded corbels. The former floor has a window recess in the N wall and a lamp shelf in the NW corner. It probably also had a fireplace in the SW corner, corresponding to the small one which survives in the NW corner of the garret above.

The parapet walk, which is supported on 2-stage corbels above a continuous corbel-course, would have continued around the wall-head, as at Bonshaw. A vestige of the crow-stepped gable at the W end survives.

It is now generally believed that the drawing of 'Robgill Tower' made in 1823 by William Graham of Mossknowe is in fact of Woodhouse, though it is surprizing that someone who was born, and grew up, in the vicinity should have added the wrong caption.[26] A ruinous tower drawn in 1823 certainly could not have been Robgill (q.v.). The drawing shows the tower viewed from the east, with a small cottage in the foreground. All that is visible at ground level is the entrance in the SE corner and, on its left, a rectangular, splayed gun-loop, while rising above the entrance are the slit-windows that served the adjacent stair. Each of the upper floors had one medium-sized window on the S side, but the windows facing E are shown as mere slits.[27] As at Bonshaw, the parapet ran around the entire wall-head, where it was supported on 2-stage corbels above a continuous course. A fragment of the crow-stepped E gable is also shown, and there is even a significant crack in the E wall. There is, however, one detail that cannot be explained: why is the entrance shown in the SE corner, when the later entrance at Woodhouse was in the SW corner? This entrance cannot have been added later, as the already ruinous tower collapsed only seven years after the drawing was made.

Woodhouse is presumably 'Ye Wythies' on Aglionby's map of 1590 showing the houses of strength in the West March.[28] The Irvings held Woodhouse until 1611, when George Irving of Woodhouse was sentenced to forfeit his life and lands for theft.[29] The lands of Over and Nether Woodhouse, with the fortalice and manor-place, were then granted to Mr. Symon Johnston, minister of Annan,[30] but there is no evidence that he got possession.

A year later, John Murray of Renpatrick, later 1st Earl of Annandale, received a crown charter of the superiority of the lands and barony of Lochmaben, together with many other lands, including Over and Nether Woodhouse;[31] and four months later

Fig. 359 "Robgill Tower" in 1823, by William Graham of Mossknowe. Although inscribed 'Robgill', Robgill (q.v.) was not a ruin in 1823, and it is thought more likely that the drawing is meant to portray Woodhouse.

he received a further grant of these and other lands.[32] In 1617 all his lands were united in the one barony of Lochmaben.[33] Following the death of the 2nd Earl without issue in 1658, all the estates passed to a kinsman, David Murray, 4th Viscount Stormont, who, in 1666, was granted a new charter of all his lands, including Over and Nether Woodhouse, which were now incorporated into the barony of Scone.[34]

Meanwhile, Woodhouse continued in the possession of the Irvings of Bonshaw. A court case in 1622 referred to 'Ritchie Irwine in Wodhous', a fugitive and outlaw.[35] Then, in 1631, William Irving of Bonshaw and his son William (d.1637) granted a liferent in the '5 merkland of the lands of Wodhous, with its tower' to Jean, sister of John Jardine of Applegarth, on the occasion of the younger William's marriage to her.[36] The young couple did not, however, live at Woodhouse, but at Rockhillhead, which William's father gave them as a wedding present.[37] The tower was apparently abandonned some time later in the century, perhaps by their son John (d.1669) 'of Woodhouse', for in the Hearth Tax returns for 1690 John's son, William Irving of Woodhouse, was living at 'The Mains' of Woodhouse, while the tower itself no longer appears.[38] There was, in fact, quite a community living on the lands of Woodhouse, as a census in 1684 lists William Irving of Woodhouse, his brother John and 17 other adults over 12 years of age at Woodhouse, and a further 12 at Nether Woodhouse.[39]

In 1696, after a long and expensive lawsuit, William Irving of Woodhouse established his right to Bonshaw as heir of line, and took up residence there. Woodhouse later passed to his son Colonel Aemilius Irving (b.1714), who is given as the owner c.1770;[40] but Colonel Irving's duties kept him away from home, so that he never took up residence on the property. Col. Irving had a distinguished military career. He held a command under General Wolfe at the taking of Quebec in 1759, later became Commander-in-Chief there, and was for a while in 1765 Acting President of the Province.[41] In 1771 he was appointed Lieutenant-Governor of Guernsey, and later he was made Governor of Upnor Castle, in Kent.[42] In 1792 the Statistical Account recorded that Woodhouse Tower had 'not [been] inhabited for many years past'.[43] Colonel Irving died in 1796, and was succeeded by his son, General Sir Paulus Aemilius Irving, Bart., of Robgill (q.v.). Sir Paulus eventually sold both Woodhouse and Robgill in 1818.[44]

There appears to be no record of who undertook the restoration in 1877. This work is itself now falling into ruin.

1 Bain III, No.1499.
2 ERS VI, 167.
3 Ibid, 275.
4 Ibid, 170, 273: ERS IX, 665.
5 ERS VI, 167.
6 ERS XII, 720.
7 Buccleuch MSS, 65 (No.134); RSS I, No.2337.
8 In 1545 'Peter Dennam of Crechane' was one of the bailies appointed by the Earl of Glencairn (superior of Crichen) to deal with Alexander Glencorse, son of Thomas Glencorse (of that Ilk) (Hamilton-Grierson, Sir P. J. 'The Protocol Book (1541-50) of Herbert Anderson, Notary in Dumfries', TDGAS, 3rd Ser., II, 193).
9 Bonshaw Charters, No.1. See also Reid, R.C. 'The Bonshaw Titles', TDGAS, 3rd Series, XXXVII, 48-61.
10 RSS, III, No.391. The relationship between John and Thomas is not stated.
11 RMS, IV, No.1574.
12 Ibid. It states that Thomas and his predecessors had held the lands by ward of service.
13 RSS IV, No.1248.
14 ERS XX, 461. The lands had been 'in the King's hands for 25 years by reason of ward, because sasine had not been taken'. The fermes for these lands were stated to be £42: 10s.
15 RMS IV, No.2364 (33s.4d = 5 merks).
16 'Acta Dominorum, 1502-58', V (3 Feb 1541/2), cited in Reid Notes. – This is not in itself significant, as Christopher had full legal title to Bonshaw as early as 1522 (Bonshaw Charters, No.2). The relationship of David is not known.
17 Irving 1907, 32, 36; Armstrong 1883, lxxiv.
18 RCAHMS 1920, No.378.
19 MacGibbon & Ross, III, 402.
20 NSA IV, 278-9.
21 The stairs were deliberately broken by the owner in the mid 20th century to prevent people from climbing up.
22 MacGibbon & Ross, III, Fig.322.
23 This doorway was partly excavated by the writer in 1968.
24 See Maxwell-Irving 1974 (II), 208-10.
25 MacGibbon & Ross, III, Fig.320.
26 The drawing was found at Mossknowe House c.1960. For the sake of clarity, a copy of the original has been inked over, but nothing has been added or omitted. Graham did a similar drawing of Stapleton (q.v.) only three days earlier, but no other drawings have come to light.
27 A comparison of Graham's drawing of Stapleton with the tower itself shows that, although he is fairly reliable as regards the numbers and types of feature shown, his drawings give absolutely no idea of either scale or proportion.
28 Hyslop, 320. It appears as 'Woodhouss' on Pont's map of Annandale c.1595 (Blaeu, 57, 'THE STEWARTRIE OF ANNANDAIL').
29 RMS VII, No.594. For some of his exploits, see Reid, R.C. 'Bonshaw', TDGAS, 3rd Ser., XX, 151.
30 Ibid.
31 RMS VII, No.683.
32 Ibid, No.764.
33 Ibid, No.1600.
34 RMS XI, No.965.
35 RPC XIV, 670.
36 Bonshaw Charters, No.16. See also Reid, 'The Bonshaw Titles', op. cit.
37 Ibid, No.18.
38 Adamson, D. 'The Hearth Tax', TDGAS, 3rd Ser., XLIX, 79.
39 RPC, 3rd Ser., IX, 621.
40 Directory of Landownership, 106.
41 Irving 1907, 87.
42 Ibid.
43 Stat Acct, XIII, 373.
44 Irving 1907, 88.

68. WREATHS TOWER
(2¼ m SW Kirkbean) (NX952565)

The lands of Wreaths formed part of the ancient barony of Preston, a large tract of flat, alluvial land beside the Solway in the SE corner of Galloway. It is not known who the earliest feudal owners were,[1] but there is a motte dating from this period half a mile to the WNW. Preston is first mentioned in 1298, when, following the Scots defeat at Falkirk, Sir John de St. John was granted the Balliol's Galloway lands of Buittle, Glasserton and Preston by Edward I; and four years later, following his father's death, John de St. John the younger petitioned Edward to recognize his title as his father's heir.[2]

The lands were subsequently granted by King Robert the Bruce to Sir James Douglas, 'The Good', presumably when he received the lands of Buittle and other Balliol lands in 1325, and in due course they passed to Sir William Douglas, 1st Earl of Douglas, who was in possession c.1360.[3] Shortly afterwards, on the resignation of Bartholomew Loon and Philippa Mowbray, David II granted half the lands of the barony to Thomas Herkers, to be held of the Earl.[4] Preston subsequently came into the possession of Sir James Douglas of Dalkeith, who was granted a new crown charter and entail of 'all the barony of Preston' in 1374/5.[5] Both the Earl of Douglas and Archibald Douglas, 'the Grim', Lord of Galloway, were witnesses. On the 2nd Earl's death in 1388, Archibald succeeded to the Earldom and estates, and it was as the new superior that, in 1393, he consented to Sir James Douglas's eldest son and heir, James, being infeft in the barony.[6]

Fig. 360 Wreaths Tower: remains of wheel-stair in S. corner.

In 1451 William, 8th Earl of Douglas, received a charter of confirmation of the lands of Preston;[7] but only eight months later he was murdered by James II at Stirling. William was succeeded by his younger brother James, who set out to avenge his brother's death; but he fared little better. Three years later he was attainted for rebellion and forfeited all his honours and estates. The lands and barony of Preston, however, remained in the possession of James Douglas of Dalkeith, known as 2nd Lord Dalkeith,[8] who presumably now held them directly from the crown. In 1456 he resigned all his lands in favour of his son James,[9] and eighteen months later the younger James, in anticipation of his marriage to Princess Joan, was created Earl of Morton. Half a century later, in 1507, the 2nd Earl of Morton resigned the lands and barony in favour of his eldest son, James, on the occasion of James's marriage to Lady Katherine Stewart, natural daughter of James IV. James and Katherine were subsequently granted a crown charter of the lands.[10]

The name 'Wreaths' first appears on record in 1529, in a letter from James V to Robert, 4th Lord Maxwell. In it the king charges Lord Maxwell's brother John (the Abbot of Dundrennan) with withholding from Katherine, Countess of Morton, 'the manys (mains) of Prestoun callit the Wrayes' and all the mails and profits of the same for the past three years, and commands Lord Maxwell to get his brother to pay the mails due.[11]

One of the more prominent, and least savoury, aspects of James V's character, however, was his treacherous disposition. An instance of this occurred in 1540, when the 3rd Earl of Morton was coerced into resigning his earldom and lands under threat of imprisonment in Inverness.[12] No good reason was given. James then granted the lands and barony of Preston, Borgue and Buittle, with the manor-places, to Sir Robert Douglas of

Lochleven, a distant cousin of the Earl.[13] Three months later James changed his mind, and forced Sir Robert to give up his new found wealth, this time in favour of Robert, 4th Lord Maxwell.[14] But no sooner was James dead in 1542, than Morton appealed to the Court of Session for the annulment of his enforced resignation. He won his case, and in March 1543 was reinstated.[15] Then, in accordance with an agreement entered into the previous year between himself and Sir George Douglas of Pittendreich, on the occasion of the betrothal of his youngest daughter, Elizabeth, to Sir George's younger son, James, Morton, having no male heir, granted all his lands of the Earldom of Morton and lordship of Dalkeith, including 'Prestoun, Borg and Buthill, with the manor-places', etc., to the said James and his wife, Elizabeth.[16]

On the death of the 3rd Earl of Morton in 1548, His son-in-law James, Master of Morton, succeeded to the Earldom, though, as he was a prisoner in England at the time, it was not until his release in 1550 that he could take his seat in parliament. In 1562 he was appointed Chancellor of Scotland. Two years later he had a crown charter of the earldom and estates of Morton, including the lands and baronies of Preston, Borgue and Buittle, with their manor-places,[17] and this was confirmed by parliament in 1567.[18] His political career, which culminated in his appointment as Regent of Scotland in 1572, is very much a part of the history of Scotland. However, in his success he made enemies; in 1577/8 he was deposed, and two years later he was accused of complicity in the murder of Darnley, tried and executed, forfeiting all his titles and estates.

Following the forfeiture of the Regent Morton in 1581, John, 7th Lord Maxwell, was created Earl of Morton and granted the lands of the earldom, including 'the lands and barony of Prestoun, the lands of Brog, with the castle, manor-place', etc.[19] Once again the Maxwell's tenure was to be ephemeral, for in 1585/6 James VI reversed the attainder on the late Regent, made during his minority, whereupon the earldom and lands, including 'the landis and barony of Prestoun, the landis of Brog, with castell tour, fortalice, maner place', etc., passed to Archibald, Earl of Angus, nephew and heir-male of the Regent Morton.[20] Three years later, on the death of Angus without male issue, the Earldom of Morton passed to the next heir-male, Sir William Douglas of Lochleven, eldest son of the Douglas of Lochleven who had held Preston so briefly in 1540; and the Earldom has remained with his descendants ever since.

It is not known when Wreaths Tower was built, nor by whom, and insufficient of the fabric remains to date it with any accuracy. The only certain fact is that the 'Cast[le] of Wraiths' was included in Timothy Pont's survey of Galloway c.1595.[21] There is a tradition that the Regent Morton used to stay here – some say with the young James VI –,[22] and as, like his contemporary Lord Herries, Morton was an active builder, it is possible that the tower was his work.[23] If, on the other hand, the 'manor-places' mentioned in earlier charters were intended to include an existing stronghold at Preston, then Wreaths would most likely have been the work of an earlier Douglas of Dalkeith or Earl of Morton, though it is perhaps significant that the word 'castle' only appears in charters after 1580.

The **TOWER** was evidently oblong in plan, with the long axis lying approximately E-W. All that now remains is a substantial part of the SW corner, including part of the well for the wheel-stair and, on the S side, the adjacent entrance doorway and passage. The door-surround itself is now missing, but M'Kerlie gives a sketch of it when it was still complete.[24] It had a semi-circular head. The S wall survives for a distance of some 26ft 4in at the base, and is 5ft 9in thick, while the W wall extends for just over 11ft before it continues as a dry-stone dyke bounding the adjacent field. The latter wall incorporates some large pieces of fallen masonry. The basement was vaulted. The stair-well in the corner, which still rises more than 40ft, served at least four storeys. It has slit windows on the S side, but none facing W. Adjacent to it on the S side, at second floor level, there is the right jamb of a large window recess, complete with part of the chamfered window surround and sockets for an iron grille, while on the floor above there are one jamb and the lintel of a doorway, both of which also have chamfered arrises.

In 1621, the year after Robert, 9th Lord Maxwell, was created Earl of Nithsdale, he received a new crown charter of many lands, including the lands and barony of Preston, with the castles and manor-places.[25] It is not clear who was living at Wreaths at that time, but a John Maxwell 'of Preston' is recorded in 1617 and 1618,[26] and a James Maxwell 'of Wraithes' in 1655.[27]

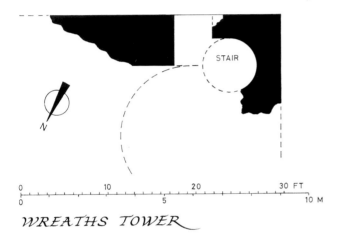

WREATHS TOWER

Fig. 361 Wreaths Tower: plan of surviving south corner of basement.

In 1663 the 2nd Earl of Nithsdale received a further charter of the lands and barony,[28] which in addition to erecting the lands of Preston into one free barony and regality, also erected the town of Preston, with twenty acres of adjacent land, into a free burgh of barony and regality, with the right to a weekly market and four fairs a year, and the right to build a free port on the lands at Glennada.[29] It is believed that by this time Wreaths had been superseded as the principal residence at Preston by a new house at Cavens. The Maxwells still held the superiority early in the 18th century.

In 1667 John Corbet, late bailie in Dumfries, had sasine of the land of Wreaths, and as 'John Corbet of Wreaths' he was still there in 1704.[30] A William Maxwell had sasine of the lands and barony of Preston c.1734.[31] He left two daughters, Mary and Willielma, who had sasine of the forty shilling land of Wreaths in 1742.[32] Then, c.1773, all the lands of Preston, Wreaths and Cavens were purchased by Richard Oswald of Auchencruive, Ayrshire;[33] and his descendants were still in possession at the end of the 19th century.

1   It has been said that the lands were at one time held by the Balliols. It is also possible that, even earlier, they formed part of the lands granted to Holm Cultram Abbey in Cumbria by Uchtred, Lord of Galloway.
2   Bain II, Nos. 1338, 1630.
3   RMS I, Appendix 2, No.1349.
4   Ibid.
5   RMS I, No.628; Scots Peerage VI, 346. Sir James Douglas of Dalkeith was a distant cousin of the Earl of Douglas and Archibald 'the Grim'.
6   Maxwell 1902, I, 236.
7   RMS II, No.472.
8   It has been questioned whether the 'Barony of Dalkeith' ever existed as a peerage in its own right – See Complete Peerage, IV, 39n.
9   Complete Peerage IX, 286.
10 RMS II, No.3160.
11 Fraser 1873, II, 2.
12 Maxwell 1902, I, 243; Complete Peerage IX, 289.
13 RMS III, No.2213.
14 Maxwell 1902, I, 244. Lord Maxwell's eldest son and heir, Robert, was married to the Earl's second daughter and co-heiress, Beatrice.
15 Ibid.; Complete Peerage IX, 289.
16 RMS III, No.2901; IV, No.1535.
17 Ibid, IV, No.1535.
18 APS II, 562.
19 RMS V, Nos.203, 269.
20 Fraser 1873, I, 263.
21 Blaeu, 66, 'The Steuartrie of Kircubright, The most easterlie part of Galloway'.
22 Stat Acct XV, 132; M'Kerlie IV, 141.
23 He built Drochil Castle (Peeblesshire) and Morton's gateway at Edinburgh Castle, and added a second tower-house at Aberdour Castle (Fife).
24 M'Kerlie IV, 153.
25 RMS VIII, No.228.
26 PRS Dumfries I (1617-71), Index, 274.
27 Ibid, 265.
28 RMS XI, No.481. The charter states that the lands had been disponed to the Earl by the Earl of Morton.
29 The township of Preston did not flourish. Early in the second half of the 18th century it had 24 farmers, but by 1793 the number had fallen to only 3 (Stat Acct XV, 127). Now only the market cross survives (see Stell 1986, 52; and Pryde, G.S. 'The Burghs of Dumfriesshire and Galloway: Their Origin and Status', TDGAS, 3rd Ser., XXIX, 115).
30 M'Kerlie IV, 144.
31 Ibid, 146.
32 Ibid, 147.
33 Ibid, 148.

CHAPTER 5

SOME OTHER TOWER SITES AND REMAINS

69.   ANNAN CASTLE
(Annan)   (NY192666)

This tower, which stood on the site of the former church, is crudely illustrated in the English Survey of the West March *c*.1565, where it is described as 'a fortelett or toure of two howse hight, unbattaled' (i.e. with a crenelated parapet, as shown).[1] The report adds that 'thei kepe one hundreith soiouris presentlie in garisone there', while another account states that, in addition to the hundred soldiers, it could also receive 'forty or fifty horses'.[2] The tower had a splayed plinth course, what are presumably intended to portray gun-loops at basement level, and a gabled roof within the parapet walk. It was built as a Crown property by Sir John Maxwell, Master of Maxwell and later 4th Lord Herries, shortly before 1565,[3] and was backed up with defensive ditches, one of which extended to the Solway. In a report to Cecil in 1565, Thomas Randolph wrote: 'In Annan town he [Sir John] has builded a fair tower'.[4] – As the town's only defence when it was attacked by the English in 1547 had been the steeple, which they undermined and then destroyed,[5] there had long been a need for something more substantial in this frontier town.

Following Mary's defeat at Langside in 1568, the Regent Moray made a progress through the West March to enforce obedience to James VI. He marched to Annan with 1000 horse, and there 'received the castle' and installed Edward Urwine (Irving) as its keeper.[6] Two years later, war again broke out with England, and in August the Earl of Sussex invaded the West

March, where he 'threw down the castles of Annand and Hodoun'.[7] Shortly afterwards, in a bitter complaint to Queen Elizabeth about Sussex's 'extreme proceedings', Bishop Ross referred to the destroyed castle of Annan as having been 'most strong'.[8] Lord Maxwell restored the castle in 1579;[9] but it was never again called upon to defend the town, and by 1600 'the hall and the towre' of the castle were in use as the local church.[10] This must have been an informal arrangement, as it was not until 1609 that James VI formally granted to the people of Annan 'The houss callit ye castell of anand, the hall & toure thairof To serue for ane kirk and place of Convenig to the heiring of the word and ministratioun of the sacramentis'.[11] The ditches associated with the former castle could still be seen in 1772.[12]

---

1   Armstrong 1883, .
2   RCAHMS 1920, xxxii.
3   It has sometimes been mistakenly attributed to the 5th Lord Maxwell, as a defence against the Grahams.
4   CSPS II, 155.
5   RCAHMS 1920, lxiv-lxv.
6   Scottish Papers II, Nos.716, 717.
7   Ibid, III, No.436
8   Ibid, No.441.
9   Fraser 1873, I 243.
10   RCAHMS 1920, xlvi.
11   APS IV, 441.
12   Pennant, 84.

Fig. 362 An English survey of 'The towne of Annand', *c*. 1565,
showing the old motte at the top and the tower in the middle of the town below.

70.   ARKLETON TOWER
(4½ m NNE Langholm)   (NY380914)

The lands of Arkleton formed part of the extensive Eskdale and Ewesdale estates acquired by the Lords Maxwell after the fall of the Douglases in 1488. Arkleton was subsequently feued by the Johnstons of Gretna, but resigned by them in 1537 and granted in that year to Ninian Armstrong in Arkleton.[1] Two years later, Lord Maxwell received a new charter of the superiority of the lands.[2] The Lords Maxwell finally forfeited the lands in 1609, when they were granted to Sir Robert Ker.[3]

Meanwhile the Armstrongs remained in possession.[4] In 1585 Archie Armstrong 'in Arkiltoun' was included in a list of those who had intercommuned with the late Earl of Morton.[5] It was presumably the Armstrongs who built the tower, which is first recorded on Aglionby's Platte in 1590.[6] Arkleton was eventually acquired from the Armstrongs by William Elliot of Falnash, who received a crown charter of the £10 lands in 1611.[7] Then, in 1643, Arkleton passed to Walter Scott in Braidhauch.[8] He was a Commissioner of War for Dumfriesshire in 1648.[9] His family were still in possession in 1665.[10]

By 1671, however, the property had evidently passed to another branch of the Elliots, for in that year a new house appears to have been built on the site by 'WALTER ELIOT'. His name appears on a stone now built into the present Arkleton House, while another stone, also built into the house, bears the initials 'WE' and 'KF' and the date '1671'.[11] Both Elliot of Arkleton and his eldest son were Commissioners of Supply for Dumfriesshire in 1696 and 1698, and six years later William Elliot of Arkleton, presumably the son, was again a Commissioner.[12]

The present house at Arkleton is said to stand just S of the site of the tower. Apart from the two inscribed stones from the later house already mentioned, it incorporates in its walls various old mouldings from the tower itself.

1   Armstrong 1883, xxxv.
2   RMS III, No.1199.
3   RMS VII, No.217.
4   RPC III, 42; RPC VII, 727; RPC IX, 713; etc.
5   APS III, 389.
6   Hyslop, 320.
7   RMS VII, No.500.
8   RMS IX, No.1289.
9   APS VI, Part II, 32.
10   RMS XI, No.709.
11   AFS Ewesdale, No.128.
12   APS X, 29, 131; XI, 142.

71.   AUCHENFEDRICK PELE I
(4m S Penpont)   (NX842882)

Little more than the foundations now remain of this tower, presumably the one known as Nether Auchenfedrick, which stood high on the hillside overlooking the Cairn valley to the SW. Built of local rubble with clay mortar, it is oblong on plan, and measures about 30ft 9in from E to W by 21ft 6in from N to S over walls some 5ft thick. The entrance was in the middle of the S wall. At the E end the tower is thought to overlie an earlier, and larger, oblong building which may have been a simple hall-house,[1] while of later date are the remains of a whole complex of buildings relating to a post-mediaeval farm settle-

ment, or fermtoun. The latter comprised an oblong building, running N-S, which abuts the SE corner of the tower; a building with two chambers and an extension and another, separate building, all running NW-SE, immediately to the W of the tower; and two further buildings and an enclosure to the S. There was also a kiln to the NE. Neither of the towers at Auchenfedrick is shown on Pont's survey of Nithsdale c.1595.[2]

In 1505, the 40 shilling lands of Auchenfathrik, together with other lands in the barony of Snaid, were sold by Sir John Hay of Snaid to John Cunningham of Westbarns, to be held of the king in feu.[3] The Hays, however, were in possession of these lands again later, as it was from Lord Hay of Yester that Stephen Laurie of Maxwelton acquired Auchinfedrikkis and other lands in 1626.[4] Twelve years later his son and heir, John Laurie of Maxwelton, had a crown charter of the lands of Over and Nether Auchinfedrickes and others of his father's lands; and this was registered in 1661.[5] Auchenfedrick does not appear as such in the Hearth Tax returns for Sir Robert Laurie's properties in 1690, but it could be one of the group of 13 hearths listed separately within 'the barony of Snaid'.[6] The Lauries finally sold these lands in the 20th century.

1   RCAHMS 1994, 14, Fig.10; NMRS Databank, 'Auchenfedrick'. The building measured about 52ft 9in from E to W by 23ft 6in from N to S, over rubble walls some 4ft thick, though little more can now be seen than the foundation platform excavated out of the hillside.
2   Pont MS. No.35 in National Library of Scotland.
3   RMS II, No.2872.
4   Gladstone, 47.
5   Ibid, 60.
6   Adamson, D. 'The Hearth Tax', TDGAS, 3rd Ser., XLVII, 171.

72.   AUCHENFEDRICK PELE II
(4m S Penpont)   (NX844881)

200 yards ESE of the first tower at Auchenfedrick, and just W of the modern cottage, there was a second, smaller tower, presumably the one known as Over Auchenfedrick. It too was built of local rubble with clay mortar, and measured about 25ft 3in from E to W by 19ft 8in from N to S over walls 4ft 6in thick. Only the collapsed base of the walls remain, with the interior a mound of rubble. A short distance N of the tower, and parallel to it, there is another building of two chambers, each with its own entrance on the S side.[1] A little further N there are the remains of a fine kiln.

1   Further details are given in the NMRS Databank for 'Auchenfedrick'.

73.   AULDGIRTH TOWER
(7m SSE Thornhill)   (NX915868)

Remains of two contiguous walls of this vaulted tower were noted by the RCAHMS at Low Auldgirth in 1913,[1] but the last vestiges were finally demolished in 1927.

The lands of Auldgirth were in the possession of the Fergussons of Auldgirth in 1531, when John Fergusson, grandson and heir of Brisius Fergusson of Auldgirth, received a crown charter of the 3 merk lands;[2] these comprised the 1 merk land of

Auldgirth, the 1 merk land of Blackcraig (Upper Auldgirth) and the 1 merk land of Fyrach. Like the Fergussons of Isle (q.v.), the family were probably cadets of Craigdarroch. Five years later, the Fergussons resigned the lands in favour of John Maxwell, burgess of Dumfries;[3] and in 1563 Thomas Maxwell sold them to John Kirko of Bogrie.[4] Then, in 1583/4, Kirko granted the lands to Roger Kirkpatrick, younger son of John Kirkpatrick of Ellisland, and his son Robert.[5] 'Aldgirth' tower is shown on Pont's map of Nithsdale c.1595.[6] In 1617, George Kirkpatrick 'of Auldgirth' was held responsible for his tenants and servants,[7] and later that year he was one of many gentlemen declared rebels.[8]

There was also a 5 merk land of Auldgirth, which was held by the Dunduffs of that Ilk, perhaps as superiors;[9] but it is not clear whether this was a separate property or encompassed the Fergussons' land. In 1557 William Dunduff of that Ilk granted a little more than half the lands to Herbert Jardine in Elshieshields,[10] and five years later he granted another portion to Roger Kirkpatrick in Clynston.[11] Herbert Jardine was succeeded by his daughter Janet.[12] She married a Charles Jardine, who was subsequently designated 'of Auldgirth'.[13]

The Kirkpatricks, however, continued in possession of part of Auldgirth, Thomas Kirkpatrick of Auldgirth being on record in 1669, when he married Elizabeth Fergusson, and the following year, when he was served heir as grandson of Janet Kirkpatrick in half the 3 merk lands of Auldgirth, comprising the 1 merk land of Auldgirth, the 1 merk land of Blackcraig and the 1 merk land of Netherhaugh.[14] Then, in 1699, Helen Kirkpatrick, daughter and co-heiress of Thomas Kirkpatrick of Auldgirth, and John Paisley, the son of Helen's sister Mary, were served heirs in half the lands of Auldgirth, comprising the aforesaid 3 merk lands;[15] and John Paisley of Auldgirth is on record in the following century.[16]

---

1   RCAHMS 1920, No.60.
2   RSS II, No.996; RMS III, No.1060. In the time of Alexander II, the lands of Auldgirth are said to have belonged to the barons of Briddeburgh (Barburgh) (Ramage, 384).
3   RMS III, No.1652.
4   RMS IV, No.1483.
5   RSS VIII, No.1799.
6   Pont MS. No.35 in National Library of Scotland.
7   RPC XI, 257.
8   Ibid, 228.
9   RSS IV, No.3301. David Dunduff had sasine of the lands of Auldgirth in 1494 (ERS X, 769).
10   RSS V, No.172.
11   Ibid, No.1103.
12   RSS VII, No.1036.
13   PRS Dumfries (1617-71), Index, 176; RMS VI, No.1775.
14   Ramage, 385.
15   Ibid. Mary Kirkpatrick's husband, John Paisley, was minister at Morton.
16   PRS Dumfries IV (1733-60), Index, 132.

---

74.   BARNTALLOCH CASTLE
(2¼ m NNW Langholm)   (NY352877)

Barntalloch Castle, or Staplegorton as it was more commonly known of old, started life as a motte-and-bailey castle, which was presumably built by Geoffrey de Coningsburgh after he was granted the lands by David I in the middle of the 12th century.[1] It stood on a cliff 100ft above the confluence of the Esk with a tributary burn, thus providing a natural defence on two sides. A considerable portion of the original castle has been eroded away, but the site occupies an area about 230ft from N to

S by 420ft from E to W, with the motte at the E end measuring about 80ft by 100ft and separated from the bailey by a ditch some 40ft wide and 9ft deep.

In 1285, the property passed to Sir John Lindsay, Chamberlain of Scotland, and it is thought probable that it was under him that the burgh of Staplegorton was established.[2] The lands were subsequently resigned by his grandson, and c.1319 granted by Robert the Bruce to the good Sir James Douglas.[3] They later passed to his kinsman Sir William Douglas of Lothian, 'the Knight of Liddesdale',[4] and from him to the 1st Earl of Douglas.[5] Archibald 'the Grim', 3rd Earl, had a charter of the lands and barony of Staplegorton in 1389, and issued summons to his vassals from 'his castell in Eskdale'.[6]

After the fall of the Douglases, their Eskdale estates were acquired by the Lords Maxwell,[7] who in 1525 granted the lands of Staplegorton to John Armstrong, better known as 'Johnnie Armstrong of Gilnockie'.[8] Armstrong was hanged by James V in 1529. Later the lands were occupied by the Littles, as tenants of the Lords Maxwell.[9] In 1550, the 5th Lord Maxwell was gifted the nonentries of the ten merk land of Stabilgortoun,[10] and in 1578/9 it is recorded that the 7th Lord Maxwell received the profits of the lands of 'Stephen Gortoun'.[11] It was also decreed in the latter year that a court was to be held at Staplegorton every month by the Captain of Langholm, and that once every quarter it was to be attended by the Warden of the West March himself.[12]

The later tower may have been built by Armstrong or the Littles, or it may have been the work of the Lords Maxwell as their local administrative centre and, perhaps, occasional residence. In 1912, the RCAHMS recorded the foundations of the tower about 20ft wide with walls 3ft 9in thick in the SW corner of the motte. They also recorded traces of stonework at the N end of the bailey and 'traces of a parapet mound'.[13] Little is now visible except overgrown mounds of rubble among the trees. The tower of 'Stablegorden' is shown on Aglionby's Platte in 1590, and also by Pont some five years later.

In 1610 the lands of Staplegorton, having been forfeited by the Lords Maxwell, were granted to Lord Cranstoun for his part in helping pacify the Borders,[14] but in 1621 they were resigned and granted to the 1st Earl of Nithsdale.[15] Later, they were purchased by the Earl of Buccleuch, whose daughter and son-in-law, the Duke and Duchess of Buccleuch and Monmouth, received a new charter of the lands in 1664.[16]

---

1   Reid, R.C. 'Staplegorton', TDGAS, 3rd Ser., XXXI, 168.
2   Pryde, G.S. 'The Burghs of Dumfriesshire and Galloway: Their Origin and Status', TDGAS, 3rd Ser., XXIX, 90.
3   RMS I, App.2, No. 523; Hyslop, 215.
4   Ibid, No.790.
5   Scots Peerage III, 149.
6   Hyslop, 217-8.
7   Ibid, 224.
8   Armstrong 1883, xvii.
9   Armstrong 1960, 116.
10   RSS IV, No.622.
11   RPC III, 80.
12   Ibid.
13   RCAHMS 1920, No.431. See also RCAHMS 1997, 200.
14   RMS VII, Nos.214, 1284.
15   RMS VIII, No.228.
16   RMS XI, No.673.

75.   BOGRIE TOWER
(4¹/₂ m W Dunscore)   (NX812850)

The Kirkhaughs – later contracted to Kirko and Kirk – first appear in Glenesslin in the 15th century, but it was not until the middle of the next century that they were first associated with Sundaywell (q.v.) and Bogrie. John Kirkhauch of Bogrie is on record in 1563.[1] It was probably he who built the tower, which, although now totally demolished, is recorded as having been larger and stronger than the one at Sundaywell.[2]

The tower, whose outline is shown on the earliest, large-scale O.S. map,[3] was still standing in 1850,[4] but ten years later it had become so unsafe that the upper floors were demolished and the masonry used in outbuildings, leaving a farm worker's house of two storeys.[5] This later fell into ruin, and was finally removed c.1974, when the later house was modernised. It was connected to the house by a doorway, now blocked, adjacent to the pend. Amongst the masonry incorporated into the surrounding outbuildings is a 16th century doorway with a QER surround. There is also a carved triangular pediment from a dormer window, which is now built into the wall of the 17th century house, and which may have come from either the tower or the house as originally built.[6]

The present house, which is a long, composite structure, now much altered, stood to the NE of the tower. It comprises a 17th century house at the N end, another building to the S, and a connecting pend in between. The house was probably built in 1660 by John Kirk, as his initials with those of his wife, Jean Maxwell, and the date are carved on a panel over its W door. The pend has been altered, and is now incorporated into the house, but it still retains its round-arched doorways with their bold QER surrounds at each end, and over the E one is an armorial panel bearing the quarterly arms of Gordon of Lochinvar and, perhaps, Maxwell, with the date 1770 and initials IBW.[7]

James Kirk of Bogrie was a Commissioner of Supply for Dumfriesshire from 1696 to 1704.[8] On his death c.1722, Bogrie passed to his granddaughter Mary, who married James Gordon of Kirklebride;[9] and on his death in 1765, it passed to his kinsman, Major Patrick Gordon of Troquain.[10]

1   RMS IV, No.1483.
2   RCAHMS 1920, No.138.
3   O.S. 25-inch, Dumfries, Sheet XXXIX.16. c.1857. It was oblong in plan, and stood immediately south of the later house, facing SE.
4   Imperial Gazetteer, 483.
5   RCAHMS 1920, No.138.
6   The style is more reminiscent of the late 16th century, but the later house at Sundaywell also has dormer windows with pediments.
7   The initials have not been identified.
8   APS X, 29, 131; XI, 142.
9   Hamilton-Grierson, Sir P. 'The Kirkos of Glenesland, Bogrie, Chapel and Sundaywell', TDGAS, 3rd Ser., VIII, 229.
10 Ibid, 230.

76.   BROCKLOCH PELE
(4m W Dunscore)   (NX802844)

Brockloch is situated on a steep, south-facing hillside, high above the Glenesslin burn, from where the tower had a commanding view down Glenesslin to Sundaywell (q.v.) and up the valley as far as the watershed. Bogrie Tower also stood on the same hillside, a little further down the glen, but out of sight.

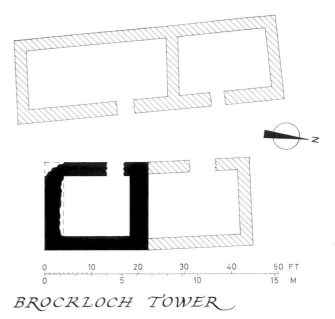

BROCKLOCH TOWER

Fig. 363 Brockloch Pele: site plan.

Only the lowest courses of the walls now survive, standing to a height of little more than 3ft. Built of local rubble, bonded with clay mortar, the tower measures some 22ft from N to S by 19ft from E to W over walls which are 4ft thick on the N and S sides and 3ft thick on the other two sides. Such a discrepancy in the thickness of the walls usually indicates a vaulted basement, but there is no evidence of this, and one would not expect it in such a primitive building using clay mortar. The entrance was on the W side.

Fig. 364 Brockloch Pele: remains seen from the SE.

Abutting the N gable of the tower, and of the same width, is a secondary building some 22ft long, with walls 2ft 6in thick and an entrance on the W side. A short distance to the W of these buildings, and parallel to them, is another building, some 57ft long and 18ft 3in wide, that is subdivided into two chambers, each with its own entrance on the E side. There are also traces of another building to the N of this complex and one to the SW, while further W there are the remains of a kiln-barn.[1]

A thumnail sketch of the tower is given in Pont's survey of Nithsdale c.1595,[2] but nothing is known of its history. It may have been in the possession of a family of M'Millans, but the

Fig. 365 Brockloch Pele: aerial view from the NW. The tower's ruins are just left of centre in the picture. (Crown copyright: RCAHMS.)

Fig. 366 Coshogle: doorway from castle re-used for cottage.

matter is confused by another Brochloch in the next valley, some 17m to the WNW, which was also apparently occupied by M'Millans.[3] Sir James Douglas of Drumlanrig gave surety for John M'Millan in Brokloch and his son Donald in 1597.[4] What is certain is that by 1711 Brockloch was in the possession of Elizabeth Kirko, heiress of Sundaywell and widow of James MacLellan of Sundaywell, for in that year she disponed the 2 merkland of Sundaywell, the merkland of Brockloch and other lands to her only son and heir, Samuel.[5]

---

1   RCAHMS 1994, 16-17, Figs.11, 14; NMRS Databank, 'Brockloch'.
2   Pont MS. No.35 in National Library of Scotland.
3   See M'Kerlie 1877, III, 301-3.
4   RPC V, 685.
5   Dumfries Sheriff Court Books (SC 15/58/1), 22 March 1717.

---

77.   COSHOGLE CASTLE
(4¹/₂ m N Carronbridge)   (NS861050)

The lands of Coshogle first come on record early in the 14th century, when they were possessed by Eustace de Lorrain.[1] Following Eustace's forfeiture for treason some time before 1340,[2] David II granted Coshogle to Hugh de Blair of that Ilk;[3] and this was confirmed in favour of his son and heir, James, in 1357.[4] The lands, which were in the barony of Drumlanrig, were 'to be held in chief of the Lord of those lands', namely William, Earl of Douglas. This grant was again confirmed by Robert II

Fig. 367 Cowhill in 1789. It was demolished later that year.

c.1372-4.[5] From James de Blair, the lands passed to his younger son, Sir John de Blair of Adamton, and they remained in Sir John's family until 1454/5, when his grandson, John Blare of Adamton, had to go to law to prove ownership, which was contested by James Lorane, presumably one of Eustace's descendants.[6]

From the Blairs, Coshogle evidently passed to the Wallaces of Crago, for in 1474 Annabel Stewart, wife of Matthew Wallace (of Crago), renounced the lands in favour of Archibald Douglas, a younger son of Sir William Douglas, 4th of Drumlanrig, who had previously leased the lands from her husband.[7] It was presumably Archibald who built the first stronghold. Archibald Douglas 'of Cowsowgill' sat on an assize in 1481/2.[8] In an entail of the Drumlanrig estates drawn up by Sir James Douglas of Drumlanrig in 1559, Archibald's grandson, Robert Douglas of Coshogle, was to succeed in the event that Sir James's grandson died without male issue.[9]

A doorway, a large armorial panel and a gargoyle are all that now survive, although in 1826 it is on record that portions of the old walls still stood to a height of 6ft, and were fully 6ft thick.[10] The doorway is built into a cottage beside the farm access road. It has a segmental-arched head, which bears the same embellished QER moulding as the jambs, while on either side there are the moulded bosses that originally supported a substantial hood moulding. The armorial panel and the gargoyle are built into the gables of another cottage, situated on the hill-

Fig. 368 Cowhill Tower: folly partly made from old ruins.

side a quarter of a mile NE of the farm. The former has two shields, the one on the left bearing the arms of Mar quartered with Douglas, and the other bearing the arms of Johnston, with the initials 'R. D. – N. J.' above, for Robert Douglas of Coschogill and his wife, Nicolas Johnston, and the date 1576 below.[11] 'Coshogill' is shown on Pont's survey *c*.1595.[12]

Sir William Douglas of Coshogle, who was served heir in 1623,[13] was often in conflict with his neighbours. In 1624 he had the lands of Coshogle apprised for debt,[14] and ten years later he was warded in Edinburgh Castle for not removing from Coshogle, whereupon he appealed to the Privy Council to be released to enable him to sell off his lands.[15] However, despite his financial hardship, he managed to build a new house for himself near Thornhill, where he also resided for some of the time.[16]

1   Reid, R. C. 'An Early Coschogill Writ', *TDGAS*, 3rd Ser., XXX, 137-9.
2   Ibid.
3   RMS I, App.2, No.1038.
4   Ibid, No.1236; Reid, op. cit., 137.
5   RMS I, No.479.
6   Reid, op. cit., 132-4.
7   Ibid, 137; Ramage, 77.
8   Buccleuch MSS, 48 (No.96).
9   Ibid, 24 (No.38).
10 Ibid, 84.
11 RCAHMS 1920, Nos.164, 165. Adams quotes Nicholas's Testament in full (Adams, App.B, No.21)
12 Pont MS. No.35 in National Library of Scotland.
13 Ramage, 79.
14 Adams 1921, 54.
15 Ibid, 55.
16 Ramage, 79.

78.   COWHILL TOWER
(5m NNW Dumfries)   (NX951825)

The lands of Cowhill originally belonged to the abbey of Holywood, by whom they were granted to Sir John Maxwell, nephew of the 3rd Lord Maxwell, early in the 16th century.[1] It was presumably he who built the original tower. John Maxwell of Cowhill was included in an entail of the Maxwell estates in 1540.[2] His son, Sir Robert Maxwell of Cowhill, pledged 91 'assured' Scots to the service of England in 1547,[3] and after peace was restored he was, in 1552, appointed one of the Queen's Commissioners in Nithsdale for overseeing the enrolment of footsoldiers for service in France.[4] When the English again invaded Dumfriesshire in 1570, the Earl of Sussex 'threw down…the castles of Tynhill and Cohill'.[5] Four years later, Sir Robert was one of those appointed to arbitrate in any disputes between Lord Maxwell and Johnston of that Ilk.[6] According to a surviving date-stone, Cowhill was rebuilt in 1579, but it was burnt again six years later during a raid by the Johnstons.[7]

Sir Robert died sometime before 1589, when his younger brother Archibald was served heir to all his lands except Dinwiddie, which was settled on Sir Robert's youngest son, John.[8] 'Couhill' appears on Pont's map of Nithsdale *c*.1595.[9] Archibald was succeeded by his son Archibald, who was retoured heir to his uncle, Sir Robert, in his lands, except Dinwiddie, in 1608 and 1609.[10] He died in 1622, when he was succeeded by his elder son, John. Later that year, John was appointed to assist the Earl of Nithsdale in administering justice in the Borders.[11] He died *c*.1665 without male issue, whereupon Cowhill passed to his daughter Janet and her husband, Dougall Maxwell, youngest son of Sir Patrick Maxwell of Newark, Renfrewshire.[12] Dougall was a Commissioner of Supply for Dumfriesshire in 1678 and 1685.[13]

Cowhill remained with the Maxwells and their descendants in the female line for another century, until 1783, when it was sold to George Johnston of Conheath, who had made his fortune as a merchant in Liverpool and purhased Conheath a few years earlier.[14]

The old tower is said to have stood some 200 yards S of the present mansion, on the knoll now occupied by the 'folly', while the house illustrated by Grose appears to have stood on the present site. He records that George Johnston started to pull the old house down in 1789 'in order to erect an elegant mansion on its site'.[15]

The building illustrated by Grose, which dates from the 17th century and has little affinity with a tower-house, was apparently built to replace the old tower, though part of it may have been incorporated in the structure. Its builder is not known. It has a central block, from which a wing projects at one end and a stair-tower at the other. According to Grose, it was originally intended that the stair-tower should be a central feature in a symmetrical arrangement, but it was never completed.[16] The main block comprises two storeys and a garret with large dormer windows. At the wall-head there is a course of embellished, chequer corbelling, which continues around the stair-tower, while at first floor level there is a string course with a cable moulding, which also continues around the stair-tower and is repeated around the dormer windows above. The stair-tower has boldly canted corners up to the level of the main wall-head, where it is corbelled-out square to support an additional storey with a low roof and probably a parapet-walk. The wing at the other end was two storeys high. It had crow-stepped gables, but no other details are visible. The Hearth Tax returns for 1690 list nine fireplaces.[17]

The house that George Johnston started in 1789 was a symmetrical building, comprising a plain, central block of two storeys with a single-storied wing with a Venetian window at each end.[18] George was succeeded first by his son, Vice-Admiral Charles Johnston (d.1856), a distinguished naval officer who sailed the world,[19] and then by his grandson William Johnston, JP, the Admiral's youngest son by his second marriage. William, who had served in the Indian Civil Service, purchased Cowhill from his late father's trustees,[20] and then, c.1867-71, he employed the architect Walter F. Lyon to remodel the central block and E wing of the house in the baronial style then in fashion.[21]

Soon after the turn of the 20th century, William's youngest daughter, Ida, married Major Henry Keswick, JP.[22] To celebrate the occasion, Henry's father, William Keswick, purchased Cowhill from William Johnston as a wedding present for the young couple. Major Keswick had joined the Hong Kong trading company of Jardine Matheson c.1894, before serving with the King's Own Scottish Borderers in the South African War.[23] He subsequently held many high offices in Hong Kong. He was also member of parliament for Epsom from 1912 to 1918, and served on Dumfriesshire County Council. In 1913-14, he increased the height of the house's W wing by one storey and added the massive tower block at the E end.[24] He died in 1928, and was succeeded by his eldest son, David.

David Keswick, CMG, JP, who became Managing Director of Samuel Montagu & Co., the bankers, made further additions and alterations to the house, principally following two serious fires, one in 1942, which destroyed the central block,[25] and another in 1972, which burned out the drawing room.[26] There

are some interesting paintings by him at Cowhill recording the building works. He died in 1976, when the property passed to his daughter, Sophia, Mrs Weatherall.

The 'folly' on the knoll to the S is a random collection of old, and not so old, masonry assembled as a typical 'romantic ruin' of the 19th century. It includes two doorways with round arched heads, one of which is 4ft wide and 7ft 4in high, and two other doorways; a corbelled-out turret base with an elaborate Renaissance moulding; a lintel bearing the date 1579 in raised lettering; two heraldic panels bearing the Maxwell saltire, one with the initials RM and BM, reputedly for Robert Maxwell of Cowhill and his wife Barbara Maxwell;[27] various pieces of QER and later mouldings; and even a mediaeval, hogbacked gravestone incised with a sword.

---

1   Macdonald, J. 'Notes on the Titles of Cowhill Tower', TDGAS, 3rd Ser., II, 225-33; Fraser 1873, I, 594.
2   RMS III, No.2164.
3   Armstrong 1883, lxxv.
4   RPC I, 132.
5   Scottish Papers III, No.436.
6   RPC II, 422.
7   Fraser 1873, I, 262.
8   Ibid, 594.
9   Pont MS. No.35 in National Library of Scotland.
10 Fraser 1873, I, 594.
11 RPC XII, 694-5.
12 Fraser 1873, I, 594.
13 APS VIII, 225, 465.
14 It was sold by Dugald Campbell of Sherrington, Co. Ayr (Burke L.G. 1886, 1000, 'Johnston of Cowhill').
15 Grose I, 148.
16 Barjarg was extended into a similar symmetrical arrangement in the 18th century.
17 Adamson, D. 'The Hearth Tax', TDGAS, 3rd Ser., XLVII, 167.
18 Gifford, 192.
19 Burke op. cit., 1000.
20 Ibid.
21 Gifford, 192.
22 Who Was Who, 1916-28, 583.
23 Ibid.
24 Gifford, 192. The architects were Peddie & Forbes Smith. There was also some work carried out by James Barbour, the Dumfries architect, in 1904, but the details are not to hand (Wolffe, A. 'James Barbour', TDGAS, 3rd Ser., LXXI, 158).
25 It was rebuilt in 1948 to a design by Antony Lloyd (Gifford, 193).
26 Gifford, 193. It was rebuilt in 1973.
27 Ibid. This could refer to Robert Maxwell, younger brother of the 3rd Lord Maxwell, who was ancestor of the Maxwells of Cowhill and who is said to have married a Maxwell of Aitkenhead (See Fraser 1873, I, 594).

---

79.   DRUMLANRIG CASTLE
(3½ m NW Thornhill)   (NX852992)

In 1357 Sir William Douglas, later 1st Earl of Douglas, received a new charter from David II of all his lands, including the lands of 'Drumlangrig', which he had recently acquired from the Earl of Mar.[1] These subsequently passed to his son, the 2nd Earl (d.1488), who gave Drumlanrig to his natural son, Sir William Douglas, c.1384-88.[2] It was this Sir William (d.1427), 1st of Drumlanrig, who built the original stronghold, presumably some time before 1400. He received a charter of confirmation of his lands from James I in 1412.[3]

Sir William was succeeded by his only son, William, who in 1429 entered into an agreement with his kinsman, William Douglas of Leswalt, concerning their respective castles. Under this agreement, Leswalt was to give up the 'Castell of

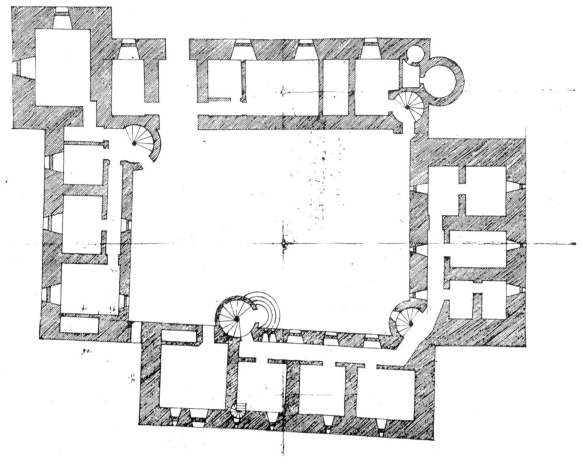

Fig. 369 Drumlanrig Castle: 'The Ground Platt of the Place of Droumlangrig as it Presendlie standis unreformed. 1615.' N is at the top.

Drumlanryge' and all the lands of the barony, which had been granted to him for ten years, but still have free access to them whenever he wished, while Drumlanrig dropped all claims he had against Leswalt and had free access to Leswalt's castle of Lochnaw.[4] This is the first mention of the castle as such. On William's death in 1444, Drumlanrig passed to his son William, 3rd of Drumlanrig. William attended parliament in 1467 and 1481,[5] but was killed three years later fighting for the Crown during the battle of Lochmaben.[6] William was succeeded first by his son James, who died in 1498, and then by his grandson, Sir William Douglas, 5th of Drumlanrig, who received a new crown charter of the lands and barony of Drumlanrig, 'with the castle', in 1492, during his father's lifetime.[7] He fell at Flodden in 1513.

Throughout this period, the castle was presumably increasing in size and importance, but it was during the time of Sir James Douglas, 6th of Drumlanrig, who was laird for 65 years, that it was either rebuilt, or extended, on such a grand scale that he could claim to have built 'the haill hous and pallice [palace]' himself.[8] Indeed, by the time of his death in 1578, the castle almost certainly comprised the various buildings shown on the earliest surviving plans of Drumlanrig; for although these are dated 1608 and 1615, showing the castle as it then was, it is evident that there had been no changes of any significance during the intervening years.[9] The plans show four ranges surrounding a rectangular courtyard, with an additional oblong block or tower projecting at the NW angle.[10] The basements were vaulted, and there were five wheel-stairs serving the upper floors, three of which were comparatively large and projected into the court-

yard. In one of his wills in 1578, Sir James refers to 'my charter hows within the bowell' of Drumlanrig, and the 'irne yet' and 'keyis of the vtter duris (outer doors)' which protected it.[11] In addition to his works at Drumlanrig, Sir James rebuilt the tower at Mouswald (q.v.), and built new towers at Ross, Kirkhope and Locharben.[12] Drumlanrig also had an enclosed game park, which is recorded by Pont.[13]

Sir James received a charter of confirmation of the lands and barony of Drumlanrig in 1540/1.[14] He attended Parliament in 1542, 1546, and 1560 and the Convention of Estates in 1561 and 1572.[15] In 1552 he was one of the Scottish Commissioners for the division of the Debateable Land,[16] and the following year was appointed Warden of the West Marches, a post he held again in 1555-6 and 1568.[17] He was also, in 1574, appointed one of the commissioners for holding wapinschaws in Dumfriesshire.[18] His only lawful son, Sir William Douglas of Hawick, having predeceased him in 1572, Sir James was succeeded by his grandson, also Sir James, who became the 7th laird.[19]

Sir James was granted a charter of novodamus in 1591/2, uniting all his estates in the one barony of Drumlanrig,[20] and in 1609 he had a further charter of the barony and regality of Drumlanrig. According to the plans already mentioned and others still retained at Drumlanrig, he was proposing further, major additions and alterations to the castle complex, but it was not until the 1st Earl's time that these changes were given more serious thought. Sir James attended parliament in 1609.[21] The following year, he was appointed a Justice of the Peace for Dumfriesshire,[22] and in 1612 he was made Judge-Delegate and Guardian of the Peace for the county.[23] He died in 1615, when he was succeeded by his eldest son, Sir William Douglas, later 1st Earl of Queensberry.

Sir William had the privilege of entertaining James VI in the castle on his last night in Scotland, in 1617.[24] The following year he had 'reformed' plans prepared to show the extensive alterations that he was proposing to make to the castle.[25] These involved the complete rebuilding of the S range, square to the other buildings, and the addition of large corner towers with new wheel-stairs at the SE and SW corners. The plans show all the rooms in detail. However, it is not known to what extent Sir William's proposals were carried out before the major reconstruction of 1679 began.

Sir William was appointed Sheriff of Dumfries in 1620,[26] a Commissioner for the Middle Shires in 1622,[27] and a Justice of the Peace in 1625.[28] Three years later he was raised to the peerage as Lord Douglas of Hawick and Tibbers and Viscount Drumlanrig,[29] and in 1633 he was raised to the dignity of Earl of Queensberry.[30] He died in 1640, and was succeeded by his eldest son, James.

James, 2nd Earl of Queensberry, was made a Commissioner for the Apprehension of Papists in 1642,[31] and a Colonel in the militia a year later.[32] In 1644 he was appointed a Commissioner of War.[33] The following year he set out to join Montrose, but he was apprehended by a force of Covenanters and taken to Carlisle, where he was held by Cromwell's forces until a large fine was paid.[34] During this time, Drumlanrig was 'plundered by a party of Sir John Brown's regiment'.[35] The castle was attacked again in 1650 and the gates burned,[36] and two years later 'Collonell Alderedge, Governour of Air, [took from the castle] tuo hundreth musquets besids piks worth tuo thousand punds Sex hundreth weight of pouder valued to four hundreth merks Three feild peices of brasse and one of yron valued to tuo thousand merks'.[37] After the Restoration in 1660, Queensberry again returned to public life, attending parliament, and serving as a Commissioner of Supply in 1661 and a Justice of the Peace from 1663.[38] He died in 1671.

William Douglas, his eldest son, who succeded as 3rd Earl of Queensberry, held many high offices of state. Like his father, he was appointed a Commissioner of Supply in 1661 and a Justice of the Peace in 1663.[39] He was also appointed Sheriff and Coroner for Dumfriesshire[40] and a Privy Councillor in 1667,[41] and a Commissioner for the Suppression of Crime on the Borders in 1672.[42] He subsequently served as Lord Justice-General from 1680 to 1682, and as an Extraordinary Lord of Session from 1681 to 1686.[43] In recognition of his services he was, in 1682, raised to the dignity of Marquess of Queensberry and Earl of Drumlanrig and Sanquhar, and was given the honour of augmenting his coat of arms with the royal tressure.[44] In the same year he was made Lord High Treasurer and Governor of Edinburgh Castle.[45] Then, in 1684, Charles II created him Duke of Queensberry and Marquess of Dumfriessshire.[46] The following year, James II appointed him Lord High Commissioner to his first parliament;[47] but his success made him the victim of intense jealousy by his rivals, and soon after he was deprived of his principal offices.[48] After the Revolution, William and Mary recalled him in 1693 as an Extraordinary Lord of Session.[49] He died two years later.

It was the 1st Duke who demolished most of the old castle and had the present, classical edifice built on the site during the years 1679-c.1690.[50] It utilised most of the old foundations and substantial portions of the existing masonry,[51] although the facades were entirely new. It also retained three iron yetts from the old castle. One of these, used to guard the main entrance, is unusually large, measuring 6ft 2in wide by 9ft 7in high; it comprises 14 horizontal and 9 vertical bars. The Duke only spent one night in the castle: being unable to make the servants hear when he felt ill, he returned to Sanquhar, where he lived for the rest of his days.[52] The great expense of the work is said to have ruined him.

James, 2nd Duke of Queensberry, also held many high offices of state. He was elected Provost of Dumfries in 1683,[53] and the following year was admitted to the Privy Council[54] and commissioned a Lieutenant-Colonel in Viscount Dundee's regiment of horse.[55] Four years later he joined the Prince of Orange, who appointed him Colonel of the 6th Horse Guards.[56] After the Prince's accession as William III in 1689, the Duke was made a Gentleman of the Bedchamber,[57] and in 1692 he was appointed a Commissioner of the Treasury, and the following year Lord High Treasurer.[58] He subsequently served as Lord Privy Seal from 1696 to 1702 and as an Extraordinary Lord of Session from 1696 until his death in 1711.[59] He is, however, best remembered for carrying through the Treaty of Union in 1707,[60] for which he was rewarded with a generous pension and the Dukedom of Dover.[61] In the new parliament, he served first as a representative peer and then as Secretary of State for Scotland.[62]

The 2nd Duke was succeeded by his third son, Charles, who, in 1706, in recognition of the services of his father and grandfather, had been made Earl of Solway.[63] He was appointed Lord Lieutenant of the counties of Dumfries and Kirkcudbright in 1721, and the following year was made Vice-Admiral of Scotland.[64] In 1726 he was appointed a Privy Councillor.[65] Although he took no part in either of the Jacobite rebellions, Prince Charles, on his retreat from Derby in 1745, billeted himself and some 2000 of his men in the castle, causing considerable damage and incurring much expense. The chamberlain indignantly reported that 'they laid straw in all the rooms for the private men to lye on, except your Grace's bedroom (where the Prince lay) and a few rooms more . . . most of them in the vestibule near the low dining room and the foot of the principal stair, which they left in a sad pickle, as indeed they did the whole house. Under the gallery they kept several of their horses, which they made shift to get up the front stair'.[66] The Duke was appointed Keeper of the Great Seal of Scotland in 1761,[67] and Lord Justice-General in 1763.[68] On his death in 1778, he was succeeded by his cousin William, 3rd Earl of March.

The 4th Duke, often known as 'Old Q', was made a Lord of the Bedchamber to George III in 1760, and a Knight of the Thistle in 1763.[69] He was also a Representative Peer for Scotland from 1761 to 1786,[70] and Vice-Admiral of Scotland from 1767 to 1776.[71] In 1794 he was appointed Lord Lieutenant for Dumfriesshire.[72] On his death in 1810, the Dukedom and associated titles, together with his Dumfriesshire estates, passed to his cousin, Henry Scott, 3rd Duke of Buccleuch, with whose descendants they have remained ever since;[73] the Marquessate of Queensberry and associated titles devolved on his cousin, Sir Charles Douglas, 5th Baronet of Kelhead;[74] and the Earldom of March passed to Francis Charteris, later 6th Earl of Wemyss.[75]

1   Buccleuch MSS, 2, 6 (No.1); RMS I, App.1, No.123.
2   Scots Peerage VII, 112.
3   Burke Peerage 1959, 1850, 'Queensberry'.
4   Buccleuch MSS, 10 (No.5).
5   APS II, 90, 137.
6   Scots Peerage VII, 116. Also known as the battle of the Kirtle, as the running battle from Lochmaben finished there.
7   RMS II, No.2099.
8   Buccleuch MSS, 5.

9   In Pont's survey of Nithsdale c.1595, he shows 'Drumlainrig Castell' as an important stronghold, but gives no specific details (Pont MS. No.35 in National Library of Scotland). See Fig. 1.

10 NMRS, DFD/58/1 'The secound Platt of the Place of Droumlangrig as it Presendlie standis unreformed 1608' and DFD/58/3 'The Ground Platt of the Place of Droumlangrig as it Presendlie standis unreformed 1615'.

11 Buccleuch MSS, 28.

12 Ibid, 5.

13 Pont MS., op. cit.

14 RMS III, No.2287.

15 APS II, 425, 468, 525; III, 77; Scots Peerage VII, 124.

16 RPC I, 120-5.

17 Rae, 241.

18 APS III, 91.

19 Whilst still an infant in 1546/7, Sir William Douglas of Hawick had been granted the lands and baronies of Drumlanrig, Tibbers and Hawick by his father, to be held in fee (RMS IV, Nos.90, 91).

20 RMS V, No.2034.

21 APS IV, 413.

22 RPC IX, 77.

23 Ibid, 419.

24 Scots Peerage VII, 134.

25 NMRS, DFD/58/5, 8 & 9.

26 RPC, 2nd Ser., I, 659.

27 Ibid, 1st Ser., XII, 650.

28 Ibid, 2nd Ser., I, 659.

29 Buccleuch MSS, 84 (No.1).

30 Ibid, (No.2).

31 Complete Peerage X, 692.

32 APS VI, Part I, 91.

33 Ibid, 200.

34 Scots Peerage VII, 135.

35 APS VII, 285.

36 Ibid, 374.

37 Ibid, 285.

38 Ibid, 91, 505.

39 Ibid.

40 Ibid, 645.

41 Complete Peerage X, 693.

42 Ibid.

43 Scots Peerage VII, 138.

44 Buccleuch MSS, 85 (Nos.3, 4).

45 Scots Peerage VII, 138; Buccleuch MSS, 173 (No.10).

46 Buccleuch MSS, 86 (No.5).

47 Ibid, 90 (No.9).

48 Scots Peerage VII, 139.

49 Ibid.

50 The names of both Sir William Bruce and Robert Mylne have been mentioned in connection with the design, but the final arrangement is thought to have been the work of James Smith, who, on the recommendation of the Duke, subsequently became Overseer of the Royal Works in Scotland. The only certain name is William Lukup, who was Master of Works until his death in 1685.

51 The vastly different thicknesses of the walls at the lower levels, and the change in masonry styles, gives some indication of where earlier work has been incorporated. A new survey of the castle by the RCAHMS in 1999 has shown that much of the masonry of the 14th century tower-house has been retained to form the centre section of the E range. Although the floor levels have been altered, the early work still survives to a height of four storeys, with walls that vary in thickness from about 7ft at the ends to 7ft 8in on the sides. The tower itself would appear to have measured about 56ft 6in from N to S by 32ft from E to W, not much smaller than Threave or Torthorwald.

52 Grose I, 151.

53 Johnstone 1889, 200.

54 Scots Peerage VII, 140.

55 Ibid.

56 Complete Peerage X, 695.

57 Ibid.

58 Scots Peerage VII, 141.

59 Ibid.

60 APS XI, passim.

61 Scots Peerage VII, 141. In 1706 he had resigned his Dukedom of Queensberry and other titles in favour of a re-grant of these dignities to himself and his heirs under a new entail.

62 Ibid, 142.

63 Ibid, 143.

64 Complete Peerage X, 698.

65 Ibid.

66 Forman, S. 'Drumlanrig', Scottish Field, June 1947.

67 Complete Peerage X, 698; Scots Peerage VII, 144.

68 Scots Peerage VII, 144.

69 Complete Peerage X, 701.

70 Ibid.

71 Ibid.

72 Ibid, 702.

73 Complete Peerage II, 369; X, 704.

74 Ibid, X, 704.

75 Ibid, X, 704; XII/2, 474-5.

80.   GLENCAIRN CASTLE
(2³/₄ m ESE Moniaive)   (NX822897)

Some of the old castle of Glencairn is said to be incorporated in the present house of Maxwelton, but even the latter building has undergone so many changes since it was rebuilt in 1641, including reconstruction after a disastrous fire c.1823, that few original features have survived.

Glencairn was an important site from a very early date, there being two mottes in the immediate vicinity.[1] One of them, Maxwelton Motte, must have got its name from a lesser member of the Maxwell family who settled here; but by early in the 14th century the lands and barony of Glencairn were in the possession of the Earls of Dunbar.[2] They were forfeited by Earl Patrick in 1335/6,[3] and later came into the possession of Sir John de Danyelston, on whose resignation in 1370/1, his son Robert, later Sir Robert Danielson of that Ilk and Glencairn, received a new charter of the barony from David II.[4] Sir Robert was succeeded by his two daughters, the elder of whom, Margaret (d. ante 1409), married Sir William Cunningham of Kilmaurs, who thus acquired Glencairn.[5] But although the Cunninghams held Glencairn for more than two centuries and either built or greatly enlarged the castle, as well as naming their subsequent earldom after it, Glencairn never became their principal residence. That position was held by Kilmaurs, in Ayrshire, while Finlayston, in Renfrewshire, was also an important residence.

Sir William's grandson, Sir Alexander Cunningham, who succeeded his father, Sir Robert, c.1449, was granted a new crown charter of the lands and barony of Glencairn in 1452.[6] Eleven years later, he was created Lord Kilmaurs.[7] Sir Alexander fought for James III against the rebel lords in 1488, for which service he was made Earl of Glencairn;[8] but he fell alongside his sovereign at Sauchieburn later that year.[9]

Sir Alexander was succeeded by his eldest son, Robert, who became 2nd Lord Kilmaurs. The earldom, however, was annulled by parliament, James IV objecting to all the later grants

Fig. 370 Maxwelton House (Glencairn): view from SE.

Fig. 371 Maxwelton from the south.

made by his father.[10] Robert attended parliament in 1484, during his father's lifetime, and as Lord Kilmaurs in 1489.[11] He died shortly afterwards. His only son, Cuthbert, who succeeded, was restored to the rank of Earl in 1503,[12] and as such attended parliament two years later.[13] In 1498 Cuthbert resigned all his estates in favour of his only son, William, whilst reserving the liferent to himself and his wife, and this was confirmed by crown charter;[14] and in 1511 William was granted another crown charter relating to the earldom and barony of Glencairn.[15] The latter charter, which still reserved the liferent to the Earl and his wife, listed all the lands within the barony, for which 'the town and mansion-house in the lands of Darnangill, near the church of Glencairn, were to be the principal messuage'. Cuthbert died c.1540/1.

Sir William Cunningham, who succeeded as 3rd Earl of Glencairn, had been appointed Lord High Treasurer in 1526, but later that year was deprived of office when his father joined the rebel Earl of Lennox.[16] He was later admitted to the Privy Council.[17] Sir William was taken prisoner at the Rout of Solway Moss in 1542, and subsequently was active in support of Henry VIII's plans for the union of England and Scotland.[17] For this act of treason he was granted a remission in 1544.[18] He attended parliament in 1546,[19] but died two years later.

Alexander Cunningham, who succeeded his father as 4th Earl of Glencairn, was a prominent supporter of the Reformation. In 1561 he was appointed one of Queen Mary's Great Council,[20] but he subsequently changed his allegiance and joined the supporters of James VI. He attended James's coronation in 1567,[21] and was one of the lords chosen to act provisionally as regent.[22] The following year Alexander fought for James at Langside, after which the Regent Moray appointed him Joint-Lieutenant in the West.[23] He died in 1574, when he was succeeded by his eldest son, William.

William, 5th Earl of Glencairn, purchased the £20 lands of the earldom of Glencairn, together with the tower and fortalice, from his father in 1549.[24] He was admitted to the Privy Council in 1569,[25] while his father was still alive, but seems to have taken little part in public affairs. He was succeeded c.1580 by his eldest son James, the 6th Earl. James, who was elected to the Privy Council in 1580,[26] attended the Convention of Estates in 1593 and 1598,[27] and parliament in 1606, 1608 and 1609.[28] He was appointed a Commissioner for the holding of wapinschaws in 1588[29] and the following year a Commissioner for keeping the peace in the Marches[30] and also a Commissioner for upholding the true religion.[31] In 1591, having been put to the horn, he was ordered to deliver up his houses, including Glencairn, on

pain of treason.[32] In 1604 he was one of the Commissioners for the projected Union with England,[33] and in 1606 he was appointed a Lord of the Articles.[34]

Little is known about the old castle of Glencairn, but c.1595 Pont shows a thumbnail sketch of a substantial tower-house with four storeys below the corbelled-out parapet walk, two turrets or cap-houses, wings on either side of the main tower, and a barmkin with a gateway.[35] It is quite unlike the symbol he normally used for a simple tower-house. Pont also shows an enclosed park. Doubts have been raised about the location of the castle,[36] because Pont shows both 'Glen-kairn Cast.' and 'Maxweltoun' adjacent to it, but a charter of 1616 clearly refers to 'the 5 merk lands of Maxweltoun with the castle of the same now called the castle of Glencarne'.[37] In the absence of the 6th Earl in 1600, the castle was surprised by John Douglas of Craigenvey, and 'stuffit with men, wictuell and armour as an hous of weir' against the King.[38]

By the end of the 16th century the family was in serious financial difficulties, and as a result the 6th Earl had to sell most of his Glencairn estate as well as the superiority. The latter was sold to Lord Crichton of Sanquhar, who received a crown charter of the lands and barony of Glencairn, with the castle and manor-place, in 1614.[39] Five years later it was incorporated into the new lordship and barony of Sanquhar.[40] Later the superiority was acquired by the Earl of Queensberry.[41]

In 1611, the estate of Glencairn, subsequently known as Maxwelton, was sold to Stephen Laurie, a prosperous Dumfries merchant.[42] He was the grandfather of Sir Robert Laurie, who was created a baronet in 1685, and Maxwelton remained in the possession of his descendants until finally sold in 1966. During that time the castle and house underwent many changes.

A new house was built in 1641, the date of which is recorded on a panel bearing the impaled arms of John Laurie, Stephen's eldest son, and his wife Agnes Grierson,[43] and most of the northern half of the present house dates from that time. The house itself occupied the NW corner of a courtyard plan,[44] with offices on the E side, an entrance pend with an arched gateway and two-leaved yett[45] on the N side, and an enclosing wall. The S wall of the courtyard was removed long ago. Both the house and offices evidently had vaulted basement chambers, but only those of the offices have survived. John Laurie was a Commissioner to the Convention of Estates in 1643,[46] and a Commissioner of War for Dumfriesshire in 1643, 1644, 1645 and 1648.[47] He was subsequently a strong supporter of the Covenanters, for which he was fined.[48] He died in 1672.

Later the house was extended to the S, while the buildings on the N and E sides were raised in height to two storeys and an attic. It is not certain when these additions were made, but a second, undated, armorial panel, which bears the arms of Sir Robert Laurie, 1st Baronet, and his wife, Jean Riddell, suggests that he had a hand in at least some of them. Sir Robert was appointed a Justice of the Peace for Dumfriesshire in 1663,[49] and served regularly as a Commissioner of Supply for Dumfriesshire from 1667 until his death in 1698,[50] as well as for the Stewartry of Kirkcudbright in 1685.[51] He was also a member of the commission appointed to act against the Covenanters in 1684,[52] and a Commissioner for Ordering the Militia in 1689.[53] It was his youngest daughter, Anna, who is the famous 'Annie Laurie' immortalized in Scottish song. Sir Robert's second son, Walter, who succeeded as the 3rd Baronet in 1702, was also a Commissioner of Supply for the county in 1702 and 1704.[54]

Sir Robert Laurie, 4th Baronet, who suceeded in 1731, was Member of Parliament for Dumfries from 1738 to 1741.[55]

He was succeeded by his eldest son, General Sir Robert Laurie, who had a distinguished military career, serving as Colonel of the 8th Dragoons, a Lieutenant-General in the army, and as Knight-Marshal of Scotland from 1785 to 1804.[56] He was also Member of Parliament for Dumfriesshire from 1774 to 1804.[57] His only son, Admiral Sir Robert Laurie, KCB, who succeeded in 1804, had an equally distinguished career in the navy.[58] It was during his tenure, in 1823, that Maxwelton suffered from a major fire, the reconstruction afterwards being commemorated on a dated lintel.[59]

On the death of the Admiral without issue in 1848, the baronetcy became extinct, while Maxwelton passed to his nephew, John Fector, who assumed the name and arms of Laurie. He died without issue in 1868, and was succeeded by his sister Charlotte's eldest son, Sir John Bayley, Baronet, who, after getting possession of the property in 1887,[60] assumed the name and arms of Laurie. It was his descendants who continued in possession until 1966.

After the Stenhouses bought the house in 1968, a major programme of restoration was undertaken under the direction of the architects Michael Laird and Partners. This revealed the great kitchen fireplace in the older part of the W range, with its fine arch and masons' marks, and many other features that had long remained hidden.[61] The restoration work won a Saltire Award. The Stenhouses subsequently set up the Maxwelton House Trust to secure the house's future.

1   Ingleston and Maxwelton (RCAHMS 1920, Nos.238, 241). The mound at Birkshaw is of dubious origin (RCAHMS 1920, No.254).
2   Bain III, 319.
3   Ibid.
4   RMS I, No.362 and App.2, No.1649. David II also granted Hugh Danielston a discharge of the castle wards in the barony of Glencairn (RMS I, App.2, No.1064). Both Sir John and Sir Robert de Danielston were successively Keepers of Dumbarton Castle (ERS III).
5   Scots Peerage IV, 230.
6   Laing Charters, No.134.
7   Scots Peerage IV, 233.
8   Ibid.
9   Ibid, 234.
10   Ibid. Notwithstanding the annulment, *The Complete Peerage* accords Robert the dignity of 2nd Earl of Glencairn for the four months before the annulment took effect (Complete Peerage V, 669), while *The Scots Peerage* does not (Scots Peerage IV, 234-5).
11   APS II, 166, 216.
12   Scots Peerage IV, 235.
13   APS II, 262.
14   RMS II, No.2416.
15   Ibid, No.3594.
16   Scots Peerage IV, 237.
17   Ibid; RSS III, *passim*.
18   APS II, 450.
19   Ibid, 463.
20   RPC I, 157.
21   Ibid, 537.
22   Ibid, 540-1.
23   Ibid, 624.
24   RMS IV, No.372.
25   RPC II, 17.
26   Ibid, III, 327.
27   Ibid, V, 94, 462, 499; APS IV, 39, 158.
28   APS IV, 280, 403, 413.
29   RPC IV, 301. He is mistakenly referred to as Alexander, Earl of Glencairn.
30   Ibid, 426.
31   Ibid, 465.
32   Ibid, 694.
33   Complete Peerage V, 672.
34   APS IV, 280.
35   Pont MS. No.35 in National Library of Scotland.
36   200 yards to the NW lies the farm of 'Shancastle', which means 'Old Castle'.
37   RMS VII, No.1546. The site of the castle is said to have been known at one time as 'Darnayngill' (Gladstone, 30).
38   Gladstone, J. 'Glencairn Castle and Maxwelton', *TDGAS*, XXVIII, 110.
39   RMS VII, No.1096.
40   Ibid, No.2061.
41   RMS XI, No.546.
42   The estate is said to have been purchased from Sir Robert Gordon of Lochinvar, whose family had held a wadset over it for some twenty years.
43   This panel is not in its original position.
44   Tranter is of the opinion that the S end of the W range pre-dates the 1641 house, and may well be a remnant of the old castle (Tranter 1935, 50).
45   The present yett is a modern replacement.
46   APS VI, Part I, 3.
47   Ibid, 53, 200, 559; Part II, 32.
48   Burke Peerage 1959, 1320, 'Laurie of Bedford Square'.
49   APS VII, 505.
50   Ibid, 544; VIII, 225, 465; IX, 70, 139; X, 29, 131.
51   Ibid, VIII, 469.
52   Fraser 1894, I, cclvii.
53   APS IX, 28.
54   Ibid, XI, 22, 142.
55   Burke Peerage, *op. cit.*
56   Ibid; Forman, S. 'Maxwelton', Scottish Field, May 1947.
57   Ibid.
58   Burke Peerage, *op. cit.*
59   Forman, *op. cit.*
60   On the death of Mrs Laurie, who, in her widowhood, had carried out numerous additions and alterations to the house.
61   Plans of the house before restoration were recorded by Miss Joan Gladstone (Gladstone, J, *op. cit.*, Figs. 12, 13).

81.   HODDOM OLD CASTLE
(2m WSW Ecclefechan)   (NY162729)

Hoddom first came to prominence in AD 573, when St. Kentigern, recalled from Wales by King Rhydderch, established his episcopal see here before returning to Glasgow.[1] It was later to become the site of an early monastery,[2] a bishopric,[3] and two churches.

After the Bruces acquired the Lordship of Annandale c.1124, they granted Hoddom to another Anglo-Norman family, who took their name 'de Hodelm' from the lands. The caput of the district is said to have been the site now occupied by Hallguards, a natural eminence on the left bank of the river Annan, and it was evidently here that the later castle also stood. Robert de Hodelm and his son Udard were witnesses to charters of the Bruces and others c.1200.[4] Udard also held lands in Cumbria.[5] In 1296 Adam de Hodolm swore fealty to Edward I,[6] but early the following century the family disappeared from the scene.

From the Scottish Crown, the Lordship of Annandale, which included the lands of Hoddom, passed first to Thomas Randolph, Earl of Moray, and then to his son-in-law the Earl of March, before being acquired by the 4th Earl of Douglas in 1409.[7] Shortly afterwards, Douglas granted the lands of Hoddom to Simon de Carruthers,[8] and in 1452 Hoddom was included with the other Carruthers lands in the new barony of Carruthers.[9] The lands of Hoddom subsequently came into the possession of Herbert, later 1st Lord Herries of Terregles, who was in possession in 1486.[10] His son had a crown charter of the lands in 1499/1500,[11] and in 1510 the '£20 lands of Hoddom' became part of the barony of Herries.[12]

After the death of the 3rd Lord Herries in 1543, all the Herries estates passed to his three daughters and co-heiresses, the eldest of whom, Agnes, Baroness Herries, married Sir John Maxwell, Master of Maxwell. Eventually, in 1548/49, Lady Herries received a crown charter of her share of her father's patrimony, and three months later she granted 'all and haill my twenty pound land of old extent of Hoddom' to Richard Irving, 'called of old Duke Ritchie', for his good and faithful services.[13] But the old castle, which is thought to have stood on these lands, was not mentioned; perhaps it had fallen into decay, or it may have been slighted by the English during their recent incursions.

Later, in 1561, Sir John Maxwell purchased the shares of the other two Herries heiresses.[14] Then, in 1563, he acquired part of the lands of Trailtrow on the opposite river bank, and it was there, two years later, that he built the new castle of Hoddom (q.v.).

It is not known who built the last castle on the Hallguards site, but the history of the site's owners suggests that it was a secondary residence. It may have been built by the Herries soon after they acquired the site, but if so it had an unusually short life. It was finally demolished in 1565, when the masonry was used to build the new castle, hence the latter's popular name of 'Hoddomstanes'.[15] The only relic of the castle is a double-checked rybat (for wooden door and yett) that was recovered on the site in 1983.[16]

1   Maxwell-Irving 1988, 185.
2   Lowe, C. E. 'New Light on the Anglian 'Minster' at Hoddom', TDGAS, 3rd Ser., LXVI, 11-35.
3   Scott, J. G. 'Bishop John of Glasgow and the Status of Hoddom', TDGAS, 3rd Ser., LXVI, 37-45.
4   Bain I, Nos.449, 606; Buccleuch MSS, 39 (No.67); Edgar, 219.
5   Bain I, Nos.154, 546. Udard was eventually succeeded in his Cumbrian properies by his granddaughter Cristiana (daughter and heiress of his daughter Cristiana), who married, firstly, Thomas de Lascelles (Bain I, No.2097); secondly, Adam de Gessemuth of Dalton (Carruthers 1934, 88); and thirdly, Robert de Bruce, Lord of Annandale, 'The Competitor' for the Crown, who also laid claim to the Cumbrian properties (Bain II, No.645).
6   Bain II, 203, 555.
7   The English also laid claim to Annandale in the 14th century. Details are given by Robert Gladstone in The Early Annandale Charters and their Strange Resting Place (TDGAS, 3rd Ser., VI, 137-145).
8   Carruthers 1934, 52.
9   Ibid, 53.
10 RMS II, No.1654.
11 Ibid, No.2526.
12 Ibid, No.3446.
13 Irving 1907, 120-1.
14 Scots Peerage IV, 410; RMS IV, Nos.405, 1393.
15 RMS IV, No.2311; VII, No.295; etc. Hallguards has sometimes been confused with Knockhill as the site of Duke Ritchie's tower, but Aglionby's Platte of 1590 clearly shows 'Knockhill – y[e] dukes howse' (Hyslop, 320). 'Duke of Hoddoms' is also shown on Pont's map c.1595, together with its 16th century deer park. Knockhill Tower was finally demolished in 1772 (Irving 1907, 127).
16 Maxwell-Irving 1988, 210.

82.   HOLMAINS TOWER
(2½ m NW Dalton)   (NY083766)

The Carruthers of Holmains, the most important cadet branch of the Carruthers family, were founded by Roger de Carutheris,[1] who was granted a charter of the £4 lands of Little Daltoun, the 8 merk lands of Holmendes and the 40 shilling lands of Fortenakerebank (Fourteenacrebank), together with the patronage of the church of Little Dalton, by the Earl of March in 1375.[2] This grant was subsequently confirmed by the Earl of Douglas in 1425,[3] and again by the Duke of Albany in 1476, when John Carruthers, 3rd of Holmains, resigned Holmains in favour of his eldest son, John, whilst reserving the liferent for himself.[4] Both Douglas and Albany were Lords of Annandale.

It was at Holmains that the family built their stronghold, on a rocky outcrop 750ft above the Annan valley, with a com-

manding view across the valley to the E. It had clearly been considered a site of great strategic importance from the earliest times, as close by stands the ancient British fort of Range Castle.[5] Nothing is known of the extent of the stronghold, unless the dotted outline of the tower shown on the earliest 25-inch Ordnance Survey map is significant; it shows an oblong tower measuring approximately 46ft by 33ft.[6] There was evidently a pit-prison, as one James Wichtman was confined 'within the pitt' c.1610.[7] John Musgrave of Bewcastle was also held prisoner here in 1544,[8] and no doubt others shared a similar fate during the course of the various lairds' duties as law-enforcement officers during the 16th and 17th centuries. 'How-mains Cast.' is shown as an important stronghold on Pont's map c.1595, which also shows a surrounding deer park.[9]

John Carruthers, 5th of Holmains, who was served heir to his grandfather in 1523, was laird for 57 years, during which time the family wielded considerable power and influence in Annandale. When John attended a wapinschaw held by Lord Maxwell in 1541, he was accompanied by 100 men,[10] and six years later, when the English gained the upper hand in Dumfriesshire, he pledged an even larger force to their service.[11] Meanwhile, in 1542, he had been granted a new crown charter of the £20 lands of Holmains, Little Dalton, Kirkhill and Butterwhat, and many other lands, all of which were incorporated into the free barony of 'Holmendis'.[12] Then in 1553, after peace had been concluded, John was appointed Stewart-Depute of Annandale,[13] and in 1567 he was one of the Border lairds summoned by the Privy Council to advise on peace and good order in the Borders.[14] The following year, in consequence of the family's support for Queen Mary and her subsequent defeat at Langside, the Regent Moray wrought vengeance by burning 'the laird of Howmanes' place' during his progress through the West March.[15]

George Carruthers, who succeeded in 1580 as 6th laird, was Captain and Keeper of Threave Castle under Lord Maxwell.[16] Five years later, he was included in a general amnesty for those previously charged with treasonable crimes.[17] He died in 1592, and was succeeded by his eldest son, John, who, in 1579, in the lifetime of his grandfather, had been granted a crown charter of the lands and barony of Holmains.[18] He had subsequently allowed his father to live there; but when his father died, and he attempted to get possession, his stepmother, Margaret Irving, and her sons 'violently intruded themselves' into, and took possession of, the houses of Holmains and Hartwood. The new laird complained to the Privy Council, who, in 1597, ordered the houses to be delivered and Margaret to remove herself to Kirkwood, the family's dower-house.[19] Five years later, John was one of the Border lairds appointed to advise the Warden on law and order.[20] He was made Stewart-Depute of Annandale in 1608,[21] and in 1610 he was one of the first Justices of the Peace appointed for the county.[22]

After the death of John Carruthers, 7th of Holmains, in 1616, his eldest son, John, perhaps mindful of his father's experience, was accused of taking an armed force to the place of Holmains, breaking into the chamber of his mother, and ejecting her. She complained to the Privy Council, who found the charge 'not proven'. They did, however, refer a second charge, of collecting and disposing of 'the maillis, fermes, and dewteis quhairupoun sho sould leive', to the Lords of Council and Session.[23] But no sooner did John set out for Edinburgh to present his case, than two of his brothers, who sided with their mother, and their accomplices raided one of his properties where two of his young children were staying, and assaulted both them and the tenants.[24] In 1625, John Murray, 1st Earl of Annandale, was granted a crown charter incorporating the superiority of all his lands and many others into the new earldom, lordship and barony of Annandale.[25] This included the 8 merk lands of 'Hoilmaynes', with the tower and manor-place, which the Carruthers held directly of the Crown. John accordingly challenged the inclusion of Holmains in the earl's charter, and won his case.[26] He was eventually served heir to his father and grandfather in 1635.[27] By that time he was heavily in debt, and had to obtain a substantial loan from John Lockhart, his eldest son's future brother-in-law.[28] He died in 1659, and was succeeded by his grandson, John. An inventory of the house's contents made by him the following year includes very little, and nothing of value: 'four old bedds, ane meikle chist, ane ambrie, two gunnes, ane uthir old little chist, ane brewing leid, ane maskinfatt and ane garner'.[29]

After the death of the 8th laird's eldest son, James, in 1657, the Lockharts obtained the ward and non-entry of the estate and assigned it to Robert Fergusson of Craigdarroch; and it was not until he resigned his interest in 1673, that the 9th laird could obtain a charter of his estates under the Great Seal.[30] John was appointed a Justice of the Peace in 1663;[31] a Captain of Foot in the militia in 1668, and again in 1689;[32] and a Commissioner of Supply for Dumfriesshire in 1678, 1685, 1689 and 1690.[33] He took the Test in 1683.[34] Three years later he was granted a Warrant authorizing him to hold three, free fairs a year and a weekly market at Meikle Dalton.[35] It was during the time of this laird that the old tower was finally abandonned in favour of the family's other principal residence, Kirkwood, 2½ miles ESE of Holmains.[36]

George Carruthers, who succeeded his father in 1694 as 10th laird of Holmains, inherited an estate still heavily in debt. Aware how much that debt had been aggravated over successive generations by minorities and their attendant debts to the Crown, he obtained a new crown charter of the barony of Holmains in 1699, with special provision to protect it against any future exactions, and this was confirmed by parliament in 1701.[37] At the same time the Crown made Meikle Dalton a free burgh of barony. Subsequent events, however, were to overtake George's precautions, when his grandson went bankrupt. In 1696, George was appointed a Commissioner of Supply for Dumfriesshire, and this appointment was renewed in 1704.[38] He died in 1727, and was succeeded, first by his eldest son, John, and then, seven years later, by John's only son, also John.

John Carruthers, 12th of Holmains, was already in debt, when he was ruined by the collapse of the Douglas Heron Bank in Ayr in 1772, with unlimited liabilities for the investors.[39] It cost him all his money and the estate. All that was left when he died in 1809 were the family muniments.[40]

By 1789, the tower that had been 'a considerable stronghold before the Union of the Crowns' had 'fallen into a total decay',[41] and in 1845 it was described as being 'totally in ruins'.[42] All that now remains are overgrown masses of fallen, rubble masonry.

1   He was reputedly a son of John de Carruthers (? of Mouswald).
2   Holmains MSS, 710, No.2.
3   Ibid, 711, No.6.
4   Ibid, No.7.
5   RCAHMS 1920, No.98.
6   O.S. 25-inch, Dumfries, Sheet L.15, 1856. The collapsed walls are now just an indeterminate heap, which cannot be measured without excavation.
7   Carruthers 1934, 97.
8   Ibid, 86-7.
9   Blaeu, 57, 'THE STEWARTRIE OF ANNANDAIL'.
10 Buccleuch MSS, 66 (No,135).
11 One account puts the number at 126 (Scottish Papers, I, No.396; Armstrong 1883, lxxvi), while another gives a figure of 162 (Armstrong 1883, lxxiv).
12 RMS III, No.2633; Holmains MSS, 712, No.10.
13 Carruthers 1934, 87.
14 RPC I, 570.
15 Scottish Papers II, No.716.
16 Border Papers I, No.334.
17 APS III, 388.
18 Carruthers 1934, 93.
19 RPC V, 379.
20 Ibid, VI, 828.
21 Carruthers 1934, 95-6.
22 RPC IX, 77.
23 Ibid, XI, 180.
24 Carruthers 1934, 98.
25 RMS VIII, No.826.
26 Carruthers 1934, 100.
27 Ibid, 100.
28 Ibid, 101.
29 Ibid, 105.
30 Ibid, 107; APS X, 316-18.
31 APS VII, 505.
32 RPC, 3rd Ser., II, 542; APS IX, 26.
33 APS VIII, 225, 465; IX, 70, 139.
34 RPC, 3rd Ser., VIII, 639.
35 APS VIII, 652.
36 Carruthers 1934, 109.
37 Ibid, 111; APS X, 316-18.
38 APS X, 29; XI, 142.
39 Carruthers 1934, 114.
40 Ibid, 114-5.
41 Stat Acct XIV, 105.
42 NSA IV, 373.

83.   KIRKPATRICK TOWER
(¼ m SSW Kirkpatrick Fleming)   (NY276704)

This tower of the Irvings stood somewhere within the grounds of Kirkpatrick House, but all that remains is an armorial panel now built into one of the barns. It bears a shield with two indecipherable sets of initials above the three holly leaves of 'Irving of Bonshaw' and with the date 1548 across the middle.

Kirkpatrick first comes on record in 1189, when it is recorded that Robert de Brus had given the church of 'Kirkepatric' to the See of Glasgow.[1] Then in 1374/5, the accounts of the chamberlain of Lochmaben Castle show that rent was being charged for 'half of the vill of Kyrkpatrick' at the rate of 40s per annum.[2] Shortly afterwards, however, in 1376, the chamberlain had to report that no rent had been received from 'half of the vills of Gretenhowe, Calfhirst and Kyrkpatryk and its mill, as the tenants were completely ruined by the Scots and English'.[3] Being almost on the Border itself, Kirkpatrick was among the first places to be burned and pillaged whenever there was a raid or dispute between the two countries, and so it continued to suffer for the next two centuries. In 1514 Kirkpatrick was one of many townships in Lower Annandale burnt or destroyed by Lord Dacre.[4]

In 1542/3 John Johnston of that Ilk received a new crown charter of the superiority of some of his lands, including the £20 lands of Kirkpatrick (viz. the £10 lands of Dunskellie with the mill and the £10 lands of Calvertsholm).[5] These were subsequently feued to Edward Irving of Kirkpatrick, who is reputed to have been a younger son of one of the Irvings of Bonshaw,[6] and it was presumably he who built the tower. If the date '1548' is correct, it would have been one of the earliest stone towers in Kirtleside.[7]

Edward appears to have been the acknowledged leader of the Irvings of Gretna, a junior, but independent-minded, branch of the Irvings of Bonshaw. In 1569 it was reported to the Privy Council that 'Edward Irwing of Kirkpatrick and Watt Irwing of Gratnohill comperand in presens of my Lord Regentis Grace, [when] the said Edward enterit plege for himself the said Watt and thair haill branche of the Irwingis of Gratno'.[8] But despite their pledge to the Regent, Lord Scrope reported two years later that he intended to burn the houses of Edward Irwen of Kirkpatrick and others, 'as they do not mind to reform themselves'.[9] Edward was mentioned again in 1583, when Thomas Musgrave drew up a list of the clans and families living on the Border,[10] and in 1586 Johnston of that Ilk referred to 'Edwart [Irving] of Kirkpatrik's house' as standing 'on my heritage'.[11] The tower is shown on Aglionby's Platte in 1590.

By 1597, Edward had been succeeded by his son Francis, who in that year was accused with his brother Watt of stealing oxen and sheep;[12] and there are various references to other Irvings of Kirkpatrick in the following century.[13]

The tower was eventually superseded in 1674 by a more modern house, the date of which, together with the arms of Irving of Bonshaw, are recorded on a lintel[14] preserved in another outbuilding, which was also believed to incorporate a part of the house itself.[15] The house was probably built by Samuel Irving (d.1686) of Kirkpatrick, who was served heir in 1649, and who was the last male heir.[16] He married Agnes Charteris. He was succeeded by his daughter Rosina, who married Thomas Williamson of Betinbush. This house was itself superseded in 1852 by the present house.[17]

1 Bain I, No.197.
2 Ibid, IV, No.223.
3 Ibid, 231.
4 State Papers, Henry VIII, I, No.2913.
5 RMS III, No.2874.
6 Irving 1907, 28. This part of the Bonshaw genealogy is, however, somewhat suspect.
7 It has been suggested that the date has been re-cut and that the '4' is suspect.
8 RPC II, 44. It has been suggested that there were two successive generations bearing the same name: Edward Irving of Kirtkpatrick, Walter of Gretnahill may have been the brother of the younger Edward.
9 State Papers, Foreign, IX, 478-9.
10 Border Papers I, 123.
11 Scottish Papers IX, 95.
12 RPC V, 380.
13 e.g. RPC XII, 360; 2nd Ser., I, 575; 3rd Ser., IV, 609.
14 RCAHMS 1920, No.375. Strangely, the lintel bears the initials 'TI', for Samuel's eldest brother, Thomas, who died in 1635 (Irving, J.B. 'List of Armorial Bearings noted in Dumfriesshire and Adjacent Counties', *TDGAS*, 3rd Ser., II, 40), suggesting that he started the new house.
15 Reid, R.C. and Cormack, W.F. 'Two Mediaeval Crosses at Kirkpatrick-Fleming', *TDGAS*, 3rd Ser., XXXVIII, 116.
16 Ibid. See also Gordon Slade, H., 'Kirkpatrick', in Mercer 1997, 142-7.
17 See Gordon Slade, *op. cit.*, for details.

84.   LOCHINVAR CASTLE
(3¼m NE Dalry)   (NX658855)

The ruins of this castle and the island on which it stood finally disappeared when the level of the loch was raised to its present level c.1970. The island started life as a crannog. It measured about 60ft by 50ft and, according to old accounts, was connected to the shore by two causeways, or 'bridges', each about 150-200ft long.[1] Little remained of the castle (Fig. 374), and nothing can be said with any certainty about either its date or

who built it. It was evidently oblong in plan, measuring about 48ft by 35ft over walls 5ft thick, and there was a circular tower, some 10ft in diameter, at its N end.[2] The masonry was local rubble. No features survived, and the remaining walls were little more than 6ft tall at their highest point.[3]

The lands of Lochinvar, perhaps originally 'Lochan-na-barr' meaning 'Lochan of the hill',[4] formed part of the extensive district known as 'The Glenkens' within the ancient Lordship of Galloway. From Alan, the last Lord of Galloway, the lands passed first to his eldest daughter, Helen, Countess of Winchester, and then to her daughter Elizabeth, who married Alexander Comyn, 6th Earl of Buchan.[5] On Alexander's death in 1290, his estates passed to his eldest son, John, 7th Earl. Not long afterwards the 7th Earl granted half of the lands of Glenkens, including the lands of Lochinvar, to John Maxwell, younger of Caerlaverock, who in turn, in 1297, granted them in feu to Sir Adam Gordon of Stitchill.[6]

During the War of Independence, Robert the Bruce gained possession of Galloway from the Baliols, while Sir Hugo de Ross obtained the lands of Glenkens.[7] Bruce then gave Sir Hugo the lands of Kinfauns in Perthshire in exchange for Glenkens.[8] There is, however, a certain amount of confusion over the possession of The Glenkens at this period due to the extent of the lands, their superiority and their feudal subdivisions. Thus one finds Bruce granting to Robert Boyd the lands of Glenkens that had belonged to Gilbert MacMalene,[9] while later, in 1368, one finds David II granting to George Dunbar the lands of Glenken and Mochrum that had been resigned by Patrick, Earl of March;[10] but it is not clear how Earl Patrick obtained possession, unless it was through his mother, who is reputed to have been a daughter of the 6th Earl of Buchan, and thus a sister of the 7th Earl. It is said to have been Bruce who first made The Glenkens into a royal hunting forest.[11] However, the earliest reference to it as such was not until the reign of David II, when John Crawford of Cumnock was granted the 'keeping of the new forest of Glenkenne'.[12] Then, in 1358, Robert, Earl of Strathearn (later Robert II), granted the keeping of the forest to William Gordon of Stitchill.[13] The Gordons of Stitchill would thus seem to have been confirmed in their rights to at least part of the lands of Glenkens, though further confusion arises in 1366, when David II granted to Walter Leslie and his wife, Euphemia Ross, a relative of the king, 'all the New Forest' with all rights pertaining thereto.[14] The lands and forest of Glenkens were subsequently included in the Lordship of Galloway given to Archibald, later 3rd Earl of Douglas, by David II in 1369; and it was Archibald's son, the 4th Earl of Douglas, who, shortly before 1410, granted a new charter of 'the lands, possessions, and lordships of the new Forest of Glenken' to Sir Alexander Gordon of Stitchill for a payment of 55 gold nobles.[15] Sir Alexander was succeeded by his elder son, Roger Gordon of Stitchill, who was succeeded c.1442 by his son, William Gordon of Stitchill and Lochinvar. William is said to have been the first of his family to reside in Galloway.[16] He was certainly the first to take the designation 'of Lochinvar', which thereafter became the family's principal messuage, and in 1450 he was infeft in the lands.[17] But whether he built the castle, or even resided there, is uncertain, as it was Kenmure that early became the family's principal residence. What is certain, though, is that the castle of Lochinvar must have existed at that time, or it could not have become the principal messuage.

The lands of Lochinvar were later merged with those of Gordonstoun, a little further west, the superiority of which was confirmed in favour of Lord Maxwell in 1507/8.[18] The charter,

which stated that the lands extended to 'half of Glenken', li-
cenced Lord Maxwell to infeft Sir John Gordon of Lochinvar in
the lands. A further charter in 1509/10 specifically mentions
'the lake and messuage of Lochinvire';[19] and there was a further
charter in favour of the Maxwells in 1540.[20] After the forfeiture
of the 9th Lord Maxwell in 1609, most of his lands, including
'the lake, manor-place and messuage of Lochinvar', were granted
to Lord Roxburgh;[21] but in 1621 they were restored to the 1st
Earl of Nithsdale,[22] and the superiority then remained with the
Maxwells until the forfeiture of the 5th Earl in 1716.

Meanwhile, the lands continued to be held in feu by the
Gordons of Lochinvar, the history of the family being very much
the history of Kenmure (q.v.). Sir Robert Gordon of Lochinvar
received a new Crown charter of the lands of Gordonstoun, 'with
the lake, manor-place and messuage of Lochinvar', in 1611,[23]
and in 1633 his eldest son, Sir John Gordon of Lochinvar, was
raised to the peerage as Viscount Kenmure and Lord Lochinvar.[24]
Early in the following century, the 6th Viscount supported the
Jacobites in the rebellion of 1715, and a year later was found
guilty of treason and sentenced to death, with the forfeiture of
all his honours and estates.[25] Six years later, his son succeeded
in recovering the lands; but the family's fortunes never recovered, and in 1787 John Gordon of Kenmure had no choice but to
sell the barony of Lochinvar to the trustees of Richard Oswald
of Auchencruive.[26] John did eventually recover the peerages in
1824 to become the 7th Viscount Kenmure, but he died without
issue. He was succeeded by his nephew, Adam Gordon, 8th
Viscount Kenmure and Lord Lochinvar, on whose death the titles became dormant; and so they have remained ever since.[27]

That the name 'Lochinvar' is so well known today is
largely due to Sir Walter Scott, for few are not familiar with the
opening lines of Lady Heron's famous song, 'Lochinvar', in his
epic poem *Marmion:*-

'O, young Lochinvar is come out of the west,
    Through all the wide Border his steed was the best'.[28]

---

1   Stat Acct XIII, 56; NSA IV, 370; M'Kerlie III, 407.
2   RCAHMS 1914, No.156.
3   Visit by writer in 1954.
4   Blaeu, 66, 'The Steuartrie of Kircubright, The most easterlie part of Gallo-
     way'; Johnston 1903, 204.
5   Complete Peerage II, 374-5.
6   Fraser 1873, I, 92; Scots Peerage V, 99.
7   Brooke, D 'The Glenkens 1275-1456', *TDGAS*, 3rd Ser., LIX, 45. — It is
     worthy of note that Eymar de Valence wrote and sealed an order to Sir James
     de Alilee 'at Glenken' in 1307.
8   RMS I, App 1, No.108.
9   Ibid, App 2, No.316.
10   Ibid, No.291; Bain IV, xxii.
11   Brooke, *op. cit.*, 45.
12   RMS I, App 2, No.910.
13   Scots Peerage V, 99.
14   RMS I, No.258.
15   Fraser 1885, III, 405-6.
16   Scots Peerage V, 100.
17   Ibid, 100-1.
18   RMS II, No.3199.
19   Ibid, No.3420. At this time the neighbouring barony of Earlstoun was also
     referred to as 'Erlistoun now called Glenken' (RMS II, No.3635).
20   RMS III, No.2164.
21   RMS VII, No.217.
22   RMS VIII, No.228.
23   RMS VII, No.502.
24   Scots Peerage V, 119.
25   Ibid, 128-9.
26   Ibid, 134.
27   Ibid, 135.
28   Canto V, Part XII, 'Lochinvar'.

---

85.   MAXWELL'S CASTLE
(Dumfries)   (NX971763)

The original castle of the Lords Maxwell in Dumfries
appears to have been built by the 4th Lord Maxwell *c.*1540, on
lands acquired by the family in 1481.[1] Five years later, he described it as his 'new house',[2] and in the English survey of the
West March *c.*1564-5 it was reported that, 'The Lorde Maxwell
haith a fare howse, battaled within this towne, but not tentable
nor strong aganis any battry or gownes'.[3] It was one of the castles subsequently 'demolished' by the Earl of Sussex when he
invaded the West March in 1570.[4]

The castle was rebuilt two years later, this time on a larger
scale.[5] Apart from the main building of four storeys, it had a
courtyard and stables. Robert Edgar, who would have known
the castle well before its final demolition, described it as a 'tenement . . [with] four large vaults with small wickers of light, and
the whole windows of this Castle were barred strongly with iron,
being of 3 large stories with Turnpike and Bartisan covered with
lead'.[6] Pieces of masonry recovered from the site exhibit various forms of moulding, including 3-stage corbels for a parapet
and the lowest course of corbelling for a round or corner turret,
of which there is said to have been one at each corner.[7] The only
other comparable, urban building in the SW would have been
the slighly later Maclellan's Castle in Kirkcudbright (q.v.).

In 1584/5, the 7th Lord Maxwell, now Earl of Morton,
was ordered to deliver up 'the house in Drumfreis',[8] and in 1588
he had to flee the house at a moment's notice when James VI
arrived in person to take possession.[9] In 1608, the council were
ordered to hand over the castle to Sir William Cranstoun, who
was to be captain of the garrison.[10] The garrison was withdrawn
in 1621.

During the Civil War, the castle was dismantled; but in
1659 estimates were obtained for its repair,[11] and between 1660
and 1687 it was frequently occupied by a garrison engaged upon
pursuing the Covenanters, while the vaults were used for stabling.[12] In 1663, as part of her marriage contract with the Duke
of Monmouth, the Countess of Buccleuch, whose family had
acquired much of the Earl of Nithsdale's property in 1643, resigned 'all and haill the Great Hous or Pallace in Drumfreis'.[13]
By 1670, the building was again described as dilapidated and
unoccupied.[14] Five years later, when it was in the possession of
the magistrates, the Privy Council ordained that a garrison of 50
footsoldiers and 12 horse should be put in the castle, which was
to be checked to see whether the vaults and second storey were
sufficient, as the other two storeys were not sufficient and the
roof was not altogether watertight.[15] In 1681 the castle was again
garrisoned.[16] Six years later, funds were again sought, and obtained, for further maintenance.[17]

Some time before 1715, the Earl of Nithsdale sold the
castle to the M'Dowalls of Logan, from whose family the burgh
acquired it in 1722 as the site for the New Church.[18] This in turn
was replaced by Greyfriars Church in 1866.

---

1   Edgar, 141
2   Barbour, J 'The House of the Maxwells of Nithsdale at Dumfries', *TDGAS*,
     2nd Ser., VI, 187
3   Armstrong 1883, cx
4   RPC XIV, 73n.
5   Shirley, 48.
6   Edgar, 35.
7   Barbour, *op. cit.*, facing p.190; McDowall 1986, 569.
8   RPC III, 725.
9   Barbour, *op. cit.*, 188.
10   RPC VIII, 73.

11 Edgar, 142.
12 Ibid, 37.
13 Fraser 1878, II, 472.
14 Edgar, 143.
15 RPC, Third Series, IV, 425, 460, 473; Barbour, *op. cit.*, 191.
16 RPC, Third Series, VII, 215.
17 Edgar, 37-8.
18 Barbour, *op. cit.*, 192.

---

86. PORTRACK TOWER
(5m NW Dumfries)   (NX939829)

Portrack Tower stood on low ground on the right bank of the river Nith, where it was defended on the E side by a tributary burn and on the S and W sides by an artificial ditch. When the RCAHMS visited the site in 1912, all that survived was a fragment of masonry, 12ft high, 8ft 6in long and 4ft thick, which had evidently formed the SW angle of the tower.[1] This has now collapsed and been reduced to the merest vestige, a heap of rubble some 3ft high with no more than a fragment of the outer face. The earliest edition of the Ordnance Survey map[2] shows the outline of a rectangular tower, which scales approximately 54ft from N to S by 47ft from E to W, but this is presumably only intended to be conjectural, especially as the surviving masonry is shown on the W side away from the SW corner and such dimensions are much greater than would be expected for such a tower.

The lands of Portrack formed part of the lordship and barony of Holywood, which belonged to the abbey of that name. In 1544, William, Abbot of Crossraguel and Commendator of Holywood, granted the 40 shilling lands of 'Porterrak' in feu-ferme to Robert Maxwell,[3] a descendant of Homer Maxwell, younger brother of the 3rd Lord Maxwell (d.1513).[4] It was presumably Robert who built the tower. Robert evidently died in 1557 or 1558,[5] and was succeeded by his second son, James, who was still laird in 1592.[6] In 1590 the laird of Portrack was included in a list of 'Landed Men'.[7] The tower at 'Portrack' is shown on Pont's survey of Nithsdale c.1595.[8]

There is a John Maxwell of Portrack on record in 1593 and 1608,[9] and James Maxwell of Portrack in 1610,[10] but it was Robert Maxwell of Portrack, described as grandson of the first laird, who received a charter of confirmation of the lands in 1629.[11] Meanwhile, in 1618, John Murray of Lochmaben, later 1st Earl of Annandale, received a crown charter of the superiority of the lands.[12]

Both Homer Maxwell of Portrack and Robert Maxwell of Portrack are mentioned in 1643,[13] and Robert Maxwell, 'elder of Portrack', in 1652.[14] The latter laird was a Commissioner of War for Dumfriesshire in 1648.[15] He married Barbara, daughter of John Crichton of Crawfordton. Their eldest son, Robert, younger of Portrack, was included in the entail of the Crawfordton and Stewarton estates drawn up by Crichton in 1657.[16] Robert supported Charles II during the Civil War, as a result of which he was 'totaly rowined'.[17] It was presumably the younger Robert whose curators are mentioned in 1674, and his father's heirs who are mentioned in 1687.[18] Robert Maxwell of Portrack is credited with three fireplaces in the Hearth Tax returns for 1690.[19] These probably relate to the old tower. Robert was a Commissioner of Supply for Nithsdale and Dumfries in 1704.[20]

The estate was later purchased by John Maxwell (1720-1814) of Terraughty and Munches,[21] whose grandson, Alexander Harley-Maxwell of Portrack, took the name and arms of Maxwell, and went to live at Portrack, when he succeeded to the estate in 1815.[22] The tower having by then been abandonned, he built himself a new house, which is now incorporated into the rear part of the mansion designed by James Barbour in 1876[23] and completed three years later.

Portrack was later acquired by Sir John Keswick, a younger son of Major Henry Keswick of Cowhill (q.v.), from whom it passed to his only daughter, the late Maggie Keswick, and her husband, the American architect Charles Jencks. Today, Portrack is internationally renowned for its spectacular cosmology garden, designed and built there by Mr. Jencks and now dedicated to Maggie's memory.

---

1   RCAHMS 1920, No.281.
2   O.S. 25-inch, Dumfries, Sheet XLI, 13. *c.*1857.
3   RMS VIII, No.1392.
4   Another brother, Robert, was ancestor of the Maxwells of the adjoining estate of Cowhill.
5   Buccleuch MSS, 74 (No.176), 75 (No.177).
6   RMS V, No.2183.
7   RPC IV, 786.
8   Pont MS. No.35 in National Library of Scotland.
9   Hope-Johnstone MSS, 35 (No.72); RMS VI, Nos.2023, 2035.
10 RMS VII, No.297.
11 RMS VIII, No.1392.
12 RMS VII, No.1817.
13 PRS Dumfries I (1617-71), Index, 262, 283.
14 Ibid, 283; Fraser 1873, I, 372.
15 APS VI, Part II, 32.
16 Laing Charters, No.2499.
17 Fraser 1873, I, 379.
18 PRS Dumfries II (1672-1702), Index, 278.
19 Adamson, D. 'The Hearth Tax', *TDGAS*, 3rd Ser., XLVII, 167.
20 APS XI, 142.
21 Fraser 1873, I, 573.
22 Burke L.G. 1863, 996, 'Maxwell of Terraughty'.
23 Wolffe, A. 'James Barbour', *TDGAS*, LXXI, 155.

---

87. STEWARTON PELE
(3¹/₂m ESE Moniaive)   (NX827883)

The ruins of this tower and an adjacent building stand on a hillside looking NE across the Cairn valley. Little now remains, but the layout appears to be similar to Auchenfedrick II (supra). The tower, which was built of rubble with clay mortar, measured about 28ft 10in from NNE to SSW by 26ft 3in from ESE to WNW over walls approximately 6ft 10in thick.[1] The entrance was on the ESE side, facing the secondary building, most of which has been robbed for dyke material.

The lands of Stewarton formed part of the barony of Crawfordton (or Crawfordstoun) (q.v.), which was held by the Crichtons of Sanquhar at least as early as the 15th century. In 1506/7, the 2nd Lord Crichton of Sanquhar received a new charter of the superiority of the lands and barony of Crawfordton, which included the 6 merk lands of Stewarton, tenanted by Cuthbert Crichton.[2] Then in 1538/9, the 5th Lord Crichton of Sanquhar had sasine of the lands of Crawfordton and Stewarton, as heir to his father.[3] Ten years later he gave sasine of the 'fourteen merkland of Craufurdtoun and Steuartoun' to John Crichton, son and heir of Andrew Crichton of Crawfordton,[4] and John Crichton was still in possession in 1569.[5] Stewarton does not appear on Pont's map of Nithsdale.[6]

In 1627, the lands of Stewarton, and others in the barony of Snaid, were acquired by John Craik, a merchant burgess and baillie of Dumfries,[7] and his descendants were still in possession in 1698, when Marion, Sophia and Violet Craik, daughters and co-heiresses of John Craik of Stewarton (the grandson of the first John Craik of Stewarton) were served heirs portioners in the estate.[8] John Craik had been a Commissioner of Supply for Nithsdale and Dumfries in 1689 and 1690.[9] His daughters all married, but the subsequent ownership of the estate is not clear. In the 1827 Valuation of the parish of Glencairn, Stewarton was evidently occupied by James Walker of Crawfordton, but 'holden of the Duke of Buccleuch and Queensberry'.[10]

---

1   NMRS Databank, 'Stewarton'.
2   RMS III, No.3025.
3   Scots Peerage III, 227.
4   Hamilton-Grierson, Sir P. J. 'The Protocol Book (1541-1550) of Herbert Anderson, Notary in Dumfries', *TDGAS*, 3rd Ser., II, 214.
5   RSS VI, No.688.
6   Pont MS. No.35 in National Library of Scotland.
7   Adams 1921, 280.
8   Ibid. The 1671 Valuation of Glencairn refers to 'The merkland of the Twa merkland and merkland of Stuartoune' held by James Craik (2nd of Stewarton), and also lands purchased from Stewarton by the laird of Crawfordton (Corrie, 32).
9   APS IX, 70, 139.
10 Corrie, 34.

88.   TANLAWHILL TOWER
(9m NW Langholm)   (NY237910)

Early in the 12th century, Robert Avenel received a charter of the lands of Tumloher and Weidkerroc (Watcarrick), in Upper Eskdale, from David I; and later, whilst reserving certain rights to himself and retaining the superiority, he granted these lands to the abbey of Melrose.[1] The lands were subsequently united with others in Upper Eskdale, including apparently Tanlawhill, to form the barony of Dumfedling, which, with the adjoining barony of Westerker (see Westerhall), passed by marriage from the Avenels to Henry de Graham of Dalkeith, who, early in the 14th century, granted them to Sir William de Soulis.[2] After the forfeiture of de Soulis in 1320, Dumfedling was granted by the Crown to the Good Sir James Douglas.[3]

It is not clear how the ownership of the various properties of Dumfedling, which by then had become 'tenantries', subsequently devolved. There are said to have been changes in ownership after the Douglases defeat at Arkinholm in 1455.[4] Certainly, it was the abbey of Melrose which, in 1568, granted the lands of 'Tynunerhill' (Tanlawhill) and Dumfedling to Alexander Balfour of Denmylne for yearly payments of £5 and £3: 6s: 8d respectively;[5] and the Commendator of Melrose who, in 1582, granted the lands of 'Tunnerhill' and Dumfedling to his father, William Douglas of Lochleven, on the same terms.[6]

The lands remained with the Douglases, Earls of Morton until 1612, when the tenantry of Dumfedling was purchased by the Earl of Buccleuch.[7] The following year, Buccleuch received a crown charter of confirmation,[8] and in 1663 the lands formed part of the marriage contract between his granddaughter, the Countess of Buccleuch, and the Duke of Monmouth.[9]

On the NE slope of Hind Fell, some 250 yards S of Tanlawhill, are the vestigial remains of the old fermtoun of Tanlawhill. These comprise the remains of a small tower, about 26ft wide and almost square on plan, six or more other buildings of uncertain date and a kiln.[10] One of the buildings, which lies just W of the tower, appears to have been a typical long-house of two apartments, and the building immediately SW of it is of similar proportions. There were also various enclosures round

about for containing stock. The tower was the home of the Beatties of Tanlawhill, the tenants of the lands. It does not appear on Aglionby's Platte of 1590, but is shown on Pont's map of Eskdale *c*.1600.[11]

John Batie of Tanlaw Hill is on record in 1598/9,[12] and in 1622 either the same John Batie of Tanlahill or his namesake was declared a rebel.[13] The lands later passed to a branch of the Scotts, though the occupier of the tower in 1691 was one Francis Elliott. In the Hearth Tax returns for that year he is credited with two fireplaces.[14] It was from Francis Scott that Anne, Duchess of Buccleuch and Monmouth, purchased the property *c*.1702.[15]

Tanlawhill was still occupied at the turn of the 19th century, but was abandonned soon after.[16]

---

1   Armstrong 1883, 147. 'Tumloher' has sometimes been assumed to be Tanlawhill, because of its proximity to Watcarrick, but the 'Tomleucher' burn, first recorded by Pont, is a tributary of the White Esk, some 9 miles further north.
2   Hyslop, 200.
3   Ibid.
4   Ibid, 201.
5   RMS IV, No.1819.
6   Melrose Regality Records, III, 308-9.
7   Fraser 1878, I, 251.
8   Ibid, II, 467.
9   Ibid.
10 RCAHMS 1997, 214; AFS, Upper Eskdale, No.140.
11 Blaeu, 55, 'Eusdail and Eskdail'.
12 AFS, Upper Eskdale, No.140.
13 RPC XIV, 691.
14 Adamson, D. 'Hearth Tax of Dumfriesshire: Part 2', *TDGAS*, XLVIII, 139.
15 Hyslop, 316.
16 AFS, Upper Eskdale, No.140.

89.   TYNRON TOWER
(1³/₄ m WSW Penpont)   (NX820939)

Tynron was an **L**–plan tower built on top of Tynron Doon, a very distinctive and prominent hilltop rising high above the surrounding country. It was the site of a pre-historic fort. The tower, which was demolished *c*.1750 to provide stone for a new kirk in the village, is presumed to have dated from the 16th century; but although the Doon is illustrated on Pont's manuscript survey of Nithsdale, no tower is shown on top.[1] It measured 42ft from N to S by 20ft from E to W, with a stair wing measuring 8ft by 10ft at the NW corner.

The New Statistical Account states that 'the foundations of an extensive building might lately have been traced on the top of this hill'.[2] The site was excavated in 1964-7.[3] However, nothing is known of the family who built or occupied it.

---

1   Pont MS. No.35 in National Library of Scotland. The Doon does not appear on Blaeu's transcription of the manuscript (Blaeu, 59, 'The Shirifdome of NIDIS-DAIL').
2   NSA IV, 474.
3   Williams, J 'Tynron Doon', *TDGAS*, 3rd Ser., XLVIII, 106-120.

Fig. 372 Westerhall: building at N corner.

90. WESTERHALL
(4¹/₂ m NW Langholm)   (NY319893)

The lands of Westerhall, originally known as 'Dalduran' (or, as shown by Pont c.1595, 'Dardarrenn')[1], formed part of the barony of Westerker, or Watstirker, which was in the possession of the Avenels by the beginning of the 13th century.[2] From the Avenels it passed by descent to the Grahams of Dalkeith,[3] who, sometime before 1320, granted one half of the barony to William de Soulis. Meanwhile, the other half of the barony came into the possession of Sir Ingram de Gynes, who leased it to William's uncle, Sir John de Soulis, Guardian of Scotland.[4] On William's forfeiture in 1320, his half of the barony was granted to the 'Good Sir James' Douglas,[5] while the other half of the lands, having become vacant after the death of Sir John, was, in 1321, granted by the Crown to the abbey of Melrose.[6] Sir James subsequently acquired the abbey's half, and in 1324 received a new charter of the whole barony under the Great Seal.[7]

It was from the Douglases that the Glendinnings of that Ilk appear to have acquired possession of Dalduran sometime during the 14th century. In 1407, Sir Simon Glendoning was granted the heritable office of bailie of the regality of Eskdale.[8] Then, in 1458, his son, also Sir Simon, acquired the lands and barony of Parton in Galloway,[9] and thereafter the family seems to have devoted an ever increasing share of their time to that property. It is not clear, therefore, what establishment they had at Dalduran.[10] Dalduran does not appear on Aglionby's Platte in 1590, which details many towers in Upper Eskdale, but it is shown on Pont's map c.1595 (supra), though without making it clear what was there. The Statistical Account refers to 'the remains of another [old tower, or castle] at Westerhall' in 1793.[11]

Glendinning and Dalduran were eventually sold by the Glendinnings in 1605 to James Johnston of Westraw, a prominent gentleman who had sold Westraw in Lanarkshire and, whilst keeping a house in Edinburgh, moved to Eskdale.[12] The following year, James Johnston 'of Westerhall', the new name for Dalduran, first appears on record.[13]

The present mansion at Westerhall has had two disastrous fires, in 1873 and 1955, after which much of the existing structure had to be rebuilt; there were also major alterations carried out under Thomas Telford in 1783.[14] Nevertheless, the shells of two, separate, older buildings can be detected in the present house, one at the E corner and one at the N corner. The former comprises an oblong block (probably only part of a building), with two vaulted basement chambers, the vaults of which run in line NE-SW, and an entrance doorway, now blocked, in the NW wall of the SW chamber.[15] There is also a blocked window with chamfered arrises in the SE wall at first floor level, but no sign of a stair. The walls are 3ft 6in thick. The other building is also oblong in plan, but with the main axis running NW-SE and a circular stair tower projecting at the E corner. It too has chamfered arrises on the original windows, but internally it has been modernized. Both buildings would seem to date from c.1600, but one cannot say with any certainty whether either existed before the Johnstones' arrival.

James Johnston received a charter confirming the sale of the 7¹/₂ merk lands of Glendonyng, the 12 merk lands of Dalduren, and others, to him by Robert Glendonyng, younger of Parton, in 1614.[16] Meanwhile, following the forfeiture of Lord Maxwell in 1609, the superiority had been held by Sir Robert Ker, Earl of Somerset,[17] before being granted to James Maxwell in 1621.[18]

James Johnston, who succeeded his father at Westerhall in 1633, was one of the Commissioners appointed for Keeping the Peace in the Borders in 1641.[19] He had, however, got into financial difficulties, and in 1643 resigned the lands of Glendinning and Dalduran in favour of Lord Johnston of Lochwood and John Alexander, rector of Hoddom, equally, under reversion.[20] He died shortly afterwards.

Five months later, Walter Scott of Arkleton also acquired an interest in the lands, 'with the castles and manor-places', for further debts.[21] The new laird, Sir James Johnston, 3rd of Westerhall, who succeeded in that year, was laird for more than fifty years, during which time he became very active in public life. He recovered possession of Westerhall in 1654, and two years later was granted a new charter of the '12 merk land of

Fig. 373 Westerhall: older building incorporated in east corner of present house.

Daldurcham, with the manor-place', and other lands, by the Protector.[22] Then in 1670, Sir James and his wife received sasine of the barony of Westerhall at the 'manor-place of Daldurhame',[23] and this was confirmed by parliament the following year.[24] Sir James was appointed a Commissioner of Supply for Dumfries-shire in 1659, and this appointment was renewed in 1661, 1667, 1685, 1689, 1690, 1696 and 1698.[25] He was Quartermaster in the Earl of Annandale's troop of horse, which was raised in 1667 for service in General Drummond's regiment,[26] and the following year he was made a Captain of Foot in the militia.[27] Zealous in the pursuit of Covenanters, he was one of the special commission appointed in 1684 to act against them.[28] In the same year, he was also appointed Steward-Depute of Annandale.[29] He attended the Meeting of the Estates in March 1689, and the first parliament of William and Mary three months later;[30] thereafter, he was a regular attender until 1695.[31] He was appointed a Commissioner for Overseeing Burgh Elections in Dumfriesshire in 1689,[32] and also a Commissioner for Ordering the Militia in the county.[33] In the Hearth Tax returns for 1690, 'The Mansion House' of Westerhall is credited with 10 hearths.[34] It is evident, therefore, that Sir James greatly increased the size of Westerhall, and it was probably he who joined the older buildings to form one large house. That being so, it is by no means clear what the *New Statistical Account* meant in 1835, when, re-iterating the comments of the *Statistical Account* some forty years earlier (*supra*), it states that 'there are remains of an old castle . . . at Westerhall'.[35]

Sir James died in 1699, and was succeeded by his elder son, Sir John Johnstone, who was created a Knight Baronet the next year.[36] Sir John was a Commissioner of Supply for Dumfries-shire in 1689, 1690, 1696 and 1698, during his father's lifetime, and again in 1704.[37] He was a Major in the Dumfries militia in 1689, and Cornet to the Earl of Annandale.[38] Sir John attended parliament from 1700 until the Union in 1707,[39] having voted in favour of the Treaty of Union in both 1706 and 1707.[40] He had also voted in favour of the colony of Caledonia in 1701.[41] He died without issue in 1711, when he was succeeded by his younger brother, William.

Sir William, 2nd Baronet, represented Annan in the Scottish parliament from 1698 to 1707, and then the Dumfries Burghs from 1708 to 1715 and the county of Dumfries from 1715 to 1722 in the United Kingdom parliament.[42] In 1717 he was made Steward-Depute of the Stewartry of Kirkcudbright.[43] His elder son, Sir James Johnstone, 3rd Baronet, following the family's tradition of public service, was Provost of Lochmaben in 1740, and Member of Parliament for the Dumfries Burghs from 1743 to 1754.[44] He died in 1772. His eldest son, Sir James Johnstone, 4th Baronet, served as a Lieutenant-Colonel in the army.[45] It was he who employed Thomas Telford to draw up plans for modernising the house in 1783.

On the death of the 3rd Marquess of Annandale in 1792, Sir James submitted a claim as heir-male of the Johnston clan and heir to the Annandale peerages, but he died two years later, before the claims could be heard.[46] His son, Sir William Johnstone, 5th Baronet, renewed the claims in 1805, but he too died before the case could be heard, and it was not until 1881 that the House of Lords finally rejected the pedigree submitted in evidence.[47] Sir William, who was an elected member of no less than seven successive parliaments, married Frances, daughter and heiress of Daniel Pulteney, in consequence of which he took the name of Pulteney.[48] He is said to have been one of the richest subjects in the British Empire. Dying without male issue

in 1805, he was succeeded by his nephew, Sir John Johnstone, 6th Baronet.

Sir John was Member of Parliament for Weymouth, where the family had an estate, as were both his son, Sir George (d.1841), and grandson, Sir Frederick. Sir Frederick, 8th Baronet, was also a Deputy-Lieutenant for Dumfriesshire.[49] On his death without issue in 1913, the baronetcy passed to his nephew, Sir George Johnstone, who sold Westerhall soon afterwards.

1   Blaeu, 55, 'Evsdail et Eskdail'.
2   Armstrong 1883, 147-9.
3   Ibid, 149.
4   M'Michael, T., 'The Feudal Family of de Soulis', *TDGAS*, 3rd Ser., XXVI, 181. Sir Ingram had evidently acquired the lands by marriage to the daughter of William de Lindsay (Bain V, No.47).
5   RMS I, App.2, Nos.227, 544.
6   Ibid, App.1, No.14, and App.2, No.75; Armstrong 1883, 150-1. It would seem that Sir Ingram's half of the barony came into the Crown's possession by forfeiture, but it is not known which half of the barony Dalduran was in.
7   RMS I, App.1, No.38.
8   Armstrong 1883, 161.
9   Ibid.
10   Glendinning was their principal residence in Eskdale.
11   Stat Acct XI, 29.
12   Burke Peerage 1959, 1236, 'Johnstone, Bt.'
13   RPC VII, 657. The name 'Westerhall' is said to have been chosen to commemorate both the old home at 'Westraw', and the local parish and barony of 'Wester-Kirk'.
14   Gifford, 562.
15   No doubt the NE chamber also had a doorway in the NW wall, as the present interconnecting doorway is unlikely to be original.
16   RMS VII, No.1423.
17   Ibid, No.217; RMS VIII, No.188.
18   RMS VIII, No.188.
19   APS V, 685.
20   RMS IX, No.1304.
21   Ibid, No.1375. As James Johnston of Westerhall died in 1643, and his son was also called James, it is not clear who was in debt and who resigned the lands.
22   RMS X, No.473.
23   Laing Charters, No.2662.
24   APS VIII, 186.
25   Ibid, VI, Part II, 881; VII, 91, 544; VIII, 465; IX, 70, 139; X, 29, 131.
26   Fraser 1894, I, ccxl.
27   RPC, 3rd Ser., II, 542.
28   Fraser 1894, I, cclvii.
29   Ibid, IX, 630.
30   APS IX, 3, 95.
31   Ibid, *passim*.
32   Ibid, 5.
33   Ibid, 28.
34   Adamson, D. 'The Hearth Tax', *TDGAS*, 3rd Ser., XLVIII, 140.
35   NSA IV, 433.
36   Fraser 1894, II, 339.
37   APS IX, 70, 139; X, 29, 131.
38   Ibid, IX, 26, 55.
39   Ibid, X, 183, 196; XI, *passim*.
40   Ibid, XI, 313ff, 404-5.
41   Ibid, X, 247.
42   Burke Peerage 1959, 1236, 'Johnstone (of Westerhall)'.
43   Ibid.
44   Ibid, 1237.
45   Ibid, 1238.
46   Fraser 1894, II, 354.
47   Ibid, 356, 388. Any claim to the peerages was, in any case, invalid, as the Johnstones of Westerhall could not claim male descent from any of the titles, and the Hope-Johnstones of Raehills had an indisputable claim in the female descent (as finally recognized by the Committee of Privileges in 1985).
48   Burke Peerage 1959, 1238, 'Johnstone (of Westerhall)'. His daughter, Henrietta, succeeded her mother in the Pulteney estates in 1782, and was created Baroness of Bath in 1792 and Countess of Bath in 1803 (Complete Peerage II, 27).
49   Ibid.

APPENDIX

(1) INVENTORY OF GOODS IN TORTHORWALD CASTLE BELONGING TO JONETE SCRYMGEOUR, LADY CARLISLE, AND TAKEN FROM HER ON 22nd NOVEMBER, 1544, BY MICHAEL, LORD CARLISLE.

12 oxen; 12 cows; 9 fedder beddis [feather beds] furnist with bowsteris, coddis [pillows], coveringis, schetis and blankettis; 24 pair of schetis by furnessing of the saidis bedis; 10 pair of blankettis; 5 arreswerkis [wall-tapestries]; 6 Inglis coveringis; 8 brasin pottis, the ane half of thame gret and the uther half small; 5 brasin pannis; 3 irne crukis [pot holders]; 4 pairs of pot bowlis; ane brasin mortar; in pewder veschell gret and small; 6 chandelaris [candlesticks]; 3 irne spetis [spits]; 8 cuschingis; tua pair of tayngis [tongs]; 6 stane of clene dicht [combed] hempt; 5 stane of clene dicht lynt; 10 stane of clene dicht woll; 7 dosane of lyning [linen] clath; 10 stane of fedderis; ane gret basing; ane meit burd [food-table] of 3 ellis lang, set in ane creddill; ane double Flanderds comptar [chequered cloth]; ane seit burd [table] with the furmi [benches] therof; tua trene [wooden] beddis of aik of carvit werk; tua lang sadill bedis, of aik, carvit werk; ane chyre [chair] of carvit werk; 4 tyrnit chyris; ane Scottish comptar of aik, schorne [planed] werk, with the furmis of the samyn; tua aikin beddis, plane werk; ane gret pres [press] of aik, caissit [cased] werk; tua schrynis [shrines] of aik;

tua gret kistis [chests] of aik; tua girdillis; ane gret baik stule; ane dressing burd; ane gret maskin fat [brewing vat]; 7 hoghedis; 6 rowbouris [casks], ilk ane of thame contenand 5 gallonis; ane boit [domestic trough] and 4 gret trene scowpis [scoops]; ane gret brewing caldroun; 3 lang meit burdis; 3 compter clathis; ane gret flesch fatt [vat]; 5 trochis [troughs] of aik; 8 burd claithis [tablecloths]; 5 vesching [washing] towellis; 24 ellis [ells] of tweill hardin [twill cloth] for sekkis [sacks]; 12 maid sekkis; ane windo clath contenand 12 ellis; ane broun ambland haiknay [hackney horse]; ane chenze [chain] of gold weyand 3 uncis; ane hingar [pendant] of gold with ane rubye stane in it; tua ringis of gold, ane of thame set with ane rubye and ane uther with ane sapher [sapphire]; 16 score bollis of sittis with the fodder; fourscoir bollis beir with the foddir; ane chalder of mele; half ane chalder of malt; 6 salt martis [from Martinmas Sales] of ky and oxin; ane dosand of wedderis [wethers] in salt; fourscoir weddir skynnis; 6 salt hydis; 34 salt salmond; 12 dry kipper [smoked salmon kelts]; 8 stane of buttyr; ane dosand stanis of cheis; ane pitcher of huny contenand tua gallonis.

---

(2) FURNISHINGS OF COMLONGON CASTLE ON DEMITION OF LAUNCELOT MURRAY AS CHAMBERLAIN AND APPOINTMENT OF ANDREW MURRAY OF MORIQUHAT IN 1624.

The quhilk day in presens of Mr Gavine Young, Minister at Ruthwall, James Murray in Hitchill, Charles Murray in Moriquhat, Thomas Graham in Blakhall, and John Murray, son naturall to umquhill Sir James Murray of Cokpuill, was producit be Andrew Murray of Moriquat ane warrant direct from the Rycht Honoll the laird of Cokpuill, ane warrant direct to Lancie Murray chamberlain for the tyme to delyver to the said Andrew the whole keyis, plenisching, furnitur and quhatsomever was in his custodie within the inner and outer gatis of the place of Cumlungen as the warrant daited at Strand June 25 at moir length beiris, for obedience to the quhilk demand and warrand the said Lancelot delyverit the keyis, plenisching, furnitur and other efterspecifeit . . .

(1) Imprimis in the long gallerie, twa stand beds quhairof the inmest has ane fether bed and ane palleis under it, ane bawster, ane pair of scheitis, tua cods and wares, ane pair of walkit blankets, ane pair of worset, ane sewit covering, ane stand of cuirtings with ane greine pand somequhat broydret. The by bed hes a fether bed, ane bowster, ane cod and codware, a pair of round scheitis, ane pair of blankets wormeitin, ane sewit covering and a course covering, a stand of grosse rid curtings and a sewit pand and a cunter clothe, a spunge, a lytle beuk and a chayre and a water pott, a lock and key.

(2) The lytle gallerie has a stand bed without curtings with a fether bed, a bouster and a pair werce ill eitin and worne blankets, a lytle buird and an old chayre, with lock and key.

(3) The sklaithous hes within it a stand of Harnessing for a man with lock and key.

(4) Inner windiehall - thre stand beds, the upmest hes a stand of zellow curtings, a sewit pand, a fether bed, a bowster, a pair of blankets somewhat moth eitin, a sewit covering unlynet and a course covering. The other twa beds bund togither having ane pand thrie single curtings of course stuff, twa fether beds, twa bawsters, four worne cods, twa pair worne blankets, twa course coverings and a chayre, this hes lock and key. Lykways in it is a gritt chest within quhilk ar tua pair linning scheitis, fyve pair round scheitis for codwairs, four coverings quhairof twa are lyned, a mortcloth, a guid buirdcloth and ane illworne, twa pands, twa braid greine curtings, one narow, fyve pair wallkit blankets quhairof one pair is worm eitin, twa pair worset and a lock and key, with lock and key on the duckat duir.

(5) Outer windiehall - four stand beds, four bowsters quhairof thrie ar filled with chaffe, four old coverings, thrie pair of skurvie worne blankets, with lock and key.

(6) The lairds chalmer hes twa plenisching in the beds bot ane fether bed and ane muskett on ane bed heid, ane gritt locket kist within quhilk are twa stand of clothes, ane stand of blak saitin the other the doublett is quhyt saitin the breikis ar welwed and ane third stand of velvet broidret and a dussone silver spones.

(7) The chappell hes a lock and key within quhilk is a lattron locket and twa locket chalmers.

(8)   Western chalmer - with twa stand beds with a stand of skurvie cuirtings, twa fether beds, twa bowsters, twa pair of worm eitin blankets, twa ill worne course coverings. A great locket kist within quhilk ar ten pair of small scheitis, four pair round scheitis, aught cods and wairis, four cuschins, fourtie serveitis, four buird clothes, four towels, twa cupbuird clothes, ane basin and a laver, with lock and key.

(9)   The scholehous chalmer - a bed with a staind of ill curtings, a fether bed, a bowster, twa pair of scheittis, four cods, twa vairis, ane covering, and ill blankets a pair, with lock and key.

(10)   The nether stair chalmer - a bowster, a pair of round scheitis, a pair of ill blankets, a coverin, with lock and key.

(11)   The hall chalmer has nothing bott a fether bed, a horse harnessing, a kist within quhilk is a waistcoit, sewin buistis quharin is leters except in one, and ane bonnet case.

(12)   The twa pledg chalmers ar weill locket, in the one are thrie locket chartour kistis the one of thir keyis viz. the inner key Lancie reservet and Moriquhat hes the other dur key. Mairover was delyvered ane purse and fyve keyis within it.

(13)   The over wall - in it are fourtreen caikis of leid, a masking fatt, a kirk bell, fyve dussone putter plaitis quhairof 29 ar resonable guid, six worse, aught altogither brokin, 10 gud coveris, sevin bad. Truncheours 29 quhairof six ar nothing worth, six chandlers quhairof twa ar lytle and brokine, four sasers, a buist with sum glasses, with lock and key. At the futt of the stair is lock and key.

(14)   In the sellar ar four brasse pott and ane yron pott, ar for no use, four pans for no use with twa gud pans boght be Lancie a yeir since for service of the hous, twa speitis, a pair of racks, thrie aill fatts, sum failed barrels, sevin old hogheids, a mortar with a pistole of bush.

(15)   In the brew hous is a masking fatt and leid and baiking buird and a kneding tubb.

(16)   In the kitchin is a cruik, nothing els.

Twa of the rounds hes lock and keyis. Thrie stables has lock and keyis. The utter yett of all a strong lock and key.

We all affirm that the fether beds ar werie worne, for that thrie wald scarse fill ane bed.

(signed by) Andro Murray resawis, M.G. Young witness, James Murray witness, John Murray witness.

BIBLIOGRAPHY

3rd Stat Acct, Dumfries *The Third Statistical Account of Scotland: the County of Dumfries*. Houston, G (ed). Glasgow. 1962.

Acts & Decreets *Register of Acts & Decreets*. Scottish Record Office.

Adams, P W L 1921 *A History of the Douglas Family of Morton in Nithsdale and Fingland*. Bedford.

Adams, T 1802 *An Elegant Collection of Interesting Views in Scotland, representing Gentlemen's Seats, Remains of Places of Antiquity, and Picturesque Scenery*. Edinburgh.

AFS *Archaeological Field Survey* (RCAHMS). Edinburgh.
The Archaeological Sites & Monuments of:-
Berwickshire District. 1980.
Ewesdale & Lower Eskdale. 1981.
Upper Eskdale. 1980.

ALCPA *Acts of the Lords of Council in Public Affairs, 1501-54*.

ALHT *Accounts of the Lord High Treasurer of Scotland, 1473-1580*. Dickson, T et al.(eds). Edinburgh. 1877-1978.

Anderson, A O 1990 *Early Sources of Scottish History, A.D. 500 to 1286*. Stamford.

Anderson, W 1868 *The Scottish Nation; or the surnames, families, literature, honours, and biographical history of the people of Scotland*. Edinburgh.

APS *Acts of the Parliaments of Scotland, 1124-1707*. Thomson, C and Innes, C (eds). Edinburgh. 1844-75.

Armstrong, R B 1883 *The History of Liddesdale, Eskdale, Ewesdale, Wauchopedale and the Debateable Land*. Edinburgh.

Armstrong, W A 1960 *The Armstrong Borderland*. Galashiels.

ASH *Atlas of Scottish History to 1707*. McNeill, P and MacQueen, H (eds). Edinburgh. 1996.

ATS *Accounts of the Treasurer of Scotland, 1566-74*, Vol XII (Continuation of *Accounts of the Lord High Treasurer of Scotland, 1473-1566*). Edinburgh.

Bain *Calendar of Documents relating to Scotland, 1108-1516*. Bain, J, et al. (eds).1881-1970. Edinburgh.

Barrow, G W S & Scott, W W 1971 *Regesta Regum Scottorum: The Acts of William I, King of Scots, 1165-1214*. Edinburgh.

Beaton, E 1997 *Scotland's Traditional Houses – from Cottage to Tower-house*. Edinburgh.

Black, G F 1946 *The Surnames of Scotland*. New York.

Blaeu, J 1662 *Atlas Maior*, VI (Scotland). Amsterdam

Border Laws 1705 *Leges Marchiarum, or Border=Laws: Containing several Original Articles and Treaties, Made and Agreed upon by the Commissioners of the Respective Kings of England and Scotland, for the better Preservation of Peace and Commerce upon the Marches of Both Kingdoms: From the Reign of Henry III to the Union of the Two Crowns, in K.James I*, by Nicolson, W, Bishop of Carlisle. London.

Border Papers 1894-6 *Calendar of Letters and Papers relating to the Affairs of the Borders of England and Scotland, 1560-1603*. Bain, J (ed). Edinburgh.

Brit Chron 1961 *Handbook of British Chronology*. Powicke, Sir F M and Fryde, E B (eds).London.

Buccleugh MSS. *The Manuscripts of His Grace the Duke of Buccleugh & Queensberry, preserved at Drumlanrig Castle*. Historical Manuscripts Commission, 15th Report, Appendix, Part VIII. 1897. London.

Buchan, J W & Paton, H 1925-7 *A History of Peeblesshire*. Glasgow.

Burke, Sir B 1883 *A Genealogical History of the Dormant, Abeyant, Forfeited, and Extinct Peerages of the British Empire*. London.

Burke L.G. *Burke's Genealogical and Heraldic History of the Landed Gentry*. 1858 (3rd Edition); 1863 (4th); 1906 (11th); 1937 (15th); 1952 (17th); 1965-72 (18th). London.

Burke Peerage *Burke's Genealogical & Heraldic History of the Peerage, Baronetage & Knightage*. 1959 (102nd Edition). London.

Caldwell, D H 1981 *Scottish Weapons and Fortifications 1100-1800*. Caldwell, D H (ed). Edinburgh.

Cardonnel, A de 1788 *Picturesque Antiquities of Scotland*. London.

Carruthers, A S & Reid, R C 1934 *Records of the Carruthers Family*. London.

Complete Peerage *The Complete Peerage*, by Cokayne, G E. Revised Edition, 1910-59. London.

Corrie, J 1910 *Glencairn: The Annals of an Inland Parish*. Dumfries

County Directory 1912 *The County Directory of Scotland*. Edinburgh.

Cruden, S 1960 *The Scottish Castle*. Edinburgh.

CSPS *Calendar of State Papers relating to Scotland: The Scottish Series of the Reigns of Henry VIII, Edward VI, Mary, Elizabeth, 1509-1603; etc*. 1858. London

Debrett's Peerage *Debrett's Peerage and Baronetage*. 1990. London.

Dickinson, W. Croft 1965 *Scotland from the Earliest Times to 1603*. Edinburgh.

Directory of Landownership *A Directory of Landownership in Scotland c.1770*. 1976 (Scottish Record Society). Edinburgh.

Discovery & Excavation in Scotland. The Annual Journal of the Council for Scottish Archaeology. Edinburgh.

DNB *The Compact Edition of the Dictionary of National Biography*. 1975. Oxford.

Dumfries Burgh Papers Original manuscript documents held in the archives of the Royal Burgh of Dumfries (unpublished). Dumfries.

Dunbar, J G 1966 *The Historic Architecture of Scotland*. London.

Easson, D B 1957 *Medieval Religious Houses: Scotland*. London.

Edgar *An Introduction to the History of Dumfries, by Robert Edgar, 1746*. Edited with annotations by Reid, R C, 1915. Dumfries.

ERS *The Exchequer Rolls of Scotland, 1264-1594*. Stuart, J, Burnett, G, et al. (eds). 1878-1903. Edinburgh.

Fawcett, R 1994 *Scottish Architecture: From the Accession of the Stewarts to the Reformation, 1371-1560*. Edinburgh.

Fitzmaurice, J T 1899 *Bonshaw Tower: the Irvings and some of their Kinsfolk*.

Forman, S 1967 *Scottish Country Houses and Castles*. Glasgow.

Fraser, (Sir) W 1873 *The Book of Carlaverock: Memoirs of the Maxwells, Earls of Nithsdale, Lords Maxwell & Herries*. Edinburgh.

Fraser, (Sir) W 1878 *The Scotts of Buccleugh*. Edinburgh

Fraser, (Sir) W 1885 *The Douglas Book*. Edinburgh

Fraser, Sir W 1894 *The Annandale Family Book of the Johnstones, Earls and Marquises of Annandale*. Edinburgh.

Frere, S S 1974 *Britannia: A History of Roman Britain*. London.

Gifford, J 1996 *The Buildings of Scotland: Dumfries and Galloway*. London.

Gladstone, I O J 1972 *The Lauries of Maxwelton and other Laurie Families*. London

Good, G L & Tabraham, C J 1981 'Excavations at Threave Castle, Galloway, 1974-78', *Medieval Archaeology*, XXV, 90-140.

Gow, I & Rowan, A 1998 *Scottish Country Houses 1600-1914*. Gow, I & Rowan, A (eds.). Edinburgh.

Gray, P 1894 *Dumfriesshire Illustrated I - Nithsdale*. Dumfries

Greig, D C 1971 *British Regional Geology: The South of Scotland*. Edinburgh.

Grose, F 1797 *The Antiquities of Scotland*. 2nd Edition. London.

Grove, D 1994 *Caerlaverock Castle*. Edinburgh.

GRS *General Register of Sasines*. General Register House, Edinburgh.

Hamilton Papers *The Hamilton Papers*. Bain, J. (ed). 1890-92. Edinburgh.

Hannay, R K (ed) *Acts of the Lords of Council in Public Affairs*. 1932. Edinburgh.

HAS *An Historical Atlas of Scotland, c400-c1600*. McNeill, P and Nicholson, R (eds.). 1975. St.Andrews.

Hist Mon NI 1987 *Historic Monuments of Northern Ireland*. Department of the Environment for Northern Ireland. Belfast.

Holmains MSS. *Manuscripts of the Family of Carruthers of Holmains*. Fraser, Sir W. Historical Manuscripts Commission, 6th Report, Appendix. 1877. London.

Hope-Johnstone MSS. *The Manuscripts of J.J.Hope-Johnstone, Esq. of Annandale*. Historical Manuscripts Commission, 15th Report, Appendix, Part IX. 1897. London.

Hyslop, J & R 1912 *Langholm As It Was: a History of Langholm and Eskdale from the earliest times*. Langholm.

Imperial Gazetteer *The Imperial Gazetteer of Scotland; or Dictionary of Scottish Topography*. Wilson, Rev. J. M. (ed). 1865. Edinburgh.

Irvine, C (Historiographer Royal) 1678 *The Original of the Family of the Irvines or Erinvines*. Unpublished MS.

Irving, J B 1907 *The Irvings, Irwins, Irvines, or Erinveines: or any other spelling of the name: an Old Scots Border Clan*. Aberdeen.

Jones, J H 1988 *Balliol College: A History - 1263-1939*. Oxford.

Johnston, J B 1903 *Place-Names of Scotland*. Edinburgh.

Johnson-Ferguson, Sir E 1935 *The Place-Names of Dumfriesshire*. Dumfries.

Johnstone, C L 1889 *The Historical Families of Dumfriesshire and the Border Wars*. Dumfries.

Johnstone, W. and Maxwell-Irving, A. M. T. 1993 *Amisfield Tower*. Amisfield.

L & P *Letters & Papers, Foreign & Domestic, of the Reign of Henry VIII. 1862-1910*. London.

Lag Charters. *The Lag Charters, 1400-1720*. Hamilton-Grierson, P.J.(ed). 1958. Edinburgh. (Scottish Record Society).

Laing Charters. *Calendar of the Laing Charters, AD 854-1837*. Anderson,J.(ed). 1899. Edinburgh.

Lawlor, H C 1906 *A History of the Family of Cairnes or Cairns and its connections*. London.

Lawrie, Sir A 1905 *Early Scottish Charters*. Glasgow.

Leask, H G 1986 *Irish Castles and Castellated Houses*. Dundalk.

Leslie, J F 1909 *The Irvines of Drum and Collateral Branches*. Aberdeen.

McDowall W 1986 *History of the Burgh of Dumfries*. Fourth Revised Edition, with Additional Notes. Dumfries.

McDowall W 1886 *Chronicles of Lincluden, as an Abbey and as a College*. Edinburgh.

MacGibbon, D & Ross, T 1887-92 *The Castellated and Domestic Architecture of Scotland*. Edinburgh.

Mackenzie, W M 1927 *The Mediaeval Castle in Scotland*. London.

Mackenzie, W & Nicholson, J 1841 *The History of Galloway from the Earliest Period to the Present Time*. Kirkcudbright.

M'Kerlie, P H 1870-79 *History of the Lands and their Owners in Galloway*. Edinburgh.

Macleod, I 1986 *Discovering Galloway*. Edinburgh.

Marchbank, A 1901 *Upper Annandale: Its History & Traditions*. Paisley.

Marwick, H 1973 *Ancient Monuments in Orkney*. Edinburgh.

Maxwell, G S 1989 *The Romans in Scotland*. Edinburgh.

Maxwell, Sir H 1900 *A History of Dumfries and Galloway*. Edinburgh.

Maxwell, Sir H 1902 *A History of the House of Douglas*. London.

Maxwell's Guide, 1896 *Maxwell's Guide Book to the Stewartry of Kirkcudbright*. Castle-Douglas.

Maxwell-Irving, A M T 1968 (I) *The Irvings of Bonshaw, Chiefs of the Noble and Ancient Scots Border Family of Irving*. Oxford.

Maxwell-Irving, A M T 1968 (II) 'Lochwood Castle - A Preliminary Site Survey', in *TDGAS*, XLV (1968), 184-99.

Maxwell-Irving, A M T 1968 (III) *The Irvings of Dumfries: Volume I - The Family Genealogy & Biography*. (MS. Copies in National Library of Scotland and Ewart Library, Dumfries).

Maxwell-Irving, A M T 1974 (I) 'Lochwood Castle II - Exploratory Excavations and Further Observations on Lochwood and its Lairds'. (MS in *NMRS*).

Maxwell-Irving, A M T 1974 (II) 'Early Firearms and their Influence on the Military and Domestic Architecture of the Borders', in *PSAS*, 103 (1970-71), 192-224.

Maxwell-Irving, A M T 1982 'Cramalt Tower: Historical Survey and Excavations 1977-9', in *PSAS*, 111 (1981), 401-29.

Maxwell-Irving, A M T 1988 'Hoddom Castle: A Re-appraisal of its Architecture and Place in History', in *PSAS*, 117 (1987), 183-217.

Maxwell-Irving, A M T 1990 'Lochwood Castle: A Résumé', in *TDGAS*, LXV (1990), 93-99.

Maxwell-Irving, A M T 1991 'The Castles of Buittle', in *TDGAS*, LXVI (1991), 59-66.

Maxwell-Irving, A M T 1992 'Lockerbie Tower', in *TDGAS*, LXVII (1992), 61-65.

Maxwell-Irving, A M T 1993 'Torthorwald Castle', in *TDGAS*, LXVIII (1993), 97-106.

Maxwell-Irving, A M T 1994 'Scottish Yetts and Window Grilles', in *PSAS*, 124 (1994), 433-454.

Maxwell-Irving, A M T 1997 'The Dating of Comlongon and Elphinstone Castles', in *PSAS*, 126 (1997), 871-879.

Maxwell-Irving, A M T 1997 'Kenmure Castle', in *TDGAS*, LXXII (1997), 41-54.

Maxwell-Irving, A M T 1997 'The Tower-Houses of Kirtleside', in *TDGAS*, LXXII (1997), 55-67.

Maxwell-Irving, A M T 'The Maxwells of Caerlaverock' in *Lordship and Architecture in Mediaeval and Renaissance Scotland* (forthcoming).

Melrose Regality Records *Selections from The Records of the Regality of Melrose and from the Manuscripts of the Earl of Haddington, 1547-1706*. Vol.III. 1917. Edinburgh. (Scottish History Society).

Menzies MSS. *The Manuscripts of Sir Robert Menzies of that Ilk at Castle Menzies*. Fraser, Sir W. Historical Manuscripts Commission, 6th Report, Appendix. 1877. London.

Mercer, R et al. 1997 *Kirkpatrick Fleming, Dumfriesshire: An Anatomy of a Parish in South West Scotland*. Dumfries.

Merriman, M 1967 'The Platte of Castlemilk, 1547', in *TDGAS*, XLIV (1966-67), 175-181.

Moffat, R M 1908 *A Short History of the Family of Moffat of that Ilk*. Jersey.

Murray, A 1989 *Discovering Dumfriesshire*. Edinburgh.

Naismith, R J 1989 *The Story of Scotland's Towns*. Edinburgh.

Naworth Household Books *Selections from the Household Books of Lord William Howard of Naworth Castle*. Ornsby, G. (ed). 1878 (Surtees Society, LXVIII).

Neale, J P 1824-6 *An Historical Account of the Seats of Noblemen and Gentlemen, in England, Wales, Scotland and Ireland*. London.

Nicholson, R 1978 *Scotland: The Later Middle Ages (The Edinburgh History of Scotland, Vol.2)*. Edinburgh.

Nicolas, N H 1828 *The Siege of Carlaverock*. London.

Nicolson, W 1705 *Leges Marchiarum, or Border=Laws* – See Border Laws.

NSA *The New Statistical Account of Scotland*. 1845. Edinburgh.

NMRS National Monuments Record of Scotland. Edinburgh.

Ordnance Gazetteer *Ordnance Gazetteer of Scotland*. Groome, F.H. (ed). Edinburgh. 1901.

O.S.Name Books *Ordnance Survey, Object Name Books*, c.1848-58, in the National Monuments Record of Scotland

Parl. of Scot. *The Parliaments of Scotland: Burgh and Shire Commissioners*. Young, M. D. (ed). Edinburgh. 1993.

Pennant, T 1774 *A Tour in Scotland, and Voyage to the Hebrides; 1772*. Chester.

Pont MSS Manuscript Maps of Timothy Pont. National Library of Scotland. (See also Stone 1989)

Post Office *Directory to Noblemen and Gentlemen's Seats, Villages, etc., in Scotland*. c.1851. Edinburgh.

Prevost, W A J 1954 *Annals of three Dumfriesshire Dales*. Moffat.

PRS Dumfries *Particular Register of Sasines for the Sheriffdom of Dumfries and Stewartries of Annandale and Kirkcudbright*, and the 5 volumes of Indexes thereto. General Register House, Edinburgh.

PSAS *Proceedings of the Society of Antiquaries of Scotland*. Edinburgh.

Rae, T I 1966 *The Administration of the Scottish Frontier: 1513-1603*. Edinburgh.

Ramage, C T 1876 *Drumlanrig Castle and the Douglases, with the Early History and Ancient Remains of Durisdeer, Closeburn and Morton*. Dumfries.

RCAHMS 1914 The Royal Commission on the Ancient and Historical Monuments and Constructions of Scotland. *Fifth Report and Inventory of Monuments and Constructions in Galloway. Vol.II. County of the STEWARTRY OF KIRKCUDBRIGHT*. Edinburgh.

RCAHMS 1920 The Royal Commission on Ancient and Historical Monuments and Constructions of Scotland. *Seventh Report with Inventory of Monuments and Constructions in the County of DUMFRIES*. Edinburgh.

RCAHMS 1929 The Royal Commission on Ancient and Historical Monuments and Constructions of Scotland. *Tenth Report with Inventory of Monuments and Constructions in the Counties of MIDLOTHIAN and WEST LOTHIAN*. Edinburgh.

RCAHMS 1956 The Royal Commission on the Ancient Monuments of Scotland. *An Inventory of the Ancient and Historical Monuments of ROXBURGHSHIRE with the Fourteenth Report of the Commission*. Edinburgh.

RCAHMS 1957 The Royal Commission on the Ancient Monuments of Scotland. *An Inventory of the Ancient and Historical Monuments of SELKIRKSHIRE with the Fifteenth Report of the Commission*. Edinburgh.

RCAHMS 1967 The Royal Commission on the Ancient and Historical Monuments of Scotland. *PEEBLESSHIRE: An Inventory of the Ancient Monuments*. Edinburgh.

RCAHMS 1990 *North-East Perth: an archaeological landscape*. Edinburgh.

RCAHMS 1994 The Royal Commission on the Ancient and Historical Monuments of Scotland. *Glenesslin, Nithsdale: An Archaeological Survey*. Edinburgh.

RCAHMS 1996 The Royal Commission on the Ancient and Historical Monuments of Scotland. *Tolbooths and Town-houses: Civic Architecture in Scotland to 1833*. Edinburgh.

RCAHMS 1997 The Royal Commission on the Ancient and Historical Monuments of Scotland. *Eastern Dumfriesshire: An Archaeological Landscape*. Edinburgh.

RCHM 1970 Royal Commission on Historical Monuments (England). *Shielings and Bastles*. Ramm, H G, McDowall, R W and Mercer, E. London.

Reg. Holm Cultram *The Register and Records of Holm Cultram*. Grainger, F. and Collingwood, W.G. (eds.). Kendal. 1929.

Reg. Scot. (Dumf.) Abridgements of Sasines and Search Books (for Dumfriesshire), Registers of Scotland. Edinburgh.

Reid Notes Note Books and MSS. of Robert Corsane Reid, LL.D., (d.1962), held in the Ewart Library, Dumfries.

René d'Anjou c.1460 *Traité de la Forme et Devis d'un Tournois*. Reprinted by Revue Verve, Paris, 1946.

Return of Landowners *Scotland: Owners of Lands and Heritages, 1872-73 Return*. 1874. Edinburgh.

Ritchie, G and Harman, M 1985 *Exploring Scotland's Heritage: Argyll and the Western Isles*. Edinburgh.

RMS *Registrum Magni Sigilli Regum Scotorum: The Register of the Great Seal of Scotland, 1306-1668*. Edinburgh. 1984 (Reprint).

Robertson, W 1798 *An Index of many Records of Charters granted by the different Sovereigns of Scotland between the years 1309 and 1413, with an Introduction giving a state of the ancient Records of Scotland which were in that Kingdom in the Year 1292*. Edinburgh.

RPC *The Register of the Privy Council of Scotland, 1545-1691*. 1st, 2nd & 3rd Series. Burton, J H and Masson, D, et al. (eds). Edinburgh, 1877-1970.

RSS *Registrum Secreti Sigilli Regum Scotorum: The Register of the Privy Seal of Scotland, 1488-1584*. Edinburgh. 1908-82.

Rutland MSS *The Manuscripts of His Grace the Duke of Rutland*. Historical Manuscripts Commission, 12th Report, Appendix, Part IV. 1888. London.

Salisbury MSS *Calendar of the Manuscripts of the Rt. Hon. the Marquis of Salisbury, preserved at Hatfield House, Part I*. Historical Manuscripts Commission. 1883. London.

Salter, M 1993 *The Castles of SW Scotland*. Malvern.

Scot. Antiq. *Studies in Scottish Antiquity*. Breeze, D J (ed). 1984.

Scots Peerage *The Scots Peerage*. Balfour Paul, Sir J (ed). 1904-14. Edinburgh.

Scottish Field *Scottish Field*. Glasgow.

Scottish Papers *Calendar of the State Papers relating to Scotland and Mary, Queen of Scots, 1547-1603*. Bain, J et al (eds). 1898-1969. Edinburgh.

Simpson, W D 1968 *The Ancient Stones of Scotland*. London.

Shirley, G W 1915 *The Growth of a Scottish Burgh*. Dumfries.

Slade, H Gordon 1987 'The Tower and House of Drum, Aberdeenshire' in *PSAS*, 115 (1985), 297-356.

SRS *Scottish Record Society* publications.

Stat Acct *The Statistical Account of Scotland*. Sinclair, Sir J (ed). 1791-9. Edinburgh.

State Papers, Domestic *Calendar of State Papers, Domestic Series*. 1895-1921. London.

State Papers, Foreign *Calendar of State Papers, Foreign Series, of the Reign of Elizabeth, 1569-71*. London. 1874.

State Papers, Henry VIII *Letters and Papers, Foreign and Domestic, of the Reign of Henry VIII, 1509-46*. Brewer, J.S. et al (eds). 1862-1932. London

State Papers, Scottish *Calendar of the State Papers relating to Scotland, preserved in the State Paper Department of Her Majesty's Public Record Office (1509-1603)*. Thorpe, M J (ed). 1858. London.

Stell, G 1986 *Exploring Scotland's Heritage: Dumfries & Galloway*. Edinburgh.

Stell, G 1975 'Mottes', 28-29, 128, in *HAS*.

Steuart, J 1932 *The Bell Family in Dumfriesshire*. Dumfries.

Stone, J C 1989 *The Pont Manuscript Maps of Scotland*. Tring.

Tabraham, C 1984 'Norman Settlement in Galloway: Recent Fieldwork in the Stewartry', 87-124, in *Scot. Antiq*.

Tabraham, C 1988 *Threave Castle*. Edinburgh.

Tabraham, C 1995 *Edinburgh Castle*. Edinburgh.

TCWAAS *Transactions of the Cumberland and Westmorland Antiquarian & Archaeological Society*. Carlisle.

TDGAS *Transactions of the Dumfriesshire & Galloway Natural History & Antiquarian Society*. Dumfries.

Thompson, 0 1986 *Drum Castle* (National Trust for Scotland Guide). Edinburgh.

Thomson, A 1902 *Lauder and Lauderdale*. Galashiels.

Thorold, H C 1993 *The Ruined Abbeys of England, Wales and Scotland*. London.

Tranter, N G 1935 *The Fortalices and Early Mansions of Southern Scotland, 1400 to 1650*. Edinburgh.

Tranter, N 1962-70 *The Fortified House in Scotland*. Edinburgh.

Victoria County History: Cumberland *The Victoria History of the Counties of England: Cumberland*. 1968. London.

Victoria County History: Lincoln *The Victoria History of the Counties of England: Lincoln*. W Page (ed.). 1906. London.

Walker, B and Ritchie, R 1987 *Exploring Scotland's Heritage: Fife and Tayside*. Edinburgh.

Watson, R M F 1901 *Closeburn: Reminiscent, Historic & Traditional*. Glasgow.

Wedderburn MSS *Report on the Manuscripts of Col. David Milne Home of Wedderburn Castle*. Historical Manuscripts Commission. 1902. London.

Who's Who *Who's Who: an Annual Biographical Dictionary*. Various editions. London.

Wilson, T & McMillan 1931 *Annals of Sanquhar*. Sanquhar.

Yester Writs *Calendar of Writs Preserved at Yester House, 1166-1652*. Harvey, C C H and Macleod, J (compilers). 1930. (Scottish Record Society).

GLOSSARY

Alba-ferme — Lands subject to blench-ferme rents (q.v.) were said to be held in alba-ferme.

Annualrent — A fixed rent payable annually in perpetuity, or for a specified period.

Apprise — Seize a property by legal order as security for a debt. The former owner might still be permitted to occupy the property, but he would no longer hold the title.

Arris — The edge or angle where two surfaces meet.

Ashlar — Squared and dressed masonry. See Fig. 2.

Attic — A room or storage space contained entirely within the roof-space of a building.

Aumbry — Mural recess usually at shelf level. An 'open-aumbry' had no door; a 'close-aumbry' had a wooden door, and is most readily identified by the surrounding rebate to house the door-frame (now gone). See Fig. 66.

Bailey — The enclosed courtyard outside an early feudal castle, such as a motte.

Barmkin — High defensive wall surrounding the courtyard of a tower-house. See Fig. 225.

Barrel-vault — A stone vault of semi-circular section. See Fig. 24.

Bartizan — A corbelled-out corner turret. See Fig. 85.

Bastle-house — A defensive stone house of two storeys with a vaulted basement and entrance at each level. See Chapter 2.

Biggings — Buildings or out-houses.

Blench-ferme — Tenure by payment of a nominal rent, such as a silver penny, a red rose, a glove, etc., sometimes only if requested.

Bolection-moulding — A moulding that projects beyond the normal surface of a wall or doorway.

Bottle-nosed treads — Steps where the outer edge is rounded and projects beyond the step below.

Brander — Gridiron.

Bretasche — See Hoarding.

Buffet — Large open-aumbry, normally with a moulded surround, used for displaying objects in a hall. See Fig. 61.

Cable-moulding — A projecting moulding in the form of a twisted rope, often with knots at each end. See Fig. 234.

Cage-grille — A window-grille in which the ends of the bars, instead of passing straight into the ingos, are fixed in the outer face of the window surround.

Cap-house — The structure covering the top of a stair where it emerges on to a parapet walk or into a garret. See Fig. 91.

Caput — The principal seat of a lordship or barony, which might be a historic site, or ruin, that was no longer occupied.

Carucate — The extent of land that could be tilled by one plough and eight oxen in a season. It comprised 8 oxgangs (q.v.), and varied from about 80 to 150 acres (it is commonly taken to be 104 acres).

Cess — A local rate or tax.

Checked — See 'Rebated'.

Chequer-corbelling — A corbel arrangement or moulding where the projecting corbels or squares alternate to give a chequered appearance.

Clare Constat — Where the heir to a feued property was quite clear, the feudal superior could issue a 'Precept of Clare Constat' to his bailie for the heir to be granted sasine.

Clencher-nail — A nail that is longer than the timber through which it passes, and which is then bent over at the end for added strength.

Close-aumbry — See 'Aumbry'.

Close-garderobe — A garderobe with no soil shaft. See Fig. 74.

Corbel — A projecting stone for supporting a beam. See Fig. 53.

Corbel-table — A series of corbels for supporting a projecting wall or parapet.

Cornice — A projecting, decorative moulding along the top of a wall or other feature.

Crenellated — Embattled.

Crow-stepped — A gable formed from staggered, square-cut stones was originally described as being 'corbel-stepped'. This gave rise to the colloquialism "corbie-stepped", and hence "crow-stepped", "corbie" also being the Scots word for a crow.

Cusping — Projecting points where the decorative foils in Gothic tracery meet.

Custumar — Collector of Customs.

Dog-legged — The well of a stair or aumbry that returns on itself.

Dog-tooth — A decorative moulding that resembles a series of flowers, each with four petals arranged in a pyramid.

Drawbar — A strong bar of timber or iron for reinforcing an entrance door and/or yett. It was slid into a slot within the adjacent wall's thickness when not in use.

Drum tower — A large cylindrical tower.

Dumb-bell — An opening comprising a narrow slot between two, larger circles. See Figs. 32, 350.

Edge-roll — A circular moulding, usually with one or two quirks, along an arris. See Fig. 16. See also 'Quirked-edge-roll'.

Ell — An old Scots measure equivalent to 37 inches.

Embattled — A wall or parapet with a series of embrasures.

Embrasure — (1) An opening in a wall or parapet. See Fig. 84.

(2) The mural recess behind a window or door.

Enceinte — An enclosing wall, or the enclosure within it.

Enriched- or embellished-corbelling — Corbelling of an ornate form, commonly comprising 3-step corbels alternating with 2-step, diminutive corbels. See Fig. 249.

Entasis — A gradual curving outwards along the length of a column to counteract the optical illusion of 'waisting' in a column with straight sides.

Entresol — An intermediate floor inserted under a vault. See Fig. 21.

Escheat — Forfeiture of goods, etc.

Fermes (farms) — Fixed yearly rent payable to the Crown or other landlord.

Fermtoun — A small settlement comprising two or more families engaged in agriculture before the agricultural revolution of the 18th century.

Feu-ferme — Tenure by payment of a feudal rent to a feudal superior.

Foil — (Trefoil, Quatrefoil, etc.) The leaf-shaped space formed between cusps in Gothic tracery.

Garderobe — A mediaeval latrine or privy.

Gargoyle — An ornamental water-spout for draining a parapet, etc. See Fig. 89.

Garret — The top floor of a building where the lower part is below the wall-head and the upper part within the roof-space. See Fig. 95.

Geometric Stair — A stair which curves in a circular or oval form around an open stair-well, without any newels. See Fig. 206.

Greywacke — A very hard, Silurian type of sandstone that is dark greyish-brown in colour. It is common in the Southern Uplands.

Gun-loop — A large shot-hole for a hagbut or similar hand-gun, more rarely for a small cannon. It was usually splayed horizontally, or very occasionally vertically, to give a relatively wide angle of fire. See Figs. 28, 244.

Hagbut, or Hackbut — An early form of portable gun, with a hook cast beneath the barrel to help support it and to take the recoil.

Harled — Roughcast and lime-coated.

Haunch — The part of an arch midway between the springing line and the highest point.

Hoarding — An overhanging timber gallery.

Hood-moulding — A projecting moulding above a doorway, arch, etc., usually following the form of the feature.

Husbandland — See 'Oxgang'.

Infeftment — Granting of Sasine, q.v.

Ingo — The return face of a wall, usually in a window or door recess or embrasure.

Insight — Household goods or furniture.

Instrument of Sasine — Legal document recording sasine.

Jamb — The side of a door or window, or the wing of a building.

Joggle — A stepped joint between two stones to prevent them from slipping. It is commonly used in flat arches. See Fig. 348.

Justice-ayre — Itinerant court of justice.

Keystone — The central stone of an arch.

Kiln-barn — A rectangular building which incorporates a kiln for drying grain at one end and a barn for storing the grain at the other.

Laird's Lug — Secret chamber or aperture which enabled a laird to overhear the private conversations of visitors. See Figs. 56, 77.

Lamp-shelf — Small open-aumbry intended for lamps.

Lawburrows — Security against doing violence to other persons.

Lug-moulded — Moulding having an "ear" projecting sideways at the top of a door or window frame.

Lymmar — A rogue or lawless man.

Macer — An officer of Parliament, the Exchequer and the Law Courts responsible for preserving order and summoning juries, witnesses, etc. His authority was represented by a mace.

Machicolation — An opening between corbels through which missiles or hot liquids could be dropped on an enemy below. See Figs. 82, 83.

Mason's Mark — A distinctive mark cut in dressed masonry to identify the mason who made it. See Fig. 106.

Merkland — See 'Oxgang'. A Merk was 13s 4d (two thirds of £1).

Messuage — The principal dwelling-house of a barony.

Motte — The mound of a Norman castle. See Fig. 165.

Mullion — A vertical partition between the lights of a window.

Nail-head — A decorative moulding that resembles a continuous string of square-headed nails. See Fig. 118.

Newel — The central pillar of a wheel-stair.

Non-entry — The profits of a feudal tenure which passed directly to the feudal superior instead of the vassal, either because the vassal had failed to register his inheritance to the property, or whilst he was unable to register his inheritance as he was still a minor. The non-entries of the estate of a minor were commonly gifted by the Crown to the ward or to the minor when he or she came of age.

Novodamus — A charter confirming certain feudal rights anew; a charter of confirmation.

Open-aumbry — See 'Aumbry'.

Oxgang — The area of land that could be worked by a single ox in one season. It varied considerably in extent, but in 1590 the Privy Council decreed that, for the purposes of Land Tax, "£1 land of old extent" = 2 Husbandlands = 4 Oxgangs (RPC IV, 543). It is commonly taken to be 13 acres.

Pediment — A classical gable above a door or window. See Fig. 98.

Pele — The simplest form of tower-house, usually almost square and often built with clay-mortar. See Chapter 2.

Pele-house — Similar to a bastle-house, but without a vaulted basement. See Chapter 2.

Pinnings — Small stones used to fill up the spaces in masonry.

Piscina — A basin with a drain set into a niche in ecclesiastical buildings. See Fig. 64.

Plenishing — Furniture.

Plinth — The projecting base of a wall, usually with a splayed or chamfered top edge.

Precept — A legal document authorizing sasine, etc.

Putlog-holes — Openings left in a wall, from which the timbers supporting a projecting timber platform or gallery can be cantilevered out. See Fig. 79.

QER — Quirked edge-roll, or bowtell, moulding (on an arris). See Fig. 16.

QERF — Quirked edge-roll-and-fillet moulding.

QERFH — Quirked edge-roll, fillet and hollow moulding (usually only on the outer face).

QERH — Quirked edge-roll-and-hollow moulding (usually only on the outer face).

Quirked edge-roll — An edge-roll (q.v.) which terminates in one or two sharp-edged channels.

Quitclaim — Formal renunciation of ownership or a claim.

Quoin — A large stone used to form the outer corner of two walls.

Rebated — An arris that is recessed to accommodate a door, or a block of ashlar masonry that is similarly recessed to accommodate another, offset block of ashlar. See Fig. 2.

Relief — A fine paid to a feudal superior by a feuar's heir on coming into possession.

Relieving arch — A structural arch incorporated into a wall to carry the weight of the wall above.

Retour — Return as heir to an estate, etc.

Reversion — Land held "under Reversion" (See Wadset)

Roll-and-hollow — An edge-roll (q.v.) with a semi-circular channel on one or both sides, but without any quirks. See Fig. 16.

Round — A corbelled-out corner turret without a roof.

Rybat — One of the dressed stones used to form the jamb of a doorway or window.

Salt-box — An aumbry for salt in, or adjacent to, a fireplace, designed to let the heat of the fire keep the salt dry. See Fig. 67.

Sasine — The formal act of giving possession of land held in feu.

Scale-and-Platt — A stair of straight flights with landings between each flight. See Fig. 218.

Scarcement — A narrow ledge formed when a wall is set back.

Scoinson-arch — The rear arch behind a window or doorway.

Segmental arch — An arch whose section is less than a semi-circle.

Service of ward — Tenure by military service when required.

Shot-hole — A small gun-loop for use with a small hand-gun or pistol. See Fig. 85.

Sike — A small watercourse.

Skewput — The lowest stone in the coping of a gable.

Slop-sink — A stone sink with a drain through the adjacent wall. See Figs. 70, 73.

Squinch Arch — An oblique arch across a re-entrant angle, usually supporting a corbelled-out stair-turret.

Squint — A peep-hole or oblique opening for discreet surveillance of a doorway, passage or public room.

String-course — A projecting moulding carried around the wall of a building.

Tenandry — The old word for a tenancy.

Test, The — 'The Test' was an oath that had to be taken by all officials acknowledging the supremacy of the Crown and renouncing the Covenants. It was instituted in 1681.

Transom — A horizontal division of a window, usually of stone.

Tusking — Stones left projecting from a wall's surface for the purpose of bonding another wall.

Tympanum — Space enclosed within a pediment or arch.

Voussoirs — Wedge-like ashlar stones forming an arch.

Wadset — The conveyance of land as security for, or in satisfaction of, a specified debt. The debtor reserves the right to recover the land on repaying the debt, commonly within a stipulated period of seven years. An early form of mortgage.

Wapinschaw(ing) — Literally a 'Weapon Show'. An armed muster for inspection of arms and practice in their use for the defence of the realm.

Wheel-stair — A spiral or turnpike stair formed around a central newel. See Fig. 43.

Window-grille — An iron lattice to protect a window, normally constructed in the same manner as a yett. See Fig. 40.

Yett — A door or gate made of interlaced iron bars. See Fig. 13.

Fig. 374 Remains of Lochinvar Castle in 1954
(seen from the W shore through a 20X telescope).

INDEX